An Enlightened Duke

Argyll, 1749 [Allan Ramsay, Glasgow Corporation, Kelvingrove Museum]

An Enlightened Duke

The
Life of
Archibald Campbell (1682-1761)
Earl of Ilay
3rd Duke of Argyll

Roger L. Emerson

humming earth

humming earth
an imprint of
Zeticula Ltd
The Roan
Kilkerran
KA19 8LS
Scotland

http://www.hummingearth.com
admin@hummingearth.com

First published in 2013

ISBN 978-1-84622-039-5 Paperback
ISBN 978-1-84622-040-1 Hardback

For
Esther Mijers and Mark Spencer
with
Respect, Admiration and Affection

Acknowledgements

I am indebted and grateful to many who for over a generation have aided me. Among them are many librarians, keepers and curators who have answered questions, checked manuscript numbers and graciously shown me things I would have missed and given permission to quote materials in their keeping.

I am especially grateful to those of the Aberdeen Town Council Archives, the Library of the University of Aberdeen, the Library and Muniments Room at St Andrews University; the National Library of Scotland, the National Records of Scotland; the National Portrait Galleries; the Royal College of Physicians, Edinburgh; the Edinburgh City Archives, the Royal College of Physicians and Surgeons, Glasgow; Glasgow University Library and Archives and the Mitchell Library, Glasgow.

At Glasgow University Library, Mr. Jack Baldwin, Mr. David Weston, Mr. John Moore and the late Mr. Peter Vasey made it a pleasure to work in that Library.

Drs. David Brown and Tristram Clarke, of the National Records of Scotland, and Iain Gordon Brown, of the National Library of Scotland, have for years patiently done more than I should have asked.

Others who have been especially helpful include Dr. Michael Barfoot, Keeper of the Lothian Medical Archives and Mr. Iain Milne of the Library of the Royal College of Physicians, Edinburgh.

Mr. John Overholt of the Houghton Library, Harvard University, gave permission to quote from a manuscript held in his keeping while at the Whipple Museum in Cambridge, Mr. Josh Nall supplied a valuable source.

Mr. Alastair Massie of the National War Museum, London, and Mrs. Penny Hatfield, the College Archivist at Eton College, helpfully responded to enquiries, as have the Librarians of the Grand Lodges of Scotland and England.

Museum Curators have been equally helpful. The National Portrait Galleries of England and Scotland, the Glasgow Museums and Art Galleries, The Twickenham Museum, and the Royal Botanic Gardens at Edinburgh and Kew have all supplied pictures to illustrate the book.

Mr. Hilary Young of the Victorian and Albert Museum, Dr. Joe Rock and Mr. George Haggarty have answered my questions about ceramics.

The 12th and 13th Dukes of Argyll generously provided information and gave me permission to use the bank records of the 3rd Duke still retained at Coutts Bank, London. There, I owe thanks to Ms. Tracey Earl and Mr. David Luck who were most helpful. So too was the staff of the Archives of the Royal Bank of Scotland.

I am grateful to the Marquis of Bute for permission to quote from papers held at Mount Stuart House, Isle of Bute.

Sir Robert Clerk of Penicuik, like his late father, Sir John, have been helpful to me over many years and with many projects.

I am in debt to others for many things.

The Reverend Dr. Frank Wyatt and Dr. Dennis C. Gilles supplied me with information about the Mausoleum in which the 3rd Duke is buried in Kilmun and with the inscription on his tomb.

Others to whom I am grateful for information or answers to questions include: Dr. Ronald Black, Professor John Cairns, Mr. Alastair Campbell of Airds of the Court of the Lord Lyon, the Reverend Dr. Alexander Campbell, Dr. Andrew Cunningham, Dr. John Dixon, Ms. Katherine C. Fairfield, Mr. Vincent Gray, Dr. Niccolo Guicciardini, Dr. Bob Harris, Ms. Elizabeth Hill, Dr. Brian Hillyard, Mr. Richard Hunter, Mr. Jonathan Kinghorn, Dr. John R. Millburn, Dr. Alison Morrison-Low, Mr. Gerald Mulcahy, Dr. Alexander Murdoch, Professor Larry Neal, Dr. Henry Noltie, Ms. Susan Patterson, Mr. Edoardo Piccoli, Professor Paul Potter, MD, Dr. Allen Simpson, Dr. Anne Skoczylas, Professor I. K. Steele and Professor Charles W. J. Withers.

Professor Daniel Szechi graciously read an early draft of the manuscript as did Professors Paul Wood and the late Frederick Dreyer. I thank them for their criticisms.

I am happy to thank Professors T. C. Smout and T. D. Devine for support and encouragement of this book.

The editors of the *Filosofia, Scienza e Politica nel Settecento Britannico* and Ashgate Publications gave permission for the reuse of portions of previously published works.

For the grant in aid of publication supplied by the Strathmartine Trust, which made the appearance of this work possible, I am deeply grateful.

I am especially indebted to Dr. John Stuart Shaw whose knowledge of the politics of Scotland during the Duke's lifetime is unrivalled and without whose aid and careful reading of my first draft, this book would not have been possible.

To Esther Mijers and Mark Spencer, whose good humour and kindness I have learned to value highly, this book is dedicated with great affection and respect.

Contents

List of Illustrations

An Enlightened Duke

Abbreviations

ARBS	Archives of the Royal Bank of Scotland
BS	Bank of Scotland
DNB	*Dictionary of National Biography*
DSB	*Dictionary of Scientific Biography*
ECA	Edinburgh City Archives
GUA	Glasgow University Archives
GUL	Glasgow University Library
EIC	The East India Company
HIKAS	The Honourable the Improvers in the Knowledge of Agriculture in Scotland
HMRC	Historical Manuscripts Commission Report
HPHC	*History of Parliament, The House of Commons*
JHL	*Journals of the House of Lords*
LPCS	Lord President of the Court of Session
NLS	National Library of Scotland
NPG	National Portrait Gallery, London
NRS	National Records of Scotland
NS	New Style (Calendar)
ODNB	*Oxford Dictionary of National Biography*
OS	Old Style (Calendar)
PCS	Principal Clerk of Session
PRS	President of the Royal Society of London
PSE	Philosophical Society of Edinburgh
RBS	Royal Bank of Scotland
RCAHMS	Royal Commission on Ancient and Historical Monuments of Scotland
SCJ	Senator of the College of Justice
SHS	Scottish History Society
SNPG	Scottish National Portrait Gallery, Edinburgh
W. S.	Writer to the Signet

Preface and Note on the Text

I became interested in the Duke of Argyll around 1980 while I was working on various topics in the Scottish Enlightenment. He is an interesting man, a great patron who, I believe, changed the nature of Scottish culture. Indeed, I came to think that he was as much a founder of the Scottish Enlightenment as anyone. I never intended to write a life of him. I am not a political historian and he had one of the great political careers of eighteenth-century Britain. He was a also very private man whose papers have vanished. Basic facts about his life are often lacking and he attracted no Boswell. There simply appeared to be too little information on which to base a biography. Yet, he needed one. Over the years I came to know more about him and became convinced he was important in ways not generally recognized. Finally, around 1994, I decided I should try to write a life of the Duke.

The sketchy, fragmentary documentation of much of his long and complex career makes it difficult to follow his personal, intellectual, or business activities over time and to integrate them into a coherent story. One has to look for patterns in action and thought in order to infer motives and intentions and to tell his story. That has made for a longer, more speculative life than I had wanted to write. The book describes all aspects of the Duke's career. I wanted to depict the man who said he was happiest when thinking about his 'gimcracks' in science and mathematics or when he was in his gardens and laboratories. Giving some sense of the non-political sides of his life has not been easy. I have had to explore the contexts in which he lived as much as what he did in them. He was a politician driven by interests in getting, retaining, and increasing his power and that of his friends but not all he did can be explained in political terms. His intellectual and improving interests allow us to see what the mature politician was attempting to do in and for Scotland and why. They also tell us about the man. One so interested in the lives of others deserves no less. His extra-political intellectual interests are mostly discussed in Part II, which divides the largely political narrative given in Parts I and III. More work will be done on him. I hope my speculations will be useful to those who do it.

The quotations printed in this work are as they appear in the sources from which they are taken. In those, spaces are often used as punctuation. They have been retained as has the spelling. Dates have been left as they appear in the texts except for a few which have been noted as Old Style [OS] or New Style [NS] when it seemed good to do so for reasons of clarity.

Part I

Archibald Campbell to c. 1725

Chapter 1

Introduction

I. The Death and Burial of Archibald Campbell

Even though he was nearly eighty in 1761, Archibald Campbell (1682-1761), Earl of Ilay (1706-1761) and 3rd Duke of Argyll (1743-61),was still vigorous and active.[1] He had been planning his annual trip from London to Scotland and had been scheming for the 1761 election. In Scotland, he expected to visit The Whim, his Peebles-shire estate, which he had been improving since the 1720s. From there he would go on to Edinburgh and Glasgow where he would see his political friends, do his politicking and perhaps spend time with booksellers and talk to professors, gardeners and botanists. Then, he would view the progress on Rosneath and Inveraray Castles, one being renovated, the under construction since 1744. He went to Scotland but not as he had planned. He died on 15 April 1761. He had been out that morning but returned home unwell. He came to the dinner table but ate nothing. There, at about 5:00 p.m., while sleeping at the table as others ate, he had a convulsion and was dead in a minute.[2] As Lord Adam Gordon remarked, his end was the kind for which sensible people wish. On the following morning, after the reading of his will, he was autopsied, embalmed, stored and then lay in state at his home in Argyll Buildings. About 1 May, he began his long journey north to his final resting place with his forebears at Kilmun, a village on the northeast shore of the Holy Loch in Argyllshire.[3]

Argyll began his last trip up the Great North Road in a funeral procession which initially included the corpse of the late Countess of Findlatter.[4] The delay between his death and the trip north was occasioned by the complexity of the arrangements to be made. Undertakers had to be engaged and the hangings from his Grace's London house, decorated with his arms, were taken down and shipped north to form an appropriate background for the places in which he was to lie in state in Scotland. Horses had to be secured, inns booked and ceremonies planned. The burial place at Kilmun had to be readied to receive him. None of those preparations could begin in Scotland until word of his demise reached there which it did by express on 19 April. Argyll's corpse was placed in a coffin to which was affixed a plate listing his offices and honours. That was 'carried ... in a superb hearse richly ornamented with escutcheons'.[5] It reached Edinburgh on Friday, 15 May. The body of Lady Findlatter had been there some days. By then, all was in order. James Gordon, a London undertaker, had done everything necessary 'for the Reception of His Grace at Holyrood'.[6]

Gentlemen met his body at the burgh limits. They conducted the body through Edinburgh to Holyrood Palace of which the Duke had been an Hereditary Keeper.

It was scheduled for a 6:00 p.m. arrival at the Palace where 'a Company are to Meet at his Grace's House half an hour after five'. [7] There, 'in the presence of a numerous company of nobility and gentry, the magistrates of Edinburgh, and the members of other respectable bodies in the city', Argyll was 'laid in state' until the following Monday in the dining room of the Ducal apartment, decked with the hangings from London.[8] There followed a reception for invited guests, 'a supper for Gentlemen f[ro] m the Country', and bread and wine given to those outside. The invited included Edinburgh's resident noblemen, the Commander-in-Chief in Scotland, the judges of the highest courts, who had been his colleagues, the Lord Provost and Magistrates of Edinburgh, the Commissioners of Custom and Excise, the Advocates led by the Lord Advocate and the Dean of the Faculty of Advocates, the King's Solicitors, the Ministers of Edinburgh, the Professors of the University, the Fellows of the Royal College of Physicians, Writers to the Signet, the Postmaster General of Scotland and others including his former secretaries, John Maule and Andrew Fletcher. Most of those invited owed their posts to him.

On Monday, 18 May, at about 9:00 a.m., 'the funeral procession, which was very grand, passed through the city, the great bells tolling all the while'.[9] The order of the marchers was probably that of the invitation list which had been worked out by his long-time aide, Andrew Fletcher, Lord Milton, Senator of the College of Justice [SCJ]. Now the notables were afforced by others from the Trades and deputations from the corporate bodies he had long assisted. Many of those people carried their banners and standards. Following them came his 'honours, the gauntlets and spurs, the sword and shield, the helmet, with the crest, and the [ducal] crown and cushion, all carried by gentlemen on horseback; after these followed the hearse, drawn by six horses, superbly ornamented with plumes and escutcheons: two mourning coaches, and the machines of several noblemen and gentlemen closed the whole'.[10] They processed though streets lined by people who watched in respectful silence. Argyll's old friend and clerical manager, the Reverend Patrick Cuming, wrote that the crowd gave 'proof of that singular importance and consideration which this great man had acquired, more by his abilities, and the lustre of his public conduct, than even by the nobility of his birth, or the eminence of his station'.[11] Cuming went on to say that, lacking official position, and sometimes the favour of the King and ministers, Argyll had made himself indispensable and respected in Scotland by his 'judgment, the talents of conversation, and graceful elocution, discernment, moderation and caution'. He noted (incorrectly) that while a partisan, the Duke had never been opposed with 'bitter enmities' which had so often marked Scottish political strife. In death, all recognized the greatness of a duke who had done much for Scotland and Britain. The procession took an hour to clear the city. The cortege went on to Falkirk where it was again met by local dignitaries who were given 'entertainment'.[12]

On Tuesday morning the procession set off for Glasgow where the Magistrates and the Duke's friends had had notice to 'meet the Corps about the end of the town and Conduct them to the place or Church where they are to be deposit'. The arrangements had been left to Provost Andrew Cochrane, the Duke's friend and political ally since before c.1730. 'Here likewise a numerous body of nobility and gentry were assembled, who with the magistrates, the professors of the university, &c. attended the corpse to

Mr. Grahams, where it lay in state that night'.[13] There was a 'supper for Gentlemen from the Country' and bread and drink for people less grand.[14]

In the morning, the hearse and its attendants 'passed through Glasgow, the Argyleshire militia, under arms, lining the streets'; their officers were in mourning.[15] The cortege reached Greenock on the south shore of the Clyde where those who met the procession were given 'cold victuals'. There the corpse was put on the Duke's Barge which took it down the Clyde and through the Holy Loch to Kilmun, the traditional burying place for the chiefs of the Inveraray Campbells. The barge was 'decorated with standards and escutcheons, and the arms and bearings of the family'. It was attended by the King's Wherry, and thirteen other properly decorated barges[16] carrying

> the relations and friends, of the family; who attended the corpse to Kilmun, the burial place of the family, where it was deposited. During the whole time of the procession this day minute-guns were fired from Dumbarton castle, from the ships at Greenock and Port-Glasgow, and on the river. The procession by water was particularly grand and solemn.[17]

Once landed, Argyll was borne to his final resting place by fourteen honorary pallbearers – on one side, principal gentlemen of his clan,[18] on the other, the Earls of Loudoun and Rosebery; Lord Adam Gordon, the Commander-in-Chief in Scotland, Lord Ruthven and Lord Milton; Andrew Fletcher (Milton's son and the Duke's last secretary) and Captain James Edmonstoune, a relative. After interment, there might have been a prayer or two at the kirk and certainly more 'entertainment'– probably more cold victuals and final drinks to the memory of MacCailein Mor, the 3rd Duke of Argyll and the best of the race of Diarmid.[19] Reflection on the man could then begin.

II. Assessments and Reasons Why Argyll Has Had No Biography

Most of those who initially wrote about Argyll noticed what they took to be his chief virtues: 'his strong natural parts', his learning and love of books and instruments, his even temper and good nature, his imperturbability and courage, his interests in improving what he could. The writers rooted his political success in those traits. Something of his restless energy was also captured in a character written shortly after his death:

> He was always contriving and always ready to listen to Schemes for promoting the Learning and the interest of his country. He had a Nice discernment a just taste in Language, History, Poetry, and was a Master in Mathematicks particularly Mechanicks; And he left the Most valuable private Library in Great Britain. The encouragement and Example he gave to all kinds of Useful improvements, Awakened the genius and excited the industry of Many. He cultivated a Garden on Hounslo Heath, att Whitam his Country Seat in England and Naturalized Many forreign curious and usefull plants and trees to the Soil of Great Brittain.

> To Demonstrate that the most barren ground is capable of improvement, he cultivated a Moss att The Whim, in Shire of Tweadale where he raised a Noble plantation of Trees.

That encomiast had begun with Argyll's political success and eloquence in Parliament; he ended, as did others, by saying: 'Rarely are so many extraordinary and excellent Qualities to be found United in one person'.[20] Two years later this image of the Duke was the one given to the European world of letters by an Italian visitor to Scotland, Carlo Denina (see pp. 358-9).

Those closer to Argyll in age and with different memories remembered a less pleasant, less accomplished man. John Dalrymple, 2nd Earl of Stair (1673-1747), no friend to the Campbells of Argyll, described the 3rd Duke as

> ... as little useful in his public character as amiable in his private one; one as mean in his conduct as in his aspect, and who acts [no] more like a man of quality than he looks like one; a man of as little weight as principle, and no more fit to be trusted with any commission that requires ability and judgment than one that requires honesty and fidelity.[21]

That was the comment of a man who had been a rival in the Army of the 2nd Duke of Argyll and had opposed both the 2nd and 3rd Dukes in politics – and had been bested by them. John, 1st Baron Hervey (1696-1743), Pope's 'Sporus' and a man who had formed part of the Campbell brother's social circle in the 1720s, described the 3rd Duke as

> ... a man of parts, quickness, knowledge, temper, dexterity and judgment; a man of little truth, little honour, little principle, and no attachment but to his interest.... A pedantic, dirty, shrewd, unbred fellow of a college, with a mean aspect, bred to the sophistry of the civil law and made a peer, would have been just such a man.[22]

Hervey, an aesthete and literary man, prized learning and intellectual activities which did not greatly concern the 3rd Duke. He, like Stair, valued different things. One can hardly imagine Hervey worrying over the linen trade, concerning himself with banking or the smelting of iron or prescribing pills to his friends. He recognized that Argyll was a considerable political figure but he did not see him as culturally significant.

Rather like them was Sir Robert Walpole's son, Horace, later Earl of Orford (1717-1797). After 1742, Horace Walpole disliked Argyll because he believed the Duke had been responsible for the downfall of his father. Those whom Horace disliked, he traduced in memorable language much read by those who prefer wit and style to truth. Argyll was scorned and Walpole's account has stuck. For Horace Walpole, his father's old friend was an 'old wizard'

> slovenly in person, mysterious, not to say with an air of guilt in his deportment, slow, steady, when suppleness did not better answer his purpose, revengeful,

and if artful, at least not in ingratiating....[By intrigue] Argyll had risen to supreme authority in Scotland; the only instance wherein he declined the full exertion of it, was, when it might have been of service to the master who delegated it; in the time of the [1745] rebellion: at that juncture he posted to London: the King was to see that he was not in the rebellion; the rebels that he was not in arms.... In his private life he had more merit, except in the case of his wife, whom having been deluded into marrying without a fortune, he punished by rigorous and unrelaxed confinement in Scotland. He had a great thirst for books; a head admirably turned to mechanics; was a patron of ingenious men, a promoter of discoveries, and one of the first great encouragers of planting in England; most of the curious exotics which have been familiarized to this climate, being introduced by him. But... though head of his country for several years, had so little great either in himself or in his views, and consequently contributed so little to any great events, that posterity will probably interest themselves very slightly in the history of his fortunes.

Horace Walpole noted that Ilay had a head for mathematics and patronized 'ingenious men' but what affected the private man seemed to Walpole to have no wider relevance. He found the Duke's interests curious but unimportant. He at least recognized his importance as a politician.[23] The Englishman thought Argyll a man of 'equivocal principles'. His 'duplicity' had cost Sir Robert Walpole his office because Argyll, then Earl of Ilay, had not exerted himself to elect MPs who would support Walpole in the House of Commons.[24] Still, in his *Memoirs of King George II,* Walpole thought Ilay important enough to give him a character and to commission a portrait of him to illustrate that book.

Others in Walpole's world were no more charitable. Tobias Smollett, who disliked Argyll and whose connections were to the Squadrone faction in Scotland and to 'the Patriots' in England, described Argyll as a 'nobleman of extensive capacity and uncommon erudition, remarkable for his knowledge of the civil law and seemingly formed by nature for a politician; cool, discerning, plausible, artful and enterprising, staunch to the minister [Walpole]'. He concluded by noting that Argyll was 'invariably true to his own interest' and not a man with principles.[25]

The Duke is briefly mentioned in every account of the politics of his time because he was a friend of Sir Robert Walpole and was the principal manager of Scottish politics for ministries between c.1725-1742 and then 1747-1761. Writers for Walpole, such as Nicholas Tindal, who gave the Duke a flattering character published in his lifetime, have not been much noticed (see p. 347). Ilay regularly shows up as important in settling the 1725 Malt Tax Riots, as a defender of Walpole's excise proposals in the early 1730s, in the Porteous Affair of 1736, and as one who did little in the '45 but more in the recruitment of Highland soldiers and in numerous elections. Still, he appears as a minor figure, simply another anglified Scot who was skilful in the management of elections. In most cases, he seems to be only a relatively minor politician neither likeable nor interesting as a man. That is not surprising among English historians for whom British history is often mostly the history of England. Scots have not interested those with whom they have shared an uneasy and unequal union.

The provinciality of the English historians should not be under-estimated. Even the great Sir Lewis Namier was content, in *The Structure of Politics At the Accession of George III* (2nd ed., 1957), to ignore most Scots. He gave more space to Saltash than to Edinburgh, more entries to John White than to the man who helped return as many as 35 MPs to the House of Commons and who was, throughout most of his career, a capable defender in the House of Lords of the governments of the day.[26] Other English historians have been even less willing to deal with Ilay since their British history seldom glances north of the Tweed. J. H. Plumb's *Walpole* mentions Ilay nine times. Reed Browning's index to *The Duke of Newcastle* lists 'Islay [sic], Lord. *See* Argyle, Alexander [sic] Campbell, duke of.' When we look, there is, not surprisingly, no entry. J. B. Owen did somewhat better but most histories endlessly repeat the sources cited above and go no further.[27] Argyll's relative lack of involvement in English affairs cannot account for these omissions.

Another reason for the Duke's neglect lies in the dominant place of foreign affairs and diplomacy in British history until c.1950. The 3rd Duke of Argyll, unlike his brother the heroic Field Marshall, could be overlooked. He made no military or diplomatic reputation. He also held no offices in any Ministry. His economic importance was not of much concern to historians taken up with the evils of enclosure or the transformation of Britain by commerce and industry. The only historian of eighteenth-century Britain with an appreciation of Argyll's importance seems to have been an American, John Wilkes, who in 1964 called the disappearance of Argyll's papers 'a most serious loss to a complete understanding of eighteenth-century political life during the time of Walpole and Pelham'.[28] Argyll was politically important long after Henry Pelham's death in 1754.

Lord Ilay sometimes appears in biographies as a hanger-on about more interesting men and women. He was a sometime friend of the Tory wits and Mrs. Howard (a mistress of George II) and her set at Twickenham. That group included writers, architects and gardeners. He had friends among British men of science but British political historians have not been interested in those aspects of his life. Some who could not appreciate his very real virtues have been vocal in denigrating his character and works. That process began early and in England but Scottish historians too have paid him little attention.

The best of the latter before 1900, John Hill Burton, has perhaps five mentions of the 3rd Duke of Argyll in the last volume of his *History of Scotland* (1853). None of them make him in any way notable. Until recently, twentieth-century historians have done little better. Sir Robert Rait's *The Making of Scotland* (London, 1929) has three mentions of 'Islay' – one to the island although it is under the Duke's entry.[29] The book which Rait wrote with George S. Pryde, *Scotland* (2nd ed., London, 1934) mentions him but does not note Ilay's presence at the Battle of Sheriffmuir where his troops were of some significance. J. D. Mackie's *The Short History of Scotland* did a little better. Ilay and his political 'machine were indispensable' but, in the end, he was only a political manager like Henry Dundas.[30] Both could manage Scottish politics because of the small size of the venal political class and its lack of interests in matters of political principle or foreign affairs. What mattered were jobs and advantages meted out to the '*People Above*'. Argyll, like Henry Dundas, 1st Viscount

Melville (1742-1811), looked after his interests and managed the region for ministries in London to which he belonged. Argyll had no greater importance.

Six years after Mackie's book, the Scottish nationalist historian, William Ferguson, quoted a 1716 letter of Ilay's which said that Ilay and his brother, the 2nd Duke of Argyll, made of politics a 'continuall petty war and game' played for stakes which translate into plunder, pounds, and power, but never into principle. Ilay, in some moods certainly thought that. Ferguson elaborated with another quotation from Ilay: 'It is enough that we can maintain an interest with some of both sides without giving up anything we must and ought to maintain, and, if I can save myself or my friends by being thought a Mohometan by a Turk, I'll never decline it.'[31] It never crossed Ferguson's mind that this anglified Scot might 'maintain an interest' in anything not personal or in anything aimed at the public good of Scotland. 'Pride, greed and avarice', arrogance and corruption, characterize the Campbell brothers in Ferguson's account.[32] Like Horace Walpole, Ferguson saw Argyll as doing little in 1745-46 'to put down the rebellion'. He says that the Duke opposed the abolition of heritable jurisdictions in Scotland for no better reason than that this would weaken his personal power – the reason that the Duke of Cumberland also gave. Argyll's death is deplored only because it left Scottish politics in confusion.[33] His intellectual attainments are derisively dismissed. The Duke is found to be only 'an amateur inventor of gim cracks in mathematics', a judgment which says more about the deficiencies of Ferguson's knowledge and scholarship than about the Duke.[34]

Rosalind Mitchison, in *A History of Scotland* (1970), managed to confuse Ilay with his brother[35] and saw the 3rd Duke as little more than a judge meant to overawe his colleagues, a party manager and placeman. In London he became a sort of 'elder statesman in the Cabinet', a patronage broker who served his class and one who 'distorted the electoral system to fit the expanding political interests of the upper classes though there are instances of distortion earlier'.[36] This led to chicanery, bogus voters and lying under oath. One would think that a social and economic historian might have noticed his role in Scottish banking, manufactures and the improvement movement, or the flourishing of the medical schools in which Ilay was interested. In the same year, T. C. Smout's *History of the Scottish People 1560-1830* gave us an Ilay who appears as the first of the Scottish political managers and as a Campbell whose family had produced hatreds in the North which led to rebellions.[37] All that is true but there is more to be said.

Why others did not say it is made partly clear in an essay by Smout's sometime colleague, Richard Savile. He noted that Scottish history until after World War II was oriented almost solely to the country's politics and religion before 1750. There were exceptions but Scots did not write much modern cultural, social or economic history until the late 1950s and then relied on borrowed ideas and methods taken from England and elsewhere. The concerns of those who cultivated those fields were not with Scottish lords who tended to be seen as heartless landlords who did little for the common Scot.[38]

Those negative opinions have coloured the works of those who have dealt with what the Duke did outside politics. One good description of his botanical garden at Whitton notes of its creator:

He does not seem to have been a particularly attractive character: slow, morose, vengeful, and careless of his appearance. His marriage proved a failure, and he established a lifelong liaison with Mrs. Elizabeth Williams, whom he set up near him at Whitton and for whom he later built a London residence.[39]

Interest in his plants, not in the facts of his life, was the only concern of the authors of that study.

Things began to change only in the 1980s with the work of three young scholars: John Stuart Shaw, Alexander Murdoch, and Richard Scott. Shaw's *The Management of Scottish Society 1707-1764* (1983) perpetuated Hervey's view but with more charity. For Shaw, the Duke was a clever politician who managed Scottish local interests to his advantage but who initiated little and whose ways were 'dark and obscure' and directed to his own survival. The key to survival was his brilliant use of patronage. Shaw told us little about the Duke's interest in science or improvements or his enlightened patronage in the universities. We hear nothing of Ilay's attitudes which helped to secularize a bigoted country which had hanged a free-thinking student in his youth but which at his death in 1761 had a Kirk run by tolerant Moderates. In Shaw's view, Ilay had virtues but few of them were civic or disinterested. Moreover, Shaw tended to see Ilay's Scottish lieutenant, Andrew Fletcher, Lord Milton, who served Ilay from 1724 to 1761, as the far less ambiguously-interested improver and the greater Scottish patriot. In Shaw's account, Ilay initiates little and seems to be distinguished by his attention in London to the details of patronage politics carried on in the interest of the governments in which he served. Shaw did, however, stress the national importance of the Duke:

> From 1725 to 1761 the 3rd Duke of Argyll was the dominant figure in Scottish affairs. He was also one of the dozen or so most powerful politicians in England. He performed the feat of holding a place in "the Cabinet Council (which usually numbered between twelve and fourteen) during five decades. He often acted as a Lord of the Regency during the King's visits to Hanover [1714, 1740, 1741, 1743, 1745, 1750, 1752, 1755, 1760]. He was matched as a political survivor only by Newcastle and the Earl of Hardwicke. His weakness was that he was too cautious. He rarely put his power on the line by interfering in the political process to help Scotland.[40]

Shaw's recent book, *The Political History of Eighteenth Century Scotland* (1999) has a better reading of Ilay's character and accomplishments but it too does not see much beyond politics. Ilay's enthusiasms are not seen to have a more than personal importance. In this respect, it resembles the account of him given by Murdoch.[41]

Murdoch's Ilay played a more principled and complicated game, particularly after 1742 when he lost the support of his old friend Sir Robert Walpole. Its complexity grew in 1743 when Ilay became the Duke of Argyll but was also deprived of most official patronage power in Scotland.[42] For Murdoch, Ilay's 'game' was always, in part, 'the study of human nature and the mastery of the intricate machinery of the day without ever questioning the value of the structure(s)' of eighteenth-century politics.[43] Part of the game involved arguing for special legislation, often for Scottish improvements, for clemency after the '15 and '45 and above all for jobs. The Duke of Argyll acted as a guardian of national interests and restrained, through his power and negotiations, the impact of English interventions in the country to prevent some policies and to weaken others.[44] Murdoch saw the Duke as representing views other than his own and interests which were national and not merely pursuing policies for his own good or that of his friends. He tells us, '... Scottish ministers were responsible to their English superiors but that relationship was not one-sided, or based on deceit... the Scottish manager represented Scottish interests within the government, sometimes successfully and sometimes unsuccessfully'.[45] Ilay was a Scottish patriot whose 'general stance of Scots jobs for Scots, no matter how self-interested politically, worked in the Scots' interest'.[46] Ilay was more civically virtuous and somewhat freer to pursue his policies than some have believed.[47] Murdoch's own judgment of the Duke is that he was an underling who made the most of his posts by keeping Scotland semi-independent but firmly in the Union.[48] Where Shaw saw much of the improving activity associated with Ilay as deriving from his Edinburgh lieutenant, Lord Milton, Murdoch gives more credit to the Duke. But even Murdoch cannot bring himself to see him as much more than a gifted politician although he quotes the Earl of Granville's comment that 'there may have been cleverer, or quicker men, but I never knew a man who had less rubbish in his understanding'.[49]

The third of the historians, Richard Scott, gave a character of Ilay which is a bit different but an evaluation of his importance which is close to Murdoch's. Scott found Ilay unimaginative and ordinary but good at management.

Unimpressive in appearance – short, slovenly dressed, walking with a limp and speaking in a high, grating voice – he had been brought up in England and then educated as a lawyer in Scotland *[sic]* and Holland and he possessed the precise, if unimaginative, mind of that profession. More important, he had the necessary qualities to master the intricacies of eighteenth century political management: he was tolerant, flexible, organized, artful, devious, ingratiating without being obsequious, and had a quick understanding and sure grasp of the complexities of patronage. Above all he was an unquestioning lover of the political system for its own sake....Ilay was neither a skilful court politician nor a powerful Parliamentary figure: his ability was to lie in being able to manipulate and cajole the bulk of the Scottish Whigs behind the administration of the day, and because he was prepared to overlook the Jacobite sympathies of many Scots, especially in the north, and do business with them, to neutralise or even reconcile for much of the time large elements of the Scottish political nation who were hostile to Whig interests. To maximise his full potential, Ilay required the support and cooperation of the Ministry, and for the bulk of patronage in Scotland to be placed at his disposal. In return he could aspire to offer the Ministry a solid bloc of support in Parliament and a solution to the difficult problem of controlling Scotland.[50]

Too unimaginative to have policies of his own and with no official position from which to push them, Ilay allowed Scotland a long period of semi-independence in which it could 'adjust to the realities of union.[51] This tolerant gradualist promoted the union of the two kingdoms but there was little else of note to say about him.[52] Murdoch, Shaw and Scott fail to ask how or in what ways Ilay's personal intellectual interests affected his political career, the patronage he bestowed, or the policies he pursued in Scotland. Those questions are worth asking; this study tries to answer them.

There are other reasons for the neglect of the 3rd Duke of Argyll and for the focus only on his politics. There is no surviving body of personal papers, only letters to others, mainly about politics. The 3rd Duke himself left no publications of substance.[53] Argyll's papers were inherited by his illegitimate son, Colonel William Williams (later Campbell) and were used by William Coxe for his lives of Sir Robert Walpole and of Henry Pelham.[54] They appear not to have been consulted by other historians since c.1803. The entry on the Dukes of Argyll in Douglas's *Peerage of Scotland* [c.1813] says that the papers were then in the possession of William Williams' grandson.[55] They appear now to be lost. The 12th Duke of Argyll assured me in 2000 that very little survives at Inveraray Castle.[56] That is not surprising since the present ducal family is not descended from the 3rd Duke who spent little time at Inveraray. There is an unsatisfactory list of the Inveraray manuscripts prepared by the National Register of Archives but that is now unavailable because the papers have been reorganized. The papers at Inveraray were effectively closed to historians for many years and were not used for this study.

There is little other surviving evidence of his achievements. Argyll's secretaries were not reflective men who kept full diaries for long periods, although several sketchy diaries survive.[57] No contemporary Scot left a substantial memoir dealing with the Duke. His great library exists only as a catalogue. The Duke's considerable collection of scientific instruments was sold to his nephew, the 3rd Earl of Bute, and dispersed at the sale of Bute's instruments after the Earl's death in 1792. Argyll's improved estates and gardens on Hounslow Heath and in Peebles-shire were not maintained and his work elsewhere has been much changed. His London house was demolished; the Palladium Theatre now stands on that site. As an improver, he has been largely ignored. Only recently has attention been paid to the ways in which he affected such institutions as the Scottish universities.[58] His effects on the Kirk, equally great, await detailed investigation. His political and some of his administrative appointments have been studied but other areas he influenced, such as the industrial and commercial life of the country, have yet to be considered.[59]

Today, few remember the man whose obsequies were almost regal. His portraits in Glasgow and Edinburgh are not now on regular display. What is also surprising is that, although he was a man often depicted in prints, few of those now appear on the market. His most familiar image is to be found on the banknotes issued by the Royal Bank of Scotland (see Plate 6) – bewigged, quizzical and pawky, the Bank's first Governor. This book attempts to rough out a rounded account of his life and its importance for Scotland. It seeks better to define his interests and how they affected his career as a politician. It argues that in many ways the Scottish Enlightenment was the lengthened shadows of this man and of the men whom he helped to places in Scotland. In doing this, it pays more attention to the favourable judgments of him by men like John Ramsay of Ochtertyre. He saw Argyll as 'not only the wisest and greatest Minister, but also the most enlightened patriot, Scotland has produced'.[60] Ramsay was not alone in this judgment. Warm but less extreme views were also expressed by admirers from David Hume to a host of men who had experienced his conversation or who had benefited from his interest and enlightened patronage. The many ordinary people who lined the streets of Edinburgh and stood in silence as his funeral procession passed on its way to and from Holyrood Palace must have felt something like that. He was genuinely mourned there and in Glasgow because he had done much, not only for himself, but for Scotland. Of the great figures of eighteenth century Scotland, Lord Archibald Campbell, Earl of Ilay (1705-1761) and 3rd Duke of Argyll (1743-1761) should be given his due. That is the purpose of this biography.

Plate 1: The Three Dukes, by Sir John Medina (c.1692), Inveraray Castle, with the permission of the Duke of Argyll.

Chapter 2

The Education of a Second Son

I. Introduction

Lord Archibald Campbell, Lord Archy as he was sometimes called until 1705 when he became Earl of Ilay, grew up to be a first rate politician who well fit the roles to which he had been born. To play them successfully required knowledge, social skills and force of character. Birth, ability and some charm made his career possible but it was his education which allowed him to be an active, knowing participant in most of what he did or which was done in his name. He could discuss, join in or direct activities which would have daunted men with less polymathic interests. Throughout his life, what he did was related to things he had learned. To understand the politician and patron, we must attend to his education which was not only academic but the product of the circumstances into which he had been born. His private actions often had public dimensions. How he got to be that sort of man is the concern of this chapter.

II. Antecedents

Lord Archy was born on 24 June 1682 O.S. at Ham House in Petersham on the south bank of the Thames near Richmond, Surrey.[1] He grew up knowing that on both sides of his family he had forbears who had had power and influence for a long time and were formidable people. Archibald and his elder brother, John (1680-1743), who became the 2nd Duke of Argyll in 1703, claimed a lineage which went back to King Arthur, Old King Cole, Joseph of Arithmathea and through him to the Trojans who descended from Japheth, the son of Noah, whose descent from Adam was set out in the Bible.[2] His family dated from the beginning of time and had always been important. In myth, the Dukes were the 'cousins' of kings, and in their own times were sometimes called 'princes.' Campbells of Argyll sometimes saw themselves in princely terms and certainly had been one of the most notable families of Scotland and the Western Highlands since c.1300. In the sixteenth century, the family had extended their lands at the expense of neighbouring clans, notably the MacDonalds, MacLeans, Camerons, Stewarts, MacGregors, Lamonts and other lesser names in the West of Scotland. The men whose lands they took and whom they continued to displace, they often confronted as Jacobites, whose support for the Stuart King rooted somewhat in resentment against the Campbells, who were old enemies as well as Whig supporters of Hanoverian Kings. Lord Archy and his brother got on socially with many Jacobites, among whom they were sometimes counted, but they opposed them both politically and in arms. Doing so was part of their heritage.

The kinship web into which Lord Archy was born provided one base from which he and his brother John constructed and sustained a political connection. The Campbells of Inveraray had a long queue in Argyllshire, one which spilled over into other counties. They counted kin among the Stuart Earls of Moray and Bute. Other relatives included the Campbell Earl of Loudoun and peers related to them by marriage: Eglinton, who like Loudoun had estates in Ayrshire; the Marquis of Lothian, the Duke of Buccleuch, the Earls of Home and Deloraine, whose estates were in the Borders; and in the North, the Earls of Sutherland, and Caithness, Lord Lovat and other Frasers from Inverness. The Breadalbane Campbells and those of Cawdor Castle were related and sometimes of Ilay's side politically. In Fife, they could find kin in the families of the Earls of Crawford and Rosebery.[3] Many cadet members of those families were lawyers and merchants in Edinburgh and Glasgow.

Another base for their influence lay in religion. Most of the Inveraray Campbells since c.1570 had proven to be more or less consistently Protestant and less willing to trim their beliefs than were many. They tended to be found on the evangelical fringe of the Kirk. Lord Archy and his brother would remain publicly committed to Presbyterianism and to that wing of the Scottish church until c. 1727. The Campbells had also been, as befitted good Calvinists, somewhat less politically reliable than their kings required. Archibald, the 8th Earl and 1st Marquis of Argyll, like his son and grandson of the same name, the 9th and 10th Earls, was never a simple royalist. A leader of the Covenanters, the Marquis was executed for treason in 1661. His scaffold speech included the following lines: 'I die not only a protestant, but with a heart-hatred of popery, prelacy, and all superstition whatsomever.' Ilay had the Marquis's final thoughts for his children published by the Foulis Press in Glasgow in 1743.[4] Ilay also remembered the Marquis and his cause in the 1749 portrait of himself by Allan Ramsay II (see frontispiece). Beheading was also to be the fate of Lord Archy's grandfather, the 9th Earl, who was executed in the Edinburgh Grassmarket in 1685 for his participation in Monmouth's Rebellion.[5] Ilay and his brother repeatedly said that the Stuarts owed his family two heads. Ilay's seal for some years bore the inscription 'MEMINI'– recollect or bear in mind. The martyrs' heirs were less religious than heroic but just as assertive politically.

Lord Archy's father, the 10th Earl and 1st Duke of Argyll (1658-1703), was often absent from the boy's life. He politicked and lived a rakish life.[6] Still, his father's career offered a model of the practice of politics which his sons would follow. Carefully use all the tools to hand; shift with the wind; look after yourself. When the Duke died in 1703, he had as many enemies as friends and was much in debt. An important part of Lord Archy's education was learning the lessons his father's career taught. Among them were: make money and incur no debts.

Absolute loyalty to one's kin, even one's father, might be impossible if wealth and position were to be kept. The Earl had opposed his own father in the Rebellion of 1685. He became a Roman Catholic,[7] then renounced that faith and fled to Holland whence he returned in 1688. Loyalty to Kings was not unqualified. Archy's father had not scrupled to rat on King James and join William of Orange at the Hague but he was not always William's man. He sat in the Scottish Convention as Earl of Argyll when it convened in mid-March 1689. Later, he was one of the delegation from Scotland to offer the crown to William and Mary and to take their oaths as rulers in

Scotland.[8] It was he who placed 'the Scottish crown on William's head'.[9] His rewards included the restoration of his titles and estates and William's gift of a line regiment.[10] However, by 1690, the Earl had begun to oppose William but went unpunished when the conspirators of the Montgomerie Plot were detected. The Earl became a Privy Councillor and an Extraordinary Lord of Session – positions his sons would both hold. About 1700, the Earl became a spokesman for the Kirk in Parliament and in the Scottish Privy Council, partly to oppose the Duke of Queensberry who favoured Episcopacy.[11] In 1701, the Earl had created his own party in Scotland, known as the Argathelians, and had been raised to a dukedom. The Duke continued to support the Kirk and a version of Whiggery until his death. That involved him with clerical politicians like the Reverend William Carstairs, a far more committed Christian but an equally skilful politician. They both knew how to play patronage politics and to win votes. Carstairs would have learned nothing from a letter from the Duke in 1700 which in somewhat uncertain prose laid out their methods:

> When I come to speak, even with those I am best with, of making a model to carry the king's business, by buying some, purchasing others, and making some places void for others, tho' those be but of the smaller sort, nor is it yet advisable; any other I meet with, this tutor has his friend to protect, the other has another, which does confound affairs; and I grieve when I see matters miscarry, where I have all the friendship in the world. However...I will send you for your satisfaction and mine, a schedule, by which I'd carry thirty members of parliament off, and so carry the affair: but you can never bring all to one in this measure, and so I fear will be the event.[12]

His practices were not novel but the calculated and methodical way he proposed to act characterised the future methods of his younger son.

Lord Archy and his older brother, John, Lord Lorn, by 1688 would have been aware that their father and the family played an important political role in Scotland. Even in the absence of their father, the boys would have watched that importance grow and would have also seen the precariousness of public life for any politician in the 1690s. From a very early age, Lord Archy appreciated that playing politics could be rough and uncertain. He grew up understanding that kings and most men could not be relied upon and that religion was political and perhaps not all its devotees said it was. His father had thought his estates and title worth a mass. His later championing of Presbyterian causes was equally political. Religion had political value but need not be taken seriously as a personal creed or as a moral guide. The Earl and his sons lacked the belief in Calvinist Christianity which their forebears had exhibited. While born a Protestant, and educated by clerics, Lord Archy grew up to despise most clerics, even calling the ministers of his own church 'priests' and 'Levites'.[13] Nevertheless, when Lord Archy and his brother came into public life, they had waiting for them a religious connexion composed of Presbyterians to whom they were often seemingly loyal but whom they secretly scorned.

By age ten, young Archy (Plate 1) had seen the risks which politics entailed and knew that the Western Highlands was a very unsettled region which needed order which could only come from force and negotiation. Campbells imposing order would be opposed by many for their Whiggish and Presbyterian principles and by others for their methods and their land grabbing. The riskiness of life was symbolized in the only portrait we have of young Archy. The Earl and his sons are posed before a Highland scene dramatically lit by a rising sun – a sun rising under storm clouds. Argyll is armed as are Highlanders in the background. The painting also tell us that Lord Archy was fair skinned, had reddish hair and was probably rather thin until late in life.[14]

The 1st Duke of Argyll was an articulate but slippery politician of some charm. His sons could be smooth and polite when they wished to be but they had hard cores. Knowing their father's experience was learning deviousness and survival skills. All his political life Lord Archy could be less than straightforward and, when it was called for, devious and mean. He could also be bold, brave and determined. Unlike his father and brother, Lord Archy grew up to be hard-working and showed 'that application to business' his father lacked.[15] Lord Archy and his brother understood Christian principles and sentiments but would not have died for them. That may not have been true of political principles but they were their father's sons.

Lord Archy's mother was in many ways like her husband. She was born Elizabeth Tollemache (1660-1735), the daughter of Sir Lionel Tollemache, 3rd Baronet of Helmingham and Elizabeth Murray (1626-1698), in her own right Countess of Dysart and later Duchess of Lauderdale. Archy's grandmother was as much English as Scottish. A clever girl, she had been 'taught philosophy, history, divinity and mathematics as well as the conventional domestic skills.'[16] Her family had also been much involved in British politics. Both sides of her family had been loyal to Charles I and II. Indeed, the Murrays of Dysart had had their loyalty rewarded with their earldom. Ham House, on the Thames near Richmond, had been built by them before the Civil Wars as their country retreat near the capital. The Countess's ties to royalist families were intensified by her second marriage in 1672 to John Maitland, 2nd Earl and Duke of Lauderdale (1616-1682). Early in his life, Lauderdale had been a Covenanter but he became a loyal follower of Charles II for whom he endured years of imprisonment in the Tower of London. Later (1668-1672), he was the 'L' in 'the Cabal' which governed the realms – one of the five most powerful men in Britain. Until 1680, he more or less ran Scottish affairs for Charles II. He urged the King to make himself more absolute and to use Scottish power to attain that end in England. Stripped of offices in 1680, he retired to Ham House.[17] Lauderdale was an example of learning and good taste but also of the opportunities and risks of playing politics. Ham House was the fruit of political victories but remembering a great-grandfather and step-grandfather was to be reminded of what political losses could mean. With connexions such as those, it is not surprising that Lord Archy could be a fairly authoritarian Whig who felt at ease with Jacobites and royalist Tories throughout his career.

Archy's mother was also a well-born Anglo-Scot and a woman whose prospects had been insured by her marriage contract worked out by the Duke of Lauderdale. When she married the Earl of Argyll in 1678, some of the Kintyre estates held by the Campbells of Inveraray were conveyed to her as jointure. It was agreed that a house was to be built for her in Kintyre. She would have in Campbeltown an establishment of her own. She was, thus, somewhat insured against the uncertainties created by her husband's political career. When her house was built, it was called Limecraigs. It was from there that she exercised a good deal of independent authority after separating from her husband in 1696.[18]

Both Lord Archy's parents were strong-willed people who led rather turbulent domestic lives. The family may have broken up into separate establishments in 1685 when the 10th Earl fled to Holland or the whole family may have lived in Holland for a time; leaving children and a wife behind was leaving hostages in the hands of James II. If Archy did not go to Holland, then he did not see his father from the time he was three until he was about six years old when his father returned to Britain with William III. When he returned, the Earl lived apart partly because his political career kept him from home but also because of numerous affairs with a series of ladies of dubious reputation. He is said to have travelled with a 'seraglio'. He and the Countess certainly had separate establishments by 1695/6.[19] When he died on 28 September 1703, it was as the result of 'black jaundice' and of a wound suffered in a brothel brawl.[20] When his will was read (and published for all to read in 1704), it was found that he had left all his personal property in England, including an estate in Northumberland, to a Mrs. Peggy Alison, one of his 'seraligio' [sic].[21] The Duchess resented the slights put upon her and sons. She and the 2nd Duke pursued Mrs. Alison for adultery in clerical courts even though this tarnished the memory of the 1st Duke who in documents was called an adulterer. They recovered the English estate.[22]

The Campbells of Inveraray had a history as improvers and entrepreneurs. By 1700 they were tree planters and the owners of, or investors in, salt works, slate quarries, lime-making facilities, iron smelting and fisheries.[23] The 1st Duke, like most Scottish notables, also invested in the Darien Company – £1,500 by 1696.[24] In 1700, he secured a royal charter for the port town of Campbeltown.[25] His Duchess was little different. She managed her estates well and planted trees at Campbeltown.[26] Active in her town, she encouraged it to 'build quays and make the harbour'. She was behind the establishment of a packet boat service to and from Glasgow. The Duchess supported the 'Lowland [English speaking] Church' with her contributions. Limecraigs became a place where young ladies of rank were put by their families to learn what polite skills and other things the Duchess had to teach. Among her lessons was Whiggery. The Duchess meddled politically in local affairs.[27] In the summer of 1711, she reported to the government that the Jacobite Macdonalds of Glencoe had imported for the Stewarts of Appin muskets, pistols and swords.[28] Limecraigs expenses contributed to the prosperity of the burgh. The burgh's gratitude was shown by its incorporation of the Tollemache family arms in the fourth quarter of its armorial shield.[29]

Unlike the 1st Duke, his Duchess kept good accounts and was a somewhat grasping woman. When her husband died in 1703, she billed his estate for many things – repairs on the house at Rosneath and Inveraray Castle, the building of her house at Campbeltown, back payments on her jointure, aliment, interest paid on a loan of £18,000 Scots made by Montrose, her husband's and father-in-law's funeral expenses, mourning for herself and her family and much else.[30] When the 2nd Duke went back to the wars in 1707, he made her one of his factors and the one with final say about decisions.[31]

She seems to have been closer to her first son than to Archy but in 1731 the 2nd Duke was suing her over something concerning her property at Duddingston. It was there that she died in 1735 leaving the property to both sons. Until the day before she died, she acted 'in all her affairs of building, and planting, and writing' either not believing she was so ill 'or else she has concealed it'.[32] Lord Archy came from tough stock but from people who had cultivated many of the interests he would pursue from politics to gardening, from fighting to improving his estates.

III. Growing up Politically

Little of Lord Archy's earliest years is known for certain. If he followed the pattern of his older brother, he spent time at Ham House as a small boy. He also spent some time growing up in or near Edinburgh. He might have been there with his brother in 1685 when their grandfather was executed in the Grassmarket.[33] The boys' sojourns in Edinburgh were likely short ones.[34] The city was not a healthy place in which to raise children; it is more likely that Archy was at the Dysart properties – Brunstane and Duddingston – both near Edinburgh.[35] The family seems also to have lived briefly c.1690 at Campbeltown in Argyllshire and at Rosneath in Dunbartonshire,[36] By 1690, they could have visited other estates which had been returned to the family by William and Mary.

The boys probably saw little of either parent. They would have been brought up mostly by servants but their mother was more of a presence than their often absent father. What impact those relationships had upon them, we can only guess. Did they worry as children that they too would go the way of their grandfather and great-grandfather? Did they wonder if they would again possess great wealth or would remain poor, as their father was throughout the 1680s?[37] The daring ambition of the elder and the habitual caution and thrift of the younger boy may reflect differing responses and reactions to the insecurity with which they had grown up.

Having a Highland background also made a difference to the Campbell boys. Neither Lord Archy nor Lorn seem to have learned any Gaelic or had much to do with the ordinary clansmen whose chiefs they were to become. They were too anglified and aristocratic for that. But, both grew up aware that their family was a Highland one despite its English homes and ties. Throughout his life, Archy would always be more at home among Highlanders than were most Scottish peers. Many of the latter, if Highlanders, surfaced in the factions of the Jacobites but others became Argathelians. As men well connected in the Highlands, the Argyll Campbells were useful to London governments which needed the loyalty of at least one great Highland family. That would have been apparent to bright young aristocrats growing up in the troubled world of the 1680s and 1690s. It cannot be documented but it is hard to deny. So too is the fact that they grew up knowing the family's enemies.

Archy and his brother inherited traditional political allies, rivals and enemies. Throughout Archy's life, his political career was made more complex by old animosities. Inveraray Campbells long looked jealously at the other over-mighty subjects who all found slippery the political ways of the times. Campbells regarded with hostility magnates like the Catholic Dukes of Gordon, the Jacobite Drummonds of Perthshire and were not very much happier with the Lowland Dukes of Hamilton. They did not always get on well with Douglasses such as the Marquises and Dukes of Queensberry. The Grahams of Stirling and Dunbartonshire were a family which had benefited by the forfeiture of the 1st Marquis of Argyll. Grahams had taken Campbell lands when the head of that house had been proscribed. They challenged the Campbells in Western Scotland into the 1730s when their head, the 1st Duke of Montrose, was still disputing control of the burgh and University of Glasgow. The Duke of Roxburghe, a Ker from the Borders, was not a local challenger of Campbell power but the Earls and Dukes of the late seventeenth and early eighteenth centuries were not usually friends to the Inveraray Campbells. When the brothers came to maturity and power, the Squadrone Whig faction was led by Montrose and Roxburghe. Growing up a Campbell from Inveraray involved knowing all that.

If politics played for power, places and profits, no one put a high premium on loyalty. Those who could move adroitly kept power and gained rewards through shifting loyalties. One had to work with many one could not eliminate but there were certainly preferred allies and the Dukes of Montrose, Gordon, Hamilton, and Queensberry would never be among them. Better Jacobites, with whom both the 2nd and 3rd Duke of Argyll at times flirted when they were out of favour, than duplicitous Whigs. Those were attitudes learned early and long held. Still, both brothers for all their tactical shifts remained at heart men committed to the Revolution Settlements of 1688-90.[38] Principle mattered to them and should not be wholly discounted as a guide to their long term policies. That meant they were willing if not eager to work with most English politicians. In doing so, they tried to preserve their power in Scotland. Interest and patriotism dictated upholding the rights of Scots and protecting their institutions.

IV. Schooling

The boys were tutored at home for the first years of their lives. If they shared tutors, then Archibald had the Reverend Walter Campbell of Dunsloskin, the Reverend John Anderson and later Alexander Cunningham of Block as his tutors. Block taught them Latin.[39] Those tutors were Whig Presbyterians who later received patronage from the family. Anderson was given a new Glasgow church in 1717, a politically significant post since it helped the Campbell brothers to control the burgh of Glasgow. If Archy was not taught by those divines, he had some other equally learned and pious teachers who would have come from the collection of men in and around Argyllshire who were associated with or dependent in some way on the family at Inveraray.

Lord Archy spent some of his early years (c.1690-?) growing up not only with his brother but with George Lockhart of Carnwath (1681-1731) who, as a ward of the house, would have shared the same tutors. Lockhart later was to be a fellow Commissioner of Union and the most important Scottish Jacobite politician serving in the House of Commons from 1708-1715.[40] Archy and his brother both liked Carnwath and protected him during the uprising of 1715 when he had been involved on the side they opposed. Their friendship continued but they never trusted him.

Lockhart was equally wary of their political statements and intentions. If those boys were like others of their time, then they early on adopted adult dress, sometimes wore small swords, had pet dogs and perhaps falcons, learned to shoot and to be assertive with the servants. They would also have spent a lot of time at their books and some on their knees as well.

Lord Archy got from his tutors a decent enough grounding in the three Rs and in Latin before he went on to Eton at an unknown date. He remarked in 1739 that he had been 'near a Year in the 6th or upper form' which tells us he finished the prescribed course. If he took all the forms at Eton, he might have gone up sometime around 1692 but, since boys progressed through the forms as they could, a good student like him, would have spent less than six years there.[41] He would have studied little but Latin, Greek and mathematics – through long division and perhaps Euclid through the seventh book. All that might have come with some classical historical background and certainly a lot of religion. He would have left Eton with a good knowledge of Latin literature, some sense of style, an appreciation of the rise and fall of nations, as exemplified by Greek and Roman history, and perhaps with some understanding of the values of a pagan, pre-Christian world. Some of the Latin he learned would have been modern and found in the *Colloquies* and *Adages* of Erasmus and perhaps works by Roger Ascham and others. His knowledge of the Greek world would have been similar but not as extensive. A tutor or governor probably went to Eton with him and might even have had him read some of the Scots Latinists such as Arthur Johnston, George Buchanan or the royal poets and their friends. That was not unusual in Scottish colleges of the time. In any case, he would have come to know the humanist heritage which educated Europeans imbibed and shared into the twentieth century. Lord Archy seems to have responded well to all that and may even have come to see himself as the little Roman Sir John de Medina painted (Plate 1).

The religion inculcated on Lord Archy by his tutors and at Eton would likely have been a perplexing thing. He would have been exposed to the version of Anglicanism which was taught at Eton in the 1690s – Latitudinarian and Low Church. It succeeded a much 'higher' form of church piety and doctrine. Knowing that, like reading an authorized version of the Bible and the royally issued Articles of Religion, would have impressed upon him the variation of faith with politics, a fact that his own Presbyterianism also made clear. If he was attended at Eton by a Presbyterian tutor, that message might have been amplified and applied to the situation of the Scots. They had a different state-established church whose ecclesiastical polity had been radically different in 1630, 1650, 1661 and 1690 and whose accepted theology was not upheld by all pious Scots many of whom disliked Presbyterian ecclesiology. Throughout Archy's life, the aim of many Scottish churchmen would be to free the Kirk from political interference. His aim would be to preserve that influence.

Lord Archy's education gave him a liking for the study of mathematics and the classics and a belief in the value of an education combining them. As late as 1738, the mature man of fifty-six, wrote to his nephew, James Stuart MacKenzie, then a student at Leiden, encouraging him to keep up his Latin and Greek, master mathematics and the sciences, and read a lot of history of every sort (see p. 274). Ilay wanted him to pay particular attention to experimental philosophy and useful knowledge. All this was urged on a boy sent to read law.[42] The letter was from a man who had liked and re-read many of the texts he was assigned as a schoolboy. It is also significant for mentioning subjects which Eton did not teach or taught badly – higher mathematics and natural philosophy. Eton was not good for those but an English education introduced Archy to many in the English political class with whom he would later deal.

Lord Archy left Eton c.1698 and probably entered Glasgow University at age sixteen in the autumn of 1698. By that time his brother had been a Colonel in his father's old regiment for four years. By then it had likely been decided that Archy would follow a political and legal career. Lord Archibald matriculated at Glasgow on 15 March 1699 in the class of Regent John Tran (?-1704).[43] Tran, probably a man in his sixties, had been a Glasgow Regent since 1669. His interests seem to have run to moral philosophy of an Aristotelian and biblically based sort, to Hebrew and oriental languages. He taught Hebrew before there was a proper professor of that subject. Tran had accommodated himself to the Episcopalian regime of the Caroline period but willingly conformed to Presbyterianism in 1690. Like all regents of the day, he taught most subjects to the boys who matriculated in his class.

Lord Archy could not have avoided doing some logic with Tran. That would have been late scholastic, Aristotelian logic. If it got a supplement, it was perhaps from the Port Royal logic book then becoming fashionable in Scotland. Tran also would have required the students to argue on their feet and to give rather formal performances both to the class and perhaps to the whole College. Lord Archibald could have come away from this course with an ability to recognize fallacies and to stand on his feet and argue with some facility. Tran's ethics prelections were said to have been derived as much from the Old Testament as from any other source.[44] They were thought good enough for him to be asked by the Visitation Commission in 1695 to prepare a textbook for all the Scottish universities on 'Ethicks, Oeconomics and Politicks.' He did this – only to be denounced by colleagues and the Visitors for having neglected '"the law of nature" and the principles of reason.... and [for trusting] entirely to quotations of Scripture, which is not at all to philosophize'.[45] What was wanted was a modern course more like that contained in Samuel Pufendorf's *On the Duty of Man and the Citizen* (1672).

The third portion of the philosophical part of the arts curriculum was natural philosophy. Tran was said to have dictated his lectures from old compends. Nevertheless, in 1699, he did mention Newton's physics in his lectures. Earlier his lectures had referred to experimental work by a number of seventeenth-century thinkers.[46] It is possible (but unlikely) that Tran was actually excited by this new material and conveyed some enthusiasm to his class and to Lord Archy. If he did, that interest would have been further heightened by attendance at the mathematics lessons given by George and Robert Sinclair, the Professors of Mathematics.[47]

George Sinclair had been a Glasgow Regent (1655-66) and again became one in 1690 before assuming the Professorship of Mathematics (1691-99). Sinclair, a strict Calvinist, wrote a notable work to prove empirically the existence of witches and spirits. It had much in common with similar books by Henry More and Joseph Glanvil. The difference was that Sinclair's father and uncle had been active in the

Scottish witch trials of the 1680s. His book was thus an apology for his family. He was also known in his time for experimental work on hydrostatics and for practical engineering feats including the invention of a diving bell. He may have taught mathematics in 1698 although he died in the following year. Lord Archy, if he did not study with him, would certainly have known of his achievements which were well publicized and significant although ridiculed by teachers at St Andrews.[48] Professor Robert Sinclair, his successor, was almost certainly his son.

The second professor Sinclair had an MD from Utrecht, (Lord Archy would later attend the law faculty there), had invented a lamp, and, like George Sinclair, had been a member of the small Scottish *virtuoso* community gathered around the Edinburgh physician, Sir Robert Sibbald, MD, and the Glasgow Principal, William Dunlop – one an Episcopalian asserter of the divine right monarchy, the other a Calvinist refugee in the 1680s. Robert Sinclair was a more modern man than his predecessor but one who, like him, knew the practical value of science well pursued. He is likely to have been the Sinclair who was rumored to be the replacement for David Gregorie as Professor of Mathematics at Edinburgh in 1690. That man had been tutor to Lord Lorn, then a boy of ten.[49] Lorn, already a colonel in the army, was taught principles of fortification and gunnery by someone. If that someone was Robert Sinclair, then Lord Archy probably took his course at Glasgow nine years later. Unfortunately, mathematics was not a required subject at Glasgow and we do not know if Lord Archy took whatever course or courses were offered by the Sinclairs. What is certain is that Archy developed an abiding interest in mathematics and its uses and that he continued to study it in both its pure and applied forms throughout his life.

From Ilay's avuncular letter to Stuart MacKenzie, it is more than likely that his Lordship read some history while at Glasgow. History was being encouraged and pursued at Glasgow. Principal Dunlop was a local historian of some note. He had interests in ecclesiastical history, which one of his son's taught at Edinburgh after 1715. His older son was once in line for the similar post at Glasgow. Lord Archy might have read some history with Tran who would normally have taught his students some Greek and possibly a bit of Greek history. Lord Archy might also have attended Thursday lectures by 'Blind Jameson'. William Jameson compensated for his blindness with a prodigious memory and lectured on both civil and ecclesiastical history at Glasgow from 1692 until c.1716. In 1699, he taught a civil history course which was probably notable for its exhibition of his ferocious Calvinism.[50] Jameson also had some interest in Scottish history and was also associated with Sibbald's and Dunlop's groups of the patriotic antiquaries.[51]

Lord Archibald enjoyed his time at Glasgow. His sentimental attachment to the College was real and is shown by a memory of him recorded by Robert Wodrow, an antiquary who was then a divinity student and University Librarian. In 1722 Wodrow sent volume one of his *Church History* to Lord Ilay and was clearly delighted by Ilay's opinion of it. Wodrow told a correspondent:

> Indeed, I could scarce think his Lordship would have minded any thing of me; yet it seems there are some secret remains of what we call school-fellowship, that have led him to a better opinion of my book than it deserves. He was then

a careful reader of the Roman authors, and hath since improved himself in all valuable parts of polite learning, to that pitch, that he is generally owned to be one of the best judges of books in Europe.[52]

Their shared 'school-fellowship' and a liking for the University may have included other common interests. By 1699, Wodrow was a proficient in natural history and other *virtuoso* topics about which Lord Archy in later life knew a great deal. Years later, one of Argyll's obituary writers also noted: 'Bred at Glasgow, he had a Strong Attachment to that university And by many instances of his Patronage and favour he promoted its interests during the whole of his life'.[53]

Going to a Scottish university like Glasgow gave Archy an introduction to subjects not taught at Eton. It also taught him about men whom he would later have to placate and lead. That was as valuable a time as the years he spent at Eton learning how to act, speak and think like an Englishman. Still, his classmates and the boys in the classes either side of his do not seem remarkable. Few, if any, of them figured in his later life.[54] This may be because he was probably older than most of them when he went up and moved in more refined social circles than was usual for undergraduates. Short as his time at Glasgow was, it would have shown him how different that college was from those in England and perhaps helped to make him the defender of Scottish institutions that he later proved to be. That did not preclude – perhaps it prompted – his thorough reform of the University in 1725-26.

By the autumn of 1700, Lord Archy, now eighteen, had surely moved on to Utrecht. In the 1690s, Utrecht was the most popular resort of Scots going to Holland because the city was cleaner and healthier than Leiden, had better law teachers, and was the most rigidly Calvinist and pious of the Dutch universities of the day.[55] Lord Archy did not matriculate which was not unusual. He studied law and seems to have stayed until 1701/2. At least part of that time, he is likely to have lived with a prominent Utrecht bookseller named Willem Van de Water to whom his mail was sent in early 1702.[56] Among Lord Archy's friends in Utrecht were Thomas Erskine of Pittodry, James Erskine of Grange and possibly Magnus Kennedy of Dunure. Archy was to be involved with those men and their relatives throughout his and their lives.[57] The four boys came from four different parts of Scotland – Stirlingshire, the Northeast, Ayrshire and Argyllshire – as did many of their classmates. In Utrecht too, he made many contacts with those whom he would later deal as a Scottish politician. And, he met a number of well-born Europeans.

The Dutch legal curriculum prescribed for Lord Archy was much the same sort of program that he recommended to his nephew nearly forty year later. It presumed or encouraged a broad humanistic education. By the end of the seventeenth century, in both the Netherlands and Scotland, that included topics like mathematics, medicine and the sciences.[58] Those subjects were seen as interesting in themselves and as useful to genteel improvers, who, in Scotland, had become important if not numerous by the 1680s. They grew in numbers and influence throughout the eighteenth century.[59] In the 1680s, the improvers included Sir Robert Sibbald and Archibald Pitcairne, both MDs, and lawyers like Sir George Mackenzie and James Dalrymple, 1st Viscount of Stair, and fashionable but lesser men like Alexander Cunningham of Block.[60] The examples set by such men, and their encouragement of the pursuit of science, helped to make the study of natural philosophy, medicine and mathematics popular with Scottish medical and law students who attended classes in Holland.[61]

Like many other boys, Lord Archy was somewhere tutored in French. While in Holland he learned a bit of Dutch and possibly some (or more of) other languages since it was later claimed that he was able to write a letter in six or seven languages.[62] As an adult, he had a reading knowledge of at least English, Latin, Greek, French, Italian, Spanish, and Dutch and a probable reading knowledge of some German and Portuguese. He may even have been able to read some Hebrew, a subject taught not only by John Tran but by Robert Sinclair.[63] Somewhere, Lord Archy acquired a good deal of science, medicine and mathematics. His interest in these subjects early in his career was substantial. Other lawyers, like the extra-mural Edinburgh law teacher John Spottiswoode, who had studied in Holland just a bit earlier, took such courses during the summers. Spottiswoode came home with a many books in chemistry.[64] Lord Archy had a good knowledge of those same subjects but it would have been very unusual for him to have acquired that without some special tuition. One guide to his academic efforts would have been Cunningham of Block.

Cunningham was a notable figure in legal and chess circles and an editor of classical works. He had the usual *virtuoso* interests and knew most of the first rate minds in London, Paris and Holland c.1700. He corresponded with Leibnitz, knew Pierre Bayle and was or had been friendly with Robert Boyle, John Locke, Martin Lister and other members of the Royal Society of London, which by c.1700 had enrolled about forty Scots. Cunningham may well have urged Archy and his brother to attend mathematics, medical or anatomical and science lectures while they were in Holland. Certainly, the 2nd Duke of Argyll, with whom Cunningham had more contacts, studied mathematics and had *virtuoso* interests which would have been picked up after his classical education and while he was advised by Cunningham in Holland. Later in life, Cunningham bought books for the brothers. Lord Archy also enjoyed playing chess with him.[65]

The law course taken by Scots normally included Roman law, natural jurisprudence and the laws of nature and of nations. There is no indication that Lord Archy did not take and enjoy such courses. He was certainly familiar with the great natural law theorists of the seventeenth century. Since Civil Law required some detailed knowledge of the history of Rome, he may well have studied Roman history as did Sir John Clerk of Penicuik who had attended Leiden about five years earlier.[66] Such courses were publicly offered or taken with a professor teaching a 'private' class for fees,[67] or taken extra-murally from a lecturer in the town who did not hold a university post. Archy might have had courses in Scots law with a teacher in some other university in Holland since those were sometimes taught. We know that he learned Scots law somewhere but probably not in Scotland or by himself. His time in Utrecht was the most likely time and place for him to have done so. His two year stay in Holland was about what future Scottish lawyers and judges got when they went abroad to study. He was better educated than most of the Scottish lawyers of his time and by the time he became a judge he probably knew as much law as many on the bench.

Somewhere along the way, Lord Archy also acquired the skills which polite gentlemen were expected to have: the ability to ride well, to fence, to dance and to behave in a polite and mannerly way. All that had certainly begun early with a variety of masters and probably continued while he was in Holland. By 1702, Lord Archy, aged twenty, had received a very good education, one which he well knew could not have been obtained in Scotland where there was as yet no university training in law or medicine. Later, he would help change that and work for the general improvement of the Scottish universities.

V. Seeing Classic Ground and Soldiering

For a complete gentleman, there were still things missing in his Lordship's education – notably, a grand tour. By 1702, he had surely seen a good deal of the Netherlands and possibly bits of Germany and France. If he made a grander tour, he is most likely to have gone from Holland through Germany to Italy sometime in c.1699-1701 returning through France.[68] The probability that he travelled 1699-1701 is heightened by the fact that his brother, with Cunningham of Block, made trips in those years. They are said to have been in Italy in 1699. Cunningham was with Lord Lorn in London, France and the Netherlands during 1700 and probably accompanied him to France in 1701. On 24 March 1701, Lord Lorn signed the visitors book at the University of Padua where several entries exist for an Alexander Cunningham, one of whom was 'of Block'.[69] Later in 1702, Lorn and Cunningham went to Rome but Cunningham was soon back in London and had returned to the Hague by 1703. By 1702, Lorn was in Germany where Archy probably joined him.

That Lord Archy visited Italy is suggested by his books. Many of them were devoted to Italian history, literature and architecture. He subscribed to Italian journals. If those tastes and interests were rooted in experience, then he made a trip to Italy sometime between 1699-1702. He probably went south with his brother and Cunningham.[70] Touring continued when Lord Archy went to Hanover and Germany in 1702. He stayed there into 1703.[71] That may be the time in which he first saw action as a soldier.

On their trips, the Campbell brothers would have attended not only to cultural novelties and sights. Travelling to and from Italy or Germany would have taken them through fortified cities and past old battlegrounds. For men like them, the fortifications and battle sites were interesting, particularly those which they might expect to see again under arms. Trips of that sort also helped those aspiring to a diplomatic career. Later (c.1711) Lord Archy, by then the Earl of Ilay, was considered for diplomatic posts.[72] He might already have seen those as a possibility. However that may be, the trips, particularly the one to Germany, would have been helpful to his family since it introduced to Europeans and the Hanoverian Electoral family the scions of one Scottish magnate family. That trip may also account for the presence of German books in Ilay's library. He probably cut short his time abroad when his father died on 25 September 1703, an event which changed Lord Archy's expectations in life. As the younger brother of the 2nd Duke of Argyll and the possible heir to one of the greatest titles in Britain, Lord Archy was unlikely ever to practice law which seems, in some sense, to have been his aim until about 1701. He 'dropt his intention of appearing at the Bar'.[73]

Sometime c.1701-03, he entered the army, in which his brother was about to become an important officer and a military hero. Lord Lorn had entered the army early and advanced from his father's Scottish regiment to ever better ones ending up as a Field Marshall and Colonel of the Scots Troop of the Horse Guards [the Blues]. A Scottish Privy Counsellor in 1701, 2nd Duke and a Knight of the Thistle in 1703, he wielded power and electoral influence which paved the way for his brother to follow both a military and political career. Lord Archy's military career was short but was not without significance.

Lord Archy followed his brother into the Army but in which regiment he was first commissioned is unclear.[74] By 1705, Captain Archibald Campbell had become Governor of strategically important Dumbarton Castle, one which he, like his predecessors, allowed to deteriorate.[75] He was made a colonel of a regiment of dragoons in 1705/6.[76] Archy, now Earl of Ilay, became 2nd Colonel of MacCartneys Regiment of Foot on 6 March 1708 and on 23 March 1709, Colonel of Charlemont's or Alnut's which became the 36th Foot.[77] He got that because he had been 'very usefull in the House of Lords in our disputes about the elections of the 16 peers from Scotland'.[78] He remained its Colonel until 23 October 1710. At that point, his political enemies may have had in mind to send him to America, either to the West Indies or Canada[79] because he had been less than useful over the Sacheverell Affair and was said to be disaffected to the Queen.[80] Ilay had been negotiating to buy Maitland's Regiment (later the 25th Foot), a Scottish regiment with a Scottish posting. That would have allowed him to escape being sent abroad.[81] He probably gave up his military career in 1712. The brothers were falling from favour so his prospects would have been bleak. By then, Army service had introduced him to many with whom he would politick, argue and associate in later years.

Little is really known about Ilay's military service. He is said to have made two or three campaigns under Marlborough in the Low Countries in 1701-5. The 1st Battalion of the 36th Foot was in Spain between 1705 and 1711 but Lord Archy was certainly not with it for much, if any, of that time.[82] He might have been in Spain for a short while after his brother was appointed Plenipotentiary to Spain in May 1711.

Two things about his military service are not without interest. In 1710 men of his regiment mutinied in England because they had not been paid.[83] That suggests Ilay was not minding the shop or was treating his regiment as a funding source and disregarding the needs of his men and the Army. He lacked cash and was not likely to have been with them. Secondly, in an obituary which obliquely refers to his period in the Army, we are told that he had 'a prodigious strength of body and surprising agility, which was so great that he would stand upright to a wall, and retiring a little backward, would at one spring, strike with his heels the mark to which his head reached'.[84] That is a very old junior officers' game in the British Army. The object is to bring one's foot to the mark but to then twist in the air and land on one's hands without spraining or breaking anything. One must be very fit to do this – and today out of the sight of senior officers who discourage this game.[85] Ilay did not lack strength or stamina. This was a man who at about this time was capable of riding over a hundred miles a day as he still could in the 1720s. Like his legal training, military service was of practical use to him in 1715 and in 1745. It enabled him to debate military affairs in the House of Lords more knowledgeably than those who had not served. By 1716, he had seen as much combat as many soldier-lords and could talk with some authority about military matters.

By 1705, Lord Archy was a well-educated man who understood a good deal about law, something about military affairs and enough about politics to begin to play it with gusto and cunning. Unlike his older brother, he did not expect to inherit the Argyll estates or to sit in the Scottish Parliament. We would not marry so well or lead and shine in the ways his brother did. He knew and accepted that he was less important than his brother John. Later in his life, he was often content to wait patiently for things to change and he was willing to take direction from others. There was a somewhat cautious and passive streak in his character which may have developed in these early years. He was not incapable of acting on his own but he did not chafe under restraints as did so many aristocratic politicians, especially his brother. He was able to wait for his moment and then act. Soldiering and politics helped this landless man to make his own way in the world. So too would investments. Sometime before 1705, he met John Law and by 1711, if not earlier, Ilay had begun to play the markets. Those speculations constituted the last phase of his education which had probably been completed by 1705-06 when he left office as Lord Treasurer of Scotland – a topic to which we will return.[86] He was now prepared to play whatever hands he was dealt. They were good hands and he played well.

Plate 2. Ilay as Earl holding his coronet, by William Aikman (c. 1723), Faculty of Advocates, Edinburgh, with permission of the Dean and Faculty .

Chapter 3

The Early Politician, 1703-1715

I. The Early Years and the Union

After their father's death, both Lord Archy and his brother, now the 2nd Duke, were caught up in the politics of turbulent times. It was in their interest to be so. They were ambitious and they had debts to pay. For men like themselves, next to marriage, office-holding was the quickest way to importance and riches. They, like all who aspired to offices, naturally sought to be with the ministers who could reward them. They changed alliances easily; opportunism was their game. The brothers were tied to a number of different ministries as they won and lost the favour of Queen Anne and then George I and the men who served them. At the beginning of their careers, the brothers played the game largely for spoils and worried little about principles until, perhaps, 1712/13. Ilay's politics were determined by his brother because by himself he was nothing since he lacked land or positions of influence. They also lived varied and interesting lives. George Lockhart, who saw a good deal of Lord Archy in his first years in England, tells us that he lived a busy social life mostly in London.

The brothers' first notable political success came in 1705 when the new Duke was made High Commissioner to the Scottish Parliament, effectively the head of a Scottish Ministry.[1] He had secured this office through the influence of the Duke of Marlborough and Sidney Godolphin.[2] With an eye to the past, the Duke of Argyll opened Parliament on the twentieth anniversary of the beheading of his grandfather. The memory of that event was never forgotten by him or Lord Archy.

Getting office was not the same as being able to use it to do something but his Ministry was expected to effect changes. Doing so would insure that they were paid off for doing the Queen's business. Doing the Queen's business meant insuring that the Crown was granted funds to meet its needs. Aiding the economy so that taxes could be passed and collected would help. Argyll was charged with the task of insuring that the Scots did not attempt to restore the Stuarts. That meant a wider settlement of outstanding political and economic issues with England.

To alleviate economic distress, Argyll and Lord Archy pushed a variety of measures designed to stimulate the economy. One concerned the fisheries – the Campbell brothers were always sensitive to the needs of the fishing industry because of the family's ports at Campbeltown and Inveraray.[3] Aid to the fisheries was helping themselves. A grander scheme to stimulate the economy by an inflation of the money supply was also supported by them.[4] It was partially worked out by John Law and had as its aim the general improvement of the Scottish economy through government action.[5] In one sense, it was another mercantilist scheme to promote trade. A central planning and credit institution was to regulate trade, increase the money supply, circulate money more rapidly and so promote the fisheries, agriculture and the linen and other manufactures.[6] The objectives of the policies were widely approved and some of the methods had been talked about in Scotland before Law made his proposals in 1704-05. New were, first, the conceptual innovations which allowed Law to see wealth as the men, materials and products of a nation, not its gold supply or trade balance and, secondly, his proposals for paper money and the degree of state control over the economy those entailed. Law also believed in freer trade, the multiplier effect and the need for better regulations which would take into account revenue needs, employment levels, the demand for money, its volume and the rate at which it circulated. His plan necessitated constant interventions in economic life which was seen as constantly changing.[7] It was hoped this scheme would engender internal developments as well as trade abroad. The scheme was defeated in Parliament but the ideas and aspirations remained with Scots and Lord Archy until the end of his life. A bill establishing a Council of Trade was passed but that did not address the grander objects of the plan. Lord Archy had been much involved with those plans since his brother had made him Lord Treasurer in 1705.[8] That gave him a seat in Parliament but the Treasury was in commission and Lord Archy was not the only one responsible for Treasury policy in this Ministry. He had ambitiously asked for a Scottish peerage; he was made Lord Treasurer.

Scotland's economic problems were more realistically dealt with in a Treaty of Union which, as the second Duke of Argyll later said, was the way to 'enrich one countrey and secure the other'.[9] A Commission to write the Treaty of Union was appointed in March 1706 after Argyll had left office but he had aided in its establishment. Initially it contained no Campbells. Argyll had lost the backing of Godolphin and the Whig Junto Lords in London. Queensberry, who replaced Argyll as High Commissioner, would give no places to men who had done him no favours.[10] Later Lord Archibald was added to the body along with the Earl of Loudoun and Campbell of Shawfield.[11]

While his brother rejoined the Army on the continent, Ilay stayed in Edinburgh looking after family interests. He was probably in London by March or April 1706 to participate in the negotiation of the Treaty of Union. His role in those negotiations is not known but it was likely not great since there are no accounts of what he said or did. He probably stayed until after the conclusion of the negotiations in late July 1706 and he certainly collected his expenses (£1,000) which had been voted by the Scottish Parliament before it permanently adjourned.[12] Being on the Commission allowed him later to speak in Parliament and in the Courts with some authority about the intentions of the negotiators and the meaning of the Treaty's clauses. He returned to Scotland for the opening of the Scottish Parliament on 3 October. There, he worked for the Treaty's passage in the last Parliament of Scotland.[13]

He attended the Scottish Parliament but again it is not clear what he did there. He played no conspicuous part in debates over the articles of Union but he may have worked behind the scenes.[14] Initially, he almost certainly worked to have popular protests against the Union ignored by the MPs but by the end of the session he had come to regard the right to protest as a 'privilege of the subject'[15] or at least said that.

He was willing that such protests should be heard in Parliament.[16] That probably attests to his working with protesters and for the Earl of Mar who came to take this view. At the end, he was important enough to be chosen as one of the Representative Peers to go to the British Parliament where he took his seat in October 1707. His brother sat in the Lords as Earl of Greenwich. Ilay now began a long career in British politics where he remained in his brother's shadow until c.1725.

Lord Archy's experience in government in 1705-06 completed his political education by exposing him to many aspects of economic affairs and banking. It schooled him in the mercantilist theory of his time and gave him a first opportunity to try to implement some innovations. Throughout his career, he pushed similar policies, and privately fostered the fisheries and supported the country's linen trade, potteries, glasshouses and manufactures. Some of those activities he later subsidized through a state agency, the Board of Trustees for Fisheries and Manufactures in Scotland (1726). Later still, he and his friends also aided the linen trade through the private development of the British Linen Company (1743-45) which became the British Linen Bank (1766). Some of Ilay's interests in banking looked back to this period since they resulted in and may have aimed at the expansion of the money supply. He was instrumental in founding the Royal Bank of Scotland (1727) whose first Governor he became. Finally, he owned a lot of pamphlets on economic matters printed around this time. Some dealt with coinage and money and the problems caused by the debased coins circulating in Scotland in the years prior to the Union.[17] Others reflected his interests in general economic problems.

The brothers' exercise of power in 1705-6 had been self-interested but it was effective and not without a few idealistic traces. Lord Archy undoubtedly believed that the Union with England was a good thing and, in general, he remained a supporter of the Union – but of a Union between theoretically equal nations and in which Scotland retained much of her old constitution, one guaranteed under the Treaty. That was a difficult position to maintain. The English encroached and Ilay remained a supporter of ministries which did so. Most Scots, for more than a generation, were unenthusiastic about the incorporating union into which many felt they had been forced by the mercenary interests of politicians like the Campbell brothers. The chicanery of his brother's time in office, to which he was party, made many always think him unreliable and double-tongued. His brother forced out of office men who did the same to him and his friends in 1706. Many remained opponents of the Campbells in Scottish politics for much of Archy's career. Still, Lord Archy must have left office in 1706 with a realization that one could accomplish positive ends, that the exercise of power was fun and that it made one richer.

The brothers were well rewarded for their brief exercise of power. The Duke was given an English peerage before the Union, which secured for him a seat in the House of Lords. He was promoted in the Army which enlarged his income, influence and ego. Lord Archibald was rewarded in 1705 with the Governorship of Dumbarton Castle which enriched him by about £200 a year and two years later that of Blackness.[18] His support for the Union, and his brother's insistence,[19] secured him a Scottish peerage (1706). He also became a member of the Scottish Privy Council in 1706. He now knew how politics was played and benefited from playing. Later his peerage allowed him to be elected to sit in the House of Lords of the British Parliament as a Scottish Representative Peer.[20] With the exception of about a year and a half (1713-1714), he was a Representative Peer from 1707 until his death in 1761. He also assiduously represented the family's interest in the Scottish peerage elections.

He had become the Earl of Ilay with the help of Lord Mar who desired to keep him happy and to see that the Campbells were placated. Lord Archibald had not made this a simple business. He originally asked to be created Earl of Dundee, a title which the Grahams thought of as family property. James Graham, 1st Duke of Montrose, begged Queensberry and Mar not to let Lord Archibald take that title. Having sufficiently annoyed Montrose and the ministers, whom his brother the Duke of Argyll threatened to desert, Lord Archy changed his mind and was content to be Earl of Ilay. Politicking by then may have impressed him as as good a way of advancing his fortune as a career in the Army. He was now as willing as the next man to annoy others or make deals with men who often had no more intention of keeping their word than did he. For many years honesty went little further than self-interest. Politics was a satisfying game and it paid.

II. Ilay's New and Larger Stage

After the Union of 1707, Scottish factions took on more stable and permanent form.[21] They had to organize more carefully to show the English that they were valuable and could provide votes in Parliament and manage Scotland for a London government. Better and more organization was needed to elect men and to control as many places and institutions in Scotland as was possible. Relatively stable groups tied to magnate interests and those of related families emerged. The Argathelians were such a group centred on the Campbells and their relatives by blood and marriage – the Marquis of Lothian, the Earls of Loudoun, Bute, Northesk, Hyndford, Morton, Deloraine, and Middleton, and Lords Lovat, Rae, and Rollo. More support came from a number of other Highland chieftains and from friends from the Army. Competing against them was a rag-tag lot of the remnants of the Scottish Court Party, the Jacobites and the Squadrone, another family interest group. Ilay managed the Argathelians. In England, the brothers tended to side with moderate Whigs and Tories who accepted the Revolution settlement but did not espouse High Anglican views. Under Anne, those Whigs were led by Godolophin and Marlborough, the Tories by Robert Harley, who resigned in 1708 but returned in 1710 to supplant Godolphin as Lord Treasurer. The brothers were not particular about their allies but they were hostile to those who would block their aspirations – High Anglicans, Bolingbroke, Whigs who had no intention of preserving Scottish institutions and their competitors in Scotland, especially Queensberry and the Squadrone interest.

After 1707, the Squadrone generally included the 1st Duke of Montrose, the Marquis of Tweeddale, the 1st Duke of Roxburghe, and the noblemen and gentlemen in their queues. The Squadrone men, often afforced by the Earls of Stair, Rothes, Marchmont and Hopetoun, had proven intractable in 1705 when Argyll was sent to Scotland as High Commissioner. That faction had refused to do all Argyll unreasonably expected of them. The 1st Duke of Montrose could also challenge the electoral interests of

Argathelians in Glasgow, Dunbartonshire, Renfrewshire, Ayrshire, Stirlingshire, and Perthshire. Old feuds, modern slights and some principles divided those men. The Squadrone sided with the Junto Whigs led by Somers, Halifax, Orford and Sutherland; the Argathelians sided with Godolphin and Marlborough.

The Campbell brothers were not too well disposed to other families which for various reason tended to cause them problems. They were fortunate that the Douglas Duke of Queensberry died in 1711 and had no active successor. The Duke of Douglas was confined for madness much of Ilay's life, as was his relative, the Marquis of Annandale. After 1712, the Douglas-Hamilton line suffered from a long minority and then from an inactive 6th Duke of Hamilton. The Duke of Gordon was a Catholic and a Jacobite. The Murray Dukes of Atholl were suspected of Jacobitism and needed friends. The Drummond Duke of Perth had been attainted and lived abroad but Ilay was friendly with others in that family as he was with some of the Murrays. Many who might have been independent players in the political world of the brothers were not.

After c.1713, Scottish politics again changed. The Squadrone men were more willing to assert Scottish independence and to protect the Kirk but were far less sympathetic to Highlanders. Problems with the Union grew more serious as it became apparent that Queen Anne would not live much longer. The Jacobite threat intensified. The Campbell brothers openly struggled for offices given by Whigs or Tories but they were not immune to solicitations by Jacobites. Their response was an old one. The Duke was more or less pure in his actions; Ilay, who had less to lose, dealt with agents of the Pretender.

As a Representative Peer, Ilay sat in what was both a legislative and judicial body. He initiated few if any measures but voted the party line and whipped others in the Commons to do so as well. He was seldom one who set policies although he changed some bearing on Scots and was among the articulate men who argued for the ministries which employed him. He usually spoke for the government at some point in long debates and did so with some skill. William Coxe, who wrote while some still remembered Ilay's speeches, said 'His speeches were replete with solid arguments and keen observations; his language plain and fluent, and his manner grave and solemn'. [22] Others agreed. His speeches, printed in the collections of House of Lords debates, tend to bear that out. They also show him often speaking at the end of a debate summing up the government's case – and, toward the end of his brother's career, sometimes answering him. Ilay was a skilled debater who could use procedure to gain his ends. He made little impact on debates on foreign affairs but seconded the policies of his brother and later of Sir Robert Walpole and the Duke of Newcastle. That distinguished him from others like Sunderland, Stanhope, Townshend, Roxburghe, Chesterfield, Newcastle, Fox and Pitt who were active in foreign affairs. Domestic affairs, particularly those of Scotland, were different.

He was also assiduous in attendance. By the end of his days, he had attended (by my count) at least 72% of the sessions of the House of Lords held while he was a member and participated in all aspects of its business except for the ceremonial occasions. He usually missed royal speeches, never went to Fast Day or other sermons and did not show up for opening and closing ceremonies. He probably avoided being chairman of committees but when he was in favour and in power, he was a member of the Lords' standing committees on customs and orders and on the privileges of peers. He was often chosen as a member of the committees to address the monarch or to reconcile the bills passed by the Commons and the Lords. He served on many committees where his legal training or his interests in technology were likely to have been helpful.[23] Ilay was almost always in the House when any matters affecting the recruiting of soldiers and sailors or Scottish legal business and legislation was before it.

From the beginning of his time in the House of Lords, his training as a Scots lawyer made him one of those who counted when cases involving Scots law were to be settled. His role in this was as great as any Scot during the time in which he sat and he was increasingly effective in adjudicating cases on appeal. Some have thought he would have served better in the House of Commons but his time in the Lords made the most of his considerable skills as a lawyer and as a politician.[24] In the Lords, he was often *the* sitting Scottish judge since for most of his career he held positions in both the Court of Sessions, the Justiciary Court and, until 1747, in his own regality courts.

Ilay's politicking after 1707 involved a great deal of routine work which must have come to seem like drudgery. It meant not only attending and speaking in the House of Lords but keeping up ties with present allies and looking after the patronage which showed the brothers had power and deserved to be supported by Scots. The latter was to be Ilay's life-long concern and is well described by Alexander Murdoch who writes of a later period what was already becoming Ilay's routine by 1708:

> ... Scottish offices [and] appointments had to be carefully shepherded through the bureaucracy by an interested party or [they] would be laid aside and lost. This task of calling at the offices at least once a week to check on the clerks and speak with the minister took up most of Ilay's time, even when he had become Duke of Argyll....It was a thankless task.... Nor was it always easy to coordinate Scottish business. 'Your Lordship has no conception what it is to settle business of this kind, betwixt a Secretary of State, and first Lord of the Treasury, whose hours, situations, and engagements, are so different and remote....' This mundane aspect of even the most successful Scottish minister's life contrasted strongly, with the viceregal status with which he was [later] credited in Scotland.... [25]

Murdoch went on to say of Ilay's later career, that, while he had responsibilities for managing Scotland, he never had ministerial offices and was reliant on his own connections, and 'personal influence' to carry him along. As an aspiring Scottish manager, and later an actual one, Ilay looked to others for protection. He needed to perform well all the time. There were many causes of frustration. It did not help that they were Scots. The Campbell brothers from the beginning of their careers were resented by many. Many of Ilay's social equals, who held places and were responsible for acting in a Ministry, found him problematic because he had power without official responsibilities. Others – gentlemen, clerics, professional men, burghs – knew others could represent them and sometimes sought their help. It is remarkable that the Earl kept up such grinding political activities until he died in 1761.

The Campbells initially supported any and all Court Parties likely to give them offices or to keep out of power the men who disliked them or who threatened their power in Scotland. The Duke was ambitious and grasping; Ilay was little better. Both were probably sincere in demanding for Scots what they thought the Treaty of Union had given them but their stance on religious issues was calculating and hypocritical. Indifference made for tolerant attitudes, Erastian policies, and a liking for practical settlements.

Political negotiations brought Ilay into contact with a wide variety of men in official London. The Earl knew most of the people about the King's court and, later, that of the Prince of Wales. He needed to know everyone with power from the Archbishops to clerks at the Admiralty and the King's Works. Over the long run, the Squadrone men and those around Stanhope and Sutherland and later Bedford, Chesterfield and Cumberland were about the only ones with whom Ilay did not work well. Both brothers worked easily with Moderate Presbyterians, such as the Reverend William Carstares, Principal of Edinburgh University, and with later men like him. The Earl dealt amicably with members of London's Dissenting community and Oxford professors. We know little about those meetings. They are mentioned in letters or as bits of gossip but they widened Ilay's circle of acquaintance and introduced him to men of interest. They were certainly of more real interest to him than many of his encounters with courtiers.

The political world in which the Campbell brothers moved was more or less co-extensive with their social world which included not only the great but their political and cultural/intellectual hangers-on. One of the families with whom we know Ilay drank tea was that of Brigadier Theophilus Ogelthorpe (1650-1702). The Earl was a visitor to the Ogelthorpes from about 1706 until at least the late 1720s. There he was probably not looking for a wife, although the Oglethorpe daughters, Fanny and Anne, were bright and Anne was said to be beautiful. They were not wealthy and the family had Jacobite sympathies which were too obvious. However, Mrs. Oglethorpe was friendly with Jonathan Swift and other Tory wits, some of whom Ilay would have met in her drawing room. Among them was Alexander Pope whom the Earl met c.1712. They would have dealings into the late 1730s when Pope broke with him over politics. With the 2nd Duke of Argyll, a far more literary man than Ilay, Pope kept up until the end of the Duke's life. Ilay moved less easily in such circles but he had an entrée.

Ilay was an eligible bachelor with an eye for the ladies but on 19 January 1713 he married for money not love. His bride was Anne, the sixteen-year-old daughter of Major Walter Whitfield, MP for Romney, the recently deceased Paymaster of Marines. Anne and her mother were thought to be worth £30,000. His marriage may have started off well – there was a large withdrawal from his bank account (£108.10,0) on the day of his marriage which suggests a big party. Later in the month there was a payment for a new silver tea service and in April his Lordship purchased some jewellery. Later that year he bought quite a lot of Scots linen and laid out £361.4.2 in plate.[26] The couple lived at 24 Great Marlborough Street which Ilay had leased in 1711 but they probably had no country house.[27]

The marriage did not succeed. Married at thirty-one, Ilay was saddled with a teenage girl half his age. His attitude toward her and his marriage is perhaps shown in a comment which he made about his brother's marriage in 1717. When Fanny Ogelthorpe suggested that the woman Argyll had married would be a risk to their security, '[Ilay] laughed and said the woman was a good plaything but in affairs of consequence they [he and Argyll] never did anything but together, and what one thought the other did also'. Argyll's wife would be no risk.[28] If he regarded his own wife as but a 'plaything', it is no wonder that the marriage was unhappy. There is no record of his young wife accompanying him to social events. It also turned out that the Treasury had claims on her inheritance. Eventually, the Whitfield estate was reduced by at least £4,000 when her mother was forced to pay money to the government.[29] He had married a small fortune which turned out not to be worth what he had bargained for. He was reluctant to part with it if not with her. He needed her money. Speculations, like politics and marriage, now offered a way to improve his fortune.

Ilay and Argyll had dealt with John Law in 1705 and they continued to be in touch. When Law tried to obtain a pardon and come home in 1712/13, the brothers and the Marquis of Annandale promised to intercede with the Queen for his pardon.[30] Law got no pardon but Ilay was fronting for Law as an investor before 1713. Ilay's friend, John Drummond, thought Ilay was investing Law's money under his own name but 'under [Law's] direction'.[31] Whatever the arrangement, there can be no doubt about the significance of their activities for the Earl.

In 1713, Ilay paid to London or Dutch bankers on his own or Law's behalf, £3,321. Another set of payments shows them spending between 28 July 1712 and 8 July 1713 an additional £5,417.1.8. What Ilay was buying for Law is not always clear but the friends were purchasing the new South Sea stock and perhaps Bank of England stock. In the same period, Ilay received £4,815 from sales and seems to have had, in addition to that, £4,420 held in stocks [East India Co., £500; South Sea Co., £1,389; East India Co., £2,216;, African Co., £115] and bonds [East India Co. £200]. He received £3,000 from one James Colebrook which may be for the sale of other assets. Finally, he collected £253 from dividends and interest. If that was 3% of what he or they held, then the capital amounted to about £8,433. Some of that money was Law's but how much is unclear.

In the same months, Ilay was probably buying for himself shares in the African Co. [£400], East India Co. bonds [£206] and he already held East India Co. stock [£500] and South Sea stock [£300]. By 30 September 1713, Ilay's holdings came at least to £1,400 with undisclosed amounts of Bank of England stock. What he had purchased in the period before January 1713 is not contained in the records. For a landless man dependent on office-holding for his income, he had done well with his own and his wife's money. He had clearly learned something about speculation and markets in Britain, the Netherlands and France where Law was then living as a gambler and banker. Like his political work, his finances must have taken up some time. Both were risky.[32]

Most of the Earl's more casual acquaintances were English but the financial men were often Jewish, something on which he never seems to have commented.[33] Ilay knew a lot of people not in the circles of Tory wits and financiers but the gardeners, botanists and men of science had not yet appeared. He impressed many as reserved, cautious and not to be trusted. His politics did not preclude socializing but it made it difficult to develop intimacy with men whom he might sell out in a month – or they him. Some, particularly Scots, already knew him as a bit of a bully whose political methods included intimidation and whose practice of politics countenanced revenge for injuries. Still, his most cordial relations seem to have been with Scots. He got on best with Highlanders being especially fond of Simon Fraser of Lovat. Ilay would be present at Lovat's treason trial in 1746 and voted to behead him.

III. Playing the Game in London and Scotland

The Earl lived mostly in London during the period 1708-1715 where what he did politically depended on his brother. The brothers quickly became active politicians. The Duke was made a Privy Councillor partly to balance Squadrone influence.[34] He tried to use his influence in 1707 to secure a better regiment for his brother but in the end failed.[35] The Earl, still keeping open the option of a military career, had to be satisfied with a promise of a future place in a Guards regiment. In the meantime, he kept busy with family politics in Scotland. In the spring of 1708, Argyll was able to name the Collector of Customs at Ayr and so secured the electoral district. Ilay managed this group of burghs. The Earl tried to set up David Campbell 'for Doeing publick business' and must have succeeded since Campbell figures thereafter in various financial transactions. A month later, Lord Loudoun, a cousin with estates in Ayrshire, was made Lord Register.[36] Arranging such things was usually left to Ilay.

Argyll's promotion to Major General and the gift of a good Guards regiment, the Blues, helped the Ministry buy his continued loyalty and support for its policies in Scotland. So, too, did Ilay's appointment in 1708 to his brother's former place on the Court of Session as an Extraordinary Lord. That paid him nothing but gave him a vote on the settlement of cases and allowed him to express opinions. Judges were political and quasi-legislative figures in Scotland, so the appointment was not an empty honour. It also allowed him to keep an eye on suits interesting to his and other families in their connexion and to their enemies. As a judge, he could watch civil proceedings against Jacobites among whom the brothers had friends and relatives. In a judicial system neither impartial nor immune to political influences, this was an important place. He held it for the rest of his life and sometimes sat with the Court.

In 1708, the brothers first opposed the abolition of the Scottish Privy Council[37] but in the end they sided with the Ministry and voted for it. It was then controlled by Queensberry, with whom they had earlier worked and then fought. It could be used by Queensberry to organize the 1708 elections. The Squadrone too believed that this body would be used by Scottish Tories, Jacobites and Argathelians to rig those elections. The Squadrone men voted for abolition.[38] Abolition made the 1708 elections less predictable but it helped neither the Squadrone nor the Argathelians. Supporting abolition curried favour with the Ministry but, in Scotland, abolition proved an unpopular move and one which in the long run deprived Scotland of an executive agency. Getting rid of the Council, the Kingdom's executive body, left the way clear for a Crown manager such as Ilay later became.

The election of 1708 was an important one for Scots because of the discontents produced by the Union and its aftermath. One cause of discontent was the earlier rumoured buying of the votes of some peers and Scottish MPs prior to the signing of the Treaty of Union. Others worried about the economy. The Union had not produced immediate prosperity but a deeper depression and more discontent. Those contributed to Jacobite unrest and to a threatened rebellion in that year, a threat which died because of poor weather and the lack of both Scottish and French support.[39] It was hoped that the election would sort things out but it did not.

Ilay was in Scotland in the spring of 1708 for the peerage election in June and for the elections for the House of Commons which occurred in May and June. He may well have been there politicking much earlier. The peerage election showed that if Ilay was not truly popular, he could manage an election. The peers who elected to the House of Lords on 17 June not only returned Lord Ilay as one of the sixteen Scottish Representative Peers but gave him 53 votes, six less than were given to the Earl of Rosebery whose 59 was the largest total for any peer.[40] Rosebery was personally popular; Ilay was needed.

Ilay was also active in canvassing for MPs both for his faction and for the government. By the end of the election, he had learned how to manage elections and win. The elections were also more corrupt than usual because of the creation of many new voters through the manipulation of tenures and proceedings in the head courts.[41] In the House of Commons, the results were not overly favourable to the Tories but suited Godolphin and the Whigs. The Court interest, led by Queensberry, returned eighteen MPs while the Argathelian and Squadrone factions elected three to five each.[42] Many of the rest owed their seats to local noblemen and town councils of varying independence.

After the election, Queensberry, Mar, and Seafield remained the leading Scottish noblemen. As Secretary of State for Scotland, Queensberry assumed some of the functions of the Privy Council and ended up handling most Scottish patronage until Harley tried to handle it through the Treasury from 1710-1713. Ilay soon began to lust for the Secretaryship and saw Mar as his rival, but it was Mar, not Ilay, who gained power and who in 1713 was made Secretary. Ilay got some patronage but he was not actively interfering in university appointments in those years which probably means he was excluded from handling minor patronage which he would later almost monopolize. In the Parliamentary session of 1708-09, the Campbell brothers did nothing either in the House of Commons or Lords to help Scots become important as a swing group as some after the Union hoped they might be. Neither brother, then, seemed much bothered by the exclusion from the House of Commons of the eldest sons of Scots peers which was voted late in the year.[43] They were willing to be bought but, in the end, they found they had joined an enterprise which was not favourable to Scots and their establishments. The Union Treaty had not put those beyond English meddling.

Before his brother fell out with the Duke of Marlborough in the autumn of 1709, Ilay had been promised a regiment.[44] Argyll, with another promotion, now began to think that he might replace Marlborough as the principal soldier of the United Kingdom, an ambition which put him at odds with the Earl of Stair. The nation was weary of war and some troops even more so. Three regiments mutinied because they were unpaid including Ilay's regiment in Yorkshire in June 1710.[45] But, Marlborough was not replaced and Squadrone men were favored for positions. Argyll was angry and was listening to Robert Harley's plans to oust the Ministry. Things were in flux as the 1710 general election approached. Into that stew were now thrown a number of religious issues on which the brothers would follow policies which showed how secular in outlook they were.

In 1709, there had been an incursion on the rights of the Established Church of Scotland by the Rev. James Greenshields, a well-born Episcopalian minister in Edinburgh. Greenshields refused to stop illegally preaching and administering the sacraments when he was asked to do so by the magistrates. He was, in effect, demanding toleration for his dissenting congregation. The Kirk was not prepared to allow this. For some ministers, the issue was the status of their ecclesiastical monopoly, which they saw as guaranteed by the Act of Union. To that extent, it was a civil matter. To allow Greenshields to continue was to violate the provisions of the Treaty of Union. It would set a bad precedent and thus had implications which went beyond religion. Others thought only the Established Church could insure that religious discipline and good morals were maintained in the country. God punished the immoral and ungodly. The Presbyterian church courts were part of His process for making men godly or at least inoffensive to those who were. For such men, this was a religious and moral concern. For yet more, it was the opening of yet another attack by Episcopalians on the Kirk, which too often in the past had been subjected to attacks by Episcopalian Scots and Englishmen. That was made even more plausible because of the oaths which were mandated to be sworn by Scottish clerics, oaths against which strict Presbyterians protested mightily because it was subjecting the Kirk to the control of Caesar. That seemed even clearer when, on 19 April 1709, the House of Lords decided that it could receive appeals from any Scottish court.[46] From the English side, it seemed obvious that if toleration was given to Dissenters in England, then a similar measure of toleration should be extended to Episcopalians of all sorts in Scotland. This was an issue which inflamed passions on both sides of the Tweed. It also produced political dangers, since it had to be argued out and settled while England was upset by another religious cause, the Sacheverell affair.

The High Church/Jacobite preaching of Henry Sacheverell in the winter of 1709-1710 had created scandal and controversy. When he was impeached, the Campbell brothers were being courted by Robert Harley who hoped to wean them from their friendship with Godolphin and his ministerial friends. The Ministry then may have tried to bring Ilay into office.[47] That did not work but in February he did find himself on the committee to make a representation to the Queen.[48]

When Sacheverell was impeached, his trial raised legal issues. Ilay had been appointed to a committee to consider the impeachment on 15 December 1709. One issue which probably remained with Ilay was the question of whether or not a man could be tried on the import of his words generally or if 'expressly specified words' alone were at issue. He voted with the Whigs not to consider only the specific words used by the divine but later in his career he insisted that indictments had to be specific. The impeachment resulted in riots. On 28 February 1710, Ilay sat on a committee which considered the riots and disturbances.[49] Argyll and Ilay made somewhat anti-clerical speeches against Sacheverell but also made clear their intention neither to vote to acquit him completely nor to punish him severely.[50] To punish him harshly would have made him a martyr and would have been to 'promote a high Tory scheme'.[51] Not to punish him at all would have done them no good with Presbyterians whose interests they claimed to uphold.[52]

Ilay spoke against Sacheverell at least twice in mid-March.[53] In the end, Argyll or Ilay proposed as punishment a short suspension from preaching and the burning of Sacheverell's sermons by the common hangman.[54] When he was sentenced on 21 March 1710, that was Sacheverell's punishment. He was not imprisoned as Godolphin and the Whigs had wanted. Godolphin was mortified that the brothers had voted with Harley. Argyll refused to accept the thanks of Sacheverell telling him that his vote 'was not at all for his sake' but for his and his brother's. The cleric's public triumph after the riots and his sentence showed the Tories would win the next election.[55] The brothers' moderation was politic in London but did not make them look good to many in Scotland.

By then, Godolophin's Ministry was struggling to keep together an alliance at home among its supporters and one abroad with wartime allies. The war had gone on too long. The Ministry was losing power. Marlborough, their military commander, was on his way out. Times were hard. The coming man was Robert Harley who had put together a group of moderate Tories and Whigs who favoured peace. The prudent thing for men on the make was to support the coming men. The brothers separated from Godolphin and Marlborough and by the end of March they were siding with the moderate Tories. Argyll and Ilay had been attracted to Harley just as the Sacheverell Case was about to force many Tories into openly extreme positions. The Campbell's shift in alliances seemed peculiar to their Presbyterian supporters but, by April, Ilay was the 'most inveterate of the whole clubb against' Godolphin and Marlborough.[56] He also had to defend the conduct of those who had let off a scandalous High Church Jacobite. For their efforts, the brothers expected to be well paid.[57]

By July 1710, the brothers were firmly in the Tory camp and working to support Harley and his friends in the coming parliamentary elections to be held in October and November 1710. Those elections put the Whigs out of power. Ilay had a 'scheme' of some sort which he wished implemented in Scotland where he spent part of the summer.[58] It probably involved his being made Secretary of State for Scotland.[59] For a 'modest' man, Ilay had not scrupled to ask for a lot but many found him able. Lord Orrery could write to Harley, 'I believe few people know the situation of affairs [in Scotland] better than he'.

I am confident you may absolutely depend upon him [Ilay] without reserve[,] that you cannot find any person more proper than he to consult upon all occasions relating to that kingdom. I could heartily wish he were well settled in some good civil post there. I know he would be pleased to be Register of Scotland if he could have the place for life, or to be Justice General in the room of Lord Cromartie, to bring about what he has formed as a scheme,[60] though I believe the first would be most acceptable to him. I am afraid he is so modest as not to have mentioned anything of this kind to you, but I beg you would take some opportunity of entering upon the subject with him. The merit of the two brothers, especially upon this occasion, entitles them to anything they can ask, and the great respect and value they have for you I'm confident will oblige you to assist them to the utmost in their demands, which I will take upon me to say will be very reasonable considering the service they have already done and their resolution as well as ability to do a great deal more.[61]

By that time, Ilay was in Scotland helping Mar and his brother manage the elections of peers and MPs.[62]

He left London on 20 July.[63] He is known to have been active in Glasgow, Aberdeen and St Andrews and would have been concerned with the seats which fell within the Campbell's own sphere of influence which covered about 3,500 square miles in the west of the country.[64] Ilay also visited men in the North going through Fife and St Andrews and Aberdeen on his way up or back. The Earl was picking candidates who were not beholden to the Squadrone. He and Mar were arranging offices for their candidates and voters – bribes for their interest. One beneficiary was Mar's brother, James Erskine, whom Ilay agreed should be made Lord Justice Clerk, the usual head of the Justiciary Court, with the title of Lord Grange.[65] Tensions were such that Ilay was corresponding with Londoners using a cypher.[66] He expected his mails to be read many times thereafter; indeed, well into the 1750s.

The elections occurred in a year when many Scots were no happier with their lot than they had been in 1708. The Union was not accepted by many; it still had not fulfilled its promises. The Treaty had seemed to guarantee to the Scots the maintenance of their legal system which, with respect to treason, was far more lenient than that of the English. The English had extended to Scotland the English law of treason (1709). That seemed to most Scots a direct violation of the Treaty and one which threatened many Jacobites to whom other Scots were related. There were clear threats to the Kirk. Both brothers had been active in lining up votes for the Tories but the management of the elections was not good. Ilay and Mar fell out over who was to do what and how much power each was to have.[67] No ministerial list of Representative Peers could be agreed.[68] Both Ilay and Mar wanted to be Secretary of State for Scotland. Mar retained influence in 1710[69] but Harley gave Ilay more of the management of Scottish affairs than he had hitherto enjoyed.[70] Before the fall elections, the brothers Campbell were bitterly campaigning against opponents in London as well as Scotland. The Duke of Argyll sent letters to various coffee houses 'threatening the utmost revenge' should the Duke of Hamilton be made Governor of Edinburgh Castle.[71] The elections gave the Campbell brothers five seats in the Commons, more than any other magnate and equal in number to those controlled by the Squadrone.[72] It was only two less than the Old Court party which was about to disappear with the death of Queensberry in 1711. The Campbells had had a qualified success but the brothers now appeared as front men for a Tory government which was not sympathetic to the Kirk which the brothers were committed to defend.

After the 1710 elections, the Tories wanted loyalty from Scottish MPs and peers but they were unwilling to treat them as equals under the Treaty of Union. The rewards of loyalty were not as great as had been hoped.[73] At the end of 1710, Argyll was still not 'Generalissimo'; Ilay still lusted for the offices of Secretary of State or Lord Register.[74]

He had only been made Lord Justice General, a life appointment then paying about £2,000. His friend John Drummond thought he might be sent as minister to Hanover but noted 'his Lordship may 'hardly think it honourable enough for him and advantageous it can never be without a very great allowance'.[75] Ilay was made a member of the Privy Council in 1711. Their friends did less well. Scottish interests could be and would be disregarded by a Parliament composed mainly of Anglicans fearful and distrustful of Presbyterians and Scots of doubtful loyalty. Offices for Scots were not numerous and there was hurtful economic legislation. Ilay concluded that allying oneself too closely to any English faction was a recipe for disaster since wheels are round and will turn. Over the next two years controversies about religious and economic issues brought him to the point where he was willing to dissolve the Union.

IV. Religion

Greenshields' case was still pending. In December 1709, Ilay canvassed the opinion of Scots in London.[76] Then, on 8 December 1709, he wrote the Reverend William Carstares, Principal of Edinburgh University and a leader in the Kirk, asking for any information which he thought would be useful in arguing the Kirk's case against Greenshields in Parliament: 'I cannot tell you of how great use it is in any public assembly to be perfect in matters of fact, and what advantage it gives one over ignorant complaints'.[77] He always wanted to have his facts right. It was debated in the Lords in February 1710 when the Tory line was that it was a civil matter. That seems to have been the genuine opinion of Ilay and Argyll. They also thought the Kirk should not oppose a limited toleration.[78] As the affair ground through the courts, Ilay assured Scots clerics

> that my Brother and I shall carie along the same inclination & Zeal for the support of [the Kirk] through any Change of Administration that may possibly happen, as our predecessors did before us or as we hope we have hither to done. I am of a temper that makes me satisfied within my self when I think I have acted right without being pleased with the vanity of telling it, or justifying myself against misrepresentations.[79]

Later, he told Carstares that toleration was in everyone's interest 'because to speak plainly, we know very well, and I am sure our forefathers felt it, the mercy of our enemies'.[80] According to George Lockhart, Principal Carstares's own position was expressed by that minister and some of his colleagues on a trip to London where he met with Ilay and some of the Tory ministers. Carstares was willing to accept the same toleration for Episcopalians in Scotland as the English gave Dissenters but he wanted everyone in the country to be subjected to the moral governance of the courts of the Established Church of Scotland. Otherwise, malefactors could claim to be Episcopalians and escape judgment. Carstares lost that fight; no one was to be compelled to submit to the courts of the Kirk. Perhaps as a sop, Ilay was willing to see the Abjuration Oath modified to become more acceptable to Presbyterians but not to Episcopalians.[81] Greenshields won his case in the House of Lords in 1711 but not before Argyll had offered him '200 l and Irish preferment for his dropping it'.[82] The outcome of the case distressed many of the 'unco guid'. Lockhart reported that the Duke of Argyll, and probably Ilay too, was very indifferent about Church government, but he and his family had been

> allwayes in good terms with the Presbyterian party, and they were useful to him, and if he did not stand by them on this occasion wher they thought ther honour as well as interest concerned theyd think he had deserted them and their cause from henceforwards would no longer be advised and directed by him, and therefore he must look to his own interest by opposing Mr. Greenshields. [83]

Another contentious cause surfaced in 1711 involving a proposed change in the 'Act concerning vacant stipends' which required patrons to use the emoluments of vacant livings for pious uses or lose the right to present to livings. Scottish Episcopalians did not want to appoint Presbyterians to the livings in their gift and were content to leave churches vacant and pocket the money.[84] On this issue, Ilay was with the Scottish Established Church. Patrons should do what the law specified.[85] The brothers also opposed the Occasional Conformity Act of 1711. Toleration was again at issue in the Bill for the Security for the Church of England which passed in late December 1711. That Bill was deeply resented by English Dissenters who saw their political power curtailed by it. They had to conform to the Anglican Church by 25 March 1712 or quit all places of public trust and profit. That had implications for English local governments, some of which they controlled, and for the elections of MPs. Scots saw this Act as a sign of what English Tories would do to them and their Kirk if they could. The bill was passed with no Scottish votes. Tories, recognizing that the Whigs and Scots could have defeated them on this issue, were later led to create a dozen Tory peers which showed Scots that they would not to be allowed to hold a balance of power between the English parties.[86] That action hurt politicians like the brothers Campbell who saw their potential value as power-brokers diminished.

In Scotland too, there were contentious religious issues to be decided. A 1712 bill restored patronage rights to heritors. The Patronage Act destroyed the right created in 1690 of congregations to choose their ministers. The right to do so was now vested in the former patrons – the greater landlords, corporations and the Crown. It would be exercised by congregations only under strict conditions. That increased the influence of the landed aristocracy and of those acting for the Crown. It also favoured Episcopalians who in Scotland were mostly Tories or Jacobites. They were now free to pick men they liked. Jacobite Episcopalians could now appoint so-called Presbyterian ministers while the Crown livings (about a third of the churches) might go to men whose appointments had been passed by politicians like Bolingbroke who despised Presbyterianism. The Tories who restored patronage were quite capable of disregarding the wishes of the Scottish majority to further ends which could only be described as English. The upshot was that some new appointees took the oaths and conformed; others did not but it took years to get rid of them. Privately, Ilay probably liked this situation since he later vigorously defended the Patronage Act which was useful to him as a patronage manager. Publicly, he and his brother supported the position of the Kirk.[87] When Argyll came back to England from Spain by May 1712, he had the Patronage Act amended to insure that appointees were at least nominally Presbyterian ministers. In forcing this concession, he helped the Kirk but also warned the English that he was unhappy with this bill and with other things. The Patronage Act passed by large majorities but was widely seen in Scotland as a violation of the Treaty of Union which had seemed to guarantee the status of the Kirk as it had been in 1707.[88] Argyll's and Ilay's London Tory allies were not now giving them enough.

The Scottish Tories and Jacobites led by Lockhart of Carnwath then moved a bill in the House of Commons for the toleration of Episcopalians in Scotland. One of the features of this bill was a new oath to be taken by all. Ilay argued that the oaths should be stated in such a way that they would be obnoxious to the Episcopalian party and to their friends in London in the hope that the whole Act could then be defeated.[89] The Earl was willing to compromise beliefs held dear by members of the evangelical wing of the Kirk with which his family had long been associated. However, he had mixed feelings about the Act of Toleration passed by Parliament in March 1712. That established toleration in Scotland by a statute which again showed that English Tories were willing to force their views on the Scots without regard to the seeming protections of the Treaty of Union. Ilay disliked English coercion but he wrote to Carstares that he and his brother were siding with the Tories and not the Whigs. He and Argyll argued for the bill which expressed their personal preferences. As two historians have put it, 'As a result of a further change in the bill, prompted by Ilay... the Episcopalian desire to be exempted from the censure of the Kirk was extended "so that no Magistrate should putt in Execution any Ecclesiastical censure of the Kirk against any person either of the Episcopal or Presbyterian Communion"'.[90] If one denied being of either persuasion, the Kirk might censure you but no civil penalty would follow.

In October, Ilay presented to Queen Anne an Address from the Synod of Glasgow which said be 'assured that such who scruple to take the [Abjuration Oath] are Her Majesty's good subjects who will not fail to confirm all under their charge in loyalty and duty to her, and in peace and concord among themselves for the real quiet of the Goverenment'.[91] At the urging of Harley, now Lord Oxford and the Lord Treasurer, he sent more letters to Scots clerics asking that they remain calm like those in Glasgow, that most orthodox of towns.[92] At the same time, he said that he and his brother were 'under the last concern at those unhappy scruples some have about oaths'. Those who scrupled to take them were imperilling the Kirk and the Succession.[93] He was asking a lot of Scots who discovered, as had he, that they were at the mercy of the English in ways they had not thought they would be.

The Treaty of Union had been made between ostensibly equal partners. Englishmen in Parliament now claimed a sovereignty that knew no limits.[94] Parliament would legislate for Scots on matters the latter did not believe it should touch. The House of Lords, as a court, now claimed an ultimate and deciding voice about Scottish affairs which a treaty with a now non-existent state could not protect. As if to make this even clearer, Alexander Scrimgeour, a layman and reputed Episcopalian Jacobite, was appointed to the Regius Professorship of Divinity at St Andrews University in April

1713. Scrimgeour had been a St. Salvator's Regent since 1691 and had the backing of the Provost of that College but his appointment came from Mar and Bolingbroke who cared little about the divinity Scrymgeour was to teach. His appointment was bitterly opposed in Scotland and created an irritant which lasted in the University, the Presbytery of St Andrews, and the Synod of Fife until the early 1730s when the professor finally died. Scrymgeour was prosecuted before the Presbytery and Synod of Fife and was held by some in 1715 to have been 'disloyal'.[95] Tory policy with respect to the Kirk had done nothing to make the country more governable or the Campbells more popular. Scotland now seemed to some a subject province.

How much that was the case was made clear again in 1714 with the passage of the Schism Act. With the Schism Act, Tories attacked dissenting schools and their masters who taught doctrines not in accord with those preached in the Established Church. English Dissenters were outraged and Scots saw this as an augury of what the English would like to do to them. The Campbell brothers, now in opposition, opposed this too. Argyll said that severity in unsettled times is no remedy for what is not an evil. Dissenters who were divided and represented no threats to the state were needed and should not be set upon.[96] For many Scots, none of the religious issues had been settled by 1715. Principal John Stirling of Glasgow was still complaining about abjuration oaths, toleration, patronage, the inequalities of treatment of Dissenters in England and Scotland and even of the 'Christmas vacance' in 1715.[97] Ilay agreed with much of that and resented the slighting of Scots, and even their country.

V. Other Issues in Play

While the religious crises played out in Scotland, the brothers struggled to preserve their own positions in a Ministry which was increasingly unpopular with Scots for other reasons. Scottish workers had been hurt by the 1711 change in the linen laws. That, and the failure of the Union to stimulate the economy, had soured many in the towns. The Convention of Royal Burghs wrote to Ilay on 9 December 1712 asking for protections for Scottish trade in the treaty then being negotiated with France. Nothing came of that.[98] At the other end of the social scale, Scottish peers with British titles granted after the Union were found unqualified to sit in the House of Lords by right of their new titles. That decision affected Queensberry and the Duke of Hamilton and Brandon[99] with whom the brothers were now on good terms. Ilay, in what was described as 'a very moving speech', argued that this was a restriction on the Queen's power, one which breached the terms of the Treaty of Union. The Queen was present at the debate and listened to him for so long that she caught a chill.[100] Ilay, Mar and Hamilton approached the Queen about the matter and were graciously received but nothing changed.[101] For Ilay and his friends, that decision seemed to close doors to social promotion for them and their friends. They dissented from the Lord's decision and justified their dissent in a statement perhaps drafted by Ilay since it used his words and arguments. It claimed the judgment violated the Treaty of Union, invaded the Crown's prerogative powers, and that by it 'the Peers of Scotland are reduced to a worse Condition in some respects than the meanest, or most criminal of Subjects'. The grounds for that was the fact that due process had not been observed. Hamilton had been denied a hearing in other courts – a right the meanest subject could claim. Their dissent was joined by a number of Tory peers.[102]

Such discontent accorded with more personal concerns. Argyll had hoped to control Scottish politics and patronage but by late 1710 he and Ilay found their ways blocked. Argyll had been made a Lieutenant General in 1709 but the chief command in the Army was not his and the Knighthood in the Order of the Garter he received in April 1710 did not make up for it. Argyll was neither to be made 'generalissimo of the British troops [nor] his brother to be Secretary of State for Scotland'.[103] While discontented, in January 1711, the Campbell brothers were still loyally 'busie mortyfing the late ministrie' headed by Godolphin and Marlborough. The issue they were pursuing was the alleged ill treatment of Jacobite peers during the invasion scare of 1708 when eighteen Scottish peers were imprisoned.[104] Ilay was said to be waiting for the right time to bring it up in the House of Lords.[105] He was also active in blaming Marlborough and Godolphin for the defeat of the army in Spain at Brihuega on 10 December 1710. Argyll had assailed Marlborough so often in the House of Lords and so violently that it seemed prudent to get him out of town. He was talked into accepting the command of the army in Spain and the ambassadorship as well. He was promised the funds to make both successful. He sailed to Spain in late February or early March 1711 and arrived in Barcelona on 4 April.[106] There he found an unpaid army in disarray.[107] And, he discovered that the Ministry's promises of support were hollow.

Amity with the Tories was not to last. The mess in Spain had been created by the former Ministry but his own did little to help Argyll. There, out of the way, he ceased to count for much in London politics and resented it. By the end of 1712, he had taken and been made Governor of Minorca, another marginal post. He returned to London early in 1713 quite unhappy with the Ministry. It made him Commander in Chief in Scotland and Governor of Edinburgh Castle but those places did not mollify him. Ilay had been made Lord Justice General (1710) and given a seat at the Privy Council (1711) – one he held for fifty years. But he suffered an unexpected insult when the Earl of Seafield, the last Lord Chancellor of Scotland, was found to still have the right to preside in any Scottish court including the Justiciary Court which Ilay now headed.[108] The Lord Chancellor of a non-existent political establishment outranked the Lord Justice General whose courts still functioned. Queensberry still held the Scottish secretaryship as he had done in 1709 and would do until his death in 1711. Rumours about this time had Ilay as a possible envoy to Spain. In either 1712 or very early 1713, Ilay was offered some sort of diplomatic assignment in Turkey which would have put him further out of the way than his brother.[109] Like his brother, the ministers found him dispensable. Mar wanted him gone.[110] When he wrote a scornful and ironic letter to Harley on 7 June 1713, Ilay noted that he had hardly had 'any opportunity of doing myself the honour to converse with you these two years' which meant from about the time of the debates over the privileges of the Kirk.[111] While the brothers stock sank, the Earl of Mar's had gone up. Control of Scottish affairs and patronage was exercised by Mar more than by anyone else.

The brothers had other problems. The Ministry insensitive to Scottish needs and desires would not always be 'in'. Indeed, it was beginning to unravel as moderate and extreme Tories worried one another and both were harassed by Whigs. The

Campbells were being openly scorned by the ministers. How were the Campbells to retain their positions and incomes, prepare for a new Ministry and the next reign? They had to break with the Tory Ministry but it was not clear where they would find friends. What was clear was that they would pay a price as defectors. Both brothers needed to keep offices. The Duke was still in debt; Ilay's income came mainly from offices. Both were alienated from the Ministry by the end of 1712 and the ministers from them. Ilay did not attend the peerage election held on 13 January 1713, but sent a proxy vote.[112] To many Scots in Parliament, it was also clear by the spring of 1713 that the Union was not worth keeping. It should be dissolved. The varied resentments of the brothers and other Scots boiled up in the Malt Tax and Union debates in which both brothers took a leading role.

VI. The Malt Tax and the Union

By the Union Treaty, Scots had been exempted from the Malt Tax while the French war lasted but it was now *nearly* over and a proposal to extend the tax to Scotland was made in 1712. That proposal was obnoxious to most Scots. Many Scots, because the war was *not yet over*, held this to be a violation of the Treaty of Union. Others said it ignored the provisions which required a recognition of the fragility of the Scottish economy when revenue measures were decided. The bill hung fire into the late spring of 1713. As late as mid-May 1713, it was not clear what Ilay's feelings about the Malt Tax really were. Balmerino wrote his friend Henry Maule to ask what Ilay, then in Edinburgh, was doing:

> ... if he be sincere in this matter he will be endevouring to promote addresses from all hands to the Queen for this dissolu[tio]n. But if all be grimace then he will only be dealing with Lords, barons and burgesses about next elec[tio]ns'.[113]

Ilay was probably doing what Balmerino wanted. George Lockhart noticed in *Scotland's Ruine* that, while Ilay was in Scotland, he was active and not just with Lords:

> Did not the Earl of Ilay in all companies make it [dissolution of the Union] his publick and constant toast, and write inscriptions on the glasses in the taverns in Edinburgh 'To the dissolving of the Union'? And did not all of his stamp and kidney declare that the Union was untollerable, and that there was an absolute necessity of hazarding all rather than it was not dissolved?[114]

The Earl's uncharacteristic emotional response suggests that his patriotism was real enough on some occasions. Many later actions reflected similar convictions. His actions had no effect on the outcome of the vote. The Malt Tax passed the Commons on 22 May.

Lord Ilay returned to London on 25 May to support the Scottish cause. By then Scots had decided to bring in a bill dissolving the Union.[115] Some of their meetings to discuss this occurred in Ilay's London house which had been made available to Scottish legislators even though the Earl was in Scotland. At a meeting of MPs on 26 May, after the Scots peers had met at his house, Ilay 'insisted very violently upon the necessity of prosecuting the dissolution be the consequences what they will'.[116] He seems also to have set out the strategy to be used. 'Scots of both Houses' were 'to join without Reserve in every Vote of whatever Concern, with the Party, which would join with us in Dissolving the Union; and to oppose without reserve that party, which would oppose us'. Scots might follow their consciences in 'Matters of Church and Religion' and could be guided by 'Motives of Conveniency or Inconveniencie' about ecclesiastical matters but they should seek a dissolution of the Union by opposing all other measures introduced by the government and other Unionists. He said the Succession had been secured and was irrelevant to the issue.[117] After that, a delegation waited on the Queen to protest the bill.[118]

Within a day or two, opinions had shifted a bit. Lockhart reported that 'Argyle, Ilay, Eglinton, Balmerino and all the Commons ... except [George] Baily and [John] Pringle, were for beginning instantly to let the Court see they could and dared to oppose them, because the Court were persons who kept the Scots under the Union and woud do so till the end of the world whilst they gained by it, and therefore it was fitt to let them see what wee durst do'. Mar, Seafield, and Loudoun were opposed to that and thought the Whigs would side with the Court. Lockhart went on, 'There are [those] here who say the 2 brothers, finding that their Court [interest] decays, are making this noise and opposition to force the Ministry into their ways'. He hoped that was not the case and thought their strategy was correct.[119]

The night before the final debate on 2 June 1713, about three months before the next elections, the Duke, Ilay, and their friends held another meeting. At the Earl of Mar's house, the Scottish peers decided on their grounds for dissolution: the abolition of the Scottish Privy Council (1708), Hamilton's Case (1711), the Treasons Act (1712) and the Malt Tax (1713). The speech setting out their grounds for the bill to dissolve the Union was to be given by Lord Seafield who would then be supported by Mar, Ilay, Argyll, Loudoun, and Balmerino.[120]

The Malt Tax was finally debated by the House of Lords in the guise of a bill to end the Union which had been moved by the Earl of Seafield and Findlatter. Argyll and Ilay led those who were for repeal of the Union. They argued that the bill violated the 14th article of the Treaty of Union which required Scottish economic circumstances to be considered when taxes were imposed. The Scottish economy was not strong enough to bear the tax which was illegal on other grounds. It came before the end of the French war and meant collecting taxes for a period in which all agreed Scots were free of the Malt Tax.[121] Ilay told the House 'that when the treaty [of Union] was made, the Scots took it for granted, that the parliament of Great Britain would never load them with any imposition that they had reason to believe grievous'. [122] The Earl also said that the analogy of a marriage between Scotland and England was absurd. [123] Like his brother, he thought the Union had failed to bring harmony to the island and that the interests of Scots had not been served by it. The Union was only a convenient arrangement, a political expedient to insure a Protestant succession and peace and not 'an ordinance of God'.[124] Scottish Calvinism and law allowed divorces.

This Union had not proven to be useful. One party had deserted it; the Union should be dissolved. The motion failed in the Lords by four proxy votes in an evenly divided chamber. It had received the support of most of the Scottish peers – Jacobites, Independent Episcopalians like Balmerino, Court Tories, Squadrone Whigs, and courtiers like Seafield. Ilay signed the dissent from the bill.

The Duke and Ilay were now telling everyone the obvious; they had broken completely with the Ministry. Harley's displeasure with the Campbell brothers' conduct was expressed on 7 June. If Oxford was trying to divide the brothers, he failed to do so. Ilay replied in an ironical defence of himself and his brother saying, in effect, that they long had been ill-used by the Tories.[125] The Earl was in the Lords on 8 June when it sat as a Committee of the Whole. Balmerino thought Ilay, Argyll and Mar all 'spoke very well'.[126] On 13 June, Ilay and his brother were listed as opposed to the Commerce bill which would have promoted Anglo-French trade.[127] They probably did not really dislike the bill so much as its sponsors whom they had determined to oppose. A month later, the brothers were reported as 'entirely of the Whig party and will join the Squadrone or anything that will join them to oppose the Court'. They were cultivating Scots for the future and presented themselves, as Ilay did to Lord Morton in August 1713, as men who had served their country 'by refusing to submit to the injuries we have received'.[128] Ilay was not asked to manage the next peerage election in 1713. Indeed, he had been left off the government's list and was not elected a Representative Peer on 8 August when the general election of peers was held. He and his brother opposed men on the ministerial list whom they knew would win. In the elections for the Commons, Scots elected about twenty-five Whigs. Among them were probably five Argathelians and four Squadrone men.[129] Opposition had not won them all that much from Scotland's bribable electors.

Having left the Tories, they had no party save those in opposition to the government. It was around this time that Ilay's secretary, William Steuart, MP, is said to have encouraged him to make overtures to the Pretender.[130] This Ilay seems to have done.

During the last months of Queen Anne's life, the Campbell brothers waited for the Queen to die and took their punishment. Their responses to the ministers were aggressive ones. Ilay kept saying that the Union ought to be dissolved and argued for constant opposition to ministerial or unionist policies.[131] He argued that this, like every thing else in politics, was 'to be directed by the Motive of Conveniency or Inconveniency of that Society, or State'. The Union was no longer convenient; he had no scruples about bringing down the government. According to Robert Wodrow, Argyll considered resigning all his posts but was dissuaded from doing so by Ilay 'who is as cunning and craft as his brother is hasty and forward'. Wodrow went on to say that had the Duke done so before the peerage election, 'he might have given a considerable turn to our election of peers'.[132] It was thought that they would not favour the Pretender although the Breadalbane Campbells might bring out 2,000 men on his side.[133]

A year or so earlier, in 1712-13, Argyll, when questioned by an agent of the Hanoverians, said that the Stuart family owed his family two heads,[134] a remark which Ilay later repeated as his own view. Now the brothers began to flirt (or appear to flirt) with Jacobites. They associated more with Jacobites and malcontents, to the glee of their old friend George Lockhart, who, with pleasure, followed their growing disaffection with the Union. He noted that the brothers 'did mention the King [James] and his interest, without that acrimony and bitterness which on too good grounds they were formerly accused of'. It was no secret that some of their close friends and dependents were Jacobites. Lockhart named Colonel John Middleton, MP from the Aberdeen burghs and brother to Ilay's banker, George Middleton, and Walter Stewart.[135] He went on:

> And so I cou'd not but think that the Duke and his brother had the same notions and opinion of my Lord Oxfords view and designs, as all the rest of mankind, and that it was certain all sides and parties did conclude that the Kings restoration was the only game His Lordship coud with safety to himself and his friends pursue; and as his Grace had contributed to enable him to bring his projects to bear, and that the Duke and all his dependents joind and concurr'd with many notorious Jacobites, who opposed the late Ministry [Godolphin's] and supported the present, because they expected the King's interest wou'd be thereby advanced; — on these, I say, and the like considerations   I was and am still perswaded, that this Duke did expect and believe the King's restauration was design'd; and as he contributed to advance the interest of those by whom it was to be accomplisht, 'tis but natural to inferr he intended to concurr in it.[136]

The brothers' contacts with the Pretender, if there were any, were part of the game. Deep down, neither Argyll nor Ilay was disposed to accept the Stuarts. They would flirt but that was all.[137] Still, the brothers were openly disaffected. Charles Cockburn, writing to the Duke of Montrose on 30 December 1714, thought Ilay was behind the continuing Scottish efforts to dissolve the union. He noted that it made him and his brother very popular.[138] However, it was unclear where their support would go.

Duke John during the spring of 1714 criticized the Ministry for making a bad peace with France and for distributing money to known Jacobite Highlanders which imperilled the succession.[139] He seems to have been telling other people that the Act of Settlement might be repealed by the government to make a Stuart restoration easier. It is hardly surprising that in March 1714 Argyll lost his Troop of Horse Guards and the Governorships of Minorca and Edinburgh Castle. Ilay in early 1714 is alleged to have offered to raise 20,000 Highlanders and to see to it that Edinburgh remained loyal to the Hanoverians. He had lost his Governorship of Dumbarton Castle and all hope of further favour while the Queen lived and Tories held power. In the long-run, the brothers would not side with extreme Tories or Jacobites but would aid the Hanoverian cause. In the meantime, they preserved a facade showing uncertainty. The Hanoverians might, in fact, not succeed to the Crown. The political issues concerning Scottish politicians in London now centred principally on the meaning of the Union the two countries had entered into and on the Succession. The Earl of Ilay, like most, was not wholly consistent in what he said and did in 1712-1714 but he had come to a position from which he would diverge only in appearance. The succession was to be Protestant which precluded a Catholic Stuart.

VII. The Transition to a New Reign

Queen Anne finally died, on 1 August 1714, but not before she had made the Duke of Shrewsbury Lord Treasurer. With neither Harley nor Bolingbroke in the chief place, there was little difficulty in getting the Privy Council to recognize the rights of the Elector of Hanover and to send for him. No one opposed the Regents named in a sealed letter. King George was proclaimed with little disturbance.[140]

The Campbells had found their interest to be with the new King. Ilay, who was in London, was ordered on 31 July, along with the Lord Provost of Edinburgh and General Wightman to 'attend their Posts'. He rode to Edinburgh where the order to proclaim George I as King was addressed to him as Lord Justice General.[141] In Edinburgh, he consulted with Montrose and other noblemen before he proclaimed the King on August 5.[142] He appears to have had ridden over 100 miles a day for three or four days to do so. Once the King was proclaimed, a great ball was held at Holyrood Palace where Ilay's mother, the Dowager Duchess, danced with John Campbell, a future Lord Provost of Edinburgh, and Ronald Campbell, W.S., a family 'doer' or solicitor. Having done what he could, Ilay went back to London and was probably there when the new King arrived in September 1714. If he was, then he had not only first hand knowledge, but perhaps even experience, of the English riots which accompanied this event.[143] George I was crowned the following month.

In the interval between the Queen's death and the arrival and coronation of George I, how politics would go in the new regime seemed undecided and some of that indecision depended upon the actions of Argyll and his brother. Mar noted in a letter sent to his brother, James Erskine, Lord Grange, a month after the Queen died, that Argyll's course of action still appeared unclear. He thought Argyll, Hamilton, Montrose, Tweeddale, and others had been dealing with each other to exclude from power in the new reign those who had served Anne. Or, Argyll might go to Scotland and join the 'Tories', *i.e.* Jacobites,[144] out of fear of the Squadrone. Or, he might make what deals he could with others. Mar worried that Ilay, resentful over the loss of his Governorship of Dumbarton Castle to a client of Montrose, would turn Argyll against himself and his brother, Lord Grange. Mar expected to be sacked and replaced by Montrose but he hoped the King would not be 'King of one partie'. Mar needed to have paid his arrears of £7,000. Mar seemed rather to disregard the fact that Argyll had helped to arrange the succession and that Ilay had made arrangements for the King's proclamation in Edinburgh.[145] The Campbell brothers remained civil to Mar and Grange but they were clearly for the King and would happily see Mar go out. Ilay wanted to replace him as Secretary of State for Scotland. The Duke had also taken up warrants for the arrest of Jacobites as early as 10 August 1714. Mar said that all were 'making interest for the new Election'.[146] This jockeying for place and power accounts for some of Ilay's time in Scotland in August and early September 1714. By September, Mar had gone but Ilay did not have his place.[147]

Not so clear were Ilay's and Argyll's positions on the Union. On 30 December 1714, Ilay and Annandale were reported to have seen the King about the possibility of dissolving the Union 'in the right way'. The King was against it but said he would leave it to Parliament. Squadrone men were not wholly opposed to that. It should also have pleased Presbyterian 'high-flyers' in the Kirk. The writer of the report thought that if the Union were dissolved, the Campbells of Argyll would become 'absolute Kings of Scotland' with the aid of the Presbyterians. Advocating dissolution made the brothers popular. Their earlier support of dissolution had been as patriotic as it sounded.[148] Another dissolution – that of Parliament was now important.

By the beginning of 1715, it was not Argyll and Ilay who gained most by the Succession but the men of the Squadrone. The Duke of Montrose became Secretary of State and the Duke of Roxburghe, Keeper of the Great Seal. The latter was a German speaker and liked by the King. Argyll was confirmed in his old posts, including that of Colonel of the Blues, and made Groom of the Stole. Ilay became Lord Clerk Register of Scotland, a precarious place from which an old family enemy, Lord Glasgow, was removed to make way for him. That made him the official head of the body which kept the Kingdom's records and insured that no official act could be transacted without his knowledge. It also gave him the right to control the elections of the Representative Peers. The post increased his income by perhaps £445.[149] The Argathelians had less power than the Squadrone men and had not been favoured with places on the newly created Board of Police – a body which was to pick ministers for royal livings, worry about non-jurors and Catholics, and promote some improvements. In reality it did little but give sinecures to those placed on it. The key to power, if the Argathelians were to enjoy it, had to be found in the elections of February and March.

For the Argathelians, the elections brought by a new reign were not a bad thing. By the autumn of 1714, Ilay was trying to secure the election of men favourable to the Campbell interests both in the county constituencies and in the burgh districts. He and his agents were active in Argyllshire, Lanarkshire, the Lothians, various parts of the North, and in the burghs. They particularly wanted to secure the election of a Lord Provost of Edinburgh and a Provost of Glasgow. Montrose's friend, Charles Cockburn, at the end of the year, thought that Ilay had been agitating to make 'the family of Ar[gyl]le as unsupportable as if they were absolute Kings of Scotland'. He acknowledged, however, that everywhere they were popular.[150] One reason for that was that Ilay and his brother supported a broad range of men as candidates. Most were Whigs but some were Tories and even Jacobites, such as their friend George Lockhart.[151] At the same time, in England they were said to be wanting the ruin of the Earl of Oxford.[152]

The Scottish elections for MPs were held in February and March 1715. The brothers proved their worth in electioneering but they were also curbed by having to work with the Squadrone men to secure the return of men on a list for the King and not just for themselves. John Forbes noted that 'Argyle and the Squadron are att dagers-drawing'.[153] To him this meant that in Scotland the government produced by the succession and the election was going to be divided and that Scots really would not know to whom to look for direction and patronage. A solid majority of the MPs returned were in favour of the succession but that probably did not reflect the sentiments of most Scots who lacked a vote. The elections confirmed that Argyll had to be reckoned with but they forced him to share power with the Squadrone which he and Ilay much resented.[154]

Ilay had played his usual role in the elections for the Commons but he may have been a bit reckless in his campaigning which tended to be as much for his family as for the monarch he and his brother served. Ilay, the letter writer in the campaign, had asked for the support of Jacobites – Lowlanders, such as Lockhart of Carnwath,[155] and Highlanders, such as Cromartie, MacIntosh of Borlum, Rose of Kilravock and others.[156] John Forbes of Culloden wrote to his younger brother Duncan: 'I truly think that if the Duke of Argyle desyres any Favours, he should be advysed to bestow them better then on such as never can be hearty to the present Government, nor firm friends to his familie'.[157] The Campbell brothers had not yet learned to be as careful with their favours as Ilay was to become. They tried too hard to buy good will for themselves and the new regime. What Ilay's electioneering did accomplish was the initial construction of a Highland interest which, in the end, would continue to prove helpful to him and to the government in 1715, 1745, and throughout his political career. Many later accusations of Jacobitism and deviousness rested on the brothers' friendships and electioneering as well as on their rumoured flirtations with the Pretender. The distrust and dislike with which they were viewed by many after the election would only be intensified by the '15 and its aftermath.

On 17 March, the peerage elections were conducted by Ilay's deputies as Lord Clerk Register, John MacKenzie of Delvine, PCS, and James Robertson, PCS. The list of those to be chosen had been brought down from London by Argyll but the elections were a mixed blessing for the Argathelians. The government got its way but the brothers, who had both been at the election, had not. The list included some not their friends.

Squadrone men were now well positioned to challenge the Argathelians. The new Secretary, Montrose, and his extended family connexions nursed old grudges over land and politics in and around Glasgow. Montrose had been Glasgow University's Chancellor for about a year. Patronage in that University was firmly in the hands of the Squadrone which had increased its influence in the Glasgow area. Charles Morthland, the Glasgow Professor of Oriental Languages, writing from London to his Principal, John Stirling, was well aware of the family rivalry. On 11 August 1715, he noted that Argyll, but also Roxburghe, had been taken into the cabinet.[158] They did not like each other. Roxburghe, the second most important Squadrone politician, had once duelled with Argyll. When a new Secretary was chosen in the following year, it was the Duke of Roxburghe and not Ilay. Many other patronage posts went to Squadrone supporters. Those outcomes can only have frustrated Ilay and deepened his certainly that the disposal of Scottish jobs depended upon Englishmen and that contests for them would involve the struggles of English politicians for supremacy. The next few years would see constant jockeying for power among Scottish Whigs. Among Jacobites, things were no better. Most Jacobites believed Ilay and his brother could not be trusted and did not think about politics in the right ways. The confused state of Scottish politics made it easy for some to think about rebellion as they were now clearly doing.

VIII. Ilay's Political Opinions

While not his own man, Ilay did have political attitudes which were fully formed by 1714. Politics was always in some sense a game for Ilay who likened it to whist.[159] You won with good cards and lost with bad. You played to win but the fact is, you must expect to lose part of the time. In the shifting alliances of the period, this made perfect sense. It expressed his political realism about how the politics of men wanting spoils proceeded. The game required bluffing and skill in play and some good cards. One should not become too emotionally committed and one should not act so that old enemies could not become future friends. This did not mean that there was nothing at stake in politics but spoils, wins and losses. The Earl had some principles.

While the books in his library suggest he had an interest in republicanism, Ilay had no interest in upsetting a state in which the powers of King, Lords and Commons were balanced in a way that gave the most influence to the class from which he came. Limited monarchy was never criticized by him. He believed in the Whig settlement of 1688-90. He was a natural conservative who was happier with small changes rather than with big ones. He was content to improve but not to abolish. Scots would have to be allowed lower taxes and given more of the benefits which the Union had promised them. The English must not hurt Scottish trade as they had done in 1711 by changing the laws governing the linen trade. And Englishmen must show greater respect for North Britons by respecting the Union Treaty.

Ilay had consistently supported a Protestant Succession and wanted some separation kept between 'Matters of Church and Religion'. Freedom of conscience should be preserved but church-men should be guided by the determinations of political bodies.[160] It is unlikely that the Earl cared much for Presbyterianism but it was established by law and protected by the Act of Union. The established Kirk was one he could manage. The alternatives to it were less protective of individual consciences and challenged necessary principles of secular order. He approved of its Erastian foundation. An Erastian regime in ecclesiastical polities meant that the land would not be plagued by enthusiasts and that toleration would be practised. The Kirk would have to tolerate dissenters openly worshiping in Scotland and to restore patronage rights to those who possessed them prior to 1690. That was his position and was pretty much the position of his clerical managers and of those who after 1753 became known as the Moderate Party in the Kirk.

Another of his most basic beliefs was that the English could not to be trusted to respect Scottish interests. In July 1710, Ilay wrote to William Carstares:

> I was always of opinion it was very obviously our interest not to mingle ourselves too much with factions here, I mean as Scotchmen; for, it being very plain that no party here [in England] has our country much at heart, the exasperating any side here might, at some conjuncture or other draw both upon us, and crush us at once.

When this letter was written, the Tories were increasing their support by promising an end to the war and more moderate government. English parties (moderate or extreme, Whigs or Tories), were all inimical to Scottish interests. In the end, the English were still the enemy who would impose on Scots what they could for English ends. In the same letter, Ilay told Carstares that he and his brother would 'be zealous for the maintaining the rights of our church' but he pointed out that the English would not show mercy to Scots and their interests.[161]

The Earl was a very pragmatic politician. He could be a Court Tory, Junto Whig or a Harleyan Tory but he would not burn his bridges to other parties in opposition, not even to the Jacobites. That meant limits to partisanship. It should never be so extreme as to preclude future deals. He had concluded that there were no constant alliances in politics and that the task of a politician like himself was to shift his support as occasions warranted and as interests and circumstances dictated. Politics, for Scots in London, had to be a matter of shifting alliances to secure benefits when and where they could be had. In Scotland, it was partly concerned with keeping out of the country as many of the English, Welsh and Irish as one could. Almost none of them were appointed by Ilay to Scottish offices and few came to Scotland while he had power. That was not just the policy of a politician keeping the goodies for the locals but the policy of a man defending a region with interests and rights seemingly guaranteed by the Treaty of Union.

The Union was a matter of convenience to both countries. If it should be preserved, Scots should not be treated badly by the dominant partner. One of the restraints on the English, indeed, on all men, was the observance of proper procedures. Ilay generally (but not invariably) wanted the terms of agreements – as he or the courts understood them – rigidly kept. He wanted due process in courts and obedience to laws. No one should go beyond his rights. The countries might grow more alike but that would be a work of time and should not be unduly forced – particularly upon Highlanders. Coercion was not an effective method to obtain that similarity of culture which a united Britain required. The convergence of cultures he desired but it could and should not be quickly achieved. This was an ideal view costly to hold at some points in his career such as after 1745.[162] It is not surprising that David Hume should have sent him his *Essays Moral and Political* in 1748.

The Earl defended Scotland's interests, such as its linen trade, but the material or idealistic needs of others usually took second place to more personal ones. Those could, and often did, include doing things of benefit to Scots generally but that was secondary to looking out for himself and his friends. His main principle as a young man was getting as much for himself, his friends and his countrymen as he could do through the sensible use of votes, the courts, place-men and whatever other tools and powers lay to hand. That also tended to mean that he was a moderate and given more to compromise than to extreme policies. He might employ irony and sarcasm and even occasionally be angry but, in general, he was a good tempered politician. He seldom invoked abstract rights and had about him nothing of the ideologue. He played according to the rules in place but he would interpret them to his own advantage and bend them if he could do so. If force had to be used, he was not squeamish unless it involved the government itself. One should put down rebellions, not make them, quell riots and disturbances, not cause them.

Still, Ilay's attitudes to politics – as opposed to his beliefs – were like his brother's – fundamentally selfish. The brothers played politics as the way to achieve their ends. They had done well by 1715. By 1711, according to an estimate by George Lockhart, the Duke of Argyll was in receipt of about '12000 l. Sterling yearlie.'[163] It came from his £3,000 pension, the remission of feu duties to the Crown worth £600, the profits of his military posts, which ran from Commander-in-Chief in Spain and Scotland (from 1712-16) to the possession of a regiment of foot, the Horse Guards and various governorships. All this probably amounted to more than the revenues of his estates and came, perhaps, to around £5,000 a year. Much of his total income of approximately £10,000 (Carnwath had exaggerated) was contingent upon remaining in office. For Ilay, the problem was much the same except that he had no landed wealth and his offices were not all for life. Ilay's income in 1714 came from offices and his market speculations.[164] He may have received something as an Extraordinary Lord of Session (1708-1761), although this post was not one which was remunerated at a later date. The Lord Justice General's place (1710-1761) was worth about £1,000 in 1715. His post as Lord Clerk Register brought in £445 and he might have had £200 for his Governorship of Dumbarton Castle. He would have found small change in other minor offices. His investments by himself and with John Law brought in more. That was a very good Scottish income for a Scottish peer, about £2,000, but a slim one for a man so ambitious. Compromising, dealing, selling one's power and talents to the highest bidder, without compromising honour too much, was the game he played. For touchy and arrogant Duke John, honour and status were more important considerations throughout his career. Ilay could not afford to be so delicate and never was, not even after he became Duke in 1743. The careers of both men were imperilled by the uprising of 1715 since it threatened their offices, prospects and possibly their lives.

Chapter 4

Ilay and the '15

I. Preliminaries to the '15

Britain in 1714 entered upon a long period of Whig rule which stretched to the end of Ilay's life. Politicians would wrangle but the '15 put an end to any real prospect of Tories or Jacobites coming into power for over a generation. Scottish politicians would attach themselves to the English political factions which they believed could help them get elected, give them offices, or in some way better their positions. The Squadrone in 1715 went with those Whigs who wished to impose a harsh policy in the North of Scotland, and they would be with their successors in 1745. Argyll and his brother consistently stuck with more pragmatic politicians who preferred order and stability even if purchased with lenity to rebels. Those men were also the ones most interested in economic matters about which the Squadrone men were less concerned. The choices each side made were conditioned by the personal interests of their leaders, by assessments of English politicians, and the prospects of their factions, but also by sheer opportunism. The '15, as much as anything, decided the future of the Campbell brothers because it allowed them to build a stable political faction and ultimately allied them with Walpole and moderate English Whigs.

There were rumours of Jacobite activity throughout Britain in the winter of 1714-15. They persisted into the spring when Ilay urged men like Maclaine of Lochbuie to stay put and be ready to do the government's bidding.[1] Lord Justice Clerk, Adam Cockburn, wrote Montrose on 22 April 1715 that the Pretender had landed at Liverpool and that various disaffected men had joined Mar.[2] About the same time, men like John Forbes in London were passing on rumours which had reached them.[3] Still, there seemed to be little enthusiasm in Scotland for a rebellion. The Jacobites, in disarray, could find no commander to lead those willing to fight. French help was necessary for the success of any uprising but it was not likely to be forthcoming. Louis XIV, nearing the end of his days, seemed unwilling to spend much to help Jacobites. Louis died on 1 September 1715, five days before the rebellion broke out on 6 September. London was, inadvertently, more helpful to the Scottish Jacobites than Paris since the Ministry's response to the rumours was inadequate. It did little to disarm those likely to make trouble and it failed to organize and arm its supporters. A few Lord Lieutenants were appointed. Argyll, hereditary Lord Lieutenant for Argyllshire, was given a commission for Dumbartonshire – a slight to Montrose. Ilay was commissioned as Lord Lieutenant of Midlothian (1715). A Scottish militia of a sort was constituted but it did not become effective partly because the commissions for its officers were slow in reaching Scotland.[4] The support of some Scots was lost when the new government issued a list of suspects who were required to turn themselves in at Edinburgh. Few had done anything overt to justify incarceration. The government neither placated those who needed to be reconciled to the new regime nor locked up those who were trouble makers. Among them was the Earl of Mar.

Mar had worked for a smooth transition of power but George I believed him to have made commitments to the Jacobites and would do nothing for him. Mar was financially embarrassed but his arrears went unpaid. The King did not reach out to him or other Jacobites. Indeed, George seemed to go out of his way to insult men like Francis Atterbury, Bishop of Rochester, who had also accepted the succession with some grace. After March 1715, Mar left London, went home and began to organize a rebellion.[5] In that he was much helped by the Scottish Episcopal clergy who were still preaching divine right theory which favoured the Stuarts.[6]

Had there been some French support and better leadership, the chances of a successful rebellion in Scotland were not all that bad. Things remained unsettled. Ordinary Scots had no love for their new King. There were few troops in the country and the castles and forts in the King's hands were not great impediments to mobile forces living off the country. Many of the likely rebels were Highlanders who held land by wardship, as did some in the southern parts of the country. This tenure obligated the occupiers of land to fight for their lords. The men of the North presented a more formidable fighting force than could quickly be mustered against them. Since the Scottish Privy Council had been disbanded in 1708, there was no authority in Scotland to organize defence other than that of the Lord Advocate and the judges. There was virtually no militia since provisions for one had not been contained in the Treaty of Union and a bill to create one had been denied royal assent in 1708. A later one, in 1713, had been opposed by Argyll who under it would have lost his hereditary Lord Lieutenancy of Argyllshire. There were few Lord Lieutenants and Deputy Lieutenants to organize or call out militia forces and not all of those were resident in Scotland. When a militia was formed, it 'consisted of a few men, Horse and foot, who never continued 3 days together, and signified nothing in the military way, the Lowland-men being a great deal more unfit for warlike expeditions than the Highlanders who had joined the Earl of Mar'.[7] Had Mar acted rapidly and more decisively, his rebellion might have succeeded. That he failed to do but his was still a considerable undertaking which mobilized as many Scots as had the Covenanting wars of the 1640s.[8]

II. The Rebellion

On 22 August 1715, the Jacobites agreed to rise and began seizing weapons. The raising of the Pretender's standard on 6 September was followed on 8 September by a failed attempt on Edinburgh Castle.[9] By 14 September, the rebels had taken both Perth and Inverness. By the middle of September, Mar had about 10,000 men in arms but he continued to sit in Perth. Argyll, now Commander-in-Chief in Scotland, and Ilay had arrived in Scotland on 14 September.[10] The Duke soon had 4,000 men with which to oppose Mar who had not occupied Stirling, the gateway to southern Scotland. Argyll made it his headquarters and waited for Mar's force to diminish and for reinforcements to come north.

Ilay was busy in Edinburgh where his activity can be followed in the nearly daily letters sent to London. As head of the Justiciary Court, an Extraordinary Lord of Session, a Justice of the Peace and Lord Lieutenant, he had a good deal of legal authority with which to defend the government. He began by holding court and locking up possible rebels. As he wrote to London, he would try to act legally but 'in time of Civil War I have no notion (Pardon the levity of the Expression) of taking the law of A Cannon Bullet'.[11] He issued warrants and then enforced them himself, notably in a raid conducted on or about 22 September. Ilay had pressed horses from Lord Leven (not one of his friends), raised a group of about 100 volunteers, including Lord Belhaven, Brigadier Grant of Grant and other gentlemen, and had ridden off to Seton House, the home of the Jacobite Earl of Winton, to search for arms. They got lost on the way. The house, when they found it, yielded twenty three old firelocks even after two searches, one conducted at 2:00 a.m.[12]

By 19 September, Ilay had ordered all boats leaving Leith to do so only with permission. He meant to keep the funds of the Bank of Scotland secure in the Castle, where they had been deposited, and he promised to 'do something at least as necessary as illegal' if the Jacobite directors or anyone else tried to remove them. He asked for a frigate or two to be sent to the Western shores and for men to disarm the Islanders. He wanted mortars and wheeled guns and told his correspondents, the Secretaries and their aides, not to buy peace as governments had tried to do in the past. When he had secured arms, he planned to go to Argyllshire. Doing that would divert rebel troops from Stirling even if his own small force was taken. His diversion might even the odds a bit for his brother.[13] At the end of September, he foiled a plot to take the city of Edinburgh for the rebels.[14] And he found time for a bit of electioneering which resulted in the selection of John Campbell, his mother's recent dancing partner, as Lord Provost of Edinburgh.[15] It is not surprising that he should have told his London correspondents that 'I am forced to be of twentie different Trades, 'tis hard [others] wont take the shadow of one to do their shere'.[16]

Ilay's intelligence told him that many rebels in the West were getting ready to invade the Argyll lands and assault Inveraray. Its defence would be difficult because of divisions among Campbells. Some were loyal to the Pretender, others to King George. Lord Ilay tried to persuade Breadalbane Campbells to side with him and his brother. That resulted in some defections, among whom Sir Duncan Campbell of Lochnell was the most prominent. Even a few defections would make the defence of Inveraray easier.[17] However, Jacobite neighbours, such as Stuart of Appin and Cameron of Lochiel, would not support him. Preparing to defend the town, he asked for more munitions. He said the government's tardiness in sending them would be seen as encouragement to the rebels. He made a quick trip to Stirling on September 24th or 25th to consult with his brother and had planned to visit Inverness but Ilay was back in Edinburgh on the 27th. There he arrested some of Mar's servants whom he intended to send to London to be held as witnesses in the trials he was sure would follow the suppression of the Rebellion.[18] He was looking into Jacobite activity in the Army, worried over the dilatory behaviour of others, especially the Squadrone lords, and tried to separate truth from fiction in the rumours which circulated. On the 28th, he ordered the Commissioners of Customs to stop and search all ships in the

Forth Estuary even though he lacked the authority. This stopped the daily dispatches sent by a Leith baillie to Mar and disrupted some rebel arms shipments. Ilay was still issuing warrants and enforcing them with men under his command.[19] He called repeatedly for arms and for the better provisioning of the Castle's complement of 120 men, to which he added sixty more. He advised the Ministry to send foreign troops to Scotland: 'We are in Scotland as fond of forreigners as the English are impatient of them'.[20] The government found neither money nor munitions and did not mobilize troops with speed.

In the first week in October, Ilay went to Inveraray and threw himself into organizing the defence of the Castle and the region which it was rumoured the rebels planned to plunder and burn. He saw to it that the Argyllshire militia of about 1,000 men, under the command of Campbell of Finab, was concentrated in Inveraray. There he armed some but put most of them to work trenching and fortifying the place. He pressed men into service, never a popular course. He and his brother seem to have borne the costs of maintaining this force. In two or three days, Ilay had razed a considerable number of houses and other structures to give a clear field of fire but also to provide materials from which to make defensive outworks and walls around the parts of the Castle and town where they were lacking.[21] To attack those without field guns would have been costly. Neither he nor the rebels had such guns. Beyond the walls were entrenchments and beyond those pickets. He would not be surprised or surrender without a fight. On 17 October, led by General Alexander Gordon, perhaps 2,400 rebels appeared. They camped about a mile away – out of range of any guns Ilay had – and stayed a week. Little happened except for a few forays and skirmishes. Rob Roy tried to pillage Inveraray but was driven off.[22] Ilay's cousin, Colonel John Campbell of Mamore, led a retaliatory raid into MacGregor country. Campbell of Finab failed to secure for the Argathelians a contingent of Breadalbane Campbells which left the seige.[23] Then, it was over. The cost was some buildings and two dead – both killed by friendly fire.[24] It was a performance which impressed even men who did not like Ilay. Robert Wodrow wrote of it:

> In the beginning of October my Lord Isla went down to Argyleshire, and gathered the militia about Inveraray. But that shire is but on ill terms with the family, and matters were like to be in hazard there for some time. My Lord Isla was obliged to entrench himself, with about fifteen hundred, near Inveraray, and about three thousand of the Camerons, Breadalbanes's and Glenorchy's men, came and viewed the camp, and saw fit to retire.[25]

When the rebels marched off, Ilay announced his intention to follow them, harassing their rear. Nothing came of that plan, perhaps because Campbells did not like the idea of killing other Campbells. Many of the clansmen, but by no means all, owed their primary allegiance to the Earl of Breadalbane whose surname might be Campbell but who was not going to take direction from the Duke of Argyll or the Earl of Ilay.

The '15 is the only time when Ilay appears clearly as a soldier. His actions suggest that he brought to Inveraray what he had learned about siege warfare on the continent and that he was enough of a disciplinarian to get his walls built quickly.

His men must have worked round the clock to accomplish that. He is also said to have been short-tempered and, by the time it was over, unpopular:

> A great many of our men deserted here because of Ilay's carriage was not satisfying to officers or sentinels. The officers received little or nothing since they came, so many would continue yet are not able. Ilay acts all with a high hand, having a greatness about him more agreable to a minister of state thane ane engadging officeer.[26]

A determined attack would have been costly but could have succeeded since General Gordon's troops outnumbered Ilay's by about two to one. Ilay saved the town and Castle and did it despite having little in the way of provisions, guns or ammunition. The rebels retreated toward Stirling where they faced Argyll whose army had been re-enforced. Ilay stayed in Inveraray for about a month before marching to Dunblane to participate in the Battle of Sheriffmuir.

While all this had been going on, bolder rebels took the citadel at Leith, most of the Fife burghs, Aberdeen, and many estates and castles in the Northeast. Attempts on Edinburgh Castle and another on the town, led by Mackintosh of Borlum, were thwarted; then, the rebels went south into England where they met with little success. When Mar did move, he was intercepted near Dunblane by Argyll's force which defeated the rebels who outnumbered them about three to one.[27] The disparity in numbers reflected the English decision to keep troops in England to suppress risings which they thought were likely and would be more critical for the Hanoverians than was the rising in Scotland. This policy was resented by Argyll and Ilay who believed they were being denied resources by men content to look after their own and let the Scots suffer the devastation of war. It would happen again in 1745.

The Battle of Sheriffmuir was fought on 13 November, the day before the Jacobites at Preston were forced to surrender. Sheriffmuir was a somewhat confusing affair fought over uneven ground that prevented the generals from clearly seeing the disposition of their troops. Ilay and his men from Inveraray are said to have arrived about half an hour before the fighting commenced and provided a welcome addition to the outnumbered force commanded by his brother. The Earl's men probably joined General Wightman's command in the centre where the foot battalions saw a good deal of action. Ilay himself is likely to have fought on the right with the mounted gentleman volunteers under his brother's immediate command.[28] The left wings of both armies were defeated and ran but Argyll's right and centre held. It was thought by many that he could have won more decisively. Rumours circulated for years that he had halted the dragoons under his command from pursuing fleeing Highlanders whom they could have cut down.[29] That became one of the evidences of the Jacobitism of the Campbell brothers and was long used against them. It should be seen as the prudence of a general low on ammunition and leading an army which, at the end of the fight, was still smaller than Mar's regrouped troops.[30] Argyll had about 500 men killed and an equal number wounded. He retired in good order to Dunblane. Mar may have lost in killed, wounded and captured as many as 1,500 but they had bought him no victory. The Hanoverian force still existed as an army of perhaps 2,500 able to fight and it held its strategic location.[31] Duke John said of his victory, 'almost by miracle; god hath begun the work and will lay it on by his own hands'. [32] Then, with more modesty than was usual, 'let the God of heaven have all the praise'. The Duke did not always share his glory.

Lord Ilay was wounded in the battle but where is somewhat uncertain. Soon after the battle, John Campbell, Lord Provost of Edinburgh, wrote to Lord Townshend that Ilay had been 'shutt throw the Right arm, and in the Right Syde'.[33] Another account says:

> My Lord *Ilay* has two Wounds, one through the right Arm, near the shoulder, and another on the upper part of the Right Side, neither of which are dangerous, his Lordship resting well and being free of Fever, May God preserve so precious a Life, for the Benefit of his Country; should he die, it would be an irreparable Loss.[34]

A third account, written after the Earl's death, says he was 'shot in one of his encles' [ankles] which would better explain why after Sheriffmuir he walked with a limp.[35]

Ilay was very likely treated by John McGill, a learned Edinburgh surgeon-apothecary. McGill served as a volunteer with Argyll's force and was later the recipient of Ilay's patronage as was his architect brother, Alexander, who worked for both Campbell brothers.[36] Until his death in the 1730s, John McGill was Ilay's 'g. p.' when he was in Scotland and was even consulted when the Earl was in London. Ilay was lucky that his wounds were well cleaned and did not become infected. Three weeks after being shot he was back in harness.

By mid-December, the Jacobite force which had invaded England had been defeated. With England secure, troops could be sent north; more arrived from Holland. The rebels realized they were beaten and began to negotiate. When the Pretender arrived in Scotland two days before Christmas, he was at least two months too late. His presence merely prolonged the uprising. When he went back to France early in February 1716, the '15 was over.

The Campbell brothers had done well. The Duke had prevailed against superior forces but he was embarrassed by the fact that many Campbell clansmen had served in the army of the Pretender.[37] While in Scotland, Argyll kept his reputation both for valour and skill, he had not done so well in London. George I believed that the Duke should have hotly pursued rebels at Sheriffmuir but deliberately had allowed them to get away.[38] Argyll did not storm towns occupied by Jacobite commanders and does seem to have allowed them to withdraw without a fight. The weather made this easier. The year 1715 ended and 1716 began cold and snowy. Toward the end of the uprising and in its aftermath, the Duke showed a willingness to forgive and pardon rebels or those who sympathized with them.[39] Why waste Scottish lives and property when it was not necessary? Argyll's conduct remains a testimony to his good sense and humanity. Some, like the Earl of Stair, an Army rival of Argyll, expressed the hope that there would be amnesty for some but severe reprisals against others because examples 'are necessary but I hope it would be carryd so that Justice may have no air of cruelty or revenge'. He too noted that harshness would engender problems, not solve them.[40] Argyll's second in command, General Cadogan, another Army rival, was not so squeamish. By the end of December, he had begun to criticize Argyll to Marlborough and others in London. Leniency toward the rebels was not what many in England wanted or what a German King thought fit. Many criticized the Commander-in-Chief for dealing gently with rebels whom they would have summarily tried and executed. The King was less concerned with mercy than with making examples of rebels. This problem was further complicated because the Ministry had given Argyll little indication of what he was to do with prisoners, especially those who were genteel.

Ilay too had served creditably in Edinburgh, in Inveraray and at Sheriffmuir.[41] He fought well enough to be noticed but was modest about his role. Lord Lovat reported that Ilay, 'got a kind letter from Marlborough congratulating him on his glorious actions' – and then he went on in a Lovat-like manner to say, 'yet he was oblig'd to own to General Wightman [he commanded the centre], yt his Ldp [Argyll] would have got nothing done in ye north without my d[ea]r. general and me'.[42] Like his brother, Ilay was for mercy which had political uses. Few bore so little animosity against those who had fought on the other side. His military experiences and his slight debility after Sheriffmuir probably set his sights more exclusively on civilian pursuits but they also show us a man willing to fight for what he believed in: the Revolution Settlement, Protestantism, and more toleration and freedom than one could expect from Stuart Kings. Of course, losing would have jeopardized his offices and his possible inheritance of a great estate. The Rebellion gave the Earl more glimpses of military life and improved his knowledge of the qualities which made a good officer and of how campaigns were conducted. Since he would for years debate military questions in the Lords, this was not time lost. He had met many military men with whom he would later deal in an official capacity as they sought places and promotions. Dealing with rebels, who in some cases were his friends, was also an experience which most of the English officers who served in this conflict lacked. Few of the Scottish politicians whom he was to oppose over many years had his sort of record or conspicuously bore wounds from conflict.

By the end of December, Ilay was gathering evidence and making lists of men who would testify at the trials which would inevitably follow.[43] In January he did not attend the peerage election held in Edinburgh but his brother did. Later in the month, the Duke and Ilay made a triumphal progress through Scotland. They were feted in Edinburgh by the Town Council which in 1716 again elected John Campbell its Lord Provost.[44] The brothers now had more influence in the burgh than they had had in the past. At the Glasgow celebration, the Duke's health was drunk at the Merchant's Hall to the accompaniment of '3 vollies of small shot by 60 men and 5 cannon'. The brothers were made burgesses and left town to three vollies of the cannon and with a mounted escort of 100 men.[45] Their friends took over the Glasgow Town Council and in 1716 Daniel Campbell of Shawfield, brother of the Edinburgh Lord Provost, was, with their help, returned as the MP for the Glasgow Burghs.[46] They were warmly welcomed elsewhere. Argyll journeyed to London to which he had been recalled because he had not seemed eager enough to punish rebels. Ilay stayed in Scotland. In February, he was travelling around the North trying to win friends for the government and to enlarge and hold together the family interest. He was probably at Aberdeen, certainly at Culloden, which he left to go on to Cromarty. He was a good horseman and this cold trip was another testament to his stamina. One outcome of his trip north seems to have been the bringing of Duncan Forbes, soon to become Argyll's personal agent in Scotland, securely into the Argathelian fold along with many of his northern friends – or put another way, Inverness-shire and Ross-shire and the Inverness burghs. Another result of the trip was Ilay's and Forbes's deepening conviction that the rebels should be dealt with gently. The Earl, like his brother, urged the King to extend mercy 'to such as he judged might deserve it'.[47] Their list would have been longer than Stair's. In April, the Hanoverian Minister, Baron Bernstorff, said Ilay 'was pushing on a general Amnesty' and recommending the parts of the Triennial bill affecting Scotland which it was thought would give the brothers more power in Scotland.[48]

III. Back to the Usual Politicking

The Campbell brothers' 'enemies' at this point were of two kinds. There were, first, their Scottish Squadrone opponents and secondly others in London. The Squadrone party faced by the brothers in Scotland in 1716 was composed principally of the politicians from the Borders, central and southern Scotland where the estates of its magnates were located. Included among them were James Graham, 1st Duke of Montrose, who had been Secretary of State for Scotland from the autumn of 1714 until the following autumn. He held other offices and had interests in Glasgow and in Dumbartonshire, Stirlingshire and Perthshire. Those made him a regional competitor with Argyll in Glasgow and the West. The other principal leader, James Kerr, 1st Duke of Roxburghe, had estates in the Borders. He was a German-speaking friend of the King. A third great landowner in this connection, John Hay, 4th Marquis of Tweeddale, was also a Border man. Other politicians in this connexion included the Earls of Rothes, Hopetoun, Haddington, and Marchmont, and landed families connected with them, particularly in Fife, the Lothians and Berwickshire. Serving them, and related to them, were men in the professions, including some with estates in the Lothians, Perthshire and Renfrewshire. Dundases, Erskines, Haldanes, Pringles and others in the Scottish administration were among them.[49] The Squadrone found supporters in some of the burghs, notably Edinburgh, but fewer in the prospering burgh of Glasgow. This faction lacked the Army connexions which had been formed by Argyll and Ilay although the adherence of the Earl of Stair and others gave them some. Collectively, the Squadrone men had a lot of the real estate in the areas around Edinburgh, the Borders and the counties of Stirling, Fife, and Forfarshire but they had very few supporters in Highland areas. They could offer counterweights to Jacobites in the Eastern Lowlands but not in the North or in Western Scotland where the Argathelians were numerous.

By 1717, Argyll and Ilay had formed a fairly stable political group. The Argyll estates themselves were extensive and were scattered in about a dozen counties.[50] Ilay could count on the relatives mentioned above (see pp. 16, 34) and sometimes on dubious figures such as Simon Fraser, Lord Lovat, a distant Campbell relative, and the Campbell Earl of Breadalbane.[51] Other connexions gave them supporters in Ayrshire, the Borders, and the Highlands. The lands of the Campbells and their friends ran up along the west coast from Ayrshire and Kintyre into Argyllshire, Inverness-shire, Ross and Cromarty, across to Nairn, Morayshire, Banff and Aberdeenshire. By the end of 1717, Ilay and his brother had ties to many landowners and chiefs in the Highlands. Among them were Brodie of Brodie, Forbes of Culloden, Rose of Kilravock and Grant of Grant. Lesser men from the North included Colonel John Middleton of Seaton who had served with Argyll in Europe. Argyll and Ilay had good relations with many Jacobite families like the Maules of Panmure who came from Forfarshire and with various of the Sinclairs in Fife. Around Edinburgh, there were some of the Dalrymples (an Ayrshire family) and Edinburgh professional men like the McGill brothers, various lawyers and medical men. Among those who would be local managers for Ilay were the advocate Charles Erskine from Clackmannanshire and George Drummond whose family hailed from Perthshire. He had worked for the Campbells since c.1705 and was a businessman, local politician and placeholder who would be six times Lord Provost of Edinburgh. The Argathelians had supporters in the town councils of Edinburgh, Glasgow and Aberdeen. More were found in the counties of Peeblesshire, Lanarkshire, Dunbartonshire, Stirlingshire and Kinross. Argyll's faction, in the long run, would be indispensable to ministries in London because the country could not be managed without having in government men who were well connected in the Highlands and able to influence politics throughout the country. Since the ownership of land in Scotland was concentrated in very few hands, and votes gave electoral victories, the Argathelians, who had more land and urban support than the Squadrone men, could usually deliver more MPs to vote as ministers might direct.

The Argathelians had other sources of strength. They attracted remnants of the pre-Union Court party once led by Queensberry. Jacobites supported them in preference to others. Among them were the Dukes of Atholl and Gordon. The latter believed he had been well dealt with by Argyll in 1716. The lenient policy toward the rebels adopted by the brothers during and after the '15 added lesser men to their Highland connexions and made it unlikely that the Squadrone could recruit there. Finally, the Campbell faction was in the minds of many still the traditional defender of the Kirk. This was so despite the fact that in 1715 many of the country's leading clerics belonged to or supported the Squadrone connexion which they saw as being harsher toward their clerical and political enemies. More older men in the Squadrone had conscientiously suffered for their religious beliefs during the repression of the 1680s than was true among the Argathelians but those men were dying out in the 1710s.

Few issues of principle divided the Argathelians from the Squadrone men. Both factions were Whig and Presbyterian. Both claimed to be defenders of the Kirk and of Scottish independence. Both had ties to English Dissenters.[52] The Squadrone men as a whole were perhaps even more openly religiously tolerant than the Argathelians but they were less willing to employ or seek accommodations with Jacobites. The Squadrone favoured a harsh, punitive policy in the Highlands in the aftermath of the revolt. After 1715, their men encouraged rumours that Argyll and his friends would, if out of power, join the Jacobites and oust the new monarch who had disgraced them. The Squadrone paid little heed to warnings such as that of James Murray to the Pretender on 7 August 1716:

I think you may depend that Mr. Anton [the code name for Argyll] is the last man you can expect any friendship of, for he is in a most entire confidence with the Gentleman I formerly mentioned [the Prince of Wales], and seems to build all his prospects upon that bottom, so there is no manner of encouragement to talk with him or his brother [Ilay] on that subject.[53]

Argathelians had few qualms about talking but many about acting. Both factions had men interested in the prosperity of the Kingdom and in its improvement but improvers were more numerous among the Argathelians. The most important thing dividing the groups was the control of patronage – the ability to get jobs for themselves and their friends in the state's civil offices, Army, Navy, the Empire, the great companies and other corporations. Each faction wanted to manage Scottish affairs so that the King's business would get done by the 'right men'.

The brothers' London 'enemies' were more formidable because they included the King, prominent Ministers, like the Earls of Sunderland and Stanhope, and their friends. Among those were many Army men who disliked or envied Argyll or who felt they had been passed over in favour of the Duke and his friends. Among them were Marlborough, Stair, Cadogan and officers attached to them. Most were not willing to be lenient to Highlanders or to give more power to Ilay and his brother. If the brothers were to succeed, they had either to placate or replace those men.

IV. Politics 1716-1719

Because the brothers were mostly in London and around the Prince of Wales's court at Hampton Court Palace in the late winter and spring of 1716, they were not involved in the disagreeable end of the rebellion in Scotland that saw efforts to hunt down rebels and disarm Highlanders. Ilay and the Duke remained busy considering who had done what? Who was to be tried, pardoned or forfeited? Who was still in the country? They were busy not finding rebels but explaining why some should not be tried. Dealing with those issues endeared Ilay neither to George nor his ministers.

The brothers' attitudes to the defeated sharply defined the differences between their Whiggism and that of the men of the Squadrone and many of their English friends. The latter long accused the forgiving Ilay of being a secret Jacobite. The main issues were stated by Duncan Forbes in an anonymous letter written to Sir Robert Walpole during the summer of 1716. Forbes's opinions were widely shared in the North and Northeast of Scotland:

It is no small cause of discontent, to such as served the King faithfully in this Nation, to find, that a Ministry can be so designing, so far imposed upon, as to quit with the Duke of Argyll; worthy in himself, but chiefly valuable for his steady adherence to his Majesty; moved by a parcel of fictions, contrived and abetted by certain politicians, who have become a proverb in this Country.... It is scarce supposible, that a Ministry could do a thing more lawless or more injudicious than to commit the Care of the Public management, at a time so critical as this is, to men so much the derision, and at the same time so much the aversion, of their Country, as those to whom the Charge is now committed in Scotland.[54]

Forbes aimed principally at the Squadrone but also at Generals Cadogan and Stanhope. Forbes was an Argathelian but he was not wrong. Squadrone Scots had no important connexions in the Highlands and could not pacify the region save through force – which was what Cadogan and Stanhope advocated. Forbes wanted the country pacified with a minimum number of trials, executions, forfeitures and recriminations. He suggested that only twenty men be executed, *if* they were already in government hands. He did not want men made desperate, and their friends and relatives soured by the new King and his ministers. He made it clear that he thought this to be the policy of Argyll and, presumably, of his brother.[55] George I, like many in Parliament, could not stomach such leniency. Argyll was replaced as Commander-in-Chief in Scotland by his second in command, William, 1st Earl of Cadogan, an Irishman prepared to follow a much tougher line with rebels. Indeed, Cadogan and others in Scotland seem not to have honoured assurances of clemency and grace which Argyll had given. Despite that, there were still rumours that the Duke would displace Marlborough in the Army.[56] They ceased after Squadrone men, including the Duke of Roxburghe, accused the Duke in the Privy Council of corrupt practices while in Scotland. By 18 March, Argyll was said to be disgraced and men like General Wightman worried about his 'Fate'.[57]

When Argyll and his brother returned to London early in 1716, they were feted by some but also attacked from unexpected quarters. Leniency won the brothers less thanks from Jacobites than one might have expected. Their old friend, George Lockhart, transcribed a verse from about this time which put Ilay in a list of 'Whig Rogues', saying ironically of him in stanzas 12 and 13:

> In making of this list
> Lord Ilay should be first,
> A man most upright in spirit,
> He's sincere in all he says,
> A Double part ne'er plays,
> His word he'l not break, you may swear it.
>
> His favours thus dispense
> On men of no merit nor candour?
> Woud any King confide
> In men that so deride
> All notions of conscience and honour?
> Hath any been untold
> How these our country sold
> And would sell it again for more treasure?
> Yet all, these very men
> Are in favour now again
> And do rule us and ride us at pleasure.[58]

Despite Lockhart, by the summer of 1716 Argathelian leniency was the talk of the London taverns where many said the Duke and Ilay were secret Jacobites.[59] Such talk was sustained for years by Ilay's seeking to reconcile Jacobites to the Hanoverian regime partly by securing pardons for them. In 1725, Stewart of Appin, Macdonald of Glencoe, Grant of Glenmorriston, the Mackinnon, Macdougal of Lorn, Rob Roy, Lord Ogilvie and several more had him to thank for theirs.[60] Others in that decade were equally in his debt.

By 20 March 1716, Ilay was trying to make the 'plotts [of the enemyes] turn upon themselves'.[61] He planned to go to Scotland in May 1716 'to manage the trials' of rebels in the Justiciary Court.[62] As head of the chief criminal court in Scotland, the Earl was well placed to slow things down if not ultimately to change them. In the end, the trials were held at Carlisle and did not involve his court which men in London thought would be unreliable. The brothers were thus untainted by involvement in the trials of rebels.

Argyll and Ilay also found other fish to fry. They were among the principal advocates in the Lords for the repeal of the Triennial Act in the spring of 1716 and voted against it on 14 April. That Act required elections for MPs every three years and annual sessions of Parliament.[63] Ilay supported repeal both for intellectual and factional reasons. He argued that the Act promoted factions and fomented disorder and corruption. He believed that the English franchise in 1716 allowed far too many small holders to vote. They were not truly independent and sold their votes.[64] Moreover, when 'gentlemen have laid out their estates in elections, they must exert their industry to find some means to make themselves amends'. Giving them seven years to recoup their fortunes from the graft that office might bring seemed only fair. He probably agreed with other speakers on his side that the Triennial Act jeopardized the country because a rebellion might occur during an election, a risk doubled by the Triennial Act.[65] In an already volatile political scene, the Act made matters worse by producing more uncertainty about who was to hold power. Of course, repeal would give him until 1722 to get his political machine in proper order to fight the next elections. After the repeal of the Act, he worked at cultivating interests in Scottish burghs and other constituencies. He made at least four trips to Scotland from 1716 to 1721 mostly to accomplish that end.

In mid-April 1716, the Duke and Ilay were still voting with the Court party. They had had a rancourous debate with the Tory Earl of Nottingham over the new Abjuration Oath for which they voted.[66] A few days later, Ilay was reported as having lobbied the Lord Chief Justice and Lord Townshend to help him get this bill dropt.[67] That took until 20 June. When it occurred, Ilay told David Forbes that he would 'propose an address from the [Scottish clergy] to the King betwixt [now] and the next session, setting forth their scruples and offering to take it [an oath] with the references [to the nature of the Kirk] left out'.[68] Another success attributable to the Earl himself was amending the Disarming Act of 1716 to make the Scottish militia and the Fencible men equivalent in duty and to increase the powers of feudal superiors to call out their vassals. His purpose was to insure a quicker and more sure response to uprisings in the future – if the government allowed the militia to be called out.[69] It was a prudent measure but it still required government action to call out the militia. That action would be slow in coming in 1745.

Since March 1716, the Earl and Duke had been under a cloud of royal displeasure. This was made worse by the increasing friendliness of Argyll with the Prince of Wales. The Duke further antagonized the King by urging that the Prince of Wales should be made sole Regent while the King was in Hanover during that summer. Argyll's tactlessness and arrogance could not be tolerated. The King told his son to drop Argyll. The Prince refused. The King said he could have no one around the Prince of Wales 'that had more interest than he had'. That was eagerly reported to Mar by Jacobites in Britain.[70] There was even talk of Argyll being sent to the Tower.[71] Until sometime in June 1716, the Campbells were still speaking for government policies. But, things were changing.

By 30 June 1716, Argyll was again no longer Colonel of the Royal Regiment of Horse Guards, Governor of Minorca or Lord Lieutenant of Surrey and he had resigned as Groom of the Stole to the Prince of Wales. By 1 July 1716, Ilay too had been stripped of offices held during pleasure but not of those he held in the Courts of Session and Justiciary which were for life. The brothers were forced into opposition and conceded, for the nonce, the control of Scottish patronage and policy to their enemies. In a remarkable display of good manners, the Campbell brothers kissed the King's hands as he left for Hanover in July. They assured him 'that their future Behaviour should show that they had been falsely represented to *His Majesty*'.[72] By the end of July, Lord Lovatt could speak of the 'Glorious fall of ye Great Argyl'.[73]

The brothers had gone out of favour for policy reasons and were now willing, for personal reasons, to be obstructive to the Ministry. They hoped to change their situation by showing they were worth buying. What they needed were London allies who could serve their purposes and with whom they could collaborate. It was not clear where those might be found. The brothers now became nuisances and disturbers but never sure allies. In 1716, they stuck to the Prince of Wales and helped exacerbate the division in the royal family which solidified while the King was abroad in Hanover in 1716.[74] But, they found it hard to find a consistent stance. In 1716, they defended the Kirk and Dissenters and sought to minimize the punishments meted out to Scots taken in the Rebellion. That won them Scottish friends but made them look Jacobitical in London – which perhaps they now were. Ilay's politics of leniency had facilitated the building of a northern Argathelian political base in Scotland to which were now added still active Jacobites. They hoped the brothers would decide to support them and oust the new King. That was contrary to the Campbell's religious professions and their continued friendship with the Prince of Wales.

They also tried to undermine the Ministry. When George I became King, four men had the leadership of the government: Sir Robert Walpole and his cousin and brother-in-law, Charles, 2nd Viscount Townshend. They were respectively Chancellor of the Exchequer and the Secretary of State for the Northern Department which handled Scottish business. The others were the Earl of Stanhope, Secretary for the Southern Department, and the Earl of Sutherland, Lord Privy Seal. The Campbells disliked both earls. Stanhope had turned Argyll out of his army posts in 1714. Sutherland was seen as little better. During the summer of 1716, Argyll and Ilay amicably dealt with Walpole and Townshend. It was suspected that Townshend, Walpole and the Campbells planned to form an opposition to the Ministry. Stanhope seems to have been convinced of that. Chancellor Walpole and Secretary Townshend denied to Stanhope that they were dealing with Argyll and Ilay to that end.[75] But, by the end of 1716, both Sir Robert Walpole and Lord Townshend were in eclipse. Townshend was driven from office early in 1717 being replaced as the Scottish Secretary by the Duke of Roxburghe, a Squadrone man. The King's friend would be hard to dislodge. Walpole, followed his cousin into opposition in the summer. They joined the Prince of Wales and his followers including the Campbell brothers.[76] Argyll and Ilay had not quite brought down a government but they had changed it and shown they were good players of the game.

Ilay was perfectly cynical about what they were doing. Interested in getting power, they followed lines of their own trying to look principled. This he made clear in a 1716 letter to his sister's husband, the Earl of Bute:

> ... we always judge for ourselves without any prejudice of any side farther than honour and interest joined oblige us ... .Thus politics is a petty war and game, and as at all other games, we will sometimes win and sometimes loose, and he that plays best and has the best stock has the best chance.... It is enough that we can maintain an interest with some of both sides without giving up anything we must and ought to maintain, and if I can save myself or my friends by being thought a Mohometan by a Turk, I'll never decline it.[77]

It is not at all clear which things could not be given up or what 'honour' really involved. A principled reading of the Earl's character would see as non-negotiable the main features of the Revolution settlement and 'honour', the position of his family in Scottish and British politics maintained by the usual means. A more cynical reading of his statement would find him with no other principles than the taking of spoils by any means. If the latter is the way to read his statement in 1716, then the former is the way to read it later in his career. What is important to note here is that this conflict had been forced on them by men who wished to savage Scots. To struggle against them was an honourable thing for a Scottish politician. Such battles Ilay seldom declined but he did not always push them to a conclusion. In 1716-17 they gained little.

Roxburghe's friends got the rebels tried and Scottish institutions filled with their men. The northern universities offer examples of this process. The Campbells had little or nothing to do with the filling of posts on the Visitation Commissions to the Universities in Glasgow, Aberdeen and St Andrews in 1716-1718. Unlike posts in the revenue services, those were for life.[78] The Commissioners entrenched Squadrone supporters in the universities in Aberdeen and seemed likely to do so at St Andrews.[79] Professors holding those places later created problems for Ilay. Concern with Scottish universities may also have accounted for his arguing against Stanhope's efforts to pass bills reforming the English universities.[80] Those schemes would have given the Crown greater control over university appointments and governance. The bills came to nothing but they touched on the independence of the corporations and the Crown's interest in them, issues important to the Scots whose own universities were being visited in 1716-18. Later, Ilay tried to assert, or threatened to assert, royal power in ways rather like those Stanhope had proposed.[81] What Roxburghe did in the universities, he tried to do generally in the civil administration of the country. Stanhope and Sunderland supported the Squadrone men in their visitations and allowed them appointees in other civil posts, notably the Customs and Excise. The new Ministry continued to follow a repressive line in Scotland which meant, among other things, confiscating rebel property.

Ilay was one of two Scots who served on the Committee which drafted the bill establishing the Forfeited Estates Commission.[82] Through the better part of two years, this made its way into law. The Earl was not much in favour of this measure but his legal skills were useful even though his views were sometimes ignored. In his opinion, the bill created an arbitrary court without clear procedures. In July 1717, Ilay, along with the Earls of Loudoun and Annandale (another trained Scots lawyer and a Tory), approached the King about the Forfeited Estates Act which Ilay thought had been ill-drafted and would produce 'inconveniencies'. They asked that it be withdrawn.[83] That did not happen. On 11 March 1718, the Campbell brothers were among those who protested the creation of the Forfeited Estates Commission. The grounds for opposition were drafted by some Scots lawyer, most likely Annandale or Ilay. The Commission was held to be an arbitrary court without formal rules of procedure. It would be guilty of countenancing perjury and would escape the jurisdiction of the Court of Sessions and even that of the House of Lords. Commissioners might be judges in their own cases if they had bought forfeited estates and they were likely to upset judgments already rendered on those estates by other courts. That would harm creditors, claimants and the new owners.[84] Such votes and protests made Ilay more respected in Scotland and had nuisance value in London.[85] Ilay and his brother were probably excluded from the appointments of men to the Forfeited Estates Commission which at first had four Englishmen among its six members and later was packed with Squadrone supporters.

In February 1718, Ilay and Argyll joined Tory lords in opposing and then dissenting from the Mutiny Bill for reasons which they never found good when they held power. The principal reasons for dissents were that the bill was novel, a violation of Magna Carta, deficient in defining what were to be capital crimes, did not provide for sufficient civilian control of the military under some circumstances and allowed the King to be a sole legislator when he decided what military courts could try. Those courts had too much power. Ilay agreed but was to say in similar later debates that the officers in the British Army and Navy could be trusted not to become agents of tyranny.[86] Ilay's motives in 1718 seem factional but seconded by his dislike for poorly drafted legislation.

In June 1717, General William Cadogan was accused of corruption in both Houses. Sir Robert Walpole, William Pulteney, Henry Pelham and the Jacobite, William Shippen in the House of Commons, and Ilay in the House of Lords, accused Cadogan of fraud and embezzlement during the 1715 uprising. Those charges garnered the votes in the House of Commons of a number of officers and many office holders who had also been extruded from their places by the ministers. The Campbells were useful to their friends in opposition and attacked a man who had been brutal in Scotland. Interest and principle here coincided.[87] The affair dragged on as did suits against the General brought by the dowager Duchess of Marlborough who accused him of dishonesty and who won in the courts. Cadogan had the King's support and in 1722 was made Master-General of the Ordnance, from which place Argyll ousted him in 1725.[88]

In 1717, the brothers attempted to defeat the government's request for funds to repel a threatened Swedish invasion.[89] The brothers argued and voted for dropping charges against Robert Harley, Lord Oxford, when he was impeached in the summer of 1717. They spoke on Oxford's behalf and both would have been pleased when the Lords voted unanimously to drop the charges against him and the impeachment failed.[90] They had little use for the fallen minister but they wished to see those who opposed them made to look badly. Both moves were supported by Jacobites and Tories.[91] By the end of 1717, Ilay and the Duke were no closer to power but they had shown they could be troublesome. The following year was somewhat similar but, in the end, they had better luck.

Given his interest in economic matters, Ilay would also have watched closely the debate early in 1718 on the shortage of silver but what he said or did is unknown except for the fact that he acquired pamphlets on those topics as his library catalogue shows. In another matter, he was successful. In 1718, Ilay secured for the Scottish Fisheries and Manufactures a small grant which eventually helped to capitalize the fund established for the Board of Trustees in 1727.[92]

The Duke and Ilay listened to Dissenters at the end of 1718 as they lobbied for the repeal of the Test and Corporation Acts passed in Anne's reign.[93] Throughout the winter session of Parliament, Ilay was in the House 85% of the time attending to such business. The brothers joined the Opposition to try to prevent the government from repealing the Occasional Conformity and Schism Acts. Ilay sargued that repeal infringed 'the articles of the Union... with respect to one church' and so might be a precedent for tampering with the rights of the Church of Scotland at some later date.[94] When the bill was amended and re-introduced, both Argyll and Ilay spoke for it and the brothers' credit with the Dissenters went up. They looked more plausible as defenders of the interest of the Kirk. When the bill passed in January 1719, the brothers had made some difference.

By early 1719, the Ministry needed Argathelian votes in Parliament and was willing to pay for them. Deserting the Prince of Wales, Argyll and Ilay were returned to royal favour on 6 February 1719. That was their payment for supporting the King and voting against Stanhope's plans to repeal the Occasional Conformity Act (1711), the Schism Act (1714)[95] and perhaps his plan to modify the Test and Corporation Acts.[96] Argyll was taken into the Ministry and his places were restored. He was also appointed Lord Steward of the Household and, on 27 April 1719, became Duke of Greenwich. The Duke and Ilay again 'took their places at ye Councill Board'.[97] The government now had the brothers' votes in the divisions on the Peerage Bill which Argyll seconded when it was introduced in the House of Lords in March 1719.[98] That cost them something in Scotland where it was widely opposed. Their return to favour also cost them the regard of the Prince and Princess of Wales who were unhappy with their conduct. Ilay was disliked by the future Queen until the end of her life. Rumours circulated that Ilay was to displace the Duke of Roxburghe as Scottish Secretary but that did not happen.[99]

V. Dealing With The Pretender

The Campbell brothers' frustrations, ambition and concerns over the insecurity of the Hanoverian regime led them to flirt with Jacobites c.1712-14. That was meant to be insurance and perhaps nothing more. Another set of contacts made during 1716-1719 deserve more notice.

In 1716, Ilay seems to have been visiting the Ogelthorpes about every day. Keeping up with the Ogelthorpes was useful. This Jacobite family provided Ilay and his brother with a connexion to the Court at St Germain-en-Laye anytime it suited them to use it. Fanny Ogelthorpe's sister, Anne, the bright and beautiful older daughter, lived at St Germain where she was said by some to be a mistress to the Pretender. Some believed she had been made a Countess. The girls' mother collected mail directed to Ilay in 1718 when she was in Paris. Ilay met with Anne when he was in France in 1719 and 1720. Between the spring of 1716 and the beginning of 1719, Ilay parleyed with the Jacobites. The Earl had talked in the past as if he was open to deals with the Pretender. Now he approached the exiled Court while his brother stayed aloof from the negotiations about which he knew. What their negotiations really meant is not clear. They were important in Ilay's political calculations and in those who knew or guessed something of his involvement with the exiled Stuarts. They used their knowledge. or suspicions, to cast aspersions on his character. In the end, the Pretender, Mar, and other Jacobites concluded that Ilay never had been sincere, a judgment which was ultimately also made by George Lockhart who knew him even better.

According to Fanny Ogelthorpe, Lord Ilay's expressions of sympathy for the exiled King dated from c.1706 when the Earl was allegedly committed to the Union.[100] She would have known that Ilay had shown sympathy with Jacobites in 1713-14 and that he and his brother had been the most merciful of those who fought them in the '15. By May 1717, Mar could write to the Earl saying '... it is a very great pleasure now to me to find that your friend [Argyll] nor you have no personal quarrel or ill will toward my master [the Pretender] or myself'. He looked forward to co-operating with the brothers and promised they would be well rewarded.[101] Part of the reward was to be a pardon for them which would come with a written promise to confirm it after a restoration. Commissions in the Pretender's army were offered in later correspondence. Those negotiations coincided with the brothers' defence of Robert Harley, Lord Oxford.[102] By the autumn of 1717, things had cooled considerably. Ilay seems to have been worried about the discovery of his correspondence. At the same time, Fanny thought Ilay was committed though he had not 'engaged'. She wrote to Mar on 24 November 1717 that Ilay had said 'that, when once he engaged in the least, he must go through, it not being fit to do things of that nature by halves, and that, whilst he had kept himself disengaged, he was free to take what party he pleased, that nothing would be expected of him'. She reported that Argyll was privy to all this and that there had been a breach of security in the handling of the correspondence, a breach which had infuriated the Duke.[103] At about the same time, Ilay [his code name was significantly 'the Doctor'] either got his pardon or learned of its terms.[104] He seems to have wanted more but he and his brother were likely told that this was all they would get until they gave more evidences of loyalty.[105]

Colin Campbell of Glendaruel wrote Mar on 10 October 1717 that Ilay and Argyll would do nothing and would stick to the Prince of Wales. By December, they had broken with the Prince and Ilay was telling Mar indirectly that they would appear to be neutral, saying that having 'ventured life and all for *King George*, and he saw the return he met with, should he venture for another, he and his brother might meet the same usage'. That looks like a play for time as did the problem he raised next. He enquired about the religious beliefs and the religious policy of the Pretender – questions which were answered by Mar and the Pretender only on 10 March 1718.[106] Ilay then claimed he needed something from Mar and the King so that his talks with the Archbishop of York and others might produce results.[107] The brothers' dissatisfaction with George I and the now arrogant Prince of Wales was shared by others who would now find it in their interest to restore the Stuarts.[108] It is most unlikely that Ilay believed what he then wrote.

Then the brothers stopped writing to St Germain and the information and the commissions which had been requested were not sent. Better Jacobites thought the brothers would create among them more troubles than they were worth. Mar's conclusion by 19 February 1718 was that, until they proved their loyalty and value, nothing more could be done. Ilay's response was to tell Fanny that George I and the Prince of Wales were 'the nations tyrants'.[109] She and Mar got sweet talk from the Earl who promised to send Fanny a new code. This impressed Fanny but Mar wrote, 'neither the King nor I can find much in Ilay's letter'– which did not contain a code book for them. Ilay finally delivered that in June 1718.[110] Despite mutual disenchantment, Lord Ilay was given a warrant for his pardon and a patent for an English Earldom 'with remainder to the heirs male of his body'.[111] By June 1718, Colonel Middleton, George Lockhart and John Walkinshaw had all pressed the brothers 'toward that branch of trade'.[112] Ilay went to France having been distracted all spring by marital difficulties caused by a wife who showed more spirit than he knew she had. In Paris, the Earl met with the Regent. By early May they had probably talked about the ongoing 1718 incursion into Scotland by Jacobites backed by Sweden and Spain and not discouraged by France and Catholic Europe. That incursion was over by the end of June so anything Ilay might have promised about that could have had no effect. The Earl returned and went to Scotland in July. In the following month, Mar asked that the brothers deal kindly with those on their lands who had rebelled against King George in 1715. Argyll had dealt harshly with some of his rebellious tacksmen and had secured part of the forfeited estate of Cameron of Lochiel. Now he made no concessions. Mar and George Lockhart gave up on the Campbells by March 1718 but correspondence probably did not cease until near the end of that year.[113] By then, Fanny's correspondence with Ilay dealt only with private matters.[114] The Earl and Duke were no longer interested in a Jacobite future – if they ever had been.

With the Jacobites there would be no rapprochement. Still, Lockhart, despite earlier misgivings, sometimes hoped for one. On 2 August 1720, he wrote to James Murray saying he had had a long talk with Argyll which might be the prelude to further discussions. Nothing came of it. In the summer of 1721, he tried again to come to some accommodation with the Duke to oppose the Peerage Bill in return for Jacobite support. That did not work.[115] Lockhart's hopes showed only that the

Argathelians were 'soft' on Jacobites and able to bargain in ways which would have been unimaginable for their Squadrone enemies.

Playing games with the Jacobites was not going to bring the Campbell brothers significant power without a successful rebellion. Still, the games had benefits and political results. Ilay had been a more than willing partner to discussions however reluctant he was to act. That gave the brothers a bit of insurance when Hanoverian rule looked shaky. It also paid off in the 1722 elections. Ilay's flexibility helped him and his brother win some seats with Jacobite support. What it did not do was to affect their usual politicking in London.

Plate 3. Duke of Argyll after William Aikman, mezzotint engraving by Richard Cooper (c.1744), with the permission of the Scottish National Portrait Gallery.

Chapter 5

A New Social Scene and the Malt Tax Riots

I. A New Social Scene

By 1719 Argyll and Ilay were seen as more interesting men than they had appeared to be in 1707. The King and country were not secure and there were divisions in the royal family which caused divisions in politics and in society. Their involvement in those currents of opinion and events gave Ilay a somewhat different set of friends. Some were in the Prince's court or were Opposition politicians. Beyond the Courts were bankers and international financiers. Some of those people were to be important in his life for many years to come. One who was not was his wife.

At some point (perhaps around 1715-17), he sent the young Countess of Ilay to Scotland to live with his mother, probably at Limecraigs, her house at Campbeltown, or at Rosneath Castle. The Duchess sometimes had girls in residence who came to learn from her manners and whatever else she could convey to shape a woman to figure in good society. There is a small chance that Ilay was educating his wife as well as rusticating her. Whatever his initial intentions, she was held against her will but escaped and was in London by February 1718. There, she was protected by his political foes. The girl had spunk. Fanny Ogelthorpe described what happened to Lord Mar:

> His wife had made her escape from his mother and is arrived in London and has sworn the peace against him and her. He has been forced to give in 18,000l. bail to commit no violence against her. She is pursuing him in Doctor's Commons for a separate maintenance. All his enemies assist her. You may imagine how thoroughly he's vexed to be linked to such a woman and so used, but why did he take her, or why did he not keep her with him? It is a pitiful revenge in his enemies to increase their division.[1]

Mar's reaction was laughter.

What this set of incidents says about the character of the Earl is hard to know. He may not have been wholly heartless in sending her off to Scotland. Educating her would have been desirable. She does not seem to have been around the Tory wits or with other of his intellectual friends. But, leaving her there when she wanted to return was akin to the usage given their wives by his friends Lord Lovat and Lord Grange[2] or by Colonel Charteris, whose rape of someone in the 1730s did not unduly distress Ilay (see p. 370, n. 18). Lovat and Grange were kidnappers who used violence against their wives. Violence does not seem to figure elsewhere in

Ilay's life and may here have been alleged to embarrass him politically. Still, his behaviour was found scandalous. Her Ladyship, when she returned, sought to do him as much damage as possible. In the end, she got her separation. He had to pay her off in some fashion but just how or with how much remains unclear. She did not live long to enjoy it. She died on 1 September 1723. Ilay never married again but had other 'playthings'.

Sometime after he had parted with his wife, Elizabeth Ann Williams (?- 1 June 1762), otherwise 'Shireburn', as she is named in his will, became his long-term mistress.[3] It is not clear when he took up with her but their illegitimate son was born c.1720 so he had probably done so by 1719. The expensive diamond ring Lord Ilay purchased on 5 December 1719 may have been for Mrs. Williams not himself.[4] What she was like, we do not know. Ilay never mentioned her to others. No letters to her survive. No pictures are known – she is almost a blank. Perhaps the best key to what she was like is offered by his grand-niece Lady Louisa Stewart who tells us

.... [Ilay] could not be supposed to share his elder [brother's] prejudice against intelligent women. He saw women (and men too) just as they were, had no toleration for fools of either sex, and felt a supreme contempt for his sister-in-law, who in return, hated him cordially, and delighted in pecking at his friends or picking up nonsensical stories about his amours.

Lady Louisa Stuart's comments are borne out by the kindnesses he showed for the bright wives of men like Lords Milton and Hervey but they seem to jar with the arrangement of his own marriage. Whatever Mrs. Williams had to offer must have satisfied him over many years. She lived close to him but not under the same roof. In London, she was in a house adjoining the Argyll House property; at Whitton she had a place near or on his estate. Since she was left all 'my Personal Estate' in England with liberty to devise that as she would, Mrs. Williams must have given him considerable happiness. It is not so clear that the Earl was a constant lover. He seems to have had other lady friends after he had taken his long-term mistress. [5]

Mrs. Williams by the 1720s had given him two children so Ilay had a family of a sort. Their son, William Williams (later Williams Campbell), was educated by tutors and in 1739, when he was about nineteen, was given a life post as Deputy Auditor of the Exchequer of Scotland, a place worth £200 a year. Ilay saw to his advancement in the Army where he rose in the end to a General's rank and to the Colonelcy in the 3rd Foot Guards, later the Scots Guards. He died in 1786. William Williams, when he was not on active service, was usually at his father's table. He was deeply distressed by his father's demise. Ilay's daughter, Ann Williams, was left a genteel income of £100 a year plus an extra £100 for three years following his death. She was probably unmarried in 1761.[6] What happened to her is uncertain. This family was well looked after since it inherited almost all of Ilay's personal estate. Mrs. Williams never figured in the circles in which Ilay moved. The most important of those was that of the Prince and Princess of Wales.

Around the Prince and his wife, Caroline of Brandenburg-Ansbach, were many young and lively people. Glimpses of the life they led are provided by the biography of Mrs. Henrietta Howard, Woman of the Bed Chamber to Princess Caroline and later mistress to the Prince. More glimpses come in the society verses of Pope, Gay and others. Mrs. Howard and Ilay had met in c.1715 and would be close until c.1727. In that year, the Prince succeeded to the Crown and Ilay tried to use Mrs. Howard to influence his policies. That was resented by the Queen – as was Lord Stair's tale that Ilay had courted Mrs. Howard.[7] Both the Queen and Mrs. Howard cooled to him but Ilay remained part of Henrietta's circle until the 1730s when politics finally divided them.

A few letters from her circle exist in the Lothian Muniments concerning Ilay's social life from 1718-1731. Most of the letters are addressed to Mrs. Howard. One in Ilay's best hand dated 22 July [1718], is finely written and might have delighted its recipient. The lady is complimented on her ability to write a good letter in a style so unlike that of her sex: 'it is void of all those pretty incoherences that charm in the writings of the fair'. Agreeable fluff. Another in this collection describes an outing to Newport in 1719, which Ilay did not make but could have. It too is a bit of rococo not unlike some of the Dresden and Chelsea ceramic figurines he would have owned:

> ... after dinner, tea partys att Cards, and by this time (little) flirtations were going forward; att ten a clock we sup'd and were not less well served than att dinner_ ___ (to bed between 12 &1) ___ next day reviewed troops, dined at Ld Mark Kerr's tent, drank, sung french songs, cards, flirting ... [8]

Then, back to London. This fits the dates when the Earl was supposedly interested in Mrs. Howard. She and Ilay would also have discussed finances since he gave her advice about investing in John Law's scheme in 1719 and 1720.[9] They were clearly more compatible than either was with their spouse. Among Henrietta's friends was Alexander Pope and the wits associated with him.

The Earl's acquaintance with Pope went back to at least c. 1712 when Pope was a celebrity poet noted for 'The Essay on Criticism' (1711), 'The Rape of the Lock' and 'The Dunciad' (1712) and for having begun his translation of Homer. Their friendship continued, at least off and on, into the 1730s. Pope's minor verse includes poems which mention Ilay and his brother.[10] Ilay's high point with the poets may have come in 1719 when John Gay penned the following quatrain to the brothers:

> See there two Brothers Greet thee with Applause
> Both for prevailing Eloquence renown'd
> Argyll the brave and Islay learn'd in Laws
> Than whom no truer friends were ever found.[11]

That was not to last but it shows the Earl in a very sophisticated literary set, one which acquainted him with men whom he would later oppose for many years. Others in this clique were leaders in architecture and gardening.

The Earl's interests in horticulture and gardens probably date from his childhood experience of the gardens at Ham House and then from his time in Holland. By the

1720s gardening, even agriculture, became for him an increasingly practical activity since he now had places where he could grow things. His first purchase at Whitton, Surrey (in the London Borough of Richmond) came in 1722. Within a few years both Whitton and The Whim, his Peebles-shire estate, had fields which allowed him to experiment and to raise large numbers of plants and seedling trees. Ilay was probably an early member of the Honourable the Improvers in the Knowledge of Agriculture of Scotland which formed in the early 1720s.[12] Ilay's friendship with Alexander Pope and many others involved gardens, plants and buildings.

By the mid and late 1720s Ilay had made many contacts with the circle of the Earls of Burlington, Pembroke and Bathurst to which Pope belonged. Colen Campbell, Lord Burlington's favourite architect, dedicated engravings to the Campbell brothers.[13] Ilay had a hand in building Henrietta Howard's Marble Hill House (1724-1729) designed by Campbell.[14] Others in this circle included notable architects and builders such as James Gibbs, Robert and Roger Morris – all of whom designed fashionable Palladian structures and could built in Gothic and Chinese styles. Interest in such novelties put Ilay in touch with architects like the Langleys, Morrises and others who were changing British taste in houses and gardens in the 1720s and 1730s. Those men were developing new-style gardens along the Thames. Ilay's garden at Whitton was fashionable with its openness, new plants, Chinese pavilion and Gothic ornaments. By the end of the 1730s, Whitton too had a somewhat Palladian villa – not on the Thames but on improved heathland.

There were other milieux where Lord Ilay mixed with men of quite another sort. He was friendly with James Brydges, 1st Duke of Chandos, and sometimes dined with him at Cannons which had considerable gardens. On one occasion in 1721, Chandos entertained Ilay and the Duke, their relative, Lord Bellenden, and several gentlemen from Scotland. Also attending were the Rev. Dr. John Desaguliers and a Mr. Hore, a man concerned with the channelling of rivers to make them navigable.[15] Desaguliers was a notable lecturer on science in London and remembered for inventing the planetarium. He was a good Whig who preached before Princess Caroline in 1717. He advised Chandos on scientific matters relevant to that Duke's business interests. Those included mines, water works, insurance companies, the 'funds' and a variety of companies, some of which he founded. Chandos was a patron and friend of Dr. Charles Stuart, Ilay's sometime companion.[16] Ilay was now at home in that world but the details of his involvement in it are not numerous. On the edges of that world were clever mechanics and artisans of various kinds and members of the Sephardic community in London which supplied many of the brokers with whom men like Chandos and Ilay dealt.

What did not characterize Ilay's life in England was hunting, visiting, going to races and indulging in the other past-times of men of his class. He is not known to have fought any duels and was not associated with any scandalous affairs or events other than political scrapes and the shenanigans of his wife. He never had a reputation as a drinker or rake and was not notable as a conversationalist outside his own house where he talked seriously to men who shared his interests in politics and business, science and the practical arts. He seemed eccentric to some but cared not a whit what they thought. He appeared in coffee houses such as Will's, a resort for politicians, and Bedford's, where book auctions were sometimes held. Both had Whig clienteles.

The Earl also had a social life on his trips to Scotland. He went there in at least twelve years between 1700 and 1720 and almost every year thereafter until the end of his life. His Scottish social life was different. It was first of all very busy with politics and the development of his estates. In 1726, Duncan Forbes warned his London friends that Ilay did not welcome visits from men who had no business with him and whom he did not especially want to see.[17] That was true of him everywhere throughout his life. When he went up, he mixed pleasure and business but he went mainly for political reasons – elections, to quell riots and to impose peace on a restive country. He met with supporters, those of other factions who were wavering, town councillors and members of corporations. All that entailed much riding and necessary socializing, much of which he may not have enjoyed but which it was his to do. It gave him a comprehensive knowledge of the country and its needs and it introduced him to virtually every interesting and powerful man in the kingdom. His trips sometimes took him to visit his mother who lived either at Limecraigs in Campbeltown or at Rosneath Castle or Duddingston House. They were not close but he seems the more dutiful of her sons. He spent time with his aide, Lord Milton, and sometimes went to northern Scotland on electioneering trips. Scottish trips were for business not pleasure until after he became an improver of two estates there.

II. Business

By c.1713 Ilay's business dealings were laying the foundations of his considerable fortune. By then he was no novice in the buying and selling of stocks but his success as a businessman was also rooted in a frugality which saw investment as more important than ostentatious living. His activities are difficult to unravel because of the paucity of records. We do not know, for example, how much money his wife brought to him in 1713. It was likely to have supplied, along with his judicial offices, the capital used in his early speculations. The best indicators of his wealth and investment income are the ledgers at Middleton's Bank (now Coutts) which begin in January 1713 but point back to earlier transactions.[18] From the ledgers and other evidence, it is clear that he was already fronting for John Law and dealing with merchant bankers in France and Holland. He may also have had Scottish accounts with private bankers. After 1724, Lord Milton held a grant of factory (power of attorney) from him and handled some funds.[19] Payments to Ilay made outside London do not always appear in his accounts at Middleton's Bank but no records of them have been found either in London or Edinburgh.[20] He also acted for others in the buying of lottery tickets,[21] stocks and bonds. It is not always possible to sort out his own business transactions from others in which he did not act for himself. That is particularly true of this period during which he and his friends were caught up in investment bubbles. Further complicating the picture is the fact that Coutts Bank lacks his 'in' and 'out' ledgers for the period 29 November 1714- 1 January 1717. Middleton's Bank nearly broke in 1720 and was effectively closed between December 1720 and 22 October 1723 which creates another gap. We also cannot say what he was worth before the bubbles in France, Holland and England or where else he is likely to have had some of his money. And, we cannot know his situation at the end of the bubbles. Finally, he both lent and borrowed monies which do not appear in his accounts or do so only sporadically. Despite those problems, it seems worth looking at his business activities since he was later to become a founder and first Governor of two banks and died a wealthy man. There is no good way to estimate his income from investments in the period 1710-1724 but one can calculate roughly what he had and was making.

As we have seen (see p. 38), by 1711, both Ilay and John Law were dealing in the newly issued South Sea Company stock.[22] Buying then was almost a guarantee of making money if the stock was sold before 1721. In 1712-13, their investments came to about £8,000 and he paid out to Law about £8,500 before the account was closed in 1714.[23] They had made money but how much Ilay profited is unclear. What is clear is that he had other investments. In 1712, he appears to have had about £3,300 in the Bank of England and East India Company stock and some lottery tickets. It looks as if he had put all his salary as a judge into the market for the previous three years. In 1713, those sums should have and did go up probably because of his marriage. He earned at least £161.6.4 in interest and dividends which means a capital sum of about £5,367 if the return was 3%.[24] He also had £281 in a 'plate account'. His 'Out book' shows a few more purchases and payments such as £361 more for plate and an East India Co. bond for £107 and some lottery tickets. While he lost £35 on an investment in the African Company, founded by his friend Chandos, he had about doubled his wealth in a year. That suggests that his wife had initially brought him at least £2,000 and the prospect of much more.

In the following year, Ilay's capital holdings look about £1,000 less but the year end entries are missing and some of the others are not intelligible. He had a larger income having been given the lucrative post of Lord Clerk Register worth £445.[25] Ilay was replaced in 1714 as John Law's agent by William Law, John's brother, a change which probably shows the Earl's preoccupation with politics surrounding the succession of George I. He had spent some time in Scotland and had been preoccupied with politicking. Law would have wanted a more attentive manager.

The Coutts accounts show the Earl to have been acting alone in the market by January 1715 but those transactions are missing from his own accounts and show only in those of the Bank.[26] In 1715, he had in South Sea stock £1,309.2.5 and at the end of 1716 £663.8.9 – he is likely to have sold some to finance his time defending Scotland or at least Inveraray. In 1717, Ilay seems to have put about £4,700 into the market while withdrawing from it about £3,000. Interest and dividend payments suggest that he had in total about £8,343 in capital. He was also enquiring that year into lead mines on the island of Islay which either looked attractive to him or which the family was going to let to an entrepreneur.[27] Finally, he had some interest in Kenwood House on which he was paying the land and window taxes.[28] At the beginning of 1718, the Earl may have had about £5,873 in the market mostly in South Sea Stock but with some East India Co. bonds paying about 4%.[29] He does not seem to have had any English dealings with Law in that year but there are transactions between the Earl and unknown others which may mask them and add to his total market involvement in England or overseas. If they do, he was, perhaps, investing something in Law's

French schemes – but then, there may have been a French account in which he and Law were working with funds left over from an earlier period. Ilay was still buying lottery tickets.[30] By the end of 1718, he seems to have owned only £1,200 in South Sea bonds. His accounts show no sales of what was earlier owned although interest and dividends are not listed for all of his earlier purchases. His 1719 'In book' accounts run only to 12 October and suggest that his holdings changed mainly by the selling of East India Co. bonds and the purchase of £1,200 South Sea bonds on 7 July just as the stock was beginning to rise steeply. His assets were now not all in English securities since he held some still rising Mississippi stock in 1719.

Ilay was in Paris in the summer and autumn of 1719 where he talked with John Law about the financial prospects. Law was using Middleton as his English agent for all his affairs in Britain which included trading in bullion and betting against the rise of the English market generally and against the East India and South Sea Companies in particular.[31] Indeed, in late August, Ilay had dinner with Law, the British Ambassador, Lord Stair, Lord Londonderry, and a speculator named Joseph Gage. Law wagered a very large amount of money with Londonderry on the decline of the English market. The others, but not Ilay, bought into the action.[32] Ilay does seem to have believed Law's forecast that the French funds would rise and the British ones would sink. He told Henrietta Howard, 'for my part, I came after all was in a manner over; and as I never meddle with those matters, I do nothing but buy books and gimcracks'. Given his next sentences that was a joke:

> I am of opinion that whatever sum you remit here may be turned to great profit. The stocks are now at 950, and if no accidents happen of mortality, it is probable they will be 1500 in a short time.[33] The money I laid out for you was 5000 livres, as a subscriber to the fifty millions of stock lately added, of which the tenth part only is paid down, so that 5000 is the first payment of 50,000 livres. The subscription was full, but Mr. Law was so kind as to allow it me: some of the subscribers have already sold their subscriptions for 230, that is their own money back again, and 130 percent profit. Whatever you think fit to do, you may bid Middleton remit to me so many livres; I shall acknowledge the receipt of them, and do the best I can. You will think the levity of this country has turned my head, when I tell you that your master [The Prince of Wales] might, within these few months, have made himself richer than his father. As late as I came, I can tell you, in secret, that I am pretty well.[34]

His cousin Jack [later the 4th Duke of Argyll] 'has got, I believe, near 10,000 l and has lost half that sum, by a timorous, silly bargain he made'. How much Ilay and Mrs. Howard invested in the Mississippi Scheme is unknown. There are from this time no transactions through his London account of large sums of money. He had had a fling but when and how much he invested is unclear as is the date on which he sold. If Mrs. Howard invested, her money went through other channels but possibly to Ilay in the end.

When the Earl returned to Paris in January 1720, his funds would have been worth perhaps eight times more and were near the height they reached in late February-early March after which they declined rapidly and became virtually worthless in the spring of 1721. In January 1720, Ilay did not think he ran much risk and was still encouraging others to invest. He joked about the risks which seemed less in France than in England where speculative fever was also rising.

> Every post I receive from England new terrors concerning it, and, what is really very diverting, some are extremely apprehensive of my losing money I have got, who, to my certain knowledge are very much mortified at my getting it: I am not insensible of distant dangers which may attend the funds here, and wish our own were absolutely free from them; but for the objections which have come from even considerable people in England, they prove more that they have learned their own business by rote than that they have any true notions of the principles of these matters. I know a pretty extraordinary instance of something of this kind, if I could venture to tell; but this far I may venture to say, that either Mr. Law knows nothing, or some who carry their heads very high in England know less than people imagine.[35]

This seems to hint at Law's belief that the English market would decline and that money could be made by selling short.

When he returned to London, Ilay began to speculate in earnest. By the end of June 1720, the Earl had invested over £50,000 in the rising market most of it in the South Sea Company but with another £8,000 in stocks such as the African Company and the York Buildings Company. He also made loans to others but those cannot now all be separated from payments to brokers and others. By the end of the year, his outlays on stocks, tallies (£7,070) and other companies came to over £92,365. To balance those sums, huge inflows were recorded in the 'In book' mostly from the sale of South Sea stock up to 2 September when it began a steep decline. His 'In book' shows increases of £103,502 up to 2 September with £25,479 coming in after that time for a 1720 total of £128,981. About £24,000 seems to have come in from abroad, mainly from someone named Formyetts. Much of the money came from the sale of South Sea Stock in late June when it was near its peak. Some of the money coming in and going out may have been invested for others who would have gotten a return which appears as the Earl's. Other credits were probably from debts called in and one payment for £10,000, in December 1720, came from John Law whose bill Ilay had accepted the previous March. Other large payments came from Dutch merchants or bankers. If he was like Law, then some of this may reflect money made by betting on the decline of the livre and Dutch florin and the rise of the pound. The difference between the 'in' and 'out' accounts, £36,616, suggests that Ilay did well during the bubbles. At their end, he still had unsold stock of an unknown amount.

He was also active in the winding down of the bubble. He is supposed to have tried to calm other investors in a speech to the stockholders – probably one he gave at a tumultuous meeting in late September 1720 when he argued against an enquiry into the behavior of the directors.[36] All that was in the interest of the Ministry but it was also in some measure self-interested since the directors included friends and those who had probably given him free or cheap stock. Later, he opposed revealing the Company's secrets (see p. 254).

How well the Earl did in the bubbles cannot be known since his English bank entries end in December 1720 and do not begin again until 19 October 1723. Foreign accounts probably existed but have not been found. He made enough early on so that he could lend money to others while the speculative mania gripped the country. Among them were the Earls of Loudoun and Kinnoull. Ilay probably lent the first £4,000 which Loudoun lost and slowly paid off at 4% out of a government pension.[37] Kinnoull in 1720 borrowed £1,000 at 4% to buy South Sea stock. By the time Kinnoull came to pay the interest and principal, the market price of the stock had crashed and Kinnoull refused to pay interest on a sum larger than it was then selling for saying that the rate asked was usurious. Ilay took him to an English court and then to the Court of Session where Andrew Fletcher, the future Lord Milton, represented him. Ilay won.[38] Others to whom he may have lent include the Earl of Bute, Col. Charles Cathcart, William Stewart, MP, and Lady Oglethorpe all of whom show up in his 'Out book'. After this period, he always had some cash out at interest as loans. Other signs of affluence can be found in his purchase of a diamond ring in December 1719 and of scientific instruments in 1720. By the early 1720s, he did not lack investment funds.

As noted above, Ilay made the first purchase of land on what was to become his Whitton estate in 1722. His correspondence with Lord Milton in 1723-24 suggests that both of them were dabbling in York Buildings Society stock and other debentures.[39] At the beginning of 1724, his accounts shows him to have had about £7,388 in South Sea funds (stocks, bonds and annuities) of which he sold nearly £3,300 during that year. Among the funds he added were debentures secured by the Equivalent Fund established at the Union. In 1724, he helped secure an Act incorporating the holders of the equivalent debentures into the Equivalent Co. This company was to collect the interest on the debentures and distribute it to holders who were mostly resident in London.[40] That was the first step toward the creation of the Royal Bank of Scotland. By the end of 1724, the Earl had bought somewhat more than £5,700 of stock and bonds. It looks as if he was then worth £14,103, plus the value of outstanding loans (£3,500?), and enjoyed an income of about £2,000, half of which was secure for his lifetime. At age forty-two, he was well off.

III. Politics During and After the Bubbles

The brothers' adherence to the Ministry in 1719 had been welcomed. In late February, Argyll took credit for proposing the expansion of the number of Scots peers from sixteen elected Representative Peers to twenty-five hereditary peers sitting in Parliament. It did not bother him that it would close the United Kingdom peerage to new creations for Scots. Argyll and Ilay knew that limiting future creations was a move partially aimed at the Prince of Wales and his friends. The Prince, when he came to power, would almost certainly create new peers who might then try to impeach ministers who had offended them. Ilay defended the bill on those grounds but he had others.[41] He claimed that the influence of Scots would be increased by their larger numbers and that sitting by right of birth would give Representative Peers greater dignity. Electing peers to the House of Lords demeaned the dignity of Scottish peers and that of the House. Ilay said he 'had long before wished to see this defect in the

Union rectified, and the Scotch Peers freed from that ignominious Mark of Distinction which made them be looked upon as dependent on the Court and Ministry, and not at Liberty to vote like the other Members, for the Good and Interest of their Country'.[42] That was special pleading from a man long used to it. He noted that the Squadrone had 'pushed' the bill in hopes of permanently excluding him from Parliament and to 'get in themselves'. He said he acted for the Scottish peers and that the whole issue had arisen because of the Duke of Hamilton's exclusion from the House of Lords years earlier – a point with which Montrose and other Squadrone members agreed.[43] In the end, it mattered more that the Ministry was said to have promised hereditary peerages to all sixteen of the sitting Representative Peers from Scotland.[44]

Squadrone members, in the end, opposed the Peerage Bill because it would, as they claimed, block the access to power of new men, a concern which Jacobites also shared although their new men would have been very different. The Squadrone members finally opposed it because they knew that Argyll wanted to sit with a precedence they were unwilling to give him.[45] They also were sure that he would name some of the new Scottish peers should the bill pass. He would include his brother but permanently exclude Squadrone families. The bill was withdrawn in April 1719 but introduced again in December 1719 when it passed the Lords only to be defeated in the Commons mainly because of the efforts of Sir Robert Walpole. The bill had set the Prince of Wales's teeth on edge and put Walpole strongly in opposition to the brothers. The Campbells did themselves more good by supporting the repeal of the Schism Act in 1719. That was popular with the Kirk which they needed to cultivate. Although active and useful to ministers, the Duke and Ilay did not get from their efforts more Scottish patronage.[46] Squadrone men were still the King's men and continued to distribute more patronage than the Argathelians. Supporting the Ministry had not done the brothers as much good as they hoped it would. The favours they had been given seemed enough to those who gave them but not to the brothers. They now did little more for the Ministry in which Sunderland too began to handle Scottish patronage.

Their reaction to perceived neglect was predictable. Would Walpole's faction give more to the brothers? Walpole and his brother-in-law, Lord Townshend, had been edging closer to the Prince of Wales. This created opportunities for the Campbells to play one set of politicians against others. To come to permanent power, Ilay and the Duke needed alliances with politicians but the English were dividing into unstable factions. One consequence of instability was that Scots were a bit unsure where patronage was to be had.[47] The brothers' position further deteriorated when the Prince of Wales made up with his father the King in April 1720. Abandoning the Prince, as they had done, meant they would now suffer. Argyll and Ilay were soon out once again.[48] Argyll was dismissed from his place as Lord Steward.[49]

Walpole had helped to bring about the reconciliation between the King and Prince. He and Townshend returned to some power as the South Sea Bubble rapidly inflated in 1720 and burst in that year. Stock, which had risen about eightfold in price, crashed between June and December. Walpole, a financial expert, was needed to help sort out the problems caused by the intense financial panic which came in September.[50]

The bursting of the Bubble produced more unity among Whigs by lessening the power of Stanhope and Sunderland (Marlborough's son-in-law) and increasing that of Walpole and his friends. Stanhope and Sunderland were both discredited by the fiasco. Sunderland had made substantial losses and was thought to be implicated in the scandal. The brothers struck a deal with Sunderland who earlier had aided Ilay's wayward wife when she took him to court.[51] The Duke and Earl agreed to support him against impeachment; he would find ways to help them. That allied the Campbells with Sunderland and Carteret against Townshend and Walpole in an unstable Ministry. Stanhope died on 4 February 1721; about a year later, so did Sunderland. By April 1721, Walpole, Townshend, and Carteret held the Treasury and offices of Secretary of State for the Northern and Southern Departments. Walpole and Townshend became the chief ministers and the Campbell brothers shifted their support to Walpole who was proving to be the strongest figure in the government. The Duke and Earl had wriggled into favour once again.

Ilay now interfered in any Scottish institution he could influence to create problems for his opponents. Political patronage usually involved securing places in posts controlled by the Treasury and Secretaries of State. By 1720, securing such posts meant accommodations with Walpole because those postings were increasingly in his gift even before he became Chancellor of the Exchequer in 1721. Places in the administrative bodies of Scotland and in the military the brothers could not easily secure since the warrants had to come through unfriendly secretaries or had to be secured with the help of Walpole. What Ilay did not have was the Scottish Secretary's position still held by Roxburghe. Between 1715 and 1725, the struggle against the Squadrone, in Scotland was waged in minor battles with the decisive action only coming in Scotland with the 1722 elections and the Malt Tax crisis of 1725. However, the minor skirmishes between the Scottish factions established the fact of Argathelian supremacy in many places.[52] The Earl made life difficult for his opponents by contesting appointments – even ones of little seeming consequence.

As early as November 1717, the rectorial elections at Glasgow University were being called a 'party business'. Montrose was Chancellor there.[53] Those elections remained of concern to politicians throughout much of Ilay's career and became a barometer of local party strength. In 1717, the letter calling it a 'party business' went on to say that it concerned 'Mr. Duncan fforbes, Mr. Thomas Kennedy & Mr. Hugh Dalrymple', all Argathelians. It was not a merely local matter but a trial of political strength involving Court of Session judges and politicians.[54] Similar battles took place in all of the universities and other corporations around this time.[55] In the Kirk, Ilay tried to affect the outcomes of elections to Synods and the General Assembly. He intervened in appointments of ministers to livings, both those controlled by the Crown and others in the gift of private patrons. He was active in the burghs. Where he succeeded, he expected to find votes in the next election. The most important of the contested places were in the two Scottish high courts, the Courts of Session and the Justiciary Court. They were about evenly divided but had to be controlled to protect one's protégés and to exhibit one's power.[56] By 1721, Argathelians seemed to be about to lose their majority among the judges but that did not happen. However, it took two years for the outcome of the struggle to be determined.[57] That conflict was not unlike others in its use of procedure, the courts, and influence in London.

In December 1721, Patrick Haldane was appointed to the Court of Session subject to the usual trials. The Court, still in the grip of the Argathelians, held that Haldane had not practised for the requisite time before his appointment. The judges believed that Haldane, a ruthless and unpopular Commissioner of the Forfeited Estates and a man known to have been touched by the South Sea Co. scandal, failed their tests of character and conduct. Ilay supported that decision. Montrose, insisting that Haldane, his relative and nominee, be appointed, took the decision to the House of Lords. Although the Lord Chancellor, Lord Macclesfield, believed the time during which an appeal by Haldane could be brought had lapsed, one was made. Ilay, Lord Loudoun and others tried to prevent the case from coming before the House. Ilay commented somewhat cynically,

> ... the warm Gentleman['s] ... conduct has astonished all sorts of people here & has done more real hurt to the worthy man ... [whose great offence was] the idle threatening of forfeiting people of their freeholds for giving their opinion according to their consciences, whether they were according to the Law or not ... those in power have too good sense too much honesty & too much A spirit of moderation to give any countenance to such billingsgate language.[58]

The Lords found Haldane technically qualified and determined he should be appointed.

Ilay then focussed his attention on the Court of Session where Haldane's enemies promptly but improbably accused Haldane of 'Jacobitism, bribery, and extortion by threats'.[59] Despite those allegations and aspersions, he was admitted but the act was protested. The case went again to London where Haldane was persuaded to accept a place as Commissioner of Customs in lieu of the judgeship. This was an humiliating defeat for the Squadrone leaders Roxburghe and Montrose.[60] Ilay won but the Court of Session lost its absolute right to veto Crown nominations to its bench and no more Extraordinary Lords would be appointed to it. Ilay said he did not care if they appointed no more Extraordinary Lords 'after the death of myself & my brethern'. The House of Lords decision was made on 4 February 1723 and the Act abolishing the Extraordinary Lords passed later in the year. Ilay spoke against making Haldane a judge but is unlikely to have opposed the abolition of Extraordinary Lords since the idea seems to have been his.[61] The Squadrone men objected to the new acts.[62] The cases and appeals dragged on into 1724 kept alive, in part, by Ilay and his brother.[63] Haldane's case was typical of the tenacious party struggles which characterized Scottish politics in those years. Many less well-known contests were as bitterly fought.

In the meantime, other issues drew Ilay's attention in Parliament. In 1720-21, the Scottish peerage bill re-emerged and became an issue in the peerage election of June of that year against the wishes of the Ministry.[64] Aberdeen, another peer trained as a Scottish lawyer, opposed the new Peerage Bill which he saw as tampering with the Treaty of Union which included provisions for the election of peers. The votes to elect him as a Representative Peer had come from the Squadrone, the Tories and Jacobites. They opposed making only some Scottish nobles hereditary peers while dis-enfranchising the rest. Aberdeen's election was a sort of referendum on the matter and embarrassed Ilay. Ilay had supported the Earl of Eglinton because he thought he could win and the Squadrone did not want him.[65] At the election, the Earl of Ilay, as Lord Clerk Register, had been not above refusing to give the oaths to his enemies to prevent them from voting.[66] That did not enhance his reputation with many Scots.

Another 1721 issue which cost Ilay some time was an assault upon English anti-trinitarians mounted by the Dean of Windsor. This was not so much an attempt to discipline Anglicans as one to divide and oppress Dissenters. Both Campbell brothers opposed the Dean's blasphemy Act and argued against it in the Lords. It failed to pass.[67]

Ilay garnered more favour with Dissenters the following year when he supported the Quakers Affirmation Bill. Bishop Atterbury had called them 'hardly Christian' and would have them given no relief of any sort. Ilay scoffed at that saying they were 'included in the Toleration Act, under the general denomination of Protestant Dissenters'. That Atterbury found an 'indecency' since 'the calling Quakers Christian by act of parliament was a sort of side-wind reflection upon Christianity itself'.[68] The Quakers got relief but Ilay's un-Christian sentiments were more exposed than he usually allowed.

Ilay's payment for his hard work was being made Scottish 'Privy Seal', an office he received in the spring of 1721. It was worth £3,000 and brought his total income from offices in 1723 to c. £4,000.[69] If things were looking up for Ilay and Argyll, Roxburghe still retained his Scottish Secretaryship. Walpole, quite reasonably, distrusted the Campbells as undependable allies but Ilay was elected to more important committees in the House of Lords. After 1721 and until 1742, he was usually named to the Committee to prepare the Address to the King and sat on the Committees dealing with Rights and Procedures; Customs; Privileges of Peers; Standing Orders, and the subcommittee on the Journals and Records which oversaw the official records. Still, the brothers did not do much better with patronage than they had been doing.[70] It was the departure of Sunderland and Stanhope and the general elections of 1722 which finally made the Campbells important to Walpole. Those showed him the value of the Earl of Ilay.

VII. The Elections of 1722

The peerage election of 1721 had been but a preliminary for the general peerage election of 1722. Aberdeen had been elected in 1721 and Tories and the Squadrone men were not expected to be excluded from the process of making a government list for 1722.[71] Ilay thought that some Tories should be elected. That would be disliked by the Squadrone but it would help some of Ilay's friends and make Scotland more manageable. However, on 13 July 1721, James Erskine, Lord Grange, wrote Ilay that the Squadrone might be wholly excluded in the next elections. There were negotiations over Ministry and party lists which Ilay described in a letter of 25 February 1722. It was delivered to Lord Grange by his cousin – the posts could not be trusted. In periods of intense conflict mail was opened by both sides.[72] Grange and Argyll were willing that the Tories (in the person of the Earl of Aberdeen) should name their own men. The Argathelians and Squadrone agreed a list but then Roxburghe, the Squadrone leader, became 'outrageous' and 'Caballed with Townshend that he and Walpole might raise the Cry against Tories & so opposed all the new men' save for the Earl of Selkirk whom the King had picked. The Ministry 'applauded moderate measures toward the Tories' but Roxburghe, would name only 'his own creatures'. In London, what was at issue were votes in the Lords on the Peerage Bill. By then, Argyll and Ilay had changed their position; any peerage bill would have to have the consent of the whole Scottish peerage. That was unlikely but was plausible as a sop to Scottish opinion. It was a way of getting the Jacobites, who opposed the bill, to help the Argathelians in the election.[73] Ilay told Grange, 'This is my real opinion', and asked that Grange burn the letter.[74] The matter was discussed at the next two peerage elections.

Argyll and Ilay both attended the peerage election held on 21 April 1722.[75] They presented the government's slate which was about equally divided between their supporters and those who opposed them or were neutral. It was a list which reflected the fact that the Ministry needed support from both the Squadrone and Argathelian factions. Before the summer election on 15 August 1722, the brothers circulated another list. They tried to do a deal with the Squadrone on the men to be returned but this fell apart when lists including Tories could not be balanced to the liking of all parties. On election day, they again faced protests over the Peerage Bill designed to limit Scottish peers to members of twenty-five families. In the end, the Court candidates were mostly elected, as was Aberdeen, but the election scuppered a Scottish Peerage Bill.[76]

Ilay also had been busy organizing to elect men to the House of Commons.[77] In a co-operative mood, the Earl had offered a deal to the Squadrone about the election of MPs. He probably proposed that the Argathelians divide the seats with the Squadrone but with some going to 'Cavaliers', *i.e.* Tories and even to some Jacobites whom he trusted. That would keep the latter from becoming desperate.[78] Like the proposal about Lords, this too was rejected. Ilay in describing those dealings to Grange wrote, 'The Squadrone would have filled up the list with whig creatures of their own & we have pleaded for the few tories that will be set up'. Squadrone men also had been spreading 'lies' and trying to win the votes of Tories. Ilay wanted the Duke of Hamilton to enquire into all that and promised, 'I shall be very ready to submit to their determination'.[79] He wanted to win but he also wanted a manageable Scotland. When agreement failed; each side sought to control as many seats as it could. That game the Argathelians won in the 1722 April elections.[80]

The Argathelian interest elected about nineteen MPs including the ten from the burghs. They won in Edinburgh, which the Argathelians had dominated since 1715, and Glasgow, which they had controlled since 1716. Since fourteen of the burgh constituencies had more than one burgh, the Argathelians controlled far more than ten town councils. That gave them additional purchase in the Convention of Royal Burghs. Walpole ingratiated himself with the brothers by backing their men in the adjudication of disputed Parliamentary election returns. Their success was noticed in 1723 by George Baillie, a Squadrone man:

[Argyll] has very near the whole Scots in the House of Commons and all of them in the House of Lords except Montrose, Rox[burghe], Tweddal[e] and

Rothes. I do not reckon Aberdeen, he acts upon another lay, and Hadinton and Hoptoun have left Rox[burghe]. Those of the Scots of the House of Commons that are not Argile's men, act as indeviduals and but very few by Rox[burghe's] interest (scarce Sir William Gordon, if any body else would take him up).[81]

The Argathelians had earlier numbered perhaps fourteen in the House of Commons and three or four in the Lords. If their supporters remained loyal, Argyll and Ilay now led the second largest interest in both Houses of Parliament, second only to the one controlled by Walpole.[82] They now were very valuable to any Ministry in London.

The brothers' relationship with Walpole now rested on mutual convenience sustained by Ilay's politicking and Walpole's access to jobs. Ilay and Walpole, at first, did business but Sir Robert listened to Ilay's advice about North Britain. The Earl became increasingly loyal. Their relationship was tinged with confidence, then liking, and finally, with affection. Sir Robert may even have tried to wean Ilay from his brother's influence in the 1720s just as he seems to have tried to detach other members of the connexion from their allegiance to Argyll.[83] Sir Robert never left Ilay free to pick Scots for all offices but Ilay made more appointments. Throughout his career, he *asked* for places and recognized that he could not give them out on his own.[84] That was one cost of not being a minister. After 1722, Ilay began to get places from ministers other than Walpole but usually through Sir Robert's intervention. Roxburghe was increasingly ignored but he remained Secretary.

VIII. The Malt Tax Riots

The next advances in Ilay's political career came with the Customs inquiry of 1722-23 and the flap over the Malt Tax in 1725. The first arose because of the mishandling of Scottish customs revenues, particularly those *not* collected in Glasgow. Smuggled imports in Scotland were estimated at almost two-thirds of legal ones, and the duties, when paid, were less than they should have been.[85] Scottish tax evasion hurt merchants trading to the colonies all down the west coast of England and in London. English merchants complained although their own ports were sometimes little better. Their complaints were important to Walpole for political reasons. He said he wanted Scottish Customs posts filled by honest and efficient men. He tried to reform the notoriously corrupt Scottish Customs service but in 1723 it was incorporated into a British service after a parliamentary enquiry. When the Customs in Scotland was reorganized, Ilay made no fuss. The Glasgow Customs men, the worst offenders in fiddling the tobacco duties and drawbacks, were not his appointees. When they were outed, Ilay filled most of their posts. That helped him to consolidate his own position. Walpole pleased the English merchants; Ilay got a tighter grip on Scotland.

The Earl had opposed the extension of the Malt Tax to Scotland in 1713 when the proposal brought on the vote in the House of Lords to dissolve the Union. Walpole decided in 1724 to apply the Malt Tax in Scotland as of 1 July 1725. Ilay now found himself allied with a minister determined to extend it and with Scots who refused to accept it. He supported Walpole.[86] His own stated position seems to have been that the country could now stand the new rates which it could not have done in 1713. Ilay supported it as a party matter but he probably thought that the revenue was needed and that this bit of unification between the economies might be good for Scotland.

Scottish protests were backed by the Squadrone, which saw this issue as one it could ride to popularity. Squadrone men fought the tax as part of a conflict with Walpole and the Argathelians which they thought they could win but they lost.[87] Initially, they had important support. On 18 December 1724, the Convention of Royal Burghs sent a representation to the House of Commons against the proposed tax and at its next annual meeting, on 7 July 1725, it passed another. The first found the 'Rigourous Exaction of that Tax' not prudent but the second, written after riots in Glasgow, urged obedience and loyalty. Other Convention letters were sent to the Commons and the King on 16 and 17 December 1725 with the latter asking for some relief from the tax.[88] Those were drawn up by a committee of eight of whom five were Argathelians. Ilay is not known to have intervened but, with his men on the committee, he did not need to.

The tax had passed easily but when it came to be collected, there were riots in the larger towns. In Glasgow, rioters sacked and burned the house of Daniel Campbell of Shawfield, MP. Troops sent to restore order were driven from the town. It took 400 dragoons to bring calm if not peace.[89] Elsewhere, brewers went on strike and then ignored court orders to resume the brewing of beer and ale with malt which attracted the tax. This was not a situation which any Ministry could allow to persist but the usual enforcers of laws were unwilling to act. Robert Dundas of Arniston, the Squadrone Lord Advocate, opposed the imposition of the tax along with his party. Until he was dismissed in the spring of 1725, he encouraged those who refused to pay it.[90] His replacement was the reliable Argathelian, Duncan Forbes of Culloden. Forbes ordered troops to Glasgow in defiance of the Town Council members whom he intended to prosecute. The Court of Session, about equally divided between Squadrone and Argathelian judges, reluctantly ordered the Edinburgh brewers to brew on 31 July 1725. The brewers refused and were then told that rioters could be charged with treason. Forbes was for harsh measures but, the magistrates did nothing; the situation became more tense.

The Earl of Ilay was sent to Edinburgh where he arrived on Friday, 15 August. He immediately set to work along lines less harsh than Forbes had contemplated. Ilay would enforce the law and uphold the power of the Crown but he dropped the prosecution of the Glasgow magistrates.[91] He would collect the tax but he also wanted beer brewed without problems and no discord which could be used by his opponents whether they were Squadrone men or Jacobites. The day he arrived, he qualified as a Justice of the Peace so that he could hold a court independent of the ones controlled by Squadrone men.[92] He also went to the Commission of the Kirk where he reminded the members that the Established Church in Scotland 'stood upon no other Right in Law but an Act of Parliament' and that a presentation of a minister to a Crown living had the same justification for it. They might not like it but laws regarding patronage would prevail.[93] All laws were to be obeyed. In a country where there was too little respect for law, he was forcing men to have some. Then, Ilay set about putting things to right.

Ilay summoned the brewers to his own court on a civil action to force them to pay the taxes they owed. Letting JPs and the Quarter Sessions sort out the problem meant, at least initially, avoiding the Courts of Session and Justiciary which were unwilling to do their duty. The JPs levied double fines on the recalcitrant. When some defied the Courts and would not pay, the Court of Session imprisoned four brewers who had led the conspiracy to strike. Ilay intimated that 130 more would be jailed if they did not go back to work. When they refused, they were held to be in contempt of the Court and some were committed on warrants given by the Court of Session which could not have done otherwise. He dispersed the prisoners so they could not concert actions while in prison. When other brewers stopped brewing in sympathy with them, the Earl had evidence of a criminal conspiracy which could be dealt with in the Court of Justiciary which he headed.[94] At the same time, he made arrangements for bringing in beer from country brewers escorted by dragoons. He also promised the brewers that the excise men would re-measure the malt which they claimed had been used earlier to brew beer. Ilay got some brewers to work again and his friend, Peter Campbell, opened two breweries which also eased matters. When a bakers' strike was also threatened, Ilay said he would turn baker and make bread which could be done without the yeast sometimes supplied by brewers. He also said he thought the bakers were well-affected and that their disaffection was only a rumour.[95] Soon, about 40 of the 68 Edinburgh brewers were at work but those in prison were not released. When their friends met on 27 August to ask the JPs in Quarter Session to delay trials, Ilay told them they had until the 31 August to pay up and that no meetings were to be allowed them. A bit later, he announced that Roxburghe had been sacked on 25 August.[96] On 31 August, he let people know that there was to be no new Secretary of State for Scotland. The Squadrone was definitely out. The Duke of Newcastle would be handling Scottish matters. Everyone knew the advice he would get would come principally from the Earl of Ilay.

By the first week in September – two weeks after Ilay had arrived in Edinburgh – the strike in the capital had been crushed. The affair was over in Edinburgh save for the trials which followed. Walpole wanted an example made of some but told Ilay he could pardon them in the end. Ilay deprived two of the four leaders of patronage jobs: one held a sinecure in the non-functional Mint, the other supplied the Castle garrison with beer. He planned to make examples of others elsewhere.[97] The Earl also began electioneering to secure a more compliant Town Council in Edinburgh. It was a settlement of things which harmed few. He had proven himself cleverer than Duncan Forbes, than Sir Hew Dalrymple, the Lord President of the Court of Session, and others who had tried to force compliance with the laws – and he had probably not spent all of the £1,500 which Walpole had given him to use at his discretion.[98] Some of that could now be spent elsewhere.

Aberdeen was coming around but other places had not yet given in. On 9 September, he wrote to Newcastle that Rothes, Atholl and Montrose had suppressed the Quarter Sessions in Aberdeenshire, Perthshire and Stirlingshire and that 'Mr. Dundass has been making A Sacheverel progress to the north but with less applause....'.[99] Ilay had to tell the Commissioners of Excise that they were to prosecute all those who were not paying the tax.[100] By November, Ilay had forced the Malt Tax on Scots. Order had been restored at the cost of some resentment. All that pleased Walpole very much. Writing to Townshend on 3 September, Sir Robert said:

I cannot say enough in commendation of lord Ilay; to set himself up in direct opposition to the spirit and wishes of the whole country, to throw off all popularity at once, and run the hazard of not succeeding, which you may depend upon it, he had not done if the duke of Roxborough had not been removed, was a desperate and resolute undertaking, and he has conducted it with admiration, and I think I can answer for him, he will not be unreasonable in his demands, or give the King or his servants any uneasiness by proposing unnecesasary charges or aiming to ingross the whole power of Scotland into his own hands. These matters have already been so fully explained betwixt him and me that I find we need be under no apprehension upon that account.

Walpole noted that the Earl had been far more moderate in his actions than Forbes would have been.[101]

By the time of that letter, Ilay had begun to try the ringleaders of the Glasgow riots. On 8 September, as Lord Justice General, he presided at the opening of their trial. The first item to be settled was the indictment. Ilay wanted the rioters tried on treason charges since they had ignored the reading of the Riot Act which constituted a treasonous act.[102] His brethren on the Justiciary Court outvoted him. They reduced the charges to misdemeanour charges of disturbing the peace. The rioters were tried, found guilty and sentenced to transportation on 14 October. Ilay tried to make their punishments as onerous as possible because they had caused a riot which resulted in deaths, property damage and hostilities with the troops. He had wanted at least some of them hanged as examples.[103]

During the fall of 1725, Ilay wrote frequently to Newcastle and his secretary, Charles Delafaye, so we have in his letters a rare glimpse of what usually occupied him both in Scotland and in England. While he sorted out the Malt Tax crisis, he was recommending men for jobs and worrying about patronage in the Kirk. He wished that ministers would 'preach for justice & against perjury, instead of pathetick sermons for mercy to the rioters'.[104] Among those appointed when Squadrone men were sacked was a Keeper of the Signet in Scotland. Ilay thought that change was necessary so that 'summonds for lawsuits' would not be blocked. He also believed that all the Writers to the Signet should be given new commissions. That would have allowed the government to purge their ranks and fill more legal offices with loyal men.[105]

He was considering what should be done with Highlanders who were still coming back from exile and making submission to the government as some of his neighbors did in 1725 (see above p. 70). And, he was thinking generally about the Highlands. James Erskine, Lord Grange, SCJ, had written two perceptive memoranda about conditions there and what could be done to change them. Ilay considered those. Grange wrote about the complexities of abolishing vassalages and feudal rights and getting rid of chieftains. He wanted military tenures converted to civil ones and recommended a programme of development and education as well as lessened dependence upon the heads of clans. Dependence was to be decreased by disarming the Highlanders – without arms they were of less use to their chiefs. Grange's solutions were not all new but his plans were more sensible than those adopted later. Ilay's own conclusion were probably given in a letter about the lawless Earl of Cromarty: 'the Highlanders can never be civilized so long as any person is tolerated in giving the publick defiance to the course of the Law, & the difficulty that attends the execution of the processes of the law in the Highlands seems to be the very essence of their barbarity'.[106] At about the same time, Lord Lovat sent a memorial to the King saying that about half the Highlanders were loyal and should not be treated so harshly as the clans who were disloyal. All this was in aid of the writing of a new Disarming Act which was passed in 1725.[107] Ilay also tried to settle disorders in Gordon territory where Catholics had been harassing Protestants.[108]

Ilay personally went to Linlithgow with some dragoons, to prevent 'A general battle' at a Head Court where the later Governor of Carolina, James Glen, was seeking election but had been strenuously opposed by Hugh Dalrymple and others. Dragoons replaced a civic guard which was supposed to be biassed to one of the sides. The Earl told the warring factions that no breach of the peace would go unpunished and that any who prevented the reading of the Riot Act would be guilty of a capital offense.[109] Ilay tried to look fair but Glen had been for the Malt Tax while his drunken opponent had been against it.

The Earl dealt with the problems posed by the mad Duke of Douglas who had returned to Scotland where he had either to be declared mad or tried for murder. The Earl had him locked up but not tried – the less fuss the better. Ilay attended to burgh elections and thought about the Visitation of Glasgow University by a Royal Commission 'to put the Government of Glasgow in to good Hands'.[110] In Edinburgh he was almost certainly doing something similar (see p. 218). He worried over the ill health of Duncan Forbes and who might replace him should Forbes die and with whom Newcastle should correspond in Scotland after he himself returned to London. What should happen to ordinary felons and to those with good connexions took a bit of his time as did Newcastle's plans for the repression of Popery. Ilay was very busy in Edinburgh but there is no indication that much of this business would not have occupied his time in London.

By December, he was eager to go back to London but a bit optimistic in saying that Scotland would quiet down when managed without ignorance and passion but with steadiness and common sense. Part of that sensible management was getting Scots something out of the Malt Tax money which they now had to pay. In December, they were promised that any surplus over £20,000 paid in malt taxes would be used to subsidize Scottish economic activities. From that promise would spring the scheme for the Board of Trustees of Fisheries and Manufactures. When he went south, he was a tired man able to point to much accomplished. It did not make him Secretary of State but he became Keeper of the Great Seal of Scotland (£2,000) which raised his income from offices to at least £3,000.[111]

Eric Wehrli saw the importance of the Malt Tax crisis as being the establishment of a new means of managing Scotland, one which found in Ilay the first new manager. There would no longer be a Scottish minister responsible to the King and able to circumvent the other ministers. There would be a principal Scottish advisor but he would be just that – an advisor responsible to the King's chief ministers. For the rest of his life, with the exception of about four years in the 1740s, Ilay would be that person. Almost all Scottish business came to him but he had no formal responsibility for it. He would go to Privy Council meetings and sometimes meet with the King but normally he worked through the Secretaries of State, the Lord Treasurer and the Secretary at War. He could propose men and measures; he could run elections but he could not act independently for himself or for Scots. The ultimate determination of Scottish affairs resided with the ministers and with institutions such as the Treasury, Army and Navy. Ilay's power would be limited. Walpole thus destroyed the independent political life of the Scots and made their parties somewhat otiose. As he did so, he changed the British political system because there would no longer be an inducement among Englishmen to try to placate Scottish parties. They would try rather to absorb them into ones which were British based and controlled by Englishmen. The politics of the magnates was at an end; there was no place for Argyll, but his brighter, more compliant brother, who accepted his dependence, had a bright future. There are reasons to doubt this account.

Ilay's system was not so much a new way of running Scotland as it was a more efficient system of management by men who knew their trade. Ilay had begun to build up an organization before the Malt Tax crisis. When he came to power, he adapted the Squadrone system but replaced their London committee by himself. He worked with and through the supporters of his brother and was still somewhat dependent on the support of his family connexion. The Campbell brothers' private means gave them some independence. No one else had used a system which worked so well and no one else was likely to be able to create one so powerful because of the geographic base the Campbells possessed. Walpole used Ilay but he could not run Scotland smoothly after 1725 without the willing help of Argyll and the Earl. The accession of the new King, in 1727, offered Ilay and Walpole a chance to entrench Argathelians because many appointments had either to be made or renewed at the beginning of the reign. Ilay's system of management had less novelty and more independence than there might seem.

The Earl did not have ultimate authority or act directly under the King but the tendency to question his judgments was self defeating. Things ran smoothly if he ran them but not otherwise. His position was secured by the satisfaction he gave Scots and by his loyalty to Walpole who was glad to have the votes Ilay produced for him. Not being a minister made little difference to Ilay's actions. He went to Council with others, acted as did ministers in the Lords and was more effective than Mar, Montrose or Roxburghe ever were. His position became increasingly less dependent on the good will of the King's chief ministers as the failure of the Duke of Newcastle to oust Ilay from power later showed. The Earl's work led ultimately to an integrated Britain but, in the short run, to what Alexander Murdoch has called it, semi-independence.[112]

As I have argued elsewhere and will here, to see Ilay as tied exclusively to the political objectives of his English patrons is to overlook much of what his Scottish politics was about. It had a cultural dimension about which the English cared little, one which remained distinctly Scottish and which owed a great deal to the Earl's own inclinations. The ability to appoint over a long period of time in every institution gave the Earl the ability to change the direction of Scottish culture and he did so. He never claimed to be doing this but his appointments had that result.

Up to 1725, Ilay's politics had been largely directed to keeping himself and his brother in office, in cash, and able to do favours for their friends. It was not a particularly ideological politics although he did believe in the principles of the settlement of 1688-1690. There is no sign that he ever reneged on a belief in limited government, the legitimacy of choosing one's rulers, and restraining both religious and political enthusiasts in a secular polity. He wanted the rule of law and he enforced laws on the books. That might create hardships but those would lead to reforms which he might not oppose. If he could achieve an orderly society through management and good legislation, that was fulfilling the mandate given to a ruling class. To achieve that, one had to improve things when necessary but reform was not for him the reason governments existed.[113] 'Peace, order and good government' came first. In disposition, he was a tolerant, moderate man who did not believe in extreme measures or bloody repressions.[114] He preferred reconciliation and management to coercion and peace to strife but he could be both under-handed and mean if crossed. Since 1705 he had been involved with economic schemes; he continued to be so. After 1725, his politics took on a more improving aspect but it would be a matter of degree, not a fundamental change in outlook. In those improvements lay the seeds of a very different Scotland from the one into which he had been born. It is now time to leave politics and to look at Ilay's other interests.

An Enlightened Duke

Part II

Knowledge and its Uses

An Enlightened Duke

Chapter 6

The Books of Archibald Campbell

I. The Libraries of the 3rd Duke of Argyll

By 1705, Lord Archy had developed intellectual interests which he pursued for the rest of his life. By 1761, he had book collections in London, at Whitton, at The Whim, at Inveraray Castle and perhaps at Rosneath Castle in Dunbartonshire and at his mother's dower house in Campbeltown. His books are a good guide to his interests and are surveyed here because they offer insights into what he thought about and how he thought. Because he was representative of those who began the Scottish Enlightenment, what he read is of more than personal interest and importance. His interests increasingly affected the policies he pursued during his long political career and influenced his conduct as a patron. Ilay became a politician concerned not only with power and patronage but with what might be accomplished with that power. About Ilay's books we know a good deal thanks to a catalogue, in which most of them are described, and from some descriptions of the libraries in which they were held.

His London collection was first housed at 24 Great Marlborough Street, the London *cul de sac* where Ilay lived after 1711. He bought the property in 1732 and demolished it in 1742 after he had rebuilt Argyll House in 1737-42. Friends such as Charles Erskine were referring to his London house as 'The Library' by the 1730s so his collection was large by that time.[1] In 1742, he added to Argyll House a new library of impressive dimensions which appears to have about doubled the ground floor size of the house. It was roofed in the summer of 1742. The new library in this now destroyed home was a two-storey gallery twenty feet in width running ninety feet across the back of the mansion to which it was connected.[2] In a letter of 1742, Ilay said that it had '2 bow windows which will there extend the breadth to 27. at the 2 ends I shall have Gallery's. in short fort magnifique'.[3] When it was finished, he called it 'one of the finest Rooms in London'.[4] By estimating the number of shelf-feet, one can see that the room would have held all or most of the books in his later catalogue. The majority of his books were housed there. Indeed, his surviving book catalogue may be only of this collection. Both the old and new library rooms held some of his instruments and curiosities and natural history specimens.

Down the Thames at Whitton, he had a sizable collection after the late 1730s, one eventually impressively housed. One visitor, around 1760, described the library: 'On each side of the great Room below stairs, is a long Gallery, in one of which are all of the Instruments which the Duke used in his Mechanical and Chymical Experiments; and along the opposite Side, are a Set of Admirable Drawings; the other is filled with Books and Drawings also'.[5] The library room would have been at least twenty feet in length and probably fifteen feet wide.[6] Such a room could easily have held over 1,000 volumes.

At The Whim in Peebles-shire, Ilay built a modest house which survives as the inside of the much altered and larger present structure.[7] It had a library by c.1740.[8] Since there were few public rooms in this house, which was likely to have been symmetrical in its layout, the library may well have been of the same size as the dining room balancing it on the other side of an entry hall.[9] That would have made it twenty five feet four inches in length by fifteen feet ten inches wide with a ceiling almost twelve feet high.[10] Or, it may been above the dining room. If it was, it would perhaps have had shelves or presses along two or three walls. By 1759, his original collection at The Whim had grown and a new room was needed. It was built over a vaulted cellar by John Adam in 1759-60.[11] The bill for the second library at The Whim shows that it probably had 168 feet of shelf space divided into sections five feet long.[12] That suggests that Argyll expected to have about 1,000 books at The Whim. How many were actually there is unknown. From the surviving list of forty titles apparently taken there in 1740, one can conclude that Ilay stocked it with volumes in at least five languages and that they fell into most of the categories under which his books were later catalogued. Book purchases recorded among the papers dealing with this estate included some on science and mathematics which either graced the shelves at The Whim or were sent west to Inveraray.[13] By 1745, he had at The Whim a copy of Blaue's Scottish *Atlas* (1662) which the Duke ordered Alexander Lind to give to the Duke of Cumberland who lacked maps of Scotland – an interesting comment on the Army's readiness to deal with the '45.[14] Blaue had printed maps older than 1662.

After the demise of the 2nd Duke in 1743, Ilay's building plans for Inveraray Castle included a library. Indeed, his secretary reported only a few days after he had inherited, that 'ye purchases for yt are sett a going already'.[15] That house remained unfinished in the 3rd Duke's lifetime and he may not have placed many books in a house damp with new plaster and without fires through the winter. He did send some books up from London as early as 1749.[16]

At Rosneath Castle, there was no known library room as such and no books are listed in the inventory made after the Duke's death.[17] It is likely that one was planned for the reconstruction which began in his last years since books were sent there too. He spent little time at Campbeltown so it may not have had many volumes but it is difficult to imagine any of his houses lacking them entirely.

II. His Collection

A catalogue of Ilay's books, *Catalogus Librorum A. C. D. A.* [*i.e.*, Archibald Campbell Duke of Argyll] was compiled by Alexander Macbean (MacBeane, M'Bean, MacBayne or MacBain), the Duke's sometime librarian, and printed by the Foulis Press in Glasgow in 1758.[18] The *Catalogus* was probably a make-work project for the Foulis brothers whom he had patronized in the past.[19] It was most likely privately printed and distributed. It allowed the Duke to see exactly what he had collected and where it was; not all of us retain perfect memories into our late seventies. He was also at that time tidying up things by listing his garden plants at Whitton and making a new will (see p. 342). A book catalogue would make it easier to sell his books after his death. The catalogue helps now to sketch a picture of the mind and tastes of this extraordinary politician. It also confirms the interests and concerns which were attributed to him by somewhat uncomprehending contemporaries.

The list probably contains only the books which he had to hand in London but we cannot be sure.[20] Because Macbean is not mentioned as being in Scotland with the Duke or even at Whitton, that points to the London library as the one catalogued. If other collections were included, the duplication of books in the catalogue might be explained by their locations. We do know that the list does not give us all of the Duke's books. The catalogue was compiled c.1750-58 and printed in 1758 so it does not include books acquired in the last years of his life.[21] Although his purchases had slowed by that time, gifts were probably coming in greater numbers. Moreover, he is known to have received books which are not on this library list. John Home's plays are not there although he was given them. Others in Scotland certainly gave him similar gifts but their names are missing suggesting that those books were retained in a library not catalogued.

The catalogue also does not allow us to estimate accurately the size of the library it lists. Many volumes would have had more than one work included in them so not every book title is listed. The problem of estimating the number of books is further compounded by the fact that some of the entries are for journals but lack the dates over which his runs extended. The catalogue gives us a sense only of the minimum number of volumes and titles which he possessed and of the kinds of books he wanted to own, not the total numbers which he held or of their locations. By 1758, the catalogued collection had at least 8,951+ titles and 12,177+ volumes. His Library is likely to have contained more than 13,000 volumes and well over 9,000 titles.

It was a large library to gather from scratch but for the times it was not a huge one. Sir Hans Sloane (1660-1753) died possessed of c.50,000 books and manuscripts.[22] Dr. Richard Mead (1673-1754) died owning about 20,000 books collected mostly in the same years in which Ilay was purchasing.[23] Ilay's nephew, Lord Bute, had at the end of his life (1792) a collection of about 30,000 which incorporated Ilay's library which he had purchased. On the continent, there were many collections formed during the years Ilay was collecting which were larger.[24] The claim that his was the largest private library in Great Britain in 1761 is erroneous.[25] The claim that it was the best may be true – depending on what is deemed to constitute a 'good' book.

The library was formed over a long time and reflected Ilay's personal interests. He himself bought many of the books at auctions like the one held in 1730 to dispose of the books, manuscripts and instruments of Samuel Molyneux (see p. 272). His Lordship frequented Will's Coffeehouse, a well-known auction site as well as a meeting place for Whigs.[26] Ilay placed bids in sales held abroad in many places from Rome to Amsterdam, Paris to Copenhagen.[27] For such purchases he would have relied on dealers or on friends. One who bought for him, as noted earlier, was Alexander Cunningham of Block (c.1650-1737),[28] an eminent dealer in rare books who purchased for a number of other lords.[29] Ilay was connected to a network of foreign booksellers and collectors who kept him informed of sales and available volumes. The Earl bought at Scottish sales as well. Until the later 1720s, he sometimes purchased books through his brother's and his mother's Edinburgh 'doer' [solicitor], James Anderson, W.S., a notable *virtuoso* and antiquary. After Sir Robert Sibbald's death in 1722, Anderson informed Ilay that he would send a catalogue of that great collector's library. A later letter indicated his lordship's probable interests in that collection:

> It has some but not many books of British Matters   The Cream of his Library being a sett of the Dauphins Variorum of Paris Edition [a complete set of the classical authors] and a large Collection of Natural History and Medicine.

Ilay purchased some of Sibbald's books, and not long after, Anderson informed him of the sale of 'Mackenzies books' but there had been no time to send a catalogue to Ilay who was thought to be on the road to Scotland.[30]

The Earl was a happy grubber in London bookstores and second-hand shops.[31] He seems really to have enjoyed the company of book-men, as an anecdote reported by the Edinburgh bookseller, Gavin Hamilton, makes clear:

> I have been taken up very much, for two or three days, with the Duke of Argyle, who comes up to the shop every day at 12, and sitts 2 hours, and yesterday he satt till three, writing letters, whereby I lost my part of a Solan goose, which was provided to entertain some friends. We had a good deal of gash conversation together; for example, on Wednesday afternoon, the Duke, looking out the shop window, saw a man standing on the Cock stool [pillory], for Perjury, 'Mr. Hamilton'. says he, 'is not that fellow there one of my countrymen?' 'No'. said I, 'he is not one of your countrymen, he is a Lochyell man'. "Well, well," said the Duke, 'that is Argyleshire, that is in my country; there are many there more than that fellow who deserve to be hanged'. [32]

Those who behaved in this fashion were likely to find that booksellers would look after them. Letters show that Argyll was regularly buying both old and new books from Edinburgh booksellers from the mid-1740s to the mid-1750s.[33] However, his Coutts 'Out books' have in his last years very few payments to booksellers. He also subscribed to books. Ilay put his name down for two copies of Colley Cibber's collected plays and bought in this way the beautifully illustrated and very expensive natural history and botanical volumes produced by Mark Catesby and Elizabeth Blackwell.[34] Another sixteen subscriptions have been found and some dedications but he was not a notable literary patron.

Although most of the books seem to have been bought before the end of the 1740s, the most recent book in the catalogue entered the collection very close to its publication date. It was likely to have been a purchase but many others obtained in his last years were probably gifts from men whom he had aided. They include books from the leading lights of the Scottish Enlightenment and from scientists in England – gifts acknowledging past favors or books sent in hopes of future favors. David Hume gave him a copy of his *Essays Moral and Political* (1748) noting that he was sending it because 'I have a Regard for his Grace, & desire this Trifle may be considerd as a Present, not to the Duke of Argyle, but to Archibald Campbell, who is undoubtedly a Man of Sense and Learning'.[35] Adam Smith sent him a copy of the *Theory of Moral Sentiments* (1759) [36] and there were other volumes from Hume's and Smith's circle in Edinburgh.

The 'man of sense and learning' was in some respects a curious buyer. His books do not seem splendid or bought for their splendor. It is a collection composed mainly of works which Ilay found useful or wanted because they had some value other than their rarity, binding or age. He bought no illuminated manuscripts and had no use for the wonderful illuminated books which Drs. Mead, Sloane or, later, William Hunter were buying – quite cheaply – throughout the century.[37] Ilay's known manuscripts numbered about a dozen.[38] Just as he did not buy manuscripts, he did not buy incunables just to have early books. If my count is correct, there are amongst his volumes only eleven published before 1500. They are early editions of Plutarch's *Lives*, Roman and Greek poets, two volumes of Cicero, the works of Angeli Politiani, and two works on language. He seems not even to have bought an immense number of books then considered very fine. There are 593 books in the library catalogue noted as being of extra weight, finely printed, deriving from some notable publisher or printer or edited by a notable scholar – less than 7% of the whole collection (see Appendix III.2). Most of those were folios and quartos. Of those books, 386 are assignable to a press or editor. Since many of the latter are represented by only one item, Ilay may have had an interest in printers and printing and could have bought some books with that in mind.[39] Other than his collection of Cicero texts and his mathematics books, he seems to have bought few very old books merely because he was curious to see what the first publication of some of the ancients looked like. He tended to buy modern editions even when he had an old copy of the same work. Of course, were we to check the list looking for fine books, we would find thousands of books which appear to us very different than they did to Macbean. He and Ilay would have perceived many only as standard editions, the best, the most useful, or the editions prepared by interesting editors and critics.

Ilay may have liked fine bindings but he did not systematically or uniformly rebind his books. The costs of binding items, when it is known, seems to have been about the cost of the books themselves.[40] That he had a good looking library would make sense given his liking for finely made scientific instruments. The Duke liked colourful decorative china, fancy wallpapers and gaudy mounted butterflies so there may have been a lot of finely bound books – but that is something we will never know since none of his books seem to have survived.[41]

We are almost equally in the dark as to the cost of his collection. In 1730, at the Molyneux sale, Ilay paid on average £0.1.6 for duodecimos and octavos, £0.2.6 for quartos and £1.1.0 for folios – £39.16.2 for 117 titles. Most of his books were collected before 1750 and those prices may well represent the usual cost of his books. If those figures are used to estimate the cost of his library then it came to £3,486. In the 1750s, Argyll was paying in Edinburgh, on average, about 9 shillings for a folio, 12 shillings for quartos and 3 or 4 shillings for octavos. The median costs were a bit lower but the sample, 76 titles, is small. If those costs are used to price his books, then they come to a total of £3,132. Neither figure may be close to the real cost of purchasing his books. Some were very rare and expensive works. Others were bought in places with lively book markets where rich collectors drove average costs to higher levels than the average cost of the volumes in Edinburgh. Many of his volumes were profusely illustrated but his Edinburgh and London purchases noticed above were not. Illustrated books would have raised the average cost of the books he purchased. The figures above must be seen as minimum estimates of the cost of his books.[42] The real figures also would have been increased by the costs of freight, some binding, insurance and possibly even customs dues – but those he usually avoided. Books from the London and, perhaps, Whitton libraries, along with mathematical instruments, an astronomical clock and some of the library fittings, were sold to the Earl of Bute on 14 October 1761 for £4,175. Perhaps about £1,000 can be assigned to the instruments. Lord Bute was a family member and may not have paid the full market price.[43] In any case, he would not have come into possession of all of his uncle's books. Only his buildings and gardens cost the Duke more. While we cannot know what the books cost, we can console ourselves with a list of the things he had on some of his shelves. The catalogue shows us a scholar with a concern for order.

III. Cataloguing the Collection

The system of cataloguing adopted for the *Catalogus* is a variant of seventeenth-century French systems. One possible origin of Ilay's system may be the account by P. J. Garnier, published in 1678, of the system according to which the books in the Jesuit College of Paris were ordered.[44] Another might be the classification system of the Bibliotheque Royale in Paris.[45] Those, like most early cataloguing schemes, go back to the first modern book on the subject and certainly the most important one for the seventeenth and eighteenth centuries, Gabriel Naudé's *Avis pour dresser une bibliothèque* (Paris, 1627). Ilay's system reflects what Naudé wrote:

> ... I conceive that arrangement to always be the best which is easiest, least intricate, most natural, most used, and which follows the subjects of theology, medicine, jurisprudence, history, philosophy, mathematics, humanities, and so on, each of which is classified into subheadings according to their several divisions, which for this purpose ought to be reasonably understood by the librarian in charge....[46]

The general categories Ilay adopted were: Theology, History, Public Law, Jurisprudence, Greek and Roman Authors, Philology, Medicine and Chemistry, Philosophy, Mathematics, and Miscellaneous. In the sub-categories, the cataloguer tended to follow Naudé. He had recommended that

> In theology all the Bibles should be placed first, in the order of their languages; next to these the Councils, Synods, Decrees, Canons, and all that concerns the Constitutions of the church, and the more since they hold the second place of authority among us; then the commentators, scholastics, learned men of various schools, and historians; and finally, the heretics.

Ilay followed this as well as a Protestant could and he was not unusual in including Islam among the Christian heresies. Some English deists also thought it to be one.[47]

Ilay, or his librarian, did not slavishly follow Naudé in the ordering of his philosophical books. Where the Frenchman wanted philosophies set out in terms of age and by systems, Ilay tended to classify his works according to the kind of philosophy they contained. Most of the moral philosophy ended up under *Jus Publicum*; a lot of the natural philosophy, particularly the most modern, was in the section on mixed mathematics while logic and metaphysics was in *Philosophici &c.* He did agree with Naudé that

> the most universal and ancient always take precedence.... the interpreters and commentators [should] be placed apart and sorted according to the order of the books which they explain... that special treatises follow the order and arrangement which their subject matter should occupy among the arts and sciences... that all books of similar designation and the same subject matter be most precisely classified and set in the places assigned them; since in so doing the memory is so much refreshed that it would be easy to find them instantly.

Ilay or his librarian managed to do that most of the time. When they did not, he could have appealed to Naudé's final comment on arrangements:

> ...the order of nature (which is always uniform and self-consistent) being incapable of application because of the wide range and diversity of books, there remains only the order of art, which every man usually wishes to establish to suit himself, according as he finds, by his own good sense and judgment, it will best suit his convenience as much to satisfy himself as from unwillingness to follow the examples and opinions of others.

The order, in the end, was what Ilay found most convenient.

His books were divided by category and subject and then shelved by size, with the folios presumably at the bottom below the quartos and the octavos. Within this order there were subdivisions. In Appendix III.1, I have tried to reconstruct the order followed. The printed catalogue's occasional disorder may be due to over-crowding on the shelves which were then described as they were, a problem afflicting other catalogues such as the first surviving manuscript catalogue of the library at Glasgow University.

Ilay's classification (Theology, History, Public Law, Jurisprudence, Greek and Latin authors, Philology; Medicine, Chemistry, etc.; Philosophy, Mathematics and Miscellaneous) gave a decent and proper priority to religion. In Baconian fashion, it allowed history to come next, followed by morality and law – the principles of order without which nothing else could flourish. Then came what might be called works on literature and the arts; that is what 'philology' seems to mean here. The sciences – his philosophy is mostly natural philosophy or science – and the practical arts using them follow in order. This was not an unusual way to order materials. James Dalrymple, Lord Stair, the great Scottish jurist, a hundred years earlier would have found it reasonable since he, like many lawyers, thought that without law there could be nothing else. Law itself rested on a theological foundations set out in the Bible and in the records of the past, both the ecclesiastical past and that conjectured past in which natural men came, through the light of reason, to see what their principles of conduct ought to be. Having established rules protecting men and their possessions, people could pursue the arts and sciences which might then flourish. Ilay, like Stair, was trained as a lawyer in Holland. He may have imbibed this scheme from the humanist law professors who taught him; or, he may have made it up himself finding it reasonable and just. The last of the sections of the catalogue is largely taken up with travel literature, modern literature in several languages and with political-economy.

The ranking of subjects which the numbers of *book titles* and *volumes* establishes is also interesting. Counting by *titles*, the largest section in the library was history. That is followed by mathematics, medicine, the ancient writers (including their historians), philology (mostly the learned literature of the sixteenth and seventeenth centuries), miscellaneous, jurisprudence, philosophy, public law and theology. This ordering of his books is close to what I take to have been his preferences for reading and study. He was interested in history; mathematics and science and their uses were his constant concerns. He needed the law books but religious materials were of interest to him only when he wished to follow controversies, was interested in languages or needed reference works dealing with religion. There are few theology books and devotions and pious works are lacking.

Counting the *numbers of volumes* and then ranking the divisions, theology still comes last but miscellaneous, not history, tops this list, followed by the ancients. Then comes mathematics, which includes here, as it often did in the century, applied mathematics and what we would call physics and astronomy. This is followed by philology, history, medicine, natural philosophy, jurisprudence, public law and finally theology. This order balances his necessary reading of contemporary materials with the books he read for the fun or used for reference. Ilay read for diversion history, the classics, modern (but not always very modern) poetry and philosophy. He enjoyed working at the medical and mathematical sciences. Because he was a judge who sat in various courts, he used his many law books. Other books served him in his political and parliamentary career. The Earl of Ilay was a serious man and this was the working library of a polymathic scholar and man of affairs. It has little in the way of light literature. Its various categories deserve a closer look.

IV. A Description of the Library

The theology books which he had included sixty-three folio titles of which twenty-two are Bibles. Among the eighty-six quartos, at least twelve are Bibles or parts thereof and thirty-four of the 313 octavo titles relate to the Bible in whole or in parts. These sixty-eight Bibles and parts thereof (15% of all the books in this category) reflect Ilay's interest in languages more than they do to his concern with his soul's salvation (see Appendix III.3). Taken with the Bibles in other sections of his library, he had Bibles or parts of the scriptures in about twenty languages and dictionaries or grammars in an additional ten or more languages.[48] He was something of a linguist who read with varying degrees of ease English, Latin, Greek, French, Italian, Spanish, Dutch, Portuguese, German – possibly even a bit of Hebrew. His curiosity extended beyond the languages included in standard polyglot Bibles (Samaritan, Aramaic, Syrian, Arabic, and Persian) to Algonkwin, Amharic, Anglo-Saxon, Armenian, Chinese, Malabaric, Russian, Swedish and Turkic. Theology was for him a convenient category under which to put a lot of linguistic material. What he really thought of religion is summed up in the sobriquets he applied to Scottish ministers: 'Levites', 'hot brethren', 'Zealots', 'enthusiasts' and, occasionally, 'fools'.

Theology was also a place to put some good stylists. He owned sets of the works of John Tillotson and Robert South, one Low the other High Church. Both were praised for the clarity and effectiveness of their writing. Pascal, Bossuet, Massillon, and Fénelon figure here partly for similar reasons. He had theologians from many camps but the majority of the theological works almost certainly formed a reference collection. He had, as, Naudé would have wished, Fathers of the Greek and Latin churches – *e.g.*, Clement, Justin Martyr, Tertullian, Clement of Alexandria, Chrysostom, Augustine, and others. They showed the diversity of belief in the early Church. He possessed what looks like a complete set of the decrees and histories of the early councils of the church in ten volumes. His collection of medieval writers was not extensive but he had purchased Bernard of Clairvaux, Thomas à Kempis, Meister Eckhart and other mystics read by Protestants. Scholastics, such as Aquinas, were to be found under philosophy. Romish material was offset by a number of ecclesiastical histories which glossed church history from a Protestant point of view. Among them might be counted books by Conyers Middleton, John Jortin, and Humphrey Prideaux; the first and last of them were much interested in religious impostures.

Argyll possessed many of the Reformation 'greats' including Luther, Calvin, Beza, Bucer and bits of Zwingli. He had Hugh Latimer's *Sermons* but not all that much else from the English Reformation. He placed in this section those Protestant writers who mixed politics and religion, such as Duplessis de Mornay, Francis Hotman (both served William the Silent), and John Selden. The library had a good selection of the early Scottish reformers – John Knox, George Buchanan, Robert Rollock and others – but not all of their works were in this section. The Scottish historians of the church – Knox, John Leslie, David Calderwood, John Spottiswoode and Robert Keith – were on the history shelves but Arthur Johnston, who had translated the 'Psams'. was here. One could also find men like Andrew and James Melville, Samuel Rutherfurd and some of the polemicists of the Kirk. Ilay bought a good deal of Scottish material in every category. His books suggest that he was genuinely interested in Scottish history and not just a possessor of materials which would be politically useful.

The Earl had a number of the works concerned with the Synod of Dordrecht and the controversialists who were there or who reacted to it. Those men included John Cameron, later Principal of Glasgow University, the Amyraldists and some of the Aberdeen Doctors. What is notable about his list of seventeenth-century divines is the irenic and latitudinarian tinge so many possessed. He had many of the works of the Oxford Rationalists and Cambridge Platonists. He owned several editions of Hugo Grotius's *The Truth of the Christian Religion,* and works by William Chillingworth, Jeremy Taylor, Isaac Barrow and by the Latitudinarians of the latter part of the seventeenth century, particularly John Tillotson, Edward Stillingfleet and Edmund Gibson. They became bishops after 1689. His list of rational, temperate theologians continued on with contemporary Anglicans like Benjamin Hoadley, Samuel Clarke, William Whiston (later a Baptist), and all the Boyle Lecturers. There were few High Churchmen and fewer Dissenters. He did not have many of the foreign 'hot brethren' but he did possess the works of moderate men like Philip Limborch, Jean Le Clerc and Jean Barbeyrac. There is no clearer indicator of his preference for moderation, tolerance and rational, moralizing religion. Most of those men argued for state established churches.

His Catholic writers included Jesuits such as Loyola, Canisius, Mariana and, Bellarmine. He had volumes on the Council of Trent including several sets of Fr. Paolo Sarpi's *History of the Council of Trent* which viewed it rather cynically. Ilay had bought a copy of the *Index of Prohibited Books*, perhaps to guide his buying. There were works by sixteenth-century Catholics from Scotland, such as Bishop John Leslie, but there were few from the following century. The eighteenth century gave him only one writer of real note, Fr. Thomas Innes. He was in the history section. He had many of the French controversialists of the seventeenth century and owned quite a few other Frenchmen, among them Cardinal Richelieu and the Quietist mystics, Pierre Poiret and Anne de Bourignon who had many Scottish followers in the Aberdeen area. The Roman Catholic opponents of his moderate Protestants were well represented.

Many of the men mentioned above were controversialists but his Lordship's interests ran to scholarly topics too. He owned works by the Johannes Buxtorfs, Louis Cappelle, John Selden, Isaac de La Peyrère, Richard Simon, Humphrey Prideaux and many more learned authors. They had worried over the pointing of Hebrew, the variations in biblical manuscript texts, differences in church traditions and the stability, authenticity, and credibility of the canonical texts. Disagreements among those men cast doubt on the veracity of the Christian religion in its various formulations. Perhaps belonging in this somewhat subversive category are some of the twenty or more folio biblical chronologies in the history section. They sometimes differed wildly from each other as did some translations and texts of the Bibles. His historical and linguistic works tended to emphasize the discrepancies among books and the contradictions among the religious authors. The deists drew on such materials. His collection had little on the sacraments. Ilay's own religious beliefs seem rooted in a skepticism of revelations and of 'priests'. His shelves were not burdened with moral theology and he did not burden his conscience with trivial matters such as fornication and adultery.

The Duke, of course, had religious works written in his own time. Those included a selection of 'wild' things by the likes of William ('Blind') Jameson and the 2nd Duke's tutor, the Rev. John Anderson. Ilay knew both men and may have been taught by them. There were also works by the Scottish Moderates, old and young. Many of those probably came as gifts. That he had them, while not generally possessing the works of contemporary wild men and 'high-flyers', is significant since his family's natural connections, and his own until c.1725, often had been with the orthodox and the rigid. He broke with the 'hot brethren' over the Simson case at Glasgow in the 1720s. In doing so, he followed his personal bent as well as what was then in his political interest.[49] Ilay's Erastian position on state-Kirk relations was supported in many of his books.

Ilay's religious books had a more subversive, darker side. Like John Locke, he possessed works which clearly objected to the doctrine of the Trinity, including those of Fausto Socinus. He owned books by the executed heresiarch, Julio Vanini, and, in other sections of the library, works by Michael Servetus and Giordano Bruno, who, like Vanini, had ended their lives at a stake. He had Richard Overton's *Man wholly Mortal* (1655), probably a Baptist work but one taken to argue for the materiality of the soul. He bought Isaac de La Peyrère's *Prae-Adamitae* from the same year. Spinoza's *Tractatus Theologico-Politicus* (1670) and Hobbes' *Works* were on his shelves. Charles Blount was represented by his *Works* (1696) and by his incomplete translation of the *Life of Appolonius of Tyana by Philostratus* (1680), a book in which parallels were drawn between the life of Christ and a pagan miracle worker who healed the sick and raised the dead. It was sometimes cited as an example of priest-craft with the implication that the life of Christ was no different. Other works dealt with Islam, which most Protestants regarded as little better than a splendid example of priest-craft. Ilay owned a Koran which would have given him the record of the 'Impostor Prophet', to use Humphrey Prideaux's description of Mohammet. The Duke had a good collection of the English deistical writers from Lord Herbert of Cherbury on. John Toland, Matthew Tindal, John Asgill, Antony Collins, Thomas Woolston, Lord Shaftesbury, John Trenchard and Thomas Gordon, Thomas Chubb, Conyers Middleton and Henry Dodwell II were all there but his interest in religious controversy did not lead him to buy many of the several hundred pamphlets by anti-deistic writers. He did own the best of them – books by Richard Bentley, Bishops Berkeley and Butler and the Dissenting ministers James Foster and John Leland. Had he been at all orthodox, he would have owned more of those writers.

Argyll's list of French and Dutch free-thinkers and sceptics is notable but most of them are not listed in the theology section. Among those who were included here were Antonius Van Dale and Richard Simon – men who had argued against superstitions and the absolute infallibility and accuracy of the biblical texts. Elsewhere he had C.- M. de St Denis de St. Evrémond, Pierre Bayle, Pierre-Daniel Huet, Jean Hardouin; the Baron La Hontan, Simon Tyssot de Patot, the Abbé de St. Pierre; the anonymous author of the *Turkish Spy*, and some of the more notable of the early free-thinking Enlightenment writers.

The library almost totally lacked books of devotions, prayers or anything else which would suggest that he had other than a professional and intellectual interest in religion. His presence in the General Assembly of the Kirk, where he was usually listed as a ruling elder after 1725, would have occasioned ironical remarks had many known his taste in religious literature.

History was something about which he felt a keener interest and in which his tastes were catholic. He had works devoted to the study of historical method, including Jean Bodin's from 1566, and Charles Rollin's in an edition from the 1730s. In between were works by Langlet de Fresnoy, Peter Heylin,[50] Degory Wheare, and Louis Thomassin. He owned both Pierre Bayle's *Dictionaire historique et critique* and Bayle's critiques of Catholic and Protestant historians but they were not in this section.

To orient himself in time, he had about 35 chronologies and world histories including such standard ones as those by Scaliger, Calvisius, Masham and the one by Sir Isaac Newton which had so upset the historians of the ancient world in the 1720s.[51] Those works came in all forms – universal, ecclesiastical, ancient, modern, devoted to nations and places – and in all sizes – in single volumes and multi-volume sets. The last acquired seems to have been Gregory Sharpe's *Introduction to Universal History* (1755) published when the Duke was seventy-three. Chronology was a long-standing interest and may relate to his and his age's concerns with time-keeping and to measurements generally.[52] One suspects that Ilay was particularly fascinated by the problems of harmonizing Judeo-Christian chronologies, not only with each other but also with those of the gentile nations, and in the principles of dating which were used by various peoples in the past. This was not an innocent preoccupation but one which he shared with anti-Christians such as Voltaire who extended historical time beyond the bounds of Genesis and made the oldest people the Chinese not the Hebrews.

Methodology and chronology were followed in the shelving by general accounts of the ancient and medieval world. Those in turn were succeeded by ecclesiastical history. Here, he favoured Protestant accounts but he possessed Cesare Baronius, Louis de Maimbourg and other Roman Catholic writers, along with Protestants such as Issac Casuabon, Jacques Basnage, Friedrich Spanheim, Jeremy Collier and more.

The Duke's shelves then went to the national histories of peoples. Those who think of him as essentially an Englishman should note that Scotland came before the other nations in Britain. It got less space than England but there was less Scottish history in print. He had, of course, Fordun's *Scotichronicon* in an edition of 1683, works by Hector Boece, George Buchanan, John Knox, and all the principal historians of the seventeenth and early eighteenth centuries. His Scottish chronology was up to date with Thomas Innes's great work on Scottish history to c.1100. Some topographical works were included here, such as George Crawfurd's *Ayrshire*, Sir Robert Sibbald's *Fife* and a number of special works like Bishop William Nicholson's *Scots Historical Library*, a bibliography, and Dr. Christopher Irving's pioneering work on Scottish place-names. Ilay had volumes on the peerage and a few on Scottish families. His collection of works on Mary, Queen of Scots, was rather good and included the apology issued for her by Bishop Leslie. He bought an edition of her *Letters* and works on the controversial Casket Letters which seemed to make her guilty of her husband's murder. He possessed other accounts of Mary's life and troubles including James Melvil's *Memoirs*. He had books on the events of the seventeenth and eighteenth century in which his family had been involved. Those included the 'Marquis of Argyll's instruction to his children', a work written on the eve of his execution in 1661 for not having been loyal enough to a worthless king. This Ilay had published by the Foulis Press in 1743.[53] One of the more curious of those more personal books was his old friend George Lockhart's *Memoirs* (1714). Scattered through this section of his collection were a few works of politics such as James Steuart's *Naphtali*, an extreme Calvinist work for which Steuart was forced to go into hiding in the 1670s. Ilay's forebears shared those views and suffered for them.

The Earl's accounts of Roman Britain were in the classical section but he had bought some of the medieval chronicles published during the late seventeenth and eighteenth centuries, editions which made possible better accounts of medieval England such as David Hume's. Ilay had both ecclesiastical and civil histories of the English in every period. From c.1600 on, his collection was good; one could find on his shelves most of the now classic works. He had purchased works by William Camden, Sir Henry Spelman, Robert Brady and Sir William Dugdale. He owned William Gutherie's *History of England* but he seems not to have in London either the early volumes of Hume's *History of England* or Robertson's *History of Scotland*. He did have at least two works critical of Hume: Daniel MacQueen's *Letters on Mr. Hume's History* and William Adam's attack on Hume's views on miracles.[54]

There were few books on Ireland but there were histories of most of the other European states. Well over 100 titles were devoted to French history and about as many more dealt with the Netherlands and the Holy Roman Empire. He had histories of the Scandinavian countries, of Poland, Hungary, Russia, and something on the Chinese, Formosans and Japanese. The Moguls, too, came into his library. If one went south, rather than north and east, then there were well over a dozen volumes on the Iberian states and twenty folios on Italy and as many more in other formats. He had a number of works by Ludovico Muratori in addition to a nine-volume set of his works published in 1744. Documents as well as narratives interested the Duke. The collection continued across the seas with a volume or two on the Serbs and Croatians and many on the Turks, Persians, and Ethiopians. He seems not to have been much interested in Africa which is surprising since he invested in the slave trade. He did have works on the Spanish conquests in the New World. Prominent among them were Garcilasco de La Vega, El Inca's accounts of Peru and Florida – works read by most of *philosophes*.

Ilay liked memoirs and biographies. No section of the library lacked them. His collection of British memoirs and biographies from the seventeenth century was good. Toland's edition of Lt. Gen. Ludlow's *Memoirs* turns up here along with others by John Rushworth, Bulstrode Whitelock and Lord Clarendon. He had lives of Cromwell and William and Mary. Among military biographies were two editions of the account of his service in the Thirty Years' War by Col. Robert Monro. Queen Christina, Louis XIV and Colbert are present and there were many more from around the world. Philosophers were not forgotten: William Chillingworth, Hobbes and William Whiston, jostle Descartes, Grotius, Spinoza, Jean de Wit (a mathematician and philosopher as well as a politician) and Jean Le Clerc.

This historical collection had been made by a cosmopolite interested in politics, religion, and philosophy but concerned with how European history could be known and how far back it ran. His tastes did not centre on wars or on providential accounts of events. They focused on the political, economic, and religious causes of events which had determined European history. He did not need religious explanations, except as they related to the beliefs which made men act. Ilay's history books suggest that he was by nature a curious man who wanted to know why things had come to be and what made men tick.[55]

Jus Publicum, the next section of the library, was smaller – 546 titles and 718 volumes. A very miscellaneous selection of texts, it included the great names in natural law theory: Vittoria, Mariana, Grotius, Cumberland, Pufendorf, Locke,

Barbeyrac, Burlamaqui, Noodt and more.[56] If these were the idealists, they were balanced by the realists: Machiavelli, Hobbes, James Harrington, John Milton, Spinoza, Algernon Sidney, Andrew Fletcher of Saltoun, John Toland and lesser British Commonwealthmen. Indeed, Ilay had most of the prominent republican writers. He seems to have been fascinated by republics in both the ancient and modern world but he had very few utopian writers other than Sir Thomas More, Thomaso Campanella, and perhaps Harrington. He preferred realistic works to utopias.

The Duke had a fair collection of other British writers on politics. Some, such as Richard Hooker, were theorists long admired. Others, like James Tyrrell, Matthew Tindal and John Toland, were his contemporaries, pamphleteers addressing current issues of interest to a peer. They shared space with the theorists of divine rights: James VI and I, Robert Barclay, Adam Blackwood, Robert Filmer and Bishop Bossuet. Competing with them on the shelves were the Calvinist and Catholic justifiers of assassination – the monarchomachs – who had forced them into print: Francis Hotman, the author of the *Vindicae contra tyrannos*, and various Jesuits. There was little more modern theory; that seems not to have interested him. He did own works by the Chevalier Andrew Michael Ramsay, Montesquieu, the Abbé Mably and Hume's *Essays and Treatises on Several Subjects* (4 vols, 1753) but there was nothing by Jean-Jacques Rousseau. Other Scots whom he may have read on politics included Francis Hutcheson, John Campbell, George Logan and his opponent, Thomas Ruddiman, and the Scottish Commonwealthman and deistical writer, Thomas Gordon, a would be protégé of Ilay's brother, Duke John.

Ilay was probably most interested in political materials which had been important in history and which had affected the laws which he knew best. That is suggested by his collections of treaties, public documents, handbooks of parliamentary procedure, statements of the rights of various churches and collections such as Sir John Cotton's on the privileges and rights of Englishmen. Many of those books would have been useful to him as a statesman. Controversial works turn up here too. Some, such as the books by James Anderson, his mother's 'doer', went back to the Union debates of his early years and dealt with English claims to sovereignty (or suzerignty) over Scotland. Those claims had been pressed by William Atwood c.1698-1705 and had been resisted by many Scots in Ilay's youth. Others dealt with the constitutions of Venice, France, and other states. Here too were L'Hopital's *Memoires*, Richelieu's *Political Testament*, and various political-economic writings by Colbert, Louvois and Vauban, and Henri, Comte de Boulainvilliers on the French nobility.

Periodicals found a place here too. Among them were *The Examiner*, *The Whig Examiner*, *The Medley*, *The Independent Whig*, *Cato's Letters*, and *The Craftsman* – all Opposition papers generally arguing against the policies which Ilay supported in the House of Lords. He may have voted with the government but he read, and saved Opposition papers which were generally better written. He needed to know his 'enemies'; changing sides was always an option.

There was a smattering of works on the political life and thought of the Hebrews, Greeks, Romans, Moguls, Japanese, Turks, Hanseatic League towns, Bohemia, Hungary, the Netherlands, Spain, Poland and Livonia, Tartary, and, no doubt, other peoples and places. While his purchases slowed down in the 1740s, he added books almost to the very end. The last book in this section of the collection entered the library in the mid-1750s and concerned European diplomacy and the boundaries of Nova Scotia and Acadia, issues in question because of the Seven Years War. He needed such information if he was sensibly to debate issues in the House of Lords.

The books in Public Law were collected by a man whose interests in politics ran to more than the sort of politics he was known for practicing – management by patronage and electioneering. He bought books which gave him arguments and which concerned political orders and their justification. There is much here on the origins of states and on the duties and obligations of subjects or citizens and a lot on rights and obligations. Many of his books advocated limited government and balanced or mixed forms. Ilay was a realist who well understood that power had limits and was best used for the betterment of larger rather than smaller groups. He read about rights and defended those of the Scots but he usually spoke about 'conveniency' and the interests of men who wanted peace and prosperity with a minimum of fuss and ideology. His legal training showed. It is remarkable that he did not put in this section much of the ephemera of politics which he possessed. That found its way into the *Miscellaneous* section. Those works interested him greatly but the ones shelved here were the books from which he could fashion arguments to use in courts, in Parliament and wherever else he had to debate policies. When he needed arguments about case law and political reality, he could go to the next section of the catalogue.

Under *Judici* he possessed 868 titles running to 1,035 volumes. Those constituted the working library of a British lawyer practicing on both sides of the Tweed. While there were some books dealing with natural law, more contained collections of laws and customs of various kinds – Roman, modern civil, ecclesiastical, criminal, feudal, Scottish, English, American colonial, Dutch, French, maritime, equity, and so on. He had collections on procedures, decisions, law dictionaries and what the Scots called 'style books' (forms of actions and models of legal instruments). There was here a good deal of history, including works by Henry Home, Lord Kames, on the development of laws in general and on the Scottish laws in particular. This section would have been useful. Here too, there were a few biographies.

As befitted a man who claimed in 1737 to read frequently some Latin or Greek,[57] Ilay had a fine collection of *Autores Graeci et Latini*, in all 1,554 volumes devoted to at least 1,080 titles. There were eighty-three volumes of folio histories of the Greek world up to the fall of Constantinople. Some of that material was duplicated in quarto and octavo volumes. Most of the great Greek historians were there. All the great names in Greek literature were present including Plato, Aristotle, Epicurus, Sextus Empiricus, Plotinus, and other philosophers. The situation was the same among Romans; he had many times over a complete history of Rome. The Romans were represented by less illustrious men but he had much on and by Cicero.

Ilay's library does not strike one in most respects as that of a collector of rare and early editions but he collected Ciceros. He owned 150 Latin octavo volumes of Cicero, thirty-seven volumes in quarto and eighteen in folio for a total of 205. All that points to his interests in oratory, rhetoric and good prose. He could not resist the urge to buy editions of orations, not only by Cicero but many others. Thirty-four volumes contained orations by Cicero in addition to those in his sets of the complete works. He had two fifteenth-century editions of the rhetorical works in folio. There were thirty-one volumes of epistles and, perhaps of more significance, as much of Cicero on religious topics as on politics. Virtually every one of those editions was marked as being by a notable editor, commentator, press or as being finely printed. His editors and commentators included Erasmus, Melanchthon, Olivet, Ramus, Turnebus and Latoni. The books themselves came from Venice, Florence, Paris, Basil, Amsterdam, Leiden, Hamburg, Cambridge and Glasgow – from the 1480s to the 1740s. More than half of the works (62%) were printed before 1600 and 35% were from the seventeenth century.

The Earl liked Latin poetry and had a good deal of it – including twelve folio sets of the works of Virgil and eight of Ovid. There was a twenty-nine volume collection of Latin poets in quarto published in Milan in 1673. He favored good editions over old ones. Among these titles, there were only four incunables and not much more than a fourth of the titles dated from the sixteenth century. In addition to the Roman prose writers and orators, he had here a few mathematical and military works but his science books were mostly shelved elsewhere.

Ilay's classical authors were what one would have found in most sizable collections but the books in the next category of the catalogue are more exciting. This was the section devoted to what he called *Philogici*, a catchall category which included 1,512 volumes and 1,074 titles, mostly on art and literature. It is a fascinating glimpse of the interests which he had and pursued with some enthusiasm. The section began with the works of learned men such as Erasmus, Cardinal Bessarion, Justus Lipsius, John Selden, Francesco Suarez and Athanasius Kircher, to cite only a few. It went on to consider antiquities generally, then those of the Greeks and other ancient peoples. This led naturally to architecture and art and to such topics as gems, numismatics, and weights and measures. Those were followed by grammars and dictionaries, criticism, ancient and modern (including that of the sceptics who found a place here as well as in philosophy), and by learned journals in English, French and Italian. Catalogues of libraries and sales rounded out the section.

Ilay collected medals, numismatic objects, gems, intaglios and sulphur casts which he probably also made. Using his books, he could pore over the objects in his cabinets which required reference materials. Those were present in over forty folios, twenty-eight quartos and a dozen or more octavos. Many were costly illustrated books. He had pictures of Roman Emperors and other famous people whose heads had appeared on such things as mural ornaments, busts, sarcophagi, and what-not.[58] Those interests led him to collect works on diplomatics, on weights and measures, and what might be called art history. There were studies of authors and aids to the study of art and literature, such as Thomas Blackwell's works on Homer and Greek mythology. This category accommodated his complete run of the Paris *Mémoires des Académie des Inscriptions et belles lettres*.

This section of the library housed his many dictionaries and grammars. Shelved with the language dictionaries were others of history, geography, antiquities, and works which included the word 'dictionary' in their titles such as the *Dictionaire universelle de Trevoux* (Paris, 1704-1771**)** or the *Dictionaire universelle des arts* *et sciences* (Paris, 1732).[59] The dictionaries of Louis Moreri and Pierre Bayle appear here. Reading several languages and having a smattering of others, it is not surprising that his interests extended to the origins of languages, universal grammar, ideal languages, and short-hands. Altogether, those volumes formed an impressive collection displaying his interests in language and miscellaneous learning. It is surprising that the early volumes of the great encyclopedia of Diderot and d'Alembert are not there, particularly since he owned mathematical works by both men.

Also shelved here were volumes on how and what to study, such as Charles Rollin's *La manière d'enseigner et d'étudier les belles lettres* (Paris, 1726-28). Among those texts were works of criticism of the ancient and modern authors. From those it was but a short jump to the journal literature of his own time. He had long, possibly complete, runs of the *Nouvelles de la république de lettres*, Le Clerc's *Bibliothèque universelle*, and perhaps a dozen more serials of a similar sort. They came in quartos in English, French and Italian.[60]

Ilay's medical library would have gladdened the heart of any eighteenth-century medical man. It was larger than most physicians could afford, 1,096 titles and at least 1,284 volumes. It was up to date but possessed classical works in fine editions.[61] It was complete in the sense that it had collections in all the medical fields – botany, pharmacy, chemistry, medical theory and practice, anatomy and surgery. It was fitting that Ilay had been given an honorary MD by King's College, Aberdeen, in October 1708 and that his code name in Jacobite correspondence was 'the Doctor'.[62] In the year the *Catalogus* appeared, he was made an Honorary Fellow of the Royal College of Physicians of Edinburgh.[63]

In botany, he possessed the taxonomic systems based on famous gardens, such as those compiled by Joachim Camerarius, Robert Morrison, Joseph Pitton de Tournefort, Johann Jacob Dillenius and Carolus Linnaeus, to name the most interesting. The Duke had most of the notable seventeenth-century British natural histories compiled by men like Nehemiah Grew and John Ray. There were also regional flora such as those of Mark Catesby on the Carolinas, John Clayton on Virginia, Caleb Threlkeld on Ireland, Albrecht von Haller on the Alps, Stephan Blankaart's Dutch plants, and those of the Paris area listed by Dion Jonquet. More covered places such as Sweden, Lapland, Silesia, Greece, Sicily, Crete, Egypt, Siberia, Canada and Madagascar. Some of those books were illustrated. The last additions to the library in those categories were made in the 1750s. That was also true of the many books which dealt with plant structure and physiology. He possessed works by Stephen Hales and James Logan of Philadelphia but earlier men, like Robert Hooke and Grew were there as well. Because Ilay was a collector of garden plants and a man who could and did botanize around his estates in Surrey, Peebles-shire and Inveraray, those books were useful. They supported his most significant and expensive scientific hobbies – improved agriculture and horticulture.

Botany in the eighteenth-century shaded off, on the one hand, into *materia medica* or pharmacy and on the other into agriculture. Books in the latter class were generally to be found elsewhere but pharmacy books were here in numbers. Nine folios were devoted to this topic. Some of the chemistry books in quarto were essentially pharmaceutical in nature and among the octavos there were pharmacopoeias from at least sixteen places, often in more than one edition. Of those sixteen places only one volume was from a period earlier than 1662. This was a largely modern collection which showed Ilay keeping up with the revisions to some pharmacopoeias. His list of medicaments was supplemented by a host of recent books on mineral waters and on medicines prepared from mineral compounds. Knowing what his books contained, Ilay could easily have made up the pills and elixirs which he is said to have sometimes dispensed to his friends. He would have appeared to his medical friends as an iatro-mechanist and iatro-chemist with spagyristic inclinations. That is, as a theorist who saw the body as a mechanism which had chemical features needing to be kept in balance by medicines derived not only from simples but also from chemical compounds in which metals, such as antimony and mercury and acids or alkalis also figured.

Ilay's collection of chemistry books was equally modern. He seems to have owned very few volumes which dealt with alchemy – only three of the folios seem to have alchemical terms in the titles. While he had some sixteenth-century texts, such as Vannoccio Biringuccio's and Giambattista della Porta's, most of his chemical books were more recent and reflected chemistry as it had emerged under the tutelage and guidance of Robert Boyle and the Newtonians. He owned most of Boyle's works, Hermann Boerhaave's chemical works and a number of systems which depended on those, such as Peter Shaw's *Lectures* and his translation of Boerhaave's *Elementa chymiae*. That he owned in more than one edition showing that he wanted the revisions. He possessed books with the same title by Johann Conrad Barchuysen, Friedrich Hoffman, James Keill, Nicholas Lemery, Georg Ernst Stahl, Pierre Joseph Macquer, and other systematizers. He had bought writers on metals, alkalis and acids, mineral waters and salts. Those shaded off into books on practical processes such as bleaching and dyeing, salt making, tanning and other manufactures. There were books on the making of porcelain, a subject dear to his heart since he was a collector and investor in potteries.

The Earl had an excellent collection of specifically medical books. Although he owned some of the classics of Greek medicine, the subject for him really began with the Renaissance anatomists Vesalius and Harvey and with the medical systematizers of the late sixteenth and seventeenth centuries. There is probably no one mentioned in Lester King's notable surveys of the history of medicine and medical theories, c.1650-1750 who is not represented in this library by a principal work or by a collected works. The folios tend to be from the earlier periods but the smaller books are later and were acquired until the late 1750s. There is a Newtonian and iatro-mechanical bias to his collection once one gets out of the late seventeenth century. Ilay's purchases probably reflected fashion as well as conviction. Less usual is the respect paid to what one might call public health issues. Ilay acquired fifty-seven works dealing with the plague, eleven of which are dated c.1720-22 – a sign of how seriously he regarded the Marseilles outbreak of those years. His interest in epidemics and public health continued.[64] One would expect him to have the books by Dr. John Pringle and Dr. James Lind on the health of soldiers and sailors, but his shelves also held books by others who had addressed similar problems in English and French. The latest book in this category seems to be Stephen Hales's 1756 work on the distillation of sea water, a tract designed to improve the water supply for ships at sea. That volume also included an account of Hales's important work on ventilators for ships, prisons and other buildings. Some of Ilay's considerable number of books on venereal diseases should be listed here as well and perhaps some of his fever treatises. At a more personal level, one might guess from the number of treatises on gout that he worried about having it. There were also a few recent medical journals, such as the *Edinburgh Medical Essays* in six volumes (1737-44). He had kept up with this field and could have earned his living as a medical man.

This peer's interest in anatomy and surgery was not as great but he possessed some of the great anatomical works. He owned books which would have told him how to prepare anatomical specimens and how to make wax moulds of the blood vessels of organs. Most of his thirty-one works dealing with surgery were not older than he was. Had he read them and gone into practice, he would have cut for stone in the manner of William Cheselden, couched cataracts as did Cheselden or the Chevalier Taylor, delivered babies as did François Mauriceau or William Smellie, done amputations as did the military surgeons of the 1740s and intervened in the body as Professor Alexander Monro I, the Edinburgh anatomist, might have advised. Other volumes taught him to pull teeth, to set bones or treat wounds. Knowing its risks, he was less averse to surgery than many in his time.

The medicine section shows Ilay to have been a careful follower of Scottish works in every field. He had botanical works ranging from the mid-seventeenth-century to his own time written by such man as Robert Morison, James Sutherland, James Douglas, Patrick Blair, Thomas Short, and Charles Alston. Among his pharmacists and chemists were the men who had produced the editions of the *Edinburgh Pharmacopoeia*. Among his other chemists and pharmacists were Matthew MacKaile, John Arbuthnot, Thomas Simpson, Patrick Keir, James Keill, Charles Alston, Robert Whytt and Francis Home. He owned many books by other Scots doctors and surgeons: Archibald Pitcairne, David Abercromby, George Cheyne, William Douglas, John Cockburn, Alexander Stuart, William Graeme, George Martine, James Russel, Alexander Monro II and his brother, Donald. Finally, there were those who contributed to the various periodicals he possessed such as the *Philosophical Transactions of the Royal Society of London*, the *Edinburgh Medical Essays*, and the first volumes of the *Essays and Observations Philosophical and Literary*. He even possessed a number of printed theses, some presented at Edinburgh by men from England and Ireland. One by Dr. Francis Home is fulsomely dedicated to him.[65] Ilay knew personally most of those Scots.

The 1,077 volumes (795 titles) labelled *Philosophici & c.* contained little but natural philosophy, a topic which extended into the next section devoted to mathematics. Ilay was not much interested in morals (which as we have seen he generally put under law) or metaphysics. For him, good philosophy dealt with physical nature and the ways one could make her reveal her secrets. If one tries to give coherence to a listing which does not seem very orderly, one should say that his listing begins with the books which discussed nature in general. Among his surveys in folio format are the works of Boyle, Pierre Gassendi, Thomas Burnet's *Sacred Theory of the Earth* (1681) Emanuel Swedenborg's *Works* (1735), and Comte de Buffon's *Cours des sciences* (?1749). In smaller formats the list would be longer. Those often cosmological accounts are followed by natural histories of particular places, things, and processes. In folio he had several of the notable English county surveys, such as the two done by Dr. Robert Plot on Oxfordshire and Staffordshire. He had bought Gerard Boate's *Natural History of Ireland* (1652) and *Scotia illustrata sive prodromus historiae naturalis* (1684) by Sir Robert Sibbald. Similar books from the seventeenth and early eighteenth centuries along with Buffon and Linnaeus found places here. Most of those books showed that nature was designed, sustained and governed by laws given by a deistical god.

Next came a section on experiments in which are considered the instruments one uses to see and measure things and the various forces that need to be considered – principally gravity, electricity, magnetism, chemical affinity and 'fire'. He included here his scientific journals since they were devoted largely to accounts of various phenomena, experiments, new instruments and their uses. As we have seen, Ilay had complete runs of the *Philosophical Transactions of the Royal Society of London*, of the Paris *Mémoires de l'Académie des Sciences* and of the academies of St. Petersburg, Berlin, and Upsalla. He had the first two volumes of *Essays and Observations Physical and Literary* published by the Edinburgh Philosophical Society (1754, 1756) and odd volumes of other journals.

His catalogue went on to list books about waters, earths or minerals. Those were followed by books which studied the forces acting in nature such as fire and electricity, winds and the forces producing earthquakes and other phenomena. The Duke seems to have believed in some form of the Great Chain of Being since these topics were followed by vegetables and the animate creation at the top of which comes man. Man is thought about from his beginnings, so we find there books such as Lord Chief Justice Hales's *Primitive Origination of Mankind* (1654, but published in 1684). Having said something about man's nature, one has to consider his practical activities – the arts he cultivates. Ilay bought books on a surprising array of technical activities, including boat-building, brewing, carpentry, deer raising, dyeing, farriery, forestry, gardening, japanning, paper-making, perfuming, and silk production. He even had ten cook-books.[66] He had books on improving and managing one's estates. Those ranged from Columella on agriculture and bee-keeping (c. A.D. 65) to John Evelyn on forest trees, from Jethro Tull to Philip Miller's latest edition of the *Gardener's Dictionary*. Other books on farming were there to aid this planter of trees and cultivator of wastelands.

At the end of the of this section, one returns to men as thinkers rather than doers, to what we might think of as philosophy. He had some philosophers in full – Renaissance men like Pico, Ficino, Pompanazzi, Agrippa –but few from the Middle Ages or from his own time. He seemed more interested in the revival of learning than in contemporary philosophy. From the seventeenth century, he had a good deal of Francis Bacon, Thomas Hobbes, Lord Herbert of Cherbury, Henry More, John Locke, Edward Stillingfleet, Joseph Glanvil, Henry More; Descartes, Malebranche and Pascal. In the eighteenth century, we find Leibnitz and the Clarke-Leibnitz controversy, Bishop George Berkeley and Edmund Law on space, time and eternity. And, as if to even the score, he bought the works of deists and a number of sceptics. He had various Scottish writers (but not Hume's *Treatise*). That shows either his interest in Scotland or the gifts which came to him as a patron – probably the latter since many of them were textbooks or elementary treatises. In this category one finds Hutcheson's *Moral Philosophy*, Archibald Campbell's *Inquiry into the Original of Moral Virtue* [67] and William Duncan's *Elements of Logic*. They had benefited from his patronage. His philosophy section ended with eighteen books on logic, rhetoric, and eloquence and with Hoyle's games of whist, quadrille, picquet, chess and backgammon. It reminds one of Hume's comment that after thinking philosophically for too long, one needed the diversion of games. Like Hume, Ilay was a whist player but apparently for stakes less high than those for which Hume sometimes played.

In his library, philosophy, the sciences and the arts display their usual continuum running from general theories to their implementation in particular ways. Attention is paid to the Baconian notion that one has to have facts before one theorizes. He gave a high value to practical human activities, such as agriculture, one not always given among the philosophers or even the *philosophes*. His interest in people is again evident here. Interspersed in the section are a number books containing biographies such as Thomas Stanley's *History of Philosophy* which contained biographies and pictures of most of the better known ancient philosophers (including some a bit mythical) and John Ward's *Lives of the Professors of Gresham College*. Still, this section of the catalogue remains a bit curious. The physics of Hobbes, Rouhault, Senguerdius, Le Clerc – even Swedenborg's *Principles of Natural Philosophy* – found places but not Newton's. Newton was in the section on mathematics although some of his followers were here.

The magnificence of Ilay's collection of mathematical books is astonishing even when one remembers that he and his brother were said to be competent mathematicians. Of the 1,164 titles and 1,276 volumes in this section, there were 305 titles in folio comprising a fine collection of the ancient mathematicians. There were fourteen editions of Euclid's works. The works of great Renaissance and seventeenth-century thinkers, both in pure and applied mathematics, seem equally complete. Many of Ilay's mathematics texts must be the first editions of the mathematicians of the ancient world and the then best editions of men like Tycho Brahe, Johannis Kepler, and secondary figures such as Jerome Cardan, Thomas Harriot, Simon Stevin, and Nicholas Steno. This was the 'oldest' part of the library since Ilay had clearly been buying first or early editions of mathematical classics. About two thirds of the folios come from the seventeenth century and only a quarter from the eighteenth century – a fact that reflects the slowing down of the printing of the heritage of the past and the increased publication of works on discrete topics only some of which he found interesting. Among the quartos, no more than 55 % of the collection dates from the seventeenth century; and, well over a third comes from the eighteenth century with most of those books being published after 1730. He duplicated in quarto works which he had in folio, presumably for the prefaces and for changes made in the later editions. Even more of the octavos were bought in the eighteenth century. Keeping up with mathematics meant that he bought many new mathematical tracts and book as they came out.

As a pure mathematician, he seems to have been most interested in geometry and in the calculus but he bought books on algebra and number theory, on arithmetic and probability theory. A smattering of works were addressed to a popular audience and some were textbooks. Those were likely to have been presentation copies since they often had as authors Scottish teachers such as professors Robert Simson (Glasgow), Colin Maclaurin (Edinburgh), Matthew Stewart (Edinburgh) and John Stewart (Marischal College). Other works, like Bishop Berkeley's attacks on the calculus in *De Motu* (1721), were addressed to a learned but still popular audience. It is more surprising to find on his shelves books like Diderot's *Mémoire sur differents sujets de mathématique* (1748). This is not of great interest to anyone now but it suggests that Ilay was buying almost anything which looked as if it might be of interest.

Given his collection, it is easy to see why he should have found it pleasant and easy to talk to mathematicians in Scotland and England. Glasgow's Robert Simson, seems to have been a special friend. Simson was nearly an age-mate; Ilay was partial to men his own age. They shared interests in ancient mathematics and concerns with astronomy and botany. Both were followers of Newton and men interested in such practical applications of mathematics as life insurance.[68] The Earl and his brother patronized Colin Maclaurin and enjoyed his company. Ilay may also have employed him to tutor his son.

The Earl had a lot of mixed mathematical books – works on geodesy, navigation, surveying, dialing and the like. Sometimes, those related to current problems like knowing the shape of the earth or finding the longitude; sometimes they were books which described the location of a place, such as G. D. Cassini's *Meridian of St. Petersburg*. At other times they are, seemingly, just works which contain odd theories or recipes. Some were books on machines and instruments, which is not surprising since he had many instruments and model machines. Other books on rational mechanics contained sections on machinery while more dealt with single machines. Most of those texts were modern but Archimedes, Nicolo Tartaglia and Galileo figure in the list. If he wished to think about ploughs, milling machinery, watches, looms and much else, all he had to do was pick a relevant book off the shelf. His numerous books on the use of mathematical and other instruments suggests that he knew how to operate all his toys and instruments and that he really could talk knowingly to the mechanics whom he employed.

Ilay was constantly building something between c.1724 and his death in 1761; it is not surprising that by the time his library was catalogued he should have had a sizable collection of books on architecture. About 10% of the mathematics books concerned this topic. They included about sixty folios, some very well illustrated. This was an expensive category. The folios included Vitruvius – in six different editions and commentaries – Palladio and Vincenzo Scamozzi, Gianlorenzo Bibiena and Claude Perrault but also works by or about Inigo Jones, William Kent, and his own architect on several projects, James Gibbs. Had Ilay not made the grand tour, he would still have known how many Italian, Dutch and French cities and palaces looked and how they had been designed and built. That was equally the case with English county seats. In quartos, he had works by Robert and Roger Morris. Perhaps of greater interest, since he built the largest Gothic structure of the time, is Batty and Thomas Langley's *Gothick Architecture*, a work published two years before work began on Inveraray Castle in 1744. As a sub-species of architecture, we should note his numerous works on military engineering, fortification, and gunnery. Cornelius Cohoern and Marshal Vauban were there and their themes would have been treated in some of the geometry books which he owned. Ilay would have been able to read about places which he had seen and as Lord Archy or as Captain or Colonel Campbell may even have fought to take.

The Duke was an amateur astronomer with seven or more telescopes. His books told him how his telescopes and microscopes were made and functioned. He had not only the predictable books on the subject but also Kepler's *Rudolphine Tables*, John Flamsteed's stellar observations, similar ones from the Paris observatory by the Cassinis as well as other tables useful to navigators, calculators, and theoreticians. He had accounts of notable observations and the systematic works of the greatest astronomers. He had even bought some manuscript observations made by Samuel Molyneux. Such items tell us that he could make astronomical calculations. Reading Ilay's folios, one could trace the debates over the system of the world and the motions of its component parts. There was even room for the ruminations on those ideas by the Rosicrucian Robert Fludd or the eccentric Newtonian, William Whiston.

Related to astronomy, but separable from it, was the work of Newton. Ilay had several editions of Newton's *Principia* and explanations of it. Those ranged from the textbooks of Petrus van Musschenbroek and Colin Maclaurin to the more popular expositions of Isaac Pemberton, Voltaire and Francesco Algarotti.[69] There were learned accounts of most aspects of Newton's accomplishment and legacy. Few of the men mentioned in Robert Schofield's *Mechanism and Materialism* (1969) are without a place on the pages of the catalogue. Here one finds works on hydrostatics, mechanics, and dynamics. He was as familiar with the work of the Bernoullis, Leonhardt Euler, Bernardus Nieuwentyt, Jean Le Rond d'Alembert, and of other Academicians in Paris and St. Petersburg as he was with their counterparts in London or Edinburgh. There were also books on music theory, on perspective, even on vision and optics, usually related topics in the eighteenth century. Among those was what the catalogue called 'Leonardo da Vinci trattato della pittura'.[70] There was little historical material in this section of the collection but the books in this section dealing with experimental philosophy constituted a history of its modern progress in Britain and on the continent.

As in other sections, many Scots were included among the authors. John Napier, George Sinclair, James, David and James Gregory, John Arbuthnot, John Keill, Robert Simson, Colin Maclaurin, John Stewart, Matthew Stewart, James Ferguson, James Stirling and Patrick Murdoch were among them. Here, as in the natural philosophy section, matters went from the most general to the particular. Ilay seems to have believed one should begin with geometry and follow on with arithmetic, algebra, fluxions, trigonometry, logarithms, and the uses of all those in astronomy, geodesy, cartography, navigation, mechanics and what we might call engineering, architecture and music theory.

The final section of the library (1,024 titles and 1,570+ volumes) was aptly named *Miscellanei*. Its largest sections were devoted to geography and travel. His librarian would have found very useful for his own work the 43 folio volumes of maps and an equal number of descriptions of countries and regions. In quarto, the maps diminish in number to nine, but the books of voyages and descriptions amounted to 58, many of which contained maps. There were 16 volumes of octavo maps and gazetteers and 118 travel books and descriptions of regions and countries. In all, this comes to almost seventy volumes of maps, plus other maps which were likely single sheets. There were at least 219 travel titles, some of which would have included more maps. There was no region of the world about which this peer lacked knowledge. For every place about whose language he had something, he also had a travel book and maps. Many of those were old and constituted the first impressions of the Europeans, but many were new. He had bought Dr. William Douglass's *State of North America* (1755) and Douglass's *Account of European Settlements in America* (1757). Those were but two items in a collection which described for the statesman the whole of the Americas from 1492 on.[71] He, like writers such as Douglass, was interested in the imperial significance of the lands they described, either for Britain or for some other country. Taken together, those books constituted something of a history of the development after c.1500 of the barbarous, exotic and colonial worlds as they were affected by Spanish, French, Dutch and British explorers, traders and conquerors.

Another large section of the miscellany, about 200 items in octavo alone, was given over to economic matters of one sort or another. Some of the works were compendia such as Jacques Savary's or Malachy Postlethwait's works on commerce.[72] Other books and booklets were specialized. Those dealt with taxes, tariffs, colonies, various trades and industries, money and interest. His Lordship's concerns with money and the problems which re-coinage had posed in Britain during the 1690s accounted for some of the items. More works dealt in a fairly systematic fashion with economies. Here one finds Thomas Mun's *England's Treasure by Foreign Trade*, the works of John Law, David Hume's *Essays and Discourses* and Josiah Tucker's *Essay on Trade*.

Virtually every trade engaged in by Britons is represented by one or more works. Among the political-economic items two kinds stand out – books on banking and others on Scotland. Ilay owned not only the by-laws of the Bank of England and literature on the Darien Company, which had also been able to engage in banking, but John Law's *Money and Trade Considered* (1705). In manuscript, he owned Law's *Essay on a Land Bank* and, in print, Hugh Chamberlain's *Proposals for a Land Credit* (Edinburgh, 1700) and William Paterson's *Proposals and Reasons for constituting A Council of Trade* (Edinburgh, 1700) – all books relevant to his concerns while Lord Treasurer of Scotland. Ilay's interest in economics was not only that of a statesman but that of an investor and speculator dealing with stocks, bonds, currency, bullion trading, mortgages and commodities. He had financial stakes in some of the businesses his books considered.

A section of the miscellaneous books was devoted to modern literature. Here is where English authors, from Chaucer on, found a place. Ilay liked poetry and there was a great deal of it here. He was definitely not a reader of novels. There are very few of them. The English novelists he possessed tended to be by older writers like Aphra Behn, and Daniel Defoe whom he might have known. He read criticism by John Dryden, Thomas Rymer, John Dennis, Alexander Pope and his Tory friends. Among these books of literature were, again, Scottish authors: *e. g.*, Sir David Lyndsay, Montrose, Drummond of Hawthornden, Sir Francis Grant, Allan

Ramsay sr., the Chevalier Ramsay, James Thomson and John Armstrong. There was even a collection of Scottish Latin verses edited by Professor John Ker. William Lauder's work on Milton, several anonymous lives, and some voyages and travels were also on his shelves. What is absent, were works by young Scots like William Robertson and John Home. They had been beneficiaries of his patronage and should have been represented in his library even though most of their works came out after this catalogue was drawn up.

After the works in English, the next largest set of literary works were those in French although the Italians ran a close second. Ilay had the greater poets beginning with Pierre de Ronsard and the rest of the Pléaide and the most notable dramatists. He had bought critics such as Boileau. He owned some humanists, like Rabelais, Jean Bodin and Montaigne and *moralistes* such as Jean de la Bruyère and La Rochfoucauld. He had some of the writings of the *érudits* such as Naudé and Le Mothe Le Vayer. Among those who wrote during his own lifetime, he possessed works by Jean Baptiste Massillon and other sermon writers. He read Fontenelle, LeClerc, the Abbé de St. Pierre, Le Sage, and the Abbé Prevost. Ilay liked fake travels and had sets of *The Turkish Spy* and Simon Tyssot de Patot's *Lettres Choisies*. Montesquieu's *Lettres persanes* was there as were the *Peruvian Letters* of Mme. de Graffigny. All of those were more than a little deistical. He owned some of the literary works of Voltaire but, in general, he was not a buyer of the productions of the *philosophes*.[73] There was no language barrier but there must have been one of age, sensibility and outlook.

His Italian authors begin with Petrach, Dante, Boccaccio and Poliziano. Ilay's list went on through Machiavelli, Guicciardini, Aretino, Guazzo, Ariostio, Bembo, Tasso, Guarini, Castiglione, Pallavincino, Botero, Sarpi, and more. He must have read Italian easily but he seems not to have read much current Italian literature, perhaps only the half dozen Italian serials to which he at some time subscribed or purchased.

Among his Spanish books were accounts of the Spanish discoverers and conquerors, the works of Antonio Perez, at least four editions of Cervantes. He had several editions of the poet Luis de Gongara y Argote, plays by Roxas and Lope de Vega, even a six-volume quarto set of the *Theatro critico* of Fr. Feijoo, the first notable enlightened Spaniard. In contrast, there were few works in Portuguese but there were some, just as there were even fewer volumes in Dutch and German.

The remaining category in the miscellaneous section of the library which deserves notice is biography. There were genealogies and peerages, accounts of notable families, memoirs, such as Gilbert Burnet's *History of His own Times*. There were royal biographies, lives of philosophers, mathematicians, physicians and scientists, artists and teachers, even one book about famous highwaymen. The listed biographies were supplemented by more in the prefaces to collected works. Altogether, biographies must have accounted for an appreciable number of his books. He was interested in people and was delighted to read about them.

V. Did He Read His Books?

The *Catalogus Librorum* tells us much about this man's mind but only if he read the volumes he owned. What evidence do we have that he read the things which filled his shelves?

The idiosyncrasies of the collection were his. The collection fits what we know of the man from other sources. It catered to his known interests in science, medicine, gardening, banking, architecture, politics and law, and certainly allowed him to study his gems and intaglios with ease. He did not purchase extensively in fields in which he had no substantial interests. This was not a collection ostentatiously heavy with classical editions. The classical writers were not all there, just as his philosophers included few mediaevals and not all the ancients. The library was not a collection with much written by men opposed to the Whiggish factions which Ilay served. When it included Tories, they tended to be men with whom he was allied c.1710. He took Opposition journals but he was not a great buyer of works by Opposition writers. In religion, it also fits what is known of his beliefs and feelings. His library had almost no religious ephemera. The library reflects his known interests in the history and in the lives of those who had made history. Ilay, although he liked ornaments, seems not to have bought ornamental volumes. He possessed rarities but did not collect rare books save in mathematics, medicine and in relation to Cicero. His was not a library full of fashionable materials but a bit old fashioned by 1761. It harked back to the *virtuosi* among whom he had grown up. All that illustrates Ilay's interests but by itself it does not establish his mastery of the texts. For that we must look elsewhere.

Ilay enjoyed the company of the learned and was reputed to be able to hold his own with them which he could not have done without much study. When he went to Scotland, he conversed with mathematicians like Simson and Maclaurin, some of the chemists and improvers. In London he knew and dealt with men like James Bradley, the Astronomer Royal, and learned instrument makers, such as James Short and George Adams sr. The surviving lists of his dinner guests are not distinguished so much by the titles of those invited as by the skills and knowledge of those with whom he chose to dine. The titled were often relatives, visiting Scots or English *virtuosi*. He welcomed his nephew Lord Bute and his cousin Loudoun, his political ally Lord Morton, PRS, the Duke of Richmond or Lord Petre – they were all men like himself. All were botanists. Richmond too held an MD. Four were astronomers and Petre was a collector of foreign plants. More often present were physicians like Charles Stuart, John Mitchell and John Clephane or gardeners and seedsmen such as Philip Miller, or visiting scientists, like the Swedish traveller Pehr Kalm. Among his enlightened visitors were ministers like the Rev. Principal George Campbell of Marischal College, Aberdeen, an institution which had a close relationship with the Earl of Ilay.[74] Ilay ate with his architects – James Gibbs, Roger and James Morris, and the Adam brothers. John Home and other literary men, such as Lord Lyttleton or Dr. John Campbell, found places at his table. He entertained Robert Nugent and Bubb Dodington and others like them who were financial thinkers and speculators like himself. At his dinner table, the talk was serious and learned. A meal at Whitton with Lord Petre, the Duke of Richmond and Philip Miller meant talk about plants.[75]

When chemists were present, only the topic changed. Offered the choice of hunting or reading while at Sir Robert Walpole's estate, Ilay opted for reading and writing letters.[76] Such a man would have read his books and, in most cases understood what he read. Certainly men who knew him well thought him learned as did those who gave him books and dedications.

Peter Collinson, another learned gardener, wrote after his death that Ilay was 'a great chemist, natural philosopher, mechanic, astronomer and mathematician'.[77] Collinson and others who made similar remarks are surely to be trusted. Their comments show us what he liked and knew best – and why men like the Earls of Stair and Marchmont, or Lord Hervey and Horace Walpole found him strange and disliked him. Ilay knew more than they did about most things but especially about topics they found boring and whose uses they did not recognize. He socialized easily outside his own rank and was not snobbish.

Ilay's books show us an inquisitive man, orderly and systematic in his thought, not much given to speculation but eager for practical, empirically derived knowledge. He had a secular outlook and was not much interested in religion. He read history and enjoyed poetry. He collected Cicero and was interested in rhetoric. As a member of the House of Lords, he spoke well but he was no Ciceronian. He knew that the modern world was a far more complex place than the ancient world had been. Politics were now more complicated; trade and commerce affected it very differently. His speeches were long on facts and solid arguments but were seldom rhetorical set-pieces. Those could be left to his brother. He had time for architecture but apparently little use for painting and music except as examples of applied mathematics. He read little modern, light, popular literature save for plays but he kept up with serious science, medicine and mathematics. Ilay spent some time with the ancients but he was clearly more fascinated by modern sciences and their employments. To him, those offered the best means for improving his own circumstances and those of men generally and Scots in particular. Knowledge, were it used as it ought to be, would do much for Britons and mankind.

Horace Walpole understood him better than many of their class. When he commissioned a portrait plate of Argyll to appear at the end of the second volume of his *Memoirs of King George II* (written between 1751 and 1763), Walpole decorated the surround of the pictured Duke with emblems of learning: a globe, a compass, a square, plants the Duke had brought into Britain, three books, a manuscript [? of a speech] and perhaps an architectural drawing. They lie on draperies. One piece of cloth appears to be a bit of a robe surmounted by a ducal coronet; another is a plaid on which is laid a sword. The bookish Scottish man of thought and action, the thinker and improver, the man of principles willing to defend them is alluded to in ways which somewhat offset the negative character Walpole gave of the Duke in the text.[78]

Plate 4. Andrew Fletcher, Lord Milton, Robert Scott after Allen Ramsay (1748), mezzotint, with permission of the Scottish National Portrait Gallery, Edinburgh.

Chapter 7

Ilay's Sciences

I. The Context for Ilay's Science

The hard decade of the 1690s evoked in Scotland many improving schemes meant to remedy the economic doldrums. Lord Archy was aware of some of those since he was at university in Glasgow at the end of that period. Schemes such as the Bank of Scotland (1695-) and the Darien Company (1696-1707) were national concerns which produced a pamphlet literature and proposals to the Scottish Parliament. What many had in common was the hope that natural knowledge, systematically pursued, would increase and result in economic benefits. For that to happen, the will to make changes had to be found. Later in life, Lord Ilay tried, both by his own efforts and those of men he patronized, to increase the store of useful knowledge and to act on it for the benefit of himself, his friends and for Scots generally.

Most of the schemes of the 1690s related to innovations in agriculture and to finding ways to a stimulate industry and trade. Some centred on the linen trade in which Scots seemed to have an advantage over the English. Other proposals called for a 'Council of Trade' and came to partial fruition in the Darien scheme and the Bank of Scotland. Both were products of the same frame of mind and the same needs, needs made manifest by the long-term decline of Scottish trade and the economic conditions of the 1690s.[1] John Law's scheme of 1705, which Lord Archy backed, was but one plan among many designed to do the same things. Less grand were schemes calling for aid to the country's farmers and the creation of a professor of agriculture, a call renewed by the Honourable the Improvers in the Knowledge of Agriculture in the 1720s and realized in the 1790s. Sir Robert Sibbald or some of his friends urged the establishment of something like trade schools in 1700-01. A proposal for a medical school associated with an infirmary in Edinburgh circulated in the 1690s and early 1700s.[2] Others advocated unifying the regional weights and measures of the country.[3]

Men like Sibbald, or the little-known *virtuoso*, Thomas Kincaid,[4] not only sought to promote the search for knowledge through experimentation but were trying to create institutions in which that would be an on-going activity.[5] Sibbald proposed c.1702 the founding of a Royal Society of Scotland. Had it come into being, it would have given Scotland an academy like others in Europe; it would have conducted experiments and recommended improvements. Sibbald himself hoped his Royal Society might survey the country and produce maps (an unfinished agendum until the 1790s).[6] His Royal Society would have been a general purpose national research institute. As he envisioned it, that was not a viable project. By c.1705 it was a dead project whose revival the Union prevented.[7] The money to fund a Scottish academy went to other things.

What Stephen Shapin once called 'the Edinburgh audience for science'[8] was, in 1700, a small *virtuoso* community which saw science as a polite accomplishment. It needed to be better established in the country to increase its wealth and to uphold its dignity. The plans and proposals of the 1690s shared that outlook and shaped ideas about the nature and uses of knowledge for Lord Archy's generation. They also set the agenda for Scots in the Enlightenment.

Ilay was very much a part of that audience, a member who sought to speak to it with discoveries of his own or those he could foster. Many of the proposals of Ilay's youth were later implemented in one way or another, often with his help or by people who shared his interests and who often owed him their jobs. Finding new and better manures, better heckles and bleaches, more effective ways of promoting trade or educating Scots were all integral to that effort. What is equally clear is that, despite a library full of books of theory, he had very little interest in scientific ideas which could not be implemented. Ilay's practical mind tended to ignore theories unless they suggested ways in which practice could be improved. Most of the men whom he patronized shared his utilitarian outlook if not always his disregard for theory. As a young man, mathematics – mixed or applied mathematics – may well have been the dearest to him.

II. Mathematics

It was not only Ilay's library which showed his aptitude for and interests in mathematics. He was appointed to a Treasury position in 1705 for political reasons but perhaps also because a Union with England required making many calculations of the sums which should be paid to Scots to compensate them for future payments on the English national debt. Those was not easy to gauge. In the end, three professional mathematicians handled the calculation of 'the Equivalent Fund' as it was called.[9] Ilay knew them all. After 1705, he enjoyed the company of John Law. Law, then a professional gambler as well as a would be banker, knew a good deal about probability theory and was noted for being able to make difficult calculations in his head. Ilay also showed a fondness for less dubious mathematicians.

By the early 1720s, Colin Maclaurin, Britain's best known eighteenth-century mathematician, was well known to Ilay and his brother.[10] Maclaurin came from an Argyllshire family long connected to the Inveraray Campbells and probably first met the brothers on a trip to London in 1719-20. He tutored one of their relatives in 1722-24. In 1732, Maclaurin sent Ilay mathematical papers to read.[11] That year Maclaurin hoped that his connexion with his Lordship would be worth a job in the Exchequer. It was not.[12] Perhaps that is why Maclaurin dedicated his *Treatise of Fluxions* (1742) to Duke John rather than to the Earl of Ilay, who seems to have been the better mathematician. When Maclaurin died in 1746, Argyll wanted Robert Simson, Professor of Mathematics at Glasgow University, to replace him in the Edinburgh chair. Argyll also found acceptable other applicants – James Stirling (a reputed Jacobite), James Williamson and Matthew Stewart. He is likely to have aided Matthew Stewart who was minister of Rosneath, a living in the gift of the Campbells.[13]

Ilay corresponded with Robert Simson occasionally after 1727.[14] The professor acted as one of Ilay's informants at Glasgow University. The 'pleasures of mathematics' which he and Simson shared would have included an appreciation of the clear and rigorous deductive structure of ancient geometry which Simson was making efforts to elucidate. Like many of Ilay's other friends and protégés, Simson was an amateur botanist.[15] Simson dedicated to Ilay his *Sectionum conicarum libri* (1735).[16] In Aberdeen, Lord Ilay knew and seems to have liked John Stewart at Marischal College. He wrote a book on Newtonian mathematics which the Earl had in his library.[17] The St Andrews mathematicians were duller men and do not appear in his letters.

Ilay also had ties to some mathematicians in England. Robert Smith, the Plumian Professor of Astronomy at Cambridge was a dinner guest and publicly referred to Ilay's 'noble collection of instruments' (see p. 396, n. 52). His Cambridge counterpart, James Bradley, was another.[18] The Earl subscribed to Abraham de Moivre's *Miscellanaea analytica de seriebus et quadraturis* (1730) and was friendly with and sometimes extended favours to other mathematicians later in his life. One should probably include here the mathematical instrument makers whom he patronized.[19] Among his noble friends, the Duke of Richmond and the Earls of Macclesfield and Morton (later PRS) were also adepts.

Those men, like Ilay, were all interested in the applications of mathematics to the real world. Simson was something of an actuary, as were Maclaurin and de Moivre.[20] Maclaurin worked on practical problems such as ventilating and draining the mines of Sir John Clerk and finding better ways to estimate easily the capacity of barrels.[21] Maclaurin, like both professors Stewart, taught practical courses which included fortification and gunnery as well as Newton's fluxions. All those Scots were competent astronomers who taught navigation and owned or had the use of at least one telescope.[22] Stirling was the inventor of a mine pump. Ilay also patronized map makers whose skills rested on mathematics. He aided James Dorrit, his valet or butler, to publish a map of Inveraray and in 1750 a general map of Scotland which seems to have had some public subsidy.[23] Ilay could have copied such things with the pantographs he owned.[24]

Ilay was very much part of their world and had made efforts to understand it. Sometime between c.1714 and 1731, he attended the lectures of William Whiston and his demonstrator or experimenter, Francis Hauksbee II. Whiston tells us that Ilay asked for and received a manuscript copy of Whiston's text.[25] The Earl may have attended other such lectures since London after c.1710 had many men who gave them.[26]

By 1737 Ilay had an impressive array of instruments, machines, toys and models but just how many he had there is no way of telling because there is no surviving inventory and few if any survive.[27] There are among his surviving papers and estate records some indications of the numbers and kinds of things he owned. Not all were 'mathematical'.

III. The Duke's Instruments[28]

One did not require any instruments to do pure mathematics but most mathematicians had sets of mathematical instruments such as the Earl bought at the 1730 auction of the books and instruments of Samuel Molyneux: 'A Case of Instruments to open like a book, made at Paris, and a Fly Catcher'.[29] The Case would have included, at the very least, straight edged rulers, protractors, compasses, and perhaps calculating devices of some description such as 'Napier's Bones' (slide rules) made by many makers. Later, Ilay seems to have owned a rotula made by James Ferguson.[30] The Molyneux instruments would have been an additional set since every mathematician had such items.

Mathematical instruments sometimes included much more. The plate showing such instruments, included in James Moxon and Thomas Tuttell's *The Description and Explanation of Mathematical Instruments* (several editions London, 1700/01-1705) has a variety of spheres, backstaffs, quadrants, astrolabes, plane tables and other surveying instruments including some used in gauging the capacities of barrels.[31] Ilay would have had examples of most of those things in his collection. He would have found them diverting but would also have seen some as instruments necessary to the pursuit of mixed mathematics having practical uses. The Earl's books told him how to use them. One such book on 'Mathematical Instruments' he purchased in April 1748, at Kincaid's bookshop in Edinburgh, presumably for use at The Whim or Inveraray.[32] There were others in his London library. Ilay possessed many instruments and encouraged the men who made them. The Board of Trustees for Fisheries and Manufactures in Scotland, run principally by his place-men under the supervision of Lord Milton, was an agency from which men like Ilay's wright and model maker, Robert MacKell, and others expected and received aid and rewards for new inventions which applied mathematical principles.[33]

Ilay as an amateur astronomer seems to have been most active in the 1730s. He came to possess most of the equipment which a serious astronomer would use and other items which were mainly ornamental toys. Among the latter was his orrery or a model of the solar system which showed the movements of the planets and their satellites. His was made by Thomas Wright and described after Argyll's death by the instrument maker George Adams as being '3 1/2 feet Diamtr. on a Table with a Glass Case. &c'. [34] The description of the orrery notes that it was made by Wright but is most fascinating for the details which it gives of its rich ornamentation:

> In a mahogany dome cover glass case. The dome to raise up occasionally by a cord or pulley. In this superb and very complete machine, all the motions of the primary and secondary planets, are exhibited by *wheel work*, on the turning simply of a winch. The earth is represented by a suitable papered globe [*i.e.* it had a map], and the revolutions of all the planets, and their satellites are performed in their due periodical times. – The wheel work is included in an elegant dodecagonal case, on which is elegantly painted and blazoned the 12 signs of the Zodiac; with 12 feet and other ornaments, carved and gilt, and contrived with taste. Upon the case are fixed 12 neat brass pillars,

supporting a large brass engraved ring, containing the ecliptic and day of the months accurately divided. The ring supports a large brass armillary sphere, with the equinoctial and solistial colures and the other circles of the sphere, all accurately divided. Upon this sphere is a large brass, moveable horizon, useful in performing many problems, and illustrating many properties.

In the dome one of the glass panes in a brass frame opens as a door, to admit the hands of the lecturer or pupil, in order to set and adjust the planets previous to use. There is also another door below that to admit the winch, when the Orrery is to be set in motion....

There are two large brass handles, to lift it out of its case if desired, for placing it on a table or other stand.

This machine, is constructed nearly after the plan of the reputed inventor *Mr. Rowley*, and originally made by *Mr. Wright*, a late Mathematical Instrument maker to his Majesty, and has undergone various emendations, and will receive further improvements by W. and S. Jones.[35]

The fate and present whereabouts of this magnificent instrument is unknown.

Another instrument noted in George Adams's inventory as being in London was 'An Armillary Sphere 19 1/2 Inches Diamtr. By [Thomas] Wright.' This was a more useful instrument defined in the first edition of the *Encyclopedia Britannica* as 'an artificial sphere, composed of a number of circles, representing the several circles of the mundane sphere, put together in their natural order, to ease and assist the imagination, in conceiving the constitution of the heavens, and the motions of the celestial bodies'. The editor, William Smellie, cross-referenced it to geography and discussed its use in explaining the motions of the earth and in finding one's position on the globe.[36]

Any astronomer who took his science seriously needed accurate clocks and the means to set them properly. Ilay had both. He possessed a splendid equinoctial ring sundial made by Richard Glynne which bore the Argyll arms. This beautiful gilt brass instrument was until the 1990s in the Time Museum in Rockford, Illinois, but on 2 December 1999 it was sold at Sotheby's New York for over a million pounds.[37] His mounted equinoctial dial allowed Ilay to establish local time precisely for such events as eclipses and transits and made his observations comparable with others. Ilay had less complex dials as well, both to set his clocks and to tell time in his gardens.[38] At the Molyneux auction in 1730, he bought for £6.1.0, 'An Astronomical Clock, used by Mr. Molyneux in his Observations'.[39] There were certainly other astronomical timekeepers.

Ilay liked clocks and had a lot of them. By 1719 he had patronized fine London clock makers like John Topping; later, he looked after Alexander Cumming (or Cuming) who worked for him both at Inveraray and at London after c.1750.[40] Bishop Pococke reported in June 1760 that Alexander Cumming was making for the Duke a clock 'to regulate time by the stars as well as sun'.[41] Included among Ilay's clocks was one which he bought in Scotland in 1725 or 1726 for £5:17.6 – clearly a fine piece.[42] For a bedroom perhaps, the Earl shipped 'an Alurm Clock' to Scotland in 1744.[43] Ilay could explain the principles of Harrison's chronometer to Dr. John Mitchell and was said to be able to repair his own watches.[44] Perhaps the Duke's 'Chest of Tools', found in his room at Rosneath Castle after his death, contained some watchmaker's tools.[45]

The Earl had many telescopes, one or more at each of his houses. By 1730, he owned at least three: 'A Reflecting Telescope of Sir Isaac Newton's [design], 8 Foot lon[g] ... Made by Mr. Molyneux, with a chair to rise and fall at Pleasure'; a Meridian Telescope, with a Regulator made by Mr. [George] Graham' and at least one other.[46] By 1733, he had acquired a 15 inch Gregorian made by James Short;[47] Colin Maclaurin, almost certainly writing of this to Robert Smith, said that the Earl's reflecting telescope of fifteen inches focal distance was impressive because of the fineness of its quicksilvering. He claimed that with it Ilay could read the *Philosophical Transactions* at a distance of 230 feet – which tells us that Ilay wanted good instruments and tested their capacities.[48] On 29 June 1745, Argyll shipped 'a little Telescope' from London to Inveraray and four years later a telescope and '2 pr of Stretchers' went to Rosneath along with a 'Telescope wrapped in a Garden mat' which was for The Whim.[49] We know nothing certain about these instruments but they do not seem to be ones already mentioned.[50] In addition, he had at London in 1761 'A Transit instrument. the Tellescope 3 feet 9 inch long of height from the Ground 5 1/2 feet. on two Mohogeney Supports' and 'A Double or rather an Equatorial Instrumt. With a Glass Case & Pedestal. &c.' [51] That may be the telescope which Robert Smith, described as 'very excellent of this kind, for taking altitudes, made all of brass except a square steel axis about 30 inches in length'. Smith did not give its maker but this equatorial telescope may have been made by James Short since he produced them.[52] The devices were useful to observers who were looking at stars for long periods and eager to make calculations.[53] If Ilay bought it for those reasons, then he was serious about his observations. None have survived and we do not know with whom he observed or who served as his time-keeper when he needed one.

Any astronomer of the time would have had more equipment and Ilay did.[54] Some things were undoubtedly picked up at auctions such as the a wooden support for a telescope and a wooden base bought at the Molyneux auction.[55] Some of those objects again suggest that Ilay was an astronomer who did calculations as well as one who just enjoyed the night skies. Much of his equipment was probably kept at Whitton where the air would have been clearer.

When one descended from the stars to the ambient air, the Duke had things to measure its qualities. The Adams inventory listed four thermometers, one of which was a spirit thermometer. One had been made by John Sisson and came with sliding scales and a level. Another, by John Bird who had worked for Sisson, is listed as a 'Boiling Thermometer' and probably belongs with the chemical instruments. Ilay also bought thermometers from Alexander Wilson of Glasgow. Among the three barometers listed by Adams is a barometer/thermometer by 'Hauksbee'. The Earl had other 'weather glasses'.[56] Some of those were made by Alexander Wilson, among them a 'portable measuring barometer'.[57] 'A Double diagonal Barometer paper Scale, Wainscot Frame – with a Level' had been made by Sisson. Lastly, the Adams inventory listed a 'Conical Hydrometer in Silver' with which the Duke could assess density of fluids like rainwater. None of those seem to have survived.

His Lordship may well have had rain gauges and anemometers since those were possessed by Lord Bute butthese are not recorded. Ilay's purchase of what appears to have been six volumes of Molyneux's weather observations suggests that he also kept records which would have included wind direction and speed, and rainfall.

Once one touched earth, instruments multiplied. Ilay owned surveying equipment of various kinds. He may well have purchased the instruments his gardeners used to level and drain his fields at The Whim.[58] This would have meant, at the very least, rods, chains, compasses, hand levels and perhaps a circumferentor. A theodolite was sent up to Scotland from London, in June 1745, probably for The Whim since the things going with it seem designed for there.[59] According to the Adams inventory, he had a plane table in London where he did not need one; perhaps he had others on his Scottish estates where they were needed. He had a way-wiser or measuring wheel at The Whim.

To work the land once it had been surveyed, Ilay had various machines. Some came from London or from Glasgow as models and were made up on the spot by his wrights and carpenters. The Whim had a smith and a wright who made machines and keep them in trim. Inveraray, a construction site for the latter part of his life, was better provided with models. They were kept in a shed used by the architect as an office.[60] Among the items sent as models were 'hurdles or flakes also a model of a 4 wheeld low Carriage for Removing of Stones, or loggs of wood'.[61] He had models of machinery used for milling. Of course, there were also the usual farm tools, some which would have been quite specialized, such as plows, drills or seeders, threshing machines, and the pruning and grafting tools, which he had and used himself.[62] Other devices included pumps and perhaps a siphon like that used by Lord Milton in his drainage system. Ilay sent from London in 1744 a model pump and bought pumps locally as well.[63] Items in the Saltoun Papers deal with water screws.[64] Additional machines are ambiguously described. Was his stone hammer to crush limestone a hand-held thing or was it a massive piece of iron mounted on a beam?[65] More special equipment would have been found in the lint yard and limekiln at The Whim, around his various quarries, coal mine and salt pans. All those fit here because, in one way or another, they exemplify the use of mechanical principles and were described by books housed in the mathematics section of his library. It is a bit more difficult to classify the novel and effective rat trap used by 'the gardiner Lads'.[66]

Ilay had many models which he insisted be built to scale.[67] They showed both the Earl and those who copied them how machines worked or how buildings and other structures were to be built. Some were made for him by Robert Mackell (or Meikle) a millwright who worked at Rosneath and Inveraray. He made the 'models of the machine mills he intended to set up when [Ilay] launched new industries in the town.... Mackell later made and installed milling machinery for The Whim and Rosneath (1749) and for the Carlundon [mill] in Inveraray (1749-51)'.[68] Mackell and other ingenious men were also employed by Lord Milton[69] and the Board of Trustees to develop new machines or to test ones proposed as useful in the linen trades.[70] None of Ilay's own models are known to have survived.[71] His book catalogue suggests that he knew how to use all his models and instruments and that he really could talk knowingly to philosophers and to the mechanics whom he employed – as one of his obituaries says.[72] The most exotic of his models may well have been one of Marshall Saxe's campaign waggon. This served as a pattern for the full-size replica which for a few years graced the garden at Inveraray until it was destroyed in a storm.[73]

The Earl of Ilay was interested in optical devices other than telescopes. In 1744 he sent to Scotland 'A Book like Camera obscura, A less d[itto]'.[74] He probably intended one for The Whim and the other for Inveraray. He had two others in London at the time of his death as well as pieces for others.[75] A year later, he sent to Lord Milton, again probably for The Whim and Inveraray, 'a little Microscope in a Shagreen Case' and 'a larger d[itto]'.[76] Two other microscopes are described as 'microscopic Spectacles'.[77] In 1730 he purchased at the Molyneux auction a 'double [*i.e.* a compound] microscope' made in Paris by Villet (Villette?).[78] Given his botanical interests, he is likely to have used his microscopes on plant materials.

To complete his interesting collection of mathematical and natural philosophical instruments, he had loadstones, magnets and compasses. The Adams inventory lists '3 Mahogy. Boxes each containing six Artificial Magnets 14 1/2 inches long'. Others had earlier been sent north.[79] Ilay, like Molyneux, was interested in magnetic variation and owned a boxed 'large Needle to find the Variation of the Compass'.[80] The Earl's interest in magnetism was oriented toward navigation. He probably had a full set of navigational instruments since his books suggest that, as does his ownership of merchant ships and a yacht, but none are listed in the surviving papers. If he did own such instruments, this would have given him a set of quadrants, compasses, and the dividers used by navigators and the masters of his ships.

Lacking in this record are teaching toys such as Newton's balls, which illustrated principles of Newtonian physics. Their omission suggests, as does the Adams inventory, that Ilay focussed on astronomy, optics and the practical applications of rational mechanics and not on other fields in the physical sciences. Argyll was not a known subscriber to Colin Maclaurin's posthumously published *An Acount of Sir Isaac Newton's Philosophical Discoveries*.[81] The most likely reason is that the professor's book paid more attention to the history of physics than to the practical application of Newtonian principles although the theory of mechanics was given. Ilay's suggestion that his nephew attend Willem Jacob 's Gravesande's experimental lectures was an endorsement of a Newtonianism oriented toward practice, engineering and improvements. 's Gravesande's natural philosophy, like that of John Theophilous Desaugliers, who translated his books into English, led to shops, mines, shipyards, factories and other enterprises.[82] Maclaurin's might lead only to reflections on the Designer of all things. Pneumatics seems not to have concerned Ilay. He is not known to have had air-pumps in London or Scotland. He also lacked electrical paraphernalia although the Hauksbee's static electrical generator had been around since 1706 and he was undoubtedly familiar with it.[83] He was aware of electrical discussions (see p. 337) but he was not an experimenter and apparently not even interested in the medical uses of electricity. That is not too surprising since electricity became of real interest to British scientists only in the 1740s by which time Ilay was sixty. His interests were already shaped and now focussed on gardening and botany.

IV. Medicine

Ilay's science collections had many books devoted to botany and chemistry. They were impressive signs of an interest in medicine which had developed early and had been acknowledged in 1708, when he received an honorary medical degree from the University and King's College of Aberdeen.[84] To give a trained lawyer a medical degree, rather than one in law, was to recognize a very special and developed interest. Fifty years later, he was honoured in a similar way when on 30 November 1758 he was made an Honorary Fellow of the Royal College of Physicians of Edinburgh.[85] That honour was most likely bestowed on him for past favours such as securing for the College in 1752 the recipe for Dr. Robert James's Fever Powders. The College prepared the editions of the renowned *Edinburgh Pharmacopoeia* so the gift of an important specific was significant. It also meant that what had been a secret remedy would now be available to benefit – or perhaps to kill – many.

Another indicator of his interest in medical topics was the frequent presence in his household for many years of notable physicians. The best known of his more or less resident intellectuals were two medical men, Dr. Charles Stewart (or Stuart), FRS (1682-1770) and Dr. John Mitchell, FRS (1711-1768). Both physicians were improvers who shared Ilay's many interests.[86] A final bit of evidence of Ilay's interest in medicine may well be the *post mortem* examination of his body. It was not surprising that a seventy-eight-year-old man should die but finding out the precise reason for that death would have appealed to the Duke. The autopsy was likely done at the Duke's London house by David Middleton, surgeon-apothecary.[87]

The Earl probably had a few surgical instruments. Certainly he had an interest in the subject and opinions about particular problems. In 1758, for example, he wrote to Milton that a mutual friend with a fistula, Sir David Kinlock, should have it cut. He opined that Scottish surgeons were too sparing of the knife although his own, Middleton, was not of that number.[88] Most Scottish surgeons were also trained apothecaries. Ilay had many mortars and pestles, pillboxes and phials some of which held what he concocted as a pharmacist.[89]

V. Chemistry

The Earl of Ilay's concerns with chemistry probably harked back to his first interest in medicine – before 1708 – and persisted into the 1750s with a peak coming in the 1740s.[90] It first becomes apparent in 1725 when we find him making invisible inks in the chemistry laboratory in his London house.[91] His interest was embodied in his several laboratories – in London, at Whitton and at The Whim in Peebles-shire. Inveraray Castle alone did not have a laboratory.[92] He was in touch with chemists including the four medical professors appointed at Edinburgh in 1726 (Andrew Plummer, John Rutherford, Andrew Sinclair, and John Innes) and their later colleagues (Charles Alston, Robert Whytt, William Cullen and Joseph Black). James Hutton and his partner, James Davy, and a number of less well known men were also in his orbit. All of them used their chemical knowledge in trying to make agricultural or industrial improvements. Since he possessed his works, he is likely to have known Peter Shaw who lectured on chemistry in London.

Little is known of Ilay's chemical laboratories in London and at Whitton but records do exist to give some sense of his laboratory at The Whim. It is likely to have been differently equipped than the ones in England where he spent more time but where it is difficult to imagine so many flues as he had at The Whim. The English laboratories may have been used to do quite different work. At a guess, it was in the south that he and his friends made inks and did medical chemistry. In Scotland, experiments tended to be conducted on peat and alkalis and were directed toward metal working and the making of pottery including porcelain.

It was not until c.1731 that a bit of drained land could sustain a house at The Whim. In that year, Ilay sent to Scotland a few chemicals and some crucibles but there seems to have been no proper laboratory there until about 1740.[93] Building records for 1740-44 suggest that the laboratory took shape during those years but it is not clear where it was located. It was probably away from the main house.[94] In 1750 'a siver [sewer] round the main house' was dug, apparently without interfering with the laboratory.[95] This suggests that it was detached from, but close to, the house, perhaps in the North Pavilion of the 'Court of Offices' which is mentioned in some manuscripts.[96] That was one story high, had outside walls, was tiled or paved and would have given the laboratory a roof of its own.[97]

In 1741, a mason was paid over £4 for paving stone for the laboratory which is measured at 258 square feet. The laboratory might then have been, as it is in the c.1731 plan, about 16 feet square. There is a bill for 480 feet of 'rough pavement'. some for the laboratory with what was left going 'in the Coach house'.[98] Another 140 square feet of 'rough Pavement' was assigned to 'the two pends [arches] in the Laboratory'. They could have functioned as hoods to direct fumes up the flues and to the chimney built in 1741.[99] If they did, then, the furnaces and stills might have sat on the rough pavement running along one side and an end – the back and the end away from the main house. One hundred forty square feet would have paved a space about four feet in width running half way around the building whose dimensions I have guessed. Such an area could have accommodated the several chimneys required by the furnaces and stills. They would not have needed a smooth floor. That would have left 220 feet of rough pavement for the coach house.

The building had an interior ceiling of 'Intaglio', by which is probably meant small glazed, decorative tiles resistant to corrosion. The roof was finished and the windows pointed in 1741 or 1742 depending on how long after the work was done the bill was rendered. More work was done by wrights in 1743 and 1744.[100] Unfortunately, the roof was not waterproof. By c.1747 it, was leaking.[101] The mason reported that 'the Inside stone work is much damnified'. It had certainly been used because, in 1744, Lord Milton wrote a memorandum to himself about repairing its chimneys.[102] In 1750, the now repaired laboratory had some more stone work added or replaced.

Other entries in the building records refer to the equipment of the building. There was a 'Sand Heat' and seven furnaces, one of them an 'are [ore] furnice'. Two furnaces were purchased in London and sent up in 1749.[103] One of them was repaired locally by James Grey of the Dalkeith Ironmiln who made for it a new door; he could have made the others.[104] One of those furnaces had a 'plate and a pot' which came with 90 bars of iron at the cost of nearly £20.[105] It cost half as much again to set up all this. It is likely that Ilay was trying to smelt and work iron with peats.

Ilay installed two stills in 1740 or 1741. One was a 'Copper Still with a pewter head' with a worm and tube of the same. They cost £5-6.[106] The records show a plumber's bill in 1740 for £5/10/2 1/4 for 'two puther worm and two Swan neck weighting 64 pound ten onces' and for 'two pip[e]s wighting 8 pound 14oz'.[107] Those may have connected to a third 'Copper' which had been fitted in 1740. In 1745, another still and a worm tube were sent up from London.[108] His Lordship intended to distill a lot of something. The only other heavy and presumably expensive piece of equipment in the laboratory was 'an Iron press'.[109] What this was is unknown but it may have been a device to compact peat into bricks from which his lordship thought more heat might be obtained than from turfs.

The laboratory had several mortars, sets of crucibles[110] and phials. There would have been more glassware and porcelain than appears in the records and perhaps some of the 'brewers' bubbles' which Alexander Wilson had made for the Duke in 1757/8.[111] There is no mention of a burning glass but with six or seven furnaces, one was not needed. There is also no mention of digesters although they were standard items in laboratories such as this.[112] It is very curious that virtually no chemicals are recorded as bought or shipped from Glasgow, Edinburgh or London. Other than slight purchases, there are only bills for a pound of mercury which almost certainly went into barometers.[113] Packages of reagents may well have travelled north with the Duke when he went to Scotland. Some of what was done at the laboratory was probably destructive distillation, experiments on calcined ores and vegetation, or attempts to smelt iron with peat and some distillation for medicinal purposes. For all that one would not need a lot of chemicals.

This laboratory was not a cheap structure to put up and furnish. The fragmentary accounts which survive show that it cost well over £56 pounds for some of the equipment and flooring alone. The cost of the structure has to be added to that. The total expenses incurred could easily have come to £200 or more.

VI. The Results of His Work

Ilay was more than the usual rich amateur devoting a great deal of time to his scientific pursuits but the results of his work are often unclear. In mathematics his Lordship is not known for proving any theorem. He appears in two twentieth-century directories of British mathematicians of the period, probably because of the richness and celebrity of his instrument collection.[114] Still, his theoretical understanding of things requiring mathematics helped to shape the things he did or had made for him. His interest in mixed mathematics and the devices, instruments, models, and machinery needed to pursue mixed mathematics made him a notable collector but he himself produced no important novelties.

His understanding of the principles of mechanics led him to some minor improvements and innovations and certainly to work by others. At Whitton, he had a notable vertical-vaned windmill which pumped water to a high tank to give his system a bit of pressure.[115] This machine took up less space than an armed windmill and was less unsightly. It was also less efficient than armed windmills. His and Milton's interest in mills and machinery led them to try to introduce more mechanization into the manufacture of linen products in Scotland. We know most about his medical and chemical interests.

Ilay used his stills at The Whim, to distill some sort of mint compound perhaps used as a cordial or digestive.[116] He made other medicinal cordials.[117] He also made 'brandy' from wine, cyder, and malt liquor. He tried to make brandy out of molasses, yeast, and burnt Rhenish tartar.[118] That would have lessened Britain's dependence on France had it been drinkable. Related to this is his recipe for 'Barbadoes Water', a sort of flavoured brandy distilled with citrus fruit and their peels and used in punches.[119] He concocted other things. 'A Receipt to Make Orange or Lemon Juice so it will keep twenty or Thirty Years' (c.1748) is found in the Saltoun Papers. The orange juice was evaporated over hot water and reduced to the point that it could be strained and then spooned into a China dish and covered. Similarly, he made a dried or 'Portable Soup' which was likely an animal broth which had been evaporated to form a dry cake. Like the orange juice, it could be preserved indefinitely and might be useful on sea voyages or to men in the Army. Those were somewhat faddish pursuits.[120] The recipes are likely to have been trivial but the one involving citrus juices may not have been.

A 1754 letter to Lord Milton from Alexander Lind of Gorgie recommended to the Duke his cousin, Dr. James Lind, who would become well known for his then recent work on scurvy. Alexander Lind, a chemist of some local note and a founding member and first Treasurer of the Edinburgh Philosophical Society, asked patronage for his kinsman noting that 'the principal Medicine mentioned in that treatise both for the prevention and cure of the Scurvy viz the inspissated Juice of Lemons and Oranges, is of the Dukes own invention, and I don't doubt his Grace will be pleased after tryal to be informed of the good effects of a medicine, the Art is indebted to him for'.[121] If this is why the Duke had been making concentrated orange juice in 1748, then he had invented a recipe which might have been of use although the credit has not gone to him but, rightly, to Lind who published after testing the effects of citrus fruits on scurvy. Both men had worked at a problem which others had tackled and for which citrus fruits had been mentioned as cures. Ilay's concentrated orange extract was likely made at Whitton, where he had an orangery and other citrus trees.[122] There he also had beds in which many simples were grown.

Evidence of his interest in preparing medicines is extensive but scattered through his surviving letters. In 1739 he had been studying Mrs. Stephens's cure for the stone. He or Alexander Wilson may have analysed it chemically, since Ilay told Sir John Clerk that hers had more soap in it than earlier but similar recipes.[123] There are suggestions elsewhere that he not only analysed but compounded things ranging from cough drops to recipes for the bite of mad dogs – another faddish problem.[124] He prepared such things as the 'Receipt by the Duke of Argyll 1760',which appears to be some sort of salve, and a pill described in the same manuscript.[125] None of this was extraordinary but it showed a level of competence notable in a peer.

Ilay's non-medical chemistry was more interesting. One of his long-term concerns seems to have been the production of inks. In the 1720s he was producing invisible ink from sugar of lead. It revealed what had been written once the paper was heated.[126] More recipes appear in the 1740s. In one, he used almonds steeped, powdered and strained with the writing made visible by rubbing it with gun powder or sand.[127] Another made black ink out of peat which Alexander Lind had pulverized.[128] He continued to be interested in inks. Sixteen years later Horace Walpole reported:

> They have found out lately at the Duke of Argyles, that any kind of ink may be made of privet: it becomes green by mixing salt of tartar. I don't know the process; but I am promised it by [John] Campbell [LL.D.,1708-1775].[129]

Walpole's reference makes it almost sound like a research laboratory. In the 1730s Alexander Wilson and others had used his facilities.

Some of his ventures had an agricultural component. He experimented on fertilizers (presumably at Whitton) at least as early as 1725. He was doing so still in 1741.[130] He continued to be interested in those and it may have been agricultural chemistry which first brought the notable Scottish chemist, William Cullen, to his notice in the 1740s. There are stories to that effect, but there is also an account, which can be documented.[131] The latter has Argyll and Cullen first meeting in 1749 to discuss agriculture and chemistry. The meeting was arranged by Henry Home, later Lord Kames, Arthur Martin or Martine and Alexander Lind. All three were interested in agriculture, particularly in soils and manures. Two of the men were also involved with clay products, Martin as the operator of a brickyard in Fife, Lind as the owner and operator of a pottery at Preston Pans which his family had run since c.1703.[132] The Earl's agricultural experiments produced, in the end, techniques for sweetening his mosses but that would have happened anyway since all the fertilizers he devised included lime or marl. His experiments probably did help to bring into the universities useful chemists. Professors Cullen, Joseph Black, Francis Home and others pursued problems dealing with agriculture. Other men associated with the Duke took chemistry into other activities seen as of national importance – the linen trade, ceramics, metallurgy and the new chemical industry.

By the late 1730s and early 1740s, Ilay's interests in chemistry focussed on alkalis, substances with which Britain was poorly endowed. There was a shortage of imported alkalis due both to rising demand and war which disrupted the provision of Spanish barilla. Alkalis sweetened fields and were essential to the potteries, glasshouses and the metal trades. They were thought potentially useful to the linen industry. Bleacheries and dye works needed cheap bleaches and mordants. Among the many who worked on finding new and native sources for alkalis were men in the Duke's orbit. One was Alexander Lind, a Leiden-educated advocate. Lind's general interests may be shown in a manuscript in the Saltoun papers entitled 'Plan of a Course of Chemical Experiments adapted to Philosophical & Mechanical purposes' and dated June 1745.[133] If it is Lind's, then he and Lord Milton were by then familiar with many reactions relevant to agriculture and industry. Everyone needed to lime fields and by the late 1720s Lind owned a bleachfield at Gorgie where, later, he also printed linen. Milton later established a bleachfield. It was thought alkalis would be useful in bleaching and dyeing so they had reasons of their own to second the Duke's interests in chemistry.[134]

Through the late 1730s and into 1750s, Lind and others worked, with Ilay's and Lord Milton's support and encouragement on problems connected to the development of alkalis for Scottish agriculture and industry.[135] The search for alkalis was joined to the search for uses of peat. Trying to find uses for Scottish peat was a very old game which went back into the seventeenth century.[136] That problem was now made interesting for Ilay by the draining of the land at The Whim which involved the removal of vast amounts of peat moss. Most of it was dried and burned on the land to create fertilizer but that seemed to Ilay to be a waste of a possibly useful material. Perhaps it could produce an alkali. Trying to get basic salts from peat was not the best use for a material which is naturally acidic but that was what Ilay and Lind tried to do.

Lind's experiments on lime began in the late 1730s since he had written a paper on lime which was read in the Philosophical Society on 2 August 1739.[137] Shortly after that he was using the laboratory at The Whim to investigate both lime and peat. He began a series of peat experiments c.1740 which continued on into 1744. Those involved trying to extract salts from the peat. In 1742, Ilay sent peats 'from Newberry for Lind to make comparisons of weight of Lixevical [water soluble] salt etc'.[138] Lind burned peat to get the salts. That work was summed up in a memoir read to the Philosophical Society in 1744.[139] Lind continued to seek a Scottish source of alkalis and in 1749 he was burning tree roots in his furnace in experiments related to the making of porcelain something in which he and the Duke had long been interested.[140]

Work on alkalis may have continued in London and at Whitton with other chemists. Dr. John Mitchell, who seems from time to time to have lived with Argyll, also tried to find cheap ways of producing alkalis. Mitchell sent the results of his enquiries on alkalis and solving the British shortage of them to the Royal Society of London in a paper of 1748. He had come into Argyll's life just before that time.[141] As those activities reached a peak, Mitchell travelled to Scotland with Argyll in 1750 where he met Cullen.[142]

In Scotland, others connected with the Duke were working on the problem. One was Lord Milton's relative, Dr. Francis Home[143] who also dealt with the Duke about agriculture.[144] For the Board of Trustees, Home and Cullen experimented with Scottish plants in the 1750s seeking native sources for alkalis.[145] Some of this work turned on the possibility that lime or plant ashes could be used to make effective and cheap chemical bleaches. When this proved to be difficult to achieve, work shifted to various acids which might also accomplish this. In 1756 Home published the results of his experiments on bleaching with dilute sulphuric acid. His work opened the way to large scale, safe, chemical bleaching in Scotland. In the end, it was not an alkali which solved the problem but it was one the Duke's men who found the solution.

Alexander Wilson may also have been working on what to do with the bleached cloth. He sought to produce better ground indigo, a dye used extensively in the textile industry already prominent in the Glasgow area.[146]

Not all the experiments on peat were to find an alkaline salt and, not all proceeded without the Duke's own involvement as is made clear by a letter which he wrote to Lord Milton on 8 July 1742. It is worth quoting at length because it is one of the few documents which shows him at work or directing work on chemical topics:

> The little bits of Peat which Lind by grinding & drying brought to the likeness of
> Indian Ink, puts in my head an experiment which I would have tryed. I would

have some wet Peat beat as they do mortar & as we did when the Pudding [a mixture impermeable to water, a putty] was to be put at the bottom of the Stop Cock, I would cast them with the help of some powder of dry Peat (if that be necessary) as they put sand to brick, into moulds & then dry them in a dry place, that the sun may not crack them, I am apt to think that Peat bricks will be much more solid than Peat cut and dryed whose fibres must produce cavities, & consequently a stronger fire, & capable perhaps of being turned to other uses. The difference of the solidity may [be] tryed pretty near by paring (?) like common dry peat into the same shape as the dry peat bricks & weigh against 5 of these.[147]

The peat bog at The Whim had produced a water fountain about which Milton and the Ilay puzzled but its peat was more important.[148] A fragment dealing with it reads in part:

Peat of the Spring of Water, retains and contains Water surprisingly as the doctors probably will say in the style of Capillary Tubes. But be yt as it will   By many Experiments made this summer   wet peat chopped & Beat into an united body stops and Damns up water as effectually as clay, and this Discovery is the more useful that the work is done less that a third of the Expense it requires to do it in clay ...

Since the Earl had three ponds and many ditches to line, this was good news. The fragment went on to note, 'Peat earth best & most natural for asparagus'[149] – which points to more experiments dealing with it as bedding material. But there might be more important uses.

Milton and Argyll wanted to know if it was possible to compact peat into bricks and burn it for fuel. One use for the peat bricks well soaked in linseed oil might be to heat the walls against which grew Argyll's fruit.[150] Other uses might be found in industrial processes such as the smelting of iron. They foresaw a future when there would not enough accessible wood in Scotland to run smelters and forges. If peat would work, it would solve a problem. Milton also had surplus peat and what appears to have been bog iron.[151] Lind had been trying since January 1741 to smelt iron with coal and peat; perhaps compacted peat might do.[152] Peat bricks would have needed a press, perhaps the one sent up from London.

Manuscripts in the Saltoun Papers from c. 1741 to 1760 suggest that some of the work done in the Duke's laboratory at The Whim related to this. By the 1750s, Argyll himself had a direct stake in finding a smelting fuel. Although there were no iron deposits in his Highland estate, an iron smelter was built by an English concern in which Argyll was a partner at Inverlechan (Craleckan) on Loch Fyne in 1755.[153] The ore was imported and smelted using the native oaks growing along the banks of the loch. Saltoun papers concerning smelting and mining equipment almost certainly relate to this venture.[154] Unfortunately, peat did not work as a smelting fuel even though it may have given the Duke a new source for ink.

Work conducted on lime and peat by Ilay's friends – Lind, Cullen, Martine, Lord Kames, Francis Home, and others in the Philosophical Society – went on in the country for over twenty years.[155] Information presented to the Society in the 1740s was shared with Milton and Ilay which suggests they belonged to the body.[156] The Duke's own contributions were not impressive but his drive to find industrial innovations continued to the end of his life. What came out of all this was a bleach for linen and the knowledge that peat was not good for much but fertilizer and fuel.

Some other work on alkalis was related to the Earl's and Lind's interests in porcelain which were deep and long lasting. Ilay had extensive collections of porcelain in London and at his Whitton estate.[157] Lind wrote of those in 1750: 'I have bestowed four days in examining them, and find I must bestow double that time in order to view them with that accuracy they deserve to be looked at'.[158] Lind made porcelain in his Prestonpans factory.[159] About the same time, December 1750, Argyll took Lind to both the Bow and Chelsea porcelain factories. The Duke was well known by those potters for he had on 28 May 1749 entertained at dinner 'Messrs of the Bow Manufactory'. That did not mean they would tell him their secrets. Lind was miffed that he and the Duke were not shown the whole process of porcelain manufacture.[160] Later, Argyll sent Lind some Bow porcelain but the Scot found his own better.[161]

Both were also involved with the Delft Pottery in Glasgow. In August 1749, Lind and his son George, at the Duke's insistence, were aiding the pottery.[162] Two years later Argyll retired Lind to the Commissary Court of Glasgow.[163] There he was to be useful to the Glasgow Delft works. The Duke bought its wares and may have had some personal financial interest in that venture since he offered the pottery clay from Islay.[164] In the 1750s, William Cullen was looking for clays which could be used in potteries.[165] The expensive 'A' marked porcelain probably made at Preston Pans did not have a long production run and did not realize their hopes to establish a porcelain industry near Edinburgh, but the Glasgow pottery flourished into the nineteenth century.

The Duke had material or intellectual interests in other industrial processes involving chemistry but he is not likely to have experimented in those areas. One was salt making. The Duke had at Saltcoats pans of his own. He owned William Brownrigg's work on the subject and corresponded with Cullen about salt.[166] Around 1750-1751, Cullen prepared memoranda for the Duke on 'fossil Alkali' and on salt-making. His letters assumed Argyll had an extensive knowledge of chemistry and of its literature.[167] Argyll's interests also related to efforts to improve the legislation governing salt taxes in Scotland.[168] Pan salt was not a good preservative for meat such as that the Scottish cattle might have provided for the Navy had they been salted in Scotland. English salt was heavily taxed in Scotland. Salting beef could not be done in Scotland at costs competitive with the English and Irish. Argyll tried to lower its rate by adjusting duties and by promoting the making of better sea salt.

At the end of the 1750s, Ilay was approached for patronage by two chemists and businessmen concerned in the new Edinburgh sal ammoniac works – Dr. James Hutton and his partner James Davie. Sal ammoniac (ammonium chloride) was used principally in the metal and cloth trades. Hutton and Davie had been in partnership of some sort since 1749 but they built their plant to produce ammonium chloride in large quantities only in 1756. Three years later, they sought Argyll's support for their venture. Sending some of their product to 'one of the first Connoisseurs of all Chymical matters', they asked the Duke's 'Opinion how they ought to Conduct Themselves'.[169] Argyll sent their sample to Doctors John Rutherford, Charles Alston and Cullen for testing, they 'being the noted Chymists of this University.... who Greatly approved of its Quality'.[170] Hutton and Davie's venture became a highly successful one since it cheapened a product which, formerly, often had been brought in from England. They would have succeeded anyway but endorsements helped.

Finally, there were little technical problems involved with the on-going construction of Inveraray Castle which required the Duke to think chemically. He was interested in the composition of putties, paints, cements[171] and plasters and made some of those.

There can be no doubt about Archibald Campbell's competency in chemistry. He worked in his laboratories, owned a lot of equipment and had on his bookshelves a lot of chemical theory – which he seldom mentioned. Experts like Cullen respected his skill. Argyll allowed others to use his laboratories for his and their purposes.[172] He would not have seen his laboratories as semi-public spaces of any sort but they served the public. His scientific interests insured that the Scottish universities employed chemists who had agricultural and industrial concerns and not merely theoretical or pharmaceutical ones. To say that is also to suggest that some of what has been urged about the history of chemistry in the Scottish Enlightenment is not correct. In the light of his career, we should be less eager to see Cullen as the man who made chemistry 'a public science'. The Duke has some claim to that honour too.[173] It was the Duke and his protégés, among whom one should count lawyers like Lind and Henry Home, who gave enhanced status to the practice of a subject useful to estate owners with lands and mineral deposits to exploit. It was men like them, as well as doctors like Cullen, Francis Home, Joseph Black, and Hutton, who made chemistry interesting and increasingly a part of a general university education in both Glasgow and Edinburgh. Chemistry was a subject tied to Argyll's own interests in improvements. He helped to institutionalize its teaching in Scotland and tied the fortunes of his country to it.[174] His other improvements had a similar effect. They all contributed to the Scottish Enlightenment.

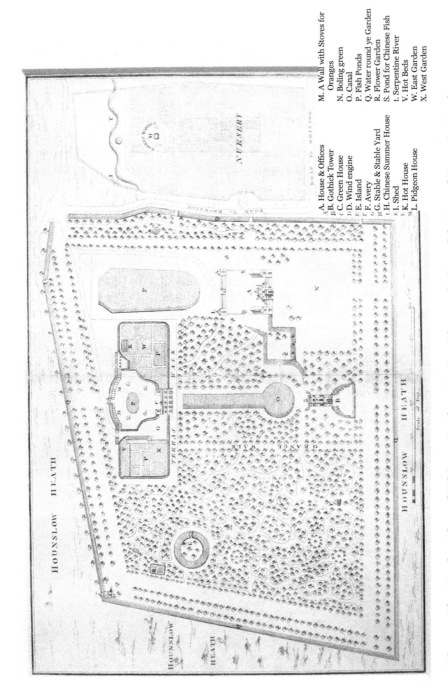

A. House & Offices
B. Gothick Tower
C. Green House
D. Wind engine
E. Island
F. Avery
G. Stable & Stable Yard
H. Chinese Summer House
I. Shed
K. Hot House
L. Pidgeon House
M. A Wall with Stoves for
    Oranges
N. Boling green
O. Canal
P. Fish Ponds
Q. Water round ye Garden
R. Flower Garden
S. Pond for Chinese Fish
t. Serpentine River
V. Hot Beds
W. East Garden
X. West Garden

Plate 5. The Garden Plan of Whitton (early 1760s), with permission of the Royal Botanic Garden, Edinburgh.

Chapter 8

Ilay as Gardener and Botanist

I. Ilay as Botanist

Those interested in medicine and chemistry during the eighteenth century were often botanists but there were other influences behind Ilay's passion for plants. Lord Archy grew up partly at Ham House where his grandmother, the Duchess of Lauderdale, had been a keen and innovative gardener. Her gardens were Dutch-influenced and among those in Britain which had a lot of colour added by newly imported flowers and shrubs. She passed on her interests. The gardens at Ham House were kept up by the Earls of Dysart who inherited them. They continued to be visited by Ilay who would have seen even more spectacular gardens in Holland. The 2nd Duke of Argyll had a fine garden at Sudbrook House not far from Whitton.[1] In their gardening there may have been a touch of sibling rivalry between Ilay and the Duke.

Beyond a love of the beauty of their plants, gardens were for Ilay objects of curiosity and a public concern. He commented on the first in 1743 when he believed he was permanently out of power: '...curiosity alone if it were not my Love of laying out Grounds & Gardening would draw me thither [to botany] especially considering, that I have now done with Political Ambition, & shall be unwilling to meddle in such of Storms, but content my self merely to satisfie my tastes in things that can occasion no disquiet'.[2] Pursuing botany was also a public concern since he believed that plants native to other regions should be cultivated in Britain for its economic advantage. By the 1740s, gardening and botany had become Ilay's most serious and expensive scientific interests.[3]

Some of Ilay's curiosity about plants could be satisfied in his library. He had the ancients and the moderns of the previous two hundred years. Those who looked for large plants and those who wondered where the line was to be drawn between the vegetables and animals at the level of microscopic organisms, they were all there. He had systematisers and taxonomists, anatomists and physiologists and those who discovered new plants in a wide variety of places. Adding to the books on gardening and natural history were the chorographies or regional studies and travel accounts which had sections on plants. He probably had 500 books which contained something on botany.

He read his books and used them in botanising. His gardens were laid out partly in accordance with taxonomic designs but the Duke's knowledge of botany was not something just picked up in books and at the dinner table.[4] In 1735, he reported finding a 'sort of wild vetch' growing in a hedgerow at Whitton. It interested him because of the height to which it had climbed.[5] This may not have been an unknown plant but he could classify a plant he had not seen before. When he went to Scotland in 1750, he and Dr. John Mitchell, a skilled botanist, looked on the hillsides for alpine plants, using as their guide Linnaeus's work on the flora of Lapland.[6] Argyll planted and grafted himself. Woollett depicted him in 1757 showing people around his garden dressed in his apron. Among his gardeners, he could be a dirty-handed fellow with a pruning hook. Even his political enemy, Lord Deskford, wrote to a correspondent in 1761 that the latter 'should talk to the Duke of Argyll about trees, for in that matter he must be allowed to have merit, even by those who might think it indecent for them to allow him merit as a statesman'.[7]

II. The Gardens at Whitton

When Ilay was in London, he lived initially at No. 24 Great Marlborough Street and then, after its construction c.1737-1742, in Argyll House, No. 7 Argyll Street. Both houses had gardens but they were neither large nor impressive. The one at Argyll House was sacrificed to his new library which covered much of it.[8] By 1722, he had the beginnings of a large garden on wasteland at the edge Hounslow Heath.

He at first bought sixteen acres from the Crown in 1722 and then added more land with purchases of twenty-two[9] and twelve acres made in 1734/5[10] and about five more in 1748.[11] In time, the place had a nine acre nursery and kitchen garden, about thirty acres of gardens and arboretum and sixteen acres of hay-fields and pasture. By the spring of 1725, he could write to Lord Milton, 'You know I live in the Garden'.[12] He did. He stayed first in the gardener's house and then in his own Greenhouse in which he had had an apartment constructed. Argyll made his wasteland bloom; indeed, he made it into one of the most notable botanical gardens in Britain but that took time.

The Earl began work on his Whitton gardens in 1723/4 and spared little expense in developing them. At first, that meant planning and then paring off the heath, levelling, grading, laying out walks, ponds, ditches, and picking the sites for structures. The sections of the garden were then fertilized and planted. Settling the plan and moving the earth took the better part of two years. Only in July 1725 did Ilay begin to build his neo-classical Greenhouse and his ornamental Gothic bird house or volary, a 'pinaccled gothick triffle'.[13] His tastes were eclectic. The Greenhouse in its original form was a single-storey, stucco-covered brick building 96 feet long. Initially, it had at each end a bedroom and closet. By December 1727, it was a more impressive two stories. The second contained a dining room and several bedrooms.[14] Flanking and behind it was a walled space for an orangery where the trees grew in the open in the summer but in winter were enclosed on the top and at its exterior sides by glass. It was heated by stoves. On either side of that walled space centred on a pool, were hot beds, hot houses, a hen house and the stables. It may have been in this area that he already kept a few exotic animals. This same area held some of his experimental gardens as well as some of his rarest and most sensitive plants.[15] Beyond the east wall of this section of the garden was a large pond. His ponds (see Plate 5) were stocked with goldfish, trout, carp, tench and possibly eels since he wanted some in 1741.[16]

Sir John Clerk of Penicuik, himself a notable gardener and the writer of an important poem on gardening,[17] visited the property in April 1727 and left the following account of it:

it stands on the South Edge of Hunts law heath [Hounslow Heath] about ten miles out of Town, he has here, a Small spot of ground well air'd & water'd but no house. His Garden consists of wilderness work   on the north side is a large Green house built of brick & finish'd with stuco without. Above this house is a dining Room & his 3 other chambers not yet finish'd the floors are of oak planks, the wainscoating is of firr carved, I think, of the Ionick order His design is to paint over the carvings with oyle colours I told him that by this sort of daubing the small cavities wou'd be fill'e up & wou'd not receive a 2d or 3d coat but to great disadvantage & that all carved work should be rather in oack or (... ??) Not to be painted above once or twice. Before the Green house is a Canal in proportion to the Little ground he has & at the end of this a Temple on a mount forced up with Earth the columns of his Temple are of wood.[18] The prospect is very good but what Scotland easily affords, viz. A great plain covered with Heath, rushes & c. My Ld din'd in the Gardner's house where he Lies we were kindly entertain'd & regal'd with a sight of his China of which he is very curious.[19]

Clerk returned again in May 1733 and again described the garden in another memoire:

On the 20 I went upon invitation to my Lord Islay's house in Honslaw heath here I was kindly entertain'd by his Losp who is a great virtuoso in all manner of things Except pictures, he has built a small house of about 28 feet in front &30 in breadth [this was the gardener's house], he has built a court of fine office houses & intends to front them with a large building [the stoves] of 108 feet in Length.[20] he has a fine Little canal of about 200 feet in Length & about 50 in breadth at one end of it is a Large green house ornamented on the outside with Stuco work especially the basse which is rustick Above the green house, are 4 or 5 convenient Rooms. at the other end of the canal is an artificial mound with a groto & above a Round Temple supported by two rowes of pillars the canal is well stor'd with Carp & Tench which thrive wonderfully. Behind his green house is a sort of Court where he has all manner of conceits & amongst other things some exotic beasts & fouls. on each side of this Area he has pieces of Kitchen grounds & fruit walls. the rest of the grounds which seem not to exceed 40 or 50 acres is laid out in a kind of natural wood planted by himself here are several little ponds well stockt with fish & wild ducks he has Living springs & rills of water which he brings from the heath which environs the whole ....

Most of those features are shown in the 1761-65 map of the property *(see plate 5)*.

By the time the Duke died in 1761, the estate was organized into three sections. The main garden, which encompassed the house, had unequal sides of about a quarter mile on each long side – about forty American acres. It was surrounded by an artificial stream which allowed for easy watering and drainage and a gravel walk of about three quarters of a mile in length.[21] Beyond the stream, to the east and across the road to Hounslow, but screened by trees from the property, lay the walled nursery bordered by the 'Serpentine River'. There, trees, and plants for re-plantings were raised. Beyond all that were the hay fields and then the waste.[22]

The principal garden had the Greenhouse as its central feature. It commanded a southern prospect overlooking the long canal which had been extended to 370 feet, partly by building a round basin at its southern end.[23] In 1761, it was nearly double the length it had been a generation earlier. One's eye was stopped not by a mound and wooden temple but by a triangular masonry Gothic Tower designed by James Gibbs c.1735. It sat on an artificial hill with a grotto under it.[24] The Canal was bordered by walks along which had been planted American evergreens. Stopping the prospect and thickly planting the borders gave the illusion of a larger property. In the southeast corner, one saw the bowling green and the back of Whitton House. The walk continued along the east side of the house past a sizeable fish pond.[25]

Scattered along the walks were ornaments in three styles: Classical, Chinese and Gothic. Gibbs may have created 'a group of cenotaphs ornamented with marble portrait medallions of Michelangelo, Bernini, Wren, and Gibbs himself – a nice statement of the Earl's appraisal of architects.[26] Other ornaments were more homely and included Colley Cibber sr.'s 'Highland Piper and his Dog'. Additional ornamental structures included the classical temple become the Gothic Tower, an ornate privy called 'the Countess of Pigsburgh's Apartment', Argyll's vertical vaned windmill housed in a classical structure (see pp. 141, 399 n. 115) and the Chinese Summer House in the rabbit warren. Over the small 'Serpentine River' and artificial boundary stream, there were a number of small bridges but the brook did not cut the entrance road into the estate.[27] At The Whim some of his bridges were Chinese in style as they may also have been here.

Akin to the ornaments were the Duke's animals. Somewhere in the garden there was a Chinese fish pond for the Duke's goldfish. His aviary contained 'Bantoms', Chinese pheasants, partridges, American king birds, a special kind of crow, rooks from the Tower of London, at least one eagle and other species.[28] This was a considerable collection.[29] Sold to the Queen after the Duke' death, the birds fetched £61.8.6. Argyll liked animals and it is no accident that William Woollett included a cat (no doubt a Maltese mouser) in his engraving of the Canal and Tower. Less exotic were his dogs. Over the years they included a Great Dane bred by Alexander Pope, 'Turkish Greyhounds', Scottish 'Highland hounds' (Scotties), terriers and wolfhounds.[30] Ilay did not hunt but liked dogs both big and small. For a while, his zoo possessed racoons and a pair of American bison.[31] He had for some time angora goats which he wanted to breed and shear. He thought they might become the basis of a profitable trade.[32] The estate, of course, raised a few chickens, ducks and geese for food; they too had their ponds and yard.

His Grace's court of offices was built c.1731 but Whitton House itself dated from 1731-39. This rather Palladian house lay on the eastern side of the great garden. To approach the house from Whitton, one had to pass the nursery and drive along the fishpond. A coach would then enter the walled forecourt of offices with small towers on the entrance side. One of those served as a dovecot housing his pigeons. To enter the house, raised one story to accommodate basement rooms looking south onto the bowling green, one went up a flight of stairs. The forty-five foot square house was in the shape of a Greek cross. The cross ends formed, on the north side, the entrance; on the south side, a window alcove and door to the bowling green accessible from the basement floor.[33] On the other two sides, the cross ends allowed for stairwells. All this was secondary to the gardens.

No garden is ever really finished but this one was more or less complete in design by the mid-1730s. Plants, of course, were added until the end of Argyll's life. The tree plantings and the walks through them would not have looked good until after the 1730s. By the 1740s, the gardens were found by many to be rather old fashioned – too geometric and rectilineal in some parts and unnaturally meandering in others – but they suited the man who built them.[34] They offered recreation and beauty. They gave him produce and fish, provided him with places to raise exotics of all sorts from the tea trees named for him (*i.e.*, *Lycium barbarum*, of the nightshade family and so not tea bushes) to racoons and goldfish. They tell us something about his curiosity and liking for novelties. His gardens reflect some of what was fashionable – the order in disorder, the efforts at naturalness and the belief that beauty lay not in right lines but in disciplined irregularity. He would have known that Roman gardens like Pliny's were thought to have embodied some of those ideas as did gardens at Versailles and in Twickenham.[35] Such ideas could also be found in the works of Sir William Temple, the 3rd Earl of Shaftesbury, and more recently in the works and gardens of Pope, Burlington, the Langleys and others with whom Ilay conversed in the decade during which this estate was planned and built. The Earl was being fashionable but, in his own mind, connecting to classical and universal norms for beautiful gardens. Men like Phillip Miller found it 'elegant' and praised its collections of rare plants, shrubs and trees in the editions of his *Gardeners Dictionary* issued between 1724-1768.

III. The Garden as a Botanical Centre

A principal feature of the garden, from one point of view, was not its ornaments and style(s) but the success with which a varied stock of plants was grown. The Duke's garden contained about 350 species of trees and other plants, about a 100 more than a good nurseryman's catalogue listed c.1760. Indeed, catalogues generally did not exceed the incomplete posthumous catalogue made of his plants until c.1770.[36] In addition to the plants catalogued, there must have been others which he had imported but lost to the climate. In the end, he probably had in this garden well over a hundred species of trees and over three hundred species of plants and shrubs.[37] The garden was most notable for its plantings of North American evergreen trees, but there were beds of exotic flowers and shrubs from many places.

Argyll made a collection of trees which was remarkable. In 1748, Pehr Kalm, the Swedish botanist and collector, was very impressed:

> Here is a collection of all the kinds of trees, which grow in different parts of the world, and can stand the climate of England out in the open air, summer and winter. The Duke has himself planted many of these trees with his own hand. There was here a very large number of *Cedars of Lebanon*, which appeared to have the best opinion of a dry and meagre earth, and it seems that it might

be suitable for planting on our great heaths and sandy tracts in Sweden and Finland.

Of North American Pines, Firs, Cypresses, Thuyas [probably an Arbor Vitae], all these and many other kinds, there was an abundance, which throve very well. There were already small groves of them. Diligence and Art have not been spared here to make everything delightful.... there is a beautiful *orangery*.[38]

Others remarked on Argyll's ability to make American conifers thrive in Britain. The architect, John Adam – as reported by his son William – 'gained more [from the Duke] than from any other person, both by the instruction he was capable of conveying on that subject (for his Grace was a superiorly skilled planter) and from the opportunity he gave [Adam], of taking from his nurseries the most useful and best trees, for the propogation [sic] of the fir tribe: so that [what by the 1830s were] the most ancient larches, spruces, and silver firs to be found on the Estate of Blair-Adam, were sent by the Duke of Argyle'.[39] The Duke may have sent to the Royal Society of Arts an account of his method for the cultivation of New England pines.[40]

The Whitton nursery raised trees and plants to be planted elsewhere on his estates or given away to his friends. It became, in time, a centre from which new items were dispersed over Britain:

The nursery at Whitton represented without question one of the largest and best collections of trees and shrubs in the country at the time. The lists show the contents of the nursery but can serve a practical purpose as a basis for period replanting .... The nursery is also important for its relationship to other collections. Since Argyll used the agency of Peter Collinson, certainly during his later years at Whitton, this bears directly on the plantings of others who dealt with Collinson, most notably the Duke of Richmond at Greenwood, Lord Petre at Thorndon Hall, and Charles Hamilton at Painshill and also at Holland Park. One can therefore see the ornamental plantings on these estates as part of a movement giving new life, shape, and colour to the previously mainly native appearance of trees in landscape gardens.[41]

Argyll's work was also significant for the planting of American citrus trees, as well as the evergreens.[42] One of the factors in his success with North American plants were his relations with Mark Catesby and John Bartram. His Grace was a regular purchaser from the nurseries at which the former worked and he got advice along with seeds and plants from Bartram between the early 1740s and the late 1750s. Both dealt with Peter Collinson, a London merchant and gardener who exchanged plants with Argyll.[43] By the 1740s, Whitton, as Horace Walpole noted, was an important source for exotic plants as well as trees.

Whitton's purpose was not just to amuse a nobleman and his botanist friends; it also served a public interest. Argyll was moved by the beauty of plants and was competitive enough to be eager to have more and more exotic ones than his friends. But, like many botanists, seedsmen and gardeners, he wanted to introduce into Britain and its colonies plants which would benefit the Empire. That activity had gone on since the introduction of Asian and New World plants in the sixteenth century. What had changed was the self-consciousness with which it was pursued by public-spirited men like the Earl.[44] Whitton was the place where he worked at that. To Pehr Kalm and to Kalm's teacher, Linnaeus, that was the real work of the garden in which the Duke was so active a figure.[45] The three men all laboured to benefit their countries economically by introducing and acclimatizing new plants.[46] Their gardens had a huge influence on what Kew Gardens were to become in the nineteenth century. The Duke wanted to domesticate plants which had value as food, fodder and as materials to be worked up. There are in the hand of Argyll's secretary, Andrew Fletcher, a number of short papers which suggest that the Duke tried to grow American plants, such as maize, and that Dr. John Mitchell was his guide in that endeavour.[47] In the end, Argyll introduced about twenty new species of plants to Britain.[48] By 1750, John Mitchell could write to John Bartram that the Duke had at Whitton 'all the [American] Plants that are common & seed of his own from most of them, he does not desire any more, unless it be any thing that is new'.[49]

The Whitton establishment represented a huge investment of money and time, far more than went into Argyll's very fine library or his scientific instrument collection. The greenhouses and nursery beds required many gardeners and much attention. So too did the plantations of shrubs and trees. Some of those were costly. The garden put Argyll in touch with the botanical world beyond his garden walls.

IV. Argyll's Botanical World

Argyll's circle of botanical friends was large and influential. One might begin with his relatives and political connexions. His brother, the 2nd Duke, had some interest in reforestation and in garden plants. So did their relatives the Earls of Loudoun and Bute and the 3rd Earl of Bute's younger brother, James Stuart Mackenzie. More distant relatives, like Andrew Fletcher (Lord Milton), Sir Henry Bellenden, and less notable relatives, shared their interests.[50] Fellow collectors at times friendly with Ilay included Frederick, Prince of Wales, and his widow, the Dowager Princess Augusta. The Princess and Lord Bute helped to found Kew Gardens. Among botanists who came to dinner at Whitton, and with whom Argyll swapped seeds, were the Duke of Richmond, Lord Petre,[51] and General James St. Clair. Among Ilay's political clients and protégés were James Justice, the author of an important Scottish book on gardening, and Sir James Naysmith of Posso, MP, who maintained a large garden and a museum.[52] Men with influence, whom the Duke invited to visit, spread the knowledge of what he had done and would have encouraged others to emulate his work. Others were probably more critical. Among them was likely to have been Sir John Clerk of Penicuik. Clerk's poem, *The Country Seat* (1727, revised 1736) had a wide circulation in manuscript among British aristocrats and recommended many of the practical things Ilay had done or was doing but Clerk could not have been pleased by the Earl's choice of location, by the buildings and by efforts at forcing nature to produce in Britain what was not native.[53] Clerk admired native beauties.

By the 1730s, the Earl of Ilay was known to a growing number of important gardeners, seedsmen and botanists. He dealt with British suppliers, such as Philip Miller of the Chelsea Garden,[54] Thomas Fairchild and Stephen Bacon of Hoxton,

Christopher Grey at Fulham, James G. Gordon at Mile End, Thomas Knowlton and his successor, gardeners to the Earl of Burlington, and Robert Furber of the Kensington Nursery. Argyll, we have seen, was in touch with suppliers, such as Mark Catesby, who had spent time in America,[55] and later John Bartram who introduced 150-200 plants to the British.[56] Joining them were American collectors and genteel gardeners such as the Reverend John Clayton for whom Linnaeus named a plant.[57] Many of those men corresponded with learned doctors or collectors who had large gardens in the London area. Among them were Sir Hans Sloane, Dr. Richard Mead, Peter Collinson, and, later, Dr. John Fothergill. Their ties, in turn, ran to men in British universities such as William Sherard and John Jacob Dillenius at Oxford University and the Scottish professors of botany and natural history – Charles Alston, John Hope, John Walker – and outside Britain to John Frederick Gronovius in Leiden, Antoine de Jussieu at the Jardin de Roi in Paris and Carolus Linnaeus in Uppsala. Those places were centres in the world network and served as clearing houses for botanical information. Argyll did not write to Linnaeus but his secretary did and the Duke happily met the Swedish botanist Pehr Kalm by whom the Duke sent plants to Linnaeus and perhaps the racoon whom Linnaeus named Sjubb [washing bear].[58] Argyll kept abreast of what was going on throughout Europe.

At one remove were the rest of the world's botanists along whose networks plants, seeds and information flowed efficiently to the seedsmen from whom Argyll bought, to other collectors and to university professors with important gardens. To Whitton and to his principal keepers, Daniel Crofts (or Crafts) and later James Lee,[59] came seeds and plants from all over the world.[60] There they were germinated, grown, planted, multiplied and shared with others. A glimpse of the networks to which Argyll belonged can be had by looking at Mark Catesby who was much involved with many gardeners and botanists until his death in 1749.

Catesby, a well-educated but not affluent gentleman, was close to the members of the Temple Coffee House Botany Club (c.1691 - c.1730).[61] To this club belonged leading London botanists and amateurs who sponsored a number of collectors in the southern colonies of America.[62] Some of Catesby's field work in the American South, the Bahamas and Jamaica in (1712-1719, 1722-1726) had been supported by, among others, James Brydges, 1st Duke of Chandos, the Earls of Oxford and Macclesfield, Lord John Perceval, Sir Hans Sloane, Sir George Markham, Col. Sir Francis Nicholson, Governor of several American colonies; Charles Dubois, John Knight, and William Sherard, the Oxford Professor of Botany.[63] Catesby dedicated a plate and a new genus of plants to Dr. Richard Mead.[64] All of them benefited from Catesby's collecting, as did some of their European correspondents. Catesby, FRS (1733), knew more botanists through connexions with the Royal Society. In America, he had made the acquaintance of the naturalists John Clayton, Cadwallader Colden and John Bartram. He was friendly with others with whom Argyll was in contact such as Peter Collinson.[65] Outside Britain, Catesby was in touch with Tournefort in Paris, whose system of classification he adopted. By the time he died in 1749, just before the publication of the second edition of his *Natural History of Carolina, Florida and the Bahama Islands* (1st ed. completed in 1735), his connexions in the botanical world ran from St. Petersburg, Uppsala, and Germany to Leiden, Amsterdam, Paris and Montpelier, and to the American colonies on whose plants he became something of a specialist.

Catesby and Ilay were not strangers. In the 1720s Catesby sold Ilay some of his first American plants.[66] The peer subscribed to Catesby's beautifully illustrated *Natural History* as did at least nine other botanists whom the Duke knew.[67] In 1749, the naturalist completed a posthumously published *Hortus Britanno-Americanus* (1763), a description of many of the plants available at Christopher Grey's nursery, all of which one can assume were growing at Whitton. Catesby worked at the nurseries of Fairchild, Bacon and Grey with which Argyll had dealt.[68]

For Catesby, collecting led to understanding plants systematically, the uses to which they could be put and to knowing how many of them lay within British domains or could be naturalized either in Britain or its colonies. Ilay, by the 1720s, shared the last parts of Catesby's vision.[69] That led Argyll and Sir Robert Walpole in 1723 to send to the colonies 'One Dr. Sinclair ... with a patent as he says for propogating Cuchinele Nutmeg Cloves Pepper Rhubarb opium with innumerable other Drugs and Spices'.[70] Catesby's reaction to this was: 'you will gues at the Man by the undertaking ...[that] ... Such an Emperick and so ignorant a person can impose on Such Men [Ilay and Walpole] is unaccountable to me'.[71] This tells us that Ilay in 1723 was already known as a knowledgeable botanist but was not yet the expert he would become. It also suggests that even before his garden was laid out, he was thinking about how botanists could serve their country. Collecting, planting and domesticating new species was desirable as his correspondence with Cadwallader Colden in 1725 showed.[72] How that work went on can be seen through the diary kept from 1746 to c.1761 by Andrew Fletcher III (1722-1779), the Duke's secretary.

Fletcher kept a list of those who dined with the Duke at Whitton. Many intellectuals came but very few of the merely fashionable and not many politicians. If one looks at the years 1748-50, the botanists attending often included the Duke of Richmond, Philip Miller, Pehr Kalm, Lord Dupplin (later the Earl of Kinnoull), Dr. John Hill, Dr. John Mitchell, General James St. Clair, John Campbell, the Earl of Loudoun; Alexander Lind,[73] Sir Henry Bellenden, Thomas Cochrane, later 8th Earl of Dundonald, and the 3rd Earl of Bute. No other category of guest was more frequently represented on the surviving lists than botanists – not even money men.

Fletcher also kept a record of botanical transactions. During 1749-1750, the record shows Argyll getting seeds from Alexandretta, Alleppo, China, Brazil, Barbados, Jamaica, Georgia, the Carolinas, Virginia, Pennsylvania, New York, Connecticut, Spain, Switzerland, Hungary and Russia.[74] Year in, year out, the Duke received seeds from colonial functionaries such as Lieutenant-Governor Cadwallader Colden of New York and his daughter Jane, from Governor Glen of South Carolina,[75] from consuls who served in the Mediterranean, from soldiers stationed in New York and Quebec, from surgeons in the employ of the East India Company who had made landfall in China, India or on exotic islands, from planters in the West Indies, from doctors in the Carolinas,[76] and from professional collectors like John Bartram in Pennsylvania. Argyll had helped some, perhaps most, of those men to obtain positions and offices. The Duke got plants, from naturalists and foreign professors like Kalm in Sweden and others in Holland and France.

Of course, he had correspondents in Scotland and in many places in England. In Scotland, the recipients of his gifts included men who were later created the Edinburgh Society for the Importation of Foreign Seeds and Plants which was formed after his death and lasted from 1764 to c.1773.[77] It, too, tried to carry on the work which Whitton promoted. From the 1720s, Ilay was very much in the network of British botanists. The Duke of Argyll's gardening and his botanising, like his science, was first for himself but also for his friends and his country. It shared that common pattern with his other intellectual pursuits.

V. Ilay's Other Gardens

Whitton was the place where the Duke's horticultural activities were centred. It was there that most of the seeds were received and whence they were sent. It was there that his abilities were displayed to the largest numbers, and from there that he influenced English gardening but it was not his only garden. Kenwood House had a garden which was later notable for its American trees. They probably came during his period of ownership or partial ownership, but one cannot be sure. About The Whim garden, we know more.

After 1729, Ilay was reclaiming wasteland at his 1,000 acre estate in Peebles-shire called The Whim. Acquired first as a leasehold property in 1729, he bought the place in three purchases – 1733, 1735 and 1739.[78] Reclamation there involved draining and planting, reforestation and the maintenance of a series of gardens one of which was walled. All this took place on what had previously been called Blair Bog or Cochrane's Bog which was then – and is now reverting to - bog land. In 1729, there was no dry place to plant or build anything. Indeed, there were problems in just standing with dry feet in many parts of the estate. Some regarded Argyll as mad for trying to improve it, an action defended in one of his obituaries: 'To Demonstrate that the most barren ground is capable of improvement, he cultivated a Moss att the whim, in the shire of Tweedale [sic] where he raised a noble plantation of Trees'. The writer added, 'this was inserted because the thing was ridiculed by those who knew not his commendable motives'.[79] In the end, Ilay showed that such land could be improved – if one had enough capital and determination. Draining just a part of the bog must have taken the labour of five or more men cutting drains in wet land nearly every day for ten years. As they did so, they discovered marl which Ilay had calcined into lime, dried for chalk and made into fuller's earth. There was also a shallow coal seam which he mined to burn the lime.[80]

Whitton and The Whim were similar. Both were on wastes with poor soils. At Whitton they were acidic and dry, at The Whim acidic and soggy. At Whitton he needed to provide water; at The Whim he needed to get rid of it. Draining it meant making an initial survey of the property, precisely laying out drainage cuts and draining a very large area into several man-made ponds. The cuts involved paring large amounts of peat so that the bog would drain and dry out. Only then could the soil be worked and gardens planted.

The peer's gardeners probably surveyed the first areas to be drained and in doing so would have followed the rules set out in standard gardening books such as John

Reid's *The Scots Gard'ner* (1683).[81] That book included most of the elementary mathematics they needed. But here, the main drains presented special problems. They required very long trenches. 'The West outward Ditch 5f deep & 7f Broad is in length 107 ch[ains] & 2 Roods or 430 Roods'. Since the gardeners were probably using a standard chain of 66 feet in length, the ditch was 7,095 feet long. The water had to move by gravity and to get it to do so, the slope of the bottom had to be carefully calculated and the depth varied to insure that the water would in fact drain away and not pool. That would have required a fancy bit of levelling. Intersecting the main drain and eight other ditches were three cuts about 2,200 feet in length. These created a grid which in the summer of 1730 cost Argyll £132.11.0,[82] many times what the 999 year right to the whole estate had cost him at 1d an acre. Those big cuts were merely the beginning. Within the blocks of land created by this grid, more cuts were made to thoroughly dry out the land. Those drains dried out only about a half square mile, 358 (American) acres – about a third of the land to be drained in the initial scheme. This was not the only grand drainage scheme planned at The Whim. An undated survey from about the same time seems to show main drains for an area of about a quarter of a square mile.[83]

Building a garden was a part of the scheme to improve the whole property. The first plans for a garden show a small area of the estate, about twenty-thirty acres, which were to be drained. It was divided into two squares with the sides taking the water off on the natural slope through ditches 6 feet in width. In the middle of this area were to be four gardens about 300 feet square – roughly 2 acres in extent.[84] By 1731, about two acres and some square rods had been pared and drained so house construction could begin. Here on the waste, house building and gardening went in tandem.

The drained land had to be made fertile since it was not likely to produce crops without a lot of attention. How the land was probably treated is outlined in a booklet published in Edinburgh in 1724 by the Honourable Society for Improving the Knowledge of Agriculture in Scotland. The Society recommended that mosses be pared and the peat dried and burned. The ashes would then be spread, the area limed, plowed and sown with barley or oats. Alternatively, it might be manured or marled and then sown.[85] Argyll had been experimenting with ways to improve poor land and tried many ways of sweetening his land in Peebles-shire.[86] In 1741, Lord Milton, after a conversation with the Duke, wrote a memo to himself which describes the methods then being tried:

> To levell some of ye moss by pairing & burning & yn cover squares of 10 foot wt. different materialls for Experiments Such as Sand Grovelly earth, Clay, Grass, Turff mix'd & unmixed wt peat ashes.[87]

The regime Argyll probably settled on is set out c.1749 in a short essay in the hand of his secretary, Andrew Fletcher, entitled 'An Essay upon Improving Moss'.[88] Fletcher nowhere says that this was the method of operation introduced by the Duke but it closely resembles what he is known to have authorized and what is said to have been practised in 'the south of Scotland' where The Whim was located. The experiments seem never to have stopped but the essay described the predominant method used.

The essay recommended cutting a large surrounding ditch going down to the clay bottom with a breadth at the top of six or seven feet and narrowing at the bottom of the ditch to about one foot. This ditch should have subsidiary ditches feeding into it from an area cross-hatched by drains made in the spring with a 'Dutch plow'. The peat which was removed was to be half burned. It should then be then mixed with dirt, clay, shingle and dung – anything really – and mounded up into a heap in the middle of the squares formed by the cross-cuts. To this mound, unslaked lime and salt were to be added in October. This should then 'smoke'. When spring came, the 'mole hills' or mounds could be spread and sown with rape or grasses or left fallow and cut. The adjacent ditches would slowly fill in and the mounded earth could be mixed into them along with as much new clay as could be added. As the mounds and old cuts drained and dried out, shrubs and trees were be planted to dry the land even further.[89] The author of this piece added:

> There is nothing but what I found from my own experience, And that I am sure will answer the Ends proposed and [be] of no great expence: the Expence never exceeds three pounds or three pound ten shillings per Acre, Ditches and planting excepted.

That procedure was close to the method followed by the gardeners at The Whim.[90] Bills exist for the 'spreading moll hills on the grass filds and cutting fell on the murland of blaur cocrean [Blair Cochrane]'. Ilay tended to plant elders and hornbeam on the newly dried land but there are no records in what now survives of the estate accounts in the National Library of Scotland for the carting or buying of salt. Perhaps he did not find salt a useful chemical to add; perhaps a man with his own salt pans did not need to buy a product he could make and cart at his own expense with his own workmen. Or, it is possible that the 'salt' was not sea salt but some alkaline salt which might make a 'smoke' on wet acidic land. Once the garden was established, it was well supplied by the nurseries of Whitton.

The Whim's gardens included a vegetable garden which seems to have been the first to flourish. In 1731, Argyll was having fences constructed around it. Those were earth works three feet high on the outside and four feet on the inside with a top four feet wide on which were planted whins or other bushes.[91] As at Whitton, the gardens were established before the house which was not habitable until 1733 at the earliest.

The first gardens had some ornamentals mixed with the kitchen stuff. If he grew at The Whim what he grew and ate in the south and at Inveraray and ordered and ate on trips, then at least the following plants and many variants were regularly grown in the fenced or walled kitchen gardens, orchards and hot houses of his various estates:

> *Vegetables*: Asparagus, Artichokes, Beans, (broad, string, yellow, Turkey large, long, white and red kidney), Beets (white and red), Broccoli, Cabbage (Annick, Dutch, green, red, Roncival, Savoy, Silesian, white), Carrots (red and yellow), Cauliflower, Celery, Cucumbers, Leeks, Lettuce and other greens for salads, Onions (white and others), Parsnips, Peas (early, hotspur, late, long, sugar, and some other kind for the pigeons), Potatoes (also a field crop), Pumpkins, Rutabagas and Turnips (yellow and white), Salsify, Spinach.

Fruits: Apples, Apricots, Cherries, ?Choke-cherries, Pears, Plums, – all in many varieties which ripened at differing times – Currants, Elderberries, Gooseberries, Mulberries, Raspberries, Rowan berries, Strawberries – again in varieties ripening over time – Melons, and Pineapples.
Herbs: Bays, Chervil, Dill, Garlic, Laurels, Parsley, Rhubarb, Sage, Sorel, Spearmint and other mints, Thyme, Tobacco.
Fungi, Morels and Mushrooms.
Nuts: Acorns, Almonds, Butternuts, Chestnuts, Hazel nuts, Hickory nuts, Walnuts (black and others).[92]

This list of nearly 100 plants and varieties is almost certainly incomplete.

Argyll ornamented the gardens as he had done those on Hounslow Heath. In 1738 he had designs for both a Gothic and a classical dovecote sent up by Roger Morris. It is not clear from the records which was constructed. He had, however, begun to grow pease for the doves.[93] In 1741, Morris designed and sent up from London a garden well. Along with it came a drawing of a pond designed to form a prospect for the house being built in the midst of this new garden. The pond was one of three created by the drainage system.[94] Like those at Whitton, this was stocked with trout, pike and eels, all fed on blood-meal. There were ornamental bridges. Some of those structures were Classical, some were Chinese. As at Whitton, 'A House of Office' or 'the Countess of Pigburgh's Apartment' was built. Somewhere in the garden, by 1761, there was a new 'ruined tower'.[95] He was still being stylish.

By the mid 1730s, Ilay was sending north from Whitton a great variety of plants, shrubs and trees. In 1731, a packet of twenty-six vegetables and spices were sent to see which of them would thrive. Along with them went twenty-one trees and shrubs, four fruit trees and three berry bushes.[96] Such shipments were often more than annual. Not everything grew but he managed to increase the variety of his plants over time although no inventory gives them all. He was trying to naturalize in Scotland new plants useful to Scots. Like his southern garden, this was to be one notable for its trees. Here they took on a greater economic significance and were planted more in the hope of gain than for show and amenity (see pp. 240-1).

At his other Scottish houses, Argyll followed much the same plan of work. When he became Duke in 1743, he set to work to improve Rosneath and Inveraray Castles. Both had gardens which benefited from the plantings at Whitton and at The Whim. At Inveraray, there was to be a large kitchen garden, walled so that fruit could be pleached against it. The extensive Inveraray gardens were for beauty and utility; they were highly ornamented. As with The Whim, the laying out of his gardens and ground required some draining of land, the making of ponds and bridges and the ornamenting of the landscape with follies and useful structures. At Inveraray, he created a salt water pond in which he hoped oysters might be farmed.[97] Inveraray's gardens have been treated at length by Ian Lindsay and Mary Cosh; it is not necessary to say more here.[98] Rosneath Castle was supplied with many of the same plants which he sent north to The Whim and Inveraray. There too, some land reclamation had to be undertaken.

Finally, to this list of gardens one should add Saltoun and Brunstane House, the homes of Lord Milton. Whatever Argyll sent north to his own estates, Lord Milton shared.

Each of the Duke's houses had greenhouses and gardeners, something in the way of nurseries and transplantation beds, and places where trees grew in various stages of development awaiting transplantation often in astonishing numbers. Each of the estates had a great variety of plants. All his gardens were places from which, and to which, new and exotic items came. They put the Duke at the heart the effort to establish exotics in new places and to beautify Scotland.

VI. Conclusions

Argyll's place in the world of British botany and gardening was one of some importance. Although he made no changes in botanical theory or taxonomy, he facilitated the exchange of information and plant materials both in and out of Britain. That speeded the introduction and growing in Britain and the colonies of some new plants. His failures in acclimatising plants showed others what might not be fit for cultivation in Britain. All that looked forward to greater efforts made with public funds by Sir Joseph Banks and Sir William Hooker at Kew Gardens. Through his nephew Bute, Kew was partly established using plant materials which Argyll had collected at Whitton.

Argyll was good at raising American evergreens which he helped to popularize and to make common by his gifts of seedlings and cones. Horace Walpole disliked him but praised him as a gardener, perhaps exaggerating his importance:

The introduction of foreign trees and plants, which we owe principally to Archibald, Duke of Argyll, contributed essentially to the richness of colouring so peculiar to our modern landscape. The mixture of various greens, the contrast of forms between our forest-trees and the northern and West Indian firs and pines, are improvements more recent than [William] Kent [1684-1748] or but little known to him. The weeping willows and every florid shrub, each tree of delicate or bold leaf, are new tints in the composition of our gardens.

Walpole found at Whitton 'one of the largest and best collections of trees and shrubs in the country at that time'. The evergreens and the often colourful deciduous trees and shrubs Argyll raised helped to change the appearances of parks, coppices and forests from essentially green spaces which went grey in winter to ones in which new plants, shrubs and trees gave colour, texture, and interest throughout the year. The Duke's arboretum at Whitton helped popularize what became known as American and winter gardens, places which American plants made green and interesting even in the winter or where sheltered imports gave a bit of colour throughout the year. For British gardeners, his significance rested on what he and his generation of collectors did to transform their gardens and landscapes.[99]

The Duke's activities as a gardener had more than an aesthetic dimension. British gardens after his time contained marginally more edible and useful plant species and varieties. The trees in his arboretum were also growing as timber on hillsides and in estate plantings where they introduced more useful woods. Had he done no more, he would have been a notable improver who had worked to acclimatize them to Britain. He did more as an improver but that topic is one for another chapter (see Chapter 11).

Chapter 9

The Religion of a Wise Man

I. A Deistical Presbyterian

As with so much of Archibald Campbell's life, his religious beliefs are more to be inferred than documented. Ilay was never notable for piety. There is no record of his attending religious services in England. Indeed, he refused to attend religious services connected with the House of Lords. Neither as Earl nor Duke did he have chaplains although his rank and wealth entitled him to them. No one seems to have said grace at his tables in England. His personal life never suggests that of a pious man who took to heart Christian counsels. He did not fear punishment in Hell. He could afford his sins, enjoyed them and sinned with no records of repentance. There is little indication that he ever turned the other cheek or took Christian moral principles seriously. He did not look for guidance from those whom he habitually called 'Levites'. He found the orthodox ridiculous and usually a problem.

Ilay developed a jaundiced view of all clerics very early. At no time were many clerics to be found among his associates. His known dinner guests in his London house or at Whitton included few ministers who were not scientists. He liked the playwright John Home but Home had resigned his Ministry. Often, Ilay's expressions of dislike of the 'high-flyers' are funny. In 1726, when he was trying to sort out the affairs of Glasgow University and bring it to heel, he visited the College and reported:

> ... I met with two things very diverting at Glasgow, one was that one Dr. Johnson had been under a prosecution before the late Commission [the standing committee and court for the Kirk when the General Assembly was not in session] for having said that the Moon was an irregular bitch, which the other party said was speaking irreverently of that glorious luminary. The other was, that there is a Professor of Anatomy there put in by our late Scotch administration [the Squadrone] who has a very extraordinary defect for one of his trade, viz. That he cannot bear the sight of blood nor of a dead corpse.[1]

The 'Levites' who tried to use a church court to punish the Professor of Medicine were as ridiculous as the Professor of Anatomy and Botany. Ilay laughed at both.

Religion may have interested the Earl as an intellectual matter but it was principally a political problem. He disbelieved in revelations or mysteries. He did not believe in the efficacy of prayer. Prayer had only a psychological effect on those praying or on those hearing their prayers.[2] He saw religious institutions principally as mechanisms of social and political control. They should promote moral conduct, care for the poor and run schools. Religion was of too great importance to be left to the clergy and the 'unco guid'. Churches had to be managed and used in the interest of and for the betterment of all. His view left intact the Kirk's traditional roles as a policing body, a welfare agency, an inculcator of good morals, an educational institution, and as a presider over the events in life which deserve some public note and ritual. It might even be a useful civiliser of Highlanders. What an established church was not to do was to challenge its Erastian foundation or countenance enthusiasm and fanaticism as some clerics did at the open air revival meetings held at Cambuslang and elsewhere in Scotland during the 1740s. Ministers should not meddle in politics by preaching jeremiads, urging intolerance or obstructing progress. Those 'hot brethren' and 'Levites' who did so could expect nothing from him. Such men were to be kept in order and allowed to do nothing harmful.

In the end, Ilay's religion was what the 1st Earl of Shaftesbury called 'the religion of all wise men', one best left unspoken and covered by conformity to the practices of the day. Archibald Campbell was, in short, probably a deist and had personal contacts with others. Like his brother, Ilay knew well Robert, Lord Molesworth the Irish politician who patronized John Toland and dealt in South Sea stock. Ilay and Argyll probably knew Conyers Middleton who wrote about impostures, heresies and miracles. Sir John Clerk found Thomas Gordon, the author of *Cato's Letters*, the *Independent Whig* and various deistical works, at the Duke's house in May 1733.[3] Did Ilay become a deist? Almost certainly.

II. The Making of a Deist

Becoming a deist usually involved a number of decisions which ended with a person shedding the Christianity into which they had been born. We cannot know those in his case but we can sensibly guess at how they came about.

Ilay would have had a good deal of Christian training early in life. As a child, Christian teachings would have been inculcated on him by tutors some of whom were almost certainly Scottish clerics. *The Shorter Catechism* and the Bible were among the first textbooks of most Scottish children. At some point, he would have memorized and learned the meaning of the doctrines of the *Shorter* and the *Longer Catechism*. At Eton, the catechism would have been that of the Anglican Church and the articles different from those of the Westminster Confession. At Glasgow, students went to church, had religious exercises in the College and were subjected to more instruction based on the articles of the Westminster Confession. By the time he left the College, he would have known the beliefs of his Church quite well. There were other influences upon him in those years likely to have been formative.

Lord Archy went to Glasgow University about the time of the trial and hanging, in January 1697, for blasphemy and atheism, of Thomas Aikenhead. He was an Edinburgh student only four years older than Archy, who was then fifteen. Archy would have had some knowledge of the heresies for which that unfortunate student died – the errors of Charles Blount and other English deists who had them from Lord Herbert of Cherbury, Thomas Hobbes, Lord Rochester, perhaps some Italian and

French free-thinkers, Baruch Spinoza, and, ironically, from a long line of Christian sceptics and controversialists.[4] The publicity of Aikenhead's trial would have given Archy in his teenage years knowledge of anti-religious ideas, a stock which was reiterated in the controversial works which appeared in the wake of the hanging. One of those, Sir William Anstruther's *Essays Moral and Divine; in Five Discourses* (1701), Archy eventually bought.

The public debate in the books and sermons which appeared after Aikenhead's death would have introduced Lord Archy to questions such as: Is the world eternal and nought but matter in motion? Is the very idea of God an invention of men? Are not all revelations and miracles but the products of clever manipulators of men's minds? Was Christ, and Moses before him, any different from that fraud whom some Protestants called 'the impostor prophet Mohamet'? Are not all religions but the scams of knowing knaves – only the 'priestcraft' of those who would eat and thrive at the expense of others? Are not beliefs in an afterlife, and punishments or rewards to be had in it, but the hopes of some and the projected fears of others? Aikenhead had died for affirming such propositions. Any bright undergraduate c.1700 would have encountered those ideas by the time he left college.[5] Indeed, they might have been heard in the colleges themselves.[6]

Atheistical ideas were addressed by James Wodrow, the Glasgow Professor of Divinity, in his 'Cases of Conscience answered...' (c.1700). Wodrow's students were asked to learn the signs of 'atheistical thoughts' which arose in our minds through 'sathans Injections' and to recognize how those differed from their own sinful thoughts.[7] Atheistical thoughts were, he said, sent to tempt us, to see if we can overcome them. They deepen our humility and enable us to strengthen our love of God. If those were discussed by divinity students, they were canvassed by others too. What is more, many of the odious beliefs were regularly attributed to those who belonged to other confessions. Anyone in Glasgow could have told Lord Archy that Roman Catholics believed in fake miracles, were cozened by their priests, deluded by pretended mysteries and canonized miracle-working holy men who were frauds. The idea that clerics sought power, and were unscrupulous in their uses of it, seemed plausible to many. The 'Vicar of Bray', as well-known verses made clear, had changed his creed with every political and religious change from the 1640s to 1690 in order to keep his living. During the breakdown in order in the 1640s, again after c.1680, and more particularly after the lapsing of censorship in 1694, debates over the status and nature of churches were common. After the execution of Aikenhead, anti-clerical and anti-religious ideas were applied by some to Scottish Presbyterian clerics. Everywhere, critical deism rooted in such contentions and the discords they fomented.

As a young adult, Ilay would have had available to him works by Blount, Lord Shaftesbury, John Toland, Anthony Collins, and other figures who made current ideas which appeared in the learned works of sceptics and Cartesians, such as Pierre Bayle, and in the writings of those who set out to refute them. If he had not read such men by 1700, he bought them later. One inducement to read them was the fact that they were scandalous, forbidden and proscribed. There is every reason to think that Lord Archy had discovered the ideas of the critical deists before he left college for the law school at Utrecht.

In the Netherlands, Lord Archy found a Calvinism more varied than that in Scotland. The Dutch Calvinists were divided into the Orthodox [Gomarists] and Remonstrants who resembled the English Latitudinarians. There were more exotic forms represented among tolerated sectaries not all of whom were even Calvinists. In Leiden, the Established Church was laxer than in Scotland but in Utrecht it was perhaps a bit more stringent than in much of Scotland. Everywhere in the Netherlands, the Established Church's powers were curtailed by the states which rigid Calvinists claimed had no jurisdiction over the Kingdom of Christ. Tolerant Holland did not make much fuss about the Catholics, sectaries and Jews who lived there. Many British visitors went to see Jews worshipping. The differences among and between religions, sects and confessions were subjects of discussion. His Dutch experience would have shown him the value of Erastianism, tolerance and perhaps the degree to which sects were human contrivances.

Studying in Holland, Lord Archy would have glimpsed the world of heresy and unbelief recently and brilliantly explored anew by Jonathan Israel.[8] For some free thinkers, critical views rooted in the history of religions; for others, philosophy and science were more important. Lord Archy probably had read enough history and the right Greek and Latin authors to notice that religious frauds were older than Christianity itself. The biographies of Appolonius of Tyana, Mohamet, various heretics and modern enthusiasts, like Cromwell and Lt.-Gen. Edmund Ludlow, all seemed to show important things about religious behaviour and belief – and how dangerous unchecked religious enthusiasm could be.

Lord Archy's intellectual world was also still one in which old arguments between the Reformers and Catholics reverberated. If he went to Italy with Alexander Cunningham of Block, Lord Archy would likely have been given an account of the evolution of popish superstition. Cunningham was a Calvinist with ties to the evangelical wing of the Kirk which enjoyed displaying the historical evolution of religious errors.[9] Pagano-papism remained alive and well and did not change much throughout Archy's lifetime. Conyers Middleton's *Letters from Rome* (1724) summarized most of what had long been said about the continuities between pagan superstitions and those of the Roman Catholic Church. Catholicism had corrupted true doctrine as its clerics sought power and control over men's minds.[10] Making the grand tour into Italy would have shown Lord Archy churches, such as the Pantheon, which were converted temples. Ilay reflected such beliefs when, in 1725, he wished Lord Milton 'According to the superstitious customs of this Place [London] ... A merry Christmas'.[11] History was not irrelevant to the English deists who saw it in very secular ways.[12]

Ilay took an interest in religious history but not for religious reasons. His history was secularized and the story of the Church was not unlike that given by his brother's friend Conyers Middleton, the deist.[13] That is even borne out by his concern to preserve the ruins at Iona. The Abbey enclosure was defined in the 1750s. He had it fenced and saved the ruins from the depredations of the inhabitants of the island and from their cattle and sheep.[14] The ruins for Ilay in 1757, were memorials of the introduction of Christianity into Scotland, that is, of a significant cultural change. Those artefacts should not be lost although Roman Catholic beliefs should be rejected. Antiquarian interests also had political uses.

Deism also rooted in philosophical developments about which he knew a good deal. English philosophers of the seventeenth century spent much of their time showing how the existence of God and truths about His attributes could be established. Christians had long seen such proofs as the preliminaries to a faith completed by revelations. The supplementary truths offered by revelation or the teaching of authoritative churches, were needed by Christians for whom reason provided no answers to so many questions — including that of our salvation. Religious men of many persuasions produced rational theologies which allegedly proved the existence of God and grounded moral and political duties. But, rational religion did not come from, or produce, one philosophy. It produced many. Cartesian proofs for the existence and attributes of God seemed good to some but for Baruch Spinoza or Pierre Bayle they were deficient. Lockeans found it difficult to credit arguments not founded on ideas coming from experience. Openly, no Cartesian questioned the creation or the governance of the world by a good God but many were called secret materialists. Newton's physics tried to show the necessity of a sovereign God but Newton's God was not quite like the one envisioned on the continent or by Trinitarians.[15] Metaphysics, which might lead to the same general conclusions, was not everywhere the same. Disagreements among thinkers undercut the efforts to assert one true set of religious beliefs.[16] Ilay was never much interested in metaphysics but he was taken by arguments from experience. Those were most commonly given in the new 'logic' of the empiricists and in natural philosophy. Natural history and natural philosophy were empirical studies but natural philosophies differed even though they came to rely more and more on experiments and observations.

Writers on every branch of natural history tried to show the providential design of the world. Many of the biological works of interest to Ilay had as part of their purpose the demonstration of the design and order of the created vegetative and animate worlds. Pious scientists, like Boyle and Newton, or naturalists, like John Ray and Nehemiah Grew, harped on those themes and set out the metaphysics which seemed to be necessary to underpin the new sciences. The Earl had most of the prominent books of that sort but it is not clear he believed their arguments. God might have made plants for specific climates but the best efforts of men like himself could make them survive elsewhere. That made for a better world than God had designed and created.

As a man interested in Boyle and Newton, Ilay shared the interest in rational accounts of the world generally expressed throughout the European learned world from the 1650s until well into the nineteenth century. But, if the world was providentially governed, providence might be general only; then, divine interventions are not much needed – as Charles Blount and others had argued. There might be agreement on the need for a God but not on the sort of God one might have. If natural philosophy showed the design and order in nature and the necessity for a creative, wise and active God, He too often seemed not very Christian and hard to nail on a cross. Rational theology was somewhat redefined by the new science of the seventeenth century. From supporting science, theology came to rely much more upon it.[17] Those who propounded heretical doctrines generally shared in the same efforts to make the world more rational which were exemplified in science. If Ilay put together critical ideas from history and the sceptics with positive ones from the scientists, and decided that they alone were sufficient to ground rational religious beliefs and morals, he would have become a fashionable deist – one of Bishop Berkeley's 'minute philosophers'.[18]

Serving in the Army was not likely to have made a young lord a better Christian but it may have made him more interested in the arguments about religion and politics which were given by deists like John Toland. The Campbell brothers were Scots of fighting age when they toured Europe and knew they would fight in a glorious religious struggle against papistry and oppression, one costly in treasure and lives. Both willingly risked their lives in such fighting. For men of their rank, doing so was probably not so much a religious duty as a way of satisfying longings for adventure and distinction. But, fighting Louis XIV was opposing a King who used religion as a means of securing and extending his power. Louis had forced consciences, persecuted religious men, both Protestant and Catholic, and used religion as a tool of statecraft and of diplomacy. His personal conduct seemed to make clear how little the King really believed the doctrines of his Gallican Church. Catholicism provided Louis with useful policemen and with a justification of his rule. For Protestant pamphleteers and deists like Toland, Louis was typical of the rulers of every age. They would stop at nothing to make their wills prevail.[19] Calvin had been right to separate sharply the state from the Church whose true head was Christ the King. As an active politician, Ilay dissented from that proposition but he agreed with much of the case made by men like Toland. Such views, between the time he entered the Army c.1702 and 1715 were made urgent by the ongoing war against the aggressions of Louis and his determination to restore Catholicism to areas from which it had been driven by the reformers. That upset the balance of power and threatened the liberties of all Europeans.

The date at which Ilay gave up the views inculcated on him as a child was probably the time when he first mastered some serious science. That would be between the late 1690s and 1708, when he was given his MD degree. Holland probably gave him an extended exposure to modern science and did so in an environment in which free-thinking was as risqué and fashionable as in London. He would have been making up his mind about religion not long after Aikenhead was hanged and John Locke and John Toland had come into prominence in the literary world by arguing for toleration and more reasonable religious beliefs. He is unlikely to have been a Christian by the time he became eligible to sit in the General Assembly of the Kirk which was probably the year in which he became an MD and an Extraordinary Lord of Session (1708).

That he never gave up deistical beliefs is suggested by his library purchases. Ilay bought many unorthodox books written by notable free-thinkers, sceptics and alleged unbelievers. His run of English deists was good. And, from France he had St. Évrermond [Charles de Marguetel de Saint-Denis, seigneur de Saint-Évremond], Simon Tyssot de Patot, the Baron de La Hontan, and some Voltaire. That critical literature implicitly questioned orthodox religion which was often presented as simply erroneous, inconsistent or unreasonable.

Christianity is not one set of doctrines or as simple as it seems on Sundays sitting in a pew. If Ilay read all the fathers of the early church whom he possessed, he would have known a lot about early Christian heresies and the reasons alleged for their appearance. He owned Socinian and Arminian works. Among the latter were those of the Aberdeen Doctors who had differed from the men at the Synod of Dort. He had Arians like Samuel Clarke and his friends, Dutch Remonstrants such as Grotius and Jean LeClerc, and a number of Latitudinarians not so different. The Earl possessed sceptical works from within the Christian tradition, such as those by Jean Hardouin, Pierre Huet, Pierre Bayle, and Richard Simon.

Books supporting Christianity are found in his library but they tended to be written by reasonable men such as those rational Anglicans who argued against enthusiasts: men like Richard Hooker, William Chillingworth, the Oxford Rationalists, the Cambridge Platonists and the Latitudinarians. Not many of his books dealt with specific doctrines; even fewer were devotional works.

III. Practising Hypocrisy and Ecclesiastical Management

In Scotland, Lord Ilay was a conforming Christian. He attended services and built churches on his estates. As a ruling elder, he sat in the General Assembly of the Kirk and at least once on its Commission. He played an influential role in church politics. He could debate religious and ecclesiastical issues and he was usually a supporter of the Kirk's independence as he understood it to be established in the Treaty of Union. Outwardly, he looked reasonably orthodox to most Scots. He even showed some distinctly Calvinist traits and agreed with some developments occurring among Calvinists, notably in England. While ambivalent about aspects of Calvinism, he may even have unwittingly kept some.

Calvinist notions of a calling and of duties to God sometimes imparted the sort of discipline of mind and will which the Earl often exhibited. They justified using one's talents in constant work and service to others, but allowed a regard for self, so long as God was served and glorified. Such ideas could imbue men with a sense of duty such as he displayed and which many of his class lacked. Works might not save but without them no one was a good Christian or a moral man. For the Earl the core of religion was moral and not salvific. While Calvinists in 1720 did not yet often believe in progress, they did believe that one should strive to improve the places to which they had been called to serve and honour God. It was for those tasks that we have been given our talents. The Earl was a constant striver.

Calvinists also tended to believe they knew little and that the ultimate secrets of the universe were not to be found although useful knowledge could be gleaned from experience. Calvin had praised astronomers and physicians as men who discovered a beneficent order while serving the needs of men.[20] Such beliefs made Calvinists hospitable to the new science of the seventeenth century. Calvin read the book of nature to be awed by the power of God and to realize that he knew little. Reading the book of nature was a pious activity which should make men aware of their inability know anything completely.

Ilay, however, was not a pious reader. He read that he might improve God's creation which he never saw as fallen – only as improvable. It could not have been well-made by the wholly good but inscrutable God of Calvin. One holding his views could encourage many innovations and hope for progress. English Dissent drifted in the direction of equating such progress with the providence of God but there is no indication that he agreed with that view.

Calvinists also believed that governments were necessary to keep order among sinful men. Ilay, like Hobbes, secularized that in his own way. He tended to see all men as knaves if not sinners; his actions as a judge and politician showed that he acted upon those beliefs. Order was to be preserved as the condition for a peaceful, prosperous and good life. Sharing such beliefs with the religious made it easier to feign belief. Covering his disbelief by affirming things pious Scots believed, made him a more plausible defender of Presbyterian interests. In the end, his mind-set was neither religious nor reflective of the doctrine of the Kirk which he was often intent on changing.

If Ilay put little store in revealed religion and was generally sceptical of its proponents, he probably thought that established Christianity was neither true, believable, nor particularly appealing. Still, it was established by law in Britain. As such, it was to be respected and preserved for social, moral and political reasons. He was always eager to assure clerics that he was a true friend to the *church established by law*, a phrase which may have masked as much as it seemed to promise. He was as unlikely to weaken the Established Church of Scotland as he was to have opposed the jurisdiction given to the courts in which he sat – and for much the same reasons. Christianity was an institutionalized fact of life having the sanction of law and necessary to the good functioning of the society. That did not prevent him from working to make both the Kirk and its law more amenable to his personal beliefs and principles. Just as he supported changes in Scottish law to make the country better and more manageable, he supported changes in the Kirk and its ways. He was for toleration and eager to see a clergy preaching good morals, not 'hot gospel'. He was willing to see the Kirk become a civilizing agency in the Highlands. The means to realizing those worthy ends was state control and the use of patronage.

Such a programme was not without problems. Family tradition, honour and loyalty to those who supported the interests of the Campbells of Inveraray, demanded that he support the Kirk. He and his brother had virtually inherited a position in the Kirk as defenders of orthodoxy. The family had supplied martyrs to its cause and had aided in the Kirk's restoration in 1690. The Duke and Ilay generally gave lip-service to the evangelicals until c.1725. Their church faction was against many of the things which polite and fashionable men personally, if privately, believed. The 'high-flyers' of 1705, when Lord Archy entered politics, would have limited the use of reason in religion, would not have tolerated dissenters in or to the Established Church, and many would quite happily have continued to make examples of others who resembled Aikenhead so that God's judgment upon a wayward people would not fall upon Scots in their time. That party in the Kirk opposed irenical ideas which they took to be weakening Calvinist doctrine. The brothers in backing them seem to have been against John Simson in his first brush with the church courts in c.1712-1719.[21] They built a new Glasgow church in 1719-1724, St. David's (often called the Ramshorn Church), for Duke John's old tutor, John Anderson. Anderson, an evangelical, had, perhaps with hope or a bit of irony, dedicated to Ilay in 1714 a work entitled 'A Defence of the Church Government, Faith, Worship, and Spirit of the Presbyterians'.[22] He was succeeded by John Maclaurin, Colin Maclaurin's brother. Ilay may have backed the candidacy of John, for the Glasgow Chair of Divinity in 1740, but, in general, he found the high-flyers objectionable. They were unmanageable. After 1743, there were few occasions when he supported those whom he had for so long called 'the Levites'. the 'hot brethren' or the 'Zealous'. Still, he made few overt criticisms of the Kirk and did not openly dissent from its beliefs or practices. It was too useful to weaken. He and his brother defended it but they mounted their defence from an Erastian position and appointed men whose actions were likely to change the Kirk.

The Church was established by law and, despite protests, its clerics functioned in an Erastian structure.[23] Moreover, it was one from which clerics could not exclude influential laymen from its management. The Crown's lay Commissioner sat in the General Assembly and was by law qualified to end or suspend its sittings and to establish when and where they were to take place. By courtesy, not law, the Commissioner followed the advice of the Assembly. About a fourth of the members at any General Assembly were laymen, ruling elders chosen by their Presbyteries to represent them. Some were titled and well-born. Others were only heritors or rate-payers in one or more parishes; some were merchants. Quite a few were lawyers. Such men also sat in the Commission, the executive/judicial body of the Church which met quarterly between Assemblies to handle legal and other business. Ilay, a ruling elder, was entitled to sit in the General Assembly and sometimes did.[24] There was nothing new about a political manager sitting in the Assembly but Ilay is listed as a ruling elder for every year from 1722 to 1760 with the exceptions of 1723, 1740, and 1744 when he does not appear on the printed lists. He is known to have been in the Assemblies of 1725 and 1754 and is thought to have been there in 1726 and 1744. He may also have attended some Commission meetings other than that of the fall of 1725 when he was in Edinburgh. Ilay, when he sat, was there to influence policy. He might not openly have called himself an Erastian but that was the brand of Calvinism he upheld. It was a Dutch divine who gave the position his name.

The Revolution settlement of 1690 restored presbyteries but gave the right to nominate ministers for vacant livings to heritors and elders with the congregation (really male heads of households) having the right to approve or disapprove of the nominees, subject to final approval by the Presbytery. Appeals could be made to higher courts. That seemed to be guaranteed by the Act of Union. Parliament changed this in 1712 allowing heritors and elders again to choose ministers.[25] Ilay supported that change and he and his brother blocked its repeal when it was urged by Scottish clergymen.[26] They argued that the Patronage Act re-establishing patronage was but giving back to landholders a property right belonging to them. Congregations had no right to pick their ministers by exercising a 'call'. He never changed his mind about that belief.

In 1723, on behalf of his brother and their London allies, Ilay intervened in the Scottish Church seeking to wrest power from the Squadrone political faction.[27] Robert Wodrow's letters and his entries in *Analecta* deplore Argathelian interventions in the affairs of individual parishes, presbyteries, the General Assembly and the universities.[28] In 1724, the Squadrone faction tried to elect the Moderator but lost by 44 votes in the General Assembly.[29] Ilay's friends then packed the Commission and got Ilay's debtor, Hugh Campbell, Earl of Loudoun, appointed as High Commissioner to the General Assembly. Ilay led a visitation of Glasgow University supported by a body made up of his friends. Ilay treated the Kirk as if it were merely another institution. It was all a part of getting a grip on all of the important institutions in the kingdom and making him and his friends more useful than the Squadrone to the politicians in London. The Earl intended to be and was in charge.

Ilay had been named as a ruling elder much earlier but seems not to have sat in the Assembly or Commission before the autumn of 1725 when he was in Scotland to sort out the problems which had arisen over the Malt Tax.[30] This time he took his seat in the Commission. He continued to do so from time to time.[31] In 1725, the Earl stated his position on patronage very clearly in a Commission meeting reported by Robert Wodrow.

The case concerned a call to fill a Renfrew church living in 1729. A minister had been named to the living but not by the Crown which had the legal right to nominate. The Commission managers put off their meeting until Ilay came up from London. They then delayed the vote until they had a majority. When a minister complained that the man appointed to fill the living had not been approved by the parishioners and that this was a case of patronage which was against the principles of the Kirk, Ilay cut him short saying:

> ... he had procured the presentation, and did think he did a service to the Church. The other said he had not his Lordship in his eye, but others; but since he had ouned his hand in it, he behoved still to be in the same mind, that it was ill service to the Church to get a man presented when people could not knou anything of his fitness for them, and without concerting matters with persons concerned.
>
> The Lord Isla answered pretty long and warm; that they sat here by an act of Parliament; the Revolution [Settlement] was by an act of parliament; patronages was nou a lau; there was an act of Parliament for this presentation; it ought not to be quarelled, otherwise the meeting quarrelled their oun powere; and much to that purpose.

Ilay was unmoved by the next speaker who told him bluntly that despite the King and Parliament, the Commission 'sat in the name and by virtue of a Commission from Christ, the head of his Church, and wished that members might speak in another stile.'[32] Ilay's side won handily because of votes cast by laymen and by the ministers who helped the Earl manage the Kirk.[33] Ilay's account of this to Newcastle was jocular. He had answered a minister who 'made A sort of an appeal to Heaven at the Day of Judgment, This was a Jurisdiction I could not indeed disown, but I took the Liberty to joyn issue with him in it'.[34]

The Earl would not have ordinary parishioners picking their own ministers. He had in essence, two arguments against their right to do so. The Kirk, like the civil institutions, was permitted to function only on terms laid down by the sovereign authority of the state. Appointing ministers ought to be managed; it was an adjunct to the political management of the country. As a political manager, he wanted the

Kirk to function under a clerical administrator who reported to Lord Milton and, through him, to himself. That was how his secular system worked. This made the clerical manager rather like his agent in Aberdeen and deprived the established Kirk of its autonomy and its divine Head. His other argument was based on property rights. Landowners had the right to appoint to the churches which they supported with their money. Wodrow quoted him as saying

> Setlements would not be readily made against my inclinations. But that is a point I'l never yield, because I take it to be my property and the right of my family, that none can take from me.[35]

It seemed absurd that those whose residence in a parish was permanent should have their ministers picked by others. Landlords might displace tenants but be forever left with a minister whom their tenants had chosen. Landowners, not congregations, had the permanent interest, one founded on property in the land. His own church patronage shows he made a compromises with parishioners. Argyll did not make the final selection of all his ministers. In 1759 he gave one parish a leet of three from which to pick their minister. He would have a man he wanted; they could have the one on his list they wanted most. Among the incumbents appointed in his time were two notable men. Alexander Campbell, minister of Inveraray from 1745 to 1764, left a large library sold by the Foulis brothers after his death. At Kilmore and Kilbride in Lorn, Patrick Macdonald, minister from 1757-1824, when he died Father of the Kirk, had been a travelling tutor and married a Roman Catholic woman. He was also a composer of minor note. The Duke's personal patronage record was better than the ecclesiastical politics for which he was known.

In other respects his record was mixed. The Duke had a dozen or more parishes in which he was sole or chief heritor. They were often large, divided by rugged terrain and with more than one place of worship.[36] Not every place had a church.[37] Argyll had built the Gaelic church in Inveraray and helped with another at Saddel in 1753. He could have done much more. Not all his ministers had manses. At Kilmore and Kilbride, neither of the two churches were well kept but a new manse was constructed in 1760. The stipends his ministers received seem a bit above average where they are known but the life was hard. The ministers seem generally to have had some additional support from the ducal family in the form of cheap rental land. In Inveraray, the two livings, for Gaelic and English speakers, had incomes from teinds his family had made over to them and possessed rental lands in lieu of glebes. By the 1790s, there were schools in most parishes which, in many cases, went back to his time or earlier. Those were likely supported to wean the majority in the Gaelic speaking population from their language. His appointees were also among those who worked to curb enthusiasm in the Synod of Argyll. Efforts to do so in the 1750s and 1760s took the form of reducing the number of communions and the 'holy fairs' associated with them. Sermons were to be preached less often and weekday services reduced.[38]

Ilay stood for the rights of heritors but he politicized church institutions in other ways. Throughout his career as a manager, he sought to determine the selection of the officers of the General Assembly. The most important of them was the Moderator, the presiding officer, who had a good deal to say about the agenda whose order was set ultimately by the Commission and the Clerk whose offices were carefully filled after advice from the politicians. The Moderator and Clerk's posts were lucrative and were politically interesting for that reason. So too were the posts of Procurator and Agent to the Kirk. To manage the choice of the men who filled them meant attending to and managing affairs in presbyteries, synods, the General Assembly and its Commission and in the universities. He expected this to be done by his clerical managers.

Lay participation in the judicatories of the Kirk was not the only way laymen interfered. The Crown appointed men to a variety of religious offices, including to some of the professorships of divinity[39], church history and Hebrew and oriental languages. The four Royal Chaplaincies, the King's Almoner and a few other offices with small emoluments and little power were in the gift of the Crown. More important was the fact that the Crown was the legal patron to roughly a third of the livings in the Scottish Church. This figure grew during Ilay's lifetime owing to the changes in the patronage rules in 1712, to confiscations of patronage rights after the Rebellions of 1715 and 1745, and to the establishment of a few new livings.[40] What changed even more was the attitude of the Crown managers:

> For a time [after 1707] the crown patronage was exercised [by the Squadrone] with a considerable respect for popular opinion, as indeed patronage was in general, but with the coming to power of Argyll and his brother Islay, in 1725 this ceased. Disgruntled congregations appealed to the presbyteries as was their legal right.[41]

Some of those appeals made their way to the House of Lords and were decided as much according to English as Scots law. That was also true of matters which Scots thought belonged to the Kirk, such as the appointment of some professors or the Greenshields case.

Ilay worked his system by picking and supporting clever, ambitious but respected clerics to be his chief clerical aids. They had to be willing to work within the Erastian framework set out in the 1690s and modified in the period 1710-1712. They had to be tolerant. They had to be effective politicians, good in debate and able to make others come around to their views of things. The men he employed had views close to those stated in a 1726 sermon by Patrick Cuming who later became his patronage manager in the Kirk:

> As we have nothing to fear from the civil Government under which we enjoy our Rights and Liberties and for the Preservation of which we are bound in Interest and Gratitude as well as Duty and Loyalty to put up our most earnest Prayers; so let us do nothing which may render us unworthy of its Countenance and Protection. Let us maintain Peace among ourselves and as we have Opportunity, instruct and persuade our People to a peaceable Behaviour and to a Chearful Obedience who ought not for some Hardships to be forgetful of greater Advantages and like peevish Children if any one thing is taken away from them, in a bad Humour cast away all the rest.[42]

Cuming seems not to have been educated in Holland but most of the leading clerics until c.1750 were and that was a message they would have heard in Dutch divinity schools.

Ilay's earliest church manager was probably James Alston. Ilay expected the Edinburgh magistrates to provide him with a city church living. He was 'look'd upon as head of that Party' in 1725.[43] By 1730, Alston had refused the principalship of Edinburgh University which went to William Hamilton who then became Ilay's chief advisor.[44] Hamilton had been given the divinity professorship at Edinburgh in 1709. He taught views very like those for which Simson in Glasgow had been banned from teaching. The difference between the professors was between a cautious, prudent man and one who was not and in cities of differing sophistication. After Hamilton's death, in 1732, Alston lived but a short time. They were followed as principal advisor in 1736 by Patrick Cuming. Always in the wings helping those clerics were others who were active in the universities and church courts and had or hoped to benefit from Ilay's patronage. They included men like James Smith who offered his services to Ilay in 1730 and succeeded Hamilton both as Professor of Divinity and Principal. Ilay saw Smith's politics as like his own and called him a man 'of the same kidney' as Hamilton.[45] Another who served Ilay in ecclesiastical politics was William Wishart II whom the Earl brought from a London church to be Principal of Edinburgh University in 1737. He was installed in his office and parish only after much difficulty.[46]

In 1730, Ilay's men probably seemed only a bit more liberal or lax in outlook than older men like William Carstares, Thomas Blackwell sr. or William Mitchell with whom his Lordship had worked easily during the previous generation. None of the new men opposed subscription to the Westminster Confession – the standard for the Church of Scotland – but they all seem to have believed, as had Simson, that there had to be some latitude in interpreting of the words of men, whether they were uttered at Westminster or as they have come down to us in the Bible. *Accommodation* was a theory which in various forms went back to Calvin and could mean many things.[47] Those clerics had things in common including a rationalist streak, beliefs in some toleration, liberty and freedom. They believed that the Christian life was a moral one and that to urge moral behaviour was less dangerous than preaching on the mysteries of the Trinity, the Incarnation and Salvation. God was more concerned that men be moral than that they have a scrupulous regard for ceremony or an overweening concern for theological niceties ultimately grounded in revelation and expressing mysteries about which men would disagree. Preaching virtue was socially and politically more important than preaching about the mysteries involved in administering the sacraments. Like others they thought true morality was possible only because of God's grace.

Those early moderate men were well described by John Ramsay of Ochtertyre in a character of Patrick Cuming:

Both he [Patrick Cuming] and the Wisharts [Principal William II and his brother George] were gentlemen by birth, – a circumstance which did not make them worse ministers, or spoil their manners and principles. [Cuming] was a man of great learning and ingenuity and worth, much admired for his pulpit talents. Less philosophical and lively than Dr. [Robert] Wallace, and less English in his strain and language than Dr. George Wishart, his own rich store of materials enabled him to shine from the outset as an enlightened useful preacher. His divinity coincided with the Standards of the Church, but his style and arrangements were more polished and pleasant than those of the highly popular clergy. But whilst his orthodoxy was unquestioned, he did not think it incumbent on him to dwell principally on certain errors of the system that lead more to strife than to edification. His sermons were pathetic, without affectation of *sentiment*; dignified and nervous in their strain, without being inflated or incumbered with words. Though he had neither time nor inclination to attend to the minutiae of language, he did not neglect the essentials of composition. He was indeed one of those pious and rational preachers whose discourses are directed more to the heart and understanding than to the fancy or humours of men. We may regard him as a happy medium between the old and the new fashioned clergy; for he had the zeal and sincerity of the one, and as much of the elegance and refinement of the other as was necessary.[48]

Ramsay remembered Cuming as one of the six best preachers of his time.[49] He thought Cuming a good teacher but added, 'Perhaps the conversations and counsels of a man who was both an excellent scholar and an excellent critic, were of much greater consequence than his lectures'. In the mind of this genteel lawyer and antiquarian, Cuming's chief attribute, which led him to 'power and celebrity', was his 'talent for business'. Professor Cuming was 'temperate and conciliatory' in his language, eloquent when he needed to be, and able to carry 'his point without producing an irreconcilable breach' when debating men whose interest and passions were engaged against him. Ramsay saw him as a man of 'common-sense', 'address'. 'prudence'. delicacy, courtesy and even humility when that was required. Cuming appears in Ramsay's memoirs as much the same sort of man as his secular counterpart, Lord Milton. Both were rather like Ilay in temper and address. Ramsay wrote his account around 1801 but he had an intimate knowledge of Edinburgh and its people which stretched back to 1753 when, as a young man, he attended the Court of Session and the General Assembly. A bit of an evangelical, Ramsay did not share Cuming's theological outlook but his opinion of the professor makes sense of Cuming's long relationship with Ilay.

Ilay's political managers in the Kirk screened clerical appointees much as Milton screened men for secular offices. They looked to the nominee's patrons, to the abilities and character of the cleric and weighed them in the balance of political gain. Would the appointment benefit the Argathelians, enhance their control of Scottish affairs and place in the office a moral man of sound theological views? Ilay wanted to appoint men who would be tractable and moderate. When he could not have them, he appointed others but with disgust.[50]

By the 1750s, Cuming, after many years as manager, was no longer so attuned to the needs of the changing Kirk as they were perceived by the Scottish elite. He was too little willing to force men on reluctant parishes and to uphold the rather stern position on patronage which Argyll had always maintained. Cuming had been willing to raise clerical stipends which were low and had fallen steadily, relative to other professions, since the mid seventeenth century. When doing that, he had been opposed by genteel politicians. Cuming eventually backed away from the demand for higher stipends.[51]

Among those who remained eager to force men on reluctant parishes and to raise stipends in the interest of improving an unenlightened people, were a group of young clerics and some of their lay friends who sat or were to sit regularly in the General Assembly. They included John Jardine (son-in-law to Lord Provost Drummond), Adam Ferguson (a tutor to Milton's son), William Robertson, Hugh Blair, John Home, Alexander Carlyle and others of less note. All looked to the Argathelians for patronage and most got it (see pp. 317, 353-4). They formed the nucleus of the Moderate Party in the Kirk and often dominated it from c.1760 until 1806 and beyond.[52] They cultivated Lord Milton who brought them to the notice of Argyll. After the mid 1750s, it was they who upheld the law as Argyll understood it and made the Kirk a more active agent of the improvement of the Kingdom.

The Duke's views and actions did not make him popular with the overly orthodox, with the literalists, with those who held that the Westminster Confession was the last word in theology, or with those who believed that the 'Levites' should offer advice to politicians which the latter were obliged in conscience to follow. Ilay appealed to the gentry, to the educated, to the modernizers and to those who thought that Scots had much to learn from neighbours, whether they were Dutch Arminians or Anglicans. To such men, the Earl's ecclesiastical regime looked good. When he fell out with government leaders in 1742, those who succeeded him did not change his policies.

IV. Making an Enlightened Kirk

Ilay's job as a manager was to appoint useful men. He worked to get moderate Erastians into the Kirk and to give them power in its courts. It was the only way to insure that the Kirk would become a body which would accept direction and would fulfil his wishes. His clerical appointments were not of brilliant theologians or of men distinguished by their piety. He appointed men with patrons whose votes he needed but he looked for clerics who were ordinarily pious, politically reliable, who knew something modern and were willing to live with the *status quo* or able to push theological doctrine toward the rationalist end of the religious spectrum. Given more than one candidate – and there usually was – the Earl could often choose among equally well-recommended men. By the time he died, Argyll and his protégés had filled about half of the churches in the land and about the same proportion of the chairs in the universities from which divinity was taught. His appointments paved the way for the Moderate ascendancy in the Kirk under Principal Robertson and his friends, a dominance which lasted more or less from 1750s until the Kirk fractured in 1843.

Patronage was the way to change the Kirk because patronage changed its personnel. That altered the ways the Kirk's institutions worked and the ends for which they were used and how its principles were construed.[53] By the end of Argyll's days, most of those who held livings in the gift of the Crown owed their posts to the Argathelians. So did many, many others. The Kirk was coming to resemble an enlightened body, one which could be used for making improvements as well as for saving of souls. It functioned more smoothly but groups within it never ceased to dissent against his Lordship's policies. Crucial to those changes were Ilay's own views, particularly his view of conscience.

Ilay seems to have sincerely believed in freedom of conscience. Freedom of conscience had a long Calvinist pedigree, even though for many who asserted it, it meant only the freedom to come to the one true conclusion without being coerced to do so. It would, after all, justify his own deviations from the orthodoxy of his countrymen. He associated freedom with Whiggism and found it to be the essence of Protestantism. He knew that it was mandated by the 'Act for securing the Protestant Religion and Presbyterian Church Government' (1707) which specifically said that

> None of the Subjects of this kingdom shall be lyable to, but all and every one of them free of any Oath, Test or Subscription within this Kingdom contrary to or inconsistent with the foresaid True Protestant Religion and Presbyterian Church Government Worship and Discipline as above established [by acts in the 1690s]: And that the same within the bounds of this Church and Kingdom shall never be imposed upon or required of them of any sort.[54]

His great-grandfather and grandfather had been killed by governments, in part, for defending views akin to those. Ilay's opposition to the Jacobite cause was partly rooted in such beliefs. Should Catholic Stuarts again exercise tyranny over the consciences of men, they would also deprive them of political liberties. Those, however, had their limits. A 1716 broadside addressed to him sums up some of the political views he is said to have argued in the House of Lords:

> That tho in matters of Church and Religion, Men are bound to follow the Direction of their Conscience, yet in all other Matters, these being only the Concerns of State or Policy, a Man is to be directed by the Motive of Conveniency or Inconveniency of that Society, or State he is instructed by.[55]

Ilay thought the 'public sphere' should be subject to the control and regulation of the state. States should not open windows into men's souls but they could determine how they were to act. His position was not so far from that of Elizabeth I.

Throughout his life, he was a tolerant man never expecting everyone to agree with him on any matter. Freedom of conscience implied some measure of toleration of others whose consciences led them to conclusions different from one's own. His attitudes to church politics were rather like those he held in secular politics. He could deal with Jacobites, be friendly with them and help them on occasion but tolerance ended when they tried to change the system to which he was loyal. The same rules applied to his conduct in the Established Church of Scotland. His support of men ended when they took seriously the anti-Erastian ideas which are inherent in Calvinism. He had the same opinions about 'high-flyers' as about Episcopalian non-jurors. By 1710 (he was then twenty-eight), he was certainly in favour of the toleration of Episcopalians in Scotland and had distanced himself from the ultra-orthodox members of the Kirk. Publically, he supported the Kirk's position that there was no right which allowed Episcopalians to openly worship in Edinburgh. He must have done so with misgivings. He found the uncompromising attitudes of the Presbyterians unhelpful and politically foolish (see pp. 41, 44).

In 1721, George Verney, Lord Willoughby de Broke, Dean of Windsor, introduced a bill extending the Blasphemy Act by forcing subscription to Trinitarian views. Ilay and his brother opposed this in the House of Lords.[56] While theirs was a mainly political stand, Ilay was surely repelled by the intentions of the Act. Opposition signalled the Campbell brothers' opposition to more restrictive terms of subscription to articles of belief in their own Church. They did not argue for the loosening of the requirement to subscribe to the Westminster Confession although around 1720 that issue was of importance to the Dissenting communities in England and to the Presbyterian Churches of Ireland and in Scotland.[57] Ilay's stand favoured the establishment party in his Church but not its most liberal members. Edmund Calamy, an eminent English Dissenter praised him for the position he and his brother took but Calamy would have gone further.[58] Others favoured allowing men to back away from their subscriptions; some opposed subscriptions of any sort. That had been called for in Scotland but had been opposed by William Dunlop, Professor of Ecclesiastical History at Edinburgh. Dunlop argued for the retention of the Westminster Confession as the statement of what his Church believed and taught. He did not think that those outside the Church of Scotland, but residing in the kingdom, should be coerced to accept such beliefs. His rather Lockean view of the Established Church (not necessarily the Church of Christ) was not acceptable to many Scots in 1720 but Dunlop's position was that of the Earl.[59]

By the 1730s, Ilay had no trouble tolerating in the Kirk men like the St Andrews professors, Alexander Scrymgeour or Archibald Campbell (see p. 182) – neither was thought to be quite orthodox. Thirty years later, men of greater laxity in doctrine were regularly being appointed in the universities and to church livings. Argyll would tolerate any who lived moral lives, preached good behaviour and who prayed for the right King and made oath to do so. Following Erastian policies was the price paid for his countenance and any power in Scotland.

The Earl's political management of the Kirk meant appointing men like William Dunlop, who could be relied upon to train clerics with modern views, and then to defend them against attempts to displace them. The Earl's period in power was marked by efforts to silence professors and to deprive them of livings. In each of those cases, he and those who did his bidding followed their own inclinations when they did what the London government wanted them to do – keep in place men who taught doctrines closer to Archbishop John Tillotson's than to those of the enthusiastic Calvinist Thomas Halyburton. The first important case during his time in power was that of John Simson (1667-1740), the Glasgow University Professor of Divinity who was twice tried by his evangelical detractors over the course of many years.

Simson was the descendent of a line of Presbyterian ministers who had been faithful to their vision of the Church since the sixteenth century.[60] He had a good education, partly at home and partly at Edinburgh where he took his M.A. in 1692. He studied theology at Glasgow under James Wodrow and then at Leiden under Johannes Markius. He was in Holland at the same time Lord Archy and James

Erskine of Grange were at Utrecht. While there (1698-1700), he was almost certainly the travelling tutor to the son of a Scottish gentleman which shows Simson was a man with good manners and some polite accomplishments. After several years as a parish minister, Simson became the Professor of Divinity at Glasgow in 1708. At that time there was no dominant political faction in Scotland but Glasgow University was closely tied to the Duke of Montrose and soon to the Squadrone politicians with whom he belonged. Those politicians had been and remained the special friends of Principal Stirling whose niece Simson married after he had been at Glasgow for two years. Simson came to office owing nothing to Ilay or to the Argathelians. Indeed, he very likely was opposed to them because his friends were.

Almost immediately Simson began to have trouble with ministers whose views were more conservative than his own. He had studied with Dutchmen who had more rational views of religion and its bases than were held by most Scots ministers. Hermannus Witsius (1636-1708), one of the professors at Leiden when he was there, tended to put the Bible into an historical context and brought to this activity some of the same attitudes employed by legal humanists when they studied the development of Roman law. Witsius separated the Gospel portions of the Bible from the legal, admonitory and historical ones. He was prepared to argue about the amount of material which was revealed and what was merely the work of men. He was also willing to state fairly, and reasonably to argue against, the views of opponents whom he tried to win over both with logic and good humour. Witsius taught divinity in a manner which Simson found appealing. Religion was a contested field. The best arguments, the best accounts of the history of the Hebrews, the best texts, the best expositions of the Word might be yet to come. We cannot be sure that we have the final word on the meaning of the biblical texts and we should not assume that there can be no improvement on the creeds we have inherited since they are but human glosses on the Bible. Witsius asserted the paramountcy of the Bible over creeds and confessions, the works of men. But, to know it and to come to a justifying faith required men to reflect rationally and then consciously act on what they believed. For the Christian obedient to Christ, good acts will be done as a consequence of both reason and the grace which the Christian has received. Those alone allow him to walk with his Saviour. Witsius' most famous book, *Irenical Animadversions*, was written to bring peace to contending British Protestants, something they needed in Simson's time.

Another modern professor whom Simson admired and taught was Jan van Marck (1656-1731) His systematic text, *Christianae theologiae medulla didactio-elenctia* (1705), was widely used in Holland and elsewhere. Marck prized the establishment of what was to be believed on the basis of critically evaluated biblical texts. His covenant theology, like Witsius's, was scholastic in form but found a greater role for reason than had the evangelicals of the early seventeenth century. Markius too found a place for the joys of prayer and the contemplation of the goodness and mercy of God. As Simson was to do, he encouraged his students to think for themselves and openly to discuss and debate issues on which the Church had pronounced. The assumption was that doing this would make them see the wisdom of their Church's theological positions.

Simson also used Benedict Pictet's (1655-1724) compend – an abbreviation of his *System of Christian Theology* (1696). Pictet had tried to write an elegant, readable

Latin textbook which expounded doctrine and sketched the principal errors of others who were then refuted. He combined this with a bit of history, both profane and sacred. He was known for his book entitled *Christian Morality* (1710) but what is perhaps of greatest interest are his discourses and sermons published in London in 1702 and 1704. Those addressed a lay audience. He asked each person to examine the grounds of his or her faith. That was traditional in Calvinism. So too was the expectation that examination would show that Calvinist Protestantism was the correct version of Christianity which alone fulfilled the needs and longings of men for solace and salvation. That alone would explain their place in the world and their destiny. Pictet offered a less routine explanation of the faith than was generally presented in Scottish classrooms by men explicating the unquestionable text of the Westminster Confession. Simson followed him in spirit but he went further.

His own teaching dealt with systems of theology and the doctrinal statements which had been made in the past but he returned to the Bible and the Fathers to show the consonance of the Westminster Confession with those texts. He forced his students to write and criticize papers. He set them topics to debate and he encouraged them to meet outside classes for prayer and discussion. Exegesis and cases of conscience occupied them in class and out. Simson thus departed from the older ways of expounding the truth. Those had tended to set it out in scholastic form and not in prose which aspired to be polite. He made instruction in divinity neither the learning of a system based on the Westminster Confession nor the mastering of works which answered the cavils of Catholics and other Protestants. He wanted his students to think matters through, to reach positions which were orthodox, which they could then politely express and defend. He wanted theologues with analytical and rhetorical skills, not boys who had the luck or grace to be born into the Scottish or Dutch Reformed Churches whose memorized scholastic doctrines were not to be questioned.

Simson was modern enough to follow the controversies and theological discussion of his time. This meant that he was personally engaged in reading and thinking about the controversies which swirled in Britain and on the continent over deism, the place of reason in religion and the degree to which natural theology might ground or buttress revealed religion. All that led on to debates about the great mysteries, the nature of the Church, and subscription to creeds. He talked about those issues with his students, hoping that they would be better prepared to defend the Church and the true faith when they became ministers. He seems to have had no doubts about the Confession he had subscribed and taught. However, he was foolish enough to vent opinions about non-essential beliefs such as that the moon might be inhabited. Such oddities and his quick temper irritated men who liked neither his theological beliefs, his speculations nor his modernity. The result was that he was criticized and delated to church courts as one who taught unsound doctrine. He was specifically charged with being an Arminian who believed that men could at least partly effect their own salvation and with being a universalist, that is one who thought that Christ called all and died for all even though not all men would or could avail themselves of God's saving grace. Others thought him a Socinian who had read the rationalist works of Samuel Clarke too carefully. If Christ was not eternally begotten of the Father and of one substance, power and eternity with Him, how has He bought our salvation?

The attacks on Simson began around 1710 when the Kirk felt imperilled by issues centred on the extension of toleration to congregations of Episcopalians, the restoration of patronage to the heritors and the interference in church affairs from English politicians who were exacting oaths. Church-men were bothered that the leading teacher in one of its two principal seminaries might be teaching things which were unsound and smacked of English divinity. All this quickly became embroiled in party politics when Simson was defended by Squadrone men and attacked by men allied with the Argathelians.[61] It was further complicated by the defence of Simson by his University which thought it should have the right to investigate and discipline its own members, and by the fact that the Glasgow Presbytery was not whole-heartedly in Simson's favour.

Between 1710 and 1717, many issues were canvassed: the possible salvation of pagan infants dying without actual sins; whether the punishment of the damned was truly eternal; the nature of justifying faith; whether or not God's providence involved Him in the evil committed in the world; the motives men had to worship – and those God might have had in the creation of the world. All of those led on to other equally cloudy issues most of which turned on what we might claim to know naturally and what came to us clearly and only from revelation.[62] The first Simson affair dragged on from the professor's first appearance in a clerical court in 1715 until 1717. When it got to court, there were many procedural disputes which raised questions about the fairness of the processes and the rights of the accused. The prosecutors were eager to try the professor generally on what he might have said and meant; the defence wanted cited precise words understood literally in their common meaning.

From 1710 to 1718 Ilay and his brother could not have defended Simson had they wished to given their position in London and their struggles with the Squadrone. However, Ilay would have noticed the passions stirred by this case and the unwillingness of men opposed to Simson to compromise. He would also have noticed that by 1717 many of the Kirk's more distinguished clerics had come to Simson's defence. They were unwilling to see the Scottish seminaries prevented from teaching in novel ways what they regarded as sound doctrine. They wanted Scots to be like the Genevans and the Dutch who had educated some of them and whose books at Glasgow, Edinburgh and St Andrews had supplanted older English and Scottish Puritan scholastics. Simson's defenders would be Ilay's future allies, men whom he patronized and placed in positions of trust in the universities and church. All that would have been recalled when the Simson case, in effect, re-opened in the 1720s.

At the end of his first trial, the professor was found to have vented opinions which he need not have stated and which had caused strife. He had been too dependent on reason and had employed 'hypotheses' which he was forbidden to use in the future. He was not found to be heretical and he was not barred from teaching since his teaching had not been unsound. He was warned to behave better in the future – to be clearer in his teaching – but no one told him to change his mind about the things which had really gotten him into trouble and he did not.[63] That he got off with a warning scandalized many.

Ilay had not been much concerned with those disputes since he lacked, until 1724, a place from which to influence them. That was not the case when Simson again got into trouble in 1726. The issues now centred on the Trinity. Again, there were procedural issues to be considered. The case went on until 1729 and agitation over it lasted until

1732. In this second case, the Argathelians were fully engaged in Simson's defence. In part, this was because they were eager and now able to sort out Scottish politics to their advantage. They attacked the 'hot brethren' who had set upon Simson. To defend Simson was to be associated with his ideas and beliefs in a more humane and rational theology. By supporting Simson, they were supporting those who were prepared to live with an Erastian Kirk and they were showing the English that intolerant Scots would not be allowed to run the Kirk. By 1729, Simson had been suspended from teaching but not deprived of his post. Ilay seems to have agreed with a memorandum sent to him by Lord Milton which said, 'It is the Opinion of all the Kings Servants [in Edinburgh], that Nothing more should be done against Prof. Simson than the leaving the affair in the state it now is till another Assembly, by which time some expedient may be fallen'.[64] It was postponed and the questions evaded. That was the solution the Argathelians supported. It left intact the University's claim to be his judge but prevented the professor from teaching what so many regarded as heretical ideas but which had not irrevocably been found to be so. Simson kept his post and salary but could not teach. It was a fairly daring settlement because the case had threatened to split the Kirk.[65] Later divinity professors had less to fear.

Simson was not the only one attacked in those years. His friends tried to have reponed Professor Alexander Scrymgeour, of St Andrews, who had been suspended from teaching divinity in 1718 because he was suspected of being an Episcopalian and a covert Jacobite. His real sins may have been his appointment by English Tory politicians and not having the backing of local clergymen. With the help of Ilay and his agents, Scrymgeour, too, continued to be paid but remained idle until his death in 1731.[66]

In the late 1730s, Ilay aided his namesake, Archibald Campbell, Professor of Divinity and Ecclesiastical History at St Andrews.[67] He was accused of being unsound on the effects of grace and of favouring a morality which lacked a scriptural base. Indeed, his views were perhaps even incompatible with scripture. Campbell had set out those views in a book dedicated to Ilay. His Lordship's party defended Campbell's right to theorize and the University's and Crown's right to have him as a professor.

Those men suffered harassment from the 'high flyers'. John Lumsden, the King's College Professor of Divinity, was set upon by Jacobites and Episcopalians. In the early 1730s, the Argathelians defended him too. At issue were the influence of Jacobites in the local Synod and the regularity of Lumsden's election to his chair. Lumsden was no heretic but he seems to have been a willing Erastian with no sympathy for 'high church' episcopacy then in something of a crisis over the remits of Scottish bishops.[68] He was kept in place; later Ilay gave him a Royal Chaplaincy.

During much of the same period in which those causes were being decided, the Kirk was upset by other theological cases. The Squadrone men had needed to deal with the problems posed by the Auchterarder Creed (1717-1720) and the 'Marrow Controversy' (1718-1722). The Presbytery of Auchterarder had tried to impose stricter doctrinal tests on those whom it licensed and began with William Craig, one of Simson's former students. Craig's responses to their questions led the Presbytery to refuse him a copy of his license. Craig took the matter to the courts of the Kirk where, after a lot of politicking, the Presbytery lost and then was exonerated. In 1743 Craig was proposed as Simson's successor but was defeated by William Leechman whose views were even more loose.

A second case centered on the compatibility of Edward Fisher's *The Marrow of Modern Divinity* (1646) with the doctrinal standards of the Kirk. To the distress of many, *The Marrow* was found to be an antinomian work. Those who recommended the book were rebuked by the General Assembly in 1722. That controversy ran from 1718 to 1723 and made very unhappy those who had been attackers of Simson. It seemed to them that the heretics were left to enjoy their livings while the pious and orthodox were disciplined. Those who refused to accept the judgment were eventually hounded from the Kirk.

When Ilay came to power c.1723-25, he showed that the lawful establishment was to be respected by enforcing the Patronage Act. That made a tense period more tense, a fact made evident in an increase in pamphlets about patronage.[69] When parishes and presbyteries were unwilling to settle a new minister, a committee of willing men was appointed to ordain the minister to his living. As we have seen, enforcement of that policy, standard after 1725, was made easier in 1732 by a clarification of the Act which allowed a call to a new minister by the heritors *only* and not by the people of the parish [*i.e.*, some or all of the heritors, heads of households and elders]. From the early 1730s, there was a variable stream of cases in church courts concerning the choosing, installation and conduct of ministers many of which related to decisions by government managers led by Ilay. The Act of 1732 sparked the 'First Secession' led by Ralph and Ebenezer Erskine in December 1733. They had been deposed from their livings by the casting vote of the Moderator of their Synod whom Ilay later patronised. The Secession Church or Associate Presbytery, led by the Erskines and others, formed in 1733 and continued to grow (and itself splinter) throughout the rest of Ilay's life. Further schisms were for many years always possible. That was vivid testimony to the belief that many still regarded as illicit any state interference in the form of oaths, patronage, laws about toleration and any resort to civil courts to deal with ecclesiastical or theological matters. Seceders generally opposed the rationalist divinity of the theological halls. Theirs was a more intensely emotional religion, more akin to German Pietism than to the tepid, rationalistic Anglicanism toward which some feared or hoped the Kirk was drifting. From Ilay's point of view the Kirk was better off without them.

Ilay prevailed in the cases of Simson, Campbell and Lumsden, partly because he was leading a united political faction. By 1740 that was no longer true. The Argathelians had split c.1737-39. Some supported Ilay and the government; others voted in Opposition with the Duke of Argyll who had gone out of power in 1738. With the Argathelian party split, unified backing or opposition could not be given to John Maclaurin, the Evangelical candidate for the Glasgow Divinity Chair in 1740 and 1743. The 2nd Duke probably supported Maclaurin whose family had for long been connected with that of the Campbells of Inveraray (who had built the Glasgow kirk in which he preached). Some of Ilay's friends in the College did not support Maclaurin but the Earl's own role is not known. The election in 1743 was more complicated because Ilay too was out of power. Maclaurin was again the candidate; the Argathelians were more united. They seem to have helped Maclaurin but that was probably to embarrass the Squadrone men who wanted no enthusiast in that chair. Ilay may have condoned the case brought against William Leechman who was the appointee backed by Squadrone men who beat Maclaurin in 1743.[70] After 1743,

Ilay, now Duke of Argyll, never backed another 'high flyer' for a divinity chair.[71] The divinity taught in Scotland would be more cool and rational.

The Earl left the handling of most cases to his underlings but those involving university men usually made their way to his desk partly because he had often been involved in the previous placements of the professors and was in some sense bound to look after his own. The sensitive cases, those which ran the danger of causing disturbances in the Kirk and in society more generally, he followed closely. He was either active in or was kept informed of the processes in all the legal cases mentioned above. In Simson's first case, the leadership of the Kirk split over the soundness of the professor's beliefs but patronage made the next round less likely to go against him. In the Marrow Case, most Church leaders believed the doctrines of the 'Marrow men' to be demonstrably unsound.[72] It was the judgement and aftermath which created the major problems.

Those cases well define Ilay's public stance on religion in Scotland. It was established by law in a form which would be preserved by the enforcement of laws and rules made by Parliament. Doctrine would not officially be touched but men would be appointed who would give it particular emphases and who would promote modern ideas and attitudes in the Kirk and universities. Those men did not include 'zealots'. To many in the Kirk, Ilay did not look like its champion but everyone recognised that he was in charge and that he wanted order, quiet and some greater latitude in theological thinking than had been usual.

By the end of his life, the 3rd Duke of Argyll had changed the Kirk in which he had prayed as a child. Ilay's views and his system of management made nonsense of the pretence of separation of church and state in Scotland. It deprived the Kirk of independence. But, that was the precondition for the appointment of moderate and more modern, if not always learned or godly, ministers. Ilay's most notable appointees were polite sermon writers, secular historians who upheld subscription but they were dubiously loyal to some of the tenets defining their faith. Argyll's Kirk became the church of Thomas Tullideph, Robert Wallace, Archibald Campbell, Hugh Blair, William Robertson, John Home, Adam Ferguson, Robert Watson, William Wilkie, George Hill and other Moderates.[73] Most of those men received patronage from the Argathelians.[74] Ilay's regime helped to make the Kirk an agency of reform and enlightenment but less a place in which to save souls through evangelical preaching. Ilay and his friends appointed men with scientific interests, literary men, and improvers. Their Kirk would twice send the botanist John Walker into the Highlands not only to count Roman Catholics but to survey the resources of the region with an eye to their development, a theme of one of Walker's books. As there were gains, so there were also losses. The divinity teachers and professors of church history Ilay appointed tended not to train theologues to defend their Kirk against those who were critical of it on historical and theological grounds. They suffered the standard of Hebrew teaching to reach a low mark. Most divinity professors wrote little or no theology but they were proud of their polite writings which often dealt with morals, politics and literary topics. They were in many ways admirable and not always bad Calvinists but they had made their religion much more compatible with a secular outlook, one which they shared with the deistical 3rd Duke of Argyll.

Plate 6. The Royal Bank of Scotland £1 Note portrait after Ramsay (1749), with the permission of the Royal Bank of Scotland Group.

Chapter 10

Archibald Campbell, Lawyer and Judge

I. Lawyer and Judge

Lord Archy had been trained as a polite Scoto-Dutch civilian and, after 1708, he was active as a lawyer and judge. Traces of his legal education remained in much that he did. Integral to the education of a civilian or Roman lawyer c.1700 was a sense that law was a construct in which the rules of legislators and the reasoning of judges embodied the sense of what a people over time had come to think was right. Laws were shaped by the circumstances which created them. Laws which did not fit a people's circumstances were not useful and would be obeyed reluctantly or not at all. That was as true of Scotland as of Rome as the first Lord Stair had shown.[1] Such a view of law might not look first to what Stair called reason, conscience and equity or to divine or even moral standards to find the immediate sources of natural law. It would look to 'human law' or the practices of men and the needs of their societies which had given rise to customs based on utility – what Ilay often called 'convenience'.[2] To see Scottish law that way was to see a complex set of practices and rules which were the products of history as well as of reason. The history of Scotland was also one of two cultures, progressing at differing rates, from primitive states to more settled forms of society – from the virtual anarchy of competing tribes, to kingdoms, feudalism, and then to a British imperial union of economically and socially complex realms. The King's law ought to run everywhere but allowances had to be made for the customs and laws of distinctive areas like Scotland or Wales.

Ilay subscribed to such a view but he wanted to see the barbarous and civilized worlds drawn into a single system. In 1725, he wrote that lawlessness and 'the difficulty that attends the execution of the processes of the law in the Highlands seems to be the very essence of their barbarity'.[3] Law could be used to push changes in the directions in which they were tending but care must be used. Highland jurisdictions might be modified but the customs and habits of a people could not, should not, be greatly and quickly changed by fiat.[4] For just compensation, Argyll was willing to surrender his regalities in 1747. The particularities which such courts introduced into the administration of justice in Scotland were not good for Scots but there were some functions of those jurisdictions which should be preserved and left to local officials.[5] Banning tartans and traditional Highland dress or the use of Gaelic was something else.

His Lordship's views on law show him to have been a 'Jacobite' only for the temporary advantages which such a pose might have in politics. His serious political attitudes were very Whiggish. They did not vary much from what had been stated in the Claim of Right and Articles of Grievances (both 1689). The Revolution of 1688 and the settlement thereafter had limited the powers of British monarchs. They no longer had the great prerogative powers they had once possessed. They could no longer act as arbitrarily as they once had and that was, or should be, equally true of the nobility and chieftains. Argyll believed in the rule of laws made by Parliaments and by the interpretations and findings of judges. The latter worked well when they worked on the laws of their own kingdom, adapting them to fit current circumstances.

Ilay's view of sovereignty put it in the British Parliament but as that had been limited by the terms of the Treaty of Union signed with Scots. Scottish laws were protected by that Treaty and should not be changed. The common law of England was not and should not become the common law of Scotland. Indeed, in Scotland, when judges referred to the 'common law', it was almost always a reference to the common law of Europe – the Roman law. Throughout his life, Argyll was sensitive to differences between Scots and English laws. The rights of men and women as persons and property owners, and the ways in which they could be asserted, were different in each country. Captain Porteous, in 1736, had to be tried for murder because Scots law had nothing comparable to what the English law defined as 'manslaughter'. His Lordship sometimes had to state such differences to the House of Lords as it sat in judgment of Scottish cases. Contracts and other obligations took different forms and led to actions pursued in very different ways. It was not such an easy thing to tamper with laws as the British Parliament often thought. Ilay seldom missed a day when Scottish cases were settled in the House of Lords acting as the court of final appeal.

Another of his permanent and underlying attitudes to the law seems to have been that the laws of Scotland and England were in many basic ways not opposed. They would in time converge – an opinion held by men like Henry Home (Lord Kames), David Dalrymple (Lord Hailes), and others whom the Duke appointed to the Scottish high courts.[6] In England, those notions were promoted by Lord Chancellor Hardwicke. When Ilay gave an opinion on the case involving the trial for murder of Sir Gilbert Eliott of Stobs in 1727, he noted that under English law, duelling resulting in death, which this case involved, was but manslaughter since Eliott had not been the aggressor. The Earl thought the Crown should and would pardon him upon conviction. He cited in support of his opinion a decision by Lord Chief Justice Holt.[7] Ilay wanted the law to be the same in both countries or rules applied to have that effect. Elsewhere, he made clear that he saw the course of legal proceedings and the content of laws becoming one in a more united Kingdom. That was the belief of many who thought that the laws of peoples of comparable social development and customs were likely to be much the same.

He had other views about the law which were not unusual. He believed, as might any in an un-policed world of poor and hungry people, that social institutions were fragile and that societies often lived on the edge of anarchy. He made a quick ride to Edinburgh to proclaim the King in 1714 but he did not issue the proclamation until all the preparations were in place to keep order and to prevent a Jacobite demonstration. He was hard on rioters because they threatened civil order whether they were rioting over taxes, elections, or the injustices which they perceived to have been done in the

Porteous case. He realized, as many historians have not, how disorderly Scotland was; enforcement of the law was the remedy he wanted employed but it had to be accompanied by long-term changes in the economy and in attitudes if future riots were to be avoided.[8] The real remedies for disorder and rebellion were economic development and improving conditions. Repression alone would not quiet regions and make government acceptable. He saw the problem of controlling Highlanders as one of making the Highlands more like the rest of Britain; that meant making men more independent and their properties more secure.

His Lordship thought and said that if a law was on the books and broken, those who broke it should be punished. Punishments should not be harsh but exemplary and sufficient to deter others. Lockhart of Carnwath, thought in 1725 that 'Lord Ilay seems to thirst after bloody processes' and said that the Earl would find men to hang after a Linlithgow riot. Ilay went to the town with a troop of Dragoons, stationed some in the town, tried to reconcile the factions and sternly warned that 'no breach of the Peace [would] go unpunished'.[9] There was no bloodshed and no hangings because there were no riots. Prevention could be as important as punishment. When it came to incorrigible traitors, such as those who in the 1750s were still trying to disturb the peace of the country, he had little compunction about hanging them. The friends of Dr. Archibald Cameron, brother to Donald Cameron of Lochiel, were said to have appealed to the Duke, asking that Dr. Cameron be spared in 1753. Argyll, in effect, told them that he could not obtain that favour from the ministers. One of the Secretaries of State, when Argyll's refusal was reported to him after the doctor's execution, denied that: 'He is our first man in Scotland, and it is not in our interest to deny him a favour when he thinks it proper to ask it'.[10] Cameron, an educated and urbane man, had been out in the '45, actively dispensed funds to Jacobites in hiding during the late 1740s and was trying to create another rebellion. When almost all hope was gone, he still wished to involve the kingdom in bloodshed for the benefit of the Pretender and the French. He was not the sort of man for whom the Duke of Argyll would ask clemency. But, the Duke might lie about it since Camerons were his neighbours and among his tenants. To Sir Duncan Campbell, he is said to have remarked, 'were I to crawl on all fours to those men, they would not grant me that favour'.[11] He could also be vindictive and in this case was. Cameron was hanged, drawn and quartered early in 1753. Ilay allowed him to be made an horrific example for other would-be traitors.

With lesser treasons, such as ignoring the reading of the Riot Act, which he thought the Glasgow Malt Tax rioters had committed, there was to be no lessening of the charges, which happened in that case.[12] Prosecution should be to the full extent of the law. Then, after conviction, the King's pardon might be sought for those who deserved it. He believed in graduated punishments but they were often unavailable. In the cases of the Glasgow rioters, he thought some should be hanged, others committed to particular places and persons under a sign manual.[13] Commitments could be used to mitigate – or harshen – their punishments. One of the Glasgow rioters he thought should be reprieved from transportation but he noted that there were no regular processes for such a graduation of punishments since the Union and the abolition of the Privy Council.[14] He believed that if a penalty seemed harsh, the remedy was to change the law so that a lighter penalty could be inflicted. As head of the Justiciary Court, he signed the sentences against the Glasgow rioters but then, as a judge, dissented from them. When it came to ordinary crimes, he believed that physical punishment was less effective than fines and imprisonment whose effects were longer lasting. In particular, he did not like whippings. In sentencing, judges should 'lean to the milder side'.[15]

In many cases where he wanted to enforce the law, there was a considerable degree of self interest and expediency behind his actions. However, that was not all there was. The Treaty of Union ought to govern relations between the kingdoms in Britain and Scots ought not to be put at the mercy of English majorities in the Commons and factional peers in the House of Lords. That was wrong. But, if the toleration of Episcopalians in Scotland was decreed by the House of Lords legitimately acting as Britain's highest court, then it had to be allowed even though it violated the Treaty of Union. If patronage in the Established Church of Scotland belonged to heritors by law, then, the patrons and heritors to whom that property right had been restored had rights to fill the livings. Their nominees should be imposed on recalcitrant parishes by the courts of the Kirk and the State. If the Excise and Customs taxes were extended by Parliament to Scottish brewers, then Scots had to be made to pay them so the rule of law might be preserved. That, in the end, was more important than the rights of Scots not to be taxed under the Union agreement unless they could afford it. If oaths were required of clerics and office holders, they should be taken and the non-jurors pursued – though perhaps not diligently in all places. In the administration of laws, political effects and utility — 'conveniency' — had to be considered if peace was to be maintained. Not to allow discretion to judges and officials was to defeat the intent of laws which was the keeping of peace in an orderly society. And, the actions of public officials were always examinable.[16] There was something self-serving in all that but there were also principled positions being consistently maintained.

Like any Scots lawyer, Ilay believed that not all laws on the books were still enforceable. Some had fallen into desuetude and would not – should not – be enforced by Scottish courts. In other cases, it was best to act so that public peace could be maintained although strict justice was not dispensed. A case of this sort arose in 1720 when two Frasers, Lovat's men, burned the house of a clan enemy. Ilay as head of the Justiciary Court asked David Erskine, Lord Dun, to look into the facts of the case, noting that 'the mutual aversions to one another in Highlands do often produce both monstrous facts & allegations too'. The Earl was 'apprehensive there has been farther views in that matter than merely bringing Criminals to Justice'.[17] The case dragged on for several years with the men being in the end convicted but pardoned. On 10 December 1726, Ilay wrote of them to Grange, 'the young men lately saved' should stay home, be quiet and 'take care that there may be no boasting or insulting over the other party'.[18] It was better to keep the region quiet than to be rigorous in executing justice if the outcome would bring more violence.[19] One would like law to be enforced but its ends might be best served not by blood and rigour but by leniency.

Ilay was not much concerned with rights and freedoms for which there was no specific legal guarantee. In 1725, he was eager to punish the writer and printer of a 'malicious libel against the Scotch members of Parliament & the malt tax'[20] and he was over forty times during his time in the House of Lords on the committee which disciplined London printers and writers for invading the privileges of the House of Lords. He was for most of his career in favour of mutiny bills which had been in place since 1717. They authorized Courts Martial in which judges had considerable discretion and crimes were not all well defined.

His Lordship was concerned that proper procedures be observed and due processes followed. That lay behind both his worries about his actions in Edinburgh during the '15, when he may have acted illegally because he had 'no notion of ... taking the law of a Cannon Bullet'.[21] In the '45 he did not raise the clans because he had no warrants to do so (see pp. 287-93, *passim*). Unless absolutely necessary, he would not overstep his bounds and he did not want others to do so either. He was also concerned about evidence. It should not be based on hearsay (admissible in many Roman Law systems) and had to be proven. In Lord Lovat's treason trial in 1747, the Duke argued that Lovat's allegation that his factor had not done his bidding was unproven and 'the house ought not to notice' it – just as it should also disregard Lovat's demand that his strong box be restored to him.[22] The House agreed with the Duke but it allowed Lovat access to his agent in the presence of an officer.[23]

The Earl was a believer in properly drawn indictments. They should not be drawn in such a manner that the person accused could have no defence. That he believed had been done by the Procurator Fiscal of the Regality Court of the Duke of Atholl in the case of some cattle thieves named Stewart and Robertson. The latter, whom Ilay called 'the genteel Whig cow stealer', had been condemned to death by the regality court in 1730. Ilay claimed the Justiciary Court would not have hanged this man since he was not a repeat offender and because his offence did not involve violence. Worse yet, the men had been tried by a court with no jurisdiction over their crime. Robertson had been selected arbitrarily as the one who was to be hanged as an example to others. Ilay applied to the King for a pardon and got him reprieved; he was presumably given justice of a fairer sort.[24] Several years later, his Lordship was outraged by a judge trying 'to enforce the Execution of his sentence & put two men to death'. He said that not to wait for the legal testing of a writ of suspension would be illegal in England and was in 'Scotland A most horrible scene'. He expected the Edinburgh magistrates to ignore the order. The victims were probably the soldiers about whose release he was 'very glad' in the following month.[25]

Ilay was an advocate of speedy trials. As early as 1711 he wrote to the Ministry that 'delays in tryalls cast A great damp upon them, & very often the speedy administration of Justice has more effect towards deterring persons from crime than the very punishment it self'.[26] He was eager to try speedily all those who offended against the Malt Tax in 1725.[27] Throughout his life, he seems to have hurried on processes but not to the point that defences could not be prepared. He allowed time for the convicted to appeal for clemency. In 1731, he was annoyed that the Circuit Justices had allowed a clerk's error to shorten the time to appeal for clemency of a woman sentenced to die. He thought allowing such cases to come for review before the courts in Edinburgh 'may be really useful.'[28] They were his 'brothers' but they were scolded for their callousness.

His Lordship was generally careful in seeing to it that advocates acted properly in his court. His interventions in the trial of the Glasgow rioters were partly to keep the advocates speaking to relevant points although he made remarks which no modern judge would allow himself. He repeatedly told the jurors that the rioters ought to have been on trial for capital offenses and not for the lesser charges voted for by the Squadrone majority of the Justiciary Court judges. He also gave 'full scope in pleading' to the advocates for the prisoners because he believed the printed versions of what they said would show how guilty their clients were.[29] In other cases, he used his discretion to keep lawyers more focussed on their tasks. In 1752, at the Appin murder trial, at which he presided, he secured as fair a jury as possible and the accused got what was considered at the time a fair trial.[30] Sometimes Argyll voted for conviction based on the facts but might also ask for a reprieve or pardon. That was the proper procedure when the punishment did not seem to fit the crime. He had no qualms about asking for those if the offender was not a violent man, a recidivist, or a danger to others.[31] The accused in the Appin trial, James Stewart of the Glen, was, in the Duke's opinion, not one of those but an old rebel and a violent man. His Lordship was also quite capable of signing verdicts which he did not like and then adding his dissent and protest against the sentences.[32]

There are other signs of his concern with formalities. In 1715, at the impeachment of his relative, Lord Stafford, Ilay argued that to deny the Lord access to his papers and the materials needed to defend himself was to act contrary to the manner of 'all civilized nations, all courts of judicature, except the inquisition... and that the house of peers of Great Britain ought not, in this case, to do any thing contrary to that honour and equity for which they were so justly renowned throughout all Europe'.[33] The House agreed. A year later, Simon Fraser, Lord Lovat, reported that Ilay wanted many legal niceties observed in the matter of clearing Lovat's name of bad intentions and of the rape of his wife prior to his scandalous marriage to her.[34] In the 1720s, Ilay's friends were eager to see to it that men like Professors John Simson and Alexander Scrimgeour were treated fairly in the courts of the Kirk. That was also the attitude which lay behind some of the clauses in the Visitation Decree given at Glasgow University in 1726. Principal Stirling had been arbitrary and high-handed. The Principal was now to act by the rules set for him and not as he had formerly done. Records and accounts were to be properly kept. Stated dates and procedures were set for rectorial elections and College meetings. Ilay was the leading figure in that Visitation and his sense of order and fairness lay behind the devising of those procedures. In the short run, they also made it easier for him to assert control over the University. His arbitration of the disputes which had divided the merchants and tradesmen of Edinburgh before he adjudicated their claims in a decreet-arbital (1729) show the same things.[35] The interests of merchants and tradesmen were balanced in a constitution which in the short run made it easier for him to control the Town Council but the Council was to be a more rule-bound body which would act less arbitrarily. The regulations lasted almost unchanged into the nineteenth century. In the peerage election of 1730, he was forced to remind the Lord Chancellor that the election warrants needed to be under the Great Seal and that no election could occur unless such a warrant was received. Nothing else could be done in the meeting and no meeting could occur without the proper documents. Argyll laughed about this and told Charles Delafaye, Newcastle's Undersecretary, that the Clerks of Session had been much 'divert[ed] by the lack of knowledge of their ways in England'.[36] In

1760, he told Lord Milton to tell the Chancellor and Masters of Marischal College that they should send up in proper form their nominations for new professorships in the gift of the Crown. Then he gave them the form.[37] Not following forms might invalidate actions and increased the risk of a successful appeal but it also offended his sense of order and the need to appear fair.

His Lordship acted in many courts including several supreme courts. His activities in the House of Lords were numerous and interesting. He sat on trials of peers for treason, including that of his old friend and creditor, Lord Lovat.[38] He voted 'guilty, upon my honour' in the trials of others found guilty of treason after 1715 and 1745. He voted to convict Laurence Shirley, 4th Earl Ferrers (1760) whose craziness had brought his marital problems before the House several years earlier (1757). He sat in judgment on the impeachment of his friend, Thomas Parker, 1st the Earl of Macclesfield, and seems to have voted to fine him £30,000. He was active in the pursuit of printers like Edmund Curll and others who infringed the privileges of peers. In 1725, he wanted to punish writers and printers who had published a 'malicious libel against the Scotch members of parliament & the Malt Tax'.[39] He was no proponent of unrestricted free speech.

Argyll took an active role in the adjudication of cases which came to the Lords on appeal. Until the end of his life, he usually attended when Scottish cases of any sorts were adjudicated[40] but he was also there when other cases from England and Ireland were decided. In Scottish cases argued there, his voice was often heard.[41] When Scottish cases came up in judicial sessions, Ilay acted as a sort of lawyer for the Argathelians and was also respected as an expert in Scots law when there were no political stakes at issue.[42]

The conditions of the Union Treaty and what they were held to allow – changes to the position of the Scottish Established Church, the imposition of oaths, the legitimacy of the Malt Tax, the Excise changes proposed in the 1730s, the settlements made after 1715 and 1745 – got his attention as a lawyer. So, too, did cases involving inheritances, land law, the penalties imposed on Edinburgh after the lynching of Captain Porteous in 1736 and much more.[43] For most of his career, he was one of the few men in the House who could speak as an expert about matters of Scots law. Indeed, he was the sitting Scottish law lord because of his membership on the Scottish high courts.

He was useful to the House because of his training in Roman Law. He was as learned as most of the House's lawyers about the law of nature or of nations and international law. That subject he may have studied in Holland; it was one which civil lawyers had developed. He sat on the *ad hoc* body called the Court of Delegates created on occasion to deal with appeals from English courts employing civil law.[44] He was picked for the Court which dealt with the £80,000 case concerning the estate of John Hawkins of Waltham Stowe, one of the largest settled on appeal in Ilay's time.[45] As a Lord Commissioner, Argyll sat on appeals from Admiralty Courts.[46] Those courts also followed Roman law with which many English lawyers were not overly familiar. Ilay had his own Admiralty Court in Scotland and knew his civil law.

If Ilay did not know much English common law when he first sat in the House, he learned a lot. The kinds of things he knew best can be inferred from the 1,197 committees on which he served. He was appointed to committees which considered procedures, evidence, and the keeping of records. Somewhat over a third of his committee assignments concerned property matters. Those committees considered cases to break entails and settlements so that estates could be sold to pay debts, find portions for children and widows, buy or exchange properties, settle wills and appoint trustees or amend the powers given to them for the benefit of the sane and mad, minors and the aged, the married and single. It is no wonder that he had a lot of English law books of every sort in his library. Other cases involved enclosures, divorces, and the granting of special rights to local bodies for improvements to fens, rivers, harbours, highways, county seats, towns, parishes, work houses, schools and universities. There is usually no way of finding out what he did on those committees but one can assume that he attended many meetings of them since they generally met in the forenoons of days when he was in the House.[47] There were other matters which came before the House on appeal which interested him. In 1751, he seconded and praised the opinions of the judges in the Anglesey Case which came to the House on appeal from Irish courts. This was a tangle of claims about kidnapping, murder, legitimacy, and the right to a peerage. Ilay like many others had followed it and cited 'several Cases in the Civil law confirming' the verdict the judges had rendered.[48]

In Scotland, His Lordship sometimes sat as an Extraordinary Lord with the Court of Session. He sat more often with the Justiciary Court of which he was a full member and the presiding judge when he attended. He seems to have sat with one or the other of those courts in 1708, 1710, 1715, 1722, 1725, 1737, 1740, 1748, 1749, 1750, 1751 and 1752.[49] From London, he occasionally sent opinions about legal matters to Lords Grange, Milton and Tinwald, the Lords Justice Clerk who presided in his absence. Some touched on what seem fairly arcane matters such as a 1759 opinion sent to Charles Erskine. Argyll told him the Commission for Sick and Wounded had no right to quarter prisoners in either England or Scotland.[50] He sometimes sat in Inveraray with the Justices of the Western circuit. He did so if he and they were both there at the ends of summers. When that happened, he entertained them. He made a point of being there for the Appin murder case. This political trial has been used to blacken the Duke's image but it is also as a case in which most of his beliefs about the law were set out and followed.[51]

In London, the case was seen as more evidence of the unruly nature of the Highlands and of the 'barbarity' and unreliability of Scots. Men like Newcastle put this murder into the context of rumours about the recruiting and arming of Jacobites in the Highlands. There were the usual worries about what the French might do to stir up trouble in Scotland. There was substance behind the rumours. In 1752, Dr. Archibald Cameron, Lochiel's brother, was apprehended in Britain while working to further Franco-Jacobite schemes. He was quickly tried and executed in 1753.[52] In 1752-53 the 'Elibank Plot', which involved a plan to mount a *coup d'etat* in London, was exposed. Corrupt Customs officials, who made it possible for Jacobite agents to slip into Scotland undetected, were then being rooted out. One principal in the Appin case, Allan Breck Stewart, a Lieutenant in a French regiment, was probably recruiting in the Highlands. The Appin case seen in that context was one which required attention from the chief law officers.

The significance of the case was quickly realized by all the important officials who would deal with it. The ministers in London wanted to find the culprits, wanted a guilty verdict and exemplary punishment. Law in the Highlands needed to be maintained. Finding the murderer was an act of justice but also symbolic of the government's determination to bring order to the Highlands and thus 'civilize' them. Argyll knew all that but also wanted it to be fair. Only if it were would its ends really be achieved.

This was not a case of judicial murder as some have argued but one where the evidence and law required the conviction of the panel or accused.[53] The trial of James Stewart of the Glen before the Lords Justices of the Western Circuit was not only for murder but for being 'art and part' of the conspiracy which led to the murder of Colin Campbell of Glenure on 14 May 1752. Being 'art and part' was a hanging offense.

Colin Campbell was the Crown factor for the forfeited estate of Charles Stewart of Ardsheal, James Stewart's half-brother. Campbell was shot from ambush while doing Crown business on behalf of the Exchequer Court which managed the confiscated properties. He was thus a government agent who had been murdered. Within two days of the crime, James Stewart had been arrested for the crime and sent to Fort William where he was held for some time without access to a lawyer or to his family. There was a strong *prima facie* case since the evidence suggested that he was the assassin. Stewart was a Jacobite who had been 'out' in the '45 and was thought to be still actively loyal to the Pretender. He once had challenged Glenure to a duel. He had on several occasions uttered threats against his life. Admittedly, he had not always been sober when he had made his threats before credible witnesses but sometimes he had been sober. Stewart had befriended others who had done the same. He had a weapon with which the act could have been committed and seemed to have had the opportunity to kill the factor with whom he had recently differed about the settling of new tenants on forfeited lands. If Stewart had not killed Campbell, then he had known of the plot to do so.

The fact that there had been a plot to kill Campbell was alleged, if not known, within days of the murder. Glenure had received recent warnings that his life was in danger. Anyone who knew details of this and did nothing about warning the victim or the authorities was also guilty of being 'art and part' of the conspiracy. James Stewart was thought to have known and he helped another likely killer in his escape, his foster brother, Allan Breck Stewart. The latter was a British deserter who had been out in the '45 but now served in a French Regiment. Allan Breck had been some time in Scotland and had been protected by Jacobites both in the Highlands and in Edinburgh. If caught, he would have been tried by a court martial and hanged. If Allan Breck had not done the killing, both Stewarts knew who had and were complicit in it. The case to be answered was a good one.

Those views were shared by the Lord Advocate, William Grant of Prestongrange; by the Lord Justice Clerk, Charles Erskine; and by Argyll, the Lord Justice General. Prestongrange recognised the importance of the case when he first heard of it and before he knew who was thought to be guilty. He was vacationing in Bath but immediately returned to conduct the case although such cases were normally left to Advocate-deputes. The Lord Advocate took a month to draw the indictment which was more detailed than usual. The family of the dead man brought a private prosecution. They pursued it and gathered a good deal of evidence in the form of precognitions which were then used by the Crown. In the end, 700 people were examined between 16 May and 11 July 1752. It took a month to get through all that but in the end the Crown had only a circumstantial case which it was unsure would lead to a conviction.

The pre-trial record shows the Duke of Argyll concerned about the fairness and the appearance of fairness of the trial. Because of where the murder occurred, the jury trial would be held in Campbell territory at Inveraray. Some thought was given to moving it to Edinburgh. Argyll assured the Lord Chancellor that the trial would be as fair in Inveraray as before monolingual Lowlanders in Edinburgh, a point with which the defence counsel concurred.[54] The defence had nineteen days to prepare for trial, four days more than the legal minimum, and was aided by the detailed nature of the indictment. When it began, it looked like a fair trial.

Argyll's role as the presiding judge was neither unusual nor unfair by the standards of 1752. Cited as an examples of his unfairness are his interventions from the bench. When the defence wished to call a witness to the good character of the panel, Argyll warned them this was not 'usual' because it meant that the character of accused could be contested and the contrary established. When they persisted after his warning, but not until, he asked if the accused had been in the rebellion. When told 'yes', that set him off:

> ...the Duke in a speech of near half an hour laid open the barbarity of the past uncivilised Highlanders, the restraints that had from time to time being [sic] necessary [to] subject [them], the wick[ed]ness of the rebellion, and concluded with showing that no rebell was intitled to a morall good character....[55]

Argyll took the side of the prosecution which had argued that Stewart's private character was irrelevant and that in this situation, only his public character as a rebel was of importance. The Duke's outburst was not outside the scope of what judges could then do and did. Neither was Argyll's final address in sentencing the convicted man. In that, he pointed out that being 'art and part' to this murder and helping Allan Breck Stewart to flee the country (the Court held him to be the murderer), the accused had been traitorous and furthered the disorder of a region which needed peace. This was what came of bad religion, wrong politics, backward social institutions and attitudes which turned men against others merely because they were of another family and clan. There was nothing new or unexpected in what he said save his vehemence. One commentator has called it an angry and bitter speech.[56] From Argyll's view, Stewart deserved his fate under the laws when he was found guilty of being art and part to the murder.[57] One should note that Argyll made no efforts to punish others such as Stewart's son who was surely as guilty. Allan Breck continued to be sought.

The trial shows the Duke taking a passionate view of actions against the government, in this case intimidating and killing a Crown agent and implicitly aiding those who would overthrow the established order. Bringing back the Stuarts, Argyll believed, would lead to tyranny. The British people had been well rid of them in 1688. Highland lawlessness and violence had long been associated in his mind with the barbarity of clan society which he had been trying to change throughout his life. The Duke was not ashamed of his remarks and, like the rest of those involved in the trial, was willing to see the trial records published as a counter to the pamphlets from the other side.[58] Argyll seems not to have edited his speeches, which were reconstructed from the memories of others, but he was willing they should be printed.[59] To the reconstructed record, the defence lawyers also contributed. Most Scots thought the accused had a fair trial even though this jury sat without a break for forty-eight hours. Argyll did later remark that the evidence given in Court had more impact than it seemed to carry on the printed page.[60]

As we have seen, there were other courts in which Argyll appeared or could appear. During 1725 some of his work concerning the Malt Tax Riots was conducted in the courts of the Justices of the Peace and in Quarter Sessions. In his own area, up to 1747, Argyll could have sat as Justiciar of the Western Isles and in the Sheriff and Regality Courts. There is no indication that he did so. There, his Chamberlain, Sheriff-Depute and others conducted business for him as they did in the various baillie courts on his estates. He appears to have been constantly involved in litigation of some sort.

Given his training and experience, it is not surprising to find that Argyll by himself issued warrants, made depositions, ordered commitments, bailed men and did much else. He sometimes offered advice to the governments he served about how to make warrants conform to Scottish usage.[61] Those orders were able to stand what judicial scrutiny and review there was in his world – one in which many would have eagerly pounced on his mistakes. He did some of his own legal business such as drawing up bills of sale and other documents. A power of attorney or a grant of 'ffactory' for Lord Milton was drafted by him in 1724.[62] In the end, he wrote his own will, having gotten a form for one from Milton in the 1730s. His legal experience and knowledge was as great as most of those who served on the courts in which he appeared. He knew the law and also knew that it could be used to effect changes.

II. The Uses of the Laws

Argyll was not backward about using laws to protect Scottish interests. New laws should be enacted to protect Scottish interests and to allow the economy to function better. He sponsored the economic legislation which created the Equivalent Company, the Royal Bank of Scotland, the Board of Trustees and the customs fiddles which helped the linen and tobacco trades. He was not in principle opposed to the efforts to 'civilize' the Highlands after the '45. Law should create the conditions in which a people might thrive. Like any politician who worked to improve his country, Argyll must have read many essays or manuscripts sent to him on such matters.

Among the known pieces were some by Dr. Sir Alexander Cunningham Dick, Bt., an Edinburgh physician and local improver. One of those concerned the repeal of the Scottish law of entails which had been upheld by the Scottish courts. Argyll and many others thought they served few good functions. He wanted an end to entails and was in favour of creating means of breaking them. He had sat on too many House of Lords committees which had had to break them in the interests of the equitable treatment of those whom the entails should have protected. That was a costly business which could be avoided. His opinions differed little from those of many men who sat in the Select Society of Edinburgh and other clubs which debated such issues. Most of them saw entails as curbs on the free use of resources which ought to be available for the development of the country. Entails restricted the freedom of present occupiers by precluding the full use of the capitals represented by the landed estates they tied up. They diminished the credit available in a poor country. They tied up funds needed by the living for many reasons not all of which could be anticipated. A Scottish bill ending entails was drafted in 1758 by Lord Kames and Sir Alexander Cunningham Dick and perhaps Alexander Tait, W.S. The Duke and Sir Alexander discussed it as they may have again in 1759. It was also debated by the Select Society of Edinburgh.[63] Argyll discussed the matter with Lords Hardwicke and Mansfield. They thought that the best way to make Scots sensible of the burden of the laws was to see them strictly enforced. That would lead, they hoped, to a general willingness to see them repealed. With more sensible policies with regard to the use of resources, Scotland would improve at a faster rate.[64] It did not happen in his Lordship's lifetime. Other legal changes to improve the economy are discussed below.

Chapter 11

Ilay and the Arts

I. Ilay's Buildings

Perhaps the most interesting aspects of Lord Ilay's involvement with the arts is how minimal it was. He was willing to be fashionable but he was generally not a trend-setter. Indeed, regarding most arts, he was a bit of a philistine very different from his friends Lord Hervey or Robert Walpole or from his brother, the 2nd Duke. Ilay cared little for most arts unless they had a utilitarian dimension. But, like most great noblemen, he was a builder. He patronized painters in London and in Scotland. His favourite art was gardening, then afforded a higher status than it has now. He was also known for his collection of porcelains and small *objets d'art*. Despite his love of books, he was not a notable supporter of authors.

It is unclear when Ilay first began to think seriously about architecture but it may have been in c.1715-1717 when Colin Campbell designed a house described in plates dedicated to Ilay and his brother the Duke.[1] The architect sought to acknowledge and flatter the leaders of his name, from whom he probably expected patronage. Ilay subscribed for two copies of Campbell's *Vitruvius Britannicus* (1717-1725). Around 1717, his Lordship may have intended to make something of Cane Wood [Kenwood] House on Hampstead Heath (see below p. 384, n. 28).[2] From at least 1724 until the end of his life in 1761, the Earl was constantly building.

The Earl's first known involvement with building came at Marble Hill House where, in 1724, as one of Henrietta Howard's trustees, Ilay handled the purchase and accounts of the property for Mrs. Howard, mistress of the Prince of Wales and later George II.[3] Her five-bay, three-story house was probably designed by the Earl of Burlington but it was built by Roger Morris between 1724 and 1729.[4] Morris belonged to a family of architects and builders then working in the Twickenham area in which many villas were being erected.[5] He was adept at working in Palladian, Gothic, and 'the Chinese style'. Morris became Ilay's favourite architect and builder. The architect was also an intellectual who could solve practical problems and was *au courant* with fashionable trends in garden design. Ilay employed Morris from 1728 until shortly before the architect died in 1749. He was then succeeded by his son James.

Marble Hill House is a wonderfully light and airy Palladian mansion. Some of its original decoration was Chinese in style and today, as in the eighteenth century, it houses a collection of Chinese and other porcelains. Its garden, was built by Charles Bridgeman who was associated with the Royal Family, Lord Bathurst, Jonathan Swift, John Gay and Alexander Pope.[6] The garden would have introduced Ilay to

Bridgeman and probably to Batty Langley who wrote on gardens and tree planting. Langley was a favourite of Charles Lennox, 2nd Duke of Richmond, another of Ilay's friends in Mrs. Howard's circle.[7] Lord Ilay may not have had great architectural taste himself but he came to know a lot about construction and had friends who could guide him in tasteful building.

Marble Hill House was close to Whitton where Ilay built his own rather plain three-bay Palladian villa, Whitton House (c.1728-1738). It is not known who designed that house. Mary Cosh, on the evidence provided by W. A. Eden, attributed the plans to Morris. Joseph Rykwert believed that the house was first designed by Roger Morris[8] and Henry Herbert, 9th Earl of Pembroke, but that the design was later modified by James Gibbs.[9] Roger Morris certainly built Whitton House which may well have resembled Marble Hill in its airiness and lightness.

Whitton House (or Place) was a three-story Greek cross about forty five feet square with each side having a pedimented projection. Its rather severe unornamented frontage was flanked by screening walls which formed the back of the office courtyard at the entrance to the house (see Plate 6).[10] It was likely to have had about a dozen rooms with guests accommodated in the first floor of the nearby Greenhouse.[11] Whitton was decorated with silk wall-hangings, a lot of porcelain and displays of natural history objects, arms and other things interesting to Ilay. As a building, it was notable for the amount of space devoted to Ilay's personal interests and pursuits.

The interior was described by Sir John Clerk in 1733: 'after a dinner which consisted of 12 dishes of meat & a desert of sweat meats...[I] was entertain'd with a sight of his Losp's curiosities, these consisted of books old china natural curiosities as shells & fossils.[12]   Odd swords & Guns & c.'[13] What is notable here is the emphasis on 'natural curiosities' since those do not figure prominently elsewhere.

About thirty years later, it was described again by Henrietta Pye:

[Whitton is] ... a regular handsome Building: There is on the Ground Floor one fine well proportioned Room, where stands a Chinese Pagoda of Mother of Pearl, of exquisite Workmanship; at the upper End of it is a Collection of China, consisting of the greatest curiosities in Porcelaine: in the Next Room is a beautiful Collection of Butterflies and other Insects, and also Drawings of Birds, Fishes, and Fruits colour'd and highly finish'd. The upper Floor is in the Chinese Taste; a withdrawing Room hung with fine India Paper, the Curtains and Chairs of painted Taffeta; next to that is a Bed Chamber in the same Manner, with the most elegant Taffeta Bed, and a Palampour [bed cover] of the same: On each side of the great Room below stairs, is a long Gallery, in one of which are all of the Instruments which the Duke used in his Mechanical and Chymical Experiments; and along the opposite Side, are a Set of Admirable Drawings; the other is filled with Books and Drawings also.[14]

If the library room in 1767 went the length of the large room, it would have been about forty feet in length and probably fifteen feet wide. It and other principal rooms had ceilings painted with grotesques by Adrien de Clermont.[15] The house pleased Ilay whose butterflies were not emblems of vanity but contributed to his obvious delight in colour and the rich diversity of the natural world. Whitton survived in some fashion until its demolition in 1847.[16]

James Gibbs, by the mid-1720s a well-known architect with something of a specialty in gardens and garden ornaments, also worked at Whitton. A genteel Roman Catholic from Scotland, Gibbs was employed at the Board of Ordnance and by Duke John as his architect at Sudbrook Lodge (1728). Gibbs too designed in Palladian, Gothic and Chinese styles. For Ilay, he designed the stuccoed brick Greenhouse which Sir John Clerk saw in 1727 and probably the Gothic volary or aviary begun in 1725 and completed by 1727.[17] It is believed that he was also responsible for the eighty-foot-high Gothic Tower which was erected between Sir John Clerk's visits in 1733 and 1748. The Tower was the most notable architectural feature at Whitton. Triangular in shape, this folly was a five- or six-story, battlemented edifice which had an observation room with furniture in the Chinese taste designed by Ilay.[18] From its top, viewers had fine prospects. Somewhere, it held a huge Chinese gong. Gibbs' other structures at Whitton included the octagonal temple, a Chinese temple in a lake with a bridge to it, the volary, and possibly some service buildings. As we have seen above, he seems also to have erected the cenotaphs to Michelangelo, Bernini, Wren and to himself and the sundial on the Greenhouse terrace.[19]

The Gothic touches Ilay gave to Whitton show him indulging himself with a new fashion, just as were Pope and Lord Bathurst, whose Alfred's Hall at Cirencester Park dates from about the same time.[20] Sir John Clerk's aesthete son, James, wrote to his father from Rome in April 1733: 'the modern architecture is now turned into the gothick manner of the most polite taste'.[21] Ilay may well have tried to catch a new trend.

After the building of Whitton Place, Ilay seems not to have had further dealings with the Pembroke-Burlington set but relied for architectural advice in England on Morris and Gibbs and in Scotland on Alexander McGill and William Adam. There is no evidence of a break with Burlington and his set but politics and aesthetics may have gotten in the way. Burlington, Pembroke and their friends were mostly Tories who opposed Walpole's Ministry. They preferred classic and Palladian forms. Ilay had no long-term aesthetic commitments of that sort and was unlikely to keep such company when it seemed that his relation with Sir Robert Walpole was to be a long one.

While Whitton was under construction, Ilay began his next building venture at The Whim. Sometime in 1730, the Earl wrote to Andrew Fletcher, Lord Milton, SCJ, 'prepare me a plan of my house which I shall revise here & consult with the learned'.[22] Like Ilay, Milton had many valuable architecture books some of which were lent (permanently as it turned out) to William Adam before 1740.[23] That Ilay trusted his aide to sketch out a house shows that they both thought they could do so with some competence. Only after Ilay and Milton had made their plans did his Lordship seek the help of the 'learned'– probably Alexander McGill and William Adam in Scotland and Morris and Gibbs in England.

McGill was the brother of the surgeon-apothecary who probably treated Ilay's wounds at Sherrifmuir and whom the Earl had wished to make King's Apothecary in 1725 and consulted about an ague in 1730.[24] He had been the partner of James Smith, the Surveyor for the Board of Ordnance in Scotland. When Smith was sacked in 1719,

McGill had been saved from disaster by being made in 1720 Edinburgh's city architect for life.[25] He was not a particularly notable or modern architect but he was one with much experience who worked somewhat in the manner of Sir William Bruce (d. 1710) with whom he may have trained. McGill and Smith had done a considerable amount of building for the government, the Campbells, their relatives and friends. McGill had worked on notable places like Dun and Yester Houses.

Plans for Whim House were drawn up by Milton before March 1730. Ilay changed details of the design; they were further amended by William Adam,[26] after conversations with David Scott of Scotstarvit in the summer of 1730.[27] Construction began in 1731 but Adam made more changes in its design in 1732. That year he was asked by Ilay's neighbour, Major Thomas Cochrane (later 8th Earl of Dundonald, from whom Ilay had bought The Whim), to help the mason get the first storey put up correctly. He was again consulted about the chimneys in 1733.[28] Adam's plasterers were working there in 1733-34. While Adam supervised the building of The Whim (1731-4), it was built by a mason from Crail, William Annan.[29] By 1734, Adam had done a lot of work for the political managers of Scotland and Ilay probably helped him to contracts with the government, town councils, and other corporations which he could influence. McGill and Adam also worked at Brunstane House for Lord Milton in 1733-34. When McGill died in 1734, Adam became Lord Milton's and Ilay's Scottish architect.[30] Until his death in 1748, Adam remained Ilay's and the government's principal architect in Scotland and was succeeded by his sons, John, Robert and James.

Whim House was another three-bay neoclassic structure with a pitched roof built over a cellar open to sloping ground at its back. It was considerably smaller than the house now on the property which extends the original house on all sides. Whim House seems not to have been finished until 1737. When it was done, The Whim is said to have had nine rooms, a servants' hall and other basement and garret rooms housing servants.[31] A library wing was added by John Adam in 1759 suggesting that the collection of books had outgrown its upstairs room. The House was taxed on thirty-one windows in 1761.[32] The furnishings of 'the farm' included mahogany furniture, chairs made of beech-wood and fir, fine china and engraved plates.[33] Ilay was here living simply.

The Whim had a fairly elaborate 'Court of Offices' containing a pavilion, stables, a wash house, possibly a kitchen/oven, dairy, hen house, barn and byre.[34] The pavilion may also have housed the laboratory built in the early 1740s. Among the out-buildings were either a crenellated Gothic or a classical dovecot designed by Morris.[35] Morris also sent plans for an oven house. Both the Earl and Lord Milton contributed to those designs. There was as at least one Chinese bridge and some Chinese fencing.[36] 'The Countess of Pigsburgh's Apartment' in the gardens was, as at Whitton, an ornamental 'necessary house'.[37] The garden well had a classical cover.[38]

In London, the Earl lived in a rather small house at 24 Great Marlborough Street from 1711 until after 1737. He acquired title to his home in 1732. When Sir John Clerk visited it in 1733, he described it as having 'several good Rooms & amongst the rest a very Large one where he keeps his Library & all manner of Curiosities particularly Mathematical Instruments'.[39] At some point, the Earl may have built a free-standing library in his backyard but no description of that has survived. If one was built, it disappeared when his larger library was erected.

In 1737, the Earl began to build what came to be called Argyll House [or Argyll Buildings] on land leased to him by his brother. The Duke was developing the area by cutting a new street, Argyll Street, through his garden and leasing the land to builders. Ilay's new house fronted on Argyll Street but was set back from it by about thirty-five feet if the map showing it is drawn to scale. That gave the house a forecourt possessed by none of the other properties on the street. It is not known who the architect for this was and it may principally have been Ilay himself.[40] The builder was Roger Morris to whom large payments were made throughout its period of construction. This was a well-lit west-east house described as follows:

[T. H.] Shepherd's view shows that the front was three storeys high [facing west], with six windows widely and evenly spaced in each upper storey, and the doorway in the third opening from the left, or north end, of the front. (On the evidence of one of the Inveraray plans the doorway had originally been in the first opening from the left.) Apart from the doorcase, composed of an architrave flanked by plain jambs with consoles supporting a triangular pediment, and the frieze-band, cornice and blocking-course below the attic storey windows, the front appears to have been quite plain. The forecourt, flanked on the north and south by the side walls of the houses fronting to Argyll Street, was screened by a wall broken at each end by plain iron gates, hung on rusticated piers, and in the middle was a blocked-up doorway, with a simple entablature head resting on long-and-short rusticated jambs.[41]

Using the description and dimensions of several rooms taken from the plans, one can estimate that the front block of the house facing Argyll Street was about 60 feet across the front and 24 feet deep. It seems to have had at the south end a drawing room of 27 feet x 21 feet entered from a parlour which was about 19 feet x 21 feet beyond which was a hall 21 feet x 11 feet. The principal staircase was behind the parlour and began an ell which ran to the east and contained two other rooms about 20 feet wide and of unknown length but probably not more that 22 feet. Behind them was a closet and a service stair case. Behind the hall to the north were the stables and coach house over which there were also rooms. The house in 1862 had a banqueting room of 43 feet x 31 feet [?21 feet]. If Ilay had one in the same place, it is likely to have been on the first floor over the two rooms in the ell and perhaps a bit of the stables. That would have made it easily accessible from the great stair and not too distant from the kitchen[42] and the service stairs. It was still far enough away to make the Earl interested in the problem of keeping his food hot. The Argyll sauceboat, which he invented, addressed that concern.[43] Where his London laboratory was is not clear but it would have vented outside to minimize the odours from chemical experiments.[44] The upper floors would have provided ample room for guests and some of his servants. In 1742-43 Morris designed the new library room added to Argyll House.

About the time he built his new library, his Lordship demolished parts or all of his old house at 24 Great Marlborough St. and a bit later, in 1747, tore down his house at No. 23. The demolitions provided a garden for his Mrs. Williams for whom he built c.1750 a house at No.10 Argyll Place. That abutted the newly opened garden space.

Two doors down was a house which he purchased in 1738 and left to her when he died in 1761. Mrs. Williams thus had a house and an income property adjoining his own in a reasonably fashionable area.

By the time Ilay, now 3rd Duke of Argyll, came to embark upon the building of Inveraray Castle in 1743, he knew a lot about architecture and construction. He came to his new project with a taste for Gothic structures which had been formed a generation earlier and shared with his brother, who c.1720 had Sir John Vanbrugh draw up a Gothic plan for the Castle.[45] At Inveraray, the attractions of Gothic were somewhat different than the ones they had at Whitton. His Gothic castle was neither merely ornamental nor did it symbolize noble liberties and freedoms. Rather, it alluded to his status as the head of a clan in what many saw as a semi-barbarous part of Britain. Contemporaries, such as Lord Kames, thought the castle fit a landscape having a 'profuse variety of wild and grand objects'.[46] The Duke's castle contributed to a sublime landscape. Inveraray Castle had battlemented towers, not the present ones with conical tops which allude to a later more civilized period in Scottish history.[47] His castle was a proper setting for a Scottish chieftain living in a half-feudal and still violent society. Propriety and fashion, dictated the design. The foundation stone was laid in October 1746 and had an inscription which flattered Cumberland but was also ironic:

CAL. OCT. ANNO DOM. MDCCXLVI POSUIT A.A. DUX
GULIELMUS CUMBRIAE DUX NOBI HAEC ITIA FECIT.

Argyll's cousin, General Campbell of Mamore, said the inscription might grace any of the 'work houses in Glasgow or Edinburgh'.[48] The Castle was under construction from 1744 until after the end of the Duke's life.

The architects employed on this project – Captain Dougal Campbell, HM Engineer for Scotland;[49] Roger Morris and William Adam – were all men with whom Argyll had long dealt. Campbell and Adam had already designed Gothic buildings and all of them shared his interest in gardening. In the end, the Castle was mostly designed by Roger Morris but built by William and John Adam. Argyll's own contribution to the design of this place were the plans to re-situate and rebuild the town of Inveraray and to make the gardens run into the romantic park and that into the waste which surrounded the Castle and town. The story of the building of the Castle has been magnificently told by Ian Lindsay and Mary Cosh; it need not be repeated here.

There was also a public dimension to this project. Much of his own building capital came from his compensation for the heritable jurisdictions he had given up in 1747. A public payment was being put to a semi-public use, that of providing work in a restive area where employment tended to make resentful Highlanders just a bit more accepting of the *status quo*. It benefited both him and the country. During its construction, the Duke was putting into the West Highland economy about as much money as the government gave it in subsidies. Purchases and employment provided benefits to men in Glasgow and the West Highlands. One indicator of how important that was are the bills for grain imported to feed his workers. In the winter of 1757 Milton ordered 800 bols of [oat]meal for Inveraray and was going to order more bear [a kind of barley] for Campbeltown and Kintyre.[50] Work helped to stabilise the area but the principal political benefit accrued to Argyll.

Argyll's patronage of William Adam by 1745 had made him Scotland's leading private and public architect and builder. He was in charge at The Whim, at Inveraray and at Rosneath Castle where the Duke made alterations mostly completed by 1757.[51] When Adam died in 1748, his sons carried on the family business in Scotland and continued to work at Argyll's projects and to receive government contracts.[52] John, Robert and James Adam enjoyed the Duke's hospitality at Inveraray and at Whitton. The Duke also helped Robert and James, after extended grand tours, to establish themselves in London. The Duke arranged for all Robert's Italian marbles and casts to be brought into the country duty free. Indeed, Argyll became one of Robert and James's early English supporters and recommended them in 1758 to his old friend George Bubb Dodington, to the Earl of Leicester and to others.[53] His patronage of Robert and James Adam helped them but they built nothing for him in England.

Argyll's buildings did not influence architectural taste in England but in Scotland they had some importance. After his time, romantic 'Georgian Gothic' would be more often built in Scotland with one of the largest and earliest structures, Culzean Castle, being built by Robert Adam for a family with many connexions to the Inveraray Campbells. There was also more construction using Chinese motifs. The Duke's plans for the new town of Inveraray and similar work done at Campbeltown, mainly by John Adam and his bothers, had some influence on later planned towns in Scotland.[54]

One suspects that the Duke was influential in other things. He was interested in having modern conveniences which other rich men copied. Inveraray had indoor water closets whose wastes were flushed into Loch Fyne. Inveraray Castle had at least one Franklin stove by 1757. Such an efficient heater would have impressed others whom he wanted to see it (see below p. 337). He also knew much about the making of plaster, putty and cements,[55] and about techniques of construction.[56] That knowledge would have been shared with others. Argyll's need to understand and his willingness to become involved in the details of the works underway was exceptional. He learned from James Morris how to join two long beams so that they would not be weakened. Morris's three solutions were illustrated with models added to the Duke's collection.[57] The carpenters who worked for him would have taken such innovations elsewhere.

The Duke's Whitton, Peebles-shire and Inveraray buildings cannot be separated from the landscapes in which they were set. Those pointed to current and later developments in landscape architecture. His garden at Whitton was a mix of formal and informal elements as one might expect to find on the estate of someone who had admired Dutch and French gardens but was also familiar with freer English ones then being designed by William Kent and others in the Burlington circle. Ilay and they would also have been quite aware of the order in disorder of *sharawaggi*.[58] Whitton had a Chinese Summer House and both there and at Whim and Inveraray there were Chinese decorative fences or other features of that sort. Ilay delighted in the colours and the textures which older gardens lacked. The Whim was similar with gardens and parkland being visually continuous. The example of the groomed landscape around Inveraray would be followed by others seeking to create more open, 'natural', even sublime, landscape settings for their houses.[59] Sir John Dalrymple's well-known *Essays on Different Natural Situations of Gardens* (1774) contained a laudatory account of Inveraray as the Duke and his architects had re-made it. Men like Lord Kames and Sir John also fostered the improvement of agriculture, reforestation projects, a liking for romantic Highland scenery and gardening styles which integrated romantic backgrounds into the parks and gardens.[60] They learned something from the Duke's work at Inveraray. In Scottish – even British – gardening, Ilay, was a more significant figure than he was as a builder.[61]

II. Ilay and the Visual Artists

Ilay patronized noted architects but he was less close to his painters. Like most aristocrats, he had vanity enough to want his portrait painted. Ilay patronized Scottish painters just as he employed Scots like Gibbs. It was what a politician did who wished to gratify his friends. In London, both brothers gave support to William Aikman when that portrait painter moved to the city in 1720.[62] Aikman was a well-connected Scottish gentleman and a good painter who quickly established a London reputation, partly by painting Campbells. His portrait of Ilay (see Plate 2) was done in c.1723.[63] When Aikman was joined in London in 1722 by John Smibert, neither brother aided Smibert nor was painted by him.[64] He worked more often for their foes than for their friends. Other painters who may have worked for Ilay are not known before 1744 when Allan Ramsay began to be patronized by the Duke.[65]

Ramsay painted at least five portraits of Ilay one of which is a great picture. Commissioned in 1747 by the Glasgow Town Council and finished in 1749 (see frontispiece), it was hung in the Glasgow Town Hall but is now in the Kelvingrove Art Gallery. It shows a relaxed Duke arrayed in the robes of his highest judicial office with his right hand on a volume of Sir George Mackenzie's works published in 1716. It is open at the page containing the advocate's speech made for the Duke's great-grandfather at his treason trial in 1661.[66] This portrait makes a statement about religious freedom, justice and the dangers of tyranny. It suggests this wise-looking head of the highest criminal court of Scotland, would not allow such a miscarriage of justice to be committed in his court. Smaller copies of this and other Ramsay portraits may have come from the painter's studio. This version of Allan Ramsay's 1749 portrait of Argyll was also engraved in reverse and sold by the Foulis Academy of Glasgow. The Foulis brothers were not only printers but between 1753 and 1775 ran an art school in the precincts of Glasgow University.[67] Argyll supported their work which he is likely to have seen in an economic, not an artistic, light.[68] The engraving of him (?1755-1757) is unsigned but attributed to François Aveline, the engraving master at Academy. It may be by one of his students.[69]

Ramsay was an accomplished scholar and writer on politics as well as an artist. He was probably the Mr. Ramsay who sometimes visited at Whitton to share the Duke's Sunday dinner as he had done at Inveraray for some time in 1748. Argyll, in the 1750s, introduced Ramsay to the 3rd Earl of Bute who brought the painter to the attention of George III who made him Painter to the King.[70] Ramsay's vogue in Britain owed much to Argyll's patronage. Aside from four later Ramsays, the only other portrait the Duke might have commissioned, is an anonymous plaster *bas relief* said to be of Lord Ilay on a house near Whitton Park in 1972.[71] What Argyll's relationship was to some others who painted or engraved pictures of him is unclear.[72]

Ilay seems to have had little or no interest in pictures other than portraits and, perhaps his ceiling paintings at Whitton. In Scotland, Ilay employed members of the Norie family to decorate two of his Scottish houses.[73] James Norie (1684-1757), the most notable of the Edinburgh landscape painters and decorators of his time, worked at The Whim (1730-1742, 1750-53) and at Inveraray (1746). The Whim had some decorative over-mantle paintings by Norie who also painted the vestibule and the arms on Argyll's carriage. Ilay had few paintings in his houses and the only painting ever known to have delighted him he paid £20 for in 1759 and kept in London. It was a fanciful oil painting of Inveraray by Agostino Brunias (1759). It had been worked up from Robert Adam's descriptions and sketches by a man who never saw the place.[74] Its novelty and its glorification of the Duke's achievement were what counted. His brother had a fine collection of paintings but Ilay was not interested in paintings.[75]

There are many other pictures of the Duke but it is not clear that they involved Argyll's patronage. Some are copies of, or after, Aikman or Ramsay and celebrate the succession of Ilay to the dukedom in 1743. It is unlikely that the 1744 mezzotint by Richard Cooper, after Aikman but with the details considerably reworked (Plate 3), was commissioned.[76] Ramsay himself did a well known 1749 portrait which is shown on the banknotes of the Royal Bank of Scotland (see Plate 6) and was later used by Thomas Chambers who has aged the Duke for his popular miniature of c.1750 (see Plate 10). John Faber did one in 1744 after Ramsay (see Plate 7). That too was probably a commercial venture on his part. William Woollett may have been commissioned to do the garden views, one of which includes the Duke (see Plates 8 and 9) but they were also part of a set of such prints sold commercially. Argyll is unlikely to have paid for them. None of those artists appear in his Coutts 'Out book'. Whoever else painted for Ilay remains to be found. For a man whose image was so common, his Lordship did little for the artists. Sir John Clerk's observation that painting did not figure greatly in his list of intellectual interests was correct.

Among his books, there were very few which dealt with painting. Some, like Vasari's *Lives of the Artists*, found a place because it was a notable and early set of biographies, not because he was especially interested in the work of the men to whom it was devoted.

III. The Duke and Other Fine Arts

Ilay also had little interest in music. When many of his friends and his brother subscribed to G. B. Buonocini's Cantate in 1721/22, he did not – and is not known to have subscribed to any later music. He did have an organ built at Inveraray by the instrument maker, Alexander Cumming, but Cumming had never before built an organ.[77] His Lordship put his music books in the mathematics section of his library. They were just another part of applied mathematics.[78]

The Duke had interests in some other arts thought of as more minor. He possessed gem and numismatic collections and over eighty books needed to understand them.[79]

Half were folios. His principal use of those was probably to help him visualize and date ancient history and the people who made it. Such materials interested others for those reasons. Medals and coins supplied motifs for decorations, for seals and whatnots. They were often struck from beautiful and finely cut dies. He would have admired the artistry with which they had been made and the dexterity which had produced the cut stones.[80] His intaglios were numerous and were lent to others so they could cast sulphur impressions of them as did Allan Ramsay the poet. Ramsay was unlikely to have been the only one who cast sulphur impressions of his Lordship's gems and intaglios. From Ramsay's account of doing this, we can infer that the Earl may have been able to cast them too.[81] It is not known what became of this collection but it was said to be sizable and would have included originals and copies made by modern jewellers or gem cutters. Some of it had been bought at auctions such as that of the effects of the Earl of Stair at which Ilay paid £245.10.0 for 'jewels'.[82] The term included things like intaglios.

The Earl of Ilay was a trend-setter in one decorative art. He was a noted collector of china and porcelain. His collections were admired by many and were valuable. In 1725, his correspondence notes the purchase of a 'China bason' valued by another connoisseur at 5 guineas – more cash than he paid many of his servants for a year's work. When, in 1733, Sir John Clerk admired the china collection at Whitton House, Ilay had enough to divide between that residence and his other in London. In 1755, Lady Mary Wortley Montagu noted his liking for china and his good taste in buying it. Three years later, she opined that his purchases 'had made all China (more or less) Fashionable' and had raised its price in Britain.[83] Argyll was eager to see Scots make porcelain and expended some effort to see that they did. If current scholarship is correct, by the 1740s he was trying to have porcelain made in Scotland. His patronage of Alexander Lind's pottery at Preston Pans near Edinburgh attests to that. There beauty and usefulness met and resulted in the delicate A-marked porcelain probably decorated by or to the designs of Richard Cooper.[84]

Lord Ilay, like his friend George Bubb Dodington, was interested in furniture design and interior decoration. We know Ilay designed some furniture, fussed over his richly hung interiors and commissioned carved wainscotting and mouldings and more of the latter in plaster. His rooms in Scotland could not depend wholly on Scots since there was too little of this fine work done in the country. William Adam's plasterers were mostly Italians and the silk hangings were probably French imports. What survives are the descriptions of rather gaudy rooms.

Ilay was more interested in practical arts and was sometimes approached by artisans catering to the needs of craftsmen or working as decorators. In 1759, a Miss Ann McLean tried to secure £300 from him to set up an enterprise to clean, touch up and varnish pictures and to gild and japan other objects and to dye cloth. She flattered him by saying, 'it is universally known Your Grace inclines to promote all useful Arts'.[85] There are no indications that he helped her or others who were not mechanics. Mechanics and wrights were patronized but most did not count as artists.

What else figured in Ilay's aesthetic life remains to be found.

IV. Ilay and the Literary Men

Argyll had a rather conventional outlook on literature. He bought many books but neither aided nor patronized many English or Scottish authors. He knew his Cicero well and probably read other ancient authors as often as he did modern men of letters. Not much recently written by Englishmen or Scots was in his library. He preferred older poets and dramatists. The Duke acquired older works, such as those of Chaucer and most of the more notable sixteenth- and seventeenth-century English poets, but he owned relatively few books by those who came later. Addison, Akenside, Gay, Glover, Pope, Swift, Samuel Wesley, Edward Young, even Stephen Duck are there but not many others. His tastes tended to be classical or neoclassical and did not get much beyond what John Dryden would have approved. The Duke read some criticism. Among the critics whom he possessed were Dryden, the 3rd Earl of Shaftesbury, Joseph Addison, Alexander Pope, John Dennis and Francis Hutcheson. Little was by Scots although David Hume was there. Being a sometime friend of Pope, Gay and Swift had not mattered much to his book collection.

There was little on his shelves to suggest that the Duke was much interested in the Scottish poets writing during his lifetime and less to suggest that he rewarded them. Among recent Scottish poets, he had works by James Thomson, but not much by other modern Scottish poets. That is not too surprising. Thomson, David Mallet, John Armstrong and others were patronized by Squadrone men or those attached to other groups in Opposition to Walpole. Ilay did not favour such men. Allan Ramsay sr. was different. His political leanings were sentimentally Jacobitical but he was also a bookseller who regarded the Duke as a friend. The Duke enjoyed his company and may well have owned his books because they had been gifts. Or, the Duke's interest in Ramsay, like his interest in 'Blind Hary the Minstrel's' *The Bruce* (c.1375) or John Barbour's *Wallace* (c.1490), may have been more antiquarian and historical and not in the poetry. Ramsay sometimes addressed his contemporaries in the language they all spoke but which for Argyll must have seemed somewhat foreign.

Late in his career, Argyll acquired a few works by young Scottish men of letters. William Wilkie sent his poems to the Duke who in the end sanctioned Wilkie's appointment to the chair of natural philosophy at St Andrews.[86] Wilkie had long-standing interests in science and he was familiarly known by the sobriquet, 'Potato Wilkie', a nickname likely to have been noticed by the Duke.[87]

Ilay liked the theatre and went regularly to London theatres and was held to be a good judge of plays.[88] He is not known to have attended operas. His library held most of the notable dramatists of the seventeenth century in French and English but he is known to have helped only three playwrights. The Earl subscribed to two sets of Colley Cibber's works in 1721 but is not known to have helped other English playwrights.[89] He may have desired to see a playhouse in Edinburgh since Allan Ramsay thought him a fit man to appeal to in 1737 when thwarted in his efforts to start a theatre in the city. He sought Ilay's protection and asked for the position of Master the Revels in Scotland.[90] His qualifications included not only his poems and editing of old Scottish verse but his ballad opera, 'The Gentle Shepherd' (1725). Ramsay was banking on Ilay's interest and his power but the year was not a good one for the Earl to go against the pious wishes of many in the country.[91] Later he aided John Home.

He liked the man and may have enjoyed Home's tragedies because they were also history plays. By 13 November 1754, the Duke had read Home's *Douglas* in draft and was 'very much pleas'd with it'.[92] Two years later, the Duke encouraged Home in his 'resolution of bringing Douglas upon the Edinburgh & Dublin stage at the same time'. Argyll was thinking about writing to General Henry Seymour Conway, then in Ireland as Secretary to the Lord Lieutenant, to ask him to use his influence with the Irish theatre managers to have it staged.[93] When his advice with respect to Edinburgh turned out badly and the Kirk moved to censure Home and his Moderate Party friends, the Duke supported them. Home reported that he had 'spoke to me in general expressing his dissatisfaction with the conduct of the brethren & that they would find themselves a little mistaken' as they sought to censure the Rev. Alexander Carlyle for his part in the business. Home went on to say that MPs and other Scottish gentlemen were organizing to quash the actions of the stiff-necked in the General Assembly.[94] After Home moved to London in 1757, he sometimes dined with the Duke. All this may not say much for the Argyll's critical judgment but it was no worse than that of most of the Scottish *literati*, including David Hume and Adam Smith. Helping John Home was also helping a political ally and sending a message to clerics with whom Ilay had long struggled. It was not just encouraging drama.

Argyll seems no more generous to prose writers. Most of his prose books were serious reads although there were some novels – mostly from the century's earlier years. He owned novels by Simon Tyssot de Patot, the Chevalier Ramsay, Alain René Lesage, the Abbé Prévost, and Mme. Riccobonni. He probably had met Ramsay, Prévost and Mme Riccobonni. Their works were as notable on the shelves as were those of their English counterparts.

Argyll's usual reading in *belles lettres* belonged to the categories of history, travels, economic pamphlets and journals like Samuel Johnson's *Rambler*. The Duke liked history and read a good deal, both ancient and modern. This is borne out by the books held in his library, by the earlier letter to his nephew (see p. 274) and by the comments of others. He may have bought the early volumes of Hume's *History of England* (1754, 1759, 1761) but they are not listed in the *Catalogus*; neither is William Robertson's *History of Scotland* (1759). There is no evidence that he aided any other historian although John Campbell may have worked in the library.

Quite a few Scots jostled others on the miscellaneous shelves. The poet John Armstrong; John Cockburn, a naval surgeon, William Douglas MD of Boston, Professor David Fordyce of Aberdeen, David Hume, Sir William Keith, William Lauder, the banker John Law, merchants like Patrick Lindsay and Ebenezer McCulloch, James Wallace, the Scottish traveller, and Robert Wallace all found places. With the exception of Lauder, a classicist and critic, their works were travels, history or economic tracts. The men were mostly dead by 1740. Whether Hume sent books other than his *Essays* to the Duke is unknown but we do know that he conveyed to Argyll Adam Smith's *Theory of Moral Sentiments* in (1759).[95] Smith was on closer terms with the Duke to whom he owed his teaching job at Glasgow[96] and whom he visited in both Edinburgh and at Inveraray.[97] Hume got no university posts.[98] Among the missing Scots were Lord Kames, and most of the learned judges and university men appointed between c.1724 and 1761. Argyll must have had more presentation copies than appear in his *Catalogus*. Only five of the men mentioned here received patronage from Argyll and it was not given principally for literary accomplishments. Argyll viewed most of his patronage through political and utilitarian lenses. His political associates had on their side few good writers and artists after 1720. It would have been natural to have tried to buy more with literary patronage but he seems to have left that to others. Still, he was expected to be a patron and enjoyed the recognition he received.

Robert and James Adam thought of dedicating to Argyll their great work on the palace of Diocletian since, as they said, dedications were 'flattery on his favorite way'. They assumed that they would be rewarded. Indeed, in the same letter, James said that William Wilkie, after dedicating to the Duke his epic poem, *The Epigoniad* (1757) had been told that 'he should have the first professorship that fell' which turned out to be the natural philosophy chair at the United College in St Andrews University.[99] That dedication repaid Argyll's past promotion of Wilkie's career in the Kirk. He got the Chair of Natural Philosophy at St Andrews in 1759 but that gift is as likely to have been prompted by his political services and his interests in agriculture and science as by his verses.[100] A generation earlier, Ilay had been the recipient of a dedication from Archibald Campbell whom he had helped to place in the Ecclesiastical History Chair at St Andrews. The Rev. Mr. Campbell dedicated to the Earl *An Enquiry into the Original of Moral Virtue* (London, 1733), a work which scandalized many because it found the origins of virtue in our self interest. Clerics like John Home, Wilkie, and Campbell seem to have been rare and only three English writers have been found.[101] What is also perhaps a bit surprising is that, once he became Duke, he had no official bard or Gaelic poet to celebrate his accomplishments although they were noticed by at least one Gaelic writer.[102]

Several works by mathematicians and scientists were dedicated to Ilay and the 2nd Duke of Argyll.[103] Among those who dedicated and sent books to Ilay were three professors of mathematics from Glasgow, Edinburgh and Aberdeen – Robert Simson, Colin Maclaurin, and Robert Stewart. Another dedication came from Robert Smith, the Cambridge Professor of Astronomy. Ilay had books given to him by medical men such as Robert Whytt, one of the foremost physiologists of the time for whom Ilay secured a share of the £100 a year given to the Edinburgh medical professors as Physicians to the King in Scotland. The medical thesis of Francis Home (noticed above, p. 121) was dedicated to Ilay. Home, after Argyll's death, was made a professor at Edinburgh through the interest of his cousin, Lord Milton. Dr. John Hill, a protégé of Lord Bute, whom Argyll entertained at Whitton, dedicated to the Duke an engraved plate prepared for his *System of Botany*.[104] There were undoubtedly more such gifts but the records found do not indicate a distinguished record of literary patronage. In all, only sixteen works dedicated to the Duke and about as many subscriptions have been found. More patronage was given by him to university men and to men who could make improvements than to literary figures. And, for some, dedications brought little or nothing. Colen Campbell seems to have gotten only two subscriptions in return for the plates he dedicated to the Earl of Ilay. James Gibbs did no better. Some of the mathematicians who dedicated texts to him are not known to have been rewarded although they may have had earlier favours. Ilay had no very good reputation for fulfilling the promises he had made to those whom he wished to use. That comes out clearly in Lord Grange's discussion of the poor peers whose votes Ilay bought or tried to buy at the peerage election of 1734 (see below pp. 258-9). It was the same with men of letters. How he regarded authors can be inferred from the interesting case of 'singing Sandie' Gordon.

An Aberdonian, Alexander Gordon studied music in Italy and had in London some reputation as a singer and composer. He had taught a bit and co-authored (with Sir John Clerk) an important antiquarian work, *Itinerarium Septentrionale* (1726; supplement 1729). In 1726, he had made some sort of survey for a cross-Scotland canal running from the Kelvin to Carron Water. Three years later, he published the *Lives of [Pope] Alexander VI and [his son] Cesar Borgia* and a translation of Francesco Scipione Maffei's *De amphitheatro*. None of those things made his fortune but they should have interested Ilay. With a wife and growing family, Gordon needed help.

Gordon told Sir John Clerk that he first sought a place from Ilay before or in 1727. The Earl gave him fair words but did nothing. Gordon thought he had

> dealt very cruelly & barbarously with me   Since   not withstanding   I've repeatedly gone to wait on him   Since I've wrote you last   Yet he consistently denys me axcess. So that I fear I've little to depend on even on what he promised of getting me some small settlement: so that if my lord Stair & Montrose my best Friends do not get something done for me I've little to hope from another corner.[105]

Anyone who asked Ilay for a favour could not then seek one from the Earl's political enemies, Stair and Montrose. It was not even prudent to seek things from men with whom Ilay got on. Gordon thought Stair and Montrose had been helpful to him; he needed to repay them. Gordon was naive and no politician.

'Singing Sandie' persisted and thought he stood well with Ilay in 1728. He now wanted to be Geographer Royal but would take a post as Collector of Customs at a port like Alloway.[106] He thought that his Lordship would have made him collector at Alloa when the post was last on offer had they been as they now were. A later letter to Sir John Clerk said Ilay had now promised him a place in the Customs in Scotland. By 13 August, 'Ila is so far softened toward my Interest that he told me himself that ye first Eassy Post that falls in Scotland I may apply to him & he'll obtain it for me & yt I may depend on't — never had said as much & offered it'.[107]

Still, Ilay did nothing while Gordon had been paying for the lying-in of his wife and then for the expenses incurred by the death of their child. He decided to dedicate his book to the Duke of Montrose and the Earl of Stair.[108] That decision taken out of gratitude was not intended as a slight to Ilay but the Earl could only have seen it in that way. Ilay could not realistically give employment to an author who had dedicated a book to his enemies. Gordon started to write a life of Leo X and a comedy.

Subscriptions to *Lives of Alexander VI and Caesar Borgia* (1729) came in slowly and Gordon kept looking for a place but he did not wait on the Earl again until 11 February 1729. Ilay then told him to be patient – as he had been for nine months. The Earl may not yet have known who the dedicatees of the Borgia book would be.

Gordon in something like despair thought he might go to Algiers to work with his cousin who was consul there.[109] When his book on the Borgias came out, he sent specially bound copies to the King, Queen, Prince of Wales and Sir Robert Walpole and those to whom he had dedicated it. None of them gave him anything. Neither did Ilay.[110] On 13 October 1729, Sir John Clerk told him Ilay would fulfil his promises and had said so as had Sir Robert Walpole.[111]

By 3 April 1730, Gordon had seen the error of his ways:

> ... as for Lord Islay, he still does nothing for me, nor   I fear Ever will for I sea my dedicating My History to ye D. of M[ontro]se & L. Stair has for Ever disgusted his Implacable revengeful spirit but ... I could not in honour or Common Gratitude do otherwise.

Gordon now waited for those whom he had honoured to help him.[112] Perhaps knowing he had sought Ilay's help, they too did nothing. Sandy continued to live on tutoring, his writings and hope.

Hope led him to apply again to Ilay and his friends in 1732. He asked Lord Milton but also Robert Dundas of Arniston (a Squadrone man) and others to recommend him for a tutor's post in an Argathelian family.[113] He did not get it. He said 'a certain Great Man' [Ilay] had complained that he had railed against him, which he admitted he had done. If 'that great man would not have people complain, he ought not to give them Cause'. Gordon went on to say that Lord Ilay had even prevailed on Walpole 'to give neither £100', which he felt was owing to him for the canal survey, nor the job he had long sought. Ilay had called him 'impertinant monster'. Gordon believed Ilay had vindictively refused to let Lady Eglinton appoint him tutor to her son.[114] It was five more years before he received an appointment as Secretary to the Governor of South Carolina, an Argathelian placement. He was glad to sail to South Carolina in 1741 as Secretary to Governor Glen. It was a dull place after London but he died in 1754 well off and respected. Gordon's experience was probably not unique.

Ilay was usually slow to reward those who sought his patronage. Those who were loyal and waited patiently often received something. Men of letters living on the margins of the genteel world could not wait; the Earl did not care. Unless they were outstanding men, they came cheap, were replaceable and could be ignored until it was convenient to help them. In 1727-1728 elections and new royal warrants were absorbing Ilay's time. Gordon was a marginal man, the kind who did well in America where men with his talents were rare. With attitudes to literary patronage so politically conditioned, it is not surprising Ilay did not play a more notable role as a Maecenas.

The 3rd Duke of Argyll's record as a patron of the arts illustrate facets of his taste and interests. Those tended to be fashionable but not trend-making except with respect to gardening and porcelain. The arts held little allure for him unless they could be made useful. If his record as a patron depended on what he did for artists, it would be of little interest. It rested instead on the great numbers of other people for whom he found places in Scotland, in England and in the Empire. That subject is treated in Chapter 18.

Part III

The Mature Politician

Plate 7. Duke of Argyll, John Faber after Allen Ramsay (c.1744), National Portrait Gallery, London, with permission of the NPG.

Chapter 12

Organising and Thinking about Improvements, 1722-1727

I. Aims

After the 1722 elections, Ilay consolidated his power in Scotland. By 1728, he had a smooth-running political machine which bore heavily on some. A reaction set in during the 1730s which led to something of a revolt against him and the government. He survived but not without difficulties. This chapter deals with the way in which he organized his political base. It also considers the improving ideas, particularly those of William Paterson and John Law, which were familiar to him as a young man.

II. Organizing to Wield Power

The purge of the Scottish customs service after 1722 and the Malt Tax Riots of 1725 enabled the Argathelians to entrench their power in Scotland. Essential to the effective use of that power was a system of management. The Squadrone lords had had one which relied on agents in the country's significant institutions to keep them informed about important developments.[1] Their informers told their betters of vacancies, the needs which made men amenable to influence, the exploitable weaknesses of others and so on.[2] Their information went to a manager in Edinburgh who co-ordinated political work at the Scottish end. He wrote regularly to a council in London which considered appointments and other business. Those were then pushed by the Scottish Secretary. By 1723 or 1724, Ilay had created a similar structure with the help of Andrew Fletcher of Saltoun (1692-1766).[3]

Fletcher was the nephew of the Scottish patriot of the same name and in 1733 inherited the Saltoun estate. Younger than Ilay by ten years, he was a well-educated Leiden-trained lawyer who had had much to do with Alexander Cunningham of Block, a friend and book-buyer for Fletcher's uncle, 'the patriot', as well as to the 2nd Duke of Argyll and Ilay.[4] In 1716, Cunningham tried to introduce Fletcher to the Campbell brothers but had not managed to do so. He did give them a laudatory account of his young friend. Fletcher passed advocate in 1717 and made his mark early. From 1718 to 1724, he was the Cashier of the Scottish Excise, an office which gave him about £300 a year – more than double what a new advocate could expect to earn at the bar – if, indeed, he earned anything. Fletcher's office showed him the economic state of the country and how its finances were managed.[5] Around 1722, he married Elizabeth, daughter of Sir Francis Kinloch of Gilmerton, a relative by marriage of the Campbells of Argyll.[6] By 1722/23, Ilay was writing to him. In 1724, he had him made a Lord of Session as Lord Milton. Fletcher was already more important to Ilay than older politicians such as George Drummond, later Lord Provost of Edinburgh. In 1726, Milton became a Lord of the Justiciary Court where from 1735 to 1748 he served as Lord Justice Clerk, *de facto* head of the Court when Ilay could not preside in person. Having a seat on both of the Scottish supreme courts gave him the clout to act as the Scottish manager for the Argathelians. Lord Milton would be Ilay's chief man of all work in Scotland from 1724 until Ilay died in 1761. He co-ordinated and conducted political business, handled some of Ilay's personal affairs and joined with him in many ventures in which it is difficult to say who initiated schemes and who supported them. Like the Earl, he negotiated well and was personally more inclined to compromise than to fight. He was also loyal – but loyal to Ilay and not to his brother. Duke John relied on Duncan Forbes of Culloden, LPCS, whose relations with Ilay and Milton were sometimes tense. The young lawyer and the Earl were kindred spirits. They shared interests in agricultural improvements and the promotion of industry in Scotland, in botany and chemistry, in banking, in architecture and building, even in the nurturing of Scottish intellectuals

The Argathelian interest was family based (see pp. 16, 66-7) and included Campbell relatives by blood or marriage. Lord Milton now added some of his kin among the families of the attainted Jacobite Earls of Middleton and Southesk but also in Whiggish families such as those of the Earls of Stair and Roseberry.[7] As noted earlier, the faction included others close to the brothers, especially Army men, and MPs and men who aspired to sit in Parliament. Along with them were others in regional offices such as Sheriffs, Sheriff-deputes, Clerks of Sheriff Courts, Justices of the Peace, other office holders and merchants.[8]

By the end of 1727, Ilay had established a presence in most of Scotland's institutions including all the universities.[9] They provided clerical politicians, men to watch local clerics and others, and places from which to watch and to influence the views people had. At Glasgow his Visitation Commission (1726-27), by reforming the corporation, reduced the power of its Chancellor, the Duke of Montrose, its Principal, John Stirling, and of their friends among the professors. In 1728, the Reverend Neil Campbell became its Principal and a Royal Chaplain.[10] From 1727 until 1761, Ilay was useful to the city and helped into office most of the College's new professors. He did favours, found jobs for professors and their sons, presented their petitions to the King and sent books to the University library and trees to its garden.

In Edinburgh, the Argathelians usually controlled the Town Council and through that had effective control of the University which was overseen by a Council committee and one of the bailies. It is likely that the Council acts of 28 August 1719, 26 October 1720 and 2 November 1720, all of which tightened the rules for the appointments of professors, were contrived to aid Argathelians. The first made professors serve 'but dureing the Councills pleasure'; the others stipulated that divines appointed to city livings would not hold chairs in the College, thus insuring that there would be more patronage to dispense.[11] Ilay had almost certainly given the University its medical school in 1725-26 by sanctioning the creation of the chairs of medicine. That gave him a faction of loyal men in the University and on the Council.[12]

At St Andrews, the Earl had made his presence felt by taking up a bit of land in the burgh and aiding the Professor of Divinity, Alexander Scrymgcour, who had been attacked in the courts. James Erskine (Lord Grange), Duncan Forbes and Charles Erskine were all active on Scrymgeour's behalf in 1726. Those lawyers kept the Earl informed of proceedings.[13] In 1727, Ilay told Newcastle that the new Chancellor at St Andrews, his friend, the Duke of Chandos, had been 'elected by the Masters of the University contrary to the right of the Crown'.[14] He used a similar threat at Glasgow to neuter the Chancellor c.1730. That argument reflected earlier discussions in England (see pp. 72-3). The same reasons probably had led to his own unwillingness to accept the Chancellorship of King's College, Aberdeen, when it was offered to him in 1716. The Duke of Roxburghe had fewer scruples. Ilay may have interfered in the choice of a Professor of Medicine at King's College in 1725. Dr. Matthew MacKaile asked him to although there is no conclusive evidence that Ilay or Milton actually did so. King's College was run mostly as a family affair and was little subject to outside influences. Dr. James Gregory, who had many relatives in the College, not Dr. MacKaile, was chosen.

At neighbouring Marischal College, MacKaile, a Regent, received Argathelian patronage and supplied Ilay and Milton with intelligence about the colleges and burgh until his death in 1734.[15] Ilay's friends tried, unsuccessfully, to determine the outcome of the election of the Professor of Mathematics in 1726.[16] In doing this, they attempted to impose not only a Campbell on Marischal College but a 'delegate' to represent the Royal interest in a corporation which they believed had no legitimate Chancellor but the King. The delegate's views would be heard when appointments were made.[17] Imposing a delegate would have deprived the men of the College of their independence.[18] What had been done in the universities, the Earl tried to do with most institutions.

The Argathelian system developed a strong urban base. In Edinburgh and Glasgow it rested on merchants, lawyers, and on Milton and Ilay's friends and relatives in the burghs. In Glasgow, Professors Alexander Dunlop and Robert Simson kept the Earl informed of developments in the town while Principal Neil Campbell watched the clerics. Patrick Duff of Premnay, an Aberdeen Advocate, was the perpetual Argathelian agent in Aberdeen from the 1720s until he died in 1763. The Aberdeen burghs chose as MP in the elections of 1727 the Campbell brothers' friend, Colonel John Middleton. By 1728, Aberdeen had an Argathelian Provost, William Cruikshanks, but it had not become entirely reconciled to the new regime.[19] Elsewhere, by 1726, most burgh councils had someone able and eager to pass on local news.[20]

Ilay's success in the burghs was reflected in the membership of the Convention of Royal Burghs which in 1726 had a near majority of Argathelians.[21] Their friend George Drummond was frequently its Praeses [chairman]. As time went on, its membership came to have fewer merchants from the burghs and more Argathelians working in Edinburgh as lawyers and place-men. They usually had some tenuous tie to the burgh they represented.[22] That body was used by the Argathelians for their purposes.

Ilay had some purchase on other institutions in the country which came from the positions he and his brother held. Duke John was an Hereditary Keeper of Holyrood Palace and so had some minor Scottish Household appointments. He controlled important regality courts and little would be done in parts of the West and North of Scotland without his or his agents' assent. And, he had military posts to grant. The Earl sat in both sovereign courts. As Lord Justice General, he could vote to determine the outcomes of criminal cases. As an Extraordinary Lord of Session, he sometimes voted and stated opinions in cases on which he sat. He was a Justice of the Peace and after 1722 was usually named to the General Assembly of the Kirk although his attendance was irregular. That of his principal henchmen – Lord Milton, Duncan Forbes (Lord Culloden), James Erskine (Lord Grange), Charles Erskine (later Lord Tinwald), Patrick Campbell (Lord Monzie) and George Drummond – was constant if they were not sitting as MPs.

The prominence of lawyers among the Argathelians meant that he could often reward them with the posts they most wanted, on the Courts of Session and Justiciary, or in the country's lesser courts – the Exchequer, Sheriff Courts, and the Commissary Courts. Between the appointment of Lord Milton in 1724 and 1736, Ilay and his friends placed in the sovereign courts seven men from five counties. In 1736, Ilay's men formed a bare majority on the Court of Session and held four of six seats on the Justiciary Court. Ilay sat as Lord Justice General. The Earl had not been able to try the Glasgow Malt Tax rioters as he had wanted, but any who came before the Justiciary Court, in the 1730s, he could deal with much as he pleased. In the Court of Session, he was not above pressing judges to find the judgments he wished to see rendered.[23] He was less successful with the Court of Exchequer, but even there he had friends such as the Englishman, Baron Scroop and, after 1748, John Maule. Ilay or his friends controlled the principal Scottish Chancery Offices while his friend, the Earl of Selkirk, was Lord Clerk Register. This gave the Argathelians a clear view of business being transacted through royal warrants and in the higher courts. They could assent, object to, or impede processes and actions. In the Customs and Excise they also had many friends.

The Earl's position was strengthened by the King's death in 1727. When a new Ministry was formed, Walpole remained chief minister and Ilay remained his man in Scotland. They filled most of the places whose warrants ran for the life of the King. Ilay doled out appointments for about a year following the death of George I. He could not control all of them but a large number went to men whom he had recommended.

By 1728, most Household officers had been re-appointed or replaced. Ilay replaced the old Court of Delegates (a body of five commissioners appointed to adjudicate claims against the Forfeited Estates) with men who would act in his favour – Lords Milton, Grange, and Minto.[24] The other two commissioners were not of his faction and Grange was sometimes thought not to be reliable, but Ilay controlled him until c.1732 through promises about the restoration of the forfeited estates of his brother, the Earl of Mar.[25] Ilay's new Court had a look of fairness about it but the majority was his. The story was much the same with the Board of Police and the non-functioning Mint, both of which provided sinecures for the loyal and deserving. That was his policy in other bodies in which, by the 1730s, he generally had a working majority because he had placed the resident and active members.

In agencies such as the Boards of Customs and Excise, his powers were more limited but within a decade the seven Customs Commissioners included two Campbells, George Drummond, The Master of Ross and George Vaughan, a Welshman with whom Ilay was friendly before and after his appointment.[26] At the Excise Office in 1736, Ilay could find among its five Commissioners his good friend

Major Thomas Cochrane and Richard Dowdeswell. They sometimes constituted a majority of those present at meetings.[27]

Where Ilay could not find loyal men among incumbents, he could sometimes replace men with those loyal to himself. During the Malt Tax uproar in May and June 1725, he ousted a number of prominent Squadrone men: the Receiver General, the Lord Advocate and Solicitor General, some men in Customs and Excise offices, some Sheriffs and other officials.[28] Ilay closely watched and manipulated the burghs' elections and the staffing of other bodies.[29] His policy was to keep happy men whom he needed to placate, even those whom he did not much like, such as the dependents and relatives of the Earl of Stair. Filling even minor offices took time but built up for the Argathelians a store of good will while at the same time making clear to others the costs of opposition.[30] The cumulative effect was the building of a political machine more loyal to *him* than to anyone else. Newcastle might sign the warrants but the English duke and Walpole appointed men who knew Ilay had nominated them. Some came to office whom the Earl did not want appointed but Ilay's usefulness to Walpole increased the Earl's personal importance just as it made him less dependent on his brother.[31] Perhaps that is why they quarrelled bitterly in the mid- and late-1720s. For a time, they ceased to socialize or speak to one another.[32]

The Kirk was little different. Ilay had friends in the Kirk since his early days but, in the 1720s, he built up a party structure in the Kirk to the distress of those who did not want to see politicians meddling in Christ's Church. A step toward that end was almost certainly the building of the Ramshorn Church, St. David's, in Glasgow (1719-24). Campbell money paid for some of it and the Rev. John Anderson, the 2nd Duke of Argyll's old tutor, was appointed Minister in 1720 despite opposition from local clerics friendlier to the Duke of Montrose.[33] That church gave the Campbells a voice in the Glasgow Presbytery. By 1724, pious George Drummond was managing elections to the General Assembly and helping Milton to fill minor offices in the Excise.[34] They were all the same to Ilay. In 1724, the Argathelians defeated the Squadrone over the Moderatorship of the General Assembly.[35] The Earl continued to cultivate men in the Kirk, a step Robert Wodrow deplored.[36] By early 1725, Argathelians in the Kirk were organizing the return of members to the General Assembly as well as to lower church courts.[37] James Alston seems then to have been tapped as the Argathelian faction's general advisor on ecclesiastical affairs (see p.175). In December 1725, after the Malt Tax Riots, Ilay promised, 'I shant forget the Levites at A proper time'. He intended to punish those who had preached against the Malt Tax and for the rioters and reward those who had followed the government's orders to castigate the rioters.[38] In May, Ilay wrote Milton of his determination to punish Professor William Hamilton for not toeing the line in the recent General Assembly.[39] The Earl's own attention usually centred on filling livings so that the Kirk would be quiet and amenable to government leadership. The King's death in 1727 completed this process.

That allowed Ilay to dignify new clerics, organize promotions and cultivate the men whom he wanted to lead the Kirk.[40] That was a rather more complicated business than it might seem. Sometimes deals were made to divide salaries and to settle successions to other posts. The succession of Moderators and professors, like moving men to better livings, took time. Professors Anderson at King's College,

William Hamilton at Edinburgh and Neil Campbell at Glasgow, all got Royal Chaplaincies as rewards for opposition to Jacobites, support for moderate policies in the Kirk and loyalty to the Argathelians. Principal Campbell's chaplaincy stipend was divided with Professor Alexander Dunlop.

By 1728, the Kirk was more docile although those who opposed him were again harassing Professors Simson and Scrymgeour. Later in the decade, the Earl added several professors to his cohort of clerical advisors which, by the early 1730s, included men in all the universities. Some now called them 'Moderate Men' and ridiculed their rationalism, moralistic stance and possible unitarianism.[41]

At the London end of his operations, the Earl had the support of ministers and of his own brother until c.1737/38. Even though they were often on bad terms, the brothers managed to work together.[42] Ilay later efficiently served diverse ministries. It was easier to do that because he did not belong to the family factions which composed their cores but he was most loyal to 'Old Whigs'. Ilay over many years also worked fairly smoothly with the officials who secured his warrants, including Viscount Townshend, Sir Robert Walpole, Henry Pelham, Henry Fox, William Pitt and finally Lord Bute. A condition of his tenure under Walpole and others was that he did not to try to monopolize Scottish patronage.[43] Some Treasury patronage always remained with Walpole; more was exercised by the Secretaries of State. Squadrone men, until the 1750s, got some gifts although they lacked much real ability to influence Scottish affairs.[44] The Earl of Ilay recognized his constraints but over time his men and his system became entrenched. Giving crumbs to others kept Ilay on his mettle. The Duke of Newcastle, however, was a problem from the late 1720s on. It also helped Ilay that governments after 1720 did not do much in Scotland that seriously antagonized the Kirk or other institutional interests. Indeed, save for crises in 1713-15, 1725, 1736 and 1745, the London government was usually willing to pass economic legislation he favoured and to let the country run itself under Ilay's supervision.

Ilay was aided in London by a personal secretary for whom he found a Commons seat and paid off with a post for life. His first secretary seems to have been an old friend, William Stewart [Steuart or Stuart], MP.[45] Stewart, like most who followed him, had trained as a lawyer. As a young man of nineteen, the Campbell brothers gave him a lifetime sinecure worth £500 *per annum*. He entered the House of Commons in 1713 and sat until 1741 for the Inverness, Ayr, and Elgin Burghs. He seems sometimes to have lived with Ilay in London.[46] Possibly someone unknown and then John Maule (c.1738) replaced Stewart. Maule served until 1748 when he was made a Baron of the Exchequer of Scotland. The secretary for the rest of Argyll's life was Lord Milton's son, Andrew Fletcher III. These men wrote some of his letters, ran errands and sometimes acted as Whip for the Scots in the House of Commons. They had been educated abroad, and shared many of Ilay's interests.

The elections which followed the death of George I in 1727 consolidated Ilay's system. He was electioneering in Scotland by the end of August. He succeeded in electing a majority of the peers whom the ministers wanted and he was even more successful in the Commons elections where probably fourteen MPs were Argathelians and twenty-five were supporters of the government among whom were only two Squadrone men.[47] That faction was now out but not finished. After the autumn elections, the Earl returned to London in late September or early October. He had ensured Walpole's continuance in office; Sir Robert would look after him.

III. Patronage Rules

Patronage was essential to the Earl's system of administration. Ilay left few statements about how he administered patronage but his practices can be inferred from his actions and from occasional comments in his letters. He did not always follow his own rules but he was usually able to do so. When nominations reached him, they had already been screened. He was then generally able to choose between men about equally well recommended and equally competent. The issue for him was to weigh political advantage as well as deserts and merits. In the end, the choice was often his and it was not guided only by political considerations. Once he had made a choice, it was seldom questioned by those for whom he worked. The Duke of Newcastle, town councils and universities were content to follow advice which, if ignored, might well bring consequences they would not like.

His first rule was that of all political managers: jobs must be dispensed so as to help not hurt the dispenser and his friends in power.[48] Secondly, all appointees were to follow generally Whiggish and religiously tolerant and Erastian policies so that the Earl might keep the confidence of his English associates. He insisted on a third rule: men should be reasonably qualified to hold the posts they sought. He was also eager to handle or review all significant patronage from his faction because he did not trust others to get right the details such as the wording of warrants.[49] Ambiguity and sloppy drafting gave rise to appeals. After those conditions had been satisfied, there were others particular to the kinds of appointments to be made.

For civil administrative posts, those in the Customs and other such agencies, he expected only reasonable competence and honesty. He would not defend peculators or the inefficient. After his death, Lord Milton [n.d. but 1761] stated this rule to Bute:

> ... your late uncle was allways attentive to this disposal of the Offices of the customs, which he gave to those who were perfectly certified by his particular Friends: By this means he knew the Characters of the persons he preferred or preferred, worthy persons, and at the same time strengthened his connections. It was an invariable rule with him never to solicit the reponing of those who were dismissed by the board [of Customs], which reliev'd him from great trouble and uneasiness which otherwise would have happened.[50]

He would not readily give a job to a man nominated by a person whose previous nominees had disappointed him. In July 1740, he told Lord Milton that an appointee who resigned, sold his place or performed badly reflected on him: 'it stand[s] in my way when I ask [for] others'.[51] He disliked making joint appointments and thought in the cases of fathers and sons, the job should go only to the son. That kept misunderstandings to a minimum.[52] He was unwilling that men, particularly university professors, should pick their successors. When James Crawford, the Edinburgh Professor of Ecclesiastical History, tried to name his successor in 1736-37, the Earl would not allow it. He picked

Patrick Cuming who became his ecclesiastical manager from 1736 to 1761.[53] Service was to be rewarded; Cuming was a satisfactory man.[54]

When it came to legal jobs, the demands were higher than for places in the Customs or Excise. The public needed good lawyers; judges ruled on liberty and property. In c.1753, he told the Earl of Marchmont that of Sessions judges,

> there are always enquiry's made how far the Candidates have been eminent in their Profession, after their Characters, & Principles to be right: I have found that the King's servants like to have several names laid before them for their information concerning those who are thought most proper to be Judges, even when there is no vacancy.   it is not long agoe that I was asked about two Gentlemen [Alexander Boswell of Auchinlech and George Carre of Nesbit[55]] and with whom I have no manner of connection but whose merit I was in Justice obliged to confess, one of these seems to be very much in favour.[56]

The Earl wished bright men to be appointed to legal offices but he worried less about their morals. A lawyer or judge who drank was not a great danger but a foolish and dishonest one was. Ilay helped into Session or Justiciary gowns Andrew Fletcher, Lord Milton; Patrick Campbell, Lord Monzie; Sir Gilbert Elliot, Lord Minto; Hugh Dalrymple, Lord Drummore; Alexander Fraser, Lord Strichen; Patrick Grant, Lord Elchies; John Sinclair, Lord Murkle; Sir James Fergusson, Lord Kilkerran; Henry Home, Lord Kames; Andrew Pringle, Lord Alemore; Thomas Miller, Lord Glenlee; Alexander Boswell, Lord Auchinlech; George Carre, Lord Nesbit; Francis Garden, Lord Gardenstone and James Burnett, Lord Monboddo. To the Exchequer Court he sent John Maule and Sir John Dalrymple. He appointed Commissaries in most of the jurisdictions and made Alexander Lind of Gorgie, Sheriff of Midlothian and Commissary of Glasgow. Collectively those legal appointees included three relatives but most were good lawyers. Five had notable interests in science and its uses. Four were leading men in banking, five in agricultural improvement and even two in industry. Two of them – Kames and Monboddo – are still read for their ideas while Dalrymple wrote a history which was long useful, an influential work on gardening, and many improving tracts dealing with topics from coal tar to soap-boiling, from entails to taxes.

Ilay filled many other civil places such as household positions – King's Smith, Apothecary, Printer[57] and positions at Holyrood House. Those places often went to men with special talents and skills whom he and Milton thought deserved recognition or support. He gave the unsalaried medical professors at Edinburgh the £100 salary of the King's Physician in Scotland. Ilay also filled very many posts not legally in the government's gift but secured by him. Of those, perhaps the most important were in the universities where he generally also named men to Regius Chairs.

In the universities, Argyll wanted polite men with brains who could use their knowledge for the betterment of the society. He liked Leiden men and improvers. He picked men who could do two or more things in preference to those who could teach only one subject. Teachers should be physically up to the job. Matthew Stewart, a fine mathematician, nearly lost the Edinburgh mathematics chair because he stuttered. Teachers ought to teach clearly and be respected by the boys. The Earl preferred not to appoint men from the same family to succeed one another and he did not wish to see relatives in the same corporation.[58] He would not appoint men who were too controversial – as David Hume discovered in 1751. Ilay was content to have lawyers choose men for legal chairs because he knew that trying to pick them himself would create ill-will even among his friends.[59] The lawyers would pick the best men since members of all factions had an interest in good legal training being locally available. Ilay often ignored the recommendations of town councillors, gentlemen and politicians preferring those which came from united faculties. When the professors unanimously recommended someone, he could be sure that faction played no part and that merit was what had mattered. A case at Glasgow shows that vividly.

In 1756 Provost Murdoch recommended Dr. John Wodrow for either the Chair of Medicine or that of Anatomy and Botany. Wodrow was a sixty-one year old physician with a Rheims MD who had long maintained a physic garden and taught botany in the town. He was otherwise notable only for being the son of a former divinity professor and the brother of the historian Robert Wodrow. Others in contention for the chairs were Joseph Black and Thomas Hamilton. The first was already a notable chemist. The second was a Glasgow-educated man who had studied in London with William Hunter. He could make fine anatomical preparations which were increasingly in demand by teachers of anatomy. He had inherited others from his older brother who had used them when he taught anatomy at the University from 1742 until 1756. Hamilton also had a fashionable Glasgow surgical practice and a local reputation as a male mid-wife. The College had no midwifery chair and needed a man like him. The professors sent up to Argyll unanimous recommendations of Hamilton and Black. Those were seconded by Professor John Anderson, who was then in London. Calling on Argyll at his levee, Anderson told His Grace that he knew 'the Merit of the persons recommended with the Rest of the World' but also 'because I had an Opportunity of knowing it thoroughly as well as their Principles and Behaviour by having been their Fellow-Student'. Argyll thanked him for this information [he had picked Anderson for a chair earlier in the year] and remarked 'the Mag[istrates] of Glasgow look upon a Place in the College and in the Excise in the very same Light, as a Thing convenient for their Friends'. That was not his view. He was involved in Black's earlier appointment at Glasgow and would have known William and Thomas Hamilton (the late Professor of Medicine) because, fifteen years earlier, when the older Hamilton was given his chair by Montrose, the Squadrone supported him. Wodrow was passed over on grounds of merit. Hamilton became Professor of Anatomy and Botany not because he was the distant relative of a duke but because, like Black, he was a better man.[60]

The rules of patronage for pastors were different. Kirks did not need bright men but they needed moral ones or those who appeared to be such. Clerics had to set good examples to their flocks whom they should make moral not enthusiastic. Ilay did not knowingly appoint bigots, enthusiasts or zealots to church livings. He and Milton were annoyed when, in 1736, to get Principal Wishart, they had also to settle for a High-flyer in another church.[61] Such ministers divided men over unimportant niceties of doctrine. In the parishes of which he was himself the patron, Ilay sometimes gave the Kirk session the names of three men and let them choose the one they wanted.[62] Ilay wanted a tolerant, moralistic and Erastian Kirk. He used patronage to get it.

Military appointments were used for mainly political ends and those who got them were scrutinized for the political value their appointments carried more than their known records and abilities. Those places rewarded the faithful and advanced Scottish interests. Army, Navy and East India Company patronage was distributed principally with an eye to keeping the Highlands loyal.

Ilay, an MD, lawyer and former soldier, knew enough about most professional men and their fields to make informed judgments about their abilities. He preferred the innovative over the merely competent. His own knowledge entered into many decisions, especially those involving the promotion of men already holding appointments. William Cullen went to Edinburgh from Glasgow because he had done well. Argyll prized his abilities as a teacher, research chemist and improver. In Edinburgh, the College men would have chosen Joseph Black or Francis Home had they been left on their own. Black was young and proven only as a chemist, not as a physician; Home was a less accomplished figure than Cullen. Neither the College nor the Town Council or any other institution was often left without guidance. Ilay's rules were not always followed but they were regularly employed.

IV. The Man in the Portrait

By 1727, Ilay was forty-five years old, his brother forty-seven. It was increasingly unlikely that the 2nd Duke would have a male heir. Ilay derived increasing personal power from that fact. Unless the Duke had sons, Ilay would inherit the largest landed estate in Scotland and would always be a figure to reckon with. The Earl's own places gave him some independence. He might live in the shadow of Duke John but the shadow was shrinking. The Earl had come into his own and was not merely the manager of a family or government connexion. If Walpole or another English chief minister backed him, he could do a great deal on his own. His long-term importance for Scotland and Scots began in 1725.

We can best picture the Earl during this period in the portrait of him by William Aikman (see Plate 2). This shows us a slim man dressed in the gown of a Scottish Earl and justifies Lady Mary Wortley Montagu's comment that Ilay and his brother 'have been remarkable for their figure'.[63] The Earl was a good-looking man with an open gaze exuding intelligence. Still, his countenance reveals little. He appears serious but not relaxed. Aikman's contemporary pictures of his brother allude to his Highland background, the Duke's military career and his Garter and his interests in plants and buildings. Ilay's portrait shows us an intelligent man, possibly a charming one, modestly asserting his status as an Earl and standing foresquare on the Saltire formed by the floor tiles. Aikman got the brothers about right.

The best description of them in these years comes third-hand from their grand niece, Lady Louisa Stuart, the daughter of Lord Bute. She remembered her father's description of his uncles in the following way:

The brothers frequently disagreed, and usually about everything else; at some times were on a foot of intimacy, at others not upon speaking terms. I have heard my father say that when he was a boy under their joint direction, [from 1723-1734], he could remember occasions where (non-intercourse chancing to prevail) all arrangement respecting him were to be made by letter. At best, there was that fundamental difference in their natures, which will rarely allow even the nearest and even the kindest relations to be partial sympathising friends. The one was properly speaking, a hero; the other altogether a man of this world. The Duke thought Lord Islay undignified and time-serving, Lord Islay thought the Duke wrong-headed and romantic. Yet both were assuredly superior men. John had genius, with all the lights and shades, thereunto appertaining; Archibald strong clear sense and sound judgment and thorough knowledge of mankind. John, a soldier from his cradle, was warm-hearted, frank, honourable, magnanimous, but fiery-tempered, rash, ambitious, haughty, impatient of contradiction; Archibald, bred a lawyer, was cool, shrewd, penetrating, argumentative – an able man of business, and a wary, if not crafty politician.... John took pleasure in wit, poetry, and the belles-lettres; Archibald in philosophical experiments, mechanics, natural history and what had no name and little existence in his days, what is now called Political Economy.... [T]he Duke of Argyll had a kind of court round him, consisting of a few sensible party-men, not a few Scotch dependents, a set of dull old officers who served under his command, and a whole tribe of Campbell-cousins....Lord Islay's humble companions were the ingenious men who assisted him in his scientific pursuits, or those whose inventions he patronised. Conversing as he did with all manner of people, yet still keeping his proper place in the best and highest society, the younger brother could not well be supposed to share the elder's prejudice against intelligent women.[64]

We should now turn to how Ilay used his power.

V. Improving Commerce and Industry

Power enabled Ilay in London to prop up Walpole's Ministry and so increase his own power, enrich himself and his friends, and accomplish ends which were desirable in and for themselves. As a political-economist, he had ideas about how to do all that. They harked back to 1705 and to the discussions of the grim 1690s. Ilay had seen Scottish economic problems at their worst because he had been in Scotland as a university student while the last of the great famines ravaged the country. If the agrarian sector was not healthy, everybody suffered. Between 1694 and 1701, crops failed and the country starved. As hard times for farmers deepened, those who worked in trades were not able to sell what they produced and soon they could not afford to buy as much food. Everyone's markets spiralled down. The country seemed on the brink of chaos as people died and wandered in search of bread and work. Perhaps 13% of the population was lost to mortality and through emigration.[65] The innovative remedies seemed to lie in councils of state, banks, protection for industries or union with England. Ilay could remember all that and would act in ways reminiscent of those which had earlier failed. He succeeded.

The crisis of the 1690s and early 1700s left a deep impression on Scots who lived through it. It stirred a few to think about economics in a more or less systematic way while at the same time thinking about some sort of a closer union with England.

The confluence of those streams of discussion led to a public debate in the 1690s and early 1700s about what should be done and what the future of Scotland ought to be.[66] One of the contributions to that debate, one which Ilay owned, was William Paterson's *Proposals and Reasons for Constituting a Council of Trade* (1701). This touched most of the themes which Ilay would have included under *improvements*.

Paterson was a mercantilist who had been involved with the founding of the Bank of England and with the flotation of the Darien Company and its ambitious scheme for banking and trading in Asia, Africa and America. In his 1701 pamphlet, he advocated the creation of a general purpose institution which would better the economy and so improve life for all Scots. His motives, he said, were patriotic; in part, they probably were. He wanted Scots to adopt a publically regulated state trading company called the Council of Trade. Its capital would be derived from taxes and incidental funds, including such things as the rents from the former Bishops' lands and the Post Office. Those funds were to be expended in trade and banking, in paying off the Darien stockholders,[67] and in enterprises meant to bring prosperity to poor Scotia:

> ... the council of trade may be empowered to purchase or build workhouses; and likewise to purchase and procure all other means and materials for employing, relieving, and maintaining the poor; and for encouraging, promoting, and increasing the manufactories and fisheries of this kingdom; to build and erect granaries for the well-keeping of stores and quantities of corn in all such places of this kingdom as they shall judge necessary; and from time to time to buy up and keep at a regular rate the several growths and manufactures of this kingdom, so as the poor in particular may not be imposed upon nor oppressed by the extreme cheapness or want of money for their work on the one hand, nor the nation in general by extreme dearth on the other.[68]

The Council was to have not only what the eighteenth century thought of as police powers – the right to regulate minor matters of trade, such as weights and measures – but also the right to 'impose, collect and receive' customs and excise duties and to oversee, protect and promote foreign trade.[69] It would regulate the mints and coin money of a better standard which would then flow freely in and out of the country.[70] The mines of the country would be improved under the 'care and inspection of the council of trade'.[71] So too would its industries. Paterson saw no reason why Scots should not do well in the woolen trade and in others. Fisheries were great employers of people and a source of income in international trade.[72] The poor, he thought, would be immediately helped when they were employed in the building of the granaries. That employment would allow them to be decently and conveniently maintained, and perpetually and profitably employed, instead of being 'as hitherto so insupportable a weight upon both the industry and morality of this nation'. If all this were to be done, the poor, whom he numbered at 150,000 [roughly 1 in 6], would be less idle and less miserable.[73] He thought in four years' time, the country could be 'for ever eased of at least three-fourths of the expense' of looking after them if granaries were established.[74] Not unrelated to this was his belief that Scotland ought to reform its criminal laws. There were too many 'unjust and unequal laws', too many 'unjust and unequal punishments'.[75] He would have ended capital punishment for theft and eased and graduated other punishments as well.

Paterson believed his measures would have the inevitable result of lowering the rate of interest, which, like the ending of monopolies, would improve economic conditions. Giving the poor work would expand industries. Fostering the fisheries would promote ship building. Promoting the wool trade would be a boon to farmers. All that would put more money in the public coffers. He saw his scheme as one of 'national improvement'. It required a national effort on the part of the talented and patriotic.[76] That was a religious obligation, a moral necessity and dictated by prudence. It was also a task to be undertaken in good humour. This visionary was a man of irenical temper who tried to convince his compatriots that 'those who are violent in everything will be constant in nothing, and [we] have had reason to know that angry men are never fit for business, but least of all in angry times'.[77] When he came to his peroration, he sounded like men fifty years later, men like David Hume and Adam Smith. Trade civilizes. Trade allows the accumulation of riches for use in wars, should they come. Trade would make Scots free. Trade is at the root of all we can do and hope. Trade can transform the world:

> We ought not only to begin with trade, as the most fundamental to us in this kingdom, and to which we have the plainest and clearest call, but as our part of a thing that at this day is capable of making greater alterations in the world than the sword, and may best enable us to strengthen the hands of our King in this dangerous time, and put us in a condition of contributing our part to the defence and support of religion and liberty, instead of being what our oppressors [the English] seems to have designed, viz. Their backdoor to let in mischief.

> Although heaven and earth call upon us at this time to defend and vindicate our rights and liberties in particular, and to take effectual care that this kingdom may be under other and more tolerable circumstances with our neighbour nation in the next age than it hath been in this, yet the measures to be taken, even in relation to them, ought not to be inflaming, but healing, since we are embarked in one common cause – the defence of religion and liberty, where every good subject ought to play his part; let therefore our deportment in this matter be such as may be capable of convincing that we are not only in the right in point of fact, but likewise in point of good conduct and management.[78]

Paterson believed that if the Parliament of 1701 would but enact those changes, it would be 'finishing a glorious work so happily begun, so as for ever hereafter to merit the name of the prudent, the wise, the healing, and happy Parliament'.[79] Paterson's pamphlet was read and discussed by men like the Rev. William Carstares, Sir Robert Sibbald, MD, and the advocate, John Spottiswoode. Surviving manuscripts and books of the last two contain references to it and other similar proposals. Paterson defined issues for the future. Was it possible to create institutions in this backward, impoverished kingdom which could raise it to prosperity? Ilay may not have shared the idealism of this merchant-banker but he shared the view that one could create institutions which would accomplish much for which Paterson hoped. Despite all the jobbery involved in the creation of the institutions which Ilay built, some of that idealism persisted. The justifications for founding of the Board of Trustees for Fisheries and Manufactures (1727), the Royal Bank of Scotland (1727) and the British Linen Company (1743), and for the Commissions which looked after the confiscated estates in the wake of the '45 Rebellion (1747-55) were not just boiler-plate but expressed a determination to achieve some of the ends which Paterson had eloquently stated at he beginning of the century and which were discussed while Ilay was young.

Ilay probably paid more attention to ideas expressed by John Law of Lauriston. Law is too often remembered as merely the man who caused or abetted the 'bubbles' which in 1720 burst first in France and then in Holland and England. He was much more than that.[80] Law (see pp. 38, 83, 85) was a long time personal friend of Ilay and his brother the Duke. Ilay possessed all of Law's works in more than one copy and he had some manuscripts including a quarto manuscript copy of the 'Essay on a Land Bank' (1703/04).

In that work, Law suggested that since money is but a medium of exchange, it might well be denominated in land rather than gold. It could then be represented by paper notes whose value and stability would be guaranteed by the stability of the value of the land against which they had been issued. The notes measured the value of the land and might be exchanged for it. The state could make them legal tender. If this were done, they would serve in commerce just as well as gold, at least within the realm. The value of the money would fluctuate with the demand for land and as its quality varied. That was to say, it would fluctuate very little in the short-run and in the long-run not as much as commodities like gold and silver had done. Other forms of money, such as stocks and bills of exchange, constantly change in value as markets decide what they are worth. Ultimately, they must have their worth fixed in the money which has become standard. Law thought the state should not issue too much paper money since the price level is determined in part by demand for money and by the supply of it. Should there be too much money in circulation, prices would rise, as they do in inflationary periods.[81] The quantity of money in circulation is, at least partially, within the means of governments to control. To monetize all land would have increased the circulating money of a state like Scotland by a great deal.[82] Law thought that would stimulate trade and bring about recovery and progress. He imagined that the corporation which would manage all this might be a Parliament-chartered body or a joint-stock company open to any who had land worth £1,000 which could be pledged against the stock or notes which they would get in exchange for their pledge.[83]

In 1705, Law may have gone beyond these proposals, which in some ways were only more imaginative variations of older versions of land banks. In one document attributed to him, he proposed to increase the Scottish money supply through the issuance of interest bearing paper currency forced upon the country and controlled by the government. The latter was also to create a Commission of Trade, a body of merchants, nobles and gentlemen, which would 'employ these notes so struck in erecting a fisherie, and in improving our manufactories'. As in Paterson's scheme, the Commission was to become the sole foreign trader for the country, which would benefit from the gold it accumulated for the state in its transactions. The portion of the national debt held in the kingdom was to be paid off in the notes issued by the Commission. That money would not stay long in the pockets of its recipients for they would set it to work to the benefit of the working men of Scotland.[84] Scots, with more money available, would spend their way out of the deep recession to which they had been condemned by bad luck and the English. Law proposed to pay the arrears of the Scottish troops with the same paper bearing 3% interest and circulating as would other government backed notes.[85] For Army men like Ilay and his brother, this inducement to loyalty would have had considerable attractions and may account partially for Ilay's willingness in 1715 to pay government troops in Bank of Scotland notes.[86] What is really notable about this scheme is that fiat money has now become the medium of exchange denominated in paper which the government issues in a controlled way:

> This, indeed, is no more than the nation lending its faith to all its private subjects, and multiplying its own credit within itself, by which it may at any time, under a well-regulated trade, employ what stock it has a mind to; and the greater the stock is that the nation is capable to employ, the greater our profit, and the greater the balance of trade on our side, and the sooner this kingdom will grow great and considerable amongst its neighbours.[87]

Another set of proposals by Law came out in *Money and Trade Considered with a Proposal for Supplying the Nation with Money* (Edinburgh, 1705), a booklet which Ilay possessed in several copies and editions and for which he is said to have written the preface when it was re-issued in London in 1720.[88] Some of the things which Law had believed in 1705, were also set out in a pamphlet published in London after the French 'bubble' had burst. There Law was derided as a spinner of beautiful but speculative schemes but the booklet contains a useful summary of things Ilay would have not only heard but thought about for years:

> The power and Wealth of a Nation consisted in Numbers of People, that the Number of a People depended on Trade, *and that* Trade depended on Money; *that* Credit was equal to Money; that Tho among Bankers and Private Traders Credit well managed is worth *Ten* times their Capital-Stock, yet the Credit of a Royal Bank supported by the whole Species of a Kingdom formed into one Great Trading Company, has innumerable Advantages over the former, and may consequently be extended much farther; that Paper might supply the place of Silver, and was even better qualified to be used as Money, as it might be made more easy for delivery, of the same Value in all places, kept or divided without Loss or Expence, capable of a Stamp, and less liable to be counterfeited; *and lastly* that France, if she would erect her whole Strength, and make use of all the Advantages Providence had bestowed upon her, might certainly become the most powerful Kingdom in the world.[89]

That had a bit more contact with the real world of 1705 than has sometimes been realized.[90] Parliament in 1705 established neither a Council of Trade nor a land bank.

What it did, instead, was to decide to negotiate a Union with England. By the 1720s that solution had not been as effective as many in 1707 hoped it would be.

If Ilay wrote the 1720 preface to Law's re-issued 1705 tract, *Money and Trade*, he must have continued to believe that Law's ideas had merit.[91] The preface praised Law's character and achievements and noted that he had enjoyed the patronage of the Argyll family in 1705. Ilay and Law helped each other financially c.1712-1720. They met in 1719 and later when Law appeared in England as an exile from France where he had become a subject of Louis XV.[92] The Campbell brothers helped him to regain his British citizenship. They spoke for Law at the legal proceedings, in 1721, when he sought to obtain and received his pardon for the murder of 'Beau' Wilson whom he had killed in a 1694 duel.[93] When Law finally left England for Italy in 1725, he went with British diplomatic accreditation and with the good wishes of the brothers. While he was in England, Law had been very much a part of Ilay's set. They had common friends, such as Henrietta Howard and a number of London speculators and bankers including Ilay's own.[94] The Earl kept in touch until Law's death in Venice in 1728.

So, from the time he was twenty-three in 1705, Ilay had probably thought about ways in which the Scottish economy might be improved. He had bought pamphlets on trade and related issues. He had a stock of notions about economics. He was interested in economic theory, even theory which was a bit utopian. He probably thought the increase of money and credit, investment in fisheries and manufactures, and the creation of special boards to direct investment and economic policy were the ways to promote economic growth in Scotland. Certainly others whom he knew thought so.

After 1705 there were a series of efforts to aid the Scottish economy of which he was also aware. The first was the Commission of Trade and Chamberlainerie established in 1711.[95] It had a yearly fund of £2,000 to disperse but it became a useless body which only provided sinecures for a few Scots. The second, created in 1714, was the Board of Police. Robert Wodrow reported that men who ought to know believed this Board was intended by Sidney Godolphin to have a general power to oversee the economy but that this had been watered down from 'a Council for Trade and Manufactures... to have some standing power, [to] the Commission of Police and a Committty of the British Council to sit at Edinburgh'.[96] In reality, the Board mainly reported on Catholics and non-jurors in the Highlands so as to control them. It gave some employment to the poor 'through the encouragement of manufactures, the repair of the highways and making rivers navigable'.[97] As an institution to aid the economy, it failed but continued to exist as a set of sinecure posts until it was abolished in 1782.[98] By 1722, this was largely a body of Squadrone placemen. After that time, it became a body increasingly filled by dependents of Ilay and the Argathelians. Its members still did little but draw their salaries. The only body in 1726 which gave direction to the Highland economy was the Court of Exchequer whose judges and officials had some jurisdiction over unsold lands taken from rebels in 1715. In short, the old ideas of a general body to regulate the economy had not been lost but its reality was unaccomplished. The economic schemes proposed between 1705 and 1716 all failed. The ones which would succeeded were less ambitious but still realized some of the old hopes and addressed political needs. They were the Board of Trustees for Fisheries and Manufactures (1726-27) and the Royal Bank of Scotland (1727).

Chapter 13

Improving Scotland, 1727-1735

I. The Board of Trustees for Fisheries and Manufactures

The Board of Trustees was established in 1727 with some funding provided by undistributed Equivalent monies. Two Acts of 1718 and 1724 specified that the interest on those funds was to be used for the improvement of the Scottish economy. Nothing had been done by 1726. At about the same time as the 1724 act, the Malt Tax was imposed on the Scots, causing the riots and disturbances which the Argathelians quelled. The quiet Ilay imposed did not keep the Convention of Royal Burghs from petitioning against the tax in 1725 and 1726. The issue was not dead but provided a grievance exploitable by Squadrone men like Robert Dundas. The fact that compensation owing to the country under the Equivalent had not been paid in the nearly twenty years since the Union also rankled. Argathelians needed to put an end to the Malt Tax problem and overcome the English lethargy which had prevented the payment of money to Scots. The answer found by Ilay's party was the Board of Trustees: 'The Board of Trustees was devised by Scots in London to answer a political emergency in Scotland and was countenanced by the Walpole administration, which relied on the management of Scotland by Ilay'.[1] The Earl may not have thought up this scheme but he supported it and made it successful.[2]

At the end of January 1726, Lord Advocate Duncan Forbes, MP, acting for himself and others, suggested to the Praeses of the Convention of Royal Burghs, George Drummond, that Scots ask for an economic improvement board. It would pay out the money owed and thus make the payment of the Malt Tax more acceptable. The Honourable the Improvers in the Knowledge of Agriculture of Scotland was induced to propose such a body to the Convention of Royal Burghs on 9 February 1726. The Convention approved it on the 17 February. It then petitioned the MPs for the Scottish burghs to seek in Parliament the creation of a development agency funded out of the unpaid funds earmarked for development. This was but asking those who had thought up the scheme to support it. By the end of the year, petitions for this body had come from several counties and burghs.[3] Those efforts resulted in two Acts which together created the body to oversee and promote the linen trade and fisheries and prescribed ways to distribute other funds compensating for losses at the Union and due under 'the Equivalent'. Its capital came from the grant to fisheries and manufactures which Ilay had secured in 1718, from the Equivalent Fund, and from the overage of the Malt Tax if that brought in more than a specified amount of revenue. That answered those who thought the Malt Tax was not in the interest of Scots and it settled an old grievance about the payment of the monies. Scots were thus compensated for taxes paid on a national debt they had not incurred before 1707.[4] The new body was styled The Board of Trustees for Fisheries and Manufactures.

The Board of Trustees was a politically useful agency. While it did not have the sweeping control of the economy which had been imagined and urged in 1701, it had substantial power although less than its Irish equivalent founded somewhat earlier.[5] For the rest of Ilay's life, Argathelian appointees controlled the Board. They approved grants and premiums to men in their faction but their work also evoked wide praise for doing what the Earl and his friends hoped it would do – help the Scottish economy.[6] It also propped up the Royal Bank by depositing funds with it – not surprising given the overlap in the membership of the Board and the Governors of the Bank.[7] Ilay's men ran those institution but with very little obvious involvement on his part. The scheme was a great success. In 1738 Sir John Clerk, a Trustee, thought that the Board had brought 'three-times, possibly five-times more money Into the nation In one year than we have mispent In Ten'.[8]

The Trustees for Fisheries and Manufactures tried first to aid the fisheries with an initial expenditure of £2,650 but that did not accomplish much because herring were not there to be caught in sufficient numbers. It soon stopped making large grants for this purpose.[9] Still, grants to fishermen had some good effects. Most of the money went to Clydeside and the western coasts which served the expanding Glasgow market – and were close to the principal Argyll estates.[10] But the fish were also there, as they were not in all the Scottish waters. The Board's efforts paid off in the West of Scotland where Ilay was a principal beneficiary. In 1772, Thomas Pennant noted that the town of Campbeltown, one of the Duke of Argyll's burghs, had 'risen from a petty fishing town to its present flourishing state in less than thirty years.' Some of that was attributable to the Board's subsidies, some to Ilay's own policies after he became Duke in 1743.[11] For a time, Campbeltown had a whale-fishing company in which Ilay and Lord Milton held shares.[12] Inveraray had also benefited. Pennant wrote of that:

> Every evening some hundreds of boats in a manner covered the surface of Loch-Fine, an arm of the sea, which from its narrowness and from the winding of its shores, has all the beauties of a fresh-water lake: on the week-days, the chearful noise of the bagpipe and dance echoes from on board: on the sabbath, each boat approaches the land, and psalmody and devotion divide the day....[13]

Romantic it may have been but the presence of skippers and kippers had raised the stated tax valuation of the Duke's property in the parish of Campbeltown. It exceeded that of his Inveraray holdings.[14] That did not include the value of burgh property but it tells us something about the appreciation which had come to the crofts and the small holdings in both parishes.

The Board did next to nothing for the woollen trade, to whose support it allocated only £700 annually. That was too much an English business for the Scots to hope that public monies could be used to help them to rival the trade of their neighbours. The industry which was principally helped by the Board was the linen trade. Moves for the better marketing of the generally poor quality Scottish linen had come in 1721 when Parliament was asked to give more protection to Scottish linen. This was done and the trade existed throughout the century behind tariff walls raised partly by Ilay and his friends. That was not the only sign of improving conditions. In 1725-27, Glasgow merchants formed a linen society which was to supervise the quality of the linen produced and to aid in the marketing of handkerchiefs, ribbon and thread. In the years while the Argathelians were coming to power in the town, in the University and exerting new influences in the Presbytery of Glasgow, spinning schools and a bleachfield were also established.[15] As we have seen (see pp. 143, 144), interest in bleaching and finishing was shown by several of Ilay's aides. Patrick Lindsay was among the Argathelians engaged in the bleaching of linens. In 1733, he noted the need not only for better Scottish-made bleaches, but a uniform product from the bleaching processes.[16] This too was taken up by the Board of Trustees.

Its first plan was to concentrate on the improvement of the linen trade. This was effected by sending Scottish bleachers to Ireland to study Irish methods, by subsidizing the laying down of extensive bleachfields, and by awarding premiums to Scottish academic scientists for researches on the production of potashes and on the various bleaching processes. On the commercial side, the Board acted on behalf of individual bleachers as an importer of foreign bleaching materials.[17]

In 1736, the Convention of Royal Burghs observed that Ilay had been 'Verry Active to Dispose the Ministry to Countenance the Bleeching Bill' and it thanked him for that and for helping to pass the linen bill against opposition in both Houses.[18] The Board of Trustees promoted the importation of flax, set up spinning schools, helped weavers, and worried about quality control and marketing. John Law in 1705 had advocated similar measures and had recognized the necessity of providing better marketing and credit facilities for manufacturers and merchants who operated the 'putting-out' systems which produced the Scottish product.[19] Those aims were later addressed by the British Linen Company. While it aided some places and people more than others – one of the first bleachfields subsidized was Lord Milton's own – the Board and later the Linen Co. contributed to the Kingdom's prosperity and future industrialization.

The story of the Scottish linen industry has been well told many times; it is a happy one. Production rose at least seven-fold between 1730 and 1790. The numbers fully or partially employed increased so that by the 1790s over a sixth of the country's working population was at least partially employed in the trade. The spin-offs in bleaching, dying and printing, in marketing and in the ability to capitalize large enterprises were to be valuable examples for the future cotton trades and did much to stimulate the scientists and engineers of the eighteenth century as well. Lord Ilay could have foreseen little of this but he was not wrong to think that subsidizing linen would be good for Scots. His own tenants got their share of the subsidies too and, through increased rents, so did he. This use of power brought a general good. So too did the Royal Bank of Scotland which also had both economic and political reasons for its creation.

II. Ilay and The Royal Bank of Scotland (RBS)

In 1716, the Bank of Scotland lost its monopoly of banking in Scotland because monopoly rights had not been included in the new charter issued to the Bank in that year.[20] At about the same time, the struggle between the Argathelians and the Squadrone intensified. Any means which would push Argathelian interests were to be found and followed. By 1723, the Argathelians could exercise a near dominance in the town councils of both Edinburgh and Glasgow; two years later they claimed it. The bank was not conceived in a neutral political atmosphere.[21] The list of investors in RBS and the early loans made by it show it to have been very much an Argathelian device for the political control of Scotland, one relying in large part on English money since the funds to capitalize it came mostly from London investors many of them well known to Lord Ilay.[22] There were Squadrone investors too but, with two exceptions, neither they nor their English friends seem to have sat on the board for any long period until 1750.[23] The Duke of Montrose was elected Governor in 1750 which probably reflects the Duke of Argyll's somewhat tenuous grip on power in 1749/50. Montrose was followed in 1756 by Ilay's friend, Beaumont Hotham, Commissioner of Customs.

Politics was served by the RBS but its main functions were economic and reflected the belief that the expansion of the money supply was a good thing. That had been stated by John Law and believed by Ilay. More money and credit fostered trade. The speculative manias of the 1720s had introduced Ilay to many bankers in London and abroad. His French and English experiences of bubbles might have cooled his enthusiasm for speculative ventures but not his interest in banking. By 1728, he knew a great deal about the operation of markets and banking. His interests in currency and in the stability of the coinage are reflected in his pamphlet collection. Others in his circle were like himself. Among those who were initial directors of the RBS were men connected with the Treasury, the Scottish Court of Exchequer, or the tax collection bodies in Scotland. Others, like Patrick Campbell, Lord Monzie, had been large if somewhat unsuccessful investors in London. Among the early investors consulted by the founders of the Bank were London merchant-bankers like George Middleton, Patrick Campbell of Greenyards, Paul Daranda and directors of the Bank of England.[24] Still other RBS directors sat in bodies essential to the governing of Scotland or were judges of the Court of Session. That was nicely symbolized by the Bank's arms. They incorporated elements of the arms of the Dalrymples of Stair and Campbells of Argyll. Ilay, the Governor, and Sir Hew Dalrymple, Lord North Berwick, the Bank's Deputy-Governor, headed the chief Scottish courts.[25]

Such men would have known that, in the period of the South Sea Bubble, there had been plans by some in London who held Equivalent Fund debentures to use those as a capital fund upon which to establish a bank.[26] That plan came to nothing because of opposition from the Bank of England. Until 1719, no provisions had been made for their redemption or for paying the promised interest on the debentures. After 1719, two Societies were formed to collect that interest on behalf of owners in London and Scotland. In 1720, the Bank of Scotland rejected a proposal to increase its capital by the amount of the Equivalent Fund debentures against which stock would have been issued.[27] In 1724, the Equivalent Fund debenture holders were incorporated by Parliament as the Equivalent Company with a capital of £248,500.[28] One of its two Committees sat in

Edinburgh, the other in London. That company was to distribute the interest on the debentures to the share-holders but it quickly evinced interest in banking operations.

That Company's directors, largely London money-men known to Ilay, sought to charter a new bank in July 1726. It would operate in Scotland. Not all of the debenture holders converted their stock into RBS stock when the Bank was incorporated under the Great Seal of Scotland on the last day of May 1727 but about half of the Equivalent Fund debentures were subscribed.[29] They were transferred to the Bank in exchange for stock. The RBS thus came, like the Bank of England, to rest on instruments then paying 4.4% annually.[30] The RBS had an authorized capital of £111,347 and an ability to increase it by £40,000. It was from the outset a larger bank than the Bank of Scotland. The RBS was given more capital against which to write notes when £22,000 was raised by a call on investors. Another £20,000 was deposited with it by the Board of Trustees in late 1727 and early 1728. Additional funds came in from ordinary savers and from those who established overdraft accounts useful in their businesses. Even so, the RBS working capital remained smaller than it needed if it was to become the only Scottish bank.

The President of the Equivalent Company wrote to the directors of the newly formed RBS, '... we are obliged in justice to my Lord Ilay to declare that the success in general and dispatch of this important affair in particular has been greatly owing to his Lordship's diligent and powerful assistance'. It was fitting that he should have been named as Governor in the Royal Charter.[31] The Earl of Ilay was not the founder, but it is unlikely that this bank would have existed in Scotland without his efforts. Its principal active directors and Edinburgh managers were his political friends as were the Directors of the Equivalent Company.[32]

Despite the fact that the Earl of Ilay's picture today graces its notes, Ilay's role in the RBS's founding and early years is not completely known but it was great. From 1720 on, he was doing things which led to its creation. He had business with an Edinburgh Society which may have been the one distributing dividends to debenture holders.[33] Four years later, Ilay and his brother the Duke were buying Equivalent Company stock or debentures and the Earl was sending money to Scotland with which to purchase any debentures available there.[34] The Earl converted his Equivalent Co. stock into debentures on 25 January 1725.[35] Other Argathelians – William Stewart, Lord Loudoun, Charles Erskine, George Drummond, Lord Milton, and men with whom Ilay had long dealt in London were doing the same.[36] Before 1727, Ilay had shown drafts of the Bank's charter to his banker, George Middleton, who was also involved with the Equivalent Company and became the largest investor in the RBS.[37] The RBS minutes of 5 September 1727 show that Ilay ordered specimen banknotes to be sent to Middleton and that the Earl was told to 'Advise with Messrs Campbell and Daranda' in getting plates made in London to print them.[38] Ilay transferred £2,200 into RBS stock by 14 September 1727 in a transaction witnessed by Lord Provost George Drummond.[39] Drummond left Edinburgh shortly after that taking with him the Bank's by-laws about which he was 'to advise there with such Friends as his Lordship thinks proper'. The Earl had been dealing and continued to deal with Bank of England officials to arrange for the RBS to open an account with it. By 23 April 1728, he was one of six who guaranteed the bond of the RBS given to the Bank of England.[40] He was still a guarantor in 1730. For some time, Ilay was the chief representative of the RBS in London.

A bank conceived by investors and politicians, and managed principally by lawyers, functionaries and gentlemen could have only a mixed agenda. Its first years, 1727-1729, were filled with moves to drive out of business the Old Bank presided over by Squadrone enemies of Ilay. Among them were the Earls of Marchmont and Glasgow and former office holders like Sir John Inglis and Robert Dundas. Its alleged Jacobite sympathies had been cited to help in the founding of the RBS and to gain it government business. The RBS soon secured a near monopoly over the handling of government funds. It collected and presented Bank of Scotland notes for redemption in large amounts which the latter could not easily pay and eventually could not pay at all. The Bank of Scotland closed for a while and was sued by one of Ilay's friends in Glasgow, Andrew Cochrane, later Provost of the burgh.[41] Ilay's roles in all that are not clear but the dirty work was done by friends whom he had helped to pick as directors and managers. He certainly followed events, asking in the summer of 1728 if the Old Bank had paid its debts and if its interest-bearing notes were passing current.[42] The legal cases ended up in the House of Lords which gave the Earl a problem. He informed the directors that he would vote on their case in the Lords or stay at home. If he did the first, he would have to resign and his letter was a resignation letter if they wished it to be one. They were free to choose a new Governor but they seem not to have done so which probably means he stayed home or voted while saying he had resigned – as he had if they needed him to. It was an unusual display of scruples on his part.[43]

Ilay was from the beginning involved with the management of the RBS investments and with other business such as selecting staff. In August 1728, he wrote letters to Lord Milton complaining of Lord Monzie, the Earl of Crawford and Paul Daranda's dealings in bank and Equivalent stocks. He thought they had been acting illegally in England and endangering the RBS.[44] He chastised Monzie, whom he threatened to 'drop' and told Milton that Daranda's offer of £11,000 of Equivalent stock should not be taken up since it would leave the RBS short of cash.[45] He intervened with the Equivalent Company whose proprietors agreed to lend money to the RBS. He did not want them to deal with the Bank of Scotland. In 1729, he gave the nomination of the RBS Cashier to Daniel Campbell of Skipness who named Allan Whiteford. Despite his 1730 illness (see p. 245), Ilay met with the RBS's London Committee about business with the Bank of England and probably saw to it that Daranda was replaced as one of the securities required by the Bank of England.[46] In 1731, Ilay was active in trying to secure arrangements which would allow the RBS to be 'Master of the Exchange'– Milton's term describing their attempts to ensure that Scotland had adequate provisions of cash by drawing on the RBS's Bank of England account to relieve a cash shortage in Scotland. That gave the RBS small profits as the transfer agent. Lord Milton went to London in 1732 to try to secure that end but Ilay warned him not to have high hopes.[47] The Earl also aided Milton in his efforts to have the RBS made a 'perpetual corporation', an end not realized until 1738 when it secured a new charter.[48] The Earl helped the RBS in buying bonds issued by the York Buildings, East India and the South Sea Companies in 1732.[49] In the fall of 1733, Ilay picked a new Secretary for the RBS and demoted the man who had held the post.[50]

While all that was going on, the RBS flourished as a bank. The RBS in 1728 simplified lending procedures by pioneering the overdraft system which allowed limited borrowing and the payment of interest only on what one needed to borrow for the time one needed to have it.[51] By 1731, the Bank was lending to the city of Edinburgh and to other Scottish corporations.[52] That meant dealing more with Glasgow banks than had been the case in the past. By the early 1730s, RBS was making more loans than had been usual at the Bank of Scotland. Some were commercial loans, such as the one of £1,000 to Lord Milton in 1734 which he laid out on his lint field. Others were for election expenses.[53] It was also remitting monies collected – taxes, fees, Crown rents – to London and handling Army funds which gave it more contacts with English politicians and with English bankers. In those operations, banking fees increased its income.[54] Its activities augmented the circulating money of the kingdom partially realizing some of the dreams of those like Law who had wanted to increase the money supply of the country and the rate at which it circulated.

By 1736, Ilay was under a cloud because of the ongoing uproar over the elections of 1734. He angered more by his role in the aftermath of the Porteous Riots (see p. 264). The RBS was still thinking about a new charter from Parliament or the Crown which would again create a conflict of interest for him in the House of Lords. All of those things probably conspired to lead to his replacement as Governor by Lord Chief Baron Lant in March 1737. Lant served until 1742 but the Deputy-Governor and effective head of the Bank became Lord Milton (1731-1766). The RBS still functioned as an adjunct to the Argathelian political machine helping him to control the country.[55] Ilay was consulted about important business until 1738 after which he disappears from the business papers. He sold all but £500 of his stock in 1739 in anticipation of war and a sinking price. Milton was told to 'take the price current' since the market for RBS stock in London was small. Even the small holding which remained, he thought of putting in trust which would leave him free to act on Bank matters before Parliament without any conflict of interest.[56] His career with the Bank, but not his use of it, had effectively ended.

There were other Argathelian involvements with the economy in those years which may have involved the RBS. In 1729, Ilay was asked to petition the King to supply more copper coins to the Scots. Rumour said bad coins were to be called in. Poor coinage and the rumours of a recall, which would make money scarce, affected the incomes and the trading of the poor for food stuffs and nearly caused riots.[57] In 1734, Ilay probably expressed the Convention of Royal Burgh's concerns over the salt duty which was important to fishermen.

III. Ilay as Agricultural Improver

Ilay's record as a Scottish improver was not confined to banking and supporting the activities of the Board. By the 1720s, he had begun at The Whim to make agricultural improvements in Scotland. It is difficult to draw the line between what he did as an individual and what was public. Few of his innovations immediately increased his revenues. They were fun and might in the end bring in more money but they were also intended to promote the emulation by others. Most were aimed at increasing over time his own income and Scottish prosperity. They aimed at making a better and a more orderly country.

The Earl is known to have been a member of only two societies, the Honourable the Improvers in the Knowledge of Agriculture in Scotland (HIKAS) (1723-1746) and the Glasgow Highland Society (1727-) (see pp. 311, 361 n. 13). The first was a national improvement society which advocated experiments with soils and manures such as he carried out at Whitton and The Whim. Throughout its existence, it promoted the sowing of grasses, turnips and potatoes. It wanted more effective rotation systems. Encouraging forestry, it looked to the introduction into Scotland of more fruit trees and exotics. It hoped to stimulate linen production and even listened to a paper on the culture of silkworms which its author, George Preston, the Edinburgh Professor of Botany, seemed to think feasible in Scotland. The Society collected and disseminated information useful to farmers and gardeners. Eventually, in 1743, it published a volume of its transactions composed of papers given to the Society over many years by its members. Robert Maxwell's introduction, almost an improvers' manifesto, called for the establishment of a chair of agriculture in Scotland so that husbandry could be developed and taught methodically. Long leases were encouraged by HIKAS.[58] Maxwell was also clear about the relation of agriculture to industry and trade:

> ... Trade and Commerce ... can only flourish as Husbandry, the Foundation on which they are built, succeeds. Trade has indeed multiplied the Number of the Rich, and made our Land-estates infinitely more valuable; but still Husbandry must furnish the Materials for Trade, as Husbandry is the Stock, and Trade only the Improvement of it.[59]

There is no reason to think that Ilay dissented from any of that or from similar statements in the 1729 and 1732 tracts of his old Jacobite acquaintance, Brigadier William MacIntosh of Borlum, tracts written while the Brigadier was a prisoner for life in Edinburgh Castle.[60] In HIKAS the Earl of Ilay was associated with about 300 Scottish gentlemen who, if they were not such notable improvers as he, at least, encouraged things he was doing at Whitton and at The Whim. His work and his example were held up to others in the Society's 1743 publication.[61] His membership endorsed HIKAS's work; the members applauded his efforts.

The Whim estate was a piece of wasteland so poor that no one thought anything could be made of it. The friend from whom Ilay bought it, Major Thomas Cochrane, thought it worthless.[62] Ilay's purchase was a sort of gamble with his friend that he would be able to make it pay. After its acquisition in 1729, Ilay 'laid out a model farm'.[63] Beside the gardens, greenhouse and nursery described earlier (see pp. 158-61), there was a working farm of some interest. Here no tenants paid their rents in kain hens and labour services; none are known to have held on wardship or other odd tenures. The place was worked largely by Ilay's paid servants who lived in tied houses and got wages or who lived as cottars paying money rents. There was no burlaw court. He had control and could run his enterprise as he saw fit.

Trees were planted to dry out the fields and to create windbreaks. Around the site of the house, various ornamental and interesting trees were planted by the mid-1730s as the bog dried out. They gave beauty to the prospects and shade to the avenues. In the remoter areas of the estate, the filled ditches and squares were being dried out by holly, whins and other thorns, by ash, maple, cypress, hornbeam, beech, plane and other species of trees. The variation suggests that the Earl was experimenting to see which dried up the land the quickest.[64] He was also diversifying the woods because of the uses which each had. Ash was good for tools; plane and beech trees were easily worked while the maples may have promised (but surely failed) to deliver sugar.

By the 1740s, Ilay had settled on forests of firs (which in Scotland was as apt to be pines as firs) and the cedars and larches mentioned below by Maxwell of Arkland. Ilay became a considerable planter. In April 1745, Argyll purchased 120,000 firs from two growers in Aberdeenshire and then 60,000 more in the following month from his friend and relative, Alexander Fraser of Strichen.[65] In 1748, the Duke had a gang of eight men planting trees and then potatoes for twenty-seven days. If half of the men planted trees for the whole time, that would represent about 110,000 trees for the year since a modern tree planter in the Canadian bush can plant 1,000 a day in soil no harder to open than that of Blair Bog. In 1751, there were about 200,000 firs and hornbeam planted on the perimeter of the estate.[66] In 1761, he was planning to have planted 60,000 more planted.[67] The planting of trees never stopped because harvesting wood was envisioned as ongoing and needing ever new supplies. While no records survive to show it, there is reason to think that 60,000-100,000 trees were planted in many years. They were very likely fenced in some manner to protect them from the depredations of deer and the tenants since that was the Duke's policy at Inveraray.[68]

Away from the house, the fields at The Whim were separated from the parks and gardens by ha-has or sunken ditches and walls which preserved prospects.[69] Crops were planted on the increasing sections of drained land and the property was slowly transformed from bog land into something resembling a potentially productive farm. As early as 1731, Ilay sent up from the south wheat, rye, oat and barley seed, along with clover, rape and grasses.[70] This suggests a multi-field system, with a rotation among grains, planted grasses and clover. As land was reclaimed, those crops were joined by pease, potatoes and turnips for stock. There are no references to an infield-outfield system or to un-enclosed rigs. By 1761, the estate's grieve was selling meal.[71] The Whim had a mill probably erected at the dam of one of the ponds since it would have needed water power.[72] The ponds contained fish and provided ornamental prospects.

By 1743, this estate had become a model of improvement. Without naming it, Robert Maxwell of Arkland noticed it in his collection of materials published for HIKAS:

The Earl of Ilay has shewn an Example of Agriculture that was much wanted. His Lordship made choice of Moss, almost every where in this Kingdom neglected, knowing that, being made of excellent Materials, it is improvable, on a moderate Expence, from a very small to a very great Value; and that it yields, and can afford to yield from its own Substance, the manure properest for fertilizing itself. Grain, Grass from Grass-seeds sown, Oak and other Planting, have already prospered upon it by the Culture given by his Directions. Besides, to his Lordship we owe the American and Balm of Gillead Firs, the Larix [larch or tamarack], and many other useful Plants, which he introduced into this Country. But, above all, we are indebted to his Lordship for the Interest he used to obtain the Appropriation of the publick Funds to the Encouragement of our Fisheries and manufactures, which is the greatest national Good that has been done this Country these hundred Years.[73]

In short, Ilay was a man to emulate; the good done by the Board was attributable to him.

No improved estate at this time was without other things. The Whim had a lint yard or bleachfield somewhere on the estate.[74] There was a smithy and a limn kiln which may have been coeval with the appearance of the stone hammer to crush limestone in 1731. That year, the Earl's men also searched for clay deposits suitable for brick making, but they seem to have failed since Whim House was made from rubble and stone.[75] A drawing for a kiln was also produced in 1739; more lime was needed for the fields.[76] Coal was found at The Whim in 1737/8[77] but the seam, eleven to twenty-five inches thick, does not appear to have been continuously worked. By 1753, Argyll was buying coal from Major Cochrane.[78] The Whim at the end of the 1730s had a flock of sheep numbering between twenty and 300 and both beef and dairy cattle. By 1761, there were fewer animals but they were imports brought in for their blood lines. Its draft animals included 'big hoarses' [Clydesdales], four 'Shalties' and oxen.[79]

By the early 1730s Ilay had a system of management, rules for picking men and had created two institutions through which he could manipulate the economic life of the country. Running an admired demonstration farm gave him credibility with improving landlords. He was well positioned for the political roles he played up to his death in 1761. He was also enjoying life.

IV. Life

A miscellany of other things engaged his Lordship's attention in the years 1725 to 1736. In 1726, he sent several pamphlets about Mary Tofts (she claimed to have given birth to rabbits) to Lord Milton. Both followed the story and seem to have laughed at its believers and the medical men who seriously investigated her case. The pamphlets went with 'A ballet [ballade] which the ladies cannot read aloud' but which Ilay clearly thought they would read and enjoy.[80] He was no prude. In London, the Earl's politicking left him time for a certain amount of tea drinking with young ladies. Since his wife's death in 1723, he was again a good catch and may have looked for a wife. He kept up with the Ogelthorpes and even loaned Mrs. Ogelthorpe £100 or so in the 1720s. But not all of his tea drinking was of an intimate sort. There is today at Yale University a picture of a tea party in 1730 at Lord Harrington's. It pictures Mrs. Howard's [Countess of Suffolk, 1731] set in which he and his brother still figured. They were present at many such gatherings. In 1727, Ilay and the Duke arranged for Mrs. Howard to elude her brutal and mercenary husband when she was forced to leave Leicester House. They spirited her away in the Duke's carriage to Argyll's house in Petersham and continued to protect her.[81]

That sophisticated society and its pastimes can also be glimpsed in letters from and to Mrs. Howard and her friends, Mary Lepel, the wife of Lord Hervey, and Mary

Bellenden, the wife of Ilay's cousin Jack. They were bright women whose reading was ambitious. In 1731, the Countess bought Bowyer's 'Wm & Q Ann' and Eachard's 'Roman History', but says she has not read the Abbé Pluche's *Les Spectacles de la nature* or *L'Histoire de Pologne sous la Ligue D Augsburg seconde* or 'the Life of Wharton'.[82] William Bowyer and Laurence Eachard were popular but learned historians. Nöel-Antoine Pluche was one of the most important and popular natural history writers of the century. The Duke of Wharton had recently died and this anonymous biography was one of several which had been quickly written to commemorate a remarkable wit, rake, Free Mason and Jacobite. *L'Histoire de Pologne sous la Ligue D Augsburg seconde* has not been traced but it would have dealt with the end of the Great Northern War (1700-1721) which reduced Sweden to a second rate power, made Poland negligible, and raised Russia to the status of a Great Power. Less learned, but perhaps no less witty, was *The Ladies Guide to dress style, gallantry and love* which was also on the list.[83] Other letters written to Henrietta refer to their reading of works of history and literature by Pierre de l' Estoile, Denis Vairasse d'Allais, Bernard le Bovier de Fontenelle, and the fashionable English journalists, deists and poets such as Alexander Pope, Edward Young, John Arbuthnot,[84] Jonathan Swift and John Gay. Some of those authors moved in their circle. In 1725, Ilay sent Lord Milton verses by George Bubb Dodington 'upon Mr. P[ope] & his brother Young'. He had earlier sent poems by 'Miss Hervey' which were actually Young's and not her's.[85] Another letter in the collection ends by saying that 'Pope is come into my roome and desires I wou'd come down and eat my breakfast with him without form, but with infinite sincerity'.[86]

Ilay still remained in contact with Pope and through him with other literary men, such as James Thomson, and their patrons – men such as Lords Bolingbroke, Bathurst, Chesterfield and Hervey. Ilay saw many of them at the courts of the King or the Prince of Wales. Pope and Ilay were friendly enough so that Pope visited Whitton unannounced in 1727, perhaps even walking over since the distance was not great between his house and the Whitton estate.[87] Before that, the Earl had given Pope a copy of the 'Corpus Juris Civilus Tomus, Primus' (1727).[88] At some point, Ilay was given a bitch which Pope had bred.[89] Many of their friends were the same people who were hosts to Montesquieu and Voltaire when they visited England in the 1720s. Ilay met Voltaire[90] and may have known Montesquieu through many mutual friends. As a peripheral member of Pope's circle, Ilay would have met in this period many of the more interesting figures in the intertwined worlds of fashion, politics and art. This was a circle taken up not only with the gossip of the court, politics and the ups and downs of members of the cosmopolitan elite to which they belonged but with more substantial concerns. Those did not preclude other interests such as cards. All seem to have been avid card players – 'whisk', loo, cribbage.

An undated letter from Mary Lepel to Mrs. Howard (c.1729) makes her compliments to Lord Ilay and goes on to say 'I really Love and esteem him, nor am I insensible of what I owe him'. Later she wrote to arrange a meeting between Mrs. Howard and Ilay. By the mid-1730s, this had changed. Relations between the Earl and Mrs. Howard had cooled; politics finally drove them apart.[91] By 1737, Lord Hervey says that Mrs. Howard, now Lady Suffolk, hated him for having neglected her in order to win over the Queen – who continued to dislike him.[92] Still, Ilay and the Countess remained in touch and, as we shall see, in the 1740s cooperated to aid Ilay's niece, Lady Mary Cook.

Relations between Ilay and Pope also soured. The good will of the 1720s and early 1730s did not last. It is not clear if he was aware of Pope's ill-natured joke on Edmund Curll, the publisher whom Pope had 'set up' to print illegally some of Pope's letters to peers.[93] Ilay managed that business for the House of Lords which involved his ordering the seizure of printed papers by Black Rod on 12 May 1735. In 1736, the poet and the politician dined to discuss legal business. By 1740, Pope was saying hard things about Ilay. Writing to Lord Marchmont in that year, Pope remarked that 'as you find Scots more honest & more honorable than the English, I think the time of your quitting them (upon those terms) must happen after my Lord I– y's arrival' in Scotland'.[94] By 1740, Ilay had few friends among the notable English literary men.

Despite his associations with literary men, Ilay was not a man who wrote much if anything for publication. He could if he wished, write a witty and gracious personal letter. His business letters said things clearly and with economy. If the introduction to John Law's republished work of 1720 was by the Earl, he could write as well as many pamphleteers. That he might also have been a pamphleteer is suggested by a story from 1730.

Lord Hervey had written a pamphlet against Lord Bolingbroke which Walpole looked at and thought libelous. It said nasty things about the peers who had protested the House of Lord's approval of the King's speech on the Treaty of Seville and did so outside the privileged space of the House of Lords. Sir Robert gave it to Ilay to work over so that it would stay on the right side of the law – an interesting judgment of his knowledge of English libel law. His emendations are described by Robert Halsband:

> In revising the essay for publication Ilay's tactic was to pretend the Lords' Protest was a forgery that had been concocted by factious Lords. To begin with he provided a title page that he headed: 'A Detection of the Late Author of A Late spurious Pamphlet intitled the Lords Protest' and beneath it a six-line quotation from Paradise Lost about the Apostate Angel. In the essay itself he struck out several long passages by Hervey and substituted his own to strengthen the pretense that the Lords' Protest', was a 'most impudent piece of Forgery & most Satyrical Libel on those Great Persons whose Names are there prostituted to this Author's [Bolingbroke's] vile purpose'. Where Hervey had written 'their L_____ships' he substituted 'The Author & his accomplices'; for 'Protesters' he substituted 'Forgers'; and he inserted 'those who personate' before 'Members of a British Senate'.[95]

It was not published. Perhaps it still ridiculed peers in ways courts might recognize even though what was asserted as the Lords' Protest was said to be a forgery – which of course it was not quite. Lady Louisa Stuart was probably correct to think that Ilay read little modern literature but it is interesting that he could find just what he needed in Milton. In the end, Joseph Spence's 1756 epigram about him probably got it right,

Argyll has wit they say, for what?
For writing? No; for writing not. [96]

Ilay's usual round was work, socializing in London, weekends at Whitton, and annual trips north. He went to Scotland most years. That could be something of an adventure. On 21 November 1725, on his return from Scotland, his coach overturned near Morpeth and rolled down a bank. Reporting this to Milton later that day, he said he had been shaken and probably would not go to bed sober – a rare allusion to excessive drinking.[97] Some trips took him almost annually to Houghton where he enjoyed himself reading while others hunted. Once he tried to find new water sources for that estate. Other trips took him to spas to drink the waters which he believed relieved his illnesses. He was in Bath in 1728. He found Bath 'tiresome' but it would be enjoyed by any 'that likes A croud'. In August 1731 he went to Scarborough.[98] Those trips were not vacations but to drink the waters for his health.

The Earl's health broke down in 1730. In the winter and spring, he had fits of fever with pain worse than he had ever felt. He was better in the summer but on 6 October 1730, he wrote to Lord Marchmont with perhaps a bit of exaggeration, 'I have been for near these 3 weeks so ill of a violent giddiness in my head after taking the bark to stop my ague which had returned, that I have been forced to avoid writing as much as possible'.[99] Three days later he told Milton that he had always been subject to heart palpitations and, in consequence, 'Giddiness's of my head & sometimes fainting in cases where people are more or less subject to them, viz upon coming from riding in the cold to A warm fire &c ...'. His spells were often accompanied by an ague.[100] The 'giddiness' sometimes prevented him from walking or riding. That autumn he had fallen down after pruning a tree. Having consulted his medical books, he treated himself with salt of vitriol (a vomit), rhubarb (a purgative), bark (given for fevers) and hartshorn (*sal volatile* or ammonia, a sudorific given for fevers). He also drank Bristol waters. While he was ill, he consulted his Edinburgh surgeon-apothecary, John McGill and possibly his regular Scottish physician, Dr. John Clerk. Ilay preferred Dutch trained men to those who qualified in England.[101] He was slow in recovering but, by the end of November, he was well enough to be up and about. He had a recurrence in July 1731 but 'no fainting fits as before'.[102] That accounted for his trip to Scarborough in late summer. While it would not be reasonable to speculate too much about the nature of his illnesses, it sounds very much as if he was a long-term sufferer from malaria and had attacks of what is sometimes called recurring positional vertigo. That is the result of small particles circulating in the inner ear. It does not usually result in much, if any, hearing loss, but it often makes it difficult to walk for some time and sometimes brings on tinnitus. The Earl's 1730-31 illness had few if any long-term physical effects and his health was generally good until 1735. In January 1735 he again became seriously ill with a fever.[103] In September of that year, he suffered another attack of giddiness for which he took 'Spaw Water' and rested at Whitton.[104] His other persistent health problem was migraine headaches which caused him pain but no visual distortions.

Ilay's mother died on 12 May 1735. That occasioned no surviving record of sorrow but it did occasion a few difficulties as the brothers settled her estate. Ilay got something out of the Duddingston properties, 'the first of any patrimnony I have ever had'.[105] Since he had some books and perhaps some furniture there, he probably had been using the estate as his Edinburgh base. In the end, the matter was not wound up for some years.[106] Intimations of mortality also moved him to make a will. He asked Milton to send him the forms which would allow the transfer of his Bank stock 'in case of my falling of the perch... to such person as I leave the rest of my stuff'. He recovered but there may have been a long-term effect of this illness. After 1735, he seems less outgoing and more content to spend his leisure time at Whitton. After c.1735, he is less frequently found in the memoirs of contemporaries– but that is an impression only. He was fifty-three and had been in general good health since he had been shot at Sherrifmuir in 1715. He was also growing rich.

The Earl improved his fortune in these years. His income from offices stayed at about £4,000 to which had to be added the return on his investments.[107] How much that was is hard to say. Some money was probably held in Scotland after 1727 although he had no account at the RBS. He is likely to have had accounts in Holland. His Coutts Bank ledgers do not state regular balances but were running accounts. The 'In book', where his income is registered, is often a peculiar record. There are years when no interest payments or dividends are entered and, in most years, some of those are not posted until a year or so after they were payable. Other years seem not to record payments from his offices. In both sets of ledgers, it is sometimes difficult to sort transactions which were really his from those which may have been transacted for others. Sometimes when a payment of principal or interest is made on a loan, it looks like any other deposit. He bought lottery tickets both for himself and others. In 1724, he may have held as much as £5,000 in various lotteries. The payments on those ancestors of the modern premium bond are hard to determine. Finally, there are gaps in the accounts for 1726 and 1727. Despite those shortcomings he was clearly richer.

In 1725, his interest and dividend payments suggest his capital was at least £25,000 and distributed between lottery tickets, Equivalent Company Debentures, East India Co. bonds, South Sea stock and loans made to Lady Ogelthorpe, Col. John Middleton, Walter Stewart, and the Earls of Kinnoull and Loudoun. In addition to an investment income of at least £777.16.1, he received what seems to have been over £400 in lottery prizes. He had an indefinite amount of money tied up in other tickets. Given his speculations of 1720, this was a very conservative portfolio. In 1729, when one can again find in his 'In book' records for what looks like a full year, his position had improved considerably. His invested capital was then about £36,467 and his investments about as diverse. No lottery tickets are listed in the 'In book' but he still had shares in the South Sea Co., a large amount in East India Co. bonds, shares in the RBS and loans to Loudoun and perhaps the Earl of Home. Perhaps unrecorded notes had been paid off and invested to account for some of the increase in his funds. During the remainder of this period, the records are so incomplete that similar calculations cannot be made. However, during the decade, he had expended money on his estates at Whitton and in Peebles-shire and was building in London. He was also living a bit more expensively. His Major Domo was getting more money, presumably to meet household expenses, and Ilay was buying, or at least recording at Coutts, the purchase of more wine.[108] That probably was a sign of increased entertaining at Whitton and his London House.

During the period of the 'bubbles'. Ilay had invested in the Bank of England but in this period there are no records of his buying or selling Bank of England stock. He may have wanted higher rates of return which were to be found in the South Sea and East India Companies whose stocks, bonds and annuities he did own. They often paid 4%. He lost some money on his East India Co. holdings. In 1728 and 1729, he bought York Buildings Company bonds and may have held them through the period since there is no record of their sale. Ilay also became a considerable lender. In addition to the loans mentioned, he lent £4,000 to his brother in 1736. On such loans he took 4-5%, a better return than he could get on his stock transactions. The once penniless Army Captain had become very well off. His book and instrument collections had also become larger and more valuable. His total worth would have been over £35,000 by 1736. With the payment from his offices, that meant an annual income over £5,000. He has few reasons to be discontented.

Plate 8. A View of the House and part of the Garden of His Grace the Duke of Argyll at Whitton, by William Woollett, coloured engraving(1757), with permission of the London Brough of Richmond upon Thames.

Chapter 14

Battles and Defeats: Politics c. 1730 - 1743

I. An Overview

The 1720s had been good years for the Earl of Ilay. He had been successful in the elections of 1722 and 1727 although there had been criticism of his methods of securing votes.[1] He had dealt with the Malt Tax crisis and got on well with Walpole. He had become more independent of his brother. The Earl had consolidated his position in Scotland partly through the founding of the Royal Bank of Scotland and the Board of Trustees for Fisheries and Manufactures. By c.1730, his control over the universities and the Kirk seemed secure and he had begun to effect changes to the country's culture through patronage appointments. He was a busy, moderately wealthy man enjoying life. This period would end differently. The years 1731-1743 were long ones for Lord Ilay.

The Earl's political life was increasingly complicated by growing resentment in Scotland at his political methods and the policies of Walpole's government. By 1733, Walpole and all those who served him were being challenged in London. Opposition to Ilay got worse with the Porteous Riots in 1736. Then, in 1737-39, his brother broke with him and with Walpole and led into opposition some of the MPs on whom Ilay and Sir Robert relied. Things worsened when the 1741 election reduced the number of Scottish government supporters to nineteen, a number too small to sustain the Ministry. Walpole was forced to resign early in 1742. When Walpole fell, Ilay was sacked as the patronage manager for Scotland but still kept his offices for life. Retirement seemed his only future. He was out but that was somewhat offset by two things. His friends were well entrenched in Scotland and could be obstructive to the inept politicians who succeeded him. The second thing which prevented his eclipse was the certainty of his inheritance of the dukedom of Argyll which would give him a larger income and more personal power and patronage than he ever had had at his disposal.

II. The Work of a Scottish Manager

Ilay's day-to-day work was recommending people for jobs in every area of life in such a manner that his political friends in London would find it easy to control Scotland and would have, after the next general election, many supporters in both Houses of Parliament. Electioneering never stopped. In London, the Earl of Ilay was an advisor; in Scotland, he seemed to be the man in charge. Scottish managers made appointments with an eye to keeping Scotland quiet. Sometimes this meant being willing to countenance Jacobites if they had ceased to lust after false gods – or gave that appearance. Supporting some was a reasonable way to control areas of the country. Ilay did not boggle at appointing Episcopalians if they would sign loyalty oaths. The loyalty of dubious others might be bought with preferment. It was better to take a risk now and then on the persuasive power of a place than to have to use force. Repression always made enemies; favours to the disaffected bought some immediate and maybe lasting gratitude. Favours were cheaper than repression. Placating Jacobites bought time to reconcile them to an order they disliked. Such views guided his Highland policies but they had little appeal in England.

Ilay's long-term Highland policy was summed up in the memoranda submitted to Ilay in 1725 by James Erskine, Lord Grange (see pp 95-6). Grange urged a lessening of the power of the chiefs, the better administration of justice in the region, the establishment of more secure and non-military tenures, economic development and education. Ilay accepted Grange's views but the London government was mostly interested in the ongoing disarming of Highlanders and in watching Jacobites and Papists. For Londoners, security took precedence over the long-term civilizing changes which would yield permanent security.[2] The commander of the disarming force, General Wade, was busy building roads in the area but he sometimes interceded with the government for those who had submitted or wished to do so. Among them was Robertson of Strowan who, in 1731, had Wade's good wishes and solicited help from Thomas Kennedy, William Stewart and Ilay.[3] Robertson was asked to give information about Papists in the Highlands and who should be arrested.[4] Cases like his regularly came to the Earl. If controlling the 'barbarous' Highlands was an essential part of Ilay's work, so too was controlling the 'civilized and polite' burghs.

After 1725, Edinburgh generally presented few problems until 1728 when the Town Council was disturbed by issues affecting the control of the city and its votes. In 1729, the Earl was picked as the sole arbiter by the parties who had suits pending in the Court of Session. In September, he wrote to Newcastle, 'My chief business at present is to reconcile or determine some disputes & mutual claims that have lately arisen between the Merchants & the Trade people of this Town'.[5] He did not take this business lightly. He heard the evidence in March 1729 and issued his decree in London on 12 March 1730:

> ... I having maturely considered the said mutual processes, with the minutes and claims, and answers, with the vouchers given in by them *hinc inde* and heard parties procurators in my presence *viva voce*, and having weighed the arguments on each side, and perused the precedents laid before me jointly by both parties; I give forth my final Sentence and Decreet-arbital....

That decree defined the sett [constitution] of the burgh and was almost unchanged until the nineteenth century.[6] Ilay's clarifications and changes gave more power to the Lord Provost and the Merchants but clearly stated and widened the electoral rights of the Trades. He strengthened his interest so that at the next election the right men would be returned by the burgh. Edinburgh gave him few problems until the Porteous Riots of 1736.

Glasgow was different because there he had to counter the efforts of Montrose and other Squadrone men. The burghs in the city's electoral district had not re-elected Daniel Campbell in 1727 although he was returned by the returning officer and his election was found good by the House of Commons. Campbell's major sin in the eyes of voters was his willingness to see the tax burden of Scots increased. Ilay had opposed the increase which was not voted. The Earl argued that the country could not afford the increase and that it would lead to riots and possibly rebellion.[7] In 1728, Ilay visited Glasgow to mend fences. The Glasgow merchants got the explanations they needed and the University men of his faction were given encouragement. The former were no doubt pleased at his opposition to the revenue reform bill in 1729.[8]

Other burghs too could be restive. In 1729, he and Milton gave jobs to the sons of a bailie at Aberdeen.[9] That smoothed feathers ruffled in the previous year or two when he had ignored some councillors' wishes with regard to Marischal College appointments and church livings. There were many cases like that.

The various agencies and courts with which Ilay and Milton were involved brought more work. Those bodies were useful so long as they served Argathelian purposes and did not become the vehicles for individuals to go their own way or try to displace Ilay's chief aide, Lord Milton. At some time, most of his under-bosses proved troublesome. Lord Monzie left the faction in the 1730s over policy differences which he had with Milton at the RBS. Lord Grange left in 1733 because Ilay would not or could not do more for his family. Charles Erskine in the 1730s and 1740s flirted with Newcastle's friends and with his own Squadrone relatives. George Drummond, who was nothing without his offices and Ilay's countenance, was disciplined on more than one occasion. Keeping them all pulling together was not an easy task and would have been impossible without the knowledge, business acumen and good sense of Lord Milton.

Control came through patronage. As we have seen, the Earl filled about three quarters of the Treasury jobs to which he nominated men and probably more in other institutions. Those men had to be made more efficient since Scottish revenues did not cover all the expenses incurred by the government in Scotland.[10] He tried to remodel the Customs and Excise Boards but that was not possible and he would never see them without English members.[11] The customs and excise revenues rose but not as much as it was hoped they might. All that took time and satisfied some but not all who expected things of him. His patronage seemed to many monopolistic and misguided.

By 1731, many in the Kirk found him odious. That made church patronage more difficult to administer. Another constant concern were the universities where posts to which he would appoint were in the gift of others. The Squadrone leader, the Duke of Montrose, had been humiliated by Ilay at the University of Glasgow. But, Montrose was still Chancellor at Glasgow and did what he could to oppose Ilay and his political faction. The Squadrone, although humbled in elections and in disarray, could not be ignored. Those who supported the 'Old Bank' did not like what he and his friends had done to it and them. Unreconciled Jacobites and Tories thought Ilay duplicitous and his brother too arrogant to bear. There was even dissension in the Argathelian ranks. Ilay and Duncan Forbes fell out over candidates in Inverness-shire, Ross-shire and the Inverness Burghs, a sign that the brothers were not co-operating as well as they had done in the past.[12]

Given all he had to do, it is not surprising that his London levees were crowded and the importuning constant. As he was waited upon, so he did a good deal of waiting upon others. And, always there were the elections for the MPs and Peers. Ilay worked constantly at those which often meant reaching out to old enemies. In 1730, he was cultivating the Earl of Marchmont and claimed to have been unable to secure for Marchmont a place for one of the latter's hangers-on.[13] Because he was ill in 1730, he did not go to Scotland for the peerage election and was absent from the election held in Edinburgh on 17 November. Despite his debility, he had organized support of the Earl of Morton who won a seat in the peerage election. It had not been easy and a lot of dispatches had been sent express. The warrants for the election were mishandled and the seals used were not the proper one; proxies seem to have been wrongly addressed.[14] The English were unable or unwilling to understand and observe Scottish procedures and forms. He had to be very vigilant. All this went on year after year.

Besides his normal managerial work, the Earl of Ilay attended the House of Lords where between 1730 and 1743 he was named to 416 committees and sat on many legal cases (See Appendix I). His work as a legislator was entering a ten-year high which saw him often looking after Scottish interests.

We know that he debated the pensions bills in 1729-1732. He argued against them because they would impede the work of managers like himself. He seems to have said on one occasion – presumably with a straight face and knowing it could not be denied – that the King honoured 'the most proper persons to be entrusted' with public business.[15] John Yorke, in February 1730, looked forward to hearing Ilay 'demonstrate that the [pensions] bill, intended to prevent bribery and corruption, will effactually establish it'.[16] Yorke's cynicism was probably justified. The pensions bill was defeated as was a Tory call for a list of those who had pensions. Ilay had the satisfaction of seeing such bills thrown out three times between 1729 and 1732.[17] In May 1731, he supported the 'English Language Law Bill' which made it mandatory to write laws in English. Archaic language and scripts had no place in the statutes or in the courts. He amended the bill so that 'the proceedings in the exchequer of Scotland, be also wrote in a plain legible hand', that in which 'the Acts of Parliament are engrossed'. That passed on 3 May.

Ilay, in 1732, supported the Salt Tax Bill. Throughout his career, he argued that it did not unduly increase royal power, had precedents in legislation enacted under William III, and would raise taxes in a more equitable manner. He did not see Britain as heavily taxed when compared to other states and tended to think taxes were good, if they did not hurt trade and spread the burdens among classes. Throughout his career, he argued that the land tax shifted burdens to the small upper class and that without excises merchants and others would pay virtually nothing for the services of the state. Allowing them to escape forced 'old families' to become dependent on the government which was not good in a system dependent on elections. 'How can this be reconciled to that justice and equality, which ought to be observed as to the imposing of taxes upon the people?' Later it was not just loyalty to Walpole which led him to support measures to use the Sinking Fund for the relief of the tax burden created by some excise and consumption taxes. Doing so might relieve taxpayers when they needed it.[18] His was a self-interested stand but there was an element of principle in it too. When the Salt Tax passed, Scots for three years were to be taxed at a much lower rate than the English.[19]

In February 1732, he spoke for the Mutiny Bill and against reducing the Army or putting new restraints on its officers. The bill in no way threatened the 'Constitution' since Parliament was to authorize it. It was a new law but so too, once, were the provisions of Magna Carta and the liberties secured by the Petition of Right.[20] A year later, on 6 March 1733, he argued for not reducing the 'Land Forces' saying, as he and his brother usually did in such debates, that the commanders of the armed forces were not and would not be threats to British liberty. The Jacobite threat was real and brought with it the threat of invasion from France and of civil war. Reduction of the force levels meant that 'we must be every now and then [be] executing or at least forfeiting some of our countrymen, perhaps some of our relations'.[21] He continued to make such arguments up to and beyond the '45.

The Earl spoke in 1733 in debates on the Excise Tax Bill and on South Sea Accounts. His brother opposed him and the Ministry on those issues which presaged a lasting split that came over the Porteous Riots and what to do about the rioters.

Scots disliked English-legislated taxes and even more Walpole's efficiency in collecting them. Many resented the fact that Sir Robert had the King's confidence and controlled the administration and policy with Parliamentary majorities which seemed bought by men like Ilay. That was the line preached by the Parliamentary Opposition and by journalists such as those writing for the *Craftsman*, sponsored by Lord Bolingbroke,[22] William Pulteney and others. Their periodical throve on its clever ridicule of Walpole, his ministers, and their policies. Its writers said they wished to see a government of good men who would truly act in the national interest under a benevolent, well-guided King. Walpole and his friends were derided in the press by Tory wits like John Gay, a protégé of the Duke of Queensberry, and Scottish men of letters like David Mallet and James Thomson – one attached to Lord Bolingbroke and the *Craftsmen*, the other to the Prince of Wales but both in the Opposition. In Parliament, Opposition grievances centred on taxes, the size and funding of the Army and Navy but extended to minor things which engendered a lot of noise. In Scotland the 'Patriot' line was echoed by Squadrone men like the Earls of Marchmont and Stair and their friends.[23] From this uproar came a concerted effort to dump Walpole and his friends in 1733. The triggers were attempts to substitute excises for customs duties on tobacco and wine and a case which upset Anglican bishops and made some of them unreliable voters in the Lords.

The Excise Bill of 1733 would have allowed excisemen to search premises and seemingly violate the right of Englishmen against illegitimate searches. Scots wanted to claim that right although it was not clear that they were entitled to do so. The bill caused an outcry in and out of Parliament in both Scotland and England. On 11 April, while it was debated in the House of Commons, a mob assembled outside which did not disperse at the reading of the Riot Act. Walpole on leaving the House braved the mob with an escort of constables and friends including Ilay. Some of them were roughed up but the Earl emerged unscathed. That incident offers another example of his friendship for Sir Robert and of the Earl's physical courage.[24] The bill had to be withdrawn the next day.[25]

In the House of Lords, Walpole's majority was now very small. It was not sure that all the bishops, on whom Walpole usually relied, would be loyal. Some lords, led by Lord Chesterfield, had defected. The issue which was used to test Walpole's strength was how the confiscated estates of the South Sea Company directors had been managed. Since the Company was then experiencing difficulties for which it was seeking parliamentary help, this was an issue which revived unpleasant memories kept alive by the flourishing condition of some directors who had been in place during the 'Bubble'. An inquiry was moved in the House of Lords on 3 May 1733 by Lord Bathurst. Ilay argued that the motion should not be voted on since there had been no notice of motion. He wanted the vote postponed so that supporters could be brought in but he failed to effect that.[26] Throughout May, Ilay was against requiring the South Sea accounts to be produced before the Lords. As a large stock and bond holder over many years, this may have been and certainly looks like a self-interested move. The South Sea matter hung fire all month until 24 May when another vote concerning this was lost by the government which secured only a tie vote on a resolution in the Lords. A tied vote was a negative in that chamber. That came despite frenzied activity by Ilay and Newcastle for the government.[27] It showed that Walpole's control of the House of Lords was very insecure. In early June 1733, the government finally won. It had managed to retain the support of the bishops and to bring in enough supporters to defeat Chesterfield and his friends. Ilay finally moved the previous question in a debate on the terms of the enquiry into the South Sea directors' conduct; that more or less ended that debate.[28] Argyll and Ilay had split over the Excise issue but Chesterfield and his friends had not persuaded the Duke of Argyll to join with them to gain control of the Lords and use it to oust Walpole.

Among the losers in this fight were Ilay's Squadrone opponents: Montrose, Tweeddale, Stair, Marchmont, Rothes and Lord Grange – all lost places or power. Ilay's reward for his efforts was the Keepership of the Great Seal of Scotland which had been held by Montrose – another in the string of humiliations inflicted by Ilay on that Duke.[29] The Privy Seal, which Ilay resigned, was given to Ilay's then friend the Duke of Atholl. All that heightened party strife in Scotland.[30] Recriminations and sackings continued with members of the armed forces being forced to resign.

The Opposition, smarting from the punishment it had taken, in 1734 introduced a bill which would have made Army commissions for life. This was presented after the King had sacked Lord Cobham and the Duke of Bolton, 'Patriots' who held commissions in the Army. Ilay and his brother opposed that bill which was defeated 100 to 62. That indicated the new balance of power in the House of Lords and the defeat of older conceptions of what Army commanders should be.[31] The next move the Opposition made was to appeal to the King to reveal who had urged him to remove from the services those who belonged to the Opposition. Ilay argued this was asking the House to again vote on the same question. It was defeated.[32]

III. Preliminaries to The Elections of 1734

If control of Parliament was to be wrested from Walpole, it would have to come in elections. But, Sir Robert and his friends controlled them. They might return a majority for themselves. The easiest majority to overturn was still that in the Lords where Walpole's grasp was slackening. Peerage elections in Scotland came when peers died and at general elections. Both were managed by Ilay so he was a man to attack. By 1733, his role in government made him subject to threats of investigating his conduct in elections. In that year, he thought he had little to worry about. Realistically, he wrote (to Newcastle?) about the coming elections in Scotland:

The only disagreeable circumstances that I forsee will attend my doing my duty here is, the being obliged too often to importune the Kings servants with applications in behalf of some, who though they are incapable of being misled so far as to joyn in the opposition, yet, through humane frailty, & the byass of self interest, are easily convinced of their own merit, & willing to think their rewards unequal to it.[33]

He was in Scotland campaigning in July and August 1733 and secured the election of Sutherland and Balcarres as Representative Peers. Ilay negotiated deals with other peers some of whom were undoubtedly paid off by Lord Milton from the Earl's personal funds or from government money given to him for this purpose.[34] Ilay did not then feel threatened but tensions were rising and conditions were about to change.

The Earl of Ilay had failed to find the money needed by Lord Grange who in exasperation had switched sides and planned to enter Parliament in opposition to Walpole. Ilay then had a bill drawn up to make it illegal for Scots judges to sit as MPs. Robert Dundas, MP, drafted it to be harmless to Grange but Ilay changed it before it was introduced. Grange chose to be an MP and not a judge although many continued to refer to him as Lord Grange.[35] His defection brought a capable manager to Ilay's opposition in Scotland – one who knew enough about Ilay's affairs to embarrass him. By the end of the year, Grange and his new friends were trusting little to the regular post fearing that the Ilay's men were opening their mail.[36]

The peerage election of 1734 everyone knew would be a rough contest. It was anticipated to be scandalous. In November 1733, disgruntled peers met in Edinburgh to organize a campaign against the Ministry and its list of those whom the government wanted elected. On 1 December, a letter was sent to voters saying that the list was 'contrary both to the letter and spirit of the twenty-second Article of the Treaty of Union' and that the writers had before them evidence of Ilay's illicit efforts to secure the return of men named on the list. He was claimed to have offered 'money... pensions, places, civil and military preferments, acts of grace, reversals of attainder' – as he had done for years.[37]

In London, Lords Chesterfield, Stair, Tweeddale and their followers renewed efforts to wrest control of the House of Lords from Walpole's friends. Marchmont on 6 March moved to give the House of Lords, not the Court of Session, the determination of Scottish peerage elections in which only the peers in 1690 would have a vote. Ilay pointed out this would prejudice those with dormant titles; it would also have deprived him and others of a vote. The motion failed by 63 to 96.[38] On 18 March 1734, the Duke of Bedford and Lord Chesterfield moved in the House that 'any persons taking upon them to engage any peers of Scotland to vote for any peer or list of peers to represent the Peerage of Scotland in Parliament is an encroachment on the freedom of elections'. [39] Two days later a lively debate ensued. It was recounted to Lord Grange by the Earl of Stair, who had long disliked the Campbell brothers:

> Lord Ilay hardly ever looked up all ye while of ye debate ... [when he spoke, he] Said it was irregular to bring in such a resolution wthout grounding it upon some fact wch had been proved. Yt witout some proof they could not believe yt anything had been done or would be done and therefore it was needless to put ye question upon which I spoke, Ld hervey, E. Cholmandoly, D. Of Newcastle, Ld Chancellor, e. Pawlet and last of all ye D. Of Argyll. Complaining of ye indignity done to ye Peers of Scotland, by suppozing they could be corrupted[;] on ye other side spoke the E. Chesterfield, Ld Easterd, ... E. Winchester and Ld Bathurst, and yn ye previous question was put [and carried] 60 to 99 ... protested.[40]

Attendance was high, a good indicator of tensions. Afterwards, Ilay did not complain when he was called the 'Scots W--p-le' but his brother said something not recorded. Argyll pretended to be above all corruption and disliked the fact that his brother was not.[41] The agitation continued and stirred up remarkable attendance at the peerage election.

Before the session was over, the Earl moved some technical amendments to bills on stock jobbing and insurance which he supported. He also showed his usual concerns over the increase in force levels.[42]

IV. The Elections of 1734

The 1734 Scottish elections repay attention since they are well-documented and likely to have been quite typical of others he managed. Ilay's surviving correspondence is full of deals in which something was given in exchange for votes. Indeed, he had been busy since 1732 giving out minor offices, church livings, and in being vindictive. In one typical deal concerning a seat in the House of Commons, the Grant Clan had one member, Patrick Grant of Elchies, made a judge of the Court of Session (1732) but the Grants were denied a desired sheriff-ship. In return, they created enough votes on their Glenmoriston estate to control the Elginshire seat.[43] They were promised that they would have no opposition in their county and that various of their dependents would later be looked after.[44]

The 'Patriots' were pushing other lines. Grange had been behind earlier efforts to get the voters in Scotland to instruct their MPs and was now trying to find candidates willing to be instructed. They were to call for the repeal of the Septennial Act which set the term of Parliaments at seven years. Frequent elections put a strain on managers and kept politics at the boil while longer periods allowed for quiet. By late spring

1734, the Squadrone had not found many MPs who would vote for a Triennial Act or candidates who were willing to be instructed.

Ilay had been active in other ways. On 11 March 1734, he secured the Act disqualifying any Court of Session judge from sitting both on the Court and in the House of Commons.[45] Earlier Grange had noted that, if it passed, 'I know I shall be trampl'd & piss'd on by every little cur of Ilays'.[46] He chose to run for Parliament and resigned his judgeship on 1 May 1734 in a document witnessed by Montrose, Tweeddale, Aberdeen, Marchmont and Stair.[47] In early April, there was a heated confrontation between Ilay's friends and their opponents in a meeting of the Convention of Royal Burghs. All the sins of his Lordship were enumerated but the Opposition failed to get a declaration of support from the body for the instructing of MPs.[48] Later, Grange managed to secure a letter of support from electors in Stirlingshire where some Erskine estates lay. Lord Milton told Ilay it was signed 'mostly by Grahame's & Erskines' and not by all the voters. Milton prevented Grange and his friends from getting a similar letter from the Quarter Sessions of Midlothian by the simple expedient of bringing in more Argathelian JPs to outvote them. He had used that tactic in the Convention of Royal Burghs when the resolution was moved and passed 'instruct[ing] their 15 Members of parliament to support the Septennial Act'.[49] Not long after the Convention of Royal Burghs had met, Ilay asked that Montrose be removed as Lord Lieutenant of Stirlingshire. That took away some Squadrone influence and prestige. Later in April, Ilay presented addresses to the King from Argathelian supporters. Those congratulated the King on the marriage of the Princess Royal to the Prince of Orange and came from the Town Council of Glasgow and the Edinburgh JPs. Petitions helped to organize groups which would be active in the elections.[50]

The elections to the House of Commons were bitterly fought. No one respected the 1729 Act against bribery. All sides wanted as many seats in the Lords and Commons as they could get. That was normal politics – as was deploring it in arguments indicting the country's chief politician and burgh-monger for corruption. When the election came, toward the end of May, the Argathelians got perhaps twenty-four seats for the Ministry. They did particularly well in the burghs. The Squadrone got four seats, other opposition Whigs five, and the Tories two.[51] The rest were independents. The election gave Ilay a new nickname – '*congé d'élire*'.[52]

The peerage election, equally corrupt, was followed by the London papers. Held on 4 June 1734, it brought out more peers than had ever assembled for an election. Eighty-seven voted but things did not go well.[53] It began badly since it was not held in the usual place, Holyrood Palace, but in the crowded 'Burrow Room of Edinburgh' which the Town Council controlled. Ilay's friend, Patrick Lindsay, was then Lord Provost. The Duke of Montrose and other peers objected to the Burgh Room because it was too confined and not the appointed place. Stair said that Holyrood Palace – perhaps a half mile away – was surrounded by a battalion of troops. By law there were to be no troops within two miles of voting peers. Ilay answered that the troops were necessary because of the threat of riots.[54] The proceedings dragged on as peers' credentials were questioned by Hamilton and Queensberry. Queensberry protested the influence used to obtain votes and told how some peers had been offered bribes.

Among those protesting was Ilay's distant relative, Lord Elphinstone.[55] It took eight hours for the speeches to be made, the votes to be cast and counted. Once it was over, six peers – the Dukes of Hamilton, Queensberry, and Montrose and the Earls of Stair and Kincardine and Dundonald – petitioned the House of Lords alleging 'illegal practices' in the election. They cited the practices about which Lord Grange later wrote in *The Fatal Consequences of Ministerial Influence* (1736) where he gave particular instances.[56] The petitioners' charges were general; they did not cite specific laws which were violated or name those bribed or the specific bribes given. The 1734 elections showed the public that the Earl's enemies were correct about Ilay's effectiveness as a corrupter of the voters.

Grange offered the evidence the petitioners neglected to give. He told the stories of poor peers approached to vote for Ministry candidates in his 1736 pamphlet which became the public statement of the required evidence. Grange showed how Ilay had 'direct[ed] his Batteries against the *weak Side* of our *Constitution*, in order to induce or *compel* the peers of *Scotland* to chuse any sixteen he should *name*'. Since his pamphlet was anonymous, Grange could speak freely to the issue and then make 'unbiased' motions in the House of Commons. The tract, which avenged his injuries, is still good reading.

Grange's London pamphlet became a manifesto for the Patriot Party in Scotland and rang the changes on Country Party views common in England and in favour with the Squadrone. Grange argued from reason and history for a limited and balanced constitution. Parliament he saw as a representative legislature having some judicial functions, but free only if its members, both commoners and peers, were left to make decisions without the influence of bribes and coercion. Corrupt practices put power in the hands of chief ministers and took it from what should have been an independent legislature and an equally independent King acting on the behalf of all. Men like Walpole no longer served their King, or the House of Commons, but were able to determine the policies of both. They had usurped the rights to make and enforce laws, determine foreign policy and give security to the lieges. Walpole's use of patronage was subversive – even treasonous. Sir Robert acted only for himself and his friends. Those who aided him were no better. Bought legislators would follow their buyer's interests, not those of the people at large. The ultimate result was arbitrary rule which weakened loyalty to the King and to the institutions of government. In such a corrupt state, honour among gentlemen, duty among military men, and civic virtue among subjects would disappear; with them would go true religion and private morality. Faction would rule all. Britons urgently needed to remedy matters before it was too late. Ilay was actively complicit in furthering all that because he led a 'Cabal' which rigged elections. The bribed voted the interest of a minister in London and not the interest of constituents in Scotland or of Britons generally. Grange's indictment was followed by an 'Appendix' in which he documented Ilay's sins. The 'Appendix' gives a glimpse of Ilay's politicking in London and on every trip to Scotland. It was direct, even brutal, but without apology and usually had the desired effects.

An un-named peer gave Grange a letter which said '[Robert, Lord Rollo] ... being poor, and needing Assistance to provide for his Children, he had engaged to Vote for the Ministerial List of Sixteen [Scots Peers] and on that Account had received a

Promise of a yearly Pension of two hundred Pounds *Sterling*, and of a Commission in the Army to his Son [Henry] and of one in the Mint to his other Son [John]'.[57] Other letters were quoted to show that this bargain had been kept.[58]

Patrick Crawford, Viscount of Garnock, was approached by the Earl of Crawford about voting in 1734. Lord Garnock claimed to have voted or given proxies in nine peerage elections since he came of age in 1718. He had been promised a £200 pension but nothing had been done for him. On 5 September 1733, when Ilay was in Edinburgh, he met with Garnock. The Earl took out of his locked cabinet £200 in banknotes and offered them to Garnock saying that this was the payment for the previous year which had not been made. The Viscount's legal agent, who accompanied the peer, rejected this money because it looked like a bribe. The election was too near. Ilay said that he would get the pension passed and pay the costs of its passing the seals. Garnock did not send his proxy. In the following year the Earl of Crawford and Edinburgh's Lord Provost, Patrick Lindsay, dunned Garnock for this. They said Ilay would make good on the promise of a pension and that a Captaincy in the Navy would be given to the Viscount's brother if he sent his proxy. The Viscount decided to vote himself which left Ilay and his friends uncertain of his vote. The Viscount probably then tried to sell his vote to the Opposition. When they failed to buy, he found Ilay had enough votes. He was told the Earl would not have accepted his proxy had he known how reluctant the Viscount had been to give it. Ilay paid the £200 he had initially promised but we hear nothing more of the Captaincy of the Man of War.[59]

A third case was that of Charles, Lord Elphinstone, a retired Army Captain who, like Ilay, was interested in science and technology and who, sometime before 1738, began to manage the collieries and salt pans at Bo'ness owned by the Duke of Hamilton. His partner in that was a member of the Dundas family which belonged to the Squadrone. Elphinstone may well have been willing to vote for the Ministerial List but he resented the implication that he was bribable and could be told how to vote. He was, however, willing to see commissions given to his sons, one of whom, Charles, served in Halket's Regiment, and the other, Archibald, in Stair's Dragoons.[60] Elphinstone was from a Jacobite family and those picked by Ilay to contact him were Lord Lovat and Charles Erskine, who came from similar backgrounds, and Colonel John Campbell (later the 4th Duke of Argyll) who descended from an Elphinstone. Ilay also introduced Elphinstone to John Sinclair of Murkle, a brother to the Earl of Caithness, whose vote, Ilay told him, had been bought by Murkle's promotion to the bench of the Court of Session. Ilay himself did not press the peer to vote with him. He offered him a place among the Sixteen and living expenses in London of about £400 and an increase of £100 on the pension he already had. When Elphinstone gave no assent to his proposals, the Earl then talked of 'Buildings, Mathematical Instruments and Experiments'. Later, Elphinstone told the Argathelians 'he was a free Man, and resolved to continue so' and that they 'might believe the Commission was by no Means a disagreeable Thing to him, or the young Gentleman; but that he [Lord Elphinstone] was perswaded his [Ilay's] and his [Lord Elphinstone's] other Friends had too much good Sense, to think a poor Pair of Colours could influence one of his [Lord Elphinstone's] long Service, to go one Step further, than returning his hearty Thanks for the Thing'. He wrote a similar letter to Ilay.[61] In the end, Elphinstone seems to have obtained a Majority for one son and an Ensigncy in Stirling Castle for the other. He also kept his pension. The Earl of Ilay sometimes looked beyond political differences when he was interested in a person and his accomplishments or when he was a relative.[62]

The fourth peer, John Boyle, 2nd Earl of Glasgow, was reminded that he had many children, debts, and not much income. Solictor General Charles Erskine offered him a place on the Ministerial List and expenses so that he could attend the House of Lords. Glasgow said he was promised '400 Pounds ready Money, with Assurance of a yearly Pension of 400 Pounds'. Glasgow thanked Erskine but said he could not entertain 'any Prospect of bettering my Family, by concurring in any Means which might endanger the National Constitution and Liberties of parliament, or Honour of the Peerage'. Erskine told him that was 'the Language of the opposing Party', who mouthed it only for their political gain. He asked what it would take to get Glasgow's vote. Erskine cannot have liked the Earl's answer:

> I told him, that if Sir [Robert Walpole] and his Friends would promote a law for frequent new parliaments, and for preventing Parliamentary Corruption, and if my Friends did not concur with such Motions, I would immediately desert them, and would give all the Votes I was capable to give, for continuing Sir [Robert Walpole] and his Friends in their Offices for Life. I desired the [Solicitor] to mention this Measure to his Friends, with my humble Opinion that such a Measure, offered by him and his Friends, would purchase them the Good-will and Assistance of all true Patriots, and would cut down all the Opposition of false ones. After some Discourse of that Nature, we parted.[63]

Glasgow then supplied a fifth account. His friend, John Gordon, 16th Earl of Sutherland, told him that he voted for the Ministerial List when he was made a Commissioner of the Board of Police, a place worth £800 a year.[64]

In those cases, Ilay played on the neediness of Scots. That left them resentful. Ilay's success with others is made clear in memoranda which detail the money, pensions and places given or to be given to the Earls of Home, Dalhousie, Northesk, Cromartie,[65] Kellie, Kilmarnock and to Lords Reay, Colville, Elibank, Rollo, Gray, Oliphant and Balcarres.[66] Of those thirteen peers, not all of them poor, at least four were former Army men but eight were thought by many to be Jacobites. Those associations did Ilay no good with many but Queen Charlotte praised his handling of this peerage elections.[67]

When Parliament met in 1735, most of those stories would have been known to his enemies in the House of Lords who were intent on using them. Ilay wrote to Milton:

> The Patriots talk of attacking me next week, they give it out that they had laid aside the thoughts of it but that upon Grange's coming up & new stating the case they will now proceed, what is in all this I don't know, but upon the best judgment I can make of it, I think their attempt will be very idle.[68]

Attack they did.

After the elections, the strategy of Bedford and Chesterfield became one of convicting Walpole and his agents of corruption so rank that they could be ousted, even impeached. Chesterfield hoped to get 'some of the lowest and of your venal [Scottish] Peers to come to the bar and confess the money they took to vote for the Court list'.[69] Such damning evidence would lead Scots in the House of Commons to demand that Ilay be impeached for 'high crimes and misdemeanours'. This plan had the support of Opposition leaders such as the Earl of Marchmont, Lord Carteret and Sir William Pulteney. No Scottish peer obliged Chesterfield in 1734/35.[70] Bedford could only present to the House of Lords, in early February 1735, the Scottish peers' petition. That he did. The Lord Chancellor, Charles, Lord Talbot, pointed out, that petition was general and vague. The petitioners only suspected laws had been broken; suspicions are not actionable.[71] Bedford had warned of corruption and had moved proposals which would reduce or eliminate it. He felt vindicated but was unhappy with the result.

The Earl of Ilay's reaction was to follow the controversy and to think of how he might defend himself by showing that he and the ministers had done nothing illegal or unprecedented.[72] He said that in his defence on 28 February 1735, noting that nothing in the peerage elections was illegal 'except as to the regiment, which is said to have been kept under arms during the time of the election; that I believe there may be some truth in. That, as I have said before, I wish your lordships would enquire into...'. He added that, not having thought about it, he had no method of enquiry to suggest.[73] Chesterfield, Carteret and Bedford had attacked but to no avail. In Scotland, the Earl of Marchmont took the lead in opposing Ilay.

Eventually the hubbub died down. It was just as well. Ilay was ill in the winter when Lord Hervey reported him unable to attend the House of Lords in the second half of January 1735. His illness lasted some time and he was only sporadically in the House until March. In April, he spoke on the sinking fund when he again deplored the burden of the land tax and argued that sinking fund monies could be used to defray any costs.[74] A bit later, in the spring of 1735, he spoke on the *habeas corpus* bill telling the peers that Scottish laws against 'wrongeous imprisonment' (1700) made the extension of the bill to Scotland unnecessary.[75] Scottish law should not be tampered with when it was not necessary to do so.

While success in 1733-35 did not mean an end to challenges in Scotland or London, Ilay was able to tell Milton, in July 1735, that his power had been increased: [Walpole] 'puts every thing upon me that is in his own province [the Treasury]'.[76] That meant that Ilay, through Milton, Charles Erskine, and his Kirk managers was now looking after most affairs in Scotland. Still, the Squadrone re-asserted itself in Glasgow University's rectorial election in 1731 and thereafter contested such elections, many successfully. There were problems in the churches and universities over patronage[77] and the orthodoxy of professors. Some, like Lord Reay, whose son still had no place in the Customs, were now dunning Ilay for the jobs promised for votes in the 1734 election of peers.

The Earl did not go to Scotland in the summer of 1735 because of illness. And, he seems to have bought no new stocks or bonds but a great deal of Bristol Water.[78] He was not very active until late April or May 1736 when he spoke for the Quaker Relief Bill. That would have made it cheaper and easier for Dissenters to pay the tithes they owed to a Church they did not attend.[79]

V. The Porteous Riots

The great events of 1736 for Scots were the Porteous Riots. Two smugglers named Wilson and Robertson had robbed the Pittenweem Customs House of tax money. They were caught, tried and condemned to die. There was considerable sympathy for them in a country where even judges bought contraband spirits and smuggled in luxury items from abroad.[80] Awaiting execution in the Edinburgh Tolbooth, Robertson, with the help of other prisoners and friends on the outside, managed to escape. Wilson was fatter and got stuck in the exit window from which he urged the other to run faster. He was to be executed on 4 April 1736. His friends tried, or were rumoured to be trying, to organize a rescue party but Wilson was duly hanged. His body was taken from the executioner and efforts were made to revive him. There was disorder despite the presence of the Town Guard, commanded by Captain Porteous, and the nearby presence of a detachment of Welsh troops. Porteous was said to have been drinking but what was clear was his exasperation with the mob around the gibbet. He probably ordered his men to fire on the mob which had attacked the executioner although the Captain denied this at his trial. The guard fired, but shot above the heads of the mob, killing observers in the windows of houses overlooking the Grassmarket. This provoked fury and troops were called upon to restore order.

Porteous was arrested, tried, found guilty and sentenced to be hanged. Ilay advised him to petition the Queen for clemency. He thought his appeal would succeed.[81] It was widely believed that the government would pardon him as it had pardoned the officers in charge of the detachment which fired on and killed rioters in the Glasgow Malt Tax Riots in 1725. Acting as Regent, the Queen stayed Porteous's execution. Things simmered down with Porteous still under consideration for a royal pardon. Then, unexpectedly, on 7 September, an organized mob rose, closed the city gates, armed itself, and burned down the door to the Tolbooth. It set all the prisoners free but Porteous. This happened over a considerable time and was watched by many but no magistrate read the Riot Act and no one called in the soldiers from the Castle or from the garrison in Leith. The mob found a convenient pole, threw a rope over its arm and made of the hapless Captain a yo-yo until someone put him out of his misery with blows from a Lochaber axe, the usual weapon carried by the Town Guard. This was an outrageous affront to the rule of law and one which disregarded the processes of royal justice. From Ilay's point of view, this riot was unforgivable. Worse yet, it happened while the chief legal officers – Duncan Forbes and Charles Erskine – were Argathelians. They investigated but found no evidence on which convictions could be secured. Those who knew the perpetrators were silent. No one saw anything; no one talked. All that was noted by the Opposition in London.

In London this 'horrible outrage'. came as agitation over the Gin Act was reaching a peak. Walpole thought both the Porteous affair and unrest in London was being stirred up by Jacobites.[82] Ilay was sent to Scotland in early October. Walpole expected him to 'exert himself to the utmost upon this occasion'. Directions were also given to General Wade.[83] Ilay prolonged his stay in Scotland to investigate the case but he could not determine who killed Captain Porteous. Witnesses were intimidated; many were willing to perjurer themselves. And, as Ilay wrote to Walpole, 'The most shocking circumstance is that 'it plainly' appears the high flyers of our Scotch church have made this infamous murder a point of conscience' arguing that the justice of God had been meted out by the mob.[84] The Earl warned the Town Councillors that if they did not do better, Parliament would make them suffer. That did not help him in the October burgh elections. By then, he had made plans to put a permanent garrison of fifty to sixty dragoons into renovated quarters at Holyrood. He worried about the peerage election.[85] The ministers and the King were pleased with all he had done but the culprits were no closer to being tried than when he went up to Edinburgh.

English outrage at Porteous's lynching, led the Opposition to push, during the winter of 1736-37, for an inquiry by the House of Lords. That Ilay offered to assist but what he could not admit was the right asserted by some to seize Edinburgh's charter or to declare the verdict in the Porteous case erroneous.[86] The first dishonoured Scots; the second abused proper legal processes. Ilay sent to Scotland for the trial records and other materials 'that I may be more learned upon the subject'.[87] He studied the materials sent and was active in the debates during which he explained differences between the laws of England and Scotland and the differing procedures of their courts.

The Lords summoned Edinburgh's Lord Provost, the Army commander and the judges of the Justiciary Court to London to explain their conduct. The judges of Ilay's own court were then humiliated by being treated not as were English judges summoned before the House of Lords but as ordinary people. That drew protests from Argyll, Ilay and other Scottish peers.[88] It raised tempers in Scotland where it was seen as yet another instance of English arrogance and ill will. His friend, Lord Milton, the Lord Justice Clerk, was singled out for criticism because he had not ordered troops to act during the riot. Ilay explained to the House that Milton had no right to do so, a point which carried weight since Ilay was himself the head of the Justiciary Court. A bill, passed over the votes of the Scottish peers, was sent to the House of Commons. There, almost all the Scottish MPs opposed it including Lord Advocate Duncan Forbes and Solicitor General Charles Erskine.

Walpole was in no hurry to soothe Scottish feelings and did not immediately lessen the harsh penalties the bill would have imposed on Edinburgh. The Netherbow Port was to be demolished and the Town Guard abolished; the Magistrates were to be punished and the burgh fined. The Duke of Argyll, in an argument sounding more like his brother than himself, argued that was punishing a community *ex post facto* for matters which should have first been argued in inferior courts.[89] Also speaking against it in the House of Lords was Lord Hervey who had been tutored by Charles Erskine and Ilay in Scottish law so he could answer a speech to be made by Carteret.[90] At that point Ilay told Walpole that

> ... he would consent to any punishment being inflicted on Scotland but such a one as would make the whole nation disaffected, and render the government of it quite impracticable; that my Lord Chancellor [Phillip Yorke, Earl of Hardwicke] abused Scotland every day in such strong invectives and behaved himself with such pride and such arrogance, that there was really no temper could bear it with patience; that if Sir Robert would suffer it, Lord Isla said he must quit and give up the whole, for he would not continue in the King's

service only to irritate people against him, when he had neither power enough to defend himself, nor interest enough to engage others to do it.[91]

The Earl would go into Opposition if Scots were not treated better. Ilay's conduct elicited praise from the Queen: 'I think my Lord Isla an excellent servant of the King, and that the complaint he makes is a just one'.[92]

After amendments, said to be devised by Ilay, Lord Hervey and the Queen acting as Regent, the Act passed second reading in the Commons by the casting vote of the chairman of the Committee of the Whole and in the end passed by a vote of 128 to 101.[93] The final Act disqualified the Lord Provost from holding any office in the Empire, fined the city £2,000 for the benefit of Porteous's widow but did not demolish the Netherbow Port. Another Act, said to be of Ilay's devising, called upon Scottish ministers to read from their pulpits for a year the Act denouncing the murder of Porteous and offering rewards to those who would delate his killers. That caused an uproar in Scotland and was ignored by many ministers well affected to the government but eager to maintain the independence of the Kirk. Ilay's purpose was perhaps not the discovery of the killers but the discovery of un-Erastian clerics. Exposed, they could then be deposed and the Kirk purged. That did not happen because so many refused to read the offensive bill including men of great moderation and distinction.[94]

The Earl's role in this case was as prominent as that of his brother who spoke often and effectively in the Lords against the penalties proposed. Ilay worked off stage and neither spoke for this Act, which he disliked, nor against it since he had helped to frame it – that is, to make it milder.[95] In the end, he voted neither for nor against the Act. His brother voted, 'No'.[96] Ilay the lawyer was offended by the crime which violated his sense of legal propriety. If Scots were to be less wild and barbarous, they must not behave as they had in Edinburgh in 1736. Ilay the politician accepted the fact that the city and its people had to be punished in some fashion. In the end he was with Walpole. Duke John was not. Argyll cared less about the lawfulness of civil society. The Duke's wavering support for Walpole's government caused a decisive break with his brother and heir. Their political courses now diverged. Divided, Argathelians counted for less and Ilay's effectiveness was impaired.[97] The Opposition had won an important round.

VI. Disquiet

Opposition efforts directed against Ilay continued with what he saw as Jacobite stirrings not unrelated to Squadrone politics. In 1737 or 1738 he wrote to Walpole

The Jacobites and Papists exert themselves more than ever I knew them since the Queen Anne's death, and though the most of those who foment this Patriot spirit here are still not Jacobites, yet I plainly for see that if they shall find that all their fancied hopes are blasted by a different turn in England, Jacobitism will be their next resource.[98]

That perception lay at the back of his mind while he enjoyed a brief period of relative quiet. Then, in the spring of 1737, Ilay and Lord Hervey stirred things up by trying to persuade Walpole that the Duke of Newcastle and his one-time protégé, Lord Hardwicke, 'were laying schemes to govern independently of him'. They should be sacked. Walpole replied, 'They don't govern me nor they shan't govern me; but you hate the Duke of Newcastle and therefore never will imagine it possible he can do anything right'.[99] Sir Robert, unwilling to sack them, let them know he was aware of their machinations; things would go on as usual. It was, however, a clear sign of the depth of Ilay's distrust and dislike of men with whom he would be associated in government until the end of his career a generation later.

The peerage election of 1736 was not disturbed despite Grange's pamphlet of that year. Similar elections held in 1737, 1738, and 1739 went well and returned the peers ministers wanted. The Earl seems to have refused to have much to do with the quarrels of the King and the Prince of Wales in 1737 although he approved of the expulsion of the Prince from St James's Palace in September 1737.[100] The Queen's death, in late November 1737, removed from politics someone who did not much like him although she was sometimes generous enough to defend his work because it was essential for Walpole's government.[101] Ilay stove off an attempt, in 1737, to reduce the salaries paid to officers of the Board of Trustees and the Commissioners of Forfeited Estates just as he had foiled an earlier attempt.[102] He visited his brother in what appears to have been an attempt at reconciliation. It did not work. Argyll said that in three days Ilay had told him he knew nothing about the government's plans and showed him only letters everyone had seen.[103] The Duke was now often in Opposition and the brothers could not speak to one another except through others or in House of Lords debates.

Duke John, still miffed by the Porteous affair, was now angry over British unpreparedness for a conflict with Spain and over diplomacy which seemed to have isolated the country. Spain, France and Austria were in alliance. Secret treaties had been signed between the Swedes and the French and the French and the Prussians. The outward and visible signs of those agreements were friendlier relations among those powers and more hostility to Britain. George II had few friends on the continent other than the Dutch, Russians and some Germans. He had outstanding issues with the Spanish. Those concerned lands south of the Carolinas, the *Asiento* Treaty, and British smuggling into the Spanish colonies in America. Spanish vessels were stopping and searching British ships and many were calling for retaliation of some sort. As British-Spanish relations became strained and tensions in Europe rose, the government was unwilling to spend on the Navy and Army what Argyll, made a Field Marshall in 1736, and others thought were adequate sums. The Convention with Spain, which tried to settle issues, did not address the problems created by the searching of British vessels by the Spanish in the Caribbean and off the coasts of South America. Those issues the Opposition took up. They and the vocal Field-Marshall were outraged by a country unprepared for conflict and unwilling to defend national honour. Duke John did not need to see Captain Jenkins' ear to fire rhetorical broadsides.

In January 1739, Ilay defended the Convention and he did so again in February when he said that the Directors of the South Sea Co. should settle their affairs with

Spain.[104] His brother replied saying that negotiations had come to nothing and that the government ought not to depend on any Company decisions when the Spanish had suspended treaties entered into in good faith.[105] Soon after, Ilay opposed the reception of a petition from West Indian merchants which the Duke of Bedford had presented to the House. The Earl said this 'serve[d] private ends and mean purposes, and inform[s] us of things already fully debated and thoroughly understood'.[106] To his arguments, Argyll replied that the government's course of action was dishonourable, would ruin trade and allowed the Spanish to close what should be open seas and to violate treaties.[107] In a two hour speech on 3 March, he reiterated things said in January. Argyll concluded that the country was dishonoured and unprepared.[108] The speech cost him his offices. He was now more firmly with the Opposition adding his voice to the bellicose chorus clamouring for civic virtue and war. Some time later, Ilay replied that Opposition speeches had too much 'wit or eloquence on all this – more proper at the other end of town', *i.e.* the fashionable section where Argyll and many of the Opposition peers lived. He thought war was imprudent. In any case, the British claimed similar rights to search and seize ships 'operating illegally'. But what was legal and illegal depended on contentious definitions of 'coasts', 'open seas' and the meaning of treaties not always clear. Besides, 'the law of nations & usage' favoured the Spanish. The debate ended in March with Ilay the last speaker for his side.[109] He had shown a lawyer's prudence and a preference for peace if it could be had. On 19 October 1739, the Ministry was forced to declare war on Spain. The split in the Argathelian party deepened. Some remained with Ilay; others joined the 'Duke of Argyll's Gang' of about ten in the House of Commons.

VII. The Election of 1741

The brothers' disagreements virtually guaranteed that the 1741 general elections would go badly. Argyll's new friends slanged Ilay in the press. About the time that war was declared, a pamphlet appeared in London called 'E[dinburg]h's Instructions to Their Member'.[110] This said Ilay was 'your Guide' in politics and foreign affairs and that Walpole would reward those who followed him. The Earl of Ilay was not like his virtuous brother. Neither Sir Robert nor his minions were patriots. Another squib of 1740, a twelve-page pamphlet called 'The Ass Race or the Secret History of Archy Armstrong, Fool to King Charles I', described Archy as 'a very wise Man, and only prostitutes his good Sense and Knowledge to divert the great Folks, or to serve a Job, which no Body else had the Art of doing so well as himself'. He would sell out his brother for 'his Place at Court' and was 'a great Hypocrite with respect to his Country'. He was blamed for the Act requiring the clergy of Scotland to preach against the killers of Porteous. Then, Archy was ironically excused since he took all his orders from 'the Prime Minister'. He was faulted for supporting a pacific foreign policy, for being inconsistent, and for being rich. He was termed a 'Vice-Roy' and the leader of the 'would-be Asses' or place seekers. His rules for the Ass race were that all should support a platform which included new taxes and excises, the employment of foreign mercenary troops, blind obedience to Walpole and a willingness to 'laugh, bully or bray' on command. The Ass race was run for money, 'a *Place for Life, a*

Pension, a Post for a Friend, a Commission for a Brother, &c.' or 'A Huge large Bladder'. That was emblematic of vain promises made to secure votes. The race was to be run by placemen who owed their jobs to Ilay and Walpole. Argyll, out of 'Sentiment of honour and Liberty', 'bravely' rejected all that Archy offered. In the pamphlet, Archy lost his race, was disgraced and then 'resume'd his Senses, and liv'd honest for the rest of his Life'. At about the same time a published speech by the Duke showed him patriotically concerned for the Cartagena expedition, with foreign affairs and with other issues that made the Opposition look good to many.[111]

In 1740 Ilay spent ten weeks in Scotland campaigning for the next year's elections. He went up in a leisurely manner dining well along the way. His meal bills show he ate 'Soup Lorrain', lobster, turkey, 'Wild Duck Larded', 'Lamb with Spirement Sauce', dried tongue, many vegetables and salad greens, morels and truffles, catchup and bottled mushrooms, 'French bread', apple pies, tarts and berries but had not all that much to drink. Sometimes he dined only with his secretary but once he got to Scotland, gentlemen and burgh councillors enjoyed the good food.[112] The government had given him £500-600 to spend on the election. That presumably paid for some of the entertainments and a few bribes.[113]

Ilay cut a more spruce figure than he does in many accounts. He is described on this trip as wearing dark clothes with gold-worked button holes and buttons. His shirts were of Scottish linen; his handkerchiefs, sometimes flowered, came from Glasgow. He wore ruffles and some lace and over it all a light blue coat. His night cap was silk.[114] He was respectably dressed and a walking advertisement for Scottish products.[115] His appearance would have contrasted with the misery which was growing around him. The harvests had been poor in 1739 and were poorer in 1740 and 1741. Grain prices rose 20-30%; wages did not.[116] In times of such distress, even in the eighteenth century, the 'ins' did not do well in elections because even the upper-class voters' costs and revenues were affected by bad times.

The elections for which Ilay was preparing would come in May and June 1741 for the House of Commons, and on 13 June for the Representative Peers. The Saltoun Correspondence from 1739 on is full of the usual memoranda and letters containing pension lists, jobs to be given, lists of committed and questionable voters and where new votes might be made and whose son could be put in which regiment and where a new tide waiter was needed. Some who agreed to run had to have their London living expenses paid from funds which had to be found. All this was complicated because Ilay could not be sure how Argathelian loyalties would divide. An example of how the brothers' disagreements affected their followers' actions over even minor places can be found at Glasgow University.

Colin Maclaurin's evangelical brother sought the divinity chair there in 1740. He seems to have been supported by Argyll and by evangelicals who included Principal Neil Campbell and some of the men in the College who owed their posts to the Squadrone. The Moderate candidate for the place was the Rev. Michael Potter. For him were men in Ilay's camp from outside the College, probably the College Erastians and one or two others who did not like hot gospellers. Against Potter were friends of Argyll and the High Flyers. Potter won but at the cost of ill will in the College.[117] There were many contests in which the supporters of the Duke and Earl divided.

To further complicate Ilay's life, Argyll bought a country house, Caroline Park, near Edinburgh and went up to campaign in the summer of 1740. The Duke entertained acquaintances such as Lord Lovat.[118] The sort of thing he was telling them is reflected in a letter the Duke wrote to his nephew, James Stuart Mackenzie:

> ... Ilay wants to make all his friends tools to Walpole because he finds his ends in so doing, Your Brother Bute and I would have all Our friends Independent of Walpole and all other Ministers Whatsoever, My Brother Ilay prefers his places to all other considerations, friendship Honour Relation, gratitude and Service to his Country Seem at present to have no weight with him, Your Brother Bute and I think it Our Honour that these considerations should weigh with us ....

He then added incongruously and probably falsely, 'tho your Relations differ in Publick affairs they live in civility with one another'.[119] The 'Patriot' spoke a new language and may even have believed it. The Field Marshall's politics was no longer a game played for offices. Ilay, who campaigned from Brunstane House at the opposite end of the city, must have been glad of the diversions provided by The Whim.

Wartime worries were compounded with the sheer fatigue caused by long endurance of Walpole and 'Robinocracy'. In the House of Lords, Carteret moved on 14 February 1741 to remove Walpole from the King's presence forever. This issue was not resolved until May. Ilay grumbled that Patriot speeches 'repeated all the Craftsmen &c have said these twenty years, found fault with all Treaties, though expressly approved by both Houses of Parliament & distribution of the sinking fund though done by Act of Parliament'.[120] His own agenda included making the Salt Bill better for Scots, just as he had the last one,[121] and supporting the importation of corn in times of dearth.[122]

Through the parliamentary sessions of 1740-41, Argyll lashed the government over corruption, the conduct of the war with Spain, expenses and diplomatic moves. His speeches made him the idol of the Opposition. Argyll (and his brother) thought, or said, the conflict was not only about British safety but 'the Liberties of Europe'. Ilay defended his ministerial friends and warded off enquiries by saying, on 1 December 1740, that they should await the ending of the present phase of the war so as not to help the enemy.[123] Chesterfield observed that Ilay was always for enquiries but never *now*.[124] Those debates continued in early 1741 when Ilay spoke in debates on the Army held on 20 January and 3 February. The second speech dealt with troop increases and ended with a flourish: 'Remember you are peers, but do not forget that you are subjects'.[125]

Argyll did not go up for the peerage election of 13 June but Ilay was there to watch and vote. The government's list was returned. The general election for MPs was more difficult. In all of Britain, only ninety-four seats were contested in the election; seventeen were in Scotland. All sides had done their work well in advance of election day. The outcome of the voting in Scotland showed how important unity had been for the Argathelian faction. The Jacobites aided Argyll's candidates, which allowed them to elect about eleven members. Other Opposition Whigs elected twelve more. Ilay's

Argathelians elected nine men and other government supporters an equal number. Tories and Independents accounted for the rest of the forty-five seats.[126] Walpole's majority in the House of Commons had been forty-two; after the election it was nineteen. Scotland had not yielded enough supporters to enable Walpole to continue long in office.[127] George Bubb Dodington, long attached to the Duke of Argyll, thought the Ministry's days were numbered. He advised Walpole's opponents to go to all meetings; they would eventually outvote the Walpoleans on some issue which would precipitate a crisis.[128] Others looking to the same end thought about the day Ilay would go out of power. Chesterfield and his friends wanted him impeached.[129] Lord Egmont, in 1741, saw him being replaced by Tweeddale but otherwise to be 'left as he is'. Presumably this meant he was to handle Scottish affairs under Tweeddale which shows how little Egmont knew his Scots.[130]

VIII. Walpole's Fall and Its Aftermath

The country's malaise was increased after the elections by the failure of the British expedition to the Caribbean. Its commander, Admiral Vernon, after doing well at Porto Bello lost his fleet and reputation at Cartagena, Santiago and Panama City. This bad news became known after the end of June. The British forces had been repulsed partly because of poor leadership but also because of the weather and sickness which had reduced their numbers. The Ministry looked worse than ever.

Between December 1741 and February 1742, Walpole's numbers in the Commons shrank; further defections seemed inevitable. He decided to resign on 31 January 1742 and did so on 11 February after losing a division on an election petition. By then, he had made arrangements for his retirement. Both Lords Hardwicke and Newcastle ratted on Walpole in the end to save themselves. Ilay did not.[131] His contempt, dislike and distrust of Newcastle and Hardwicke seems to have hardened after Walpole's fall. For the rest of Ilay's career, they would sporadically make efforts to minimize his influences on Scottish affairs and to exclude him from government when they thought they had a chance to do so. In the end he prevailed.

After Walpole resigned, those who had been the Opposition were in; Ilay was out. He told Lord Milton in February that 'the Political Game is over'.[132] By the end of February 1742, patronage in Scotland was no longer administered through Ilay and Lord Milton but had been taken over by Squadrone politicians. Carteret's friend, the Marquis of Tweeddale, replaced the Earl of Ilay as manager in Scotland. Ilay seemed reconciled to that asking only that his friends holding offices there be left in place as they were.[133] In March, John Drummond reported to Baron Clerk that 'Lord Ilay keeps still all he had & makes his Court well but some of his old friends have been unkind in their characters of him as he was a harsher minister & slower & indolent in the last Elections, but he could not make bricks without straw'.[134] Ilay seemed resigned to a retirement that would still allow him a few places and some influence on legislation. He even offered to support Tweeddale's candidate, William Mure, in the Renfrewshire by-election.[135]

The Duke of Argyll came back to seeming power in Carteret's and Newcastle's Ministry. The ministers willingly restored his offices in February 1742. He was again

Colonel of the Blues, Master-General of Ordnance, Commander-in-Chief of all the Forces in Southern England and in Scotland. His was a loud voice in the Lords, while in the Commons, Argyll's 'Gang' of MPs reinforced by a few more of Bubb Dodington's supporters gave him some purchase on the new government. What he did not have was power. The ministers allowed him little influence in policy making or what he regarded as his share of patronage. On 16 March 1742, the mercurial old soldier again resigned all his places. He bitterly retired from politics. Richard Glover, whose pen had served the Whig Opposition, claimed that when Argyll left London he described his brother's character to Lord Chesterfield

> in the most infamous and diabolical colours, and then said, can your Lordship blame me for not seeing such a brother as this. He went down to Sudbrook, and in about a month sent for his brother, by whose intervention all matters were adjusted between Argyle and the late detested Lord Carteret, who had certainly deluded him with expectations of putting the army into his hands, which was his favourite passion.... [136]

The 2nd Duke had been forced into retirement and did not enjoy it. When he decided to support the ministry again, he was talked out of it by Chesterfield and his friends. The Duke's health failed not long after. He was physically and mentally ill.[137] Ilay described him as having 'low spirits' and thought he needed exercise and a good purging.[138] The Duke refused to follow his physicians' advice and a trip to Bath did him no good. Toward the end of his life he was partially paralysed.[139] The half-mad Duke remained for Ilay a political and personal problem, one not made easier by the Duke's knowledge that Ilay would inherit his dukedom.

While Ilay remained on bad terms with his brother, he was on polite or good terms with Carteret and Henry Pelham. The Earl did not side with any of the new factions which developed. He defended Walpole in a notable speech given on 25 May 1742, one in which he spoke last and effectively. At issue was whether or not 'to indemnify Evidence against Robert Earl of Orford', Walpole's new title. Ilay called this measure 'a bad end by bad means'. 'The intention of the Bill is cruel and oppressive; the measures by which that intention is promoted are contrary to law; and without precedent; and the original principle is false, as it supposes a criminal previous to the crime'. Peers should be guided by justice and not popular clamours. He saw those as the results of passion and a desire to win at all costs. We want too much what we contend for. The bill was not committed and died.[140]

The Earl may have ceased to politick in London but, in Scotland, Argathelians continued to battle. Ilay may not have been much involved with that since Lord Milton's correspondence with him is virtually denuded of patronage requests – even of minor places in the Kirk and universities. It remained that way from late 1742 through early 1745 but party struggles went on between old enemies. Appointments were contested and even the way men voted in meetings of the stockholders of the Bank of Scotland was reported to Tweeddale.[141] By 1744, there was an Edinburgh club ironically named the 'Patriot Club' which 'daily lash'd' Tweeddale, Robert Dundas, Robert Craigie, Thomas Hay and other supporters of the Squadrone. It also circulated scurrilous poems about them.[142]

In the summer of 1742, Sir Robert's son, Horace Walpole, believed Ilay only professed not to be disappointed by his loss of power but he coupled that opinion with a glimpse of a man now more distant from the fashionable and literary world than he had once been. Walpole, then on a grand tour, was the person on whom Ilay relied that spring to arrange for the shipment to England of his latest new animals – six Maltese cats which Walpole did not find extraordinary, just larger than the usual moggies.[143] 'I believe they will be extremely welcome to Lord Islay now, for he appears little, lives more darkly and more like a wizard than ever; these large cats will figure prodigiously in his cell: he is of the mysterious dingy nature of Stosch'.[144]

Ilay, now sixty, busied himself in the summer of 1742 with his new library at his London home, with Alexander Lind's peat experiments and other sciency things. He did not go north that summer, but stayed in London and at Whitton, doing things he enjoyed and previously had too little time to do.[145] He tried to effect a reconciliation with his brother, as Richard Glover reported, and he maintained amicable relations with Carteret and Henry Pelham.[146] Ilay could not get many jobs for friends and clients but he could not be ignored. His and his brother's stocks rose when Ilay reported to the government, at his brother's request, that the Duke had been approached with offers from the Pretender. Horace Walpole said that Ilay showed letters supposed to have been sent him by Col. Cecil, a Jacobite agent, to Sir Robert Walpole and the King. Those offered Argyll the command of the Pretender's forces in Britain. Argyll a bit later admitted they had come from Lord Barrymore, an old comrade in arms.[147] The Duke had hesitated to delate him but his loyalty to the King eventually trumped that to an old companion in arms. Because he was ill and out of office, he let Ilay take the message.

When Argyll finally died, Ilay regretted that he would be 'confined at home till the Funeral is over' and supposed that by his brother's will 'every thing is done to my prejudice that the Law allows'. For the shortest time decency allowed, he used a mourning seal with an odd design and possibly a Hebrew motto.[148] It was soon replaced by one with the ducal arms. Within days of his brother's death, he planned to rebuild Inveraray Castle, replace its gardener with a new one, relocate the town, build a new harbour and create there an industry of some sort.[149] His succession made possible projects about which he had long thought and all but one of which his brother never conceived.

IX. A Changed Social Scene

The political struggles of the decade and perhaps increasing age had changed Ilay's socializing. When George II became King in 1727, Ilay and his brother were good friends of Mrs. Howard through whom they may have tried to influence the King's policies. It did not work and they switched their attentions to the Queen who had more influence on policy and patronage than the mistress had or wanted.[150] As the first connexion lessened, so did Ilay's ties to the literary world. Opposition to Walpole and his government in the 1730s pushed away others. Old acquaintances were replaced by new friends who shared his interests in gardening and science. He spent more time at Whitton where the gardens reached their final size in 1734 when he bought twenty-two additional acres.[151] They were maturing and more activity arose from them. They were now notable and even noticed in a scurrilous poem about the Earl which painted him as an irreligious thief of public lands while musing on the ends met by others of his name:

> Old Islay, to show his fine delicate taste
> In improving his garden purloin'd from the waste,
> Bid his gard'ner one day to open his views,
> By cutting a couple of grand avenues.
> No particular prospect his Lordship intended,
> But left it to chance how his walks should be ended.
> With transports of joy he beheld at one view-end
> His favourite prospect, a church that was ruin'd!
> But alas! What a sight did the next view exhibit!
> At the end of the walk hung a rogue on a gibbet!
> He beheld it and wept, for it caused him to muse on
> Full many a Campbell had died with his shoes on.
> All amaz'd and aghast at the ominous scene,
> He ordered it quick to be clos'd up again,
> With a clump of Scotch firs by way of a screen![152]

That is not likely to have bothered him; he was much thicker skinned than his brother. And, a gallows in Inveraray probably would have been visible from the Castle. Every regality was entitled to one.

His instrument collection was expanding as was his library. We know that he paid instrument makers from 1 January 1728 to the end of 1743 at least £145.2.6 but most of what he bought is unknown.[153] However, some information on both collections is given in the record of one of his auction buying binges. It is preserved in the auctioneer's notes to the sale catalogue of the library and instruments owned by Samuel Molyneux (1689-1728).[154] This was a notable sale of the effects of a well known and competent amateur scientist whom Ilay would have known as a politician, a courtier about the Prince of Wales, and as a man of science who made telescopes and used them to record observations to determine annual stellar parallax which it was hoped would determine distances to stars. The sale ran over thirteen days, from January 20 to February 2, 1730. Ilay attended one or both of the two daily sessions on eight days skipping one day for a debate in the House of Lords but remaining in town over a weekend to attend on other days. He probably bid for himself since he paid for some of his purchases by a 'note' drawn on Campbell and Middleton dated the day of the sale.

Ilay spent on instruments a total of £48.7.6[155] and £39.16.2 on books. The Earl purchased 117 titles (46 duodecimos and octavos; 42 quartos, 29 folios) coming to over 122 volumes. An additional £2.14.10 went on manuscripts, some containing Molyneux's astronomical and weather observations. The total, £90.18.6, represented a sum at least twice as great as the money income of an average Scottish cleric for a year or the half-pay of a junior Army officer. The sale testified to his interests in most aspects of knowledge but especially the sciences of astronomy, chemistry and medicine. Other books dealt with botany, history, languages, classics, poetry and travels.

His Lordship must have attended many auctions of this sort. At them, he met bibliophiles, learned instrument makers whose works he used, physicians, and men of learning of all kinds. Bidders at the Molyneux sale included learned dissenting clergymen, Fellows of the Royal Society, such as Sir Hans Sloane, PRS and Martin Folkes, V-PRS; Fellows of the Royal College of Physicians, like William Cockburn, Samuel Horseman and Thomas Pellet, and science lecturers, such as William Whiston and the instrument maker George Adams, sr. At other auctions, he purchased coins, medals and objects of *virtù*. His collections of seals, intaglios and cameos took him time both to acquire and to study. Some of his many pieces of porcelain had come from auctions.

While he still saw and was helpful to old friends like Lord Lovat, those men were aging; his new associates were different. Many were younger men not of his class but men with scientific, not political and investing interests. From the mid-1730s on, more were seedsmen, gardeners, mechanics and chemists. Among them were Alexander Wilson and later James Lee. In 1736, Ilay, like about half the House of Lords, was even a subscriber to the schemes of Joshua 'Spot' Ward, a quack doctor and sensible chemist who had recently started at Twickenham a chemical works producing sulfuric acid.[156] Ilay supported Ward's medical scheme to treat the London poor. With his new friends, he stood on little ceremony but even with aristocrats, he used less ceremony than was customary.[157]

He was presumably very much a part of the Whig political and financial community. He dined with men at the Treasury, or connected with the London banks. And, when the Bank of England had a reception in 1736 to show Sir Robert Walpole its 'new House', Ilay but not his brother was in attendance.[158]

The Earl was also a family man. Mrs. Williams and her young or teenage children never appear in the records but his Coutts ledger entries show more purchases of silver, china, jewellery and small art objects, and even (in 1727) a 'wood horse' which could be either an exercise machine or a toy for William Williams then about six or seven.[159] His illegitimate children must have gotten some attention since he was later fond of his son and in the end looked after him and his sister very well. He also had an avuncular concern for the children of the 2nd Duke and for those of his sister, the 2nd Countess of Bute. Family feelings show us a warmer side than he often displayed. He, like his friend Gwynn Vaughn, probably also paid some attention to Lord Milton's bright daughter Elizabeth, who, after 1741, attended for several years a boarding school in Chelsea. The girl went to plays and was popular with others Ilay knew.[160]

To John Stuart, who became 3rd Earl of Bute at the age of ten, Ilay was helpful in a variety of ways. He and his brother saw to it that the Earl was given a good education. Like Ilay, Bute went to Eton and then to Leiden where he studied law. He got there, and from tutors his uncles employed, a love of learning and competence as an astronomer. He became a fine student of 'fossils' and natural history and a better botanist than his uncles.

In 1736, Bute married against the will of his and his wife's family. His wife was Mary, daughter of Lady Mary Wortley Montagu. Her family opposed the union because Bute had too little money. The bride's parents would not attend the wedding. Ilay tried to smooth matters by having the young couple to dinner within two weeks.[161] A bit later, his uncles found a pension for Bute and had him elected a

Representative Peer. As a parliamentarian, he was a disappointment. He was seldom in the House of Lords and took little part in debates. Part of the reason for that were the disagreements between his uncles over political matters. Bute sided with Argyll and adopted the outlook and rhetoric of 'the Patriots'. Still, Ilay continued to be nice. He tried to help Bute in his political career but he was often rebuffed by his stiff-necked nephew who preferred the politics of Bolingbroke and the elder Pitt to the non-ideological practical burgh-mongering of his uncle Ilay. As late as 1746, after advertising the place and probably renting it for some time, Argyll conveyed Cane Wood [or Caen Wood or Kenwood House] to the Earl (see above p. 384 n. 28).[162]

Bute's younger brother, James Stuart Mackenzie, experienced similar attention as he was groomed for a career in politics and diplomacy. In a remarkable letter written to him by Ilay in 1738 as he was going off to Leiden to study law, the Earl told him,

> ... you are to consider that this is the only time in your life you can have for laying such foundations of knowledge in the several sciences which you may afterwards improve yourself farther in as your inclination or interest may lead you. I would advise you to make yourself master of General History both antient & modern, this will make every book of History agreable to you when you shall find it only an enlargement of the general History you have learnt the dates of the great Periods commonly called Epoch's you should have by heart. You should continue to improve your self in the Civil Law, & with the Roman History read some abridgement of the Roman Antiquities, all which will explain one another. Read often the Classicks such as you learnt at school which will revive what you got there & perfect you in them. Whatever Greek you learnt at School you should take care not to forget, this is done by reading over your Grammer & the books you were taught, I am so sensible of this that I do it to this day. You are now of an age that Your studying the Mathematicks will be proper, learn arithmetick & and some Algebra & go carefully over Euclid making yourself a perfect master of every proposition, this is so necessary that one single proposition not being well understood will throw all the rest into obscurity & confusion, this must be done by the help of ye master for some time till you are able to read alone, & you cannot conceive what pleasure & use you will find in it. Gravesends Lectures of experimental Philosophy are very proper for you to attend, you will find them very entertaining & afterwards very useful in many things. Let me know what Colledges [intra- and extra-mural lecture courses] are given this winter & which you propose to attend....[163]

The young man heeded his advice and became in time a skilled amateur astronomer, a naturalist, agricultural improver and chemist. Lady Mary Wortly Montagu found him in 1740 'a very pretty Youth with a turn of Head very like his Uncle Islay'.[164]

In one respect, Stuart Mackenzie was different; he was far less discreet. By 1741, he had taken up with a beautiful ballerina, Barbera Campinini (1721- 1799). He met 'la Barberina' when she danced in London or possibly earlier in Venice. It was fine to have such a mistress but James wanted to marry her. They planned to meet at Venice where he was to be posted as a diplomat. At that point, his uncle Ilay stepped in. It simply would not do to have the family embarrassed by such a marriage. It was one thing to have a shady mistress, quite another to marry her.[165] Lady Louisa described Ilay's role in the affair:

> [Ilay,] instead of feeling due pride in the connection, or leaving a man of his age to secure his own happiness, officiously took measures to disturb it. Though the lovers were to be united far off in Venice, where they hoped they might defy his authority, yet having long hands, and putting many irons in the fire, he discovered that before the lady formed her present plans of aggrandisement, she had signed articles binding herself to dance that winter at the Berlin theatre. This being ascertained, his friend Lord Hyndford, then our ambassador in Prussia, easily induced that Court to demand of the Venetian Government that she should be compelled to fulfill her engagement. Accordingly she was arrested by order of the Senate, and, on the very day fixed for her marriage, sent off under guard to Germany.[166]

Stuart Mackenzie followed her there only to be told by the Prussians to leave. The affair soon went cold. La Barberina found a long series of other protectors. Stuart Mackenzie went on to a diplomatic and political career which made him richer if not distinguished. In the end, he married his cousin, Lady Betty, a daughter of the 2nd Duke of Argyll. Family feelings show us a warmer side than Ilay often displayed.

In 1743, the only insoluble family problem was posed by Ilay's brother, now a bitter, sick, perhaps mad, old man. Ilay was enjoying life and prospering; the Duke was not and was probably still in debt to Ilay for £4,000 at 5% borrowed in 1736.[167] It contributed to the Earl's net worth which in 1740 was at least £31,400 in stocks, bonds and mortgages.[168] His properties had increased in value and his total income, now over £6,000 a year, would be increased by his brother's death.[169]

X. The New Duke as Landowner and Improver

The 2nd Duke of Argyll died at Sudbrook, his estate near Petersham, on 4 October 1743. Ilay at sixty-three succeeded to one of the largest estates in Britain and became the greatest and richest landlord in Scotland. However little formal power he might have as a politician in London, he now had much more power in his own right. No government could ignore a Duke. After Duke John's funeral, Ilay went on a book buying spree. There was little he could not now afford.[170] By November 1743, he wrote to Milton in the wake of Tweeddale's appointment as Scottish Secretary, 'I am now too old and have too great a Stake to wish to set myself up again as a Cock to be thrown at, and farther I have not health and constitution and I shall not have time on account of my private affairs, and my amusements to enter into any to any Political scheme that required application, attendance or bustling, and every year at my age I must expect to be less capable of it'.[171] He seemed content to be done with politics.

Ilay and the Dowager Duchess of Argyll left the settlement of 'all questions that may arise from my Brother's succession between the Dutchess, my neices & myself' to Andrew Fletcher, Lord Milton and Duncan Forbes, Lord Culloden – respectively his and his brother's chief agents in Scotland. As he told Forbes, 'no man knows [the 2nd Duke's] intention as yourself, & whatever that was, I shall think right'.[172] One can imagine Duke John generously and impulsively doing this; Ilay did not want to deal with his sister-in-law whom he had long disliked. The new Duke expected his cousin, Major General John Campbell of Mamore and his sons, and his more distant cousin, Alexander Fraser of Strichen to help.[173] Ilay wanted some of the lands his brother had bought to round out the Argyll lands and a share of the Duddingston estate, including its coal. Whatever sums were at issue, would not have amounted to a great deal in comparison with the lands and honours which passed to him now. A 'Decreet Arbitrall' was issued by Lords Milton and Forbes.[174]

The new Duke had long been a Representative Peer, Privy Councillor, Lord Justice General (£1,000), an Extraordinary Lord of Session and Keeper of the Great Seal (£3,000).[175] He now became Duke and Earl of Argyll, Earl of Arran, Lord Campbell and baron in a number of regalities, Lord Lieutenant of Argyllshire and Dumbartonshire, Bailie or Stewart of Tiree, Balinbabb, Arrist, How, Salgo, Islay, Kamis in Jura and a whole lot more. Among his subsidiary titles and offices were Justice General of Argyll and the Isles, Admiral of the Western Coast, Hereditary Sheriff, Chamberlain and Coroner of Argyll, the holder of the Tack of Teinds in the Bishopric of Argyll and of twenty-five Hebridean islands and Heritable Grand Master of the King's Household (that gave him an apartment at Holyrood Palace and £1,000) – the list goes on in archaic profusion. The reality was that each of those posts gave him something (often not much) in the way of rights and income. His lands or rights now lay in about 2,500 square miles and ran into the counties of Ayrshire, Renfrew, Dunbarton, Argyll, Inverness, Perth, Sterling, Fife and Midlothian. Some of this was directly under the Duke's control but most was held of him by vassals. Merely to convey all this to him was a substantial undertaking and an interesting one.

In order for him to be served heir and possess those lands and rights, an inquest had to be held. The peers who sat on that were mostly old friends or relatives but were also chosen for their knowledge of the matters at issue. The six judges who joined them had all been appointed by Ilay. Once he had been served heir, his 'doers' or Writers had to go over the instruments by which men held land of him. All of them would pay an entry fine. He had at least sixty-six major vassals who paid feudal dues to their new lord with whom they had to work out new arrangements. His chamberlains and 'doers' ascertained the terms on which lands were held, calculated the value of the holding and determined what should be levied as an entry fine. Many lesser obligations were not paid in money but in kind and services. Ilay had rights to bolls of meal, firkins of butter, wedders and ewes from some vassals, and from others services such as keeping a boat so that he could cross a loch at the usual place. Others paid rents or held on tenures which obligated them to serve him as soldiers should he need them. To make the most of all this was the new Duke's intention but he also recognized that he needed to change the somewhat feudal conditions he had inherited to something resembling the estate he was creating at The Whim. There, traditional ways had been abandoned from considerations of utility and efficient farming. When he inherited the dukedom, he inherited some on-going plans which envisioned those ends but his plans and dreams were bolder and more thorough. As Eric Cregeen has pointed out, both brothers shared the desire to improve conditions so that they might make money:

> ..the domain lands in the neighborhood of Inveraray and Rosneath, [the 2nd Duke] ... exploit[ed] them fully by grazing cattle for the market, by selling farm produce and growing timber for sale to the new iron foundry on Lochfyneside. Domainal rights were extended to include minerals, fishings and timber wherever they were on the estate. Rents, too, could be increased, now that the tacksmen were removed, though the increase was governed by the resources of the tenantry....Since feu-duties and teinds[176] were relatively static, most of the increase is attributable to rents and domainal products. In the eighteen years of the 3rd Duke's administration, the increase in rents was of the order of 40 per cent and over the whole period from 1703 to 1770 rents on the average roughly tripled.[177] In the long run such measures improved the fortunes of the family and produced in Argyllshire a pace of development which was seen in few places in the Highlands.[178]

The Campbells commercialized farming to the point that some leases were let by open, competitive bidding and without regard to bidders' families or names. Those policies Ilay helped to popularize among other lairds but they were also the policies of HIKAS. The only exceptions made to this policy were dictated by politics. The 3rd Duke would not have disloyal tenants. He preferred men of another name to disloyal Campbells and he was willing even to abate rents a bit to have them.[179] His terms did not make him popular with all his tenants. Knowledge of his intentions may have prompted some to join the rebels in 1745. In detail, all this was a vastly complex business. He was still signing charters when the '45 began.

The 3rd Duke sat atop an organization which had reporting to him Lord Milton, the chamberlain at Inveraray, stewards elsewhere, country lawyers, his 'doer' in Edinburgh, Alexander Campbell of Succoth, W.S., Glasgow merchants, friends and relatives. They in turn used not only their eyes but heard all that the gardeners, grieves, shepherds, and minor managers of all sorts who lived on the estates had to tell them. Little of any note escaped the attention of someone willing to send news of it to Milton or directly to Argyll. If it was crucial to the success of his policies to act as a rational capitalist and to rent to the highest bidder, and not to give land to those of his own name for non-economic ends, it was equally so to deal reasonably with all the men who wished to help him often for ends very much their own.

The plan of modernization, which the 3rd Duke everywhere employed, would, he hoped, introduce into the Highlands industry, towns, civility, peace and an end to Jacobitism. Essential to its realisation were the removal of the tacksmen and the introduction of tenant farmers who would try to make the most of the land.[180] Tacksmen were tenants or others who often held large farms on terms which did not give the landlord the return on his investment which he might have gotten had he rented it for what it would fetch in open bidding. Excluding them entailed social disruption because tacksmen were the local middling men who held land of their feudal superior and rented it out to ordinary clansmen. They generally managed things for the Dukes, including their clan regiments and companies and whatever took some skill and education in a part of the world lacking in those things. Displacing them meant removing a level of Highland society which had structured and managed it for a very long time. Argyll clearly thought many of them inessential. Their functions could be as well filled by men paid by him – men who were dismissable. He continued a policy with which he had been associated since his first experience of estate management in 1717 when he and the Earl of Bute set leases in Morven. Those were granted for nineteen years and went to reliable men. That policy had been followed in Tiree in 1737 by Duke John and his agent Duncan Forbes. It was now more thoroughly pursued with some leases tied to requirements for improving the properties.[181] The new Duke also wanted managers and tenants who were competent and met his standards of knowledge – even Englishmen. It mattered less if they were his relatives or bore his name – as many continued to do.

To carry on this work, he needed to know what he had and where it was. John Cowley, a map maker was or had been one of his brother's factors.[182] Cowley's 1734 map of Scotland showed the progress made in the mapping of the Kingdom since the seventeenth century – just the sort of thing which Argyll would encourage. In 1744, the Duke took with him to Scotland, probably for the first time, James Dorret. He was skilled as a valet and genteel enough to serve in the dining room but he was most useful as a surveyor. Dorret worked for some years drawing estate maps and made land surveys around Inveraray and for the County. In April 1750, he published, by Act of Parliament, a map of Scotland. Dorret was made a burgess of Inveraray in 1744 and remained employed by the Duke for at least eleven years leaving his Grace's service in 1755.[183] Argyll knew more about his properties than had earlier dukes.

Another requisite of modernization was the connecting of Inveraray with the world. In 1743, it was accessible by boats coming through the Firth of Clyde or Kilbrannan Sound but Inveraray lacked good port facilities.[184] Inveraray was also cut off from the rest of Scotland by a lack of roads. The land route from Dumbarton to Inveraray in 1743 required one to ride horseback or walk for part of the way. That forty-five mile stretch of road had never been surveyed until 1744 despite its importance to the military men. By 1745, 300 soldiers were constructing a road beginning at the Dumbarton end. Delayed by the '45, by the terrain – 'REST AND BE THANKFUL' was the inscription on a monument at one of the steeper passes – and by difficulties with lairds over rights to cross fields, the road was pushed to its conclusion in 1750. By then the soldiers had cut into many steep hillsides and built many bridges – eighteen in 1747 alone. The final bridge over the Aray was constructed by the Adam brothers following designs by Roger Morris in 1749. By 1750, the land journey could be made in a vehicle but it was not a pleasant one. Road work continued for years and only in the late 1750s was this journey undertaken by many. Goods still moved mostly by water.[185] A new town and port were needed and planned.

The scope of Argyll's business is sometimes breathtaking. Again, it is useful to quote Cregeen on the reforms of the island of Tiree, only one of the places where Argyll was engaged in similar reforms:

Between 1737 and the end of the century the instructions of successive Dukes to their chamberlains in Tiree range over a wide variety of 'improvements'; the construction of a harbour and roads and the provision of wheeled transport (unknown in Tiree at that date, as in most of the highlands); the drainage of peat-mosses and the building of sea-walls to preserve the land from inundation; the division and enclosure of farms and commons; the improvement of the blood-stock and seed grain, and the introduction of new crops; new domestic industries, schemes for training craftsmen, encouragement of fishermen, and much else.[186]

Among 'much else' were planting and reforestation schemes. Large numbers of trees, both for amenities and profits, were planted on the Inveraray estate. Like the plantings at The Whim, those at Inveraray were to yield materials for building, for axe handles and other things needing tough ash or hickory, for the making of baskets and creels and more. Argyll tried to change the crops grown by introducing flax. He encouraged stock raisers. Cattle farming was not subsistence agriculture but looked to an English market. Like the expanding linen industry, this too was eventually aided by the new banks. The Duke's plans necessitated the building of new farm buildings and the employment of more workers. Even so, they were a small proportion of the nearly 600 men who were working in and around Inveraray in 1763.[187]

Essential to the Duke's success was his determination to enforce his wishes through generally long but restrictive leases.[188] Those became common on the estates. Scottish tenants and peasants, like those in most places, had to be forced to make changes perceived by them, but not always by their landlords, as risky. Restrictive leases were a means of achieving that.[189] Among the things which he did in 1756 was to force his tenants on the Tiree estate to pay part of their rents in spun yarn: 'I'm resolved to keep no tenants but such as will be peaceable and apply themselves to industry. You'll cause intimate this some sabbath after sermon'.[190] One proper role of the Kirk was to encourage the linen trade. By the 1760s, there were 'over a hundred women and girls' spinning for the rents.[191] Argyll knew that to improve Scotland was to give it jobs which could supplement incomes from agriculture for both the farmers and the lairds. Rural industry had to be increased. He tried in many ways to increase it and was not reluctant to have his managers allow the tenants little choice but compliance.[192] At Inveraray, the new planned town envisioned by Ilay in 1744 was to be a nicer, better administrative centre, and a place of commerce. To effect those ends, he built a chamberlain's residence and other houses for the more important members of the community, an inn (run by an English innkeeper), a church and a new courthouse – all laid out in a pleasing and rational way. In 1758, the Duke's chamberlain hired Robert Dobson, a Glasgow mathematics teacher for the town.[193] He taught in the English school of this predominantly Gaelic-speaking town. That too was, from the Duke's point of view, a step toward civility for which industry and commerce were necessary.

Industry in that part of the world meant primarily linen production. That was planned as soon as he inherited.[194] Spinning, weaving and stocking-making were all promoted. By 1751, there was a Board of Trustees subsidized spinning school in Inveraray enrolling forty girls. By 1753, the number had increased to 122 spinning wheels. A 'bletchfield for thread & Stockings' was to serve a stocking manufactory which he hoped to settle there but never did. Weavers had been introduced. Despite subsidies from the Board and from the Duke, his ventures had failed by the early 1760s. Flax could not be economically grown there. By 1758, the spinning school had educated all of the available local talent for whose skills and talents there was little demand.[195] Nothing came of his plans for a stocking factory although one was set up in Rosneath. Elsewhere, such efforts did increase the prosperity of Lowland areas, areas which often bordered the Highlands and Glasgow.

Flax growing seldom succeeded in Scotland but linen production could and did. The Scottish manufacture of linen depended on imported flax and yarn. Even then, it needed the protection of the tariffs, small government subsidies and an imperial market in which cheap, rough Scottish linens could clothe slaves and provide sail cloth. For this to be achieved, better ways of marketing Scottish linen had to be found and tariff walls erected to make certain that it would sell against foreign competition. The Duke played a role in effecting those conditions.

He helped to organize the national trade which was promoted through the British Linen Company (later Bank). He encouraged the efforts of chemists and bleachers working in the universities and for the Board of Trustees (see p. 144). Finally, he advertised Scottish linens by using them. Many if not all of his own shirts, handkerchiefs, nappery, and sheets were of Scottish manufacture. In all that he had the indispensable aid and cooperation of Lord Milton. They were among the greatest of the century's agricultural improvers and ones who clearly recognized that they were modernizing an archaic society. The Duke's promotion of industry and commerce through the protection of tariffs and state subsidies was just what one might expect of a statesman of his age. But to do it through the creation of new, largely private, marketing and credit institutions was innovative. To apply scientific research to the problems of farmers, bleachers, potters and other manufacturers was somewhat uncommon in Britain. His Scottish estates, in the 1740s, led him into all those fields and established patterns which others would apply as they emulated him.

Inveraray's linen schemes and the town's busy building sites are graphically described by Lindsay and Cosh but they were repeated in smaller ways wherever he made substantial improvements – at The Whim, Rosneath or Campbeltown. However, Inveraray was different. Improving his principal estate became something of a make-work project which helped to keep up his political interest during years 1742-47 when he was out of power or had but a tenuous grip on it. After the '45, road work and construction supplied needed employment and an infusion of cash into the Western Highlands still in a state of shock. Building gave him the means to keep many men dependent upon him while he increased the visible power of his family. How bustling a place his town became is well captured by Cregeen:

Inveraray now [c.1747] presented a scene of industry such as it had not known for many years, excepting the hectic days when the General's troops had been quartered there. Besides the masons and labourers for the castle, a host of wrights with their own labourers were making sheds to house men, tools, carts and barrows; the smith and his men at the forge turned out quarry-tools and other ironwork, and there were a wheelwright's shop, a shed full of sawyers making planks and scaffolding, lime-burners at the kilns, carters hauling up stone from the quarries, not to mention the increased staff of gardeners' men improving the parks. Further, military parties were now working on the King's Road, and some of them were quartered near at hand. Another road had to be built to Creggan's quarry down the loch, where a hut was built from its stone for the quarriers to live in and a stable for their work-horses. The stone itself, however, was carted only the quarter mile to the loch-side and then ferried up to the town by water.[196]

The pace of regional change was forced by the Duke's expenditures on his town. The results of this appear in an account a generation later, the entry on Inveraray in Sir John Sinclair's *Statistical Account of Scotland* (1792):

Since the beginning of the of the present century, the several successors to the estate and honours of Argyle, have been particularly attentive to extend their plantations, and to embellish the place. About the year 1745, the present castle was begun, by Archibald Duke of Argyle, and, after a short interruption during the rebellion, it was resumed and finished. Since that time, a great sum was annually expended by him, by his successor, the late Duke, and by the present, in making extensive enclosures, in building, planting, improving, making roads, (which in this parish are highly finished, and kept in excellent repair,) and in other works of utility and decoration. It is said that the sums laid out at *Inveraray*, since the 1745, do now amount to the enormous sum of £250,000, and that the present Duke, since his accession to the estate [1770], has expended at the rate of at least £3,000 *per annum*.[197]

The money Ilay expended yearly probably came to roughly a third of the value of the expenditures of the Crown for the Scottish economy through the Board of Trustees for Fisheries and Manufactures.

By the 1740s, the Duke was using his official and personal economic power to promote development in Scotland. Pursuing his own inclinations on the scale he indulged them, required a large income. That he had from lucrative offices, from the Argyll estates and from the payments for his feudal rights surrendered in 1747. He spent that money not on wild, high living but principally on improvements in Scotland and his Whitton estate. He pleased himself, increased his power and made Scotland better and richer. His power, connexions and economic base helped to decide what Scotland's future was to be. His 'gimcracks' paid off and were not merely idle diversions. He had not wholly ceased to politick and in 1744 was described as neutral only waiting for Tweeddale and his friends to fall out.[198]

Plate 9. A View of the Whitton House Garden and Gothic Tower by William Woollett (1757), by permission of The British Museum Co. Ltd.

Chapter 15

Ilay and the '45

I. Preliminaries

The 3rd Duke of Argyll did well in the '15 but is sometimes said to have done little or nothing in the '45.[1] This chapter considers that charge. But first, we need to get to 1745.

After Ilay was stripped of patronage power in 1742, he found distraction in his gardens and, after his brother's death, in new enterprises. Andrew Mitchell gives us a somewhat cynical glimpse of the Duke in April 1744, prior to his first visit to Inveraray since c.1715.[2] Argyll was told by Sir James Campbell of Auchenbreck, in the presence of Mitchell and others, that he was too old to 'begin such laborious projects' as his plans for Inveraray involved. The Duke replied that 'were he to dye tomorrow he would do all the good he coud today'. Mitchell went on, 'Give me leave to say my Lord [Tweeddale] that no Hero of Antiquity, nor no Plutarch for him, ever said a better thing, but alas how fickle is man, and how late is it before he arrives at the summit of Virtue'.[3] Mitchell's reference to Plutarch was not much amiss; Argyll in retirement was consciously, perhaps sincerely, burnishing his image as a virtuous man.

The Duke remained politically active and generally supported the Ministry. He still went to some Privy Council meetings. His attendance in the House of Lords was about as usual. He was busy in the peerage election held on 30 April 1742. The Marquis of Tweeddale, who now managed Scottish patronage, replaced the deceased Earl of Hopetoun. Argyll, along with twenty-eight others, voted for Tweeddale.[4] In January 1743, he was opposed to the recent place bill but discretely took his grievances 'to the King's Servants'.[5] He seems not to have been initially much involved with the Scottish Elections bill of 1743, perhaps because Scottish MPs generally supported it. Argyll went along with changes clearly thinking his period as an important player in the political game was over.[6] By the following year, he wished it had not been passed.[7]

He supported the Ministry and probably enjoyed attacking some of its critics. In mid-February 1743, Argyll had exchanges with Chesterfield in the House of Lords over the Gin Act. Chesterfield would have levied high taxes on gin and rigidly enforced them. In debate, he ridiculed the proposals of those who wanted the Gin Act to levy lower taxes which could be collected. He laughed at the poor who drank it and at those who would make sin profitable. Argyll supported the government which wanted the taxes lessened and collected. In Samuel Johnson's recounting of his speech, Ilay said, 'Every man that could foresee any thing, foresaw that it was a law that could not be executed; but as the poor had run gin mad, the rich had run anti-gin mad, and in this fit of madness no one would give ear to reason...'. Lessen duties, collect them but in the future raise the tax as men became accustomed to paying it. England would be more lawful and orderly. Chesterfield was wrong to laugh at the misery of the poor which legislators should alleviate. Johnson made him eloquent: 'Yet being now arrived at a time of life in which the passions grow calm, and patience easily prevails over any sudden disgust or perturbation, I forebeare to disconcert him [Chesterfield], though I have known interruption produced by much slighter provocations'. Chesterfield had used humour but that 'is less defensible in this practice, when we are contriving the relief of misery, or the reformation of vice.... he that can divert himself with the sight of misery, has surely very little claim to the great praise of humanity and tenderness; nor can he be justly exempted from the censure of increasing evils, who wastes in laughter and jocularity that time in which he might relieve them'. The ideas may have been Argyll's but the prose is surely Johnson's.[8] The Duke had risen earlier in the debate to point out that what was before the House was a motion to delay and not a substantive issue but then added that the Lords should not make the tax on British distillery products so high as to favour foreign spirits.[9] Whisky would be protected if he had his way.

In Scotland, too, he claimed to be a supporter of the Ministry hoping to make things 'go smoothly'.[10] However, the old Argathelians there remained divided between his and his brother's former followers and without strong leadership. In 1743-45 the Argathelians on the Town Council of Edinburgh split over the selection of David Hume as Professor of Moral Philosophy and at Glasgow over the appointment of a theology professor.[11] The new Duke's friends had diminished but that did not diminish his reputation. By the end of the year it was rumoured that he was to receive a Garter.[12] His opponents thought him still playing politics but he probably was not fully engaged until the spring of 1744. What brought him back were concerns about inadequate provisions for the defence of Scotland and by what he saw as the foolishness of the Scottish politicians.[13] He could do better.

Rumours of Bonnie Prince Charlie's arrival in the Highlands escorted by a squadron of French warships circulated in late 1742 and were reported by the King to Parliament in February 1743. A French invasion led by Prince Charles was planned and rumours that it was already under way were reported by Sir John Clerk of Penicuik.[14] Lord Milton was employing a McDonald to report on Jacobite activity in the regions north of Argyllshire.[15] Other reports came to Milton from the islands of Islay and Mull and from fishermen. Invasion rumours became more frequent and plausible. By February 1744, Argyll was worrying over the activity of the French fleet.[16] Tweeddale received such reports and was advised that it was necessary to raise troops in the region for the defence of Scotland. That became urgent with the declaration of war by both France and Britain in March. The War of Jenkins' Ear (1739-) had become the War of the Austrian Succession (1740-1748) and was a wider conflict. Argyll sympathized with Maria Theresa while Tweeddale, Carteret and their friends did not. The Duke of Argyll now sided with Old Whigs not the New – with Pelham and Newcastle who were increasingly uncivil to Carteret. They would be his colleagues from now on.

War raised the demand for soldiers in Britain and increased Argyll's importance. In January 1744, Argyll spoke in the debate about the employment of Hanoverian troops: 'we must have those troops or none'. It was the Ministry's view but it would not last.[17] The recruitment of soldiers in Scotland for Britain was becoming urgent. The Highlands, where under-employment left many wanting posts which the Army could provide, was a better source than foreign mercenaries. Getting rid of surplus men was seen as likely to make for less cattle stealing and violence in the region.[18] The drawback was that it seemed to many to be training soldiers for a Jacobite rising. Still, after 1743, it became British policy to recruit for line regiments in the Highlands. That did not involve whole units such as would shortly be raised and raised again in the Seven Years War. The Campbells were the largest clan in the region, they and their nobles [Argyll, Breadalbane, Loudoun] cadets, and chief tacksmen were essential to this activity. Tweeddale, no Highlander, could not effectively meddle in recruitment save to impede it. The Duke became increasingly important as this conflict and the Seven Years War (1756-1763) required more men.[19] Like his brother and Duncan Forbes before them, he and his friends used the recruitment of officers to wean men from Jacobitism. That opened them to the charge that they were favouring Jacobites.

Throughout most of 1744, Argyll urged the formation of Independent Highland Companies to keep the peace in the hills. The London response was not the organization of northern defences but the passage in May of a bill making it High Treason to correspond with the Pretender or his son.[20] Argyll supported that but is not reported as speaking to it in the House of Lords. He had already argued for more sensible measures and did so again when he got to Scotland in July. Staying at Holyrood, he held daily levees and was asserting his political authority.[21]

The Squadrone Lord Advocate, Robert Craigie of Glendoick, thought he should meet with Argyll in Edinburgh during the summer of 1744 to secure his approval of changes in the Justiciary Court.[22] When the Duke held court at Holyrood Palace in July and August, he embarrassed those who had displaced him. An irate Squadrone man wrote to Tweeddale that there 'were great numbers of all ranks (as lord Garlies says) clean & unclean... our Provost [John Coutts], Th[omas Allan, the senior Bailie?] & some of the Bailies were of the number who had not noticed him the last time he was in Scotland'.[23] In August, Tweeddale promised not to name JPs for Renfrewshire and Glasgow until he talked with Argyll. The Duke's response was to tell the Marquis that he also should not fill up the list of Lanarkshire JPs until Argyll had talked with him in London. The same letter asked for more troops for Independent Companies in the Highlands.[24]

What bothered Argyll most may not have been patronage concerns but the progress of the war and English nonchalance about defence of Scotland – but Argyll did begin to seek more places for his friends. In August, the Duke got permission to arm the Argyllshire 1744 militia but Newcastle did nothing to secure him a warrant which would make it legal. Milton wrote his patron that an invasion was expected.[25] Not long after, Robert Craigie was warning Tweeddale of unrest in the Highlands.

Having felt the pulse of Scotland, the Duke renewed his calls for the recruitment of loyal clansmen so that the Highlands would have a standing force of armed and loyal men: 'The nearer view I take of this Country I am the more convinced that the want of a sufficient force in this wild part of the Country will have bad consequences sooner or later'.[26] Argyll wanted at least two additional Highland companies of seventy men each to police the region. They were to be commanded by two captains and two ensigns drawn from the western and northern regions. They were not to be half-pay men but active men of credit in the Highlands, men who would have his confidence but also that of Breadalbane and his son Lord Glenorchy, Atholl, the Duke of Gordon and Duncan Forbes of Culloden – of men across the Highlands from Inveraray to Inverness.[27] That was necessary because the disarming of the disloyal had never been very successful.[28] When the '45 came, the region lacked such a rapid reaction force to counter the initially small number of men who gathered around Prince Charles.[29] The Ministry ignored Argyll's advice but Tweeddale did invite him to meet with the Dutch minister in December 1744.[30] The Dutch were trying to recruit men for their army in Scotland. The Duke was not in favour of that even though he was asked for a list of men who might command the companies they were raising.[31] He wanted Scots soldiers at home to keep order and to defend their own country not that of an unreliable ally. Argyll refused this invitation.

When two Independent Companies were formed in 1745 to police the Highlands, Tweeddale and other Squadrone men delayed and obstructed that business because they believed that it would enhance Argathelian power. Argyll named half of the officers.[32] Meanwhile, Prince Charles's men were being organized. John Murray of Broughton returned to Scotland from France in October 1744, where he had promised Prince Charles 4,000 Highlanders in arms should he come to Scotland. Less sanguine men later said that would happen only if the Prince came with 6,000 French troops.[33]

By mid-1744, patronage issues had become important and Argyll again was acting as a factional leader. Late in the summer, it was apparent that there were to be changes in the courts. In the second week of November, John Maule sent word from Edinburgh by express that Lord Royston had died. Argyll would try to fill the post. Robert Craigie soon told Tweeddale that if Argyll named Royston's replacement in the courts, then he would continue to have a majority of one in both the Justiciary Court and in the Court of Session if the same man was given both places. Later he reiterated this message writing that if Argyll picked the new judge, 'our lives and properties [will be] at his Disposal'. Argyll supported Charles Erskine of Tinwald for Session and Justiciary gowns in November 1744 and gave the impression he had secured him the post although the Squadrone too had been for Erskine.[34] The impression stuck. Erskine's cousin, Robert Dundas of Arniston, then Solicitor General, wrote to Tweeddale that he 'had no aversion to Charles being a judge, but this way of his coming in [without Tweeddale's visible help], is terrible fatal to your interest and renders your friends here contemptible'. The minister had been weakened.[35] Two weeks later Argyll exclaimed about the astonishing 'Imbecility of the Scotch Ministry'.[36] He was fully back in the game – partly because of the incompetence of his old enemies.

Parliament generally showed little real concern about Scots but worried about the English coasts. MPs continued to debate bills on pawnbrokers, annual parliaments, the municipal government of London and other such things while the Ministry unravelled.[37] Argyll thought Carteret and the Tories might try to strike a deal but that they would fail and Henry Pelham and his brother, the Duke of Newcastle, would remain.[38] A few days later, the Duke was approached by Tweeddale and Carteret, now Earl of Granville, who spoke to him of the 'Civil war at Court' in the 'handsomest manner'.[39] They wanted him for a new Ministry but, as General John Cope reported, Argyll had 'drawn strongly with the Pelhams'. The Duke urged Milton to help Cope 'so as to be useful to the publick'.[40] A bit earlier, Argyll got permission from the King to arm his militia but still was granted no warrants to make it legal. Tweeddale, opposed issuing them so Argyll could do nothing until the political situation in London was clearer.[41]

Clarity came late in November 1744 when the Pelhams forced Carteret out of power and a new Ministry formed. The King's new chief ministers were the Duke of Newcastle, Secretary of State, Henry Pelham, Lord Treasurer, and Philip Yorke, 1st Earl of Hardwicke, Lord Chancellor. When the '45 came, they would deal with it. They also had to deal with Argyll, with whom only Pelham worked well, and with resentful inefficient men like Tweeddale who thought they should not be in power.[42] His Edinburgh aides, Lord Advocate Robert Craigie and Thomas Hay of Huntington, were bumblers. The ineptitude of ministers helped Argyll but made the '45 a more difficult affair.

II. The Uprising

By early 1745, Prince Charles and the French were concerting a descent on the Scottish coast – a bid by the Prince to claim his own, for the French a minor diversion in a World War. By May, Argyll was making up lists of officers for the new Highland regiment whose colonel was to be his twenty-two-year-old cousin, Lieutenant Colonel John [Jack] Campbell, MP, eldest son of Major General John Campbell of Mamore, later 4th Duke of Argyll.[43]

On 15 July, Norman McLeod of Skye wrote to Lord President Duncan Forbes that he had observers out in the Hebrides seeking to verify reports that Prince Charles had landed but he had been unable to do so.[44] By the time the letter was received, Argyll was probably in Edinburgh at Brunstane House with Lord Milton. The Prince landed on Eriskay on 23 July but for two more days sailed around the islands before landing on the mainland on 25 July 1745. The first important politician with confirmed knowledge of the landing was Argyll who learned of it on 6 August from men of his clan. He immediately informed officials in Edinburgh and London. The Duke's message reached London on 13 August, the same day on which the commander at Fort Augustus realized there was 'serious trouble brewing in the Great Glen'.[45]

Newcastle, on 1 August, had written to Argyll telling him that he and Pelham, 'are fully convinced, That Your Grace's great Influence, and Power enable you to be of the greatest Use for the Support of the Government, if it should be attack'd in that Part of the Kings Dominions'.[46] He told Argyll that arms had been ordered for Scotland but not everyone in London wanted them distributed. Scots could not be trusted. The Duke of Cumberland was putting together a force which would go north. Tweeddale had put a £30,000 bounty for Prince Charles's head.[47] Newcastle's colleague, Lord Stair, who was in charge of the Army, thought the 6,000 troops in Britain would be enough but as insurance he called over to England seven battalions in the Dutch service; an eighth would be sent to Scotland.[48] The priority was the defence of England, not the quashing of a rising in Scotland before it became dangerous.

That reflected intelligence which said the French would make an incursion on the southern coasts.[49]

Once in Scotland, Argyll and Lord Milton made a progress to the west of Scotland. On 1 August, they were in Glasgow, the next day in Dumbarton, on the 3rd in Rosneath where they stayed. There they met Lt. Col. Jack Campbell, the newly appointed commander of Loudoun's Highlanders.[50] Under the Earl of Loudoun, Jack would lead troops of that now forming regiment throughout the Rebellion.[51] Jack had been using Inveraray as a base from which to recruit soldiers but with little success. At Rosneath, or perhaps earlier, Argyll discovered how few men Jack had raised. He was so angry that he threatened to take the awarding of commissions away from him and give it to men who were more diligent.[52] Jack's idleness made the Campbells look badly, left their lands unprotected, and might cost them commissions.[53] Milton mockingly said Jack's efforts had amounted not to the men of three independent companies but three men.[54] West Highlanders were unwilling to enlist because it was nearly harvest time, after another year of scarcity. Some in Morven, Ardnamurchan, Appin, Mull and Tiree were disaffected enough to later join the revolt. Those areas were in the end severely punished for their doing so – and so was the Duke who collected rents and dues from the regions devastated.[55]

On 5 August, the Duke again wrote letters urging the raising of troops and money and the gathering of intelligence. Argyll and Milton intended to move on to Inveraray. By 6 August, the Duke had learned from a message sent by an old friend, the Rev. Lauchlan Campbell, minister in Ardnamurchan, that Prince Charles had landed on the Scottish mainland.[56] On 8 August the Duke was uncertain about going to Inveraray because of the risk. As he told Lord Advocate Craigie, '... if the matter grows serious I shall not be in safety there'.[57] He would have made a fine political hostage for the Jacobites. On 10 August, Argyll's old friend, Lord Lovat, offered to suppress 'any Disturbances that Highlanders will make this year' for 'a moderate reward'.[58] He held a commission from the Pretender so this was likely meant to buy time as well as to save his skin should things go badly for the Prince. Later, some of Lovat's friends suggested the whole affair might be ended by a general pardon.[59] Argyll on 9 or 10 August laid out £5 for the gathering of intelligence.[60]

In Rosneath, Argyll began a flurry of activity designed to make Inveraray defensible enough to at least delay the enemy. The Duke ordered guns to be cleaned and readied. Money was gathered in. Strong points were garrisoned. Roads and the paths over the hills were to be blocked by troops. People were ordered to watch and report. Later, the Duke asked for two sloops to be sent to the Sound of Mull to patrol the waters into which men and supplies would have to come if a substantial invasion force were to land there.

Sometime after he got to Rosneath, the Duke had received the letter Newcastle had written of 1 August. It said that Cope was to 'concert with the Lord Justice Clerk [Lord Milton] and the Lord Advocate, what may be proper to be done'. The minister went on to say'. We do not presume to point out to your Grace, any particular measure to be taken at this juncture, as your judgment will direct you infinitely better than we can do; but if there is any thing, that you may think proper to be done by us here, I shall hope you will be so god *[sic]* as to let me know it'.[61] Argyll was now of importance to the Ministry which still did not give him the right to arm his or other Highlanders. The Duke also correctly believed that the Disarming Act prevented his calling out and arming Highlanders such as the men of Argyllshire certainly were.[62] While he had an hereditary commission as Lord Lieutenant for Argyllshire, he was not empowered to act and he had no deputy-lieutenants (the effective recruiters and directors of forming militia units) and could not by himself make them since their warrants came only from the Crown.[63] Argyll could not call out the militia. Illegally raised troops would not have had to obey. And, Argyll might not be given expense monies for illegal acts for which he could have been held responsible. That and other laws could not be quickly changed because Parliament had been prorogued and could only be recalled by the King who was in Germany.[64] He had not given the Regents the right to recall it. The Duke's interest in acting legally and for his own security prevented any action which was what he told Craigie on 12 August.[65] If the Duke did not act, the law and the Ministry were more responsible than he for his inaction.

It is likely that he did infringe the law in his own locality. He probably distributed some arms around Inveraray. The Duke did not have enough weapons at Inveraray to supply many and if the men called out had brought their own, this would have demonstrated to all that he had winked at the illegal possession of guns by those on his and other estates. Still, some were told to fortify their houses but he knew this to be illegal and said so.[66] He did keep his labourers working on the new Castle so that they could be pressed into service should that be necessary and if arms came for them.[67]

In the rest of Scotland the same legal situation obtained. There were few Lords Lieutenant or deputies, so no militia units were immediately embodied 'to assist the regular forces against the Young Pretender' in the summer of '45.[68] Tweeddale was aware of the problems posed by the warrants but he seems to have regarded this as a Highland and not a general British problem. He wrote to Lord President Forbes on 17 August,

> I am sensible of the want of legal authority in the Highlands to call forth the King's Friends to action in case their should be occasion for them but your Lordship will remember the difficulties that occurred about naming Lord Lieutenants of certain Counties at the time of the last Invasion which were the reasons that prevented any nominations being made at that time.[69]

Fearing protests from slighted men and not yet believing in the seriousness of the crisis, he waited to see if the warrants were really necessary. Squadrone men had not conceded anything in this crisis to men whom they had long struggled to oust from positions of power in Scotland. Argyll's fear of acting illegally and not being pardoned later has to be read in the light of that and earlier factional fights, including the efforts made in 1734-36 to impeach him. As Argyll told Newcastle and others, he was 'very sensible of the inconveniences arising to the Government and to the country' but he was 'unwilling to subject himself to penalties and trust to pardon'.[70] The lack of arms and munitions imposed another limit to what could be done. The Marquis thought there were reasons not to issue them until absolutely necessary.

While he waited, the Duke was not idle. Lists of those who were to become Deputy Lieutenants in Argyllshire were made out and given to Archibald Campbell of Stonefield, the Sheriff-depute of Argyllshire and himself later a Deputy Lieutenant. Commissions for militia regiments were also made out. Milton could have the warrants for the first issued and Argyll would sign them when 'the Government make it Lawful for them, to act'. On 11 August, Argyll sent to General Cope what intelligence he had and on 13 August asked for ships to be sent to the west coast and Western Isles, a request Craigie immediately passed on to London.[71] Two days later, Thomas Hay told Tweeddale that he believed Argyll had sent two navy ships to the Sound of Mull where they could support the garrison at Fort William and patrol vital waterways.[72] That would have been a proper response to the reports that French ships had taken prizes in the Clyde Estuary but it was beyond Argyll's power to order.[73] On about 17 August, Argyll did order all boats in the region to be secured which he could lawfully do.[74]

As Inveraray was being made as defensible as possible, more intelligence activities were organized. Argyll approved Cope's decision 'of keeping his little army together' and seconded Pelham's suggestion that the rebels be attacked before they had gathered in numbers. Developments were not encouraging. On 12 August, Argyll had received Craigie's letter of 11 August telling him that Sir John Cope had confirmed the Prince's arrival in Scotland. Plaintively Argyll wrote

> I have little to say but that I hope it is not true, if it is, I have nothing to do but to return. I wish it were in my power to give any assistance to the friends of the Government, or that I could flatter myself that my advice was of any use. I shall wait here till I hear from Argyllshire, which will determine my journey one way or other.[75]

The next day Lt. Col. Jack Campbell went to Inveraray and the Duke, at Cope's request, hurried back to Edinburgh by chaise. There he heard rumours that the Jacobites had sought to capture him.[76] Argyll spent the next few days with Lord Milton at Brunstane House giving advice to Cope and to others. Among them were the Edinburgh magistrates and civil officials, bankers, army men, clerics and the Lord Advocate. To him, Argyll complained of the Ministry whom Craigie said he treated like 'intruders'.[77] Writing letters to London was sending useless letters.[78]

By 16 August, there had been a skirmish near Fort William. Three days later the Prince raised his standard at Glenfinnan. Cope marched north with a small force to carry 2,000 muskets to Fort William to arm the loyal clans in the Northwest. He turned back a little beyond Dalnacardoch fearing ambushes in the passes over the mountains. Argyll ordered that all the intelligence from Inveraray be sent both to Milton and to Cope and again urged that two sloops of war be sent to sail off Moidart and to intercept any French vessels plying the Clyde Estuary. For those he offered pilots.[79] By then the government, with the King's permission, had allowed the Campbells to be raised but that news came only after Argyll had returned to London.

By 21 August, the day Argyll left Edinburgh, Newcastle had received at least four letters from him which he said 'contain the chief intelligence that has been received from any quarter, relating to the arrival and proceeding of the pretender's son and his adherents'.[80] Newcastle, not knowing the Duke had gone south, gave him a warrant to act backed by 'their Excellencies' – the ministers.[81] The Secretary of State was candid enough to admit that 'if your Grace's proposal [arming Highlanders] had been pursued, we might now have had a much more considerable number, in arms, for the government, than in all probability can be brought against it'. Argyll still lacked arms to distribute, or the warrants to embody a militia or any right to act in ways which required explicit formal authorization from London.[82] Since he had been on the shelf for three years, and was dealing with men who had ousted him, and did not make Scotland a priority, it is not surprising that so little was done.

Argyll's secretary, John Maule, writing on 24 August and knowing of Cope's defeat at Preston Pans, thought the 'Scots Ministry' was principally at fault but also said that the King had not until that battle admitted there was a rebellion. The English wanted to believe that rumours of French troops landing in sizable numbers were just that. Rumours required no action.[83] Until the '45 ended, rumours circulated by Jacobites had large numbers of French soldiers either being landed or about to be and of French gold and arms sent to men in the West or North.[84] It was easy in London to disbelieve those and think not much was happening in Scotland. However, events developed faster than anyone imagined they would.

By the time the Duke went to London, he had probably made up his mind to push for quicker action and a policy of leniency toward the Jacobites as the most feasible plan to pacify the country and to reconcile it to Hanoverian rule once order had been restored. Those views, if they were to matter, had to be pressed in London. In Scotland, Lord Milton and Lord President Duncan Forbes secured his power; he would anchor it in London. Together, they would pursue the same ends. Jacobite plans by then included asking Argyll to lay down arms, accept the Prince's pardon and join them for the good of all Scots.[85] Being beyond capture made those schemes impossible to fake.

The Duke's actions appeared very differently to others.[86] A Scottish correspondent of Robert Dundas of Arniston faulted 'a Certain Great Man' for leaving Scotland

> without giving the least advice to Any Body how far it was lawful to Arm that he did not care to want a Indemnity Not knowing who might be sitting sheriffs That he did not think it safe to commit Treason against two kings   did Great Mischief heere & gave great discouragement. his Words have been quoted as oracles by our Provost of EDr. & the Town of Glasgow   the first opposed all he cd doing any thing in Ed   the last have done nothing & Indeed cd do little when Sir John [Cope] was on his Pilgrimage wch has done Infinit Mischief to Particular persons as well as to the General Cause.[87]

Arniston's correspondent said that the Duke had urged the raising only of the Highland Militia. If true, that may well have reflected Argyll's low opinion of Lowland military forces – a view he shared with many including David Hume.[88] For the letter writer, it had another meaning: 'What tht wd have produced we may guess fm what we have seen. It wd have been so Many Raised for another Use'.[89] Squadrone men and that writer had a deep suspicion of armed Highlanders. None of the clansmen were to be trusted. Argyll could not even count on the loyalty of his own or on that of Whig clans like the Raes, Sutherlands and Monros. Few of them had joined Cope when called to do so.[90] Others wondered why Argyll had not raised the Campbells. They distrusted Argyll whom they were inclined to see as a crypto-Jacobite. Tweeddale characterized the Duke's return to London as 'a long and safe retreat'.[91]

That was also the judgment of the King and other Englishmen. George II thought Argyll should have remained in Scotland and that he had done too little.[92] The King had no sympathy for Argyll's long-held views of Jacobites and how to deal with them. He did not share Argyll's views of the law and what lawful government required. Others, like Horace Walpole, went further. Argyll's decision to return to London was a sign of fence-sitting, a secret favouring of the Jacobites or even cowardice. Argyll's return was a dereliction of duty. Walpole quipped 'the king was to see that he was not in Rebellion; the Rebels, that he was not in arms'.[93]

The judgments of Walpole, Dundas, Tweeddale and the King have stuck but are unfair. Had Argyll stayed in Scotland he could have mobilized men no faster than did the law officers (Lord Advocate Craigie, Solicitor General Robert Dundas, Lord President Forbes and Lord Justice Clerk Milton). They also did not call out the militia. Argyll had given them a list of those who should be chosen as deputy-lieutenants; those men were the ones principally employed. From Edinburgh he could not have pressed his arguments about the conduct of affairs where it mattered most. There was simply no point in staying. If Argyll was to have an effective voice in policy, or to look after the interests of his friends and country, he needed to be in London. Milton later remarked that 'something like ye old Scots Privy Councell in times like this would ben of use for when we get orders at 300 miles distance the opportunity is lost'.[94] The next best thing was to have a sensible advisor in London. Having done all he could, Argyll left for London to be heard.

He left knowing what others would think. In a letter to Norman McLeod written on 19 August, two days before he left for London, he said:

> I wish it [the Prince's arrival] may not turn to the prejudice of us all by producing severities that the most moderate amongst us may not be able to prevent. What will they not say to us in England, who have all along endeavoured to give the English a better notion of the Highlanders than they had, and it will particularly fall upon me who have relieved all those who were in my power, from the distresses that the last affair [the '15] brought upon them.[95]

He knew what the future held.

Even though absent, Argyll's presence was felt in Scotland. Prince Charles was said to have written the following to his father the Pretender:

> There is one man in this country whom I could wish to have my friend, and that is the Duke of Argyle, who I find is in great credit amongst them on account of his great abilities and quality, and has many dependants by his large fortune; but I am told I can hardly flatter myself with the hopes of it. The hard usages which his family has received from ours has sunk deep into his mind.[96]

That gives meaning to the motto on the seal Argyll used for some years. 'Memini'.

The Duke arrived in London on 31 August after an unpleasant trip. He also arrived a sick man. He had been ill with migraines, had suffered a bout of his recurring malaria, had rheumatism and what sounds like diverticulis. His illnesses showed the strain he had been under.[97] On his return to London, he was bled and confined to his bed for some time. That gave his enemies more doubts about his real allegiances. Some now found his pretensions to be 'Governour of the Highlands' ludicrous.[98]

By then, Prince Charles's forces, almost without opposition, had made great gains. After contact with Lord Lovat in Inverness-shire, they headed south to the Lowlands bypassing Cope's forces. It was feared that the Murrays of Atholl and the Breadalbane Campbells would join the Prince whose forces were growing and arming themselves as they went along.[99] They seized powder where they could – 1,000 pounds at Dundee.[100]

On 29 August, General Cope was in Inverness having failed to reach Fort William to distribute arms. The loyal men in the Northwest would not be armed. By early September, the government's inaction had created problems which made the defence of Scotland problematic. Milton summarized them:

> it is with difficulty I can walk the Streets of Edinburgh, from the Attacks of most zealous Friends of the Government, asking why the Offers of the well affected to the present happy Establishment are not armed and properly supported and impowered to appear in a legal way for the defense of His majesty's person and the Support of his Government. I am sorry I have not been impowered to say anything satisfactory to so faithful subjects... I do all I can to encourage and keep alive so Laudable a Zeal for his majesty's Service.... But my Credit that way will soon be exhausted unless some Salutary Measures be laid down & followed out, or that kind providence once more interpose in our Behalf.[101]

In London, Argyll, now writing often in cypher and using invisible ink,[102] still urged the issuing of warrants to raise and arm the loyal clans and the militia everywhere. Milton wrote to Tweeddale to the same effect and could not forebear adding, 'Had legal strength been given to the friends of the Government in the Highlands, no such Insurrection could have happen'd as this without a Landing of foreign Troops; and if it had [it] must have been crushed in the beginning without endangering or harrassing His Majesty's Troops or taking them from Ports where they may be wanted [to thwart an invasion of England]'.[103] Argyll made available to the government maps from his collection which were better on the Western Highlands than any the government possessed.[104] The Highlands had been worried over for a very long time but no London government had mapped regions where it might have to send troops or even collected existing maps in any quantity. The militia still could not be embodied; the loyal clans could not be raised. Even Lord Stair foolishly thought the rising was not beyond the capabilities of the meagre forces in Scotland.[105] Tweeddale, still reluctant to recognize the seriousness of the situation is said to have called it the equivalent of the 1744 mutiny in the Black Watch Regiment.[106] By October 1745, he still had given no permission to arm Campbells or to call out loyal clansmen.[107]

Scottish cities had been ordered to defend themselves but they could not have defended themselves had they chosen to do so. By the end of August, Aberdeen had no significant defences, only 500 stand of arms and no troops to use them.[108] Glasgow, a larger city, was worse off. The town council had asked for arms; no arms had been sent. It was allowed to arm only on 12 September – when it was found that the city of 17,000 people had only about 300 muskets.[109] The next day, it was warned to contribute £15,000 to Prince Charles who had already raised money in other towns. Andrew Cochrane, Provost of Glasgow, wrote Argyll asking him to intercede for the burgh which had raised and paid the Prince £5,500.[110] It was not then assaulted or occupied as were Aberdeen and Edinburgh on 16 and 18 September.[111] Edinburgh's Lord Provost, Archibald Stewart, and its Town Council were faulted by Tweeddale for not having defended themselves and for not earlier having taken up more suspects. The city was indefensible despite the efforts of Colin Maclaurin to brace its walls and point its guns.[112] The loss of Edinburgh and Glasgow disrupted normal trade and banking operations affecting the transmission of government funds. For the rest of the conflict there were difficulties in paying troops and buying needed supplies. Meanwhile, Prince Charles held court in Edinburgh's Holyrood Palace and debated the feasibility of invading England; Glengarry raided in Berwickshire and four French privateers landed arms, a few soldiers and money at Peterhead and Montrose.[113] French arms came more quickly than those of the London government.

It was not until 22 October, that Argyll was legally allowed to call out the Argyllshire militia and his clansmen. Even then, there were not arms for all of them. On 24 October, Lord President Forbes was allowed to raise men in the North. On the same day, 500 muskets, 500 broadswords and powder was ordered to be sent to Inveraray from Liverpool. The munitions were sent only on 12 November and went down in the care of Neil Campbell, son to the Principal of Glasgow University. The guns and swords arrived in Inveraray on 29 November. In the meantime, the Jacobites had occupied Carlisle on 18 November and pushed deeper into England.

In late October or early November, Argyll was said to be about to return to Scotland but he did not.[114] Instead, on 2 November, the Duke wrote to Archibald Campbell of Stonefield that he had signed the commissions and the Scottish militia might now legally be embodied and called out. Further recruiting was to be done without compulsion.[115] Argyll also ordered the arrest of Sir James Campbell of Auchenbreck who since 1743 had held the Pretender's commission as a Major General.[116] Stonefield was to be diligent in watching the rebels and their sympathizers and should seize whatever evidence he could find of the guilt of rebels.[117] On 25 November, Argyll gave further instructions to Stonefield about the Militia Act. He was to look up the powers stated in the Scottish Acts of Parliament anent the militia and follow the 'Old Law' which, 'though obscure [,] Imperfect, & not explicit, yet is sufficient in Times like these to do great service to the Government'. It, and the amendments Argyll had made to the Disarming Act of 1725, allowed more men to be quickly called up by loyal lairds. Whatever ambiguities there were could be faced later. Argyll had perhaps returned to his 1715 position – he would not be too nice about legal ambiguities when rebels threatened him and his. The letter concluded with the hope that the guns distributed at both Inveraray and Campbeltown 'will remain with them after this bustle is over'– in short, he wanted the Disarming Act modified so Scots could defend themselves.[118] The Jacobite forces at that time were at Standish, about 25 miles south of Lancaster but the organization of Scotland to fight the rebels was still not complete.

In London, Argyll received reports on affairs in the North from Milton and his various friends and servants such as Principal Campbell of Glasgow University, Patrick Duff of Premnay in Aberdeen and even Alexander Kincaid, the Edinburgh printer. Those were supplemented by others from Lt. Col. Jack Campbell and later from his father, Major General Campbell. The Duke named officers for the Edinburgh and Glasgow regiments and asked for more arms as the Jacobites pushed south, reaching a bit beyond Derby on 5 December. He pressed for more adequate naval patrols, more munitions and more troops. A bit later he intervened to aid his cousin when the government was unhelpful.

By late November the Navy was making problems about the moving of General Campbell's troops which had come over from Holland. Those problems were severe enough so that on 8 December John Maule wrote to General Campbell that 'The Duke of Argyll has cried Murder About ye delays of ye Admiralty and has complained both to ye Duke of Newcastle and L. Harrington in my hearing – when you get to Inveraray write to Shawfield'.[119] Argyll may no longer have been going to Council meetings since his advice had been too often ignored.[120]

The Duke needed money to support Campbell troops whose expenses were unpaid.[121] He asked for rent money so that he would not have to sell securities in a low market. Some of that money went to General Campbell of Mamore who had reported that his troops were ill supplied and lacked meal. Lord Chesterfield, Lord Lieutenant in Ireland, had refused on 10 December to send any meal and told others he did not care if all the Scots starved.[122] Three weeks later, the General complained that he lacked money to pay his men and had little in the way of provisions. They were burning Argyll's building timbers for their fires.[123] By 1 February 1746, Argyll was sending provisions and money was being supplied to the General by Argyll's bankers. This may have gone on for some time since, on 8 September 1746, the General told Lord Milton that Argyll 'gave me an unlimited Credit for drawing Money for the Publick Service' with the Duke's bankers.[124] The Duke, in effect, invested in the repression of the '45.

Probably in February, the Duke wrote to Lt. Col. Jack Campbell that 'guarding the Coast on the Western Sea seems to me to be the last Importance at present'. He wanted General Campbell of Mamore to base himself at Fort William and to give commissions in the Argyllshire Regiment only to Campbells.[125] The Duke was still concerned with the General's financial problems. Mamore had had bills refused by the Paymaster General, Thomas Winnington, and by someone named Wilson who was, probably, in the Office of the Treasurer of the Navy. Neither had bothered to speak with Argyll before they did so. Within two weeks, Argyll had sorted out the problems.[126] A few days later, he was thinking about the Edinburgh burgh elections and writing about supplies.[127]

As the Jacobites turned north from Derby, it was still not clear what, if anything, the French might do. The southern British coasts could not be denuded of troops lest there be an invasion through the Channel ports. However, the Jacobites found Scotland better prepared to fight them. Argyll had helped General Hawley to the position of Commander-in-Chief in Scotland. The Army in the West had been put under the command of Major General Campbell of Mamore who arrived in Scotland and was acting by 22 December. He had come with better armed and experienced troops and now also commanded the militia troops which had been fully activated. He was not, however, in constant contact with the troops raised in the Northeast by Duncan Forbes and under the command of Major General John Campbell, 4th Earl of Loudoun. Lord Lieutenants had finally been named for Scotland by mid-January. There were now more troops and militia men. Ships were on patrol but the government had sent larger ships than the Duke requested and kept them mostly in the Clyde Estuary. Ships of shallower draft would have been more serviceable in the islands and coastal areas.[128] Such ships could supply places on the sea lochs such as Fort William, Inveraray and Campbeltown. Still, defence was better organized but Squadrone civil officials had made no lists of those out in the Rebellion.[129]

At Christmas the Jacobite army was coldly received in the undefended city of Glasgow where the inhabitants were forced to provide it with 6,000 coats, 6,000 waistcoats, 12,000 shirts, 6,000 pair of shoes, and 6,000 blue bonnets. It stayed for Hogmanay. Glasgow was much hurt by the exaction of goods and money but, later, also by the fact that it had done or seemed to have done so little to resist the rebels. Provost Cochrane told the Duke, 'we confide solely in your Grace for obtaining relief from the great distress our corporation and inhabitants at present are labouring under'. Argyll spoke to the ministers. It took a while but in 1749 the Duke secured a grant for the burgh of £10,000.[130] Earlier, Cochrane had written to Lord Milton that they all regarded the Duke as their 'patron'.[131] Toward the end of 1745, the Provost made requests of Argyll for University patronage and did not send them to Montrose, the University's Chancellor. It was a sign of power returning to Argyll – at least for a time.

After fighting well at Stirling (7-12 January) and Falkirk (17 January), the Jacobites headed further north and west to seek shelter in Aberdeen and Inverness and to take Forts Augustus and William.[132] The forts secured entrances to the Great Glen. Taking the latter would open Argyllshire to the rebels and would give them a coast on which supplies could be landed. This shifted the focus a bit from troops to the Navy. By the second week of February, instructions were being given to ship captains.

In London the King and his ministers were still at odds with one another. Tweeddale benefited from this since the government needed the votes of his friends in the Commons. William Pulteney, now Earl of Bath, and John Carteret, Earl of Granville (he had resigned as one of the Secretaries of State in November 1744) had the King's ear more than did the ministers. The Pelhams wanted William Pitt to be Secretary at War but the King would not have him any more than the Pelhams and their friends wanted to work with Bath and Granville. Those disagreements continued into 1746. The first to go was Tweeddale whose judgments, usefulness and power had been brought into question. He informed the King in late December that because he was not consulted, he could no longer serve. He resigned his seals on 9 January 1746 and was replaced by Newcastle.[133] Argyll told the ministers he would not deal with Lord Advocate Craigie 'directly nor indirectly'.[134] Tweeddale's underlings in Edinburgh were on their way out.

Those changes solved no problems in London. By 10 February, Newcastle, the Secretary of State acting as Scottish Secretary, was relying on Argyll to correct some of his orders sent to Scotland.[135] Argyll would had been under no illusions about the meaning of that. It was meant to butter him up and induce him to resign with Pelham, Newcastle and Harington on the following day. The Old Whigs wanted him to go out with them but he did not. In the midst of war and rebellion, Argyll commented that he could not 'help pitying the King'.[136] Argyll seems to have intended to keep in with both the Pelhams and with Granville and Bath. On 11 February, Bath and Granville were given the Treasury and the Secretary of State's position; Argyll remained in place as an advisor.

Argyll's staying on created a dilemma for himself. Be loyal to Newcastle and the others and lose his interest in Scotland and possibly the support of some Scots fighting the Pretender. Or, work with the new government and hold onto his Scottish positions at the expense of his character. Argyll set that out in a letter to Lt. Col. Jack Campbell.[137] He thought it was in his and the country's long term economic and political interest to stay but it would not sit well with Newcastle and his friends and it seemed dishonourable. Two days later, the new ministers were out; Newcastle and the others were back. We do not know if Argyll was overjoyed but his secretary celebrated with the Old Whigs at 'a Drum & a Consort of Musick; Monticelli & tout cela' at Lady Townshend's.[138]

The politician who most benefited from the change in government was perhaps the King's son, the Duke of Cumberland whom Argyll on 1 February described to Milton as 'a most amiable Young man'.[139] His voice in Scottish policy became stronger as he took command of troops in Scotland and found more friends in London. He generally opposed all that Argyll wanted done and soon saw the Duke as little better than a Jacobite. In Edinburgh, Argyll's stock was higher. On 13 February 1746, the Convention of Royal Burghs sent their address to the King through him.[140] Ten days later, Argyll was sending for lists of rebels and lining up posts for his friends.[141]

By the Spring of 1746, information came to Argyll from the towns and counties, from Lord Milton, still coordinating an intelligence operation from Edinburgh, and from others, including his cousin General Campbell of Mamore.[142] Some of their news was passed on to Newcastle who then took it to the King.[143] Mamore answered the Duke's enquiries about the behaviour of the Argyllshire men and worried that he still had no money to pay them. That led to frequent absences without leave. In early April, grain for the troops had to be taken from Argyll's tenants. The General was buoyed by the approval of his superiors.[144] Cumberland promised he would pay the General's out-of-pocket expenses.

Fighting in Scotland now focussed on the North where Lord Loudoun and the Independent Companies from Argyllshire had not done so well but the Jacobites had had no sustained successes. They could briefly hold Aberdeen and Inverness but they could not keep them. They might control much of the Highlands but that would not make them victorious in the long run. They needed to clear the Great Glen and establish a port on the west coast if the French were to help them significantly – a faint hope at best. To do that, the rebels had to capture the forts which controlled the Glen, especially Fort William on Loch Linnhe from which it was possible to sail into the Sound of Mull or the Firth of Lorne and then into the Atlantic. The geography which made it possible to bring in supplies for the rebels also made it possible for the government to support Fort William by artillery fire from small ships anchored off shore.

Fort Augustus was weak. It was taken on 5 March 1746 after a short siege and a bombardment which exploded its magazine. The siege of Fort William was abandoned by Prince Charles's troops only on 3 April. By then, its Governor, Alexander Campbell, had been superseded by a more aggressive and bloodthirsty Lowlander, Captain Caroline Scott. Control of the shores and of the water ways was important. In the course of fighting for the latter, and to prevent the Jacobites from supplying their troops and to retaliate against the rebels, a fourteen-mile stretch of the Morven coast was devastated between 10 and 28 March. Over 400 houses in the sparsely settled region were destroyed. General Campbell of Mamore, who had overall command of this theatre, was told by John Maule, surely speaking for Argyll, that Campbells should not be involved in such activities and recommended that 'more distant clans or ye Regular Troops' be used if they were to follow that policy. He also expressed the belief that reprisals would do no good but would induce rebels to be more destructive in retaliation.[145] Highland policy left to Englishmen and bigoted men like Scott was brutal and caused useless misery. Argyll had opposed such actions in 1715 and he did so now.

Responses to the burning of houses and the looting of farms came from MacDonnell of Keppoch and Cameron of Lochiel. They asked, or were rumoured to have asked, for permission to plunder Argyllshire in revenge for what the troops had done to them and their people.[146] Argyll knew that by 5 April when he wrote to Stonefield that it was 'a pity the Rebells should impute to you or me the burning which I am sorry for & never would have advised'. On 8 April, he wrote again wanting to know who had issued the orders to burn the district and 'what foundation they had for that which they assert relating to intercepted letters of Yours & [Campbell of] Airds. I am very sorry for the whole affair, but I cant help it'. He also asked for a list of the Argyllshire rebels. Two days later he asked for more information about 'the burning that I might be better able to discourse upon that subject'.[147] It was unusual for him to treat any topic with three letters in five days. The burnings in Morven were but the first of many instances which cost his tenants and him dearly.[148] They set a precedent for Cumberland who needed little inducement to harry rebellious Scots. Those actions blackened the name of the Campbells because most of the burnings were carried out by the Argyll Militia. What is clear is that the Duke had taken no part in planning those actions and condemned them. What was equally clear to his principal man of business at Inveraray, Archibald Campbell, was that 'The Duke of Argyll will be under an absolute necessity to New Model his Estates in Morven & Mull & other Countrys possess'd by the Rebells'. Stonefield was not sorry that the Army was rooting out Jacobite tenants.[149]

From mid-March until the Battle of Culloden on 16 April 1746, the Jacobites were a viable fighting force but generally in retreat and in some disarray as their funds ran out and the French failed to relieve them. The Battle of Culloden reduced Jacobite numbers to about 2-3,000 rather leaderless men. It was also a battle in which the Argyll Militia distinguished itself by being the only regiment of foot to pursue the fleeing rebels. Cumberland praised it.[150]

Subsequent months saw the devastation of more Highland and Island areas by troops under the command of both the Campbell Major Generals, Mamore and Loudoun. Lochiel's residence was destroyed and many more of the tenants' houses were also. Argyll's lands and tenants were not spared. Mamore had given amnesty to Jacobites in Glencoe and Appin which later was more or less ignored. He, at least, was a reluctant brute. Argyll tried to get Cumberland's policy changed in London so that there would be no more driving off of cattle and burning of homes but no one was interested.[151] Men like the Earl of Chesterfield, again a leading figure in the House of Lords, believed or said Argyll's actions showed that the Duke was not a sincere Whig. Many did not understand his belief that if you want laws obeyed and Crown authority respected, then 'favors & disgraces rightly applied' do more than legislation and soldiers to preserve 'publick peace'.[152]

As the fighting ended, Argyll could look back on the previous two years and be pleased that his initial assessment of the danger had been correct and that his responses to the '45 had been more sensible than those of others in London. His advice had been good, his conduct difficult to fault. Even before the '45 ended and the guilty were punished, the debate about the future of the Highlands had begun. He would be active in those discussions but not as effective as he wished to be. Had it been up to him. there would have been fewer recriminations in the aftermath of the rising. Argyll thought laws should be enforced but ones dealing with political offenses should be enforced with great discretion. Argyll was less at odds with the English over parts of the aftermath – the punishment of captured rebels.

The Duke did nothing to save any of the four condemned Scottish peers, three of whom were executed – not even for Lord Lovat whom he had known for over forty years and with whom he had sometimes been quite close. He is not known to have done anything for the 120 ordinary men who were executed. He did nothing for genteel rebels, such as Lord Elcho, who appealed to him.[153] He made no objection to the trials of commoners being held in England or to the selection by lot of those who were tried. He did not object when those who were found guilty and then reprieved were transported to America and the Caribbean colonies. He would find much to object to in the settlement proposed for the Highlands.

ARCHIBALD Duke of ARGYLL.

Plate 10. The Duke of Argyll by Thomas Chambers after Allen Ramsay (c.1750), mezzotint, Scottish National Portrait Gallery, Edinburgh, with the permission of the SNPG.

Chapter 16

The Aftermath of the '45

I. Uncertainties

The aftermath of the '45 was a tense and uncertain period for the Duke of Argyll. When Tweeddale resigned in January 1746, it was not clear who, if anyone, would succeed him as Secretary of State for Scotland. No one in the Squadrone faction looked fit for his office but Argyll's restoration as Scottish manager was difficult because of his perceived role in the suppressing of the Rebellion and the leniency with which he was likely to regard the rebels. For the Duke, the keys to peace in Scotland were order and prosperity which could only be achieved through a policy of leniency. He was where he had been in 1716. As had been the case then, many regarded his position as a sign of secret Jacobite leanings. The Duke's survival as a cabinet level politician was doubtful but he could not be ignored. In Scotland, not much functioned well without his countenance because his supporters were entrenched in so many institutions. In the West of Scotland, his economic power counted for much. His place in British politics might not be settled but Glasgow thanked him for the aid he had given the burgh and sought patronage through him and not from Montrose, the local Squadrone leader.[1] In July 1746, the Convention of Royal Burghs asked Argyll to present their address to the King. Perhaps to make his interest visible, Argyll 'by Special orders' told General Campbell of Mamore to 'take up his Lodgings at the Abby' in the ducal apartment. The person who wrote that noted that 'the Duke is in the absolute Disposal of civil posts in Scotland & he has acquainted the General to lett him know who he looks upon to deserve notice within the Shire [Argyll] for Eyr [either] Civil or military Employs that he might Embrace what Opportunities will Occur to do for them'.[2] If that was really so, it did not last.

Once the rebels had been defeated, most Scottish corporations obsequiously honoured the Duke of Cumberland. He received honorary degrees, the freedom of burghs, praise from the right thinking and those who had suddenly joined them. Argyll wryly joined this chorus since the foundation stone of Inveraray Castle said that Cumberland had made its erection possible (see p. 204). Four months earlier, Argyll had complained that people had been turning Cumberland against him.[3] That shift in opinion was not good for most Argathelians.

When the municipal elections came in the autumn of 1746 and again in 1748, Edinburgh returned George Drummond as Lord Provost. Drummond claimed that ministerial influence, not that of Argyll, had elected him. Ministers could not elect Drummond to the House of Commons[4] but little patronage was going through the Duke's hands. Argyll's position in London was made more uncertain by tensions in the Ministry itself which had not been fully resolved during the crisis of February 1746. Some ministers seemed reconciled to working with the Duke and his friends, others were not. Still, Argyll and his friends were given a few plums. Milton, then ailing from the long strain which the Rebellion had imposed on him, resigned as Lord Justice Clerk in November 1746 and was made Keeper of the Signet.[5] That was payment for his activity in organizing resistance to the Rebellion but it was also, perhaps, for Milton's having shown some independence of Argyll.[6] The post involved virtually no work, paid him more and gave him some patronage. Charles Erskine succeeded him as Lord Justice Clerk, but earlier he had Squadrone support although Argyll seems to have secured this warrant.[7] 'Old Charles Erskine', as Argyll called the man two years older than himself, would now be a more distant friend.

Argyll found the next two years ones of ups and downs. In January 1747, it was reported that he had 'nobody to support him in the House of Commons' because he was willing to see too many punitive measures applied in Scotland.[8] Pelham and Newcastle curtailed Argyll's authority in Scotland. They made it clear that jobs could be had through men who were not Argathelians. Newcastle and his brother wanted a broad-bottomed Ministry which in this case meant power-sharing between Argyll and his old enemies. Argyll would have some patronage but Scottish jobs would be shared. Involving more Scots in the management of Scotland would make English politicians the arbiters of what happened there. Newcastle and Pelham, but particularly Newcastle, began to shape the Squadrone and Patriots into a group which could partially replace the Argathelians in the next elections.[9] To lead this opposition, Newcastle and Hardwicke tried to set up the Earl of Marchmont and his twin brother, Alexander Hume-Campbell, MP. The English lords also had notions about re-organizing Scottish institutions such as the courts and the laws they administered. They aimed at Argyll's power, his friends and his beliefs about what the Union had guaranteed to Scots. There would be a fight and not a clean one.

In late March 1747, Alexander Hume-Campbell wrote his brother, Marchmont, that Argyll had always supported the Jacobites and was doing so still. The King would no longer see Argyll because he had been convinced that the Duke was a Jacobite. George derisively called him the 'Viceroy' of Scotland.[10] The Earl of Chesterfield, the Dukes of Cumberland and Montrose and the remains of the Squadrone faction all hoped to oust Argyll and Milton using that allegation. Their Highland policies would be punitive. Old friends of Argyll, including Lord Tinwald and Lord Advocate William Grant, were being weaned away.[11]

With less support in Scotland and with many of his London associates thinking him a Jacobite at heart, it is not surprising Argyll's prospects were bleak.[12] Newcastle, Hardwicke, Bedford, Chesterfield and Cumberland wished him out.[13] Cumberland was particularly against Argyll for being willing to employ former Jacobites or men from families which had been Jacobite and because he disliked Argyll's opposition to his European policy which was one of aggressive war against the French and their allies in Europe. Such opposition made the Duke of Argyll unpopular with others in London.[14] Well into 1747, Argyll's standing was unclear. What Lord Stair referred to as 'a Lowland party' opposing 'the Highland Party' seemed to be working for the Pelhams in 1747.[15] At the end of October, Alexander Hume-Campbell told his brother

Marchmont that Argyll was no longer attending Council meetings 'but acting just as he did last year'.[16] Once again electioneering saved him.

Henry Pelham saw Argyll as someone with whom he could and needed to work because he needed votes in the House of Commons where Argyll's men could not be ignored.[17] In the municipal and parliamentary elections of 1746 and 1747, Pelham opposed Argyll's candidates in some burghs while helping others. On the whole, they found it possible to co-operate. Argyll's pre-election comment was that Cumberland was having his way and that 'Pelham is the only one of the Ministers who seems to know what they are doing'.[18] Cumberland did not have it all his own way. In the general election for the House of Commons, held at the end of July 1747, thirty-five of the forty-five MPs were elected from a list prepared by Pelham and Argyll. Of the men elected, eleven were Argathelians, six came in because of Pelham and seventeen more were government supporters; only nine seats went to the Whig Opposition – along with one to a Tory and one more to an Independent. In most cases, Argyll had advised on, but had not determined who ran.

Argyll did not feel good about the elections and seems not to have gone up to campaign. He wrote to Milton that he would not come until after the elections were held because 'I should only draw of people about me & make a most wretched figure, by being neither able to reward, punish nor in some cases to protect my friends, all which would appear in a more glaring light if I was now at Edinburgh than here at London... I might easily have made matters worse, but not better...'.[19] Despite that, he counted. In Dumfries, when the Duchess of Queensberry told him her friends 'did not care to go [into office] by me, I asked her pardon for troubling her & said I would take care that they should not go by me'.[20] A Johnston won, not a Douglas. In Berwickshire, Argyll set up a candidate against Marchmont's brother backed by Pelham and came close to defeating him at the polls.[21] In Aberdeenshire, a place where he had enjoyed unquestioned dominance for many years, Argyll was pressed into accepting Andrew Mitchell, the former deputy to Tweeddale.[22] In other elections, the Duke was supposed to have had been up to old tricks which Marchmont described in a letter to Cumberland which should not be taken too seriously:

> ... all askt in Scotland of any man to be preferr'd was whether he would devote himself to the Duke of Argyle and whether he were the King's friend of foe, if he would go to Hell for the Duke of Argyle he was sure of preferment; that all this summer the King's service had been betray'd and all those who had joyned the English ministry in the Jurisdiction Act had been opposed by what was called the Court interest in Scotland and unless his Royal Highness threw his weight into had shown some independence. the scale it was like to continue so.[23]

Marchmont went on to worry that all the new sheriffs to be appointed in 1747 (see pp 306, 308) would be Jacobites. Paranoia and lack of realism of this sort made the Squadrone and the Patriots ineffective politicians. Such men made conditions in Scotland after the Rebellion worse than they need have been. Their complaints went to the willing ears of the King, Cumberland, Newcastle and Lord Hardwicke. Argyll could not have things his own way but excluding him would be costly and difficult. In some places he created new votes by selling superiorities and secured others by gifts or offices. The Duke drew the line at giving anything to Archibald Grant of Monymusk, Lord Prestongrange's brother and a onetime swindler who had been extruded from Parliament in 1732.[24] The Earl of Bute received an £800 pension – his uncle remarked, 'so this world of ours is made'.[25]

The peerage election of 1747 showed the same trends. The Squadrone men and Cumberland hoped that the elections would be managed for their benefit but Argyll and Pelham picked most of the government's list of representative Peers.[26] Cumberland chose five of the peers on the list but things did not turn out well for them.[27] Those opposing Argyll and his friends planned to exclude from the elected Peers, the Duke of Atholl and the Earl of Sutherland. The Earl of Home was to be re-elected but he was no longer to be Argyll's man. The vacant places were to go to Montrose and Marchmont. Should Argyll object, he was to be told he was being obstructive and would lose power with no open fight or quarrel.[28] Argyll was present at the election held on 1 August 1747.[29] Of the replaced peers, only one or two seem then to have been Argathelians. Nevertheless, his friends filled about half the sixteen seats while a slightly smaller number of old Squadrone men were elected. Marchmont was elected only in 1750 and Montrose not during Argyll's lifetime.

The election of 1747 stopped Argyll's slide from power. He now had to be given more consideration. By the end of the year Pelham was acting 'a kind part' but Newcastle was accusing the Duke and Milton of shielding an un-named Jacobite. Argyll told him that he could hang the Jacobite and oblige them both but Newcastle could not or would not name him.[30] Newcastle's new system of management was failing. Its long-run outcome was the building up of networks of Scottish correspondents by Newcastle and Hardwicke and the hope that those correspondents could, in time, be made into a group to replace Argyll and the Argathelians. That constrained Argyll's actions for some time to come and it helped to revive the hopes of the Squadrone and their Scottish friends after the death of Henry Pelham in 1754. Argyll lacked the power he had formerly had. Pelham and Newcastle would never restore that.[31] The Duke of Argyll could not exclude Patrick Boyle of Shewalton (December 1746) or James Graham of Easdale (June 1749)[32] from the Court of Session or Robert Dundas of Arniston from the Lord Presidency (September 1748). All three came from Squadrone families which had long opposed him. However, Pelham was consulting on most appointments; even that of Robert Dundas involved favours for Charles Erskine, Lord Milton, and his son Andrew. Of that deal, the Duke said, 'the whole is a good bargain'.[33] A bit later, Argyll got the Crown to make Erskine's post, Lord Justice Clerk, one held not at pleasure but for life. Milton, Erskine,[34] John Maule, and William Grant of Prestongrange all got something. Pelham himself seems to have chosen men to sit on the Court of Exchequer and in the offices controlled by the Treasury. All that was in the background as the settlement of the Highlands was worked out 1746-1748. That showed Scotland could not be managed without Argyll. He slowly gained more power. While his enemies worried about Jacobites and included among them Argyll, Milton, Patrick Grant, Lord Elchies and even Charles Erskine,[35] Argyll worried that Argyllshire would be further ravished by Jacobite raiders and insurgents.[36]

II. The Settlement of the Highlands

Argyll suffered from the '45 not only as a politician but as a Highland landlord. He would be affected by the attempts to settle and civilize the Highlands which for the next decade preoccupied Scottish politicians. The popular solutions were the old ones – introducing better agriculture, promoting fishing and industries, trade and towns in a region no longer dominated by over-mighty subjects leading subservient clansmen. That prescription changed only in the details, the force to be used, and the thoroughness with which remedies were applied.[37] To realize those ends, the region had to be changed culturally in ways like those which Lord Grange had suggested years earlier (see pp. 96-7). The politics involving those policies was difficult and some of the decisions bore heavily on Argyll's personal interests.

The first step toward a Highland settlement was the Act of Attainder which came into full effect on 12 July 1746 and was not opposed by Argyll. It outlawed forty-one principal rebels and confiscated their estates. It removed many clan chiefs. Collectively, that Act concerned the lives of about 150,000 people in an area of about 5,000 square miles.[38] Some army commanders in Scotland, particularly the Duke of Cumberland and the Earl of Albemarle,[39] wanted whole clans proscribed and moved out of Scotland to British colonies. Their successor, General Humphrey Bland, was little better even though Argyll had recommended him, approved his appointment, and seems personally to have liked him.[40] Bland worked in Scotland until 1763. Such Englishmen were not appalled at the North being devastated. English lords like the odious Chesterfield were worse. The bloody-mindedness of some important English political players was appalling and made the pacification of the Highlands more difficult.[41]

The Disarming Act of 1716 had proven impossible to enforce. The Disarming Act of 1746, like the earlier one, was widely disregarded. Lord Milton feared this, too, would disarm the friends of government but not its enemies.[42] The Disarming Act was followed by an Act banning Highland dress – the wearing of plaids and tartans, the only sort of clothing owned by many. Milton thought this was necessary although it would create hardship among such people.[43] Highland dress was to be only for the loyal soldiers of Scottish regiments. Gaelic was not to be spoken in schools in the region and non-juring ministers were to be put out of their livings. Such acts attacked the culture and morale of the Highlanders but the Tenures Abolition Act was meant to change the way things were run and realized very old hopes.[44] The military tenures or ward holding were made into feu and blench tenures as Lord Grange had called for in 1725. That ended the obligation of tenants to fight for those from whom they held their land. Other changes simplified the obligations of vassals and reduced the services which could be demanded of them. Milton and Argyll approved of this.[45]

The Heritable Jurisdictions Act of 1747 was complicated – indeed, it was complex enough for English Lords to ask that the judges of the Court of Sessions draft it.[46] Argyll would not support that. The Act tampered with the Treaty of Union and asked those committed to defend Scotland's laws to subvert them. The Duke took a principled stand consistent with others he had taken over time and not a particularly self-interested one. It won him friends in Scotland. The bill Argyll was willing to support and see passed was not that which had passed the House of Commons by a slim margin in April much less that of the Dukes of Cumberland and Bedford or their friends the Earls of Marchmont, Hopetoun and Findlater.[47] They envisioned something harsher and more punitive.[48]

The opposition to the bill mounted by Argyll and others was such that the government feared losing the bill in the Commons and so made concessions to Scots.[49] 'The Scots Bill' brought to a head the animosity against Argyll but also showed that he was needed. On 10 April, Horace Walpole wrote his friend Horace Mann that 'The Ministry are now trembling at home with fear of losing the Scotch bills for humbling the Highland chiefs: they have whittled them down almost to nothing, in complaisance to the Duke of Argyle; and at last he deserts them....'[50] The next day Newcastle wrote the same thing to his friend the Duke of Richmond.[51] The compensation for the confiscated property was increased so lords did not lose so much; the baron and burgh courts were left to function to preserve order locally. After he had made it less onerous, Argyll was willing to support it.

In the House of Commons some of Argyll's friends voted against the bill just as they had voted against one or another of the previous acts. Some simply stayed away. That was taken as more proof of the Jacobitism of the Argathelians.[52] The Ministry's revenge for this seeming obstruction and the Duke's amendments was partially to exclude him and his friends from the choice of the new Sheriffs necessitated by the confiscation of the hereditary sheriffships. Excluding Argathelians from the picking and appointing of Sheriffs was no minor matter. Sheriffs in the future would be more important judicial figures and they remained the returning officers in elections.[53] Sheriffs might be persuaded to return as elected, men who had actually lost at the polls, or men whose voters were dubious because their votes had been recently (and often illegally) created.

When the bill was introduced in the Lords on 17 February 1747, Argyll would not move or support that measure in debate but 'sat by in a corner silent, and complained of the headache'.[54] He had never been opposed to the ends envisioned by the Act although those violated the Treaty of Union albeit in the interest of Scots. The final version of the Act included many of his suggestions. It abolished, with compensation, all rights to heritable jurisdictions save those of High Constable of Scotland, some of the hereditary Vice-Admiralties and rights exercised by burghs.[55] The regality rights of Scottish lords were taken and their jurisdictions given to the ordinary civil and criminal courts of the kingdom. They were to be compensated for their losses. Argyll offered opinions on the technical aspects of the bill so that appeals might be avoided and the processes simplified.[56] Holding a baron court was still possible. In those, lords or their deputies could adjudicate minor criminal cases where fines amounted to less than a pound or decide civil cases where the sums at stake came to twice that or less. Baron courts could still collect rents and dues. Most had fallen dormant by 1800. The Act ended jurisdictions which were impedimenta to the uniform government of the country and which gave undue legal powers to the tiny class of landlords who already had so much economic power over their dependents.[57] Argyll also argued that all the Jacobite Bishops, preachers and teachers in Scotland should be forced to conform to the acts requiring them to swear allegiance to the proper King or be replaced. Opinion governs all; they could not be allowed to pervert it.[58]

Fights over the bill went on to the end. Lord Hardwicke noted on 21 May 1747 that Argyll claimed in the House that it 'carries a reflection upon the people of Scotland, as if all were disaffected', and that the new regulations came from prejudices. Heritable jurisdictions were not the cause of the Rebellion and abolishing them would not touch all its roots. The jurisdictions had a thousand year old history and were part of a complex social fabric. Their abolition should not be a hurried matter. 'It would be happy for all who have estates in the Highlands, if all the powers of Clanship were abolished'. Then estates could be run with only economic ends in mind. The Duke was equally clear about the ways the Bill violated the Treaty of Union:

> I was at the meeting where the 20th article [treating of feudal jurisdictions] was proposed. It was proposed in the same words by the Scotch Commissioners, proposed by us in different words for the very next article of the royal burghs, Reserved as rights of property, and therefore only purchased now.'

Not to pay for them would be unjust and would go against many English precedents such as the paying for advowsons or compensating the owners of the Darien Company which was put out of business at the Union.[59] Archdeacon Coxe described his speech as a 'long argumentative speech [which] ably combatted all objections which had been adduced'. Others did not find it so good.[60] Chesterfield asserted that payment for confiscated rights was not an obligation since they were not protected by the Union Treaty which, therefore, was not violated. The heritable jurisdictions had contributed to the Rebellion; Scots deserved to suffer.

Argyll could not but have ambiguous feelings about the Highland Settlement. He was one of the principal speakers on the government side in the Lords for this bill but there could be no doubt about his reservations.[61] The bill reaffirmed the acts disarming Scots, banning the tartan and the confiscation of estates. Collectively the Scottish acts were meant to break up Highland culture by eradicating its language, changing its manners and customs, even the religious, economic, and political regimes under which it ran. It changed tenures and the ability of the chiefs to wage war. Argyll was caught in the position of wanting Scottish 'barbarism' to end but not liking the ways or speed with which some Lowlanders and Englishmen were prepared to end it. He had spoken for the Highland Jurisdictions Act but he also argued that the measure ought to be delayed while passions raised by the Rebellion cooled. He recognized that punitive schemes designed for the guilty inflicted hardships on the poor and innocent. He saw that aspects of the attempts to settle the Highlands violated the Treaty of Union and that they were meant to further integrate Scotland into a Britain in which his country's peculiarities and distinctiveness would eventually be lost. At the same time, the Duke was not opposed to all aspects of the settlement. He willingly surrendered jurisdictions which introduced particularities into the administration of justice in Scotland and which were not of benefit to Scots.[62] He expected compensation for the loss of his property, possibly at a greater scale than others would receive.[63] The Duke asked for a compensation payment of £25,000. He received £21,000, far more than anyone else in Scotland.[64]

About a month after the Heritable Jurisdictions Act passed, the management of the forfeited estates was given to the Barons of the Scottish Exchequer Court by the

Vesting Act of June 1747. That made the Court of more interest to all politicians. However, the Vesting Act did not provide particular means for administering the annexed estates. Those came only in 1752.

The votes and attitudes of the Argathelians may have cost them places just before the summer elections of 1747. The choices of Sheriffs and Sheriff-deputes in 1747 were often made by local interests and military officers like General Bland who had few political ties in Scotland. Those appointments gave Pelham and Newcastle a way of balancing the powers of those in Scotland with whom they dealt. After the elections, Argyll's political prospects brightened and continued to improve. In the autumn he made his annual trip to Scotland, one reported in the London papers.[65]

III. Assuming Power Again

The next steps in Argyll's political career were to do what he could to smooth things over with old foes. In England, this was somewhat out of his hands since it depended on Pelham, Newcastle, Hardwicke and William Pitt the elder and on their willingness to protect him from the Dukes of Cumberland and Bedford, the Earl of Chesterfield and their supporters. However, tensions between the Pelham brothers allowed the Duke of Argyll an increased importance. Chesterfield left the Ministry in 1748. The Duke of Bedford became less important and Argyll had a bit of revenge as he helped to defeat a turnpike bill the Duke wanted.[66] The winding down of the war, which Argyll had opposed, also helped. Even Cumberland was less of a problem for a year or so. The Duke of Argyll had enough political capital to settle scores and make some gains. He kept out of government men he disliked such as the Earl of Marchmont.[67] In the summer of 1748, he secured for the Justices on circuit an increase of £50 in their expense money.[68] He spent six or seven weeks in the autumn in Scotland mending fences and tending his estates. To thank the soldiers building the road from Luss to Inveraray, he gave them an ox to eat and ten guineas to divide. By the end of the year, his health was drunk at celebrations of the birthday of the Prince of Wales.[69] Some popularity could be bought but he also had to come to terms with men who might be won over. That was in his power. We have glimpses of how he worked at it.

Argyll met Marchmont in a bookstore at the end of January 1748. Initially the Duke mistook the Earl for his twin brother, Alexander. After apologies and compliments, he asked if Marchmont thought he had blocked his election as a Representative Peer. Marchmont, as good a liar as the Duke, said, 'I had made no enquiries about it but it was natural to imagine so since my brother and I were known to lie under the misfortune of his disapprobation'. Argyll then denied that he had aimed at him – only at the Marquis of Tweeddale, now discredited. Marchmont went on

> ... he [Argyll] had refused being a minister when it was offered him some years ago and would not be so now on any account. I said it could not be that he suspected himself deficient in abilities for it. He said when he got to his gimcracks in mathematics he was the happiest man in the world, and bid me believe everything he had said was spoke plainly as he meant, and so he left me as I thankt him.[70]

This did not make a convert but the meeting told Marchmont that Argyll was willing to be friendly and had less concern with aggrandizing himself than was often thought. One could bargain with him.

Argyll's soothing of Jacobites had a similar function and was generally more effective. As an old man, Alexander Carlyle remembered them in his *Autobiography*:

> ...the Duke of Argyle... and Fletcher [Lord Milton] very wisely gained the hearts of the Jacobites, who were still very numerous, by adopting the most lenient measures and taking the distressed families under their protection, while the Squadrone party continued as violent against them as ever. This made them [the Argathelians] almost universally successful in the parliamentary election which followed the Rebellion, and established their power till the death of the Duke... in 1761.[71]

Not quite an accurate or nuanced account of events, it shows how the Duke was perceived to have acted after the '45. He continued to procure places for men whose families had suffered because of their role in the uprising. That generated gratitude and popularity which was not irrelevant in later elections. He had always said that leniency and buying men was cheaper and more effective than coercing them.[72]

Argyll's other steps can be seen in things discussed earlier and below – the development of his estates, the encouragement of industry, fishing and banking. In the long run, it was such things, along with the acceptance of Highlanders into the armed services in greater numbers, which changed Scotland and make further rebellions impossible.

IV. Argyll's Own Reconstruction Plans for Scotland

Argyll spent time on measures designed to make Scots more prosperous, content and less rebellious. His principal concern was the promotion of the linen trade and resuming his own projects for the improvement of the ducal estate. At The Whim in the 1730s, he raised sheep and had women spinning his yarn on a model estate.[73] Now he could work on a larger scale.

Lord Milton had been involved in the linen business privately and through his work on the Board of Trustees for nearly a generation. In the 1730s and 1740s, he had owned stock in The Edinburgh Linen Company, an enterprise founded by William Dalrymple of Cranston which was principally an importing, bleaching and marketing business. It failed in the early 1740s.[74] Milton's experience taught him that the trade needed more capital, quality controls, better technology and more efficient marketing. Given those, the economic prospects of much of the Lowlands and the margins of the Highlands could be improved. Thousands of spinners and weavers might be employed in the industry. Any improvements providing more employment and income would help to stabilize the country. In the autumn of 1744, Milton and others created a new firm, the Edinburgh Linen Co-partnery also known as 'The Company for Improving the Linen Manufactury in Scotland'. This was capitalized at somewhat more than three times the value of Dalrymple's enterprise.[75] Absent from the list of stockholders was Argyll but many Argathelians were there including Alexander Fraser, Lord Strichen; Charles Erskine, Lord Tinwald; Archibald Stewart and John Coutts, both sometime Lord Provosts of Edinburgh, and other business and professional men long associated with Argyll. In London, the stockholders included Dr. Charles Stewart; Argyll's banker, George Middleton; William Beckford and Galfridus Mann.[76] This company was to be managed by two men, Ebenezer McCulloch and William Tod, who were to own 10% of the stock; they had every incentive to make the venture a success.[77]

By April 1745, the managers and Lord Milton found that they were faced with a credit problem created by the apparent unlimited liability of shareholders in England. Under Scottish laws, the company already had limited liability in Scotland but only there. An additional problem had been created by Milton when he secured a grant of public monies from the Board of Trustees to be used to finance some of the work of the new company. He appeared to be using his official position on the Board of Trustees to benefit himself as a businessman. That might provoke suits against the company. The managers in 1745, and the London based investors in January 1746, resolved to petition the King for the formation of a royally chartered company.[78] Such a charter could legitimize the dubious deal which Milton had arranged. It could give limited liability in England and thus assurance to English investors who believed they might be liable for damages should the company be sued.[79] By June 1745, William Tod was writing letters which assumed that a charter would be granted.[80] The charter application was approved in January 1746. Argyll gave 'advice and approbation' for what was admitted to be Milton's project.[81] The petition for the royal charter for the British Linen Company was presented in the spring of 1746 and granted on 5 July 1746. The new company was a limited liability company able to operate in England as well as Scotland and was not excluded from banking. When it became a bank in 1765, it was probably the first one ever established and devoted to the financing of a single trade.[82]

Argyll's politicking for it in London is hardly surprising since the linen trade had already benefited from his support for duties and subsidies in 1742, 1745, and would again find him supportive of duties in the 1750s. In 1744, he had been somehow involved with a Glasgow linen company and later he encouraged those who sought new bleaches and dyes. He now subscribed £3,000 toward the British Linen Company's capital of £50,000 and became its first Governor.[83] Milton served as Deputy-governor and combined that with the headship of the Linen Committee of the Board of Trustees. Among the Company's original Directors, were Patrick Crawford of Auchenames, MP, two Edinburgh merchants and John Coutts – all old Argathelians. The Duke of Argyll may not have been personally active in the new body but in every meaningful sense it extended his connexions and offered him and his dependants more opportunities to help their friends. It was as much his as was the Royal Bank which gave it loans, the Board of Trustees which co-operated with it, and the Convention of Royal Burghs which furthered its work. He and Milton took an active personal interest in experiments on bleaching, and the dyeing of linen. Indeed, at Saltoun, Milton's estate, there was, after 1746, a large bleach-yard, and workers engaged in other aspects of the trade.[84] Argyll, Milton, and the Board of Trustees fostered the linen trade in Argyllshire after 1748. For a time in the 1750s, Argyllshire produced 'more than half of the stamped linen made in the Highlands'.[85] Similar interests and concerns had led to Argyll's membership in the Highland Society of Glasgow which dated from 1727.[86]

By 1751, the British Linen Company had £46,000 of working capital and £55,000 of borrowed money. By the end of the Duke's life, it was circulating notes to the value of £96,000. Involved in every aspect of the linen trades, it had brought greater employment and added income to much of the country. 'In short, the British Linen Company was by contemporary standards a very substantial enterprise, rivalled in the manufacturing and trading sectors of the Scottish economy only by the largest of the tobacco partnerships and perhaps not even by them'.[87] The Duke had again helped promote the economic forces which shaped a more modern Scotland and, for some, eased the economic pain caused by the '45. He and his friends used the Linen Company to remit Post Office money to London. Politics and private gain marked most of what they did.[88]

On his own estate, one of Argyll's responses to the devastation of his lands was to secure in 1749 an Act which produced a new valuation roll for Argyllshire. Argyllshire was the first Scottish county to be subjected to such a re-appraisal of values since 1700. It was probably sought primarily to reduce his own taxes which he thought were higher than those levied elsewhere.[89] It lowered the taxes of some in Argyllshire while raising them in areas not devastated. This also represented a bit of modern management since it established titles,[90] set fairer values which took account of the damage done in the region during the Rebellion, and did all this in pounds sterling and not pounds Scots. Neither he nor the tenants in devastated areas would be paying taxes on value no longer present. At the same time, he could collect more rents elsewhere calculated on valuations which had increased. Raising rents added incentives to be more efficient to those who had to pay them. The new roll went into effect in 1751. A decade later one of his obituaries called it 'the standard for raising the Cess'. [91]

Among old projects to which he returned were the creation of his new town, the promotion of agriculture, manufacturing and fishing. The first is treated elsewhere but here we should note that he was employing a wright (one of the Meikle family) to make mill models for new enterprises.[92] He supported the Free British Fishery Society which did not flourish but manifested his belief in development as an antidote to disorder, rebellion and poverty.[93] Argyle also, sometime in the 1740s or in 1750, became a partner in an unsuccessful whale fishing venture centred on Campbeltown. This gave him a part-interest in a snow named *The Duke of Argyll*. After 1750, the ship was engaged in both whaling and trading in the Caribbean and to the northern colonies in America. It was finally captured by the French and taken as a prize to Martinique.[94]

Finally, he had a hand in the Land Tax Bill which affected Scots. The Convention of Royal Burghs in 1749 tried to have changed provisions of the bill.[95] Argyll agreed to take this up with the Lords of the Treasury but he told the Convention that they would be better off with a separate Scottish bill than with one designed for England which they had modified to fit Scotland. Scotland should be kept separate.

In 1749 and 1750 when he visited Edinburgh, he lodged in Holyrood and held court symbolizing his return to power.[96]

IV. Glimpses of a Personal Life

In the 1740s and early 1750s the Duke of Argyll was busy with his own families. His brother's demise made him head of the family and with that role came responsibilities to his nephews and nieces. He had a hand in adjusting the Earl of Bute's marriage settlement in 1749.[97] His Bute nephews probably presented fewer problems than his brother's daughters, the 'bawling Campbells'. The worst of the lot was the youngest daughter, Lady Mary Coke.

The 3rd Duke arranged her marriage on 1 April 1747 to Edward Coke, Viscount Leicester, heir to the Earl of Leicester. Married after a difficult courtship, the couple had serious troubles. She refused her husband his marital right on the marriage night. Viscount Leicester was a drunk, a gambler, and a violent man.[98] Lady Mary was an obstinate shrew. One thing led to another. Lady Mary was struck and confined to the house and abused in other ways – or thought she was abused. The Earl of Leicester reproved his son and promised Lady Mary that, as 'a man of honour', he would look after her.[99] Argyll, who had been informed about all this, told the girl, whose face still hurt, to live with her lord.[100] He interceded for her with her husband's family and obtained promises of better usage. Lady Mary said he had been very good to her, better than her mother and sisters.[101]

Despite the Duke's interventions, the husband did not keep his promises. He continued to persecute his termagant wife. The Viscount visited Argyll but the interview went badly. Gossip about this now public scandal made the situation worse. Colonel Henry Bellenden, a cousin by marriage of Lady Mary, drunkenly argued with the Viscount and challenged him to a duel which the Viscount seems to have declined. The charitable reading is that he asked time to arrange his affairs. The Colonel forced the young man to defend his words and conduct in a duel which he meant to make a deadly affair fought with two pistols each. Horace Walpole described the encounter to George Montague on 14 July 1748. Walpole clearly thought Argyll was behind an attempt to kill Viscount Leicester:

> ...two or three wicked circumstances on t'other side, never to be got over, are Ballenden's stepping close to him after Coke had fired his last pistol and saying, 'You little dog now I will be the death of you.' and firing, but his pistol missed– and what confirms the intention of these words, is its having come out, that the Duke of Argyle knew that Coke, on having been told that his Grace complained of his usage of Lady Mary, replied very well, "Does he talk! Why it is impossible I should use my wife worse than he did his." When Harry Ballenden left Coke on the road from Sunning, the day before the duel, he crossed over to the Duke, which his Grace flately denied but Lord Gower proved it to his face. I have no doubt but a man who would dispatch his wife, would have no scruple at the assassination of a person that should reproach him with it.[102]

Lady Mary Coke wrote to Argyll that her husband 'had accused her of endeavouring to get him murdered, and told me (before his father and their clergyman) that to his knowledge Mr. Bellenden came to tell me of the duel the night before'. To some this affray suggested that the seventy year old Duke was too cowardly to fight his own battles.[103]

The duel solved nothing. The Viscount again abused and confined his wife, searched her belongings, and forbade her to write to her mother.[104] The Earl's father now supported his actions. Lady Mary sent her things to Argyll's house. Her husband demanded them back saying he would 'use the means the law puts into my hands to recover what is my right'.[105] This scandalous affair ended in court. Lady Mary was ordered to be produced in the Court of King's Bench on a writ of *habeas corpus*.[106] Argyll probably initiated that action. Eventually, a divorce action was initiated but no dissolution was effected.[107] The couple separated in 1750 when Lady Mary went to live at her family home, Sudbrook Lodge. She agreed to remain married as long as her husband lived. The 3rd Duke of Argyll was willing to look after his relatives and did so at some cost to himself.[108] Family honour was important to him and it must have galled him to have this affair noticed in the papers.

The Duke's illegitimate 'family' also concerned him. About 1749-50, as we have seen, he erected a house at 10 Argyll Place for Mrs. Williams. This adjoined his own garden at Argyll House and looked out on a new garden made for his lady by tearing down 24 Great Marlborough St. where he once had lived. No. 23 had been demolished in c.1747. She was now provided with a nice little property and later would inherit No. 22 Great Marlborough St. which he had bought in 1738. He must have had something of a private domestic life across his garden.[109] That was unlikely to have kept him fully satisfied. Before 1735, a scurrilious poem circulated in Scotland about Ilay's womanizing there. He was accused of cuckolding both Milton and 'T-m' 'C- n' to which the husbands consented in order to have political power. At least two copies still exist. His enemies would have been titillated by this doggerel.[110]

After leaving politics in 1742, Ilay seemed to be enjoying his life. His new library was ready to fill with books. His buildings went up; his improving schemes were underway. In 1744, Argyll had planted at The Whim 700 spruce trees and 300 at Rosneath. There was already a nursery at Inveraray where laburnum seeds, yellow roses and other plants were raised as they were at Brunstane. Interrupted by the '45, he was back at it in 1746, planting more spruce and other plants.[111] His gardens were maturing nicely.

In 1746, Argyll had been unwell but he was usually in the House of Lords up to its proroguing on 12 August by which time the Disarming Act and the Heritable Jurisdictions Act had been passed. He stayed in London for the trials of the Jacobite Lords – Kilmarnock, Balmerino and Cromartie – which began on 28 July 1746 and ended with two executions on 18 August after the remission of the penalty for Cromarty. He and Kilmarnoch had been Ilay's pensioners (see p. 266). Travelling north would have been difficult.[112] By 1747, he had recovered and went to Inveraray with a party which included John Maule, Roger Morris, William Adam, Lord Deskford, Charles Erskine (Lord Tinwald), Hugh Dalrymple, Harry Barclay and others of less note. They were all made free of the burgh of Inveraray. The ceremony was one the Duke seems to have encouraged but did not undergo. He attended as his friends – peers, lawyers, merchants, physicians and skilled artisans – joined more humble masons, schoolmasters and soldiers as burgesses of the town. It was part of the festivities which marked his trips to Inveraray.

The next year saw more guests of a similar sort including Henry Home (later Lord Kames), Allan Ramsay jr., Joseph Tuder [or Tudor, Ilay's spy at the Board of Customs], Lord Milton (his wife often served as Argyll's hostess), Lord Tinwald, and the usual hangers-on. When the Circuit Judges came to Inveraray, Argyll presided at the opening of the Court as Justice General and sometimes sat if there was business. He did so during the trial of James Stewart of the Glen in 1752 – which impressed one of his later guests, Signor Gastaldi, Minister to the Court of St James from the Republic of Genoa and Burgess of Inveraray.[113] Later that autumn, the Duke was visited by Corbyn Morris, Secretary to the Scottish Customs. Morris was an economist 'who had writ some papers relating to the funds with great applause'. He probably had not been recommended for his post by Argyll.[114] The Duke sometimes used his time in Inveraray to woo those not of his camp. It was also a time when he did estate business and made plans for future projects and inspected work already done on old ones. He was investing in the grandeur of his family.

His fortune was also growing. The Duke's personal net worth had risen by 1749 to something in the order of £52,000.[115] His income from offices was about £5,000 with the rest coming from the ducal properties and his investments. Again, we cannot be sure of the totals because for some years there are no dividends and interest entered in the Coutts accounts and in other years sums are missing which he must have been paid. All that is a bit baffling but the trend was upward.

Chapter 17

Argyll's Last Years, c.1750-1761

I. Politics: Scotland

The last period of the Duke's political life did not start auspiciously. After 1747, the Ministry was led by Henry Pelham as First Lord of the Treasury. His brother, the Duke of Newcastle, the Secretary of State, handled Scottish business and conducted the most important foreign affairs. The first did not quite trust the Scottish Duke; the second neither liked nor trusted him. Newcastle's one-time protégé, Philip York, 1st Earl of Hardwicke, the Lord Chancellor, also distrusted Argyll. By 1749/50 the Pelham brothers were not on good terms which enhanced Argyll's position but Hardwicke, like Newcastle, continued to believe Argyll was secretly some sort of Jacobite enemy of the King. So too did George's son, the Duke of Cumberland, who still alleged that Argyll and Milton were Jacobites and that they had appointed Jacobites to offices in Scotland and were protecting them. Hardwick and Newcastle continued, until 1760, to cultivate Scottish networks of their own with the hope of ousting Argyll from his position in Scottish affairs. All three ministers influenced events in Scotland directly or through men other than Argyll. They found allies in Scotland among those who had belonged to the now weakened Squadrone faction and sometimes among those who were not with it. Squadrone men impugned Argyll's honesty and spread rumours of the Duke's secret Jacobitism and, more justly, of his care for those who shared such loyalties. Such comments prompted him to write, 'The Scotch have of late been so liberal in calling one another Jacobites, that it is no wonder the English incline to believe them without distinction & none have practised that Calumny more than the very people who brought in the Tory Magistracy'.[1] That remark glanced at Cumberland and his friends including George Drummond. Argyll's position was shaky. The Convention of Royal Burghs sent their address to the King in July 1749 through Newcastle.[2]

Despite difficulties he continued to appoint many to the forces and in the early 1750s, Argyll mounted something of a Scottish campaign to show his power and to increase it. When the Duke held court at Holyrood in 1749 and 1750 and was waited upon by local notables, he was signalling his return to some power and advertising his ability to do business.[3] In Glasgow, the magistrates hung his portrait which they had commissioned the previous year (see frontispiece). That was reported in the London papers.[4] Argyll's London support in the early 1750s was problematic and throughout most of this period Argyll's prospects remained somewhat uncertain but his hand was not weak and he was a skilled player. He worked to show his influence at the peerage election of 17 January 1750 when Lord Marchmont, a 'Patriot' with whom Argyll seemed to have made his peace (see pp.308-09), replaced the deceased Earl of Crawford who had been useful to Argyll since at least 1733-34. Marchmont did not lead a substantial faction but he was not a man Argyll would have chosen had the choice been his alone.

Argyll's politics turned on his ability to manage Scotland for ministers in London. Scotland could not be managed without London backing; ministers in London increasingly needed the parliamentary support of Scots which Argyll's political machine provided. After the 1747 election, Pelham, impressed with Argyll's ability, did not, could not, ignore him. Argyll's men in the Commons were a group of about a dozen whom Pelham, and later even Newcastle, had to treat gingerly since they did not know when their votes might be crucial to the survival of the government. Argyll also had friends in the House of Lords. The Duke also managed to keep a working majority in the various bodies essential to the running of Scotland – the Courts of Session and Justiciary, the Exchequer, the Board of Trustees, and after 1755, the Forfeited Estates Commission.[5] He was less successful with the Customs and Excise offices controlled by the Treasury but his men were entrenched in most institutions of the kingdom. The King, who overestimated the Duke's ability to appoint the men he wanted, still derisively referred to Argyll as 'the Viceroy of Scotland'.[6]

The simmering conflicts between old enemies continued into the late 1750s and were at work in many patronage matters. Argyll nominated Henry Home of Kames as the replacement for Lord Monzie as a Senator of the College of Justice in 1751. Sir Andrew Mitchell, Tweeddale's old Under-secretary, then told Newcastle that Kames should not be made a judge because his father had been out with the Jacobites in the '15 and that the son was little better. This rumour the Duke refuted after getting an account of the facts from Kames.[7] Charges against Kames bit but had not stuck. Absent from Kames swearing in ceremony were three judges associated with the Squadrone: the 4th Marquis of Tweeddale (an Extraordinary Lord), Lord President Robert Dundas and John Pringle of Haining.[8] In Edinburgh, the younger Robert Dundas and other lawyers with long memories stood ready to thwart the Duke's schemes.

By 1752, Squadrone men left most minor patronage in Scottish institutions to Argathelians and local families but places were contested if there was the slightest chance that an Argathelian candidate might be defeated, embarrassed or a man sympathetic to the Squadrone faction could be elected. Candidates of that faction were regularly elected by the students to the Rectorship of Glasgow University under a constitution made by Argyll and his friends in 1726 which had given students more rights. The Duke of Montrose could still challenge Argyll in Glasgow partly because, in 1743, when Lord Ilay seemed out of power for good, a new Duke of Montrose had been chosen Chancellor of Glasgow University, a lifetime post. Montrose and his friends tried to assert some control over Glasgow University, the burgh and its hinterland. Montrose in 1750 became Governor of the Royal Bank of Scotland. Old tensions continued until the end of Argyll's life. However, most of the professorial appointments made in Scotland between 1747 and 1761, even those at Glasgow, went to men with Argathelian backing.[9] That was true of many other minor jobs.

Another front opened in clerical politics. That saw Argyll after c.1750/51 supporting the young men who formed the Moderate Party. They addressed a set of problems centred on patronage, the character of ministers, their functions and the nature of the message which ministers should preach. The enthusiastic evangelical revivals at Cambuslang and Kilsyth of the early 1740s still resonated with many.[10] Those who approved them found the increasingly moralistic preaching of the men appointed by heritors and politicians not only unedifying but dangerous to the state which would be exposed to God's wrath – as many preachers of jeremiads warned.[11] The Moderate Party was for moral preaching and no enthusiasm; it supported the Erastian ideas which Argyll had long held. That put them at odds with Evangelicals. The Kirk, periodically riven by dissension, needed stronger leadership from men who looked not to their Bibles for guidance in ecclesiastical affairs but to the politicians.

After the 1750 General Assembly of the Kirk, Argyll and Milton began to help the Moderates. Their party had formed c.1751/52. By the end of the General Assembly of 1752, they had made their mark because of their debating skills in the General Assembly. Like the Duke, they wanted laws obeyed and errant men forced into obedience to Kirk law. They pursued their policies in the lesser church courts and in the General Assembly. From 1752 on, they took a consistently more radical line regarding the government of the Kirk than had Argyll's earlier managers. Eager to be recognized as genteel, learned and responsible clerics, they were tolerant promoters of learning and good morals.

Most of the leading Moderate clerics had or came to have ties to the Argathelians. Some were promoted to better livings, others to places in the universities.[12] John Jardine, Lord Provost Drummond's son-in-law, received an Edinburgh living in 1750 and a better one three years later.[13] By 1753, William Robertson had come to Milton's attention as a bright man who wanted an Edinburgh church. It was noted that he was a relative of the late William Adam and his sons whom Argyll employed as architects.[14] William Wilkie was already asking for good livings.[15] Adam Ferguson, an Army Chaplain, had likely met the others by 1751 during a long vacation from military service. He and John Home were intimates of Milton's family by 1756. Home had been introduced to Argyll before 1755 by Lord Bute who also advised him on the writing of three of his plays. By the mid-1750s, Lord Milton and the Duke appreciated this new coterie for its performances in the General Assembly.[16] Over the next generation men like Jardine, Home, Robertson, Wilkie, Alexander Carlyle, Hugh Blair and their secular counterparts, who sat in church courts as ruling elders, shaped the Kirk in ways which Argyll had seen as desirable since he first entered politics. The Moderates were fully active by 1752, a year marked by other important events.

Argyll mended fences with old foes. Marchmont, not on the best of terms with the Ministry, seemed by 1751 to be on good terms with the Duke.[17] Still, when the latter solicited a Court of Session judgeship from him in 1751, Argyll replied that he meddled little with such things because he did not wish to be refused appointments for which he had asked.[18] That was hardly true but its plausibility was based on some refusals such as that of Henry Home in 1750-51. The Duke's statement rang a little hollow after Kames was appointed in February 1752. The Duke and Marchmont stayed on speaking terms and discussed other appointments including others to the Court of Session.[19] By 1753, they were bargaining. Argyll agreed to help one of Marchmont's friends to a Customs House place while the Earl was to help elect

Gilbert Elliot of Minto, the son of an old Argathelian, to the House of Commons. By August 1753, Marchmont was calling Argyll his friend and invited the Duke and his illegitimate son, Captain Williams, to spend a day with him at his home.[20] Mutual interests triumphed but such friendliness did not mark Argyll's dealings with men like Robert Dundas of Arniston (son of the late Lord President Dundas), the Marquis of Tweeddale,[21] Andrew Mitchell or the Duke of Montrose.

Argyll cultivated his interest in Edinburgh by doing favours for the burgh. When he was approached in 1750 by Lord Provost Drummond about improvements to be made in the burgh, Argyll took the proposals to Henry Pelham who 'was not well pleased to hear of such a Project'.[22] They would have looked like a 'Scotch job' for people putting up little money themselves. The following year the Town Council mounted a public effort for improvements led by Drummond and supported by the town's professional men and intellectuals. By 1753, plans included a Royal Exchange (1753),[23] port facilities at Leith (1753), plans for the North Bridge (not built until after the Duke's death) and a police bill which allowed for better lighting and paving.[24] Acts were necessary not only to secure Crown money but also to enable property to be taken by eminent domain proceedings from owners reluctant to sell. Drummond, sent to London to lobby for the schemes, was told by Argyll not to use subscribed funds to defray his costs.[25] In the end, Argyll secured Crown contributions to those works and for the Royal Infirmary.[26] The Duke was one of those who drafted the Leith Harbour Act in 1754.[27] In 1755 he subscribed £200 toward the projects.[28]

Glasgow was not forgotten. In 1751, Argyll was concerned with a tobacco bill which he thought should not give Scotland exceptional treatment. To do so was politically imprudent since the English would resent it and probably stop it. He thought it also not in accord with the Act of Union.[29] About the same time, the Convention of Royal Burghs appealed to him to preserve the bounties on Scottish linen which he tried to do.[30] That too was a Glasgow worry. Despite his efforts, the bounties were allowed to lapse in 1754. That reduced the sales of Scottish linen by about two thirds and quickly brought hardship to many.[31] Argyll was not then in a position to secure favours: Newcastle was again trying to oust him from power. The Scottish Duke tried through his own example to aid the linen and wool industries by buying, using or giving away Glasgow handkerchiefs and plaids.[32] He got the linen acts changed and, in 1757, he sought an exemption from tariffs for the Glasgow soap and rope makers – a move in aid of the cloth finishers and the merchant fleet.[33]

Other interests were not neglected. When Parliament in 1752 considered bills for the improvement of the harbours and roads in Berwickshire, Argyll was named to sit on their committees.[34] In 1752-53, the Duke was active in trying to get more favourable treatment for the Scottish fishermen in legislation then pending in both Houses.[35] He had been asked by the Convention of Royal Burghs to secure a better Act concerning the 'Herring Fishing in Open boats'. Scots wanted those who cured and packed fish relieved of 'foreland Dues' – the expenses incurred by the use of beaches and shores by fishermen. They wanted regulations on barrel manufacture and some provisions of the salt laws repealed so that fish cured with Scottish salt could find a market in England. Salt laws were a constant irritant. The Convention's London agent was told to take Argyll's direction in his every step. When by 20 November 1753, the Convention drafted a new bill, it was sent for approval to the Duke who was to direct their agent.[36]

The Saltoun Papers show Argyll and Lord Milton doing favours for the Royal College of Physicians of Edinburgh,[37] deciding which boys Glasgow University should send up as Snell Exhibitioners to Balliol College, Oxford; helping Alexander Lind in his pottery at Prestonpans, as well as making him Commissary of Glasgow where he could advise the Delft work (see p. 146) and much more. Numerous letters and memoranda from Sir Alexander Cunningham Dick to Lord Milton, and Dick's reports of conversations with Argyll himself, suggest that the Duke was asked to act on proposals for turnpikes, roads and industrial projects such as a paper mill and the changing of the acts governing entails.[38] Such activities went on for years. Political debts continually accrued to the Argathelians. It was hard to oust from power a man to whom so many owed so much.

By the summer of 1752, the Duke was back in the saddle but riding more cautiously. He managed the peerage elections of 1752 and was present at them. The first, held on 9 July 1752, saw Breadalbane replace the Earl of Dunmore. Although Breadalbane was a Campbell, this was not much of a victory for Argyll who had long regarded that more Jacobitical branch of the family with suspicion. In 1752, the Duke still suffered from charges that he and Milton were Jacobites. Breadalbane left an account of this election:

> Arch. D. of Argyll had the nomination, but acted in a different manner, [*i.e.* he did not himself write or have the Ministers write to the electors] but for some persons here [Milton and others] — who did his dirty work — took care to let all Peers know who would be agreeable, and the knowing from whence the authority came almost always acquiesced. This was influencing but was not done in so open a manner.[39]

The Duke was playing old games more civilly. A second peerage election went as he wished: Lord Cathcart, a Glasgow-area man, replaced the deceased Duke of Gordon.

Argyll and Milton continued to work well. Milton increasingly looked after matters in Scotland with Argyll saying 'yes' or 'no' to his suggestions but initiating less. Milton's son, Andrew Fletcher III, became the Duke's London secretary and was provided with a seat in Parliament and, in 1751, a life sinecure worth £1,200. Argyll's team was able to make life difficult for any Ministry which disregarded their interests.

II. Politics: London

In London, Argyll's big issues in the early 1750s still centred on the Highlands and their settlement. There was no consensus on how military, economic and cultural issues should be resolved. Many Englishmen saw repression and the total and rapid changing of Highland society as the solution to Highland ills. Men with attitudes such as Cumberland had held in 1746, were, like Cumberland himself, still very active in London. Lord Milton and Argyll wanted substantial changes to 'civilize' the region but they wanted them made slowly and with restraint. Inaction was an option for others who saw the likelihood of another rebellion receding; they would not spend money uselessly. The long awaited bill to deal with the problems came with the Forfeited Estates bill, introduced on 23 February 1752.

The Vesting Act of June 1747 had given the Barons of the Scottish Exchequer the management of the Highland estates which had been forfeited. In 1747, Milton and General Bland drafted a plan calling for the sale of some forfeited lands and the management of the remainder by a new body.[40] Milton wanted most of the estates either forfeited to the Crown or purchased by it. The bill was, revised by Argyll and presented to other Scots in London.[41] It then waited a long time for parliamentary action.

Eventually forty-one of the estates were sold; thirteen were annexed to the Crown by the Annexing Act of March 1752.[42] In the long wait were reflected the intensity of debates in Scotland, the paranoia of some in England who feared the settlement would aid or employ Jacobites,[43] and the dithering of English minsters who did not see it as an urgent matter and could not find the money for it.[44] By 1752, urgency had returned with plots and a threatened uprising (see p. 194).

The Act proposed changing Highland society by undercutting the chieftains and making their tenants more independent. It gave the task of managing the forfeited estates to unpaid Commissioners of a new Annexed Estates Commission. They were to use the rents and other incomes from the estates, and the proceeds of sales, to pay off creditors and 'for the Purposes of civilizing the Inhabitants upon the said Estates, and other Parts of the Highlands and Islands of Scotland, and promoting amongst them the protestant Religion, good Government, Industry and Manufactures, and the Principles of Duty and Loyalty to his Majesty his heirs and Successors, and to no other Use or Purpose whatsoever'.[45] In the end, the programme of reconstruction involved using small sums to improve roads, teach English, introduce new men to lands formerly worked only by clan members and trying to introduce new agricultural practices, new industries and fishing stations.[46] It resembled what the Duke was doing privately.

Once introduced, this bill immediately evoked Opposition charges from the Duke of Bedford and the Earl of Bath that it was 'a job, devised to gratify the Duke of Argyle, and to afford the means of providing for some of his numerous dependents'. At first reading, the Dukes of Bedford and Cumberland accused Argyll of keeping in government employment or planning to place many Jacobite friends. By March 1752, Argyll favoured a bill but not one which contained provisions for colonizing the Highlands with Englishmen or ex-service men. Argyll and Milton scuppered those provisions.[47] Their friends argued against those plans in the House of Commons.[48]

In the Lords debate, Argyll opposed Bedford and the Earl of Bath who were for amending the draft bill. Argyll responded to his critics with a 'positive disavowal of any view or personal interest in the bill'.[49] He was not opposed to Crown ownership of large tracts and even the buying of more land from mortgagees. That would aid in 'civilizing' the Highlands which would prevent future rebellions. Two weeks later, when it was again brought up, Argyll replied to his critics in a speech which was 'short and confused.' According to Horace Walpole, who also thought the plans 'a notable job', Argyll neither defended it nor answered Bedford's charges in the House of Lords but made 'a strange, hurt, mysterious, incoherent speech' which ended with an irrelevant attack on Lord Bath and the window tax in Scotland.[50] Argyll had been confined by illness in March 1752 so his speech may not have an easy accomplishment. He wrote to Lord Milton that he had had to pull his punches:

> I was actually affraid if I launched out to far that I might have been engaged in altercations with one too much above me and whatever reflection I had thrown on the D. Of Bedford would all have been construed to have been levelled at his superior [the Duke of Cumberland].[51]

Argyll said of their 'new malicious work', 'it [made] doubtful point with me whether I can with prudence advise the scheme'.[52] The attack by the English lords delayed the matter and discredited Argyll and Milton in some eyes until the autumn of 1752. Indeed, Bedford's opposition forced an inquiry into the charges that it was a 'Scotch job' and a Jacobite scheme hatched by Argyll, Milton and their friends. The investigation came in the summer of 1752. While the King and Newcastle were abroad, Pelham himself conducted this enquiry which cleared the Scots of all charges. In the end, the Act passed with difficulty without provisions to acquire more land or to change radically the culture of the area as Lord Milton had initially hoped it would. Neither Newcastle nor Hardwicke had been strong in defence of Argyll or the bill.[53] Horace Walpole claimed Argyll himself did not vote for the bill.[54] After its passage, Argyll was happy to report that Bedford was attacking the government with 'despair and rage'.[55]

To implement the Act, Commissioners had to be picked. That was delayed by opposition in London, led by Cumberland and Bedford. Also causing delays was the uncertainty of Argyll's position in the last years of Henry Pelham's life and following his death (c.1752-1756). Then a new war focussed attention not on the civil reconstruction of the Highlands but on recruiting. One suspects that delays also came because there was no agreement about what was to be done or how to do it.[56] The Act was probably not signed and sent to Scotland until Argyll had taken a final look at it in late 1754.[57] Commissioners approved by Milton and Argyll were appointed only in 1755.[58]

Once appointed, the Commissioner's long-term record was a mixed one. It could not have been otherwise given the ambitions of the projectors, the size and complexity of their tasks, opposition in London, and the little capital and income with which they had to work. Most of what was accomplished before 1763 was the result of the work of Lord Milton and other Argathelians. What chiefly hampered them was the fact that they could only propose policies and plans; they could not act on them without the approval of the Treasury in London. Until Argyll's death in 1761, the Treasury 'failed to acknowledge their reports'.[59] This again is testimony to the effectiveness of those in London who distrusted Scots and disliked Argyll but also of the disordered state of British politics following the death of Henry Pelham. Had Argyll himself been whole-heartedly in favour of the schemes, things might have happened more quickly. Delay protected Highlanders, particularly chiefs with votes, from the extensive reforms which the initial drafters had intended to make and make quickly. None of those were imposed while Argyll lived.

There were other things which one would have expected Argyll to be concerned with between 1751 and 1754. He is not known to have spoken on calendar reform in 1751 – indeed, he was not in attendance the day on which it passed.[60] Calendar reform was a project of the Earl of Chesterfield but one would expected Argyll to have spoken for it. The Duke, well known to many of London's Jewish brokers, is not known to have spoken about the Jewish naturalization bill of 1753 or its repeal in 1754. He had sat on naturalization committees which had probably recommended that some Jews be allowed to become subjects. It would be surprising had he not favoured allowing them the rights of subjects, particularly the right to own landed property.[61] He also seems to have said nothing on Hardwicke's Marriage Bill of 1753. That should have engaged his attention since it arose partially out of Scottish cases, one from Campbeltown and one involving a relative.[62]

III. The Elections of 1754

By 1753, foreign affairs and the possibility of war began to dominate discussions in London but, for the Duke, practical matters turned on the 1754 elections and the death of Henry Pelham.

When Henry Pelham died in March 1754, Argyll lost a protector and the Ministry its leading spirit. The Duke of Newcastle, now chief minister, tried again to make more Scottish decisions in London and to have them depend on advice drawn from a wider set of Scots, principally his own correspondents. He sometimes said, and may even have believed, that this was to complete the Union; it was certain to curtail the power of Argyll. Again, it was the management of elections which showed the need for the Scottish duke.

Henry Pelham died while he and Argyll were preparing for the elections of 1754. In 1753, they agreed a list of the Representative Peers and they were picking MPs and noting voters who could be bought with offices and favours.[63] After Pelham's death, the elections would be fought by Newcastle and Pelham's old assistants. Foremost among them was Lord Dupplin who had been Pelham's man in overall charge of English elections. Argyll was now subordinated to him in managing the Scottish elections. Newcastle hoped the election would help him but its results, from his standpoint, were mixed. At the peerage election of 21 May 1754, the government's list was returned. Argyll had been there to vote and watch others. Seven of his friends were elected to the sixteen places, more than the number of old Squadrone men.

The elections of MPs, also in May, were well managed: the government had to contest only two county seats. Scotland came cheap. While £3,000 were spent on elections in Oxfordshire, Argyll had for his activities in Scotland only £1,000 to disperse [another source says £1,800[64]], along with favours.[65] Argyll's friends won fifteen seats with old Squadrone men holding only two or three. The remainder were mostly won by men sometimes willing to be led by Argyll. Now it would be more difficult to disregard the Duke in London. Newcastle and Pelham had deprived Argyll of two seats his friends might have won without ministerial interference. One, after weeks of obstructive bickering, went to Andrew Mitchell.[66] Newcastle's Ministry had a majority but he led Scots who were unhappy with him and were made more so by his diplomacy and by his conduct of the war which began in 1754-55.

Argyll understood that things had changed after the elections of 1754. He had been useful but Newcastle wanted to be rid of him. When the parliamentary session of 1754-55 began, Argyll did not receive his usual committee assignments as a member of the House of Lords committees on customs and orders and the privileges of peers. Neither was he asked to serve on the committees which replied to the King's speech given at the opening of the session. By 20 December 1754, Argyll wrote to Milton that plans were being made for 'a new Scotch Ministry' but with Tweeddale and most of his old followers being left out as was he.[67] The Duke noted that it was not much liked by Scots.[68] He had no intention of going quietly and formed plans with Henry Fox and William Pitt to frustrate Newcastle.[69]

Newcastle's new management team was composed of Newcastle's and Hardwicke's correspondents – mostly old Squadrone men – and Lords Dupplin and Deskford. Thomas Hay, Lord Dupplin, was the son of the 7th Earl of Kinnoull and later succeeded to the title as 8th Earl. Dupplin was a Scot but he had spent his life in England and would never be an effective Scottish politician. He was not well known to Lowlanders and had few significant Highland contacts although his estate was in Perthshire and his father had been imprisoned as a Jacobite. He was not a Presbyterian but a Scottish Episcopalian. Bookish, and polite, Dupplin was unlikely to win fights with a rougher man like Argyll.

James Olgivy, Lord Deskford (later 6th Earl of Findlatter and 3rd Earl of Seafield), was no more of a Highlander than his relative Kinnoull. He was, however, related by marriage to the Murrays of Atholl since he had married the eighteenth child of that Duke. He also had Grant cousins. Deskford's father, like Kinnoull's (see p.87) had earlier unhappy dealings with Ilay. The 5th Earl of Findlatter sought patronage from Ilay in 1727 but had failed to obtain it. That may have rankled.[70] Lord Deskford was also grave, brusque, officious and something of a blunt tool. He had attacked the Argathelian influence in some of the northern burghs which incurred Argyll's dislike. Milton and Argyll in correspondence ironically called him 'Honest Deskford'.[71] Deskford was appointed to the Boards of Trustees (1749), Customs (1754), and the Annexed Estates Commission (1755). Those places gave him points of observation and action. Like Milton, whom he was preparing to replace, he had interests in improvements and the linen trade. To aid Deskford and Dupplin were men like Lord Hopetoun and other Squadone aristocrats. They were seldom efficient. Those who served them, men like Lord Advocate Robert Dundas who received that office in

1754, were often able but Dundas was soon in financial trouble and unwilling to be troublesome to Argyll.

Argyll might be seventy-two but he and his friends frustrated Newcastle's efforts to manage Scotland through Lords Dupplin and Deskford. When the latter tried to be effective at the Board of Trustees, he found he was blocked by men loyal to Argyll who were unwilling to follow Deskford's lead. At the Customs and Excise Boards, Argyll's friends resisted the removal of officers whom Deskford thought corrupt. Full control of the Boards by Newcastle's appointees was not achieved.[72] In 1754, Deskford complained that his enemies were plotting to exclude him from appointment as Commissioner of Customs. He was appointed but soon complained to his London sponsors that Mr. Joseph Tudor, a Commissioner of Customs since 1751, frustrated his efforts. Dupplin told him Tudor would be reminded that his loyalty should be only to the Treasury. Tudor persisted and was defended by Argyll. Dupplin told Deskford, on 19 December 1754, to 'go on gently' and influence would come to him.[73] It did not.

In 1755, Dupplin continued to explain to Deskford that Argyll had to be treated well by Newcastle and it would not do to have Argyll complaining of Deskford's 'disrespect' by, for example, 'shewing such a distrust as intimated that you thought him capable of imposing upon the Publick' in some matter concerning the sale of Argyll's yacht to become a coast guard vessel.[74] Argyll had spoken of this to Newcastle with 'warmth' and intimated that he would do business with Deskford but expected some politeness.[75] Argyll had begun to seek allies among others left out of the 'new Scotch Ministry.' Nine days earlier he had recommended Lord George Hay, Tweeddale's brother, to Newcastle for membership on the Board of Police.[76] Some weeks later Dupplin again urged Deskford to

> wait upon the Duke of Argyle when he comes to Scotland and shew him that civility & respect which is due to his station & his Grace [Newcastle] is well assured that you will meet with a suitable return. Yr Lp will consider the Duke of Argyle not only as a person in high rank in the King's Service, but as one that professes to carry on the measures of Government in friendship with the Duke of Newcastle.[77]

Deskford was told that his good humour would be a help to the Ministry. By 2 November 1755, Newcastle had been obliged to promise Argyll 'to make me easy about honest Deskford'.[78] By the end of 1755, Argyll thought Deskford would find 'that he is not to govern as he had hopes to do'. Deskford was eventually removed from the Commission and given a place on the Board of Police, a sinecure position paying less and conveying no power.[79] Argyll blocked a pension for Deskford in 1758 and was still opposed to giving him one in 1761 when Deskford formally left the Board of Customs.[80]

Meanwhile, the Argathelians continued to embarrass Newcastle. The appointment of David Ross as Sheriff-depute of Banff upset Deskford's father and divided Newcastle's northern supporters. Since Newcastle and Hardwicke's intentions were not always made clear to Scots, Argyll urged others to push for the appointments of men whom he knew could not be placed. By the summer of 1755 Newcastle was liked and trusted by fewer Scots than had approved of him at the elections of 1754.[81] Argyll also opposed the appointments of Englishmen to offices in the Excise and Customs and the Court of Exchequer. Like most Scots, he wanted no Englishmen in Scotland as he made clear in a short letter to Lord Milton:

> This goes by Provost Cochran of Glasgow I find some very bad schemes going on, such as sending an Englishman to Scotland in place of Baron Clerk when he dies, this was proposed to Mr. Pelham by Baron Edlin & much pressed, also to make more English Commissioners of Customs & Excise, in short one would think their heads are turned & that they want to try to what degree of ill humour they can bring the People of Scotland to; all I can do is to play every card with prudence & decency, & leave all accidents & consequences to Fate. The Secretary of the Excise must also be an English man. Adieu.[82]

Defeating some of those schemes, Argyll continued to pack the courts and other agencies with men with Argathelian sympathies. Among the Senators of the College of Justice were Robert Pringle, Thomas Miller, Thomas Hay, Alexander Boswell, Peter Wedderburn, Andrew Pringle and Andrew Macdowal all of whom his correspondence shows to have had his support.[83] By the end of 1756, Argyll and his friends had made Edinburgh so unpleasant and frustrating that Deskford left it. He gave up his hopes of political importance for the time being.[84] Newcastle could do nothing for him since he needed Argyll's support in London. Dupplin also became a casualty of Argyll's ripostes.

As in 1750, Argyll reached out for new friends. He effected a reconciliation with Tweeddale and some of the Squadrone men attached to him who had been left out of the planned new 'Scotch Ministry'. The Duke of Argyll had never regarded opponents as necessarily permanent enemies. His reconciliation with Tweeddale showed how flexible His Grace could be when he needed to find friends. It was said to be easier now because Tweeddale was tutor to the future Duke of Buccleuch, the son of Argyll's niece.[85] Lord Milton soon found a distant relation to the Marquis which might make him seem more friendly.

It is not clear who made the first move,[86] but, by August 1754, the Duke had told Tweeddale that he would recommend one of the Marquis's protégés to Newcastle for a place.[87] On 4 September, Argyll apologized to Tweeddale for not being able to meet with him since he was about to go to Rosneath and Inveraray where guests awaited his arrival.[88] On his way back in November, he stopped in Edinburgh. There, on 9 November, Milton had a long conversation with Thomas Hay who had been nominated for a Court of Session judgeship. Hay had been Tweeddale's agent in Edinburgh and came from a family tainted with Jacobitism.[89] It might do Argyll no good in London to back such a man but he did.[90] That course of action came after a long and almost candid interview between Hay and Milton. Hay acknowledged to Milton that there had been 'deep rooted...old animosities on both sides' and that he had long acted against the interests of the Argathelians but that he 'had no notion that his Grace resented that'. Lord Milton assured him that was true. The Duke would have thought the less of him had he not done so given his position as a manager. Hay then asked for their help in securing his gown and for an opportunity to meet the Duke. He asked Milton to introduce them.

Argyll was not then at Brunstane but in Edinburgh celebrating the King's birthday with General Bland. Milton advised Hay not to attend Argyll's levee as it would 'serve for nothing but to raise a cry'. It was arranged for Alexander Tait, WS, to act as a conduit for messages between Hay, Milton and Argyll. Hay was Keeper of the Signet; Tait did the work as Substitute-Keeper. The Taits had long done business with the Dukes of Argyll. Hay left his interview able to say, 'I have no sort of doubt of Lord Milton's friendship for me'. At some point, Hay told Lord Provost William Alexander and Lord Justice Clerk Charles Erskine that he would leave the bar if he failed to get his gown.[91]

On the following day, Sunday, November 10, Hay went again to Brunstane House where he met Argyll who was gracious. Hay summarized for Argyll the letters Tweeddale had written for him to Lord Chancellor Hardwicke and to the Lord Justice Clerk. Argyll dismissed the rumours of Jacobitism levelled against Hay as malicious and somehow linked to the appointment of Newcastle's friend, Attorney General William Murray. Milton opined that they had owed something to Deskford and Corbyn Morris but Hay himself named no one and the naming of 'Tom Cochran was of no consequence'.[92] Milton and Argyll apologized for the zeal and officiousness of some of their friends and noted they were not much connected with the Dalrymples, who seem to have been among those critical of Hay's candidacy. Argyll thought Hay's father had done 'nothing but what others had done'. He said even he himself had been unreasonably attacked as being a Jacobite.[93] As for a Jacobite servant employed by Hay, Argyll 'was served three years by a fellow who had at the long run was discovered to be a Jesuit'. He had kept him on out of charity. His Grace had Milton read to Hay a letter he had already written to Newcastle recommending Hay for the judgeship. He assured Hay that the London inquiry into his character and credentials would be only to satisfy formal requirements. Argyll expressed his disposition 'to oblige your Lordship [Tweeddale] & to be in friendship with you'. Hay responded that the Marquis of Tweeddale was equally determined to be obliging. Hay was invited to dine with Lord Somerville, Frederick [later Lord Frederick] Campbell, David Kinloch, Mr. [Andrew] Fletcher [III] and the rest of Milton's family. 'The Conversation was generall about trifles, after the Duke was asleep Lord Milton & I had conversation in another room till I took leave'.[94] He had been there from 11:00 a.m. until about 4:00 p.m.

To Tweeddale, Hay wrote that he spoke with 'the same ease & frankness that I used to do wt your Lordship without saying all I suspected or anything that could offend nor laid your Lordship or myself too open'. He thought Argyll would be friendly in the future but he would 'proceed upon his plan with a discreet Caution without showing suspicion but so as to be safe untill his Graces practise proved the sincerity of his profession'. Later that month, Thomas Hay, took his seat on the Court of Session as Lord Huntington. Thanking Milton for the appointment, he wrote: 'I will endeavour to do Justice to His Graces recommendation & to behave myself in every instance in such manner as may be acctable to His Grace'.[95]

By 1755, Tweeddale had been made a friendly supplicant. Over the next few years, Argyll obtained more places for Tweeddale and recommended his protégés to some posts they did not get. Tweeddale's brother was provided for at the Board of Police; other relatives got smaller plums. Mr. Bertram, a family tutor whom the Marquis had tried to place in a university for years, was nominated for the Chair of Ecclesiastical History at St Andrews but failed to obtain it. In this case, Argyll claimed to have complained to the Duke of Newcastle about the man who received the place, William Brown, a nominee of the Duke of Cumberland. Newcastle promised that the appointment would not be made if it could be stopped.[96]

As Argyll mended his fences and became more necessary to the Ministry, the Argathelians had some legislative achievements. The House of Commons refused to extend the tenure of Sheriffs-depute from seven to fifteen years as Newcastle had wanted. After that, the Ministry dropped its other Scottish legislation for the session.[97] Argyll's men and Robert Dundas, the Lord Advocate, wrote legislation which improved the collection of Scottish taxes and incidentally created more places in the gift of the Barons of Exchequer. Those went mostly to Argyll's friends.[98] The bounty on exported linen, which, despite Argyll's efforts, had lapsed in 1754, was restored in the autumn of 1755.[99] Argyll had threatened to introduce a bill for this purpose but, in the end, Lord Dupplin moved it in the Commons. Newcastle had not wanted the bill passed then but it was. It drew support from Argyll's allies, Henry Fox, William Pitt and Charles Townshend, whose speeches all disparaged the conduct of the Ministry.[100] It was fully implemented by June 1756.[101] The restored bounties helped the British Linen Company and was for Argyll and Milton an interested measure. It also helped other Scottish estate owners, businessmen and thousands of ordinary Scots. Contemporaries estimated that as many as 8,000 Scottish linen workers had been put out of full employment by ending of the bounty which curtailed sales, exports and production and hurt other businesses and the payments of rents.[102] The industry boomed as the Seven Years War saw the purchase by the Army and Navy of a great deal of Scottish shirting and sail cloth.

IV. Instability and War

Newcastle had made the last peace with France which many thought disastrous. In August 1754, news came that Major George Washington had been defeated in his attempt to stop French incursions into the Ohio valley. Britain was not ready for war. By the end of the year, the news was worse. On 9 July 1755, Major General Edward Braddock was defeated not far from where Washington was forced to surrender his small fort the previous year. Many Scots died with Braddock. That was known in London by the autumn. Other defeats followed. The Ministry rapidly lost credibility. Newcastle had not made a success of his time in office.

As Newcastle lost power, his Ministry became unstable. In the Commons, Newcastle had few effective defenders and no replacement for his brother other than the unreliable Henry Fox and Pitt who distrusted or disliked Newcastle. By the summer of 1755 only a handful of Scots willingly voted with the Ministry.[103] The English Duke, under attack in the Commons, needed the votes Argyll could deliver. Newcastle's embarrassments were made more acute when he learned that Argyll was thinking about going into Opposition.[104] How Argyll viewed the developments of the

1750s is perhaps put best by him: 'My Lord', he told Viscount Stormont, 'I have now been a dabbler in politics near fifty years, and my way has been to do there what I do at my party of sixpenny whist, I lose nothing for want of attention and do what I can to play the game, but am very indifferent after that whether I win or lose'.[105] His game was to stay in power if he could; he did so.

From 1754 through 1757, tensions between ministers worked to the advantage of Argyll. While on his summer trip to Scotland in 1755, he was approached by Fox and Newcastle who were eager for his support and that of Lord Bute, now a fixture at Leicester House, the centre of the Opposition. Argyll offered help to Fox and Lord Mansfield but he did little to influence Lord Bute. By October 1755, Newcastle was calling him an 'enemy'.[106] The Ministry again asked the Duke in the Spring of 1756 to wean Bute from Pitt, to reconcile him with the King and get him to vote with the government. Bute was not weaned from his patron, the Prince of Wales, but, in the end, pleased his uncle by becoming Groom of the Stole to the Prince despite the wishes of the King and Newcastle. Fox helped to arrange that appointment.[107] Newcastle was forced to concede Argyll's demands for more patronage and administrative control of the Scottish governing agencies. He acquiesced in the sacking of Deskford. By 1756, Argyll was again the dispenser of most Scottish patronage. Even bodies which Argyll and his friends had not controlled, such as the newly appointed Commission of Forfeited Estates, came into their hands as influence shifted away from the appointees of the English Duke and Lord Hardwicke. That Argyll was not a minister helped him to play English politicians against each other and to retain his standing both then and in the following years.[108] That play did not make ministries more stable.

War required more men for the armed forces. Proposals for Highland regiments were made in 1754, 1755 and 1756 but stalled as men debated whether or not it was better to use European mercenary troops, Irishmen or Scots.[109] Argyll was understandably opposed to the use of mercenaries when Scots could be employed.[110] With the war going badly, troops and sailors were needed more than ever – as Pitt, now in opposition, kept saying.[111] They could be recruited from the Highlands and Borders of Scotland where there was a surplus of un- and under-employed men. For the government, this had the advantage of draining from the first area men who might make trouble. For Scots, it meant employment in ways which were traditional, honourable and sometimes lucrative – if one survived. Most English politicians recognized that efforts made to raise Highland regiments would not be very successful without the co-operation of the Duke of Argyll. The alliance between Argyll and Henry Fox, Secretary of State and Paymaster General in the mid-1750s, rested partly on that perception. Old obstacles to raising Scottish soldiers and sailors had been overtaken by events. That gave the Duke new confidence.[112]

That those troops might be turned against the state which had armed and trained them, as the King, Cumberland and their friends thought, was unlikely – particularly if they served in America or India. Putting military commissions in Argyll's hands increased his powers but without doing so the numbers raised would have been smaller and taken longer because fewer would come from the Western Highlands. Given the necessities of the times, Argyll could not be outed. By early February 1756, Argyll's place in the war effort was assured. He had his Highland Regiments and now made arrangements about commissions which he hoped would satisfy other Highland lords such as the Duke of Atholl and the Earl of Breadalbane. With Major General John Campbell, Earl of Loudoun, he settled on a list of officers to be appointed. He sent letters north to support the recruiting drive then under way.

His recruiting gave him more interest than in the past in foreign affairs. The Duke was not generally active in the discussions of foreign policy and often in the past was on the side of the diplomats and peacemakers. He now wanted the French soundly beaten. Only a defeated France would restore a balance of powers in Europe. He later applauded Frederick II's shifts away from France to other allies and his victories over the Russians and Austrians. Argyll also followed events in America and India with interest.[113] What he thought of the situation of the country in October 1756 is probably shown in a 'Letter From London' which may not be his but was copied and sent to Lord Milton. It depicted a Britain standing without allies, disarmed, 'divided at home', and ruled by squabbling ministers who had no popular mandate and only wavering support in Parliament where 'all threaten to resign'. 'A total Revolution must soon ensue'.[114] The Duke was not sanguine about the prospects of Newcastle and his followers. The English duke and Fox had left office by the end November 1756.

William Pitt and the Duke of Devonshire came to power in December 1756 with Pitt as Secretary of State and Devonshire at the Treasury. Argyll survived the shuffle with his power and position intact even though he did not like Pitt's policies. For Argyll, Pitt was too much a Patriot who might try to enact 'an equal Assessment of the Land Tax, including Scotland,— triennial parliaments, a reduction of Pensions and — un-necessary or overgrown Salaries'.[115] What Pitt did immediately was to plan for the sending of troops to America some of which would have to come from the army in Europe unless more Highlanders were raised.[116] That convinced Cumberland, who commanded in Europe, not to oppose recruiting regiments in Scotland.

Argyll likely felt no sense of loss when Pitt left office in March 1757 due to Newcastle's machinations. That change did not affect the Scottish Duke's standing with other politicians, particularly Fox. He recognized how useful Argyll was and offered him a ministerial position more or less equivalent to that of the old Secretary of State for Scotland. It was rejected – but then Fox never got to form his Ministry.[117] When a new Ministry was created by Newcastle and Pitt in the spring of 1757, Argyll's importance and standing again did not change.[118] Pitt and Newcastle thought about excluding Argyll from all government responsibilities but decided they needed his ten or so votes in the House of Commons.[119] This was the last real threat to his power until 1760. He was simply too useful to everyone.[120]

For the Duke of Argyll, perhaps the most important change of 1757 was the political demise of the Duke of Cumberland. Cumberland by April 1757 had come to terms with Argyll whom he recognized as essential to the quick expansion of the army.[121] Several months later, on 26 July, Cumberland lost the battle of Hastenbeck and signed the Convention of Kloster-Zeven on 8 September 1757. The Convention required him to disband his small army in Germany. His actions were repudiated by the King and his ministers. Cumberland, called home in disgrace, resigned his places. By the end of the year, he was a spent political force no longer able to bother Argyll or Scots generally.

The Duke's increased importance rested on his grip on recruitment for the forces. Pitt wanted fifteen regiments, twelve for America and three to be used elsewhere.[122] The men were to be raised by the Captains, Lieutenants and Ensigns who would lead them, *i.e.* by their own clan leaders.[123] Argyll expected the field officers to be the most experienced Scots. Among the prospective commanders was Simon Fraser, Lord Lovat's heir.[124] By early 1757, some of Argyll's favourites – the Earls of Home, Eglinton and Loudoun and some Campbell tacksmen – were or had recently been engaged in raising men.[125] Lieutenant General James St. Clair wrote toward the end of January 1757, 'The Man of the Library is at present in more power with regard to our Country than ever I knew him'.[126] He had known him since they had served as young officers in Europe c.1704. By the fall of 1759, most of the commissions had been issued though some captaincies remained unfilled[127] as did some places in Scotland.[128] Argyll staffed the Highland Regiments with men whose families would be grateful. The Duke's influence spread in parts of the Highlands where he had not been welcomed earlier – among the Breadalbane Campbells and the Gordon clan. Some Gordons came to like him very much. Among them was Lord Adam Gordon, the future Commander-in-Chief in North Britain who would serve as one of the Argyll's honorary pallbearers.[129] By 1761, Argyll had named 40% of the commissioned officers in the Highland regiments, many more men than the 8% he had been able to name to the Salt and Customs services in the same period.[130] Others owed places to Argyll's friends and relatives, particularly to the Commander-in-Chief in America, the Earl of Loudoun; and to General John Campbell of Mamore. Those regiments went a long way to make Highlanders more acceptable to the English public and its politicians.

Another kind of recruiting interested him less. During those same years, plans were made in Scotland to create a Scottish militia. Those were not liked by the Duke although Lord Milton had a hand in framing a militia bill. Argyll supported the creation of fencible regiments in Argyllshire, Sutherlandshire and Perthshire. The first two were created.[131] They were not to be new modelled but created according to seventeenth-century legislation. 'Argyll wanted to use the old Scottish laws and institutions to meet the problem when nothing but the same law and the same militia that operated in England would satisfy the younger members of the ruling class'.[132] The Duke was still trying to preserve the country's distinctiveness. Argyll was willing to see one Lowland militia unit in Marchmont's region of influence but he had the Earl of Home, not Marchmont, made Lord Lieutenant of Berwickshire. Were the county to call out a militia regiment, the reliable Earl of Home, not Marchmont, would name the officers. That was to annoy one who had again opposed the Duke in patronage cases and whose brother, Alexander, MP, had been disloyal to the Ministry he was meant to serve.[133]

In 1759-60, the French Captain François Thurot raided on the Scottish coast. Argyll worried that the French would land in Ireland or burn west of Scotland towns. Those worries increased after a raid on Islay early in 1760. Thurot drove off the islanders' cattle to feed his men. Horace Walpole said he had burned 'two ships belonging to King George, and a house belonging to the King of Argyle'.[134] A day later, one of Lord Holderness's clerks in the Secretary of State's office wrote the Lord Justice Clerk that 1,000 French troops were reported to have been landed at Carrickfergus. Others worried that the Pretender would come over backed by French arms. On 8 April 1760, the Convention of Royal Burghs asked Argyll and other politicians in London to improve the posts and express service. They mentioned the 'Trade of the Country' but its security was also on their minds. They were advised to 'secure the countenance and assistance of the Duke of Argyll' and afterwards to approach Newcastle. Argyll was named after others who had already supported a Militia Bill.[135] To many, he must have seemed ancient and less effective; to others, a man trying to determine their next MP against their wishes.

Pressures for a better postal service and to create a Scottish militia increased. The latter were focussed by the debates and activism in Edinburgh of the Select Society and in London by rather independent MPs associated more with Bute than with his uncle.[136] The Edinburgh men included many of the Moderates and younger *literati*. Their London friends included James Oswald, Gilbert Elliot and William Mure, all MPs.[137] These men solicited support for a militia from the Convention of Royal Burghs, some of the counties, and other groups but their efforts came to nothing. The Militia Bill was defeated although some Scottish MPs voted for it – to please their electors, said the Duke.[138] Horace Walpole said of it, 'the Duke of Argyll was not cordial to the bill, and it was rejected'.[139] This business and contentious appointments drove the Duke and Milton again to code their letters which they had avoided most of the time since their struggles with Lords Deskford and Dupplin.

V. Preparing for a New Reign

George II was nearing his end and Argyll, a year older, was thinking about the succession.[140] The new monarch would be a man very different from his grandfather and opposed to his ways of ruling. The future George III was naive enough to think that he could be a 'Patriot King' and truly respect the balance of powers in the British constitution. That view he owed mainly to his tutor, the 3rd Earl of Bute, who became tutor to Prince George in 1755. Bute became a favourite of Prince George and his mother.

Bute was not his uncle's favourite. Argyll had not been close to this nephew since Bute sided with the 2nd Duke in 1737. Ten years later, Argyll had been reluctant to rely on the Earl's help in the general election of 1747. A decade further on, Bute was closer to Pitt, Argyll to Fox. Argyll supported every Ministry which would countenance him and served them with his management of Scottish patronage. Bute, no burgh-monger, wanted to support the virtuous although he had not refused the £800 pension which his uncle had arranged for him in 1747 when he needed money to live in London. He probably saw Argyll as an unprincipled old fellow, who, like the King, was nearing his end.[141]

By 1760, Bute was an Opposition politician who had had more than decade-long association with Leicester House and the court of the Princes of Wales. He had played some role in bringing about the coalition in 1755 but that annoyed the King, Cumberland, and men who would later get even. Not a Representative Peer, he was still seen as an important politician. Because of his relation to the Prince of Wales, he was potentially more important than Argyll. When, in the spring of 1756, Argyll asked him what it would take to wean him from the Opposition, Bute made it clear he would not leave his friends. He only wanted a place in the Prince's household. Bute rejected a further pension and a role in government but later claimed he had been 'slighted and passed over'.[142] The pure are always aggrieved. The Duke tried to give him sensible advice while protecting his own position as Scottish manager.

Argyll's advice to him was, 'prepare a Plan of Administration in case of the old King's Death' and the sudden accession of Prince George. Since 'his Majesty might possibly disappoint them by living longer than they expected', the plan was to be kept up to date 'which would oblige them to form new Plans according to times & Circumstances... some regular system should be always in Readiness.'[143] There is no indication that Bute did this. What did happen was a coalescence of the new, younger Scottish politicians with Bute whose regard for his uncle, never high, cooled further.

By 1755, ambitious men who would be involved with the Militia Bill had already turned to Bute as a leader of a Scottish faction not dependent on Argyll. Among them were Alexander Montgomerie, 10th Earl of Eglinton; Bute's brother, James Stuart Mackenzie; Gilbert Elliot of Minto, William Mure of Caldwell, and Patrick Crauford of Auchenames. Several of them would be annoyed by Argyll's lack of sympathy for, and unwillingness to support, a Scottish militia. Mure and Craufurd had electoral hopes which were incompatible with the Duke's plans for the 1761 election. Their friend Charles Townshend was eager to contest another Scottish seat. Townshend, Mure and Craufford wanted seats in Edinburgh, Renfrewshire and Ayrshire. Argyll had already picked candidates for those places. As their ambitions played out, the chilly relationship between uncle and nephew became colder.

Townshend's marriage to Caroline, daughter to the 2nd Duke of Argyll and mother of the Duke of Buccleuch, had given him a considerable electoral interest in Scotland. Friendship with those who urged the formation of a Scottish militia gave him a claque while his conviviality and wit made him agreeable to Edinburgh Town Councillors who were the burgh's electors. They were restive under Argyll's leadership and had found in William Alexander a Lord Provost who looked as if he might lead them to freedom. Alexander's forces were defeated in the civic elections of 1755. From then until 1759, the Duke of Argyll intended to have Alexander Forrester elected as MP for Edinburgh. Forrester, a Scottish lawyer working in London, was a frequent guest at Whitton, and a friend of the Maules of Panmure. The Duke's choice was opposed by some Edinburgh councillors who proposed Townshend. The latter showed an interest in being MP for Edinburgh. His association with the militia schemes gave him Edinburgh friends. Townshend also looked good to them because he was willing to forget the '45 and see North Britons as Britons like himself.

Townshend was not a man of consistency or even short-term purpose. In the end, he supported Pitt's version of a Scottish Militia Bill which excluded the Highlands. That false step lost him the support of Militia Bill agitators while it gave Milton and Argyll, with whom Townshend had spent much time in January 1760, reasons to reject the plan altogether. Scots soon thought of Townshend much as they might have thought of the last comet – a meteor splendid for a time.[144] Townshend's candidacy lasted only to 1760 but his ridicule of Argyll's candidate and the Town Council's wishes forced the Duke to back someone other than Forrester. In the end, he chose George Lind, an Edinburgh merchant and a nephew of Alexander Lind,

Argyll's chemical friend of the 1740s. The Duke's opponents put up an Edinburgh banker, John Fordyce, who lost the contested election held after Argyll's death.[145]

William Mure was Bute's Scottish agent. It was he who in 1758 urged Bute to secure the Ayrshire and Renfrewshire seats for the interest of the Prince of Wales. They moved to do this without asking leave of Argyll or the Earl of Loudoun. Both then opposed them. Suddenly Mure himself faced a contested election. By 1759-60, Mure was trying to work out deals with Argyll which would save his Renfrewshire seat and reconcile Bute and Argyll. The Duke, at first, resolved not to interfere in Renfrewshire. Then he backed Mure and later allowed Mure to exchange his seat for a place on the Scottish Court of Exchequer so that Patrick Craufurd could be elected. Argyll prevailed, but at a cost.[146]

The Ayrshire seat was held by James Mure Campbell, a cousin of the Earl of Loudoun, whose interest was challenged in 1759 by the Earl of Eglinton. So long as George II lived, Loudoun and Argyll supported the incumbent but they gave up this seat when George III and Bute came to power.[147]

As electioneering heated up in the autumn of 1759, the break between uncle and nephew centred on symbols which would be read as signs of favour and of present and coming power.[148] Was Lord Eglinton, once a favourite of the Duke, to have the Governorship of Dumbarton Castle? Or, was he to be refused and General John Campbell of Mamore appointed? Argyll insisted on the latter and even threatened to go to the King about the matter. He would have argued that Bute had set up the Prince of Wales's friends in Scotland against the King's. Newcastle was more afraid of the King than of the coming favourite. Argyll had his way. But not all patronage matters went Argyll's way. He tried (perhaps half-heartedly) in March 1760 to secure the Lord President's chair for his old friend Charles Erskine but could not. Hardwicke would not appoint an octogenarian to an office requiring diligence.[149] Argyll told Erskine that this was the 'only thing of that kind which I met with this winter'.[150] If he was not lying, he had secured every appointment he asked for from December 1759 to March 1760.

Argyll and Newcastle together drew up the tentative lists of candidates for Parliament without Bute's help or knowledge.[151] Those lists continued to be revised as new deals were made. The Duke wanted to make the lists acceptable to his nephew and to the Prince of Wales. He tried to make peace with his nephew so that the 1761 elections would go smoothly. When Bute rejected his proffered overtures, Argyll went to George II. The King was happy to support Argyll's candidates since he had come to see Bute as a man who was perverting his grandson. The King and Argyll would not have Bute on the next list of Representative Peers. Their breech was now open; the old Duke was the winner. It must have been very gratifying to succeed in fights of this sort at his age but his victory was fleeting.

Argyll continued making deals and drawing up lists of men to stand or benefit from the 1761 elections. He interfered in municipal elections to insure that the right men voted the right way when burgh electors were chosen.[152] He meddled in the Dumfries election to protect the interest and honour of Charles Erskine whose supporters had rioted in the town.[153] In June 1760, on behalf of the Convention of Royal Burghs, he congratulated the King on his recent victories.[154] Later in the month he and Lord

Hardwicke went through the list of candidates for the coming election.[155] Then, on 25 October 1760, everything changed. George II died in Germany while Argyll was in Scotland. George III became King. Bute was the new favourite. Argyll's status was again in doubt. Despite that, he went on making election arrangements. He vetted lists of new Justices of the Peace to be named as a consequence of the succession of George III. Those lists came to him from the Lord Justice Clerk but others also made suggestions.[156] Still, until late December it was not clear what would happen to Argyll.

Newcastle and Hardwicke would have had him out and the problem of managing Scotland solved by appointing fewer Scots to Scottish offices and making all in Scotland more dependent on English politicians. Bute decided that his uncle was still useful and sent Gilbert Elliot, once an Argathelian MP, to work out a reconciliation. Argyll, according to Elliot, was willing 'to be the instrument to execute your Lordship's [Bute's] commands in Scotland, provided you are inclined to employ him, to treat him gently, and to protect him from the oppression of the Duke of Newcastle, which though he has struggled with in former times, yet he is now too old and too unambitious any longer to endure'.[157] He would stay but on his own terms. Bute visited him the next day and the reconciliation was completed. Argyll then advised Bute to take on the responsibilities of first minister. The nephew had qualms which his uncle dismissed saying he should 'not quit the Service for I see no good & much evil may arise from it'.[158] A few days later Argyll kissed the King's hand on receipt of his new commission as Keeper of the Great Seal of Scotland. On the following day, 27 December 1760, both Argyll and Newcastle went to Pall Mall 'flattering Bute with the King, and offering to act under him'.[159] Among Argyll's earliest acts was a satisfying meeting with Newcastle to tell him that he would no longer have any influence over Scottish business which he would conduct under Bute's supervision but without a ministerial office. Argyll then went back to his electioneering.

In Argyll's election plans, there was now a place for William Mure on the Court of Exchequer, seats for Crauford of Auchenames and a compromise candidate for the contested Ayrshire seat, but no Edinburgh seat for the Duke's friend, Alexander Forrester. In late November, the Town Council wrote to the Duke asking whom they should choose as MP. On 16 December, the Duke wrote Milton a letter to show to the Town Council. The Council was fulsomely thanked and told that he would have to consult with 'some considerable persons here' which would benefit the city.[160] His nominee, Forrester, was no surprise but not liked by the Town. By early April, Argyll had been forced to accept someone else.[161] By then, he changed his good advice to Bute – it would be better to stay out of office and to influence things from behind the curtain much as he himself had done for so long.[162]

Then, suddenly, when his preparations for the elections in Scotland were nearly complete and as he was preparing to go north, Argyll himself died on 15 April. His preparations and deals were all but done but not all were clearly written out. At his death, there was panic among those who now had to run the elections because they could not find the Duke's lists or his election papers. They did not know all the promises which had been made, all the deals struck. Hardwicke lamented that the papers concerning the peerage election were lacking although arrangements for it had been made.[163] As late as 1 May 1761, Gilbert Elliot wrote the Lord Justice Clerk that the MP lists were still incomplete and might be with Hardwicke.[164] Their concerns were a sign of Argyll's importance to the very end and perhaps show how he insured himself. Bute said he had lost more than anyone else by his uncle's death.[165]

His last years had not been without political successes. His men, by 1761, controlled the Kirk and Scottish universities as never before. The economy was doing well and Argyll proved to be a first rate recruiter of Highlander troops. He had stayed in power and gradually increased his importance. By April 1761, he was as well situated as he had been since 1742.

VI. The Duke at the End of His Life

Argyll worked at politics but he also happily pursued his building schemes, improvements, 'mathematical gimcracks', and horticultural activities. Until the end of the 1750s, he was still buying instruments and books and watching his fortune grow. He did all that in an ordered way with his life following the seasons and the political year.

While Parliament sat, he was in London with weekends usually spent at Whitton. When the session ended, he spent some of the summer in London and at Whitton. Then, in late summer or autumn, he headed north, taking generally more than a week to reach Scotland. The trip, which had once taken ten to fourteen days by carriage, could now be done in five or six.[166] He sometimes went first to Edinburgh where he stayed at his apartment in Holyrood Palace or with Lord Milton at Brunstane House. From there he went to The Whim, his Peebles-shire property. Sometime between late August and October he would go to Rosneath and Inveraray to see the progress made on his projects in both places. At Inveraray, he entertained guests. After two or three weeks of that, he returned to Edinburgh or The Whim and then headed south. He arrived in London late in the autumn and resumed his duties.

In London, his mornings seem to have been devoted to business. He held a levee at Argyll House to which supplicants came and business was done. He sat with them at the end of his audience chamber at a distance from the crowd gathered at its other end and in the parlour beyond. During the 1750s, he seemed especially active in the Scottish universities and met many of their professors at his London house or at Whitton. His appointments to the colleges burnished his reputation.[167] On other mornings, he visited those whom he needed to see or found time to deal with correspondence. Some days, he would have gone to the House of Lords for committee meetings. Until 1760, he was still a somewhat active market trader buying and selling stocks, bonds and annuities. He was not bothered by 'insider trading'. In 1756, he sold 'funds' anticipating the fall of Minorca and a market slump.[168]

His afternoons and evenings were given over to the sessions of the House of Lords, to some visiting and dining out or entertaining. Little survives to show what sort of social life he lived in the city. His intimate life must have involved Mrs. Williams who lived next door and had an entry into his London garden. Their daughter too must have figured in his life but of her nothing is known save that she was probably now in her thirties. Argyll's circle of friends had always included pretty and witty women but not much is known of those whom he entertained in the 1750s. He liked Mrs. Boscowan and Col. Jack Campbell's wife and presumably still saw some old friends but many, like Mary Bellenden, once a favourite, were long dead or old and out of circulation like Lady Mary Wortley Montagu.

More is known about his male friends. By the 1750s, his son, Captain and then Colonel Williams, was very much a part of the Duke's life. When Argyll could, he travelled with him and his son often dined with him and his friends. Bubb Dodington's *Journal* from 1749-1754 shows Argyll and Bubb Dodington dining and visiting with a variety of politicians many of whom were connected with the Treasury, the Navy Treasury, the East India Company or the Bank of England. Economic policy, markets, investments and trade would have been among the topics canvassed at their meals. Some, like Bubb Dodington himself, were attached to the court of the Prince of Wales. Bubb Dodington was invited to Whitton but their usual meetings seem to have been in London, casual after dinner talks when Bubb Dodington 'dropped in'.[169] There were probably many evenings in the Duke's life like his last one. He dined that night with the Edinburgh banker and speculator, Adam Fairholm, with one of the Couttses and with others who had interests in money and politics. Fairholm described him on the eve of his death as 'chearful as ever he was in his life, when we were rising to go away he called for a Bottle of Burgundy and [kept] us up till one in the morning'.[170] The Duke still enjoyed his food and ate well. While not a very deep drinker, he liked claret and hearty wines and still had a taste for champagne.[171]

In London, the Duke was active in all the usual ways. His china collections grew. Given his scientific interests, it is surprising that he was not a member of the Royal Society of London to which so many of his friends belonged. Another body to which he gave some attention was the British Museum, founded in 1753.

There is no evidence that Argyll played a part in its founding but he was the first non-founder elected as a trustee. At the first general meeting, he was put on the executive committee of the Museum but he did not become an active manager. Between December 1753 and his death in April 1761, the Trustees' Standing Committee - the management - met over fifty times, but the Duke was there for only ten of the meetings and at none of them after 10 December 1756.[172] The meetings he attended dealt with finding a meeting place, hiring a surveyor for Montague House,[173] with bookcases, and with electing new trustees. He missed discussions of most matters before the Committee. Argyll was appointed to special committees but his record there was probably no better; there is no evidence that he attended.

The Duke's presence at General Meetings was also spotty and ended on 21 June 1759.[174] He was present on 12 December 1753 when Sir Hans Sloane's collections, which formed the nucleus of the Museum's natural history collection, were considered and he was named on 4 January 1754 to the committee to inspect them. He did not attend on 2 February 1754 when the committee's report was submitted. He attended on 13 February 1754 when it was decided to buy the Cottonian and Harleian Libraries and arrangements were made to fund their acquisition. He went several times when surveyors' reports, finances and fire insurance were discussed.[175] The appointment of Gowin Knight as Principal Librarian - the Director - drew him out to another meeting. Knight would have interested Argyll because of his work on magnetism and nautical compasses whose accuracy he improved. The same meeting also dealt with the Museum garden whose plantings had cost £205/16/8.[176] On 17

May 1757, the Duke turned up to approve the Harleian catalogues and to discuss Museum rules and finances. His last appearance, on 21 June 1759, was to consider money matters, tickets of admission and a Persian type font. He skipped sessions on issues like the plumbing of the building and most other housekeeping details. As he was no active trustee, neither was he a great benefactor of the Museum. None of his library books were given to it. He presented no instruments and he left no bequest to the foundation. He did make two substantial gifts of plants and trees. On 14 May 1756, the Standing Committee thanked him for 'having presented a great Variety of Exotic Trees, for the Garden'.[177] That was likely to have been a sizeable gift since his 'servant' was given a guinea – as was the servant of Peter Collinson who had made a similar donation. Both were thanked again on 6 May 1757 for gifts of plants but this time their servants received only a half guinea.

Despite his laxity as a trustee, Argyll was keeping up with some scientific discussions and works. In 1750 he commented that the recent London earthquakes might have been caused by underground 'Phenomena' or 'from the Atmosphere'. Those resolutely secular explanations reflected current scientific thinking about earthquakes. The atmospheric theories appealed to electrical discharges setting off great underground explosions; the underground explanations usually involved some sort of chemical reactions or combustion.[178] He had no interest in the religious explanations commonly given at the time. In 1755, he was probably studying some aspect of botany, natural history or chemistry with a teacher found for him by Lord Bute.[179] But, there are few references to chemistry after the mid-1750s. The Duke's last known activity as a chemist came in 1756 when he sent a sample from a 'burnt haystack' to the Royal Society to ascertain its alkali content. It had almost none.[180] There are, however, at least three payments in his Coutts 'Out book' to instrument makers – Alexander Cumming (1757), James Ferguson (1758), and Benjamin Martin (1760). All of those exceeded £10 so he was buying complicated or expensive items. However, there is nothing more about his astronomical devices which, after his death, seemed not to be in good repair. When he travelled, he still took with him a case of mathematical instruments – and sometimes forgot to bring take it home.[181] He was still interested in science and improvements and was circulating among men dedicated to both. A curious document from the British Museum papers shows that.

In the summer of 1761, an 'Examination' of a Mr. Stephens was held at the Museum.[182] He was accused by Gowin Knight of saying that an improved Franklin stove was not of Knight's contrivance. Knight asserted that Stephens had told Argyll that Knight had seen such a stove at the studio or home of Richard Wilson, RA, and had copied it. Stephens admitted this to be true. He added that he had drawings made of it and was selling it but giving Knight a 5% commission or royalty on each sale. Knight wanted credit for the design. Both men had made contact with the Duke whose interest in 'hooded stoves' went back at least to 1748 when Benjamin Franklin had sold him one.[183] Argyll had such a stove copied in 1757 [by Stephens?] and sent to Scotland for Lord Milton to 'deposit in the Abbey for inspection of friends'.[184] Argyll may not have been an FRS but he knew some of its useful members.

His Whitton, gardens flourished and his plantings approached maturity. There he had time in his gardens and talked during long dinners with men whom he wished to see and not those who wanted or needed to talk to him. Among his guests were Drs. Charles Stewart and John Mitchell and others who could talk to him about a range of scientific and improving interests. Mitchell's great map of North America (1755) dates from these years and would have engendered discussions because of its relevance to politics and rival claims to empire in America.[185] Most of the friends invited to Whitton were still either relatives, Scots in London, politicians and others with interests in financial matters, like Bubb Dodington and Gwynn Vaughn, or scientists, physicians, botanists or learned gardeners like Phillip Miller. Argyll gave away plants and trees from his sizable nursery, enjoyed his animals and worried about their condition.[186]

When Argyll went north, as he did nearly every year after 1708, he still followed old routines. He might limp from his wounds of 1715 but he did not fear riding 400 miles both ways in his chaise or coach and still more while he was there. Sometimes he went up in considerable style. The London *General Advertiser* reported that on 9 July 1752 'Argyll passed through [Newcastle], with a grand Retinue'.[187] His usual travels were more modest. His travel expenses on those trips seem to have amounted to about £2 a day with his suppers costing him 20/- to 30/- depending on who and how many he entertained.[188]

Once he got to Scotland, his costs shot up. His meals still included lots of vegetables, not too much wine or beer but enough meat to clog anyone's arteries.[189] One recorded in November 1759 included 'Supe, Roast Beef, a Goose, Boild pudding, a Tongue & Greens, a frigacy of Chickens and Celery'[190] Not too fancy and only one 'remove'. At Inveraray, he enjoyed venison shot in Cowal and brought to Inveraray by boat. His meals usually included a 'salat' and ended with fruits or tarts or another sweet such as almond or sugar biscuits. At The Whim, he had built, in 1759, 'a Fir press for the sueat meat room with Drawers and the Doors covered with gauzes'. It cost £2.[191] He had a sweet tooth though perhaps not many teeth.

His usual itinerary was from London up the Great North Road often with stops in Darlington and Newcastle. Then, it was on to Morpeth, Alnwick and Berwick. He visited along his way and entertained and politicked once he crossed the Tweed. In 1751 (not an election year) he dined with the Town Councils of Lauder, Jedburgh, Haddington and Edinburgh. His trips near the end of his life – 1758, 1759 and 1760 – seem no different. He politicked and looked after his properties. When he reached The Whim, there was much to look into. There were always men draining land, quarrying limestone to be burned to sweeten it and planting more trees – some now along fences or avenues in the park, gardens and approaches to the house. The Whim accounts show men hedging the fields, shearing the sheep he had introduced,[192] spreading 'mole hills' on the drained land, haying, digging potatoes, putting a bridge over the 'high pond' and building pond walls and a 'Cole house'.[193] The place constantly employed somewhere between thirteen and twenty-three men on the land alone.[194] Inside, he had more servants, headed by the cook.

On the way to and from his western estates, Argyll usually stopped at Edinburgh for politicking and visiting old friends. Argyll less often held court at Holyrood Palace after 1752. He found the throngs who had waited on him there a bother. Instead, he stayed with Milton at Brunstane where he could avoid many who wished to see him and had more peace. Lord Milton and the Duke took an active interest in the linen trades, improved their estates and were happy with their 'gimcracks'. Some of those in the 1750s were probably new devices to process flax or linen promoted by the Board of Trustees. Sometimes he sat as a justice in the Courts of Session and Justiciary as he had long done.[195] He also met those his politicking required him to meet. Alexander Carlyle in describing his 1759 visit with the Duke, noted that Argyll was polite in not pressing him about his relations with Charles Townshend or his promotion of a Scottish militia.[196] The Duke's Edinburgh visits sometimes involved things somewhat unusual. In 1759-60, his friends interested him in the settlement of a long running dispute between the painter Allan Ramsay, whom he had long patronized, and John Davidson, WS, to whom he had given a post. Their disagreement was over the land on which Ramsay had built Ramsay Garden.[197] Their arbitrators sent him a report saying that a fair settlement had been proposed and the two men should accept it.[198] Despite Argyll's efforts to reconcile the men, they ended up in court.

Glasgow was usually his next stop. He visited with gentlemen, the Provost and merchants, clerics and professors. A spring memorial of 1754, offering Glasgow University trees and plants for its physic garden, seems to have been prompted by such a visit.[199] His more usual meetings were likely to have been about appointments and the things Alexander Wilson and other natural philosophers had to show him.[200]

From there, it was on to Rosneath to see the progress of work on the Castle. At Inveraray, where the Castle was still unfinished, he was busier. There, since 1747, he had built a breakwater, quay and a dock, 'a Square or Court of Houses in the Cheery Garden', other slate-roofed houses, a tolbooth, an inn and a mill. Piped-in water would drain away in sewers under the new town streets. The Castle property had been parked and fenced. One wall carried seventy pleached trees which would make it about 500 feet long. There was a 'Spring of physical & mineral waters in the meadow'. A bleach-yard had been laid out, trees planted and other improvements made. One entered the town on new roads and over a new bridge.[201] The Duke may occasionally have visited Salt Coats in Ayrshire where his salt pans kept twelve men working and fourteen more mining the coal needed to fire them.[202]

Alexander Carlyle gives us a picture of him at Inveraray in 1758 enjoying his old age. He limped in to dinner (served at 2:00 p.m.) when he liked and did not make others await his coming. Carlyle says that he sat in whatever chair was left at the table. Carlyle noted that the company had 'sea and river fish in perfection, the beef and mutton and fowls and wild game and venison of both kinds' were 'in abundance' and the wines were 'excellent'.[203] Argyll drank few healths but downed his bottle of claret and talked readily to all who were there. Carlyle was more impressed by the fact that he also listened to everyone. He talked well and addressed the interests of his varied guests. The Duke was a good story teller but of stories he had often told. After the ladies left, 'he retired to an easy-chair hard by the fireplace: drawing a black silk nightcap over his eyes, he slept, or seemed to sleep, for an hour and a half' while his male guests plied themselves with wine. At about 6:00 p.m., he roused himself and had tea. After that, he often played whist with the ladies. His stakes were low enough so that all could play with him. This seems also to have been his custom in London, but there were few ladies at Whitton and The Whim. Carlyle does not mention chess games which had amused Argyle as a young man. At about 9:00 p.m., supper was served. During and after that he drank another bottle of claret and retired at about 1:00 a.m. He was either not an early riser or a man who needed little sleep. The Duke attended church services when at Inveraray. Carlyle preached to him and was pleased that the Duke had approved of what he said and how he said it. He also noted that 'without him no preferment could be obtained in Scotland'.[204] Carlyle's picture accords with the reports of others.

At Inveraray, Argyll played host to old friends and relatives, political allies, soldiers, and intellectuals such as the playwright John Home and Benjamin Franklin.[205] He was happy when Colonel Jack, a very eligible bachelor, was married in 1759 to the twenty-five-year-old dowager Duchess of Hamilton, his junior by ten years. The noted beauty and her husband were often at Inveraray after they married. Argyll had given them a house in Rosneath. The Duke seems to have liked most of his relatives but he was especially fond of Jack's wife on whom he settled a jointure during his lifetime. Should her husband die before her mother, from whom she could expect only a small inheritance, she would be well off.[206] When he was not in residence, guests might be entertained by his Chamberlain and given a tour of the house and the policies.

When the nights got cooler and the sun set earlier, he went back to London often stopping in Glasgow, Edinburgh, at The Whim and then at towns along the way. It took him sometimes two or three weeks to return to London from Peebles-shire. Sometimes he went by way of Newcastle, York, Hull, Lincoln and Northampton.

VII. Domestic Arrangements

As Argyll pursued his usual routines he was catered to by people many of whom worked for him for years. It is difficult to discover how large his London household was but from his letters and papers one can infer that it had besides his secretary and maybe Dr. Stewart at least twenty-five others. They included Henry Pujolas, his 'major domo' or steward, a valet, butler, about six footmen [the number in 1748], a cook, under-cook and probably at least two kitchen helpers, a housekeeper and maids, the coachmen, grooms and stable boys, a gardener and, for some years, his part-time librarian. He had no chaplain. Many of those people had skills other than those they exercised as servants. Pujolas, who had been with him since at least 1714, seems to have had some legal training as was common among stewards. The valets, butlers and footmen sometimes had been and continued to be surveyors and map-makers. His one known librarian had qualified as a minister and had been employed as a hack writer in London (see p. 104). His head gardeners were able to do elementary surveying. One at Whitton had run a commercial nursery. In addition to those people, his guests (and perhaps Pujolas) would have had servants of their own living in or near Argyll House. If Argyll's servants averaged £10 a year cash wages and a suit of livery and their keep, the cost of his London establishment alone would have come to at least £400-500, with more for Pujolas. When the Duke travelled, he took with him at least one footman, often a valet, sometimes a cook and butler and of course his coachman and grooms. He travelled in a coach often followed by a second coach and a wagon.

At his other homes there would have been the same sorts of people in the household but with variations. Whitton certainly had fewer in the house but there would have been many gardeners. Probably the whole complement of servants there was more than in London since the gardens and nurseries needed many hands. The Whim had the figures one would find on any bustling estate – a grieve, people to look after sheep and cattle, ordinary agricultural workers and always ditchers making drains and fences. There were overseers and a smith, often a mason, sometimes a miner and his helpers. In 1759, the outside staff numbered twelve plus the gardener but many casual seasonal workers were hired to plant potatoes or trees (five to twenty-two), shear sheep (up to seventeen men) and to do other chores. Inside, he had more, headed by a cook to whom he paid £5 a year even though his Lordship was seldom in residence. She would have had a lodging, shoes and her board. At Rosneath there was a housekeeper and maids, someone to oversee the reconstruction of the castle, a mason, a wright, a man to oversee the making of bricks and labourers.

At Inveraray the number of servants was much larger partly because this was his principal seat in Scotland. There, the hierarchy of servants began with his Chamberlain and Deputy Chamberlain who looked after the business of the estate – legal, economic and political. In the old castle, there was a housekeeper, cook and a staff large enough to look after the perhaps four to fourteen guests and their entourages who showed up when he arrived in the summer. There would have been a butler and footmen – perhaps twelve in all but not all kept on throughout the year.

Outside there were the usual estate figures for a place of this kind: a park-keeper, a gardener and their staffs; a grieve to look after the farm; a shepherd; a pond keeper for his fish and the pond in which he tried to farm oysters; boatmen for the Ducal Barge and other ordinary workers. They must have numbered over twenty-five when he was in attendance. There were also men involved year in year out with the construction of the new castle. They included a clerk of works and an accountant, overseers of the contracted labourers – head quarriers, 'the Duke's mason', dyke, bridge and quay makers, mill, wheel and wagon wrights, smiths, joiners and no doubt others. He employed a clockmaker who also built his organ. He subsidized the schoolmaster who had been brought in from Glasgow to teach mathematics in the town.

The total workforce at Inveraray, without counting the casual construction workers, certainly comes to over sixty. Some of the skilled workers were highly paid – £50 or more per year. Argyll constantly employed perhaps 150 servants in the 1750s at his places of residence and varying numbers of other workers temporarily engaged in building, farming, mining and on other particular projects of one sort or another. In addition to those servants, he had a 'doer' in Edinburgh and probably retained a lawyer in London.

His establishments were expensive to maintain. Altogether, he must have spent well over £1,000 a year on his household staffs. The additional costs of his London household can be very roughly gauged by the payments made to his 'major domo'. Those included Pujolas's salary, some wine costs, and a miscellany of other bills. They ranged in the years examined from about £130 in 1720-21 to about £720 in 1725 and then to about £1,300- £1,700 for the years up to the 1750s. They reached £2,000 in 1758-59. More expenses would have been attributable to Whitton and his Scottish houses. Perhaps altogether they reached £4,000. There were perhaps added costs for wine. Those seldom went over £150 a year and some years those costs are absent from the 'Out books'. Some years, wine cost him less than his instruments. His Grace's pocket money, or the sums he drew from the account for his own uses, for the years looked at, were between £700 (1755) and £2,480 (1738). If it averaged £1,650, then his usual costs late in his life came to about £5-7,000. Politicking and living as he would took more.

Building at Whitton, The Whim and Inveraray was a major expense every year after c.1725. Whitton and its gardens were costly but there is no way to estimate those costs. The Whim took more than £1,000 a year as the scattered expenses in his and Lord Milton's letters show. It was a never-finished work. Drains were continually dug. The new library was finished by John Adam in 1759 at the cost £160 plus the cost of a stove – about £200 in all.[207] In 1760, he sent to The Whim a number of maps and possibly put on its shelves the finely bound copy of Fordoun's chronicles which he bought in May of that year for 3g.[208] Those were trivial costs but they piled up. At Inveraray, about £3-4,000 a year seems to have been spent on the castle and its surrounds after 1743. The £21,000 received for his heritable jurisdictions was expended on building as were thousands more from his yearly income. That increases his annual expenditure to about £10-12,000 in the 1750s. Even so, it is hard to see how he could have used all his income in any given year since he did not live as grandly as many peers or have their debts.

To defray the expenses of these establishments and activities there was a large income. His offices paid him handsomely – Keeper of the Great Seal of Scotland (£3,000), Lord Justice General (£2,000), Heritable Master of the King's Household (£1,000).[209] Small incomes derived from many minor offices, fees and perquisites. To that £6,000+, one has to add his estate revenues which have been estimated as £6,687 in 1743 and at about £10,000 for 1761.[210] That included rents and something from the woods, quarries, salt pans and coal mines worked on his behalf. He sold some sheep, cattle and meal from The Whim. Finally, he had income from his investments and personal loans. During the last year of his life, his investment income came to at least £1,251. All in, his final income was probably in the range of £15-17,000 annually.[211] His income was larger than that of any Scottish peer but smaller than many English peers and business men. The difference between the income and expenses is difficult to explain given the surviving documents. He may have made new investments but after 1750 he seems to have sold more securities than he bought and ten years later he had stopped trading except for the purchase of small amounts of plate on which he paid fees at the Excise Office.[212] He did however take from his Coutts account on 7 May 1760 £10,000 whose disposition is unknown.[213] Earlier, he had bought annuities; perhaps more money than now appears was used for that purpose for his illegitimate family or for others. Perhaps it was used to provide his promised jointure for the former Duchess of Hamilton mentioned above (see p. 339). That may account for some of the difference between what he seems to have spent in many years and what he received. Still, he was worth much more than appears from his bank statements.

In the 1750s, life went on but it was slowing down. His lifetime attendance rate in the House of Lords was 72% but in the Parliament of 1754 that fell to 47%. In 1760 (a year of good health), the percentage was 45%. He was also less active in the House as a speaker. Cobbett's *Parliamentary History* records very few speeches by him after he turned sixty-five in 1747. His committee assignments did not much diminish but we do not know if he attended as regularly. Seeming inactivity may be the artefact of partial reporting but the record is slim and is more likely to reflect his age and varying health. Throughout most of his last years the Duke's health was good. His active life kept him in reasonable physical shape. He was ill before and during the Annexed Estate debate in 1752 but was not often sick again until 1754. In 1754 he had a sore throat ('my family distemper') which confined him to the house for a month although he had little 'swelling, suppuration or the least degree of fever'.[214] In 1756 he had what seems to have been a leg infection which developed from a scratch and another in August 1758.[215] In January 1759, he complained of a 'a sore leg' which kept him house bound for some weeks.[216] Those took long to heal – possibly because of his treatments of them, possibly because he was diabetic. Illnesses account for some of his more frequent absences from the House of Lords. If one looks to the last portraits of the aging Duke, he had become florid of face and a bit jowly (see Plates 11 and 12). Montrose, who saw him not long before he died, said, 'He looks red but old and feeble and surly'.[217] The Duke's last weeks belied that judgment as do his final portrait and the study for that made by Allan Ramsay. He was – despite age, forgetfulness, an unsteady hand, malaria, migraine headaches, vertigo and other ailments – still an active, effective man enjoying life. It is surprising that he continued to work at his political tasks when he could have led an easier life. It is not clear whether he kept at it from a sense of duty, a need to exercise power and to count, or if working gave him pleasure as he manipulated men and circumstances for the benefit of himself and his friends.[218] He had long likened politics to a game.[219] Perhaps he was just addicted to play.

He was thinking about his end. William Woollett's pictures of his garden appeared in 1757 and his last portrait was painted about then. His book catalogue was published in 1758. He also made a new will on 14 August 1760. There was much to leave.

His known personal fortune recorded in the Coutts records came to at least £42,000, mostly in East India bonds. In addition there must have been about £2,000 in British Linen Company stock since he had to have £2,000 to remain as its Governor.[220] He had on his person or in his houses when he died another £315 in notes and cash. The sales of books, instruments and sundries listed in the Coutts 'In book' come to £5,310,18.5. That adds to about £49,626.[221] Left unsold were most of the expensive furnishings and his collections of porcelain, small art objects and curiosities. And, there were the houses in London and the estate at Whitton and The Whim. His improved estates were stocked with valuable trees, plants, animals, books and other objects. Those would have added hundreds more. His personal estate, exclusive of the entailed ducal properties, must have come to between £55,000 and £67,000. Also, the £10,000 he withdrew from Coutts remains unaccounted for.

Argyll's will was eccentric; family and kinship did not mean to him what they meant to many aristocratic Scots. When his will was published in the papers and the *Scots Magazine,* the whole world knew that he had preferred his mistress and their illegitimate children to his legal heirs who by the will got only what was entailed. Personal affection counted with him. He left 'Mrs. Elizabeth Williams otherwise Shireburn of Witton Dean in the County of Middlesex and of Marlborough Street in London' all of his 'Personal Estate in ... [England] of what kind or Nature Whatsoever'. If she died, all would go to his illegitimate son, Captain William Williams of the 3rd Regiment of Foot Guards. This was a more generous settlement on his 'family' than had been made in his will in the 1730s and surely reflects a greater fondness or appreciation of his dependents. His illegitimate daughter, 'Mrs. Ann Williams now residing near Maidstone in Kent', got an annuity of £100 and a further £100 for each of three years following his death. Since his personal estate was left to Mrs. Williams without conditions, she could increase her daughter's share of the estate should she choose to do so. Mrs. Williams and her children were well taken care of in a way reminiscent of the Duke's father's care for Mrs. Alison, his last or favourite mistress. The 3rd Duke gave The Whim to John Maule[222] and may have given annuities to others. Argyll's other legacies seem to have involved only small sums.[223] He left the customary year's wages to his servants but cut his cook off with nothing because his 'wages were too high'.[224]

Having made a will in 1760, the Duke set off for Scotland for the last time.[225] He visited Inveraray as usual but he was never to occupy his unfinished castle or see completed the new town he had planned. He did the usual things and returned to worry about the new reign which had begun.

VIII. The Duke's Death

The Duke's end was quick and came at a peak in his career. On 14 April, he had dined out (see pp. 3 and 334). The next day he visited Mr. Coutts but came home at 2:00 p.m. feeling unwell.[226] He sat down to dinner with his son, John Maule, and Dr. Charles Stewart but was not hungry. He 'eat none', said 'he woud take a Camomile puke'. While they dined, he fell asleep but 'soon after [he] had a convulsive motion over his body, & died in a minute'. His surgeon and physician were sent for but he could not be bled and was gone.[227]

Argyll's papers were sealed and his effects secured against the settlement of his estate.[228] On 16 April his will was read. That afternoon the Duke was anatomized and embalmed. His mistress and their children, in due course, inherited as they were to do.[229] The long business of the funeral began. His successor was surprised to find that he was expected to pay for Duke Archibald's funeral for which no money had been allocated. That was unlikely to have been an oversight. The Great Duke would have enjoyed the joke on Jack, a less brilliant version of himself.[230] In the end, Mrs. Williams bore the costs of the arrangements in England and the 4th Duke those in Scotland.

Baron John Maule wrote to Milton on 16 April, 'There is justly an universal lamentation for him, & every body speaks of it, as an event of ye greatest consequence yt coud have happened in this Kingdom'.[231] That certainly was true for the Duke's circles in London and Scotland but the English did not care so much and it is unlikely that Lord Bute felt much but the inconvenience of having now to manage Scotland.[232]

Chapter 18

Appraising the Man

I. Memories and Obituaries

Although the Duke of Argyll was an old man, his sudden death was an unexpected blow to his London family. Mrs. Williams, surprised and unable to comprehend the magnitude of her inheritance, was unprepared to be a rich woman. It was explained to her that she now needed to make a will of her own, something she had not formerly had. Her son and principal heir was now certain that he would be a wealthy man and not just the holder of good commissions in the Army and a sinecure post in the Exchequer of Scotland. Colonel Williams was stricken by his father's death and seems to have been depressed and inactive for some time.[1] About his sister Ann's reactions, nothing is known.

The family of the 4th Duke mourned. The new Duke, who had been close to his predecessor for about fifty years, sent his condolences – along with his annoyance that he was being charged for funeral expenses – to Lord Milton who was treated almost as a family member.[2] General Campbell's older son, now Lord Lorne, and his second son, Lord Frederick Campbell, both expressed their grief to Milton.[3] Many other Campbells were saddened. John Campbell, 4th Earl of Loudoun, and Daniel Campbell of Shawfield were typical of them. Loudoun described the Duke's death as a 'general loss' while Shawfield wrote of the 'melancholy if unexpected accounts of the Duke of Argyll's Death [which] affected me in a manner I want words to express'.[4] He owed his seat in the Commons to Argyll but his letter expressed sadness as well as regret at the loss of a patron.

Beyond the family, others mourned. Baron John Maule, the Duke's one time secretary, was very upset. The splotches on his letter to Milton informing the latter of the Duke's death may indeed be his tears as Ian Lindsay and Mary Cosh suggested.[5] Many noblemen, gentlemen and politicians expressed their regrets. Men like Alexander Forrester, whom Argyll had tried and failed to bring into Parliament for Edinburgh, wrote that 'my course & habitudes of life are broken without possibility of repair'. He called himself one of the 'Whitton Party' now forever sundered. That was the set of men asked out for Sunday dinners to discuss topics of interest. Affection for the Duke and intellectual interests had united them. Sir Harry Erskine told Milton,

'Nobody cou'd be more seriously affected with grief than I was when I received the melancholy news of the loss which your Lordship, Lord Bute and this Country have sustained. His Grace's abilities were far superior to those of the rest [of] Mankind. His friends were justly very numerous. And none of them:

will more sincerely feel from Affection, this blow, than you and Your family will do'.[6]

Andrew Cochrane, Provost of Glasgow, banker and political economist, described the Duke to Lord Milton as the 'late worthy patron and friend to the corporation and country' – and said that to honour his memory the city fathers would in the elections do 'what is obliging to my Lord Bute'.[7] Lord Adam Gordon wrote to Milton,

> You'll forgive me, since no man has had a greater loss than my self, for condoling with you, and this Country. Alas! Where shall I ever find such a friend? At the same time I am pleased to know the good Man departed, with such ease & tranquillity – and in a manner every sensible man would wish.[8]

He noted that Argyll's Scottish enemies, such as the Duffs of the Northeast, were joyful. An election was coming. Bankers sent in letters which were more than formulaic expressions of sentiment. Most said, in one way or another, what Sir Alexander Cunningham Dick told Milton: 'we may really say the Country has lost a father whose place it will not be easy to supply.[9]

Argyll's obituaries stressed his talents and learning, his judgment and moderate use of power. The Duke was praised by his clerical manager, Patrick Cuming, for being a friend to the Kirk, to Highlanders, to manufacturers and fishermen, indeed, to Scots of all kinds. Cuming found him 'patient 'when out of power', 'steady' when he had it, and 'always contriving and always ready to listen to Schemes for promoting the Learning and the interest of his country'. He described him as calm in the midst of struggles and not one to excite enmity or to nurse grievances. Taking a final leave of his old friend, Cuming wrote, 'Rarely are so many extraordinary and excellent Qualities to be found United in one person'.[10] *The Scots Magazine* quoted the 'Edinb. papers':

> His great abilities and learning early pointed him out as a patron and protector of this part of the kingdom. Which character particularly showed itself in the latter years of his life. Happy in the esteem and friendship of his sovereign, he supported a firm character in the midst of faction, and could boast alone in the transitory revolution of state affairs, that he still remained invariably the same.[11]

An anonymous writer (c.1762) from Inveraray or its environs praised the transformation Argyll had effected in his own county.[12] He was a great man who had developed Inveraray by building the Castle and town, extended and bettered the highways to them, and had carried out a new valuation of the county in 1751.

A London pamphlet of 1763, mostly on Bute, contained a laudatory character of Argyll. He was learned. He 'could write a letter in six different languages'.[13] He understood not only mathematics, philosophy and law but also 'the construction of watches, and clocks, nay of all the machines depending upon mechanics'. He was a 'stedfast friend, and no cruel enemy'. Through his improvements and schemes, 'thousands have had bread, and millions unborn may find entertainment'. Argyll had been a very great man – the implication being that neither the 2nd nor 4th Dukes of

Argyll, nor Lord Bute, could or would match him as a benefactor of North and South Britons.[14]

Not exactly an obituary (it was published in 1759), but probably meant to serve a similar function, was the character of the Duke given by Nicholas Tindal. He noted that Argyll was born in England and resided there until he was about seventeen. A good student, he 'studied hard as if he had ... to get his livelihood by his learning' and became learned in the civil law. Disliking the Stuarts, he used his power

> to gain over to the government as many of the deluded followers of that house, as he possibly could, and to his wise moderation it was owing, that in Scotland, few besides men of desperate fortunes, were then jacobites. He united, if ever man did, the characters of a philosopher and a politician. For, notwithstanding the torrents of unsupported personal abuse, poured forth against him in public, he never was known to revenge his own quarrel, or to desist from his own plan. The pursuit of power in him never diverted him from that of knowledge; of which he had a greater variety, than perhaps, any man of his age. He despised money, even to a fault, and the larger his estate was, the smaller was his income, for he expended it before it came to his hands, in the encouragement and quickening of national industry and the promoting public improvements. Nothing more shall be said of this great man; nothing has been said, that his greatest enemies have not at all times confessed.[15]

Here Tindal was far more flattering than in the preceding character of the Earl of Stair.

Obituaries usually exaggerate the merits of their subjects and gloss over short-comings but the feelings expressed in those for the Duke were real enough to be shared by a wider public. Argyll's engraved portraits were the most common images possessed by those in Edinburgh and Glasgow who could afford pictures of any sort.[16] The great outpouring of affection and respect in Edinburgh and Glasgow as his cortege passed through the burghs, was more than gratitude for an effective defender of Scottish interests or respect for a clever man.[17] That affection was aroused by other qualities. He had brought employment to many. As a landlord he had asked for conformity to Whig politics and to his directions but he racked no rents. As Eric Cregeen noted, 'contemporary accounts are agreed in praising his moderation and humanity'. He was willing to divide farms to accommodate people. He continued renting to old tenants when new would have paid more. He evicted few.[18] In an age which prized rank and exerted its privileges, his informality and graciousness to those beneath him must often have seemed remarkable. Usually genial to those around him, he could be conniving and unpleasant to those whom he opposed politically but when nothing political was at stake, he was generally a considerate man. He cared little for appearances and willingly learned from clockmakers and gardeners. Some found his preference for nursery owners at his Sunday dinners baffling when he could have dined with his social equals. Bantering with Gavin Hamilton in his bookstore was not the style of every earl or duke. The discrete and laconic Duke committed to paper little which was truly personal but his actions explain some of the sense of loss occasioned by his death.

II. Argyll's Political Legacies

Argyll's public legacies have seemed clear. Many have seen the Duke's importance and his legacy mainly as a political one. Under his leadership, Scots remained semi-independent led by a manager who in many ways replaced the Privy Council abolished in 1708. Argyll provided a buffer between Scotland and the government at London. That gave Scots time to adjust to the realities of Union. The system of management which Lord Ilay created and Henry Dundas would more or less follow, while not wholly novel, was effective and ran smoothly. One condition for this was the small size of the Scottish electorate and the venality of urban voters. Without an office, Argyll managed Scotland so that ministries were backed by Scottish votes in Parliament and Scots were paid with patronage positions. Argyll's power depended upon the support given him in London by men who used him to keep Scotland manageable, relatively peaceful and useful for the purposes of imperialists. Those ends were generally also his. He was not in the end his own man. His Lordship did not oppose many changes but he wanted them to be gradual and he never wished the Union with England to be as close as some would have had it. As much as he could, Argyll, preserved the integrity of Scottish institutions. No Scottish politician would have placed men who were not useful in maintaining his position but Argyll did not want Englishmen in Scotland subverting Scottish law, government and culture. Few were appointed on his watch – and some who found places were made uncomfortable by him and his friends.[19] On those points I am in substantial agreement with Alexander Murdoch, Richard Scott, John Shaw and Eric Wehrli.

To that, we need to add more stress on his Highland policies – moderate, forgiving, reasonable and looking to the changing of customs and ideas through economic betterment more than through coercion. He was for compromises and moderation, for legality and order – supplied by Scottish, not English, law. He slowed the pace of the political change but not that of the economic integration of the United Kingdom. By the end of his life, the Scottish and English economies were more closely linked by banking ties and imperial trade although some industries in both countries were still given special protection.

Within the limits in which Argyll was free to work, there was also a minor politics being played out which was very much the work of Scots and in the long run as important to Scots as the political issues which revolved around elections to Parliament or the expansion of the Empire. That minor politics dealt ultimately with the kind of place Scotland was to be and what Scots were to think and do. In that scheme of things, Argyll was a more significant figure, not just another good Scottish election manager and 'fixer' upheld or trammelled by English politicians. The length of his service, his character and interests, and the patronage he dispensed changed his country. His political career must be seen from Scotland and in a cultural perspective for his significance to be fully appreciated. When it is, his economic and cultural importance becomes greater and he looks rather different from the politician described by so many. To appreciate that one must again consider his patronage.

III. Patronage Politics

One of the 'characters' of Argyll which appeared after his death says that 'he at a moderate computation settled fifty-four thousand individuals in civil and military employments'.[20] That is to say, he either appointed, approved or did not block the appointments of that many men. The author of this statement probably thought, 'His Lordship was in office for about fifty four years; he must have made or agreed to 1,000 appointments a year of some sort'. This seems exaggerated and unrealistic. It may not be. Consider the following very rough calculation.

The principal source for any biography of Argyll is the Saltoun Correspondence's collection of letters and other items written to and by Andrew Fletcher, Lord Milton, and other members of his family. The letters to and from Argyll run from c. 1724 to 1761 and fill about 200 boxes with perhaps an average of 100 documents a box. That is 20,000 items most of which probably deal, on average, with at least one appointment. Argyll had been appointing people as early as 1705 but those people do not appear there. Much of his business was transacted in face-to-face meetings in London, where he lived, or in Scotland, which he visited in at least forty-three of the years from 1705 to 1760, sometimes more than once. Many appointments considered in those meetings are not found in the Saltoun Correspondence. Lord Milton did not deal with all Argyll's military patronage, so other appointees exist who are not all mentioned in the Saltoun letters. The anonymous author mentioned explicitly the soldiers of the Independent Highland Companies and those employed in the linen trade and fisheries. He was thinking about quite ordinary people whose names seldom surface in the Correspondence – those who were employed because of the tariffs and the subsidies which Argyll had secured for the fisheries and linen or other industries. When one includes all those, the figure of 54,000 is perhaps too small – even when one discounts those who received more than one post or none at all.

His patronage power and the length of time he exercised it allowed Argyll to be an important force in the shaping of modern Scotland. In time, his nominees came to dominate most important institutions in the country. No other politician in the period had a record of this sort because none were involved for so long and interfered with so many institutions. Argyll's periods of political power totalled about thirty-six years. In Scotland, only Henry Dundas, for about twenty-seven years, came close to exercising the influence he wielded.

While Argyll patronized men in London, the most important patronage he exercised was given to Scots who stayed at home. It came in the appointments of men to the institutions in Scotland which mattered to many people – the Kirk and universities, the civil administration and courts, places in the burghs and counties and in the many civil institutions in which politicians traditionally interfered. Those appointments over time shaped the outlook and values of Scots. He did not appoint with that clearly in mind but it was an unintended consequence. The values and methods which guided Ilay's patronage made a difference.

Ilay prized useful knowledge, broadly defined, and he expected such knowledge to be sought and used. He saw improvement in secular terms. The means to improvements he found principally in science and the applications of empirical knowledge. He shared the desire for progress and betterment of all sorts which was characteristic of the best minds of Europe after 1650. Like many of them, he found the application of science to problems the best means to attain his own ends. It went with accommodations and piecemeal political reforms. He would have understood the Baron de Montesquieu, a tolerant political theorist and improver who did experiments and extended his vineyards and sold his own wines; or M. de Voltaire, who ran a watch manufactory on his estate; or Denis Diderot, the man of letters who produced the *Encyclopédie* to make France, Europe and the world more productive through the spread of knowledge. In a similar manner, Argyll's patronage forced the pace and determined the directions of change in ways which facilitated the Scottish Enlightenment.

Ilay's improvements were made to benefit himself and his friends, and to sustain political interests by satisfying and improving the lot of his countrymen. He wanted to make Scotland more self-sufficient but also a trading nation. The men he tended to appoint were men who knew the value of new knowledge and sought to apply it. Active men who pursued new ideas and applied them were put into the universities which they helped to make among the best in the world by 1761. Others by c.1760 had made Scotland a hotbed of improvers in agriculture, industry and banking, in natural philosophy, even history and economics. When we look at the institutions which Ilay controlled or manipulated through patronage, we see them gradually filling up with men interested in remaking the Scottish world along the lines he thought right. Ilay was an initiator in all that but he need not have done this – as the patronage of the Duke of Newcastle makes clear. Newcastle too appointed a lot of men and was Chancellor of Cambridge University but how many of his appointees count in the intellectual, social or economic history of eighteenth-century England? At best, they were literary bishops. Argyll's men ran the Royal Bank of Scotland, the British Linen Company, the Board of Trustees for Fisheries and Manufactures and for many years dominated the Convention of Royal Burghs which also nudged the Scottish economy in directions he approved. The kinds of Scots whom the Duke favoured can be seen in the many he chose who belonged to and led the country's most distinguished literary, philosophical and improvement societies and clubs. A look at Edinburgh illustrates this.

The Duke and Lord Milton had many friends in the Philosophical Society of Edinburgh, to which they may even have belonged.[21] About a third of the 150 or so known Scottish PSE members were connected with them. Among them were the botanists Charles Alston, Sir James Naysmith of Posso, MP, and Professor John Hope. Argyll liked mechanically minded men and helped William Crow of Netherbyres, James Grey 'of the Iron Miln'.and Major Dougal Campbell, His Majesty's Engineer in Scotland. The Duke patronized mathematicians and astronomers such as James Stirling of Keir, Colin Maclaurin and Alexander Wilson. The Edinburgh University teachers of medicine appointed in 1726 were given small pensions which supplemented their fees and incomes from a pharmaceutical concern.[22] PSE chemists patronized by him included Andrew Plummer, Alexander Lind, William Cullen, Joseph Black, and James Hutton. Lind, Cullen, Francis Home, probably Arthur Martine (he may have been a PSE member), and Black all dealt with Argyll and worked for the Board of

Trustees. The Duke may have had something to do with the establishment outside Edinburgh of the sulphuric acid works of Dr. John Roebuck. Argyll took an interest in Lord Milton's experiments in the bleaching and dyeing of linen. William Adam, Alexander Cumming, Sir Alexander Cunningham Dick, Duncan Forbes of Culloden and Colin Maclaurin were among other PSE members who contributed items on economics, technology, or chemistry to the files of Lord Milton and the Duke. Altogether, about a fourth of the members of both the Philosophical and Select Societies are known to have owed Archibald Campbell some job or favour. Those memberships are a significant indicator of the sorts of men he wanted in office. If one looks at a wider sample, Squadrone men were in all such groups but they were present in smaller numbers and were less active if one measures their personal involvement with innovations against that of Argyll's friends.[23]

In assessing the Duke's legacy, it is worth looking in some detail at the men he appointed and the differences they made. The clearest indicator is found in the universities where future leaders were taught. Argyll's patronage generally came in the form of recommendations to others who had the legal right to appoint. His influence can be measured in several ways. Between 1 January 1724 and 1 January 1763, 151 appointments were made. Argyll backed 46%-49% of them, 69-73 appointments. That is, he agreed to one man rather than another when he had the power to block an appointment. He sometimes made the final selection himself. Most of the other appointments were made by college men or local men of influence. They often appointed men he would have favored because the electors were his appointees or supporters. His appointees between 1724 and 1761 included most of the principals and divinity professors, most of the regius professors and almost all those put into the teaching chairs of medicine. In the eighteenth century only Henry Dundas came close to having Ilay's influence, accounting for 56-62 appointments made in larger institutions between about 1778 and 1806.[24] Dundas often chose men who were reactionaries or less brilliant and innovative than those whom he passed over. In both cases, the men recommended for appointment to those politicians came in time to resemble in their interests the politicians who picked them. Many of Argyll's appointees were improvers or had interests in chemistry and other sciences which intrigued him.

Glasgow, the best arts college in Scotland, was the university in which Argyll had the most influence and where the direction of his patronage is most clearly shown. At Glasgow the chairs were, throughout this period, all in the hands of either the University and College or the Crown but few appointments were made without the approval of the managers of Crown patronage in Scotland. That meant that Argyll from 1725 until his death in 1761 was the dominant influence on the selection of Glasgow professors. During those years the Principal of the College was his distant cousin and Argathelians usually had a majority in the College and University meetings which chose new professors. Appointments made there were of enlightened men who had effects on their society which are not always noticed.

In the Divinity School, Ilay kept in office until 1740, John Simson, the Professor of Divinity who was tried for his heresies in the 1710s and again between 1727 and 1731, when he was suspended from teaching.[25] His heresies were teaching that less emphasis should be placed on notions of damnation and more on the love of God, that less emphasis should be given to documents like the Westminster Confession, a creed devised by men. Men should be captive to the word of God as they understood it from their Bibles. Understanding the Bible required reasoning as well as faith. Ilay could not dictate Simson's replacement in 1740 or in 1743 but in other years he placed moderates in the chairs of ecclesiastical history and oriental languages. In those chairs, the Duke allowed a succession of secular-minded men who did not teach theologues the history needed to defend their creed or the rightness of Protestantism. He appointed no distinguished Hebraists. In 1761, neither chair was well served by the men who held them. The Professor of History, William Wight, was a polite, conservative man interested in political economy and in improving Scotland. The Professor of Oriental Language, James Buchanan, was a mathematician whom Argyll had found the best qualified of the several who sought the post. He was destined for the mathematics chair but died before it came to him. The Kirk was changed and weakened by those appointment and ones like them made elsewhere.

In law things were different. Argyll had at first opposed the appointment of William Cross (1746) but supported him in the end to gratify the Town Council and other politicians. Hercules Lindsay, who replaced Cross in 1750, was a more competent law teacher with much experience whom Ilay had supported for some time.[26] Argyll appointed more and better medics.[27] William Cullen, one of the great European medical teachers of the century, came to his teaching posts at Glasgow (1747) and Edinburgh (1756) with Argyll's help. After his appointment, Glasgow's medical school began to thrive. In the future, more men like Cullen were appointed to fill its chairs.

In the Glasgow arts chairs, the Duke's record was equally distinguished. Ilay personally chose and told the College to elect Francis Hutcheson as Professor of Moral Philosophy in 1729.[28] In the 1750s, the Duke was able to replace most of the faculty members. Among the notable professors he was willing to see hired was George Muirhead. He worked as an editor for the distinguished Foulis Press which operated within the University precincts. Argyll befriended the Greek Professor, James Moor, not his appointee but another Foulis editor. They shared common interests in mathematics, numismatics and the classics. That was also the case with Robert Simson, the Professor of Mathematics and an amateur botanist. Ilay approved Professor Simson's choice of a successor c.1759 and thus placed in the College another religious moderate, a man of whom David Hume approved.[29] When Argyll created for Alexander Wilson a Chair in Practical Astronomy (1760), he kept in the city a distinguished type-founder and his lucrative business.[30] Argyll helped to place Adam Smith in the Chair of Logic in 1752. Smith was the son of a man whom Campbells had patronized as they had other members of the Smith family.[31] Later, in 1752, Smith assumed the Chair of Moral Philosophy.[32] Argyll was a backer of John Anderson who became one of the most interesting and influential teachers of Natural Philosophy, in eighteenth-century Britain.[33] Anderson, the grandson of a tutor of the 2nd Duke of Argyll, was a chemist, botanist, antiquary and the inventor of munitions, as well as a lecturer on Newtonian science. Andersons and Campbells had a long history but the men's abilities were what the Duke respected. Argyll first got him into the College as a Professor of Hebrew even though Anderson was then hardly qualified for the post.[34] The Duke expected him to be promoted to a useful chair, as he was when he became Professor of Natural Philosophy.

The list of other distinguished university men who owed something to Argyll is a long and interesting one. At Glasgow, it includes Robert Hamilton and William Rouet (or Ruat). At Edinburgh, he aided professors Charles Erskine, later Lord Tinwald; the medical professors appointed in 1726 – John Innes, Andrew Plummer, John Rutherford, and Andrew St. Clair (Sinclair) – and later Professors Robert Whytt, Francis Home, James Russell and Matthew Stewart. In addition to the principals and divinity professors, he and Milton helped Adam Ferguson. At St Andrews, his appointees included Alexander Morton (a noted travelling tutor), William Wilkie and perhaps Robert Watson. At King's, Argyll's influence was of little importance because only one Regius Chair existed and most of the livings were in the hands of the masters who appointed their relatives. Still, he had two appointees, George Gordon II and John Lumsden. The first he reluctantly appointed to succeed his father when he learned that Gordon was competent, had for some years been teaching for his father and had become responsible for their large family which had no other means of support.[35] Lumsden was a moderate cleric. At Marischal College most of the livings were in the gift of the Crown. There, Squadrone men had replaced nearly all the professors in 1717/18. They lived long lives so Argyll appointed few men. Those he placed included Dr. Matthew MacKaile, Principal George Campbell, William Duncan, Francis Skene, George Skene and James Beattie – two scientists of minor distinction, a notable rhetorician and philosopher, a translator and man of letters with numerous publications, and a moralist who became George III's favourite poet.

The transformation of the Scottish universities in the eighteenth century owed much to the Duke. Change had already begun and would have come to them anyway but he speeded it up and made the colleges more science-oriented and practical in outlook. That was especially the case where he was most active – at Glasgow University, Marischal College and Edinburgh University. The colleges appointed good moralists. Hutcheson, Smith and Adam Ferguson need not have been appointed, just as some of the bright physicians and anatomists need not have found places. Few of his university appointees were mere place-men. Those who held sinecure chairs were in divinity faculties or non-teaching medical chairs in Aberdeen. The often praised practical outlook of the universities stemmed from the work his men did.

In the Kirk, his record seems equally clear. He supported all of the early moderates. Men such as William Hamilton and William Wishart II were promoted by his interest. They became Moderators (1727, 1728) with his help as did others like them – James Alston (1729), James Smith (1731), Neil Campbell (1732), John Gowdie or Goldie (1733), John Lumsden (1746), George Wishart (1748), Patrick Cuming (1749), Robert Hamilton (1754), and William Leechman (1757). Less distinguished men like them served in years unmentioned. All of them helped to make the Kirk more liberal in outlook. After 1750, the men who formed the Moderate Party pushed it even further in directions Argyll approved. John Home, William Robertson, Principal George Campbell, William Wilkie, Adam Ferguson, and Hugh Blair all got something from him because they shared Argyll's attitudes in ecclesiastical matters.

He knew how they would vote in the General Assembly. Filling for about thirty years the 300 or so Scottish livings to which the Crown appointed put his friends in many of them by 1761. Many of his appointees were promoted to other livings. When he solicited favours from others with the right to appoint, he was often successful – which affected local church courts and the membership of the General Assembly.

The Duke's long encouragement of the attitudes espoused by the Moderate Party changed the Kirk's ethos and behaviour. While his men claimed to be and perhaps were sincere Calvinists, the love of God and the moral obligations He has placed upon us, not a limited atonement by Christ and Him crucified, were the usual subjects of their preaching.[36] By 1761, the Kirk had come a long way from the one whose leaders had urged the hanging for blasphemy and atheism of Thomas Aikenhead only sixty-four years earlier. Argyll's clerics were Erastian moderates who let polemical divinity wilt as they pursued polite letters in the form of histories, plays, epics and criticism. Moderate ministers were ridiculed by the orthodox for their interests in politeness and good literature.[37] The Kirk's better places were filled with moralists who might believe mysteries but did not preach about them. They were also the ones who sent the Rev. Dr. John Walker on expeditions to the north to count Roman Catholics and to carry out a natural history survey of the region expected to yield economic benefits.[38]

Scots had long been of two minds about the relation which should obtain between the church and the state. By the late 1720s, the Kirk was dividing. Argyll's men were prepared to see some driven out of the Established Church and tolerated rather than to have them in it making trouble. The long run consequence of this was to make it easier to deprive the Established Church Kirk of independence. Ultimately that would lead to the 1843 Disruption, but in 1761, it seemed to be leading to a more peaceable and manageable country in which the Kirk was chiefly a moral guide and not a salvific force. His patronage helped force that transition. Peace in the Kirk was maintained but at the cost of later schism and division. However, increased toleration would now be supported by tolerated fanatics because they benefitted from it. Argyll's Erastianism and patronage weakened the Kirk in precisely the ways Voltaire would have applauded.

The Duke's civil appointees are harder to assess since his merit tests for them differed. As we have seen (see p. 224), he picked some very bright men for judicial offices. Some were also bankers, investors, improvers or had notable interests in science and its uses. They tended to be among the lay-managers of the Kirk. His Customs and Excise appointees were not so often men of ideas but mere functionaries. Still, among them were improvers like his neighbour, Major Thomas Cochrane, and Lord Provost George Drummond, whose record as an improver of Edinburgh was unequalled by anyone. What is important to remember is that there were limits to what men in those offices could do, and say – limits set by their offices and by his and the government's outlook on politics, religion, and conduct.

Military appointments accounted for much of Argyll's wartime patronage. It was mainly used for political ends. Commissions rewarded the faithful and converted Jacobites and so advanced Scottish interests. How important he was has been made clear by Andrew Mackillop:

That Argyll was able to engross a substantial part of what amounted to an extremely lucrative branch of imperial patronage illustrates something of the metropolitan perceptions that helped shape the British-Highland military and influence its later development. Even prior to 1745, whilst officially no longer in government and facing a challenge for control from John Dalrymple, second Earl of Stair, as well as the Atholl family, Argyll nonetheless established primary if not exclusive right over appointments to Highland units. This continued even when, after Culloden, he faced considerable hostility in other areas of Scottish administration. For example, he was automatically entrusted with the supervising commissions for the Highland companies sent to India in 1748.[39]

The protracted periods of warfare at the mid-century increased his importance in this sphere. Mackillop estimates that 40% of the men commissioned in Scottish Highland raised regiments in 1761 owed their ranks to the Duke. In addition to those places, more were found in regiments such as the 3rd Foot Guards in which his own son served. Argathelian officers such as Generals James St. Clair, John Campbell, Earl of Loudoun; or John Campbell of Mamore had long placed in their regiments Scots whose families belonged to the Argathelian faction and came well recommended. When Argyll died, his grip on the Highlands depended partly on his ability to find commissions for the sons of Highland gentlemen.[40] That task had become easier during his career because war and imperial expansion increased opportunities for military service but also because he was willing to trust Highlanders. Others came to do so when they had served with the Scots.

Military patronage included far more than infantry places. During the period of the 2nd Duke's administration of the Army and the Ordnance Office, men like Major Dougal Campbell of the Engineers, found it relatively easy to get a place if they had the training in mathematics which was required. After 1712, that was given at all the Scottish universities save King's which did teach navigation. Among the problems which Colin Maclaurin tried to solve for his Edinburgh mathematics classes were classic problems such as the angle at which a ship's masts should be stepped to make maximum use of the wind or the length at the waterline which would give the fastest speed. Mathematics was useful. So too was the medical training of Scottish surgeon-apothecaries which included training in both surgical and medical skills. Scots found many places in the medical departments of the services as surgeons. Judging from the names given in the lists for the 1740s and 1750s contained in *Commissioned Officers in the Medical Services of the British Army 1660-1960* (London, 1968) about a third of the medics were Scots or of Scottish descent. Many more trained in Scotland.[41] The cumulative value of this to the country was great. Support for science and medicine kept Scots at the leading edges of those fields until c.1830. Much of Argyll's scientific and medical patronage was possible because he had fostered medical education and insured that good mathematicians were employed as teachers.[42]

Argyll had far less influence in the Navy than in the Army but in the East Indian Company services he had more. Scots whose poverty and demographic pressures had always sent them abroad were willing to serve in East India Company ships and armies. Argyll himself seems to have had little to do directly with East India Company patronage but he had access to some through friends – notably John Drummond of Quarrell. Drummond was from the margins of the Highlands and a man much like Ilay. Both had spent time in Holland. Both had been Tory supporters of Harley in 1710 and both were interested in trade and banking. Both befriended John Law; both speculated in the 'Bubbles'. Between 1725 and his death in 1742, Drummond was a leading director of the East India Company. 'He linked the Argyll interest in the north with EIC contacts in London and the Walpole connection which increasingly depended on an amenable phalanx of Scottish votes in the Commons for support.'[43] By 1731, this connection allowed Ilay to place men, particularly Jacobites, in the Company's civil and military service.[44] Ilay also placed medical men in the East India Company's service which he once remarked was 'overloaded with Scotch Surgeons'.[45] That patronage also had the effect of weaning families which had been 'out' in 1715 or 1745 from the cause of the Pretender. By the time of Drummond's death, Scots had begun to form their own networks in the Company. Increasingly they supplied servants and directors most of whom were allied with the Argathelians. It was this base laid by Drummond and Ilay on which Henry Dundas later built his own position in East Indian patronage.[46]

Outside Scotland, Ilay placed some men in the colonial civil service[47] but he complained that 'American places are generally picked up by A certain species of people who ought not to have them'.[48] Still, placing Scots in the services and abroad led to their enhanced presence in the Empire, to a greater interest in it and, perhaps, for some, eased the problems of later emigration. It certainly made them more acceptable to the English who came to know them better by serving with them in the armed forces.

III. An Economic Legacy

Most Scottish political leaders in the period were keen to see the Scottish economy stimulated and developed but it is not clear that all of them would have been so effective. It mattered that the Dukes of Argyll had been improvers and tree planters and investors in commercial concerns.

Agriculture in all old regime countries except the Netherlands mattered most to the economy. Few followed the programme of the Honourable the Improvers in the Knowledge of Agriculture as far as did the 3rd Duke of Argyll. Like some men in his youth and those in HIKAS, he wanted agriculture taught. He patronized Scottish university professors who taught it. Among them were Cullen and Francis Home who taught courses on agriculture partly because that was approved by Argyll. Argyll read Cullen's unpublished lectures from the 1740s almost as soon as they were written. Those ideas did not die. By 1790, there was a Professor of Agriculture in Edinburgh, Dr. Andrew Coventry. There was also a Professor of Natural History, the Rev. Dr. John Walker, who taught young men how to make the most of the natural resources on and under their estates.[49] Walker became a proponent of Highland development, one with a sympathetic view of Highlanders.[50] Like David Hume, who thought one of the most beautiful things in the world was improved farmland, Argyll would have understood Faust's dying wish – that the moment in which he enjoyed the prospect of improved land might be prolonged.[51] What the Duke was doing was well symbolized in the plate introducing the section on agriculture included in Diderot's *Encyclopédie*.[52] Improving agriculture along the lines they urged led to the prosperous Scottish farms of the early nineteenth century – often owned by Walker's former students.

The rents of the principal Argyll estate rose 40% while managed by the 3rd Duke. To achieve that required the rationalization of land use and the introduction of new methods, new stock, and new management techniques. What they were to be, Argyll showed at The Whim and imposed on his Highland tenants. The costs in Scotland were considerable. A way of life was changed for many – but the mortality experienced by some in the nineteenth century was not visited upon Scots. We should ask what would have been the costs of leaving in place the poor who were evicted in this last British enclosure movement. Was it better they should starve in Morvern or be homesick on farms in New Brunswick or Vermont? The Duke, by running estates modern in their management. showed what might be done to make all estates more profitable. Some of his increased farm incomes went for further improvements.[53] Scottish fishing never became what Argyll hoped it might but his efforts to improve that too were impressive and were continued after him.

It took not only a desire for more income but perhaps an acquaintance with John Law and his ideas to promote the linen industry as Milton and Argyll did. The Board of Trustees and the British Linen Company partially fulfilled Law's old schemes for the better capitalization, production and marketing of linens.[54] The resulting expansion of the industry created employment in Scotland and it helped to settle the country after the '45. After 1753, the importance of the Linen Company as a producer of linen declined but the importance of the Scottish linen trade did not decline until the coming of cotton. Argyll's support of the trade kept Scots employed at the expense of Germans, the Dutch and the Irish. In 1758, he was still acting for the Board of Trustees to keep the protection of the tariffs which disadvantaged 'foreign Linnens'.[55] That raised the cost of linens sold in Scotland but much of the commercial product was sold abroad in protected markets. The trade expanded within an empire having more slaves and kept Scots regularly employed and more prosperous than they might otherwise have been. In Argyll's lifetime, the linen producers, encouraged by the Board of Trustees, continually experimented with new machines, bleaches and dyes, techniques, and even patterns of organization and marketing. Setting premiums for such things elicited novelties. The spin-offs of those innovative activities led to chemical works producing a variety of products that gave employment to mechanics and wrights who could do other things as well. The inventor of new heckles was a maker of threshing machines.[56] When, in the 1760s, the Linen Company became principally a bank, its value to the trade increased. When linen was displaced by cotton, there was less to learn in Scotland than elsewhere.

Agriculture and related industries were not the whole story. The Royal Bank of Scotland, created for private and political ends. was more than a political tool by 1761. Through innovations, like the overdraft provisions introduced by 1728, it lowered the costs of borrowing and made the process less complicated.[57] The Bank kept small cash reserves but issued more notes against its assets than did the Bank of Scotland. It supplied more money to the economy than the 'Old Bank'. By 1761, it had much increased the circulating money of the country. Other Scottish banks followed the Royal Bank's example. Collectively, the Scottish banks constituted a more adaptable system than was available anywhere else but in Holland.

More available capital for farming and business raised employment and may have marginally increased wages in some sectors. While often wages did not rise, they nowhere declined drastically in the face of substantial population growth.[58] When the American Revolution led to a decline in the importance of the Scottish tobacco trade, Glasgow was already a city with a diversified economy served by modern banks. That had happened partly because Argyll and his friends had supported trades other than tobacco through the Board of Trustees, the Convention of Royal Burghs and private members' bills aiding development in Scotland. Argyll played a role in the founding of the Board, of two banks and he frequently aided the Convention, dominated for many years by his friends. By 1761, Scots were poised for a rapid expansion of the economy. Had the country found its patronage managers in Montrose or Marchmont, it is hard to believe that would have happened.

IV. The Effects and Cultural Importance of Patronage

Most patronage managers would have overseen the integration of Scotland into Britain and have done much that Ilay did but few could have had his cumulative impact on the country. Few politicians could have stayed in power for so long a time. To do that required having a large Highland estate. To do that required health, energy and longevity enjoyed by few of his contemporaries. To do that required having political skills lacking in most men. Argyll's regime was unique and its impact on the country the greater for that. While he served English Ministers, aspects of his politics and patronage were his alone. He had clear personal goals which were furthered by his appointments.

Through his appointments, Argyll became as much the real creator of the Scottish Enlightenment as *virtuosi* like Sir Robert Sibbald or philosophers like Francis Hutcheson, David Hume and Adam Smith. He and they resembled the *philosophes* and *physiocrats* who were intent on making similar changes. The continentals were seldom political radicals but, like Argyll, pushed their societies toward tolerance and a more secular society, toward more settled and uniform conditions, and toward the promotion of natural knowledge as the means of improvement even though it might challenge church doctrines and long held traditional views. Power should be used to improve. When it was so used, it justified itself; when it was not so used, it was arbitrary, coercive, and wrong. They all sought to change their worlds – to make them more productive, happier, gentler and more open to change guided by what they took to be reason and utility. Argyll and his friends were utilitarians before the word was coined. The Duke left no great written works but he did leave remarkable monuments. If the Scottish Enlightenment was a 'Hotbed of Genius', it was in one of his gardens. Unlike those at Whitton Place, this lasted to become his principal memorial.

One contemporary who looked at Scotland in his time saw this. In 1763, the Italian traveller, Carlo Denina, cited Argyll and Hutcheson as the men who had been primarily responsible for what we now call the Scottish Enlightenment:

> HUTCHESON, an IRISHMAN, zealous for the advancement of literature, and the generous ARCHIBALD duke of ARGYLE, seem to have been particularly destined by heaven to raise, and to bring to maturity, in the cold regions of the north, what had heretofore been foolishly supposed incapable of taking root but in the warmer climes of ASIA MINOR, GREECE, AND ITALY ... [Argyll] patronised the ingenious with a bounty worthy of himself, and paid particular attention to the university of Glasgow, which has since become one of the most renowned in EUROPE.[59]

Denina went on to say that a 'spirit of literature... nobly animated LONDON' but 'of late, the principal ornaments of the BRITISH literature have received their birth and education in Scotland'.[60] He singled out for special mention natural philosophers and mathematicians: Robert Simson, Colin Maclaurin, [?James[61]] Ferguson and William Cullen. The poets James Thomson and Willliam Wilkie got honourable mention as did Thomas Blacklock, David Mallet and John Home. Among the historians he cited were Tobias Smollett, William Robertson and David Hume, of whom he asked: 'Is there a man of letters in Europe unacquainted with the works of HUME?'[62] Denina praised the Scots for writing the purest English and for being erudite and elegant and enjoying the patronage of a man who valued the ingenious. Seven of the twelve men praised by the Italian had had Argathelian patronage.

Denina also placed the Scots and Argyll in a European context. Hutcheson and the Duke shone as enlightened men and Scotland as a place enlightened by them although no one would talk about a 'Scottish Enlightenment' until c.1900. Everywhere, men such as the Duke, openly or surreptitiously, defended their views and values. Patronizing and protecting men who shared their outlook was a principal means of fostering those values and ideas and allowing them to flourish. Such a process needed the support of men with power. As the eighteenth century wore on, state offices and bureaucracies in much of Europe became centres of enlightened thought and activity with great bureaucrats using their influence to cultivate interests of their own which they believed would benefit their states.[63] Most of the so-called 'enlightened despots' in Italy, Germany, Scandinavia, and Eastern Europe were only as enlightened as their chief ministers. Government functionaries mattered most in states which were not particularly 'enlightened'. Everywhere men like the Duke of Argyll affected the societies in which they lived. How much was changed depended on circumstances. The influence of Anne-Robert-Jacques Turgot, Baron de l'Aulne, as Intendant in the Limousin and then as France's chief minister and later as an advisor to others, was felt in French education, in the development of French science, and in the political and economic spheres.[64] Turgot, unlike Argyll, was in power for a relatively short time and could not change his church or many other institutions. Argyll, effective over a longer time, changed a great deal in a small country.

With the Duke's death, a remarkable man left the scene. He was learned, brave, an astute politician and kind to his friends and family. He did not disavow his illegitimate children or their mother. He put on no airs and stood not on ceremony except on public occasions – which he tended to avoid. He was capable of great generosity but, in political conflicts, he played to win and not always by fair means. As a judge, he was usually intent on being just to those who came before him. Argyll had taste but it ranged over few fields. He possessed a large stock of secular learning and good sense. He adopted fashionable styles but his gardens were not just ornamental; they were for the nation and his own kitchens. He was forward looking and worked at improving schemes all his life. Those brought him into contact with all sorts of men to whom he talked affably and without condescension – unless they cheated him or thwarted him in what he took to be right or necessary. He liked pretty, clever women and Lord Ilay was not unattractive to some of them. He may have seemed dowdy and unkempt to men who dressed more fashionably but few of them mended their own watches or made medicines for their servants. He was very discrete but to intimates displayed a wry and cynical humour. As a young man he had moved easily in the circles of the London wits; as an old one, he promoted the careers of the men who made a great deal of the Scottish Enlightenment. Even in temper, he lived a life which benefited others while it gave pleasure to himself. Complex, but very private, he was what some called him, the Great Duke of Argyll.

Memini!

Notes

Book and newspaper titles are in italics. Dissertations, pamphlets, articles and other short works are not italicized but put in quotation marks. Manuscripts have neither italics nor quotation marks

Chapter 1

1. Throughout the book, references to Archibald Campbell use the title appropriate to the time.
2. Ian Lindsay and Mary Cosh, *Inveraray and the Dukes of Argyll* (Edinburgh, 1973), pp. 177-78; Horace Walpole to Lady Mary Wortley Montagu, *The Yale Edition of the Correspondence of Horace Walpole*, 48 vols, ed. Wilmarth S. Lewis, *et al.* (New Haven, Conn., 1941), 9:358.
3. *Scots Magazine,* 23 (1761), p. 222; [London] *Public Advertiser*, 1 May 1761.
4. *Edinburgh Evening Courant,* 6 May, 1761.
5. [London] *Public Ledger,* 20 May 1761.
6. Gordon to Andrew Fletcher, Lord Milton, SCJ, 1 May 1761, NLS 16720/190. Most of the *Scots Magazine* account of this funeral is given in Alexander, Murdoch, *The People Above: Politics and Administration of Mid-Eighteenth-Century Scotland* (Edinburgh, 1980), pp. 101-102. Murdoch saw this funeral as a 'ritual demonstration of the continued influence and importance of the Argathelian party' but the popular tribute to the Duke rested on affection and recognition of a long career caring for local interests.
7. William Alston to Charles Erskine, Lord Justice Clerk, 14 May 1761, NLS, 5081/128.
8. Memorandum about the late Duke of Argyll's funerals, NLS, 17612/202-209.
9. *Scots Magazine*, 22, p. 222.
10. *Caledonian Mercury,* 18 May, 1761.
11. Patrick Cuming, Of the late Duke of Argyle, NLS, 17774/270.
12. Memorandum about the late Duke of Argyll's funerals, NLS, 17612/202-209. This includes draft lists of those specially invited to attend.
13. *Scots Magazine*, 22 p. 222. Mr. Graham may have been the proprietor of 'the Black Bull Hotel, then known as the Highland Society's House, in this street, which but a short time previously had been named in his [the Duke's] honour'. The hotel stood between Glassford Street and Virginia Street. Hugh Macintosh *The origin and history of Glasgow streets* (Glasgow: "Citizen" Press, 1902 and Glasgow Digital library), unpaginated.
14. NLS, 17612/212.
15. Memorandum about the late Duke of Argyll's funerals, NLS, 17612/202; *London Evening Post*, 23 and 28 May 1761.
16. Lord Milton had organized the Collectors of the Customs to find them.
17. Josiah Corthine to Milton, 13 May 1761, NLS, 16719/155; *Scots Magazine*, 22, p. 222.
18. Among the gentlemen of the clan was Sir Duncan Campbell of Lochnell who in 1754 had raised a memorial to those of the Clan who had died in or as a result of involvement in the uprising of 1685. Among them was Argyll's grandfather.
19. The undertaker had listed as a necessary expense the funeral 'entertainment yn by the Road At Glasgow, Grenock and the place of Interment for the friends of the family and other Gentlemen that voluntarily Assembled to Pay their last duty to so great a man'. NLS, 16719/30.
20. Anonymous, 'A Character of His Grace Archibald Duke of Argyll 1761', NLS, 17612/218-221.

21. Quoted from Edmund and Dorothy Berkeley, *Dr. John Mitchell: The Man Who Made the Map* (Chapel Hill, 1974), pp. 145-46.
22. John, Lord Hervey, *Memoirs of the Reign of King George II*, 3 vols, ed. Romney Sedgwick (London, 1931), I: 296.
23. Horace Walpole, *Memoirs of King George II*, 3 vols, ed. John Brooke (New Haven, Conn. and London, 1985), III: 178-186. The others so honoured were George II, Prince Frederick and his brother, the Duke of Cumberland, Henry Fox, the Duke of Bedford, William Murray, Lord Mansfield, the Duke of Newcastle, Henry Pelham and William Pitt. All save Argyll have been the subjects of much historical writing and editing.
24. That was not Sir Robert Walpole's view. He defended Argyll for having tried to keep his Ministry from falling. Walpole, *Memoirs of King George II,* I:187-88.
25. Tobias Smollett, *The History of England from the Revolution of 1688 to the death of George II*, 6 vols (London, 1810), III:344.
26. *The Structure of Politics in England in the Age of the American Revolution*, (2nd ed. London and New York, 1961). Namier's remarks on Argyll deal almost exclusively with his relationship to Argyll's nephew, the 3rd Earl of Bute.
27. J. H. Plumb, *Sir Robert Walpole*, 2 vols (London, 1960); Reed Browning, *The Duke of Newcastle* (New Haven, Conn., and London, 1975); J.B. Owen, *The Rise of the Pelhams* (New York and London, 1971; 1st ed. 1951).
28. John Wilkes, *A Whig in Power: the Political Career of Henry Pelham* (n. p., 1964), p. 247.
29. The Earl of Ilay never spelled his name with an 's'. Moreover, it was spelt without the 's' in the London newspapers of the time. The persistent use of 'Islay' by historians points to an unfamiliarity with his letters and with him.
30. J.D. Mackie's *The Short History of Scotland* (Edinburgh and London, 1962), p. 282.
31. William Ferguson, *Scotland:1689 to the Present* (Edinburgh and London, 1968), pp. 137-38.
32. *Ibid*, pp. 143-44.
33. *Ibid*, pp. 151, 155, 236.
34. *Ibid*, p. 147.
35. Rosalind Mitchison, *A History of Scotland* (2nd ed. London, 1982), p. 371.
36. *Ibid*, pp. 326, 343.
37. T. C. Smout, *A History of the Scottish People 1560-1830* (2nd ed., London, 1970).
38. Richard Savile, 'Banking Archives and Scottish History', *Scottish Archives*, 3 (1997), pp. 12-19.
39. Michael Symes, Alison Hodges and John Harvey, 'The Plantings at Whitton', *Garden History*, 14 (Autumn, 1986), pp. 139-40.
40. Shaw, *Management*, pp. 123, 48. Shaw cites other contemporary estimates of Ilay provided by the Rev. Robert Wodrow, Professor William Cross, Henry Pelham and his brother, the Duke of Newcastle; and Alexander Hume, 2nd Earl of Marchmont. Of those men, only Cross was a friendly witness – and he may have been hoping for patronage. See also, Edmund and Dorothy Berkeley, *Dr. John Mitchell*, pp. 108-11, 144-51, 244.
41. Murdoch's account, *The People Above: Politics and Administration of Mid-Eighteenth-Century Scotland* (Edinburgh, 1980) has affinities with Eric G. J. Wehrli's 'Scottish Politics in the Age of Walpole', unpublished Ph.D. Dissertation (Edinburgh University, 1983). Like Murdoch and Scott, Wehrli underestimated Ilay's power.
42. Murdoch, *People Above*, p. 34.
43. *Ibid*, pp. 38, 50-51.
44. *Ibid*, pp. 32-33.
45. *Ibid*, p. 83.

46. See, *E.g.*, John M . Simpson, 'Who Steered the Gravy Train, 1707-1766?' in *Scotland in the Age of Improvement*, ed. Rosalind Mitchison and N. T. Phillipson, (Edinburgh, 1970), p. 34. Some contemporaries did see Ilay both as a monopolist of power and the servant of English masters; see Thomas Somerville, *My Own Life and Times, 1741-1814* (Edinburgh, 1861), p. 380.
47. Murdoch, *People Above*, p. 34.
48. *Ibid*, p. 33.
49. Richard Scott, 'The Politics and Administration of Scotland 1725-1748', unpublished PhD dissertation (Edinburgh University, 1982), pp. 357-59.
50. *Ibid*, pp. 357-58.
51. *Ibid*, pp. 553-560.
52. He may have prepared a paper on the planting of pine trees for the Royal Society of Arts; Berkeley and Berkeley, *Dr. John Mitchell*, p. 149. He also produced a judgement, 'The Decreet-Arbitral of Lord Ilay' in *Set of the City of Edinburgh: with the Acts of Parliament and Council Relative thereto*, ed. John Robertson (Edinburgh, 1783), pp. 40-51. There are other short essays which may be by him; (see below pp. 154, 160, 404 n. 47).
53. William Coxe, *Memoirs of the Life and Administration of Sir Robert Walpole, Earl of Orford*, 3 vols (London, 1798) and *Memoirs of the Administration of the Right Honourable Henry Pelham*, 3 vols (London, 1829).
54. Sir Robert Douglas, *The Peerage of Scotland, containing An Historical & Genealogical Account of the Nobility of that Kingdom*, 2 vols (2nd ed. revised & corrected with a continuation by J.P. Wood; Edinburgh, 1813), I:115.
55. Personal letter from the Duke of Argyll, 24 January 2000. The following books, partly written out of that archive, contain almost nothing on the 3rd Duke: *The Argyll Papers*, ed. Thomas G. Stevenson (Edinburgh, 1834); *Intimate Society Letters of the Eighteenth Century*, 2 vols, ed, John Douglas Sutherland Campbell, 7th Duke of Argyll; *The Clan Campbell: Abstracts of Entries relating to Campbells in the Sheriff Court Book of Argyll at Inveraray*, ed. Henry Paton (Edinburgh, 1913); Alastair Campbell of Airds, *A History of the Clan Campbell*, 3 vols (Edinburgh, 2000, 2002, 2004); *Fourth Report of the Royal Commission on Historical Manuscripts, Part I. Report and Appendix... The Manuscripts of His Grace the Duke of Argyll, K.T.* ed. William Fraser (London: 1874). The last item notes that the manuscripts at Inveraray were then ill preserved and of little interest, a comment recently borne out by the paucity of references to them contained in Robert McGeachy's *Argyll 1730-1850* (Edinburgh, 2005) and even in Alastair Campbell of Airds's account of this period in *A History of Clan Campbell*, Vol. III.
56. Diary of Andrew Fletcher, Auditor of Exchequer, NLS, 17745- 17750.
57. Roger L. Emerson, *Professors, Patronage and Politics: the Scottish Universities in the Eighteenth Century* (Aberdeen, 1991), *passim*.
58. This is not true with respect to banking; for Ilay's role in this field see Chapter 13.
59. John Ramsay, *Scotland and Scotsmen in the Eighteenth Century*, 2 vols, ed. Alexander Allardyce (Edinburgh and London, 1888), I:87. The uncut manuscript of this work is in NLS 1635.

Chapter 2

1. This well preserved seventeenth-century house is now a National Trust property open to the public and easily accessible from London. In Lord Archy's childhood, the house was much darker. The centre hall was not opened until sometime between c.1698 and 1728 when the ground floor hall ceiling was cut away to form a first floor gallery lit by large

windows. Ham House was renowned for its gardens which are not so impressive today. In Lord Archy's childhood, it had many exotic shrubs and flowers displayed in formal beds but it also included a 'wilderness', an orangery and was graced by summerhouses and statuary. 'Ham House Surrey' (National Trust, 1995).

2. D. H. Sellar, 'The Earliest Campbells', *Scottish Studies*, 17 (1973), p. 114; Alastair Campbell, 'The House of Argyll: the Rise of Clan Campbell' in *The Argyll Book* (Edinburgh, 2006), pp. 140-150; 140. Another mythical account has them coming into Scotland with 'Fergus the Second from Ireland to assist the Scotch against the Picts in 404', Robert Campbell, *The Life of the Most Illustrious Prince, John, Duke of Argyll and Greenwich...*, (London, 1745), p. 5.

3. More are listed by John Stuart Shaw, *The Management of Scottish Society 1707-1764* (Edinburgh, 1983), p. 46.

4. *Instructions to a Son, Containing Rules of Conduct in publick and private Life, Under the following Heads: Religion. Marriage. The Court. Friendship. Travelling. Housekeeping and Hospitality. Tenants and other Concerns of Estate. Study and Exercise. Of Pleasure, Idleness, &c. By Archibald Marquis of Argyle. Address'd to his Children, and to his eldest Son in particular. Written in the Year 1660, during his Confinement. To which are added by the same Noble Author: General Maxims of Life. Maxims Political and Military, under the following heads: The Prince. War. Courage. Command. Fortune. Victory. Miscellaneous Observations* (Glasgow: Printed by R. Foulis, and sold by him there; at Edinburgh, by Mess: Hamilton and Balfour, 1743).

5. His 'Declaration ... to conveen for the Defence of ther Religion, lives and liberties' is printed in *Culloden Papers*, no editor (London, 1815), pp. 11-12. The 9th Earl was a Fellow of the Royal Society of London and interested in natural history.

6. John S. Shaw, 'Archibald Campbell, 1st Duke of Argyll', *ODNB*, 9:724-25.

7. Like many such conversions, this may not have involved much more than appearing to conform to the King's religion. Had there been more to it, he would not later have been so acceptable to Presbyterians.

8. Alastair Campbell, *A History of the Clan Campbell*, 3 vols (Edinburgh, 2000, 2002, 2004), III:64-65.

9. Christopher Whately, *The Scots and the Union*, (Edinburgh, 2006), p.81.

10. That the Earl used to pacify the west of Scotland and to punish those who had devastated his lands. In 1692, it was soldiers from the Earl's regiment who massacred the MacDonalds of Glencoe. That act was officially censured and long remembered by the victims.

11. The Earl of Argyll to William Carstares, 8 August 1700, in *State-Papers and Letters Addressed to William Carstares...*, edited by Joseph M'Cormick (London and Edinburgh, 1774), p. 599.

12. *Ibid*, p. 600.

13. Quoted in 'Archibald Campbell', in Robert Chambers, ed. *A Biographical Dictionary of Eminent Scotsmen*, 4 vols (Glasgow, 1856), IV: 489. Those were names which in England went back at least to the 1660s.

14. 'Inveraray Castle' [a tourist brochure for the Castle](Derby, 1982), p.11; James Holloway, *Patrons and Painters: Art in Scotland 1650-1760* (Scottish National Portrait Gallery, Edinburgh,1989), p. 36; *see Plate 1*

15. Robert Campbell, *The Life of John, Duke of Argyle*, p. 89. For other similar assessments, see Alastair Campbell, *A History*, pp. 100-01 and Sir Robert Douglas, *The Peerage of Scotland*, 2 vols, ed. John Philip Wood (Edinburgh and London, 1813), I:106.

16. Rosalind Mitchison, 'Elizabeth Murray, Duchess of Lauderdale' in *ODNB*, 39: 892-93

17. Ham House had been his wife's since the death of her father in 1655. Some of its present decoration is thought to have been designed by the Countess and Duke. When the Countess died in 1698, the house went to the 3rd Earl of Dysart. Lord Ilay visited his relatives and their splendid garden even though Ilay and the 4th Earl did not share the same political views.

18. Argyll Papers, NLS, Adv. 29.3.5/75.

19. After her separation from the 1st Duke, the Duchess of Argyll and her two sons lived at Brunstane and perhaps in Duddingston. The first house was bought by the 2nd Duke of Argyll in 1736 and inherited by the 3rd Duke in 1743. In 1747, he sold it to Andrew Fletcher, Lord Milton, who had lived in it for some time. He had it extensively renovated and enlarged by William Adam between 1735 and 1744. John Gifford, Colin McWilliam, David Walker and Christopher Wilson, *Edinburgh* (in *The Buildings of Scotland* series, London, 1984), pp. 557-58; For Brunstane see also, John Gifford, *William Adam 1689-1748* (Edinburgh, 1989), pp. 155-158. On 23 January 1726, the dowager Duchess made over Duddingston to Lord Dysart as security for a debt owed to Montrose. NLS, 2967/6. For records of the ownership of Duddingston House, see Dennis B. White, *Exploring Old Duddingston and Portobello* (Edinburgh, 1990), Appendix III, pp. 212-216.

20. One commentator calls it a 'private brothel', Paul Hopkins, *Glencoe and the End of the Highland War* (Edinburgh (1986; 2nd ed. 1998), p. 16.

21. *The Argyll Papers*, ed. Thomas G. Stevenson (n.p., 1834), p. xliv; A. Campbell, *A History*, p. 101.

22. *The Argyll Papers*, pp. xlvi.

23. Christopher Whately, *Scottish Society 1707-1830* (Manchester and New York, 2000), p. 27; Ian Lindsay and Mary Cosh, *Inveraray and the Dukes of Argyll* (Edinburgh, 1973), p. 121-22.

24. *The Clan Campbell Abstracts of Entries relating to Campbells in the Sheriff Court Book of Argyll at Inveraray* [and other places], 8 vols, ed. Henry Paton (Edinburgh, 1913), IV:278.

25. *Ibid*, IV:278.

26. Anderson, *Scottish Nation*, I:564. There are letters concerned with the management of her estate in the papers of her 'doer', James Anderson, W. S., NLS, Adv Ms 29.5.1.

27. Col. Charles Mactaggart, 'The Limecraig Duchess', *Kintyre Antiquarian & Natural History Society Magazine*, Web Edition, 13 January 1998.

28. Scottish Papers, Scotland Series II, Vol, IV, held at NLS in Adv. Ms. 22.2.20 and at the National Archives, London.

29. Mactaggart, 'Limecraig Duchess', *Ibid*.

30. Argyll Papers, NLS, Adv. MS 29.3.5/24.

31. The others were Patrick Campbell of Monzie, later a SCJ, Colonel Allen Campbell of Finab, who had fought in the family's regiment, John Campbell, merchant and later Lord Provost of Edinburgh, and Ronald Campbell, W.S. By 1718/19, the Duchess was no longer on his list probably because relations between her and her sons were troubled. The new commissioners for the Duke were John Campbell, Duncan Forbes, depute-advocate and MP, George Drummond, merchant and government official, and Ronald Campbell, W.S. Argyll Papers, NLS, Adv.Ms. 29.3.5/82, 89.

32. Lydia Maria Menzies to Lord Milton, 12 May 1735, NLS 16562/152.

33. It is not clear that John, then aged five, saw the beheading of the his grandfather but he may well have done so. Children were not always spared such sights. Indeed, such events inured them to conduct they might well be expected to emulate and certainly established in their minds ideas and standards which they were uphold. John is said to have fallen out a third story window that day. Patricia Dickson, *Red John of the Battles: John Second Duke of Argyll and First Duke of Greenwich 1680-1743* (London, 1973), p. 20.

34. *Ibid*.

35. John Stuart Shaw, *The Political History of Eighteenth-Century Scotland* (London and New York, 1999), p. 65.

36. Dickson, *Red John*, p. 22.

37. Improvement of the Inveraray estate began long before 1700 since both the 9th Earl of Argyll and his son, the 1st Duke, were improvers and planters of trees, partly because they had mounting debts. The 2nd Duke worked as an improver because his estate was encumbered with debts in his youth.

38. Christopher Whately has many references to Ilay's career and to his role in Scottish development in the period 1707-1761, *Scottish Society, passim*. See also, Whately's *Scots and the Union* (Edinburgh, 2006), pp. 365-66.

39. Dickson, *Red John*, p. 22; Alexander Murdoch, 'John Campbell, 2nd Duke of Argyll', *ODNB*, 9:814. This says Cunningham was tutoring Lord Archy as late as 1698. If that was the case, then he may have accompanied him to Eton for some of his time there. It is likely that John also had some tuition from Robert Sinclair, who became Professor of Mathematics at Glasgow University; Roger L. Emerson, *Academic Patronage in the Scottish Enlightenment: Glasgow, Edinburgh and St Andrews Universities* (Edinburgh, 2008), pp. 35-36, 214.

40. *The Lockhart Papers*, 2 vols, ed. Anthony Aufrere (London, 1817), I:394. What is known of Lockhart's early education is told by Daniel Szechi, *George Lockhart of Carnwath 1681-1731*, (East Linton, 2002), p. 18-19.

41. Eton College has 'no complete list of boys who were not King's Scholars. R. A. Austen Leigh compiled *The Eton College Register 1698-1752* (Spottiswoode & Ballantyne, 1927) using a variety of mainly non-Etonian sources and he says the Duke was here in 1698. However, he gives no original source for this statement and there are no archival records from which I can confirm it'. Letter to me from Mrs. P. Hatfield, the College Archivist, 2009. If Archy was there in the spring of 1698, then he could have entered Glasgow in the autumn and matriculated, as was usual, in the following spring. Staying two years would have put him in Utrecht in the summer or fall of 1700.

42. Ilay to James Stuart MacKenzie, 29 September (o.s.) [1738], Bute Papers, Mount Stuart House. I thank Alexander Murdoch for drawing this letter to my attention. Ilay had a dim view of English Universities which he thought taught well only classics. Ilay to Milton, 5 January 1739, NLS, 16776/73. He 'attacked their sinecure Professors' in a Lords debate in 1736. Ilay to Milton, 29 May 1736, NLS, 16564.

43. *Munimenta alme universitatis glasguensis: Records of the University of Glasgow from its Foundation till 1724*, 4 vols, ed. Cosmo Innes (The Maitland Club, Glasgow, 1854), III: 166. Lord Archy is said by the author of his entry in the *Scots Peerage* to have gone up to Glasgow at age sixteen but no source for this information is given. That is a rather late date and one which suggests that he was at Eton from about age nine or ten until he was fifteen or sixteen.

44. J.D. Mackie, *The University of Glasgow 1451-1951* (Glasgow, 1954), pp. 139, 144.

45. *Ibid*, p. 144.

46. Christine M. Shepherd, 'Newtonianism in the Scottish Universities in the Seventeenth Century' in *The Origins and Nature of the Scottish Enlightenment* ed. R. H. Campbell and A. S. Skinner (Edinburgh, 1982), pp. 74-75.

47. Robert Sinclair succeeded George Sinclair as Professor of Mathematics on 13 March 1699.

48. Emerson, *Academic Patronage*, pp. 35-36.

49. Papers of David Gregorie, Edinburgh University Library, EUL, Dk.1.2. 21 /B/23 -28. If Sinclair had taught Lord Lorn, then he almost certainly owed his Glasgow place to the Earl of Argyll, who would have been anxious to take care of a former family tutor with the College's money.

50. T*he Correspondence of the Rev. Robert Wodrow*, 3 vols, ed. Thomas McCrie (Wodrow Society Edinburgh, 1842, 1843), I:470-72.

51. Emerson, *Academic Patronage*, p. 30.

52. Wodrow to James Fraser, 26 February 1722, in *The Wodrow Correspondence*, III:628.

53. Memorandum about the ffamily of Argyll May 1761, NLS, 17612/214-224. That includes A Character of His Grace Archibald Duke of Argyll 1761 (f.218).

54. The lists can be found in *Munimenta*, III:155-165.

55. Sir John Clerk claimed that in 1694 there were nearly 80 Scots at Utrecht but only 10 at Leiden; Kees Van Strien and Margreet Ahsmann, 'Scottish Law Students in Leiden at the End of the Seventeenth Century: The Correspondence of John Clerk, 1694-1697', *LIAS* 19 (1992), pp. 281, 318; Esther Mijers, *News from the Republick of Letters: Scottish Students, Charles Mackie and the United Provinces, 1650-1750* (Leiden, 2012), pp. 91-92, 193-96.

56. Van de Water, the Utrecht University printer, published many modern philosophical and religious works and some translations of English books. He was an associate of the Rotterdam Scottish book-dealer, Thomas Johnson, an important link between the learned in Britain and the Netherlands. Mijers, *News*, pp. 138, 145. See n. 59.

57. Mar and Kellie Manuscripts, NRS, GD124/15/222/1-5; 'Letters from James Erskine, Lord Grange to Thomas Erskine of Pittodry', ed. John Stuart, *Miscellany of the Spalding Club*, 5 vols (Aberdeen, 1841-52), III:25. I thank Dr. Anne Skoczylas for the last reference.

58. John Cairns, *The Teaching of Law in Eighteenth Century Scotland*, forthcoming;
___, 'George Mackenzie, The Faculty of Advocates & the Advocates' Library' in *Oratio Inauguralis* eds. John Cairns and A. M. Cain, (Edinburgh, 1989); pp. 18-86;
___, 'John Spotswood, Professor of Law: A Preliminary Sketch', *Stair Society, Miscellany Three*, ed. W. M. Gordon,(1993), pp. 131-159.

59. What is being described here roughly fits the pattern of development sketched by Morris Berman in *Social Change and Scientific Organization: The Royal Institution, 1799-1844* (London, 1978). Berman saw science as 'part of the aristocracy's hegemonic apparatus' and tended to see science teaching during the eighteenth century as 'a type of finishing school education' for the gentleman amateurs who pursued it (pp. 22-23). It may have been so in England but for Scots, like Sir Robert Sibbald or Sir John Clerk, it came earlier than 1700 and was more than a polite amusement. Their vision of knowledge-based improving schemes enlisted increasing support throughout the eighteenth century and led to a significant amount of professionalization in chemistry which was expected to contribute to both industry and agriculture from at least c.1740.

60. Roger L. Emerson, 'Natural philosophy and the problem of the Scottish Enlightenment', *Studies on Voltaire and the Eighteenth Century*, 242 (1986), 243-291;
___, 'Sir Robert Sibbald, Kt., The Royal Society of Scotland and the Origins of the Scottish Enlightenment', *Annals of Science* 45 (1988), pp. 41-72.

61. Esther Mijers, 'Scots Students at Utrecht', unpublished paper given at the 2000 joint meeting in Toronto of the Canadian Society for Eighteenth Century Studies and the Eighteenth-Century Scottish Studies Society.

62. Argyll was said in 1763 to be able to write a letter in six languages; *A letter to the Author of the North Britain... with a Striking Character... of the late Duke of Argyll* (London, 1763), p. 41.

63. Hebrew was an arts subject although it was taken mostly by those intending to become ministers.

64. Nicholas Phillipson claims that Lord Archy studied chemistry with Hermann Boerhaave in Leiden but he gives no evidence for this implausible claim. Boerhaave began to teach medicine in 1701 and gave a chemistry course in 1702. Lord Archy almost certainly

spent part of the winter of 1701-02 in Utrecht. He went to Hanover early in 1702. It is likely that he was travelling outside Holland during those summers. Phillipson in Robert Anderson, Michael Lynch, and Nicholas Phillipson, *The University of Edinburgh: An Illustrated History* (Edinburgh, 2003), p. 63.

65. John Cairns, 'Alexander Cunningham's Proposed Edition of the Digest: an Episode in the History of the Dutch Elegant School of Roman Law (Part I)', *The Legal History Review*, 69 (2001), pp. 81- 117 (37); Shaw, *Political History*, p. 25.

66. *Memoirs of the Life of Sir John Clerk of Penicuik ...*, ed. John M. Gray, Scottish History Society, 1st Series, vol. 13, 1892; pp. 15-16.

67. Those were classes he was not required to teach but offered in the university for a fee. Many Scottish professors by the 1730s were giving them too.

68. Alexander Murdoch puts his Italian tour in 1699-1700. If he went then, Lord Archy would not have gone with his brother and Cunningham. 'Archibald Campbell, 3rd Duke of Argyll', *ODNB*, 9:726-733.

69. Horatio F. Brown, *Inglesi e Scozzesi all' Universita dall'annon 1618 sino al 1765. (Monografie Storiche sullo Studio di Padova* (Venezia, 1922), p. 183, No. 1132. This book shows at least eleven Scots visiting from 1 January 1699 - 1 January 1703. They included a number of men with whom Ilay would later deal. An Alexander Cunningham was there for the third time in 1702.

70. For the information about the movements of Cunningham and Lord Lorn, I thank John Cairns.

71. Mar and Kellie Manuscripts, NRS, GD124/15/222/3.

72. In his political career, foreign affairs seem not to have greatly concerned him. He had no qualms about fighting Louis XIV and during peacetime he was concerned with foreign trade. Serving Walpole, he advocated peace in 1739 when his brother was for war with Spain. In the 1740s and early 1750s he was for balancing powers by aiding Austria and destroying the alliance between France and Prussia. After 1754, his support went to defeating the French and seeing to it that Scots were enrolled in the forces doing that. The Empire concerned him because it offered opportunities to Scots.

73. Memorandum about the family of Argyll, NLS, 17612/214-224; 214, 218.

74. The *Scottish Peerage* says he got a commission after his father became the 1st Duke in 1701. Murdoch, too, thinks he took his first commission in 1701 following his father's elevation to the dukedom. Alexander Murdoch, 'Archibald Campbell, 3rd Duke of Argyll, *ODNB*, 9:725. Ilay was still in Holland in early 1702 and does not appear in the scant surviving correspondence with a military title.

75. As Governor, Ilay probably was paid about £200 a year but the Crown did not get much for that. In 1710 the Castle was ruinous, its walls were reported breached and its twelve brass guns dismounted. It had no shot or powder and lacked its full complement of about eight officers and 100 soldiers. William Cobbett, *Parliamentary History of England From the Norman Conquest, in 1066 to the Year 1803*, (London, 1810), Vol. VI, Column 773.

76. If he had served in the dragoons before, it was probably with the 4th Dragoons or Royal Scots Greys since this was the Scottish dragoon regiment with the longest history and most prestige. If this was his unit, then he fought close to his brother. Under the command of Thomas, Lord Tiviot, the Scots Greys fought in the sieges of towns in the border area between France and Holland. For most of the campaigns of 1702 and 1703, it was mostly used by Marlborough as cavalry for reconnaissance and raiding. In 1703, it captured a supply train with a large amount of bullion and, in 1704, it played a notable part in the Battle of Schellenberg or Donauworth. Some weeks later, it fought at Blenheim and then returned to the Netherlands. Two other dragoon regiments were then

commanded by Scots, the 7th and 9th, but they were not Scottish regiments. This Captain
Campbell is unlikely to have served in them.

77. Henry Scott, 1st Earl of Deloraine, a friend and ally of the brothers, succeeded
   MacCartney as Colonel. See also *The Marlborough-Godolphin Correspondence*, ed.
   Henry L. Snyder, 3 vols (Oxford, 1975), II:755; *Letters of George Lockhart of Carnwarth
   1698-1732*, ed. Daniel Szechi, Scottish History Society, 5th series, vol.2; p. 26. I thank the
   Rev. Dr. Alexander Campbell for the date of Ilay's commission in the 36th Regiment of
   Foot.
78. Sidney Godolphin to John Churchill, 1st Duke of Marlborough, 30 January 1709,
   Marlborough-Godolphin Correspondence, III: 1212.
79. The regimental history suggests it was Newfoundland; Richard Cannon, *Historical
   Record of the Thirty-sixth or the Hertford Regiment of Foot ...1701...1852* (London,
   1853), p. 19.
80. Godolphin to Marlborough, 20 and 28 April, 1710, *Marlborough-Godolphin
   Correspondence*, III:1459, 1475.
81. *Ibid*, III:1446, 1459, 1464, 1475.
82. *HMCR, House of Lords Manuscripts*, New Series, 1710-12, ed. M.F. Bond (London,
   1949), IX:52. Lord Castleton thought Ilay had resigned his Colonelcy two years after the
   battle of Almanza which was fought on April 25, 1707. Castleton to the Earl of Oxford, 4
   June 1712, *HMCR Portland MSS*, X:79.
83. J.H. Plumb, *Sir Robert Walpole The King's Minister,* 2 vols, (London, 1960), I:157.
84. Anon., *A Letter to the Author of the North Briton*, p. 41-42.
85. I thank Mr. A.M.J. Hyatt for this information.
86. Ilay's earliest financial records begin 20 January 1713 and are to be found in his 'In' and
   'Out' books at Coutts Bank in the Strand.

Chapter 3

1. *The Coltness Collections*, ed. James Dennistoun, Maitland Club, vol. 58, (Edinburgh,
   1842), p.86. For accounts of his tumultuous time in office, see P. W. J. Riley, *The Union
   of England and Scotland* (Manchester, 1978), pp. 114-161; Michael Fry, *The Union:
   England, Scotland and the Treaty of 1707*, (Edinburgh, 2007), pp. 153-198; Christopher
   Whately, *The Scots and the Union*, (Edinburgh, 2006) pp. 226-269.
2. Angus MacInnes, *Robert Harley Puritan Politician* (London, 1970), p. 95.
3. The Convention of Royal Burghs survived the Union as a body made up of representatives
   from the sixty-six Royal Burghs many of which were insignificant and decayed towns. It
   met yearly and, when not in session, was represented by a standing commission. It acted
   as a lobbying group for the Scottish business community but its members were often not
   merchants but local lairds who had interests in the prosperity of their towns. Argathelians
   like Duncan Forbes, Charles Erskine, George Drummond, Patrick Lindsay and others
   often sat for the burghs near their estates of those from which they came. The Campbells
   virtually appointed the men who sat for Inveraray and Campbelton and, with their relatives,
   could usually count on naming representatives to Rothesay and Ayr. The larger towns
   were generally represented by merchants but the Convention as a whole was composed of
   politicians who spoke as much for their political factions and interests as for the merchants
   and tradesmen whom they nominally represented. Argathelians tended to be less important
   in its affairs from 1705 to 1720 but from 1723-1746 and from 1748-1761 they more or less
   dominated its proceedings. There is little evidence of Ilay's direct interference in it. He was
   an administrator who believed that his men would act in his interests if they knew them.

That they did. Argathelian influence and direction in the Convention came from men like George Drummond and the provosts of the important towns who often also sat as MPs. The Convention of Royal Burghs approached Argyll for more help in 1707; Minute Books of the Convention of Royal Burghs, ECA, SL/30/1/1/8 1705-1712. p. 65.

4. Antoin Murphy, Law's most recent biographer, says that Argyll was not a supporter of the scheme but that Lord Archy was; Murphy, *John Law Economic Theorist and Policy-Maker* (Oxford, 1997), p. 72. That claim seems disputed by George Lockhart of Carnwath who wrote that Law was a favourite of both the Duke of Argyll and the Squadrone who backed his plans. *The Lockhart Papers*, 2 vols, ed. Anthony Aufrere (London, 1817), p. 117.

5. Law's mother was a Campbell but it is not clear that she was related to the ducal family. Law's father, an Edinburgh goldsmith, had lent money to the Campbells of Argyll in the 1670s and 1680s. The brothers kept in contact with Law for the rest of his life. Murphy, *John Law*, p. 15; Law to the Duke of Montrose, 29 September 1712, Montrose-Lennox Papers, NRS, GD220/5/380.

6. I have described this elsewhere in more detail. See, Roger L. Emerson, 'The Scottish Setting of Hume's Political Economy' in *Essays on David Hume's Political Economy*, ed. Margaret Schabas and Carl Wennerlind (New York, 2005), pp. 1-32.

7. These are all noticed in Law's 1705 pamphlet 'Money and Trade Considered with a Proposal for supplying the Nation with Money' (Edinburgh, 1705); see also, Michael Fry, *The Union: England, Scotland and the Treaty of 1707* (Edinburgh, 2007), pp. 133-136.

8. Mar to David Nairn, 19 October 1706, NRS, Mar and Kellie Papers, GD124/15/449/38.

9. *Lockhart Papers*, 1:435; The 'authorized' view of Duke John's remit and success can be found in Robert Campbell, *Life of the Most Illustrious Prince, John, Duke of Argyll and Greenwich...* (London, 1745; Belfast, 1745), pp. 96-100.

10. P.W.J. Riley, *The Union of England and Scotland* (Manchester, 1978), pp. 175-177. Riley says that neither the Duke, Ilay nor Lothian, their uncle, had places on the Commission much to the Duke's chagrin.

11. Lord Archibald was 'one of the Commissioners of the Treaty' by the time the Earl of Loudoun solicited his earldom from Godolphin. Patricia Dickson, *Red John of the Battles: John Second Duke of Argyll and First Duke of Greenwich 1680-1743* (London, 1973), p. 169, n.1. Campbells voting for the Union are listed in Alastair Campbell, *A History*, III:101.

12. William Cobbett, *Parliamentary History of England From the Norman Conquest in 1066 to the Year 1803* (London, 1810), vols VI: Appendix, p. clxxxi.

13. Riley, *The Union*, p. 256.

14. Had he done much, he would have appeared in the accounts of the debates given by Sir John Clerk and George Lockhart: *'Scotland's Ruine':Lockhart of Carnwarth's Memoirs of the Union*, ed. Daniel Szechi (Aberdeen, 1995); *History of the Union of Scotland and England by Sir John Clerk of Penicuik*, trans., ed. and abridged by Douglas Duncan (Scottish History Society, 5th series, Vol. 5, Edinburgh, 1993).

15. Christopher Whately, *Scots and the Union*, p. 287.

16. Nearly all the petitions were against the Union; many were inspired by clerics who preached against it. Argyll called the petitions 'paper kites'; T. M. Devine, *The Scottish Nation*, (New York, 1999), p.9.

17. His library catalogue shows that he possessed works by most of the notable 17th and 18th century economic writers – Scottish, English and foreign; see *Catalogus librorum A.C. D.A.* (Glasgow, 1758), section 10, 'Misscellanei'.

18. Blackness probably paid him about as much as Dumbarton and was what the Earl got after asking for an appointment in a Guards Regiment. David Nairne to ?Lord Mar, 9 May 1707, Mar and Kellie Papers, NRS, GD124/15/517/2. Ilay had earlier been in debt to

the notorious Col. Francis Charteris who had written the Duchess of Argyll that he was unwilling to extend the time of his loan to Lord Archy but would have him imprisoned for debt. Charteris to the Duchess of Argyll, 11 January 1705, *The Argyll Papers*, ed. Thomas G. Stevenson (Edinburgh, 1834), p. 124. Charteris in 1724, when in legal trouble, had the Earl's support (NLS, 16529/13). More importantly, in 1730, when Lord Milton told Ilay that the Colonel was guilty of rape, the Earl said he would have him fined not hanged. Ilay joked, saying that he would 'do the fellow any good I can' but that the only way to do that was by making light of him and his case. 25 February, ? February, 14 March 1730, NLS, 16542/34, 36, 42. One suspects he liked this distant relative despite his evil propensities. In 1739, Ilay was a guardian to Charteris's grandson whom he sent to Eton, then abroad, and finally had confined on a Chancery warrant because he would not obey his tutors. Ilay to Milton, 13 August 1739; 3 June 1740, NLS 16576/117; 16580/85.

19. A. S. Turberville, *The House of Lords in the XVIIIth Century* (Oxford, 1927), p. 148.
20. Mar to David Nairn, 8,13 and 19 October 1706; Mar to James Erskine, Lord Grange, 29 October 1706, Mar and Kellie Papers, NRS, GD124/15/449/31, 34, 38, 39 and 47; Riley, *The Union*, p. 256; Fry, *The Union*, pp. 222-23.
21. The clearest short account of the Scottish politics of the period is that of John Shaw, *The Political History of Eighteenth Century Scotland* (New York and London, 1999), pp. 23-62.
22. William Coxe, *Memoirs of the Life and Administration of Sir Robert Walpole, Earl of Orford*, 3 vols (London, 1800), I:235; 'Lord Islay speaks very well and solidly [he has] a great knowledge of the law civilian' [1730]; Joseph Spence, *Observations, Anecdotes and Characters of Books and Men*, 2 vols (Oxford,1966), I:283.
23. See Appendix II in which his attendance record is tabulated and his committee assignments are categorized in general terms.
24. While he might have had more general influence as a minister sitting in the Commons, that role might not have allowed him such a long run as the Scottish manager during which he did much permanent good.
25. Alexander Murdoch, *The People Above: Politics and Administration in Mid-Eighteenth Century Scotland* (Edinburgh, 1980); pp. 9-10. Duke John certainly saw it as drudgery. The brothers' grand niece, Lady Louisa Stuart, in writing of the brothers said, 'The Duke thought Lord Islay undignified and time-serving' and, in return, 'Lord Islay thought the Duke wrong-headed and romantic'. *The Letters and Journals of Lady Mary Coke*, 4 vols (facsimile ed New York,1970; 1st edn. Edinburgh, 1889-1896), I: xxiii.
26. These and later comments about his finances are taken from the typescript transcript records of his 'In' and 'Out book', ledger accounts with George Middleton, his banker, whose firm survives today as Coutts Bank. The expenditure on plate may point to his trading in old silver since he later did deal in precious metals.
27. I thank John Shaw for that information.
28. *Calendar of State Papers Belonging to His Majesty The King Preserved at Windsor Castle* [no editor listed] (London, 1902). V:232.
29. *The HPHC 1690-1715*, 6 vols, eds. Eveline Cruickshanks, Stuart Handley and D. W. Hayton (Cambridge, 2002), V:858.
30. Law to Montrose, 29 September 1712, Montrose Muniments, NRS, GD220/5/380.
31. Among the first entries in Ilay's bank account in January 1713 are monies received from and sent to 'Mr. Law'. John Law had been convicted of murder in 1694 and sentenced to death. He fled. As an outlawed felon, he could not act in Britain in his own name.
32. The Coutts ledgers do not seem to show Ilay buying books and instruments but it would be surprising if he had not begun to collect his library and purchase instruments before 1718 when the first of the purchases were made from an instrument maker who can be identified.

33. He voted for the 'Jew bill' in 1753 (it allowed Jews to be naturalized and to hold landed property) but he does not seem to have spoken for it (see p. 322).

34. P. W. J. Riley, *King William and the Scottish Politicians* (Edinburgh, 1979), p. 117.

35. Mar and Kellie Manuscripts, NRS, GD124/15/517/1 and 2.

36. Nairne to Mar, 1 June 1708, NRS, GD124/15/840/3; 831/8, 34; *The Letters of Joseph Addison*, ed. Walter Graham (Oxford, 1941), p. 90.

37. Joseph Addison to Charles Montague, 7 February 1708 in *Letters of Addison*, p. 90.

38. Murdoch, *People Above*, p. 28.

39. Bruce Lenman, *The Jacobite Risings in Britain 1689-1746* (London, 1980), pp. 88-90.

40. William Robertson, *Proceedings Relating to the Peerage of Scotland from January 16. 1707, to April 29, 1788* (Edinburgh and London, 1790), p. 31.

41. *HPHC 1690-1715*, ed. D.W. Hayton (Cambridge, 2002) I:228-29.

42. *Ibid*, I: 228-29.

43. *Ibid*, I:511-12; 515.

44. P. W. J. Riley, *English Ministers and Scotland* (London, 1964), p. 146. *The Marlborough — Godolphin Correspondence*, ed. Henry Snyder 3 vols (Oxford, 1975), III:1212, 1225, 1227.

45. J. H. Plumb, *Sir Robert Walpole*, 2 vols (London 1956), I:157.

46. A. S .Turberville, *The House of Lords in the XVIIIth Century* (Oxford, 1927), pp. 95, 140.

47. *The Correspondence of James Clavering*, ed. H. T. Dickinson, The Surtees Society, 178, (1968), p. 108.

48. *Journals of the House of Lords 1707-1761*, vols 18-30 (London, 1709-1763); *JHL*, vol.18, 3 February 1710; he was again elected to the committee to address the Queen on 15 February 1712; *JHL* 19. By then, he had also begun to appear on committees to consider engineering and building projects. By the end of his career, he had probably sat on over 200 of those (see Appendix VII, Table II).

49. *JHL*, 18, 28 February 1710.

50. Angus McInnes, *Robert Harley Puritan Politician* (London, 1970), p. 95-96; Geoffrey Holmes, *The Trial of Doctor Sacheverell* (London, 1973), pp. 212, 227-28, 240; Riley says the brothers were consistent in not supporting the Tories and not voting against the Junto to which the Squadrone men were allied. *English Ministers* and Scotland, p. 147, 150; Cobbett, *Parl Hist*, VI: column 886.

51. One of Argyll's speeches on this was 'a general attack upon clerical influence. In all ages the clergy had delivered up rights and liberties of the people, and preached up the royal power, in order to control it themselves. The moral was that they ought not to be allowed to meddle in politics'. Turberville, *House of Lords*, p. 95.

52. Holmes, *Sacheverell*, p. 228; Lord Orrery to Robert Harley, ?14 March 1710, *HMCR of the Manuscripts of His Grace the Duke of Portland* (London, 1891), IV:537.

53. *The Correspondence of James Clavering*, p. 73. He and his brother were said to have been effective in this debate. Clyve Jones and Geoffrey Holmes, *The London Diaries of William Nicolson, Bishop of Carlisle 1702-1718* (Oxford, 1985), p. 97.

54. Holmes, *Sacheverell*, p. 228.

55. On 1 March, Argyll commanded the troops of the 1st Foot Guards and the Horse Guards who were kept in readiness to resist the rioters who had created disturbances in the city. Holmes, *Sacheverell*, p. 172.

56. Godolphin to Marlborough, 17 April 1710, *Marlborough-Godolphin Correspondence*, III: 1464.

57. *Ibid*, III: 1459; Holmes, *Sacheverell*, p.240. That would have been Ilay's stance as well.

58. *Letters of Addison*, p. 232.

59. Peter Wentworth, writing to his brother Thomas on 8 December 1710, said that it was rumoured that Ilay was to replace Queensberry in that office but it went to the Earl of Mar. *Wentworth Papers 1705-1739...* ed. James J. Cartwright (London, 1883), p. 161.

60. This was probably to do with the elections but it might have concerned the reform of the courts and administration since he later seemed interested in that. Ilay to Mar or Lord Grange, 1710, NRS, GD124/15/1004/2.
61. Orrery to Robert Harley, 31 July 1710, *HMCR Portland Manuscripts* (London, 1891), IV:553.
62. Mar to Grange, 22 and 29 July 1710, NRS, GD125/15/975/8, 11. Mar thought Argyll was out only for himself and was probably playing up to the Squadrone.
63. James Erskine, Lord Grange, to Mar, 12 and 20 July 1710, Mar and Kellie Papers, NRS, GD124/15/975/5 and 7. Mar to Grange, 6 June 1710, NRS, GD124/15/975/2.
64. Ilay to Mar or Lord Grange, n. d. [1710] and August 1710, Mar and Kellie Papers, NRS, GD124/15/1004/1 and 2; Ilay to Principal John Stirling of Glasgow, 6 July 1710, GUL, Murray Manuscript 651/100. Ilay promised in this letter to defend the Kirk, to help the universities and not to 'deviate from such steps' as his martyred grandfather would have taken were he still alive.
65. P. W. J. Riley, *English Ministers*, p. 171.
66. Mar to Grange, 22 January, 12 July 1710, NRS, GD124/15/975/3, 5; 18 February, 12 July 1710; NRS, GD125/15/ 975/3; 5; 7.
67. Their families and supporters had clashed earlier in elections; *HPHC 1690-1715*, 1:154.
68. Mar, Argyll, Hamilton, Ilay and Loudoun tried to make a list but could not agree even though the Queen was told there was one. Mar to Harley, *HMCR Portland Manuscripts*, X:349-50.
69. *Lockhart Papers*, I:344; Mar to Harley, 7 November 1710, *HMCR Portland Manuscripts*, X:349- 50.
70. Orrery to Harley, 29 August 1710, *HMCR Portland Manuscripts*, IV:568; Peter to Thomas Wentworth, 8 December 1710, *Wentworth Papers*, p. 161.
71. William Stratford to Edward, Lord Harley, 6 September 1710. *HMCR Portland MSS*, p. 198.
72. *HPHC 1690-1715*, I:517.
73. *Ibid*, I:521-22.
74. Riley, *English Ministers*, p. 147.
75. Earl of Orrery to Harley, 31 July 1710; Duke of Hamilton to Harley, 19 October 1710, *HMCR Portland Manuscripts*, IV:553, 616. Ilay was being mentioned for a diplomatic post by John Drummond on 8 August 1710, *Ibid*, 4:560. A bit later, Drummond thought he might be sent as minister to Hanover, 25 November 1710 or 1711, *Ibid*, 5:110.
76. Ilay to Carstares, 8 December 1709; *State-Papers and Letters Addressed to William Carstares...*, ed. Joseph McCormick (London and Edinburgh, 1774), p. 779. Lockhart described this meeting: ' ...there was a meeting betwixt some of the Scots Tory members and the Earl of Ilay, attended by Mr. Carstairs and two or three more Presbyterian brethern [William Mitchell and ?], who had been sent to negotiate the affairs of the Kirk, expecting some blow would be levelled at it'. He went on to say that Ilay and his cousin, the Earl of Loudoun, argued for modifying the Abjuration Oath to make it acceptable to more Presbyterians while still being difficult for Episcopal dissenters, mostly Jacobites, to swear. *Lockhart Papers*, I:379-380. For more on the religious issues see, Robert Story, *William Carstares....* (London, 1874), pp. 314-350.
77. Ilay to Carstares, 8 December 1709; *State Papers*, I:799.
78. Mar to Grange 18 February 1710, NRS, GD124/15/975/4.
79. Ilay to Principal John Stirling of Glasgow University, 6 July 1710, Stirling Letters, 3 vols GUL, MS 204, p. 100.
80. Ilay to Carstares, 5 July 1710, *State Papers*, pp. 786-87.
81. *Lockhart Papers*, I:379-81; Jones and Holmes, *Nicolson Diaries*, p. 5.
82. *Ibid*, I:531.

83. *Ibid*, I:523.
84. Lord Balmerino to Henry Maule, *Letters of Lord Balmerino to Henry Maule*, ed. Clyve Jones, Scottish History Society, Miscellany 12, (1994), p. 124.
85. *Letters of Balmerino*, p. 124. Argyll seems not to have had a position on the question at that time.
86. Turberville, *House of Lords*, p. 114f.
87. *HMCR, House of Lords Manuscripts, New Series 1712-1714*, ed. M. F. Bond, (London, 1949), IX:235.
88. A. Ian Dunlop, *William Carstares* (Edinburgh, 1964), p. 135.
89. *The Correspondence of Robert Wodrow*, 3 vols, ed. Thomas McCrie, Wodrow Society (Edinburgh, 1842, 1843), II:111.
90. For the background to their views see Story, *William Carstares*, pp. 328-335; Jones and Holmes, *Nicolson Diaries*, p. 573.
91. Principal John Stirling to Lord Oxford, 11 October 1712, *HMCR Portland Manuscripts*, X:282. Ilay also delivered addresses from the Synods of Perth and Sterling. Principal Stirling to Lord Oxford, 11 October 1712, *Ibid*, X:439, 282.
92. Ilay to Principal Stirling, 30 October 1712 and 1 November 1712, Stirling Letters, GUL, Murray MS 651/3:156-7.
93. Ilay to ?, 13 October 1712, NLS, 2208/24.
94. For a discussion of the issues involved here and how they changed over time see, Colin Kidd, *Union and Unionisms Political Thought in Scotland, 1500-2000* (Cambridge, 2008).
95. There is no evidence that he was either. See Anne Skoczylas, 'The Regulation of Academic Society in Early Eighteenth-Century Scotland: The Tribulations of Two Divinity Professors', *Scottish Historical Review*, (88) 2004, pp. 171-195; pp. 178-187. Ilay became one of Scrymgeour's defenders. See also, Wodrow, *Analecta*, 1:197,198; 2:587; William Dunlop to Andrew Dunlop, n.d. (? 1718), GUL, Gen. 83; PRO, SP54/20 item 22.
96. Robert Campbell, *Life of the Most Illustrious Prince, John, Duke of Argyll and Greenwich* (London, 1745), p. 283.
97. Stirling to Montrose, 10 March 1715, NRS, GD220/5/472/7.
98. Minute Books of the Convention of Royal Burghs 1705-12, ECA, SL 30/1/1/8, p. 191. The resolution referred to here said that this task would have fallen to the Duke of Hamilton had he survived the 1712 duel in which he was killed by Lord Mohun – an event which rid the Campbells of a competent, adult competitor.
99. Hamilton's case was hard. Because he was a British peer created after the Union, he could not sit in Parliament. Because he was a British Peer, he was excluded from the Scottish Peerage elections. Nowhere had he a vote.
100. Peter Wentworth to Thomas Wentworth, 21 November 1711, *Wentworth Papers*, p. 229; *HMCR, Papers of the House of Lords, New Series 1710-1712*, ed. M. F. Bond, (HMSO, London, 1949), XIX:346. He later moved to make the sitting of Peers alterable by Parliament 'at the request of the Peers of Great Britain who were Peers of Scotland before the Union'. *Ibid*, XIX:365.
101. George Baillie to Patrick, 1st Earl of Marchmont, 1 January 1712, *HMCR on the Manuscripts of Lord Polwarth* ..., ed. Henry Paton (London, 1911), I:5. Ilay, Hamilton and Mar drafted the memorandum to the Queen. Ilay had proposed in the debate in the Lords that the rule baring Hamilton from sitting in the House be made amenable to the Treaty of Union by being specifically requested by the Scots peers whose titles existed at the time of the Union which would have meant a veto by the Scots. *Lords Manuscripts, New Series, NS 1710-12* (London, 1949), IX:174.
102. *JHL*, Vol. 18, 20 December 1711.

103. *Lockhart Papers*, I:394. Many wanted him out of the way, they were not willing to give him much to go.
104. Balmerino to Maule, 16 January 1711; 3 April 1711, *Letters of Balmerino*, pp. 123, 128.
105. *Ibid*, p. 123.
106. Alastair Campbell, *A History*, III:103-4.
107. Shaw, *Political History*, p. 52.
108. This had happened as Harley, now the Earl of Oxford, tried to funnel patronage not only through Mar but Seafield; Murdoch, *People Above*, p. 29.
109. Riley, *English Ministers*, p. 240; Murdoch, *ODNB*, IX:725. John Shaw thought this was more likely 1712; certainly it would have been before May 1713. Whatever it was, Ilay could not have afforded it without a salary larger than would have been provided.
110. Ilay to Harley, 14 April 1711, *HMCR Portland Manuscripts,* IV:673.
111. Ilay to Harley, 7 June 1713, *Ibid*, V:294.
112. Robertson, *Proceedings*, p. 61.
113. Balmerino to Maule, 12 May 1713 OS, *Letters of Balmerino*. pp. 99-168; p. 152.
114. Lockhart, 'Scotland's Ruine', p. 276. This also tells us that Ilay either wore a ring cut with a pointed diamond or had a fob or other device holding a diamond with which to cut the glasses. Those were things for dandies. His accounts show him occasionally buying rings, some with diamonds.
115. Balmerino to Maule, 26 May 1713, *Letters of Balmerino*, p. 153.
116. *Ibid*, pp.152-53; *Letters of George Lockhart of Carnwath 1698-1732*, ed. Daniel Szechi, (Edinburgh, Scottish History Society, 5th series, 1989) pp. 76-81, 76;
117. 'A Letter from a P[e e r]. In North Britain to the Right Honourable the E. of I _ _ a'. (n.d. but 1715 or 1716) in National Library of Scotland Pamphlet Series, 1.10, No. 131 and in *The Argyll Papers*, NLS, Adv.Ms. 29.3.5/109.
118. Cobbett, *Parl. Hist.*, VI: column 1215.
119. *Letters of George Lockhart*, pp. 80-1.
120. Balmerino to Maule, 2 June 1713, *Letters of Balmerino*, pp. 155-56.
121. *JHL*, Vol. 19, 8 June 1713.
122. Reported by Tobias Smollett, *The History of England from the Revolution in 1688 to the death of George II...*, 6 vols (London, 1810), II:465.
123. Cobbett, *Parl. Hist.*, VI: column 1217.
124. The analogy had been offered by Lord Peterborough, another General who had been in Spain and was a rival to Argyll. Smollett, *History*, II:465; Balmerino to Maule, 2 June 1713, *Letters of Balmerino*, p. 155.
125. Ilay to the Earl of Oxford, 7 June 1713, *HMCR Portland Manuscripts*, V:294-95. Duke John could also be ironical as he was when he congratulated Francis Atterbury, Dean of Westminster for being made Lord Privy Seal. William Stratford to Edward, Lord Harley, The same writer said that in November 1714, Argyll and Marlborough wanted to ruin Oxford. 2 August 1714; *Ibid*, VII:198, 208.
126. Balmerino to Maule,6 June 1713, *Letters of Balmerino*, p. 60.
127. Editor's commentary, *Letters of Balmerino*, pp. 115-16.
128. Ilay to Morton, 20 August 1713, Morton Papers, NRS, GD150/3/3466//9; 'A letter from a P --- in North -Britain' claims that Ilay had been wholly sincere in his arguments and that he had not 'pursued it only in Resentment against the then Ministry'.
129. Riley, *English Ministers,* p. 251.
130. *HPHC 1690-1715*, V:567-68.
131. 'A Letter from a P — in North-Britain'.
132. *Intimate Letters of the Eighteenth Century*, ed. George Campbell, 8th Duke of Argyll, 2 vols (London, n.d.), I:15. This work relies heavily on Wodrow's *Analecta*.

133. Captain John Ogilvie to Oxford, July 1713, *HMCR Portland Manuscripts*, X:282.
134. I thank Daniel Szechi for this information.
135. This was probably William Stewart, MP, who lived sometime with Ilay but served both brothers for many years. However, it might be Walter Stewart, Lord Blantyre, who inherited his title in 1710. Lockhart reported that Ilay regretted having been opposed to the Pretender; *Lockhart Papers*, I:395, 435.
136. *Ibid*, undated but 1710-13, I:394-95.
137. Riley, *English Ministers*, p. 244; Basil Williams, *Stanhope: A Study in Eighteenth-Century War and Diplomacy* (Oxford, 1932), p. 138.
138. Montrose-Lennox Papers, NRS, GD220/5/382/13.
139. Turberville, *House of Lords*, p. 130.
140. Ragnhild Hatton, *George I Elector and King* (Cambridge, Mass., 1978), p. 109.
141. John Hill Burton, *History of Scotland*, (Edinburgh and London), 1898, VIII:250.
142. Montrose-Lennox Papers, NRS, GD220/5/339; 340/1; 340/2.
143. Ilay was in the Lords for the debates on the Riot Act passed in July 1715 which became effective on 1 August of that year. He would later invoke it more than once.
144. Duke John has been claimed for the Jacobites by Evelyn Cruickshanks in *Political Untouchables* (New York, 1979) but her evidence is not convincing.
145. Mar to Grange, 10 August and 1 September 1714, NRS, GD124/15/1129/8 and 9.
146. Mar to Lord Grange, 7 August 1714, Mar and Kellie Papers, NRS, GD124/15/1117. Mar expected to be sacked and replaced by Montrose.
147. Peter to Thomas Wentworth, 24 September 1714, *Wentworth Papers*, p. 422.
148. Charles Cockburn to Montrose, 30 December 1714, NRS, GD220/5/13.
149. John Chamberlayne in *Magae Britanniae Notitia of the Present State of Great Britain...* (London, 1723; Part II, p. 12) gave its value as just over £444.
150. Cockburn to Montrose, 30 December 1714, Montrose Papers, NRS, GD220/5/382/13.
151. Duncan Forbes to CP, *More Culloden Papers*, II:68. Forbes was an Argathelian. Others said there was 'much crying against a[gyll] and I[lay] both by Whigs and Jacobites over their partial distribution of places, esp[ecially those that have always stuck fast to the Protestant Succession]', Cockburn to Montrose, 12 October 1714, *HMCR Montrose Muniments*, p.369. In a letter two weeks later, Cockburn complained about the number of Campbells running for election; pp. 371-72.
152. William Stratford to Edward, Lord Harley, ? November 1714, *HMCR Portland MSS*, VII:208.
153. John to Duncan Forbes, 4 March 1715, *Culloden Papers*, p. 37.
154. Shaw, *Political History*, pp. 54-56.
155. Montrose-Lennox Papers, NRS, GD 220/5/340/3.
156. In a surviving letter to the Earl of Morton which may be typical of those he wrote, he said that for the past three years he had tried to serve 'in all matters where our Country has been concerned'. He had opposed injuries to Scotland which he hoped 'will not turn to my prejudice'. Ilay to Morton, NRS, GD150/3466.
157. John Forbes to Duncan Forbes, 4 March 1715, *Culloden Papers*, p. 36.
158. Morthland to Stirling, GUA, 27115.
159. See Murdoch, *People Above*, p. 34.
160. 'A Letter from a P— in North-Britain'.
161. Ilay to Carstares, 5 July 1710; *State Papers*, pp. 786-89.
162. See Murdoch's perceptive comments on this, *People Above*, pp. 37-39.
163. *Lockhart Papers*, I:393.
164. Ilay perhaps received something as an Extraordinary Lord of Session (1708-1761), although this post was not one which was remunerated at a later date. The Lord Justice

General's place (1710-1761) was worth about £1,000 in 1715. The Earl would have had perhaps £200 for his Governorship of Dumbarton Castle and probably found small change in minor offices. By May 1713, and very likely earlier, he was investing with John Law. He continued to do so for the next decade. John Drummond to Harley, 8 May 1713, *Portland Manuscripts*, V:287.

Chapter 4

1. Ilay to MacLaine, 4 April 1715, NRS, GD174/1217/2.
2. Montrose-Lennox Papers, NRS, GD220/5/455/52.
3. John Forbes to Duncan Forbes, 30 April 1715; *Culloden Papers*, no editor (London, 1815), p. 38.
4. John Robertson, *The Scottish Enlightenment and the Militia Issue* (Edinburgh, 1985), p. 51-52.
5. Daniel Szechi, *1715 The Great Jacobite Rebellion* (New Haven, Conn., and London, 2006), pp. 40-101. Szechi's study supersedes earlier ones.
6. Bruce Lenman, *The Jacobite Risings in Britain 1689-1746* (London, 1980), pp. 130-39; ____, 'The Episcopal Clergy and the Ideology of Jacobitism' in *Jacobitism and Conspiracy: Aspects of Jacobitism (1689-1759)*, ed. Eveline Cruickshanks (Edinburgh, 1982); *Ibid*, pp. 202-03; Bruce Lenman, pp. 36-48.
7. *Memoirs of the Life of Sir John Clerk of Penicuik ...*, ed. John M. Gray, Scottish History Society, 1st Series, vol. 13 (1892), p. 89.
8. Szechi, *1715.* p. 119.
9. Szechi, *1715*, pp. 202-03.
10. Patricia Dickson, *Red John of the Battles: John Second Duke of Argyll and First Duke of Greenwich 1680-1743* (London, 1973), p. 189. Montrose had been dismissed as Scottish Secretary before Argyll was appointed in the hope that there would be less friction between those who had to repress the Rebellion. Montrose's replacements as the Secretary of State, was General Charles, Townshend. 2nd Viscount Townshend. After the Rebellion was put down, the Duke of Roxburgh became Scottish Secretary. Basil Williams, *Stanhope: A Study in Eighteenth-Century War and Diplomacy* (Oxford, 1932), p. 181.
11. Ilay to My Lord [Townshend], 20 September 1715, NRS, SP54/8/72.
12. ?Charles Cockburn to Montrose, 23 September 1715, Montrose-Lennox Papers, NRS, GD220/5/468/28.
13. Ilay to My Lord, 20 September 1715, NRS, SP54 8/72. He also told his correspondent that had the government spent one twentieth of the money the Rebellion cost to avoid one, they could have done so.
14. Szechi, *1715*, p. 170.
15. Ilay noted in a letter to London that the previous Lord Provost, Sir George Warrender, was not of their side and had not taken sufficient steps to defend the town. Ilay to My Lord, 29 September 1715, NRS, SP54/8/120.
16. Ilay to My Lord, 26 September 1715, NRS, SP54/8/106.
17. Ilay to My Lord, 26 September 1715, NRS, SP54/8/104.
18. *Ibid*.
19. Ilay to My Lord, 26 September 1715, NRS, SP54/8/112. This letter also says that he wanted the troops paid in Scottish bank notes. This looked back to a nostrum of John Law but, as Ilay noted, the troops would know that the money would only be good if the Jacobites were defeated.
20. Ilay to My Lord, 29 September 1715, NRS, SP54/8/120 and 121.

21. 'A Letter from a Gentleman in Fife to his Friends in Edinburgh' in NRS SP54/9/80; Robert Campbell, *Life of the Most Illustrious Prince, John, Duke of Argyle and Greenwich*, (London,1745), p. 185.

22. Szechi, *1715*, p. 191.

23. Those men claimed to have been pressed into service and ill-used. James Cockburn to Mr. ? Pringle, 4 November 1715, NRS, SP 54/10/20. Alastair Campbell believes Ilay was really angry at Finab's failure; Szechi thinks Ilay may have feigned anger and 'quietly negotiated an armistice in the west that preserved Argyllshire and the Jacobites' clan territories there pretty much inviolate throughout this period'. Neither Argyll nor Ilay were above making or conniving at such a deal which would have been to everyone's advantage – as the devastation of the region thirty years later showed. Finab remained a favourite of Ilay. Alastair Campbell, *A History of the Clan Campbell*, 3 vols (Edinburgh, 2000, 2002, 2004). III:112-14; Szechi, *1715*, p. 191-92.

24. A. Campbell, *A History*, III:113.

25. Robert Wodrow to Robert Black, 8 November 1715; *The Correspondence of Robert Wodrow*, 3 vols, ed. by Thomas M'Crie, (Edinburgh, 1842-43), II:87. Evidence of the disaffection of the gentlemen of the Campbell lands can be found in Campbell, *A History*, III:106-110.

26. Unattributed source cited in A. Campbell, *A History*, III:113.

27. William Ferguson, *Scotland:1689 to the Present* (Edinburgh and London, 1968), pp. 67-69; Szechi agrees with the ratio and gives about 9,000 as the size of Mar's force, *1715*, p. 15; Sir John Clerk thought Mar had about 12,000 men and Argyll 4,000. Clerk, *Memoirs*, p. 92.

28. This battle was notable for the presence of Scots noblemen. For the Jacobites: Mar, Huntley, the Earl Marischal, Lord Sinclair and many Highland chieftains were on the field. For King George, the noblemen included Argyll, Ilay, Loudoun, Lauderdale and Belhaven - all Argathelians - and for the Squadrone, Roxburghe, Rothes, Haddington and Montrose. Among the volunteers and officers were many with whom Ilay would work (or oppose) for the rest of their careers.

29. That was the opinion of Andrew Henderson, the biographer of the Earl of Stair and a soldier in the '15. *The Life of John Earl of Stair* (London, 1748; printed 1747), p. 167.

30. See, for example, Henderson's *Life of Stair*, p. 167; Szechi, *1715*, p. 158.

31. *Ibid*, p. 159.

32. *The Argyll Papers*, ed. Thomas Stevenson (Edinburgh, 1834), p. 15.

33. The following day Argyll wrote to Lord Townshend saying that Ilay had been twice wounded in unspecified places; Argyll to Townshend, 14 November 1715, NRS, SP54/10/48. There are other accounts of his wounds. Alexander Carlyle said he had a foot wound *(Autobiography*, p. 401). Another story had him taking three bullets: one in the leg, thigh, side or arm and being left on the field, probably in the centre. Another says he was hit in the side and leg. The Earl was important enough so that the London papers carried reports of his being shot, *E.g., The Daily Courant* for 19 November 1715.

34. 'A Copy of Three Letters, giving an Account of the total Defeat of the Rebels at Preston in Lancashire' (Edinburgh, 16 November 1715), p. 3. An Argyll letter of the same date says Ilay was in 'a fair way'. NRS, SP54/10/54.

35. 'A Breaft acct. of the life of Archd Duke of Argyll'. NLS, Acc 8168/1/3.

36. Alexander McGill worked on buildings at Brunstane, The Whim and Inveraray Castle. He was employed by the government and by Lord Mar. John Gifford, *William Adam 1689-1748* (Edinburgh, 1989), pp. 127-28; Ian G Lindsay and Mary Cosh, *Inveraray and the Dukes of Argyll* (Edinburgh, 1973), p. 25.

37. Dickson, *Red John*, p. 182.

38. Mar said dragoons under Argyll's command gave no quarter for some time after the

breaking of the rebel line. NRS, SP54/10/45.

39. Argyll went south with letters from a number of rebels asking for a 'general indemnity'; Dickson, *Red John*, pp. 192-94.

40. Stair to Montrose, Paris, 28 and January 1716, Montrose-Lennox Papers, NRS, GD220/5/624/1 and 2.

41. Anonymous, 'A Letter to the Author of the North Briton' (London, 1763); p.41. One of the Earl's obituaries says that Ilay led '5,000 men in arms for the government'. If he did so, it must have been successively and at the different sites at which he saw action.

42. Lovat to Duncan Forbes, 5 March 1716, *Culloden Papers*, p. 41.

43. Adam Cokburne, Lord Justice Clerk, to Ilay, 6 December 1715, SP 54/10/112; NRS, SP54/10/146.

44. *The Lord Provosts of Edinburgh 1296-1932* (Edinburgh, 1932), pp. 61-62. His men won again in 1719 and 1723.

45. ?Charles Morthland to ? Mungo Graham of Gorthy, [Montrose's chief agent in Scotland], 9 January 1716, Montrose-Lennox Papers, NRS, GD220/5/1918/2.

46. Charles Morthland to Montrose 24 January 1716, Montrose-Lennox Papers, NRS, GD220/5/628/2. This election was a defeat for the Hamilton interest and for the Duke of Montrose.

47. This phrase from the House of Lords' address to the King is quoted from J. H Plumb, *Sir Robert Walpole*, 2 vols (London, 1960), I:220.

48. *Diary of Mary Lady Cowper.... 1714-1720*, no editor (London, 1744), pp. 102-03. He was not supporting yearly Parliaments but advocating the repeal of the bill.

49. John Stuart Shaw, *The Management of Scottish Society 1707-1764*, (Edinburgh,1983), pp. 41-85. There is also much on this topic scattered through Alexander Murdoch's *The People Above: Politics and Administration in Mid-Eighteenth-Century Scotland* (Edinburgh,1980).

50. A more or less comprehensive list of them is found in 'Abstract and Condescendance of His Grace the Duke of Argyll's Titles...' (Edinburgh, 1748). This document was drawn up to show what jurisdictions the government had bought in 1747.

51. Shaw lists 'Lothian, Sutherland, Lauderdale, Bute, Buccleuch, Loudoun, Breadalbane, Crawford, Home, Moray, Caithness, Eglinton, and Rosebery.' *Management*, p. 46.

52. Members from both groups had opposed the Occasional Conformity Act (1711) and the Schism Act (1714) which was meant to close Dissenting schools in England.

53. Dickson, *Red John*, p. 199.

54. Duncan Forbes to Sir Robert Walpole, August 1716, *Culloden Papers*, p. 65.

55. *Culloden Papers*, pp. 61-65.

56. *Calendar of Stuart Papers belonging to His Majesty The King preserved at Windsor Castle* [no editor listed] (London, 1902), II:200.

57. Major General Joseph Wightman to Duncan Forbes, 18 March 1716, *Culloden Papers*, NLS, 2965/75; Dickson, *Red John*, pp. 196-200; Shaw, *Management*, p. 59.

58. *Lockhart Papers*, I:594.

59. *The Diary of Dudley Ryder 1715-1716*, trans. and ed. by William Matthews, (London, 1949), p. 267.

60. Ilay to Milton, 9 December 1725, NLS, 16531/55.

61. Ilay to Lovat, 27 March 1716, *Culloden Papers*, p. 44.

62. Sir Hugh Paterson to ?, 28 May 1716. *Stuart Papers*, I:193.

63. Culloden Papers, NLS 2965/37; *Diary of Mary Lady Cowper... 1714- 1720* (London, n.d.), p.102-03; *A Collection of Parliamentary Debates*, ed. William Cobbett, Vol.VI, (Dublin, 1741), pp. 379, 381.

64. Joseph Addison, *The Freeholder*, ed. James Leheny (Oxford,, 1979), p.1, n.4; William

Cobbett, *Parliamentary History of England From the Norman Conquest, in 1066 to the Year 1803* (London, 1811), vols VI-XV, VII: 302-3.

65. Ryder, *Diary*, 15 April, 1716, p. 220; A.S.Turberville, *The House of Lords in the XVIIIth Century* (Oxford, 1927), pp. 164-65.
66. *Stuart Papers* II:122; The brothers had clashed with him earlier over those bills in 1711 and 1714; Edward Calamy, *An Historical Account of My Own Life,* ed. John T. Rutt (London, 1829), II:243.
67. George Drummond to Duncan Forbes, 19 April 1716, *Culloden Papers* NLS, 2965/130.
68. David Forbes to Duncan Forbes, 21 June 1716, *Culloden Papers*, NLS, 2965 /133.
69. Ilay to Archibald Campbell of Stonefield, 25 November 1745, Campbell of Stonefield Papers, NRS, GD14/48.
70. Walkinshaw of Barrowfield to the Earl of Mar, 29 July 1716, *Stuart Papers*, II:316.
71. Dickson, *Red John*, p.197; ? to Montrose, 30 June 1716, Montrose-Lennox Papers NRS, GD220/5/821/12a; *HMCR Polwarth MSS*, I:36.
72. Lady Mary Cowper, *Diary*, 7 July 1716, p. 111.
73. Lovat to Duncan Forbes, 28 July 1716, Culloden Papers, NLS, 2965/157.
74. Ragnhild Hatton, *George I Elector and King* (Cambridge, Mass., 1978), pp. 198-99. Basil Williams thought the plot was real and that Sunderland was using it to play off Townshend and Walpole against Stanhope. Williams also thought Townshend favoured Argyll. Williams, *Stanhope*, pp. 242, 245.
75. William Coxe, *Memoirs of the Life and Administration of Sir Robert Walpole, Earl of Orford*, 3 vols (London, 1798), II:143,145-46, 158-62. If Ilay was not dealing with them, he certainly looked for the ouster of Stanhope and Sutherland, Coxe, *Walpole*, II: 148.
76. Coxe, *Walpole*, II:143.
77. Ilay to Bute, 1716, Quoted in William Ferguson in *Scotland:1689 to the Present* (Edinburgh and London, 1968), pp. 137-38. *Bute Manuscripts in HMCR Report 5*, p. 618.
78. There are full accounts of this in the sections devoted to the individual universities in Roger L. Emerson, *Academic Patronage in the Scottish Enlightenment: Glasgow, Edinburgh and St Andrews Universities* (Edinburgh, 2008). It was feared that Argyll would protect the Principal of King's College, Aberdeen, because he was a relative of the Duke's friend, Brigadier John Middleton. David Brown to Robert Wodrow, 2 November 1716, NLS Quarto Letters of Wodrow, XI/256. That did not happen it but may explain why Ilay was offered the Chancellorship of King's College and University at this time. He turned it down. He probably thought the right of appointment belonged to the King and not to the University Senate which had made the offer. Roxburghe had reservations but accepted when it was then offered to him. *Officers of the University and King's College Aberdeen*, ed. Peter J. Anderson (Aberdeen, New Spalding Club, 1893), p. 5; See also Emerson, *Professors, Patronage and Politics*, pp. 42-43.
79. Emerson, *Academic Patronage*, pp. 414-16.
80. Tobias Smollett, *The History of England*, II:580.
81. Emerson, *Academic Patronage*, pp. 92-94.
82. The committee reported on 22 June 1716; *Culloden Papers*, NLS, 2965/137.
83. George Drummond to Duncan Forbes, 2 July 1717, *Culloden Papers*, NLS, 2965/251.
84. *JHL*, Vol. 21; 11 March 1718; Cobbett, *Parl. Hist.* VII:553-4.
85. *JHL*, Vol 21, 11 March 1718.
86. *JHL*, Vol. 21; 20 and 24 February 1718; Cobbett, *Parl. Hist.*, VII:548- 48. Sunderland, Stanhope, Cadogan, and Roxburghe supported the bill.
87. See: P. W. J. Riley, *English Ministers and Scotland 1707-1727* (London, 1964), p. 271.
88. *HPHC 1715-1754*, 2 vols, ed. Romney Sedgwick (Oxford and New York, 1970), 1:512-13.

89. *HPHC 1715-1754*, I:26. Ilay seems again to have opposed Stanhope and Sutherland in 1720 when they proposed an aggressive policy toward Sweden. Ilay supported Townshend and Walpole who favoured aiding Prussia and minimizing Hanoverian influences. Unlike his brother, he was often on the side of less bellicose. Basil Williams, *Stanhope*, pp. 246-250
90. Williams, *Stanhope*, p. 174.
91. *Stuart Papers*, IV:452, 482; Lovat thought their speeches 'were ye strongest [that] were made [in] the debate'. Lovat to Duncan Forbes, 25 June 1717, *Culloden Papers*, NLS, 2965/244. Less creditably, Ilay also intervened on behalf of the rakish thief, gambler and rapist, Col. Francis Charteris, a cousin of Lord Mar and a distant relative of Lord Milton.
92. Murdoch, *ODNB*, 9:730.
93. Edmund Calamy, *An Historical Account of My Own Life*, 2 vols (London, 1829), 2:394.
94. Turberville, *House of Lords*, p. 167; Cobbett, *Parl. Hist.* VII:568-70.
95. The brothers had not protested this in 1714; Cobbett, *Parl. Hist.*, VI:1358.
96. Basil Williams saw those as part of a larger reform package which was enlightened but much watered down but did improve the condition of English Dissenters. Williams, *Stanhope*, pp. 384-418.
97. Montrose reported this to Mungo Graham of Gorthy on Friday, ? February 1719. He noted that he 'could not find it in my heart to answer my Summonds to Councill this morning'. Perhaps it helped to be able to add that the Campbell 'brothers had a verie dour look both'. Montrose-Lennox Papers, NRS, GD220/5/828/13; see also Hatton, *George I*, p. 243.
98. Calamy, *My Own Life*, II:421-22.
99. Duke of Gordon to ?, 18 February 1919, NRS, GD248/562/55/6.
100. Fanny's father, General Ogelthorpe, MP, had served Charles II and James II but took the oaths to William and Mary. His wife and three children were Jacobites; the fourth, General George, was not.
101. *Stuart Papers*, IV:255.
102. *Stuart Papers*, IV:256-60, 270, 317, 396-97, 456, 513; *Parliamentary Debates*, ed. John Torbuck, vols 6-17 (1736-1741)[some volumes were printed in London, some in Dublin, but the places are not always noted,]; VI:477 (n. p. [Dublin], 1741).
103. *Stuart Papers*, V:229-231. Ilay worried about the opening of his mail and later learned to make invisible ink; he had good reasons for sending sensitive letters by courier.
104. *Stuart Papers*, V:230.
105. Fanny Oglethorpe to Mar, 16 December 1717, *Stuart Papers*, V:284.
106. *Stuart Papers*, VI:132.
107. The Archbishop was Sir William Dawes, Bt.. He held the See from 1713-1723. A High Anglican and Chaplain to both William III and Queen Anne, he was an unlikely Jacobite. See Stephen Hadley's entry in *ODNB*, 15:531-33.
108. Anne Oglethorpe to Mar, 27 December 1717, *Stuart Papers*, V:336.
109. *Stuart Papers*, V:336-37, 432, 457, 495, 500-01.
110. *Stuart Papers*, VI:118, 7:10, 48,159.
111. *Stuart Papers*, VI:132. Archibald Foord believed the patent showed that Ilay was serious in his Jacobitism. Foord, *His Majesty's Opposition 1714-1830* (Oxford, 1964), p. 92. Accepting it was only playing the game, nothing more.
112. *Stuart Papers*, VI:131, 164, 535f, 539, 491.
113. Lockhart to Mar, 8 April 1718, *Letters of George Lockhart of Carnwath, 1698-1732* , ed. Daniel Szechi, Scottish History Society, 5th Series, vol 2 (Edinburgh 1989), p .130.
114. Fanny Oglethorpe to Mar, 21 November 1718, *Stuart Papers* 7:554.
115. Lockhart Letters, pp. 149.

Chapter 5

1. Fanny Ogelthorpe to Mar, 19 March 1718, *Calendar of the Stuart Papers Belonging to His Majesty The King preserved at Windsor Castle,* Vols I-VII (London, 1902- 23), VI:168. The Countess would have been a welcome charity for Ilay's enemies of the time – Stanhope, Sunderland and their friends. Ilay's 'Out book' at Coutts Bank shows an expenditure of £1.3.6 on 21 February 1718 to the 'Lords Justices' – probably the cost of his posting bail in the Court of King's Bench which had jurisdiction in his case.
2. For Grange, see the forthcoming biography by Anne Skoczylas; Lovat's actions are succinctly recounted by David N. Mackay, *Trial of Simon, Lord Lovat of the '45* (Edinburgh and Glasgow, 1911), pp. xvi-xxi..
3. Lady Louisa Stewart, called her Elisabeth. The name Shireburn or Sherburn was also used by Ilay and others when referring to her. A descendant of the Duke's son tells me that Ilay went through a 'marriage' with Mrs. Williams posing as a 'Dr. Williams'. This sounds very like a joke of some sort. Personal communication from Katherine L. Fairfield, 2008. Lady Louisa's account of Mrs. Williams is found in *The Letters and Journals of Lady Mary Coke,* 4 vols, ed. J.H. Thorne, (Edinburgh, 1889; New York, 1970), I:xxiii.
4. It was said to cost £600; Coutts, 'Out book', 5 December 1719. Of course this may have been for the Earl who had been writing on windows with a diamond in 1713 (see pp. 49, 375 n.114).
5. Copy of Argyll's will dated 14 August 1760, NLS, 17612/178. A will of 1735 (NLS, 16559) made similar arrangements.
6. In Argyll's will of 1760, she is listed as Mrs. Ann Williams and was living in Kent not in London with her mother. The 'Mrs.' may be an honorific title. Her mother could have left her more money when she died in 1762.
7. If he did so, it is likely to have been sometime between 1720 and 1728. R. L. Arkell, *Caroline of Ansbach George the Second's Queen* (Oxford, 1939), p. 200.
8. ? to Mrs. Howard, 1 September 1719, Lothian Muniments, NRS, GD40/ 9/ 139/20.
9. See below pp. 85-6.
10. *E. g.,* 'The Court Ballad' and 'Epigrams Occasioned by An Invitation to Court' (1717) and 'Six Maidens' (c.1732) who were anything but; *The Poems of Alexander Pope*, ed. John Butt (New Haven, Conn., 1963), pp. 305-308, 815-16.
11. Quoted in Norman Ault, *New Light on Pope with some additions to his Poetry hitherto unknown* (London, 1949), p. 173. Peter Martin attributes the verses to Pope: *Pursuing Innocent Pleasures, The Gardening World of Alexander Pope,* (Hampden, Conn., 1984), p. 154.
12. He is on the list of members for 1743 but was not added in the period 1731-1736; Robert Maxwell, ed. *Select Transactions of the Society of Improvers in the Knowledge of Agriculture of Scotland....* (Edinburgh, 1743; reprinted Glasgow 2003); transcript minutes of HIKAS, 1731-36, Library of the Royal Highland Society, Edinburgh, APS 4.9632.
13. Those appear in *Vitruvius Britannicus, or the British Architect...* (London,1715), pp. 53, 54. The house designed for Ilay was not commissioned by the Earl who subscribed for two copies of the work.
14. Tracy Borman, *Henrietta Howard King's Mistress, Queen's Servant* (London, 2007), pp. 131-36.
15. C. H. Collins and Muriel Baker, *The Life and Circumstances of James Brydges First Duke of Chandos* (Oxford,1949), p. 195. Friendship with Ilay may account in part for Chandos's selection as Chancellor at St Andrews University in 1724. The masters there were thanking a generous donor but this appointment is also likely to have had the approval of the

government which in university affairs at that time mean Lord Ilay. Roger L. Emerson, *Academic Patronage in the Scottish Enlightenment* (Edinburgh 2008), p. 417.

16. For the roles Desaguliers and Stuart played in Chandos's life, see Larry Stewart, *The Rise of Public Science: Rhetoric, Technology, and Natural Philosophy in Newtonian Britain, 1660-1750* (Cambridge, 1992), pp. 130-33, 213-220. Stewart's book contains the best account there is of the inter-connexions of science, technology and money in the period covered by this chapter.

17. Duncan Forbes to Baron Scrope, Mr. Delafaye, Ilay and Milton, 2 September 1726, NLS, 2967/10.

18. Ilay's bankers belonged to Scottish families patronized by the 1st and 2nd Dukes of Argyll. John Campbell of Lundie (?-1712), a goldsmith, started the company in 1692 and was joined in 1708 by another Scottish goldsmith, George Middleton (?-1747). He was a cadet of the Middletons of Seaton and brother to Col. John Middleton one of the brothers' friends from the Army. The Middletons were related to the King's College Principal, George Middleton, and were tied to many of the Jacobite families in the Aberdeen region which the Colonel represented in Parliament (1713-39). In 1712, banker George married his partner's daughter. His bank became Coutts Bank in 1755. Ilay banked with this firm all his life and it handled his most important transactions. But not all of his known income went through Middleton's accounts. For Middleton and his operations during the bubbles see Larry Neal, ' "For God's Sake, Remitt me": The Adventures of George Middleton, John Law's London Goldsmith-Banker, 1712-1729', *Business and Economic History* 23 (1994), pp. 27-60.

19. Ilay to Milton, 21 April 1724, NLS, 17610/37. He retained this power until the end of the Duke's life in 1761.

20. Other London or Scottish accounts would explain why the Earl's account at Coutts has so many missing sums in the ledgers. A likely bank would be Drummond's Bank which was later absorbed by the Royal Bank of Scotland but there are no accounts of the Earl surviving in its records. The Earl was sometimes associated with Andrew and John Drummond, bankers related to the family of the exiled Jacobite Duke of Perth (but also to good Whigs such as Colin Drummond, an Edinburgh professor who raised a company for service in The '15). John had been Ilay's friend at least since 1710 and was brought into Parliament by the Argathelians in 1727. Ilay had no account at the Royal Bank. Some of his money in Scotland was held by Lord Milton from time to time.

21. Those were roughly the equivalent to present-day state-issued premium bonds. You had a chance to win but your principal was safe and might even yield a little interest.

22. I thank Professor Larry Neal for this information. See also NLS, 17614.

23. Neal, "Remitt me", pp. 32-33.

24. That is the rate I have applied to his investment income to establish his capital holdings. Where other holdings are known they have been added to that sum. The figures given should be read as minimum figures not likely to be precise.

25. John Chamberlayne, *Magnae Britanniae Notitia of the Present State of Great Britain...* (London, 1723), Part II, p. 12.

26. I thank Tracy Earl, the Coutts Bank Archivist, for this information.

27. Henri Pujolas [Ilay's 'major domo'] to James Anderson, WS. 18 March 1717, NLS, Ad.v Ms 22.2.20/61. Pujolas served Ilay for about fifty years and a younger man of the same name later became a member of the English College of Heralds.

28. There are several stories about Ilay's involvement with this property. In one the Earl of Bute bought the property in 1715 and in 1720 sold it to William Dale, a London upholsterer, who mortgaged it to Ilay who foreclosed in 1724 and retained title until 1746 when he sold

it to the 3rd Earl of Bute; Edna Healey, *Coutts and Co. 1692-1992* (London, 1992), p. 59. Another account on the web dealing with Camden and North London seems to make this more specific. Dale bought the property before 1720 and in that year mortgaged it to Ilay for £1,675. He foreclosed in 1724 and took the property for £1,907.7.6. He is then said to have sold all or part of it to his brother in 1724/5. The 2nd Duke left it to Lord Bute in 1743. Ilay's 'In book' at Coutts shows payments of £1,575 made in 1720 by a Mr. Dale. Another story has the 2nd Duke giving Ilay title to Kenwood in 1715. The latter gave it to the 3rd Earl of Bute in the 1740s when he moved to London (c.1745). That story seems false. Yet another says that it was 'bought by the 2nd and 3rd Dukes of Argyll who later jointly owned it with their brother-in-law the 2nd Earl of Bute. His son bought out the brothers because he needed a London home when he received a position at the court of Frederick Prince of Wales. The author of that account thinks the 3rd Earl of Bute built the orangery; Anonymous, *Middlesex, biographical and pictorial* (London, 1906). p. 45. The House, which Ilay called Cane Wood, figures in his Coutts accounts between March 1717 and 1724 and may have done so earlier in records now lost. Tax payments on Kenwood disappear from his Coutts 'Out book' in 1720. That suggests some change was made in arrangements. Perhaps Bute, the Duke and Ilay each had a share. Ilay did convey all or part of the property to the 3rd Earl of Bute in 1746 so he owned some of it until then; *Complete Letters of Lady Mary Wortley Montagu*, ed. Robert Halsband, 3 vols (Oxford, 1965-67), II:348 n.2.

29. It seems likely that some ledger entries for 'bonds' refer to stocks.

30. He was hedging his position with lottery tickets.

31. Larry Neal, ' "I am not master of events." John Law's Bargain with Lord Londonderry, 1717-1729', 2008 draft paper provided by its author; __"Remitt me", p.37.

32. Personal letter from Professor Neal.

33. His optimism was likely rooted in Law's schemes of to take over some tax collections and to fund the national debt through the Mississippi Co.

34. Ilay to Mrs. Howard, September 1719, *Letters to and from Henrietta Hobart Howard, Countess of Suffolk ? 1681* [sic, 1688]- *1767*, ed. John Wilson Croker (London, 1824), pp. 92-99.

35. Ilay to Mrs. Howard, 16 January 1720, *Ibid*; Neal, "Remitt me", pp. 36-39.

36. *Applebee's Original Weekly Journal*, 1 October 1720; *Weekly Journal or Saturday's Post*, 22 October 1720.

37. Later entries in the Coutts 'In book'. Loudoun was one of several in the Campbell circle to invest; see Patrick Walsh, 'The Bubble on the Margins: The South Sea Bubble in Ireland and Scotland', forthcoming.

38. Ilay to Duncan Forbes, 18 July 1723, NLS, 17610/15-32. Ilay told Forbes that he 'had ordered all manner of diligence to be carried on against him in the most effectual manner, & if he pleases to make me an offer I can accept of its well but I beg nothing be omitted or delayed that can distress him'. Another undated letter to Forbes says that he needs the money having already spent it – probably in buying The Whim. 'Let me know how his estate stands in Scotland & whether he did anything lately to defraud me'. NLS, 2970/172. That he lent to Kinnoull is somewhat surprising. On 7 June 1713, Kinnoull had told Lord Oxford that Argyll and Ilay should be turned out and the next peerage election better managed. *HMCR Portland MSS*, V:294. Kinnoull's son, Lord Dupplin, would be one of Ilay's political opponents in the 1750s.

39. NLS, 16525- 16531.

40. Murdoch, *ODNB*, 9:730. This was an important step toward the creation of the Royal Bank of Scotland.

41. A portion of his speech is recorded in Robert Campbell, *The Life of the most Illustrious Prince, John, Duke of Argyll and Greenwich....* (Belfast, 1745), p. 308.
42. Cobbett, *Parl. Hist.*, VII:591. Campbell, *Life of Argyll*, p. 308; Turberville, *House of Lords*, p. 172.
43. Ilay to Grange, 25 May 1721, Mar and Kellie Papers, NRS, GD124/15/1221/1.
44. William Coxe, *Memoirs of the Life and Administration of Sir Robert Walpole, Earl of Orford*, 3 vols (London, 1800), I:117.
45. Montrose to Mungo Graham of Gorthy, 21 March 1719, Montrose-Lennox Papers, NRS, GD220/5/528/25. Montrose claimed he had defeated this attempt.
46. Shaw, *Political History*, p. 60.
47. Eric G.J. Wehrli, 'Scottish Politics in the Age of Walpole', unpublished Ph.D. Thesis (Edinburgh University, 1983), p. 17.
48. Plumb, *Walpole*, I:289.
49. Wehrli, 'Scottish Politics'. p. 23.
50. The standard source on the 'Bubble is still, John Carswell, *The South Sea 'Bubble'* (London, 1960).
51. Wherli, 'Scottish Politics', pp. 19-24.
52. Wherli's 'Scottish Politics' (pp. 17-94) gives the best account of this complex development.
53. For the growth of the Argathelian interest in the colleges see, Emerson, *Professors Patronage and Politics*, pp. 45-47. On 27 December 1716, Robert Pringle wrote to Principal Stirling that the Visitation Commission report for the Aberdeen colleges, written by Squadrone men, would 'come into the hands of the Duke of Roxburghe, under whose direction the concerns of North Britain, doe more immediately fall....' Most university business until 1723 was funnelled through him. Stirling Letters, GUL, 204 [a copy of the GUL 651], I:13; Montrose to Gorthy, 15/16 January 1722, Montrose-Lennox Papers, NRS, GD220/5/838/8a-b.
54 ? to ?, 28 and 30 November 1717. GUA, 27146.
55. Emerson, *Professors, Patronage and Politics*, pp. 34-77;
___, *Academic Patronage*, [see index entries for 'Argathelians' and 'Squadrone'].
56. In 1720, Ilay had intervened to have an indictment changed so that it would not read in a way that questioned Lovat's very dubious claim to his title which had been secured through lying and the forced marriage of an heiress. Ilay to Lord Grange, 15 October 1720, NRS, GD124/15/12/3.
57. Duncan Forbes to John Forbes, 19 December 1721, *Culloden Papers*, no editor, (London, 1815), p. 75. See also the discussion of this case in Wehrli, 'Scottish Politics'. pp. 19-23; 130- 137; 156-161.
58. Ilay to Lord Grange, 9 February and ?February 1722, NRS, GD124/15/1224/1 and 2.
59. *HPHC 1715-1754*, I:95.
60. Haldane, formerly a sinecure Professor of Ecclesiastical History at St Andrews, was a government lawyer active in the confiscation of Highland estates. He was disliked in Scotland because he had prospered by selling up Jacobite families. Montrose to Gorthy, 15/16 January 1722, Montrose-Lennox Papers, NRS, GD220/5/838/8a-b.
61. Ilay to Milton, 25 February 1724, NLS, 16529/24-5; John Hill Burton, *The History of Scotland*, Edinburgh, 8 vols (Edinburgh,1898), VIII:350-352; *HPHC 1715-1754*, ed. Romney Sedgwick, (Oxford and New York, 1970), p. 95; Wehrli, 'Scottish Politics', p. 90.
62. Ilay to Milton, 4 March 1724, NLS, 16529/31-2.
63. Ilay to Milton, 25 and 28 January 1724, NLS, 16529/12-13 and 14.
64. *Letters of Lord Balmerino to Henry Maule*, ed. Clyve Jones, *Scottish History Society, Miscellany 12* (1994), pp. 99-168; p. 117.

65. Ilay to Grange, 25 May 1721, NRS, GD124/15/1221/1.
66. Robertson, *Proceedings Relating to the Peerage of Scotland ...* (Edinburgh and London, 1790), p. 82.
67. The background to this included the Salter's Hall controversies of 1718-1719; see, Duncan Coomer, *English Divines under the Early Hanoverians* (London, 1946), pp. 71-77.
68. Cobbett, *Parl. Hist.*, VII:938.
69. Wehrli, 'Scottish Politics'. p. 19. George Logan told James Erskine, Lord Grange, it had been dearly bought, presumably because it curtailed his independence. The value of Ilay's places is given in John Chamberlayne, *Magnae Britanniae Notitia: or the Present State of Great Britain...* (London, 1723), Bk III, pp. 11, 12. No place was worth exactly its face value since fees were extracted by those who paid out the monies.
70. See Wehrli, 'Scottish Politics', pp. 19- 94.
71. JK to Ilay, 13 July 1721, NRS, GD124/15/1221/2.
72. Ilay had earlier shown a familiarity with codes; now he devised a seal which could not be counterfeited. It involved using red wax under a seal - a bearded classical head – super imposed on it in black wax. An example of this is to be found on a letter of Ilay to Lord Grange,16 December 1721, NRS, GD124/15/1221/3.
73. Lockhart to Henry Maule, 12 April and 17 May 1721, *Letters of George Lockhart of Carnwath*, ed. Daniel Szechi, Scottish History Society 5th series (1989), pp. 159-60; Robertson, *Proceedings*, pp. 8, 103-4; Ilay to Lord Grange, 27 February 1722, Mar and Kellie Papers, NRS, GD124/1215/1224/4.
74. Ilay to Grange, 27 February 1722, NRS, GD124/15/1224/4.
75. There is a detailed account of this election in the *Letters of Balmerino*, pp. 116-120.
76. *Ibid*, p. 120.
77. Duncan Forbes thanked Argyll on 18 July 1721 for 'the choice your Grace has been pleased to make of me to represent your Borrows'. *i.e.*, the towns of Fortrose, Inverness, Nairn, and Forres, *Culloden Papers*, p. 74. Forbes had sat since 1721-22 for the Ayr burghs which were then in the gift of Argyll.
78. Ilay to Lord Grange, 19, ?, 25, 27 February 1722, Mar and Kellie Papers, NRS, GD124/1215/1224/1-5.
79. Ilay to Grange, 9 February 1722, NRS, GD124/15/1224/1. Amongst Ilay's Tories was Balmerino who was surprised to be asked by the Earl to stand. Balmerino to Maule, n.d.[1723], *Letters of Balmerino*, pp. 165-66.
80. Duncan Forbes to Argyll, 18 July 1721, *Culloden Papers*, p. 74; Wherli gives the numbers in May as 16 Argathelians, 11 Squadrone men, 1 Tory, 13 other Whigs of whom 8 were for the government and 2 unclassifiable and 2 undetermined. Later, appeals raised the Argathelian total by 4. Wehrli, 'Scottish Politics', pp. 144, 150-51.
81. Baillie to Polwarth, 10 July 1723, *HMCR of the Manuscripts of Lord Polwarth*, ed. Henry Paton (London, 1931), II:282.
82. Scott, 'Politics and Administration', p. 317.
83. Wehrli, suggests this but the evidence for it is not overwhelming, particularly since he thinks the brothers had a serious argument around 1723 and thereafter tended to go their own ways while sharing similar political views. 'Scottish Politics', pp. 169-170.
84. See the discussion of this by J. H. Plumb, *The Growth of Political Stability in England 1675-1725* (London, 1967), pp. 180-82.
85. T. M. Devine, *Scotland's Empire 1600-1815* (London, 2003), pp. 75-77.
86. Ilay to Milton, 15 February 1724, NLS, 16531/24.
87. Ilay to Milton, 10 July 1725, NLS, 16531/22.
88. Minutes of the Convention of Royal Burghs, ECA, SL 30/1/1/10, pp. 30, 51, 67, 71.
89. *Glasgow*, 3 vols, ed. Gordon Jackson and T. M. Devine (Manchester, 1995), I:95. That section was written by Jackson.

90. Robert Dundas, the best Squadrone lawyer, failed to become a Court of Session judge until 1737.
91. This cost him the good will of Duncan Forbes who thereafter periodically made trouble for Ilay; *ODNB*, 20:271.
92. Coxe, *Walpole*, II:456. This was written in a long letter of 24 August to 'Mr. Stewart'. *Ibid*, pp. 456-461.
93. Ilay to [? Charles Delafaye], 19 August 1725, NRS, SP54/15/69.
94. Coxe, *Walpole*, II:454.
95. *Ibid*, II:459-61; his interest in simple chemistry and 'gimcracks' here had a minor payoff.
96. Walpole had decided to dismiss him around the middle of August and did so on 25 August; *Ibid*, II:443, 449.
97. Ilay to Newcastle, 31 August 1725, NRS, SP54/15/79.
98. Coxe, *Walpole*, II;454.
99. Ilay to Newcastle, 9 September 1725, NRS, SP54/16/7.
100. Ilay to Newcastle, 16 October 1725, NRS, SP54/16/ 45.
101. Coxe, *Walpole*, II:467-68.
102. That was his position about other riots too.
103. Ilay to Newcastle, 23 September 1725 and 14, 16, 21, and 28 October 1725, NRS, SP54/16/23, 44, 45, 53 and 63.
104. Coxe, *Walpole*, II:462-64; Ilay to Newcastle, 9 October 1725, NRS, SP54/16/41. He made a similar plea in 1736 when the Porteous Rioters were defended by clerics.
105. Ilay to Delafaye, 16 October 1725, SP54/48.
106. Grange to Ilay, 16, 17 and 24 December 1724, NRS, GD124/15/1262/1-3.
107. Charles B. Realey, 'Early Opposition to Walpole', *Humanistic Studies*, Vol. IV, Nos. 2 and 3, 1931, pp. 143-44.
108. Ilay to Newcastle, 7, 9 and 14 October 1725, NRS, SP54/16/38 and 41.
109. Ilay to Newcastle, 7 October 1725, Transcript Copies of Letters from Ilay to Newcastle, NRS, GD215/1657. A note on this letter says that Ilay in 1738 promoted the career of James Glen but only when he got assurances that Glen as Governor of South Carolina would not cause problems for General George Ogelthorpe in the colony to the south of him.
110. Ilay to Newcastle, 5 October 1725, NRS, SP54/16/38.
111. Murdoch, *ODNB*, 9:730; Coxe, *Walpole*, I:234. Robert Wodrow believed that Ilay's brother had opposed his appointment as Secretary because Ilay had been too forceful in handling the Malt Tax crisis; *Intimate letters of the Eighteenth Century*, ed. George Campbell, 8th Duke of Argyll, 2 vols (London, n.d.), I:18.
112. Alexander Murdoch, 'Management or Semi-Independence? The government of Scotland from 1707-1832', unpublished paper given to the Association for Scottish Historical Studies, 1996.
113. In a 1743 House of Lords debate on a 'Bill for the further quieting of Corporations' he set out principles which guided his reforming actions: 'it has never been the custom to introduce new regulations or to make alterations, but some evil has been really felt, or some attack actually been made; and I hope, this custom will be always observed; for if we should give loose to our imagination, and resolve to provide against every evil, and every attack, which might be suggested by a fruitful but gloomy imagination, we could never be a moment at ease, nor a session without making some material alteration in our form of government'. When it suited him, he found the reasons he needed. Cobbett, *Parl. Hist.*, (London, 1812), XIII:96.
114. In the spring of 1725, Ilay and his brother spoke and voted for the bill to allow Lord Bolingbroke to return to England. It passed on 24 May 1725 and was intended to allow him to return but without being able to play an active role in politics. Still attainted and

unable to hold office or to sit in the House of Lords, he became through his writings a very real force of opposition to Walpole's Ministry. Realey, *Early Opposition to Walpole.* pp. 143-44.

Chapter 6

1   It is not clear when this nickname became current but by the early thirties he, Lord Milton, and other friends were calling it that. Charles Erskine to Lord Milton, 24 February 1735; NLS, 16560/242.

2. It replaced the one which Sir John Clerk described in 1733 as being large, full of instruments and books 'Lying in a very careless phylosophic manner' which suggests Ilay had then no librarian. Clerk's description also suggests that already there was not enough shelf space. A Toure into England in the year 1733, Clerk of Penicuik Papers, NRS, GD18/2110/1. Ilay to Andrew Fletcher, Lord Milton, 8 July 1742, NLS, 16587/85. By that winter Ilay exercised by walking in it. Ilay to Milton, 30 October 1742, NLS, 16587/113.

3. Ian Lindsay and Mary Cosh, *Inveraray and the Dukes of Argyll*, Edinburgh, 1973), pp. 10, 354 n. 43; Ilay to Milton, 8 July 1742, NLS, 16587/86.

4. Ilay to Milton, summer 1743, NLS, 16591/54.

5. The instrument room had chemical apparatus, one or more telescopes, models of machines and curios. Henrietta Pye, *A Short Account of the Principal Seats and Gardens in and about Kew* (London, 1767), pp. 30-32; see also the account of the estate and its buildings by Mary Cosh, 'Lord Ilay's Eccentric Building Schemes', *Country Life*, 20 July 1972, pp. 142-145.

6. Views of the house and garden at Whitton can be found in Plates 6 and 8.

7. *Peeblesshire : An Inventory of the Ancient Monuments*, 2 vols (Royal Commission on Ancient and Historical Monuments of Scotland, (1967), II:326-331.

8. Cosh (n. 5; p. 145) says The Whim lacked a library until 1759/60 but a letter to Lord Milton of 17 May 1740 says books were sent to The Whim library which as yet had no shelves. NLS, 16580/81. A memorandum from June 1741 also lists books to be taken to The Whim Library; NLS, 17646/2-2.

9. On 1 November 1735, Ilay wrote to Lord Milton that he would send all his books from Duddingston, where his mother had recently died, to The Whim where the library was then 'above stairs'; NLS, 16559/162.

10. NLS, 17651/12.

11. *Peeblesshire: An Inventory*, p. 328.

12. NLS, 17647/152; 17650/164. The last item is Adam's account for the building of the library which had '56 yards 5 feet in the shelves being 3/4 wood & wrought on both sides at 3sh p yard.' The cost is given as £158/18/5 but he was later paid £200; NLS, 17628/12.

13. *E.g.*, Book Bill from Alex Kincaid 4 April 1748, NLS, 17819/37. Books there are noted as being for Inveraray and The Whim.

14. NLS, 17617/220-21.

15. John Maule to Lord Milton, 22 October 1743, quoted in Lindsay and Cosh, *Inveraray*, p. 10.

16. NLS, 17611/119.

17. Rosneath Inventory, NLS, 17630/275.

18. Macbean came from the Aberdeen area but is neither among the matriculates of Marischal College nor the MAs of King's College. He worked on one of the republished editions of Ephraim Chambers *Cyclopedia* (1738, 1741, 1743) and later was employed as an aid by Samuel Johnson when he was preparing his *Dictionary*. Johnson wrote the preface to Macbean's *A System of Ancient Geography* (1773). Some of the geographer's

work is likely to have been done while he attended the Duke's library which had a fine collection of geographical works. Macbean had stopped working for the Duke by 1759 and received no legacy when the Duke died. According to James Boswell, the poor man died a pensioner of the Charterhouse to which he had been admitted on the recommendation of Johnson to Lord Chancellor Thurlow. He is mentioned by Richard Yeo, *Encyclopaedic Visions: Scientific Dictionaries and Enlightenment Culture* (Cambridge, 2001), pp. 37

19. I thank Mr. David Weston, Keeper of Rare Books at Glasgow University Library, for this suggestion.

20. The catalogue is described in Philip Gaskell, *A Bibliography of the Foulis Press.* (London, 1964), p. 220; and, in the corrected edition of this catalogue issued by W. T. Johnston as an Officina compact disk.

21. The Coutts 'Out book' shows a payment to Macbean on 23 July 1750; more begin in the summer of 1753 and run to 14 September 1759. Macbean was paid over that time £207. Several entries for 21 guineas suggest that was his yearly salary and that he was not employed after the last payment. There was no reason to leave him a legacy.

22. M.A.E. Nickson, 'Books and Manuscripts', Chapter 17 of *Sir Hans Sloane: Collector, Scientist, Antiquary*, ed. Arthur MacGregor (London, 1994), pp. 263-294.

23. Paul Potter, ' "Taste Sets the Price:" Mead, Askew, and the Birth of Bibliomania in Eighteenth-Century England', *Canadian Bulletin of Medical History*, 12 (1995), pp. 241-257, 245. For other collections, see: *British Book Sale Catalogues 1676-1800: A Union List*, compiled and edited by A.N.L. Munby and Lenore Coral (London, 1977). Mead's collection is noticed on p. 81.

24. Antonio Magliabecchi (1633-1717), Librarian to the Grand Duke of Tuscany, died possessed of c.30,000 volumes, while the personal library of Cardinal Domenico Passionei (1682-1761), the Vatican Librarian, was twice that size. *Encyclopedia of Library and Information Science*, 64 vols (New York, 1968-1995), XXIV:137, 139. The library of the Charles Spencer, 3rd Earl of Sunderland (1674-1722), a man with whom Ilay was associated in politics, ran to c.20,000 volumes; *Ibid.*, XXIV:158.

25. 'A Character of His Grace the Duke of Argyll 1761' in NLS, 17612/218.

26. Munby and Coral, note that many auctions occurred there; *Union List, passim*. Ilay is known to have been frequenting it in 1716; See: *More Culloden Papers*, ed. Duncan Warrand, 5 vols (Inverness, 1923-1930); 1:117-18.

27. The book catalogues he possessed would have allowed him to compare his collection with others formed in the past. Catalogues for sales held long before the time he began collecting, if annotated, would have given him an idea of the increased value of his books, perhaps of the provenance of some, and of the relative importance of his own collection. Other catalogues appear to have been guides to collections and not to sales. Among his fifteen quarto catalogues were those for the following libraries: Corbin, Hemmiana, Norfolciana, Vander Walle [Van de Water], Slusiana, Bentesiana, and Gudii. Of the fifty-seven octavo catalogues he possessed, forty-six fall into the period 1700-1753 with perhaps thirty before 1730. Most of his collecting seems to have been done 1710-1740.

28. NLS, 16531/188.

29. See: Robert Wodrow, *Analecta or Materials for a History of Remarkable Providences Mostly Relating to Scottish Ministers and Christians*, 4 vols (Edinburgh 1842-43); IV:152-53; John Gordon to Lord Milton, 7 July 1725, NLS, 16531/188; John Cairns, 'Alexander Cunningham's Proposed Edition of the Digest An Episode in the History of the Dutch Elegant School', *Tijdschrift voor Rechtsgeschiedenis*, vol. 69, (2001) pp. 81-117, pp. 307-359.

30. James Anderson to Ilay, n.d. [1722/23], NLS, Adv. Ms 29.3.4/134, 139.

31. Lindsay and Cosh, *Inveraray*, p. 10.

32. Barbara Balfour-Melville, *The Balfours of Pilrig*, (Edinburgh, 1907), pp. 131-32.
33. Book Bill from Alex Kincaid 4 April 1745, NLS, 17819/56; Kincaid & Donaldson Acct. 1749-1754, NLS, 17624/83-85; Acct. of Gavin Hamilton, 8 December 1753 - 11 November 1754, NLS, 17624/89-91.
34. David R. Brigham, 'The Patronage of Natural History' in *Empire's Nature: Mark Catesby's New World Vision*, ed. Amy R. W. Meyers and Margaret Beck Pritchard (Chapel Hill and London, 1998), p. 141; Elizabeth Blackwell's *Curious Herbal*, 2 vols (London, 1737-39) was published by subscription and is listed in his catalogue. Its value lay in its beauty and in its very accurate depictions of plants. He also subscribed to James Justice's *The Scots Gardener's Directory* (Edinburgh, 1754). This book was dedicated to Lord Milton but its dedication referred to Argyll as 'the Great Maecenas of the present Age'. Argyll and Milton had arranged for Justice to retire honourably from his legal post although he was bankrupt.
35. Hume also humorously noted that the Duke should be pleased that he had not had the *Essays* dedicated to him or been burdened with Hume's presence among the other job seekers at the ducal levees. The letter was sent before the Duke had excluded him from a Glasgow professorship; *The Letters of David Hume*, 2 vols, ed. J.Y.T.Greig (Oxford, 1969; 1st ed. 1932); 1:113.
36. David Hume to Adam Smith, 12 April 1759, *Letters of David Hume*, 1:303.
37. See *The Glory of the Printed Page*, ed. Nigel Thorpe (London, 1987).
38. *Catalogus,* and *A Catalogue of the Library of the Honble Samuel Molyneux...* (London, 1730). The auctioneer's copy of the latter is held at The Houghton Library, Harvard University, B1827. S78*. Ilay's manuscripts were on bleaching, the construction of sundials, mills, a copy of John Law's 'Essay on a Land Bank', on fortification and gunnery, the making of sun-dried sea salt and several by Samuel Molyneux containing observations of stars, the dipping needle, and weather.
39. This also may not have been the case. The dispersion of printers of learned materials was characteristic of the sixteenth and seventeenth centuries. A learned printer would flourish near a university town for a few years and then die or move so the learned, medical, and other scholastic works of the period were often printed outside major cities and by men with short careers in particular places. If you wanted a certain work, you might buy one of the few publications of such a firm or printer. If you had a particular interest, you would have books about the subject from printers from all over Europe. I thank Dr. Paul Potter for this information.
40. This is the inference I have drawn from the accounts with Kincaid noticed above, n. 33.
41. The books purchased from Mrs. Williams by Lord Bute were destroyed in a nineteenth century estate fire. The 11th Duke of Argyll assured me that the library at Inveraray Castle has no books which belonged to Ilay. The librarians at Aberdeen University know of none among the books gifted to Marischal College by the 3rd Earl of Bute. His gift almost certainly included some of his uncle's books. Those facts suggest that Ilay did not bind his books uniformly, that he had no special book plate and that he did not sign his books. That fits the character of a man not given to ostentatious displays.
42. The cost of books at the sale of Dr. Francis Bernard in 1698, about the time Ilay would have begun collecting, was around 18s per folio, 4s per quarto, while 'a typical octavo' could be bought for 10d. Mead's sale, in 1753, brought in £5,499.4.5 for over 20,000 volumes of which there were 101 manuscript items. Potter, "Taste", pp. 241-57; 242, 243.
43. Lord Bute also bought all the instruments and models which were in Ilay's library. Personal communication from the 11th Duke of Argyll, 24 January 2000.
44. P. J. Garnier, *Systema bibliotheca collegii parisiensis* (Society of Jesus, Paris, 1678).
45. An outline of this is given in L.-A. Constantin, *Manuels-Roret, Bibliotheconomie ou*

Nouveau Manuel Complet pour L'Arrangement, La Conservation et L'Administration des Bibliotheques (Paris, 1841), p. 130-132.

46. This and the quotations which follow come from Gabriel Naudé, *Advice on Establishing a Library*, trans. Archer Taylor (Berkeley and Los Angeles, 1950), pp. 62-69, the chapter called 'Arranging the Books'.

47. John Toland, for example, wrote of 'Mohametan Christianity' in *Nazarenus*. See Robert E. Sullivan, *John Toland and the Deist Controversy* (Cambridge, Mass., 1982), p. 136.

48. See Appendix II, Table 3.

49. For an account of all this see, Anne Skoczylas, *Mr. Simson's Knotty Case, Divinity, Politics and Due Process in Early Eighteenth-Century Scotland* (Montreal & Kingston, 2001).

50. *The Christian Magazine* 2:333 (1767) There had been a family connexion.

51. See, Frank E. Manuel, *Isaac Newton Historian* (Cambridge, Mass., 1963).

52. The most notable Scottish example of this is found in the unfinished work on measurements by James Stirling of Keir, a man whom Ilay would have known as a theoretical and applied mathematician and as the manager of the Earl of Hopetoun's mines at Leadhills (see p. 133). Stirling's manuscript is retained by his descendants.

53. The Foulis Press started in 1742/3 so this is likely to have been a book given them to help along their new venture. It also came out just after Ilay had been displaced by Squadrone men as the manager of Scottish affairs and, perhaps, just after his brother had died and the dukedom became his. It was a nice reminder of the family's commitment to Whiggism and Calvinism. It would also have reminded Scots that among those clamouring for the Marquis's death in 1661 were men whose present representatives were members of the Squadrone faction who had displaced Ilay in 1742.

54. Anonymous, [Daniel MacQueen], *Letters on Mr. Hume's History of Great Britain* (Edinburgh, 1756); William Adam, *Essay on Mr. Hume's Essay on Miracles*, (London, 1752). Argyll denied Hume a job at Glasgow in 1752 because he knew what Hume stood for. Roger L. Emerson, *Academic Patronage in the Scottish Enlightenment: Glasgow, Edinburgh and St Andrews Universities* (Edinburgh, 2008), pp. 128-29.

55. Alexander Murdoch has also noticed his curiosity about human nature; The *People Above: Politics and Administration of Mid-Eighteenth Century Scotland* (Edinburgh, 1980), p. 34.

56. For a recent discussion of the term as Ilay would have understood it, see: Merio Scattola, 'Before and After Natural Law: Models of Natural Law in Ancient and Modern Times' in *Early Modern Natural Law Theories: Contexts and Strategies in the Early Enlightenment,* eds. T.J. Hochstraser and P. Schroder (Dordrecht, 2003), pp. 1-30.

57. Ilay to James Stuart Mackenzie, 29 September 1738, Bute Papers, Mount Stuart House.

58. One by-product of all this may have been the baroque plaster relief once at Whitton and in 1972 still on a house near the location of the estate; Cosh, 'Lord Ilay's Eccentric Building Schemes' has a picture of it; p. 142.

59. This notable work on the arts and machines was begun in the 1680s and was pillaged by Denis Diderot and his illustrators for the *Encyclopedie* edited by him and Jean LeRond d'Alembert.

60. His catalogue listed among those serials: *Giornale di letterati d'Italia* 1710-?, *Osservatione letterarie* (4 vols.), *Ang. Cologra raccolta d' opuscoli scientifica* (5 vols.), *Bibliotheca volante di Gio. Cinelli Calvoli*, 1677-? (? vols.).

61. Sampling of the titles appearing on two pages each from the lists of specifically medical folios, quartos and octavos suggests that the distribution of his octavos was: 4% from the sixteenth century; 47% from the seventeenth century; 49% from the eighteenth century. Of the seventeenth century books, most were published after 1670. In the eighteenth century, most were from the period 1730-1755. Only five came into the collection later.

Those were likely gifts from grateful Scots but not all the later works fall into that category nor are they all by British authors.

62. This is likely to have come as a result of his campaigning there in the election following the Union.

63. Ilay as a scientist is discussed below in Chapters 7 and 8.

64. Some of that was likely prompted by his connexions with the South Sea and African Companies and by the similar concerns of his friend James Brydges, Duke of Chandos; see, Larry Stewart, 'The Edge of Utility: Slaves and Smallpox in the Early Eighteenth Century', *Medical History*, 29 (1985), pp. 54-70.

65. I thank Michael Barfoot for this information.

66. From the food bills included in the accounts found in the Saltoun Papers at the NLS it is evident that Ilay had a real interest in his food and liked variety. He liked most meats but seems to have especially enjoyed tongue – hot, spiced, dried and sauced. He ate Virginia hams procured in Glasgow and most kinds of fowl. He willingly ate fish and oysters. None of the bills for meals paid by him on the road is without vegetables. These came in many forms and kinds – artichokes, asparagus, beans, kidney beans, cabbages of several sorts, cauliflower, carrots, cucumbers, peas, salads, spinach, sorel, turnips, and more. His own vegetable gardens were even more diverse. All that was garnished with capers and 'Morrells and truffles', India Catchup, and bottled mushrooms. The list of fruits and deserts is also long: apples and apple pies, berries of all kinds, sago, white Confits and 'China oranges', lemon puddings, sillabubs and tarts. He liked English cheeses but also ate crowdy. The bills have entries for ale, beer, wine and sometimes spirits but he does not himself seem to have been much of a drinker. When the bills are only for him and his travelling companion, the bar bills are small. Sometimes the bills included 'burnt coffee', *E.g.* NLS, 17614/150, 17616/120, 17616/87 17617/279, 17818/279, 17819/37.

67. This would have been a gift since it is dedicated to Ilay; another of Campbell's books was dedicated to the 2nd Duke. They had secured his university post.

68. In the 'Miscellaneous' section of the library, Ilay possessed the principal works of political arithmetic, bills of mortality, and pamphlets on insurance.

69. He knew Voltaire and Maclaurin in the 1720s, and probably Pemberton and van Musschenbroek. Algarotti spent time in London and was a friend of Lady Mary Wortley Montagu.

70. This treatise was first published in 1651 but an edition which Leonardo might have recognized as his was not printed until the eighteenth century; see,Victoria Steele, 'The First Italian Printing of Leonardo da Vinci's Treatise on Painting:1723 or 1733?', *Notiziario vinciano*, 13 (1980), pp. 3-24.

71. Not long after Dr. Douglas died in 1752, Argyll ordered, through Peter Collinson, Douglass's various works. Collinson to Franklin, 7 March 1753, *The Papers of Benjamin Franklin*, ed, Leonard W. Labaree, *et al.* (New Haven, Conn., 1961), 20 vols, 4:456.

72. A. O. Hirschmann, in *The Passions and the Interests* (New York, 1977), called the first a textbook for French traders of the seventeenth century but one notable for its interest in trade as a polisher of manners and morals. That was a view Ilay shared. Many Scots had long wished to civilize the Scottish Highlanders by introducing industries and trade. That was hardly a new idea in the eighteenth century.

73. Forty years after Ilay had met Voltaire (c.1727), the latter praised him and his brother to Lady Lousia Stewart, *The Letters and Journals of Lady Mary Coke*, 4 vols (London 1889-96; Facsimile ed., London, 1970), III: 159

74. Campbell was also a botanist.

75. Diary of Andrew Fletcher, 18 July 1748, NLS, 17891.

76. Ilay to Milton, 12 November 1735, NLS, 16559/162. In that letter, Ilay says that while at

Walpole's estate, Houghton, he spent half his day reading in the library and half with '20 or 30 Foxehunters'. Half their days were spent hunting and the rest eating and drinking. Although he limped, it was likely to have been his preference for bookish leisure which kept him from the field.

77 Quoted by Edmund and Dorothy Berkeley in *John Mitchell: The Man Who Made the Map* (Chapel Hill, 1974), p. 244.

78. This plate is printed in *Memoirs of King George II*, 3 vols, ed. John Brooke (New Haven, Conn.,1985) III: 182.

Chapter 7

1. The list of proposals comes from the papers of John Spotswood held in NLS, 658, 2933, 2937; for a discussion of the Councils of Trade and the Darien scheme see *The Writings of William Paterson...*, 3 vols, ed. Saxe Bannister (London, 1859), I:2-160. For other proposals and initiatives see, W. R. Scott, *The Constitution and Finance of English, Scottish and Irish Joint Stock companies to 1720* (Cambridge, 1911) and Roger L. Emerson, 'The Scottish Setting of Hume's Political Economy' in *Essays on David Hume's Political Economy*, ed. Margaret Schabas and Carl Wennerlind (N.Y., 2005), pp. 1-32.
2. Roger L. Emerson, 'The Founding of the Edinburgh Medical School: The Real Story', *Journal of the History of Medicine and Allied Sciences*, 59 (2004), pp. 183-218.
3. R. D. Connor, and Allan Simpson, *Weights and Measures in Scotland: A European Perspective*, ed. Alison Morrison-Low, (Edinburgh, 2005).
4. Two of Kincaid's diaries exist. One for parts of 1703-06 describes the improving activities of some of his friends who were intent on making better measuring devices, machine-tools and machines. NLS, Adv Mss. 22.2.10 (11) and 32.7.7. Part of the second has been published: 'An Edinburgh Diary', ed. Henry Meikle, *Book of the Old Edinburgh Club*, 27 (1949), pp. 111-154.
5. Roger L. Emerson, 'Sir Robert Sibbald, Kt., The Royal Society of Scotland and the Origins of the Scottish Enlightenment', *Annals of Science*, 45 (1988), pp. 41-72.
6. Charles W. J. Withers, 'Geography, Science and National Identity in Early Modern Britain, The Case of Scotland and the Work of Sir Robert Sibbald', *Annals of Science*, 53 (1996), pp. 29-73.
7. Emerson, 'Sir Robert Sibbald', p. 59.
8. Stephen Shapin, 'The Audience for Science in Eighteenth Century Edinburgh', *History of Science*, 12 (1974), pp. 95-121.
9. They were the former Edinburgh professor, David Gregory, his brother James, who succeeded to his Mathematics Chair in 1692, and Dr. Thomas Bower who held the short-lived Mathematics Chair at King's College, Aberdeen.
10. His family had been patronized by the Campbells since c.1660 when his grandfather had moved from the island of Tiree (a Campbell domain) to Inveraray; [Patrick Murdoch],' An Account of the Life and Writings of the Author' in *An Account of Sir Isaac Newton's Philosophical Discoveries...* by Colin Maclaurin, ed. Patrick Murdoch (London, 1748; New York and London,1968), p. i. See also: Judith Grabiner, ' "Some Disputes of Consequence": Maclaurin Among the Molasses Barrels', *Social Studies of Science*, 28 (1998), pp. 139-168; ___, 'Maclaurin and Newton: The Newtonian Style and the Authority of Mathematics', in *Science and Medicine in the Scottish Enlightenment*, eds. Charles Withers and Paul. B. Wood, (East Linton, 2001), pp. 143-171.
11. *The Collected Letters of Colin Maclaurin*, ed. Stella Mills (Nantwich, 1982), p. 32.
12. *Ibid*, p. 32. In the early 1730s, Walpole's government was under attack; Ilay would have reserved his patronage positions for those who could do more than Maclaurin for the

interest the Earl served. Given the political realities of the 1730s, it is not surprising that Maclaurin failed to secure a job in the Excise.

13. Roger L. Emerson, *Academic Patronage in the Scottish Enlightenment:Glasgow, Edinburgh and St Andrews Universities* (Edinburgh, 2008), pp. 327-28.

14. NLS, 17819/56.

15. Ian N. Snedden, 'Robert Simson' in *Dictionary of Scientific Biography*, 16 vols, ed. C.C. Gillispie (New York, 1970-1980); XII:445.

16. E. G. R. Taylor, *Mathematical Practitioners of Hanoverian England* (London, 1966), pp. 48, 131.

17. Ilay had vigorously opposed the appointment of this man in 1727 but, once he was appointed, the Earl had no difficulty dealing with him. Aberdeen University Library, MSS. 399; M93; M 108/359; PRO, SP54/17 item 20. For the last reference, I thank Dr. Andrew Cunningham.

18. Emerson, *Academic Patronage in the Scottish Enlightenment*, p. 134.

19. Roger L. Emerson, 'The Scientific Interests of Archibald Campbell, Earl of Ilay and 3rd Duke of Argyll', *Annals of Science*, 59 (2002), pp. 52-56. The makers included at least George Adams, senior and junior, John Bird, Alexander Cumming, James Ferguson, Francis Hauksbee jr., Richard Glynn, George Graham, Benjamin Scott, James Short, Edward Sisson, John Topping, Alexander Wilson and Thomas Wright.

20. Maclaurin's actuarial work is touched on in Judith Grabiner, 'Maclaurin and Newton', pp. 155-58.

21. For Scottish interest in such uses of mathematics see, Roger L. Emerson, 'The Philosophical Society of Edinburgh 1737-1747', *British Journal of the History of Science*, 12 no.41 (1979), 154-191, *passim*; Judith Grabiner, see n.10.

22. At Maclaurin's death in 1746, he had the use of two instruments loaned to him by Lord Morton. F.F. to the Earl of Morton, 10 July 1746, Morton Manuscripts, NRS, GD150/3487/59.

23. The map says it was 'Published by Act of Parliament'.

24. George Adams inventory of 'My Uncles Instruments Purchased by me ... October 3rd 1761', Mount Stuart, Isle of Bute. The collections was valued at £360.7.0 and the instruments were said to have come from 'the late Duke of Argyll's Library'. I thank Dr. Alison Morrison-Low for a copy of this document. If the instruments were all from London, Bute did not purchase all his uncle possessed - perhaps only half.

25. They advertised a 'Course of Mechanical, Optical, and Pneumatical Experiments, to be performed by Francis Hauksbee, and the Explanatory Lectures read by Wm. Whiston, M.A.'. Those included 'experiments on the 'qualities of air', others 'concerning the vitreous phosphori', and 'relating to the electricity of bodies'. Demonstrators employed an 'electrical machine to revolve a sphere of glass with the air exhausted', and showed the 'effect of electricity on strings of yarn'. It was pointed out that the electric light had a 'purple tint': Larry Stewart, 'Francis Hauksbee', *ODNB*, 25: 841-2; William Whiston, *Memoirs of* ..., 2 vols (London, 1753), I:135.

26. Larry Stewart, *The Rise of Public Science: Rhetoric, Technology, and Natural Philosophy in Newtonian Britain, 1660-1750* (Cambridge, 1992), *passim*.

27. The collection was notable enough for Alexander Wilson and Robert Smith to record their reactions to it: NLS, 17747/71-72 [1751]; NLS, 17617/271.

28. A list of those known is given in Appendix III.

29. *A Catalogue of the Library of the Honble Samuel Molyneux* (London, 1730), p. 57. He paid £3. 1.0. The flycatcher was probably just what it seems to be since the *Oxford English Dictionary* gives no esoteric meaning for this term.

30. This device was an adding machine. One is shown in D. J. Bryden, *Scottish Scientific Instrument Makers 1600-1900* (Royal Scottish Museum, Edinburgh, 1912), p. 5.

31. Some of Moxon's plates are shown in D. J. Bryden, 'A Dictionary of Mathematical Instruments;' in *Making Instruments Count: Essays on Historical Instruments presented to Gerard L'Estrange Turner*, ed. R.G.W. Anderson, J.A.Bennet and W.F.Ryan (Cambridge, 1993), pp. 365-82. Many of the instruments referred to below are described and shown in: Mary Holbrook, R.G.W. Anderson and D.J. Bryden, *Science Preserved: A Directory of Scientific Instruments in Collections in the United Kingdom and Eire* (HMSO, Science Museum, London,1992) or in works listed in their bibliography. One wonders if Ilay's barrel measures were bought before or after Maclaurin had done his memoir for the excisemen of Scotland. See Grabiner, n. 10.

32. NLS, 11819/56.

33. In 1754, one James Hog wrote to Lord Milton about his newly invented horse- or water-driven mill 'for fining and beating flax'. That, he claimed, would produce 15% more flax and have less wastage. NLS, 16688/41-42 and 51. Other items from men Ilay employed at Inveraray and elsewhere are mentioned in the Saltoun Papers and in Board of Trustees' Minutes, NRS, NG/1/1/2-14.

34. George Adams' Inventory, Mount Stuart House. Its probable appearance can be seen in the plate which served as the frontispiece to the tenth edition of Joseph Harris's *The Description and Use of the Globes and the Orrery* (London,1768). Sold to Lord Bute, this instrument may be the item described in the W. & S. Jones Advertisement for the sale of the Bute's instruments in 1794. There, the item is said to be 'four feet in diameter' and five and a half feet from the floor to the top of the glass case. If it was Ilay's orrery, it had been modified or re-cased. Or, the diameter of the instrument may have been measured and later the total diameter of the case.

35. The Harris advertisement notes that Wright had made a similar one for the 3rd Duke of Argyll. The first appearance of this notice seems to have been in 1745. I thank Dr. Alison Morrison-Low for these advertisements. See also: Dr. Alison Morrison-Low, (note 53 above), p. 199. A similar orrery is described in *Science Preserved*, p. 64.

36. *Encyclopedia Britannica*, 3 vols, ed. William Smellie (Edinburgh, 1168- 1111), I:425; II:615- 682.

37. This piece is described and pictured in 'Sotheby's Sale Catalogue 1395' for the auction held in New York on 2 December 1999. I thank Dr. Alison Morrison-Low for bringing this to my attention.

38. Another instrument thought perhaps to have been his has recently been purchased by the Royal Museum in Edinburgh. It is described by the seller as a: 'PORTABLE SILVER COMPOUND ASTRONOMICAL DEVICE...The instrument thus functions as a universal ring dial, telling time anywhere on earth without need for compass. It also shows the right ascension/declination coordinate system...The instrument ... shows the observer's altazimuth coordinate system, within the celestial system'. Other rings allowed the instrument to function 'as a solar demonstration/armillary sphere' ...'This is one of the most sophisticated little astronomical devices we have seen'. This in compact form would have duplicated what the Duke possessed in London. I thank Alison Morrison- Low for this information. Sun dial bottoms are listed in the Adams inventory and there are references to an unknown number of sundials in Ilay's surviving papers.

39. *Molyneux Cat.*, p. 61.

40. Mary Cosh, 'Clockmaker Extraordinary: The Career of Alexander Cumming'. *Country Life*, 12 June 1969, pp. 1528, 1531.

41. Ian G. Lindsay, and Mary Cosh, *Inveraray and the Dukes of Argyll* (Edinburgh, 1973), p. 106.

42. NLS, 17614/71.

43. NLS, 17617/141.

44. Edmund and Dorothy Berkeley, *Dr. John Mitchell :The Man Who Made the Map* (Chapel Hill, 1974), p. 147.
45. NLS, 17630/275.
46. *Molyneux Cat.*, p. 66; the second came with '4 Books of Observations'.
47. *Letters of Colin Maclaurin*, p. 252; David Bryden's exhibition catalogue, 'James Short and His Telescopes' (Royal Scottish Museum, Edinburgh,1968), does not show a telescope matching this description but he does show others which must be very like it, *E.g.*, items 15 and 16.
48. Colin Maclaurin to Robert Smith, 28 December 1734, *Letters of Colin Maclaurin*, pp. 252-53.
49. NLS, 17617/271.7; 17619/286.2 and 5.
50. NLS, 17617/141;17619/286; 17619/286.
51. Adams Inventory, n. 24 above.
52. Robert Smith, *Optics*, 2 vols (London, 1738), II:329.
53. One of those telescopes is depicted and described by Bryden, 'James Short', item 25; see also T. N. Clarke, A.D. Morrison-Low and A.D.C. Simpson, 'James Short the Optic', in *Brass & Glass* (National Museums of Scotland, 1989), pp. 1-6, 46.
54. See Appendix II.
55. *Molyneux Cat.,* p. 60.
56. NLS, 17645/ 218 (1737); 17627/91 (1756).
57. NLS 17620/70; Wilson, trained as an apothecary surgeon, met Ilay and worked in his London laboratory in c.1737-39. It was obviously equipped to blow glass since Wilson there made thermometers of various sorts. The Duke patronized him until 1761, finally making him Professor of Practical Astronomy at Glasgow. Patrick Wilson, 'Memoir of Dr. Wilson read at the Royal Society of Edinburgh, 2 February 1789', pp.3-4, 8, 10.
58. His chief gardener probably laid out the drains which would have required a surveying instrument capable of sighting distant marks and noting the angles between the surveyor and the marks. NLS, 17647 and 17642/116 -130 .
59. Inventory, 29 June 1745, NLS, 17617/271.
60. Some were destroyed when the shed burned. Lindsay and Cosh, *Inveraray*, p. 86.
61. NLS, 17747|71-72 (1751); NLS, 17617|271.
62. NLS, 16533/162,188; 16591/ 48; 16604/170; 16670/153-7; 16671/ 134; 16684/26; 16695/108; 16591/48;17747/72.
63. NLS, 17617/141; 17646/65, 84; 17670/23.
64. Ilay to Milton, 30 June 1743, NLS, 16591/47.
65. NLS, 17642/130.
66. They were paid two pence for every mole and in one night took 34, about half the number of rats which the special trap caught at Whitton on one occasion; Method of Catching Rats, NLS, Saltoun Misc.54 /G 1756. Moles appear also in NLS, 17646/173 and in 17650/142 where the boys were paid one penny (?Scots) for each dead mole.
67. Ilay to Milton 12 January 1745, NLS, 17617/170].
68. Lindsay and Cosh, *Inveraray*, p. 360 n.166, a note on the Meikle (or MacKell) family of wrights.
69. *E.g.*, Alexander Cumming examined for Milton a model steam engine which Milton thought of using to drain his coal pits. NLS, 16694/108.
70. Many of those men are to be found in the Minutes of the Board of Trustees which sometimes commissioned them to build certain things or judge the usefulness of machines the Board wished to adopt and use in the linen trades. See: Minutes of the Board of Trustees, NRS, NG/1/1/2-14.
71. It is possible that 'A Modell to shew the Scaping of a pendulumm' which Adams noted in

his inventory, is what is described in Cosh, 'Cumming', p. 1528. Models were commonly used in the natural philosophy courses taught at the universities in Holland and in Scotland by men whom the Earl had helped into their chairs - Robert Dick jr. and John Anderson at Glasgow and Matthew Mackail and Francis Skene at Marischal College, Aberdeen. The most famous model of the time was the steam engine James Watt repaired at Glasgow. Models like theirs are shown in Peter de Clercq, *The Leiden Cabinet of Physics: A Descriptive Catalogue* (Museum Boerhaave, Leiden, 1997). Some of those used later by Patrick Copland have survived at Aberdeen University.

72. 'He could talk with every man in his own profession, from the deepest philosopher to the Meanest but ingenious Mechanic'. NLS, 17612/218.
73. Lindsay and Cosh, *Inveraray*, pp. 98-99. Ilay had met Marshall Saxe who was to have commanded the Jacobite soldiers who were to have accompanied Bonny Prince Charlie from France. They were not sent. His waggon was later taken and there were other models and reconstructions of it around Britain.
74. NLS, 17617/141.
75. Adams inventory (note 24).
76. NLS, 17617/271.7.
77. NLS, 17620/70.
78. *Molyneux Cat.*, p. 57; several types from the early eighteenth century are shown in Marian Fournier, *Early Microscopes: A Descriptive Catalogue*, (Museum Boerhaave, Leiden, 2003).
79. Adams inventory (note 24); NLS, 17617/271.
80. *Molyneux Cat.*, p. 57.
81. A publisher's note suggests the list is incomplete. *Account*, p. 21.
82. For s'Gravesande, see: *Physices elements mathematica,experimentis confirmata, sive introductio ad philosophiam Newtoniam, 1720-21*; (2nd ed. 1725; 3rd ed. Enlarged, Leiden, 1742) and *The Leiden Cabinet of Physics* which shows some of his instruments and more like those he used in demonstrations. For the teaching of physics in Holland see Edward G. Ruestow, *Physics at Seventeenth- and Eighteenth- Century Leiden: Philosophy and the new Science in the University* (The Hague, 1973), pp. 116-7, 141; Stewart, *The Rise of Public Science*, pp. 220, 236.
83. J. L. Heilbron, *Electricity in the 17th and 18th Centuries: A Study in Early Modern Physics*, (Mineola, N.Y. 1999; 1st ed.1979), pp.230-249; 233 and pp. 290-305.
84. He received his degree in October 1708 and had as his sponsor or promoter the King's University Mediciner, Patrick Urquhart, M.D., whose daughter Elisabeth decorated his diploma. *Officers and Graduates of University & King's College Aberdeen*, ed. Peter John Anderson (The New Spalding Club. Aberdeen, 1893), p. 125.
85. NLS, 26223; William Craig, *History of the Royal College of Physicians, Edinburgh* (Edinburgh, 1976), p. 1072.
86. Stuart [or Stewart] was the same age as the Duke and held an MD from Leiden (1706). He later studied at Padua and again at Leiden where he was said to have been a favourite of Boerhaave. He was in the entourage of the Duke of Chandos during the 1720s as a tutor to his son. He was also a man friendly with the 2nd Duke of Argyll, Ilay and Lord Lovat who may not have been jesting when he called him a Jacobite. Stuart had shares in the Sun Fire Insurance Company. Later he functioned as a travelling tutor to the Earl of Galloway. By the late 1730s or early 1740s, after Chandos had died, he probably became for a time a member of Argyll's household. In 1743 he travelled to Scotland with Argyll who introduced him to professors such as Robert Simson at Glasgow. John Mitchell was a chemist and botanist born in Virginia but educated at Edinburgh and at Leiden where he took a medical degree. He too may have lived some time with the Duke in the 1750s. A

well-travelled medical man, he was a congenial companion for the Duke because he was a botanist and chemist who had sought to solve the British alkali problems by finding new sources for potash production. He had a wide scientific correspondence and was the author of a notable map of North America used to define boundaries after the wars ending in 1763 and 1783. E. Ashworth Underwood, *Boerhaave's Men at Leyden and After* (Edinburgh, 1977), pp. 149-150; Stewart, *The Rise of Public Science*, p. 377; Lindsay and Cosh, *Inveraray*, p. 376 n. 4; Berkeley and Berkeley, *Mitchell*, pp. 102-105; Peter J. and Ruth V. Wallis, *Eighteenth Century Medics* (Project for Historical Bio-bibliography, Newcastle-upon-Tyne, 1988), p. 413.

87. Lindsay and Cosh, *Inveraray*, p. 78.

88. Sometime later, Alexander Carlyle reported that Sir David was cured of his fistula c.1758/9 by a course of the waters at Barege. *The Autobiography of Alexander Carlyle of Inveresk*, ed. John Hill Burton, (London and Edinburgh, 1910), p. 368.

89. The pillboxes sent to Scotland at one time came to more than eight bundles. If they were full, he was stocking a pharmacy; if not, he was looking to make a lot of something. His Scottish medicine chest had in it at least: spirit of hartshorn, 'Dr. Eaton's Stiptick', '14 phials wt Sp.V.C.', liquid laudenum, more stiptick, nox vomica, ipecacuanha, tartar, and probably increasing numbers of simples made from plants in his herb gardens. Ilay was growing in his gardens by 1748 what he thought was 'the true rhubarb'. That he would have dried and ground to make a laxative. It was one of the most common medicines of the time but one which had not been successfully raised in Britain. Domesticating it eventually saved the country a very large sum - it was worth up to about £5 a pound and thousands of pounds were imported annually. See, Clifford M. Foust, *Rhubarb The Wonderous Drug* (Princeton, 1992); NLS, 17619/286. 2, 4, 6.

90. Interests in medicine and botany were family interests. Ilay's father and a cousin of the same name, Archibald Campbell (?-1744), Bishop in the Scottish Episcopal Church, shared them. The latter left a huge collection of medical recipes which is held at the National Library of Scotland whose catalogue wrongly says that it was compiled by Ilay (NLS 3773). Ilay is not even among those listed as having contributed to this volume. Most who did were High Church Anglicans and Jacobites. The Bishop was more notable for working out the terms of inter-communion between English Non-jurors and some Orthodox Churches.

91. Lindsay and Cosh, *Inveraray*, p. 50.

92. The 12th Duke of Argyll informs me that there is not even a tradition of one having been created there.

93. '[A] nest of Crucibles', four small pans, 14 pounds of 'Green Vitriol', two ounces of 'Spirit of hartshorn and two ounces of 'prepared Corall' were shipped to Scotland at that time. NLS, 17614/124. The chemicals were probably for the painters.

94. NLS, 17648/67.

95. NLS, 17648/318.

96. *E.g.*, NLS, 17641/79. The North Pavilion was located in the complex of offices which flanked the house. The laboratory could have been in a free-standing building elsewhere on the estate to whose decoration it might then have contributed. There is no indication of it on the surviving plans at the National Library of Scotland or the Royal Commission on Ancient and Historical Monuments.

97. National Monuments of Scotland, MS PBD/286/43. This was a tentative plan of the Court drawn c.1730.

98. NLS, 17646/315. 17647/78, 130.

99. The last chimney seems to have been installed in 1741 by which time the laboratory was substantially complete. NLS, 17646/311.

100. NLS, 17646/67, 152; 17636/21. More pointing was done in 1746/7; 17648/131.
101. The mason wrote: 'The Laboratorie Roof is Intaglio Gon so as Non can be sarfe [safe] to stand under Both it the timbers being all Consumed and Rotten If it had Not bin Propt It would all of It ben In the Bottom Long Ago'. NLS, 17648/67. Corrosion as well as rain may have been at work.
102. NLS, 17647/152.
103. NLS, 17619/286-7.
104. NLS, 17646/285. Ilay had an account with Gray who was himself a *virtuoso*. A member of the Edinburgh Philosophical Society, Gray possessed microscopes, a telescope, a *camera obscura* and other apparatus. He wrote on weights and measures and in the 1750s was, like other of the Duke's associates, working on lime and limewater. Ilay made him King's Smith in Scotland (1757), an office with no salary but the perquisite of supplying all the Crown's ironwork. NLS, 17628/173.
105. NLS, 17646/284.
106. Ilay to Milton, 13 March 1741, NLS, 16584/58.
107. NLS, 17646/286, 282.
108. NLS, 17617/271/12.
109. NLS, 17619/286/8.
110. NLS, 17619/286/2, 4.
111. 'Brewers Bubbles' were hollow glass balls which floated at known specific gravities. They were widely used in the brewing industry but not restricted to it. Their re-discovery by Wilson (they had been known earlier but he thought he had invented them) was announced at a meeting of the Glasgow Literary Society in 1757/58. 'Biographical Account of Alexander Wilson M.D.', *The Edinburgh Journal of Science* 10 (1829), pp. 1-17, 8.
112. A digester - a sort of pressure cooker used to analyse substances - was one of the first purchases made by the Edinburgh Philosophical Society in 1743. British Library, Additional MS 6861/66.
113. NLS, 17624/91.
114. Taylor, *Mathematicians*; Ruth and Peter Wallis, *Biobibliography of British Mathematics and Its Applications, 1701-1760* (Letchworth, n.d. [1986]).
115. Berkeley and Berkeley, *Mitchell*, p. 111. His windmill is shown in a cutaway print in the *Gentleman's Magazine*, 19 June, 1749, pp. 249-50. It is not clear what his contribution to this device was.
116. Mint to be distilled, NLS, 17650/260. This is undated but before 1758.
117. NLS, 17889/35.
118. NLS, 17889/2.
119. These can be found in NLS, 17797/11 [1748] and 'Barbados Water', in NLS, 17889/34-5; 'Portable Soup' in NLS, 17889/1. The last may not have been his invention since a similar soup was for years advertised in the London papers where it was said to have been concocted by his brother's cook in c.1719, *E.g., General Advertiser*, 26 January 1748.
120. NLS, 17797/11; NLS, 17889/34-5; NLS, 17889/1.
121. Alexander Lind to Milton, n.d. (1754), NLS, 16688/98.
122. Argyll's recipe is given in NLS 17797/11. The house was notable for citrus trees; Symes, Michael, Alison Hodges and John Harvey, 'The Plantings at Whitton', *Garden History*, 14 (1986), pp. 138-172; Ilay to Milton, 30 June 1743, NLS, 16587/47.
123. Ilay to Sir John Clerk, 1 September 1739, Clerk of Penicuik Papers, NRS, GD18/5426/1. Ilay said he found her basic recipe in a book printed in 1655. The problem was of interest to him because members of the Walpole family suffered from the stone.
124. Green parchment bound book, NLS, 17889.
125. NLS, MS 17851/109.

126. Cosh and Lindsay, *Inveraray*, p. 50.

127. This does not sound like something he invented but made; NLS, 17889.

128. NLS, 17646/311.

129. Horace Walpole to Richard Bentley, 9 January 1755, *The Edition of Horace Walpole's Correspondence*, ed. Wilmarth S. Lewis, *et al.*, 48 vols (New Haven, Conn., 1937-1963); 35 (1973), pp. 200-04. It is interesting that Walpole should refer to more than one chemist working in Ilay's London laboratory but it is not clear that John Campbell was among them. Walpole had chemical dealings with Argyll in 1743 when he sent to Ilay to ask where cobalt and zinc might be purchased; Walpole to Horace Mann, 10 June 1743, 18 (1954), p. 247.

130. [Milton's] Memorandum Whim Saturday 6th June 1741, NLS, 17646/193. For the ambiance in which these studies were pursued see: Charles Withers, 'William Cullen's Agricultural Lectures and Writings and the Development of Agricultural Science in Eighteenth-Century Scotland'. *The Agricultural History Review*, 37 (1989), pp. 144-156.

131. The most interesting of those accounts dates from just after Cullen's death in 1790 and informs us that Argyll did chemical experiments in Scotland. According to the author, the Duke one day had found himself in need of some apparatus. Cullen supplied it. He was accordingly 'invited to dine, was introduced to his Grace - who was so pleased with his knowledge, his politeness and address, that he formed an acquaintance which laid the foundation of all Doctor Cullen's future advancement'. The author is likely to have been the paper's editor, James Anderson, who knew both men. One would like this story from c. 1745 to be true but it is indeed doubtful. *The Bee*, 22 December 1790, I:1,4.

132. George Haggarty and Sheila Forbes, 'Scotland: Lind and A-Marked Porcelain', *Northern Ceramic Society Journal,* 20 (2003-4), pp. 3-4.

133. This seems to be in his hand. NLS SC Misc. 54.

134. Lind's career is discussed by Haggarty and Forbes, 'A-Marked Porcelain', pp. 1-10.

135. 'Copy of a Memoire or paper upon Lime read in a Meeting of the Philosophical Society at Edinburgh Aug:2 1739 containing an Account of the Materials of which it is made, the way of burning or calcining Limestone, and the Natural properties and Uses of Lime by Mr. Lind member of the said Society'. This is among the papers of Lord Milton, who should not have had it unless he himself were a member of the Society. NLS, Saltoun Misc. 59b.

136. George Mackenzie, Earl of Cromarty, 'An Account of the Mosses of Scotland', *Philosophical Transactions of the Royal Society of London*, [1710] 27:296-301.

137. 'Memoire upon Lime', NLS, Saltoun Papers, S Misc 59b.

138. Ilay to Milton, 8 and 24 July 1742; NLS, 16587/5-7. The latter letter describes Ilay's library at Whitton, notes details of his planting techniques, and suggests experiments to make peat bricks which might burn with more intense heat than did loose peat.

139. The paper, 'Of the nature & Vertues of Peat'. mentions many experiments mostly from the summer of 1744. NLS, S Misc.54.

140. Lind to Lord Milton, 10 April 1749, NLS, 16667. Lind's work was published by the Philosophical Society in 1756; Joe Rock, 'The "A" Marked Porcelain: Further Evidence for the Scottish Option', *Transactions English Ceramic Circle*, 17 (1999), pp. 60-78; 72. Another of Argyll's friends working on peat was Henry Home who would himself later clear a substantial bog by floating his peat away to the Forth where it destroyed oyster beds. Ian Simpson Ross, *Lord Kames and the Scotland of His Day* (Oxford, 1972), p. 362; John Thomson, *An Account of the Life and Writings of William Cullen*, M.D., 2 vols, (I Edinburgh, 1832; I and II Edinburgh, 1859). I:63.

141. Berkeley and Berkeley, *Mitchell*, p. 102.

142. *Ibid,* pp 106-248, *passim*.

143. The best general account of these activities is still that given by Archibald and Nan Clow in *The Chemical Revolution* (London, 1952; reprinted, Freeport, N. Y., 1970); see the sections on ashes, kelp, soap, bleaching, glass, pottery, and 'social personnel'; see also Roger L. Emerson, 'The Philosophical Society of Edinburgh, 1748-1769', *British Journal for the History of Science*, 14 (1981), pp. 133-76, 162-5. Francis Home's experiments were conducted at Milton's estate; see Alastair J. Durie, *The British Linen Company, 1745-1775*, Scottish History Society, 5th Series, 9 (1996), p. 56.

144. Arthur Donovan, *Philosophical Chemistry in the Scottish Enlightenment*, (Edinburgh, 1875), p. 85.

145. Berkeley and Berkeley, *Mitchell*, pp. 102-5; Donovan, *Philosophical Chemistry*, pp. 79-83.

146. Lind to Ilay, 17 December 1741; Argyll to Milton, 24 July 1742; NLS, 16585/211-12; 16694/108; Wilson to Cullen, 19 May 1760, Thomson/Cullen Papers, Glasgow University Library, MS 2255/ Box 3.

147. NLS, 17687/85-86.

148. In the summer of 1732, when he visited Sir Robert Walpole at Houghton Hall, Ilay's knowledge of springs and water led him to attempt to find a new water source for the estate. 'Account of a Journey ... in September 1732, 2nd E. Oxford', *HMCR of His Grace the Duke of Portland* (London, 1851), VI:161.

149. Lind, 'Of the Nature and Virtues of Peat [undated but probably 1742-44]'. NLS, Saltoun Papers, S Misc 54.

150. Ilay to Milton, 18 January 1742, NLS, 16587/54.

151. Haggerty and Forbes, 'Lind and A-Marked Porcelain', p. 5.

152. Lind to Milton, 19 December 1741, NLS, 16585/211-12.

153., Memorandum about Iron, 1757, NLS, Misc SB; Robert McGeachy, *Argyll 1730-1850: Commerce, Community and Culture* (Edinburgh, 2009), pp. 151-66.

154. Some Remarks on the Nature & Qualities of Iron (c.1757?), NLS, Saltoun Misc 54.

155. 'Of the Analysis and uses of Peat.' *Essays and Observations Physical and Literary*, 3 vols, II: (Edinburgh, 1766, Essay 10); Lindsay and Cosh, *Inveraray*, p. 372 n. 42. In 1761 James Stuart Mackenzie, Argyll's nephew, was still doing peat experiments at Belmont. Uncatalogued James Stuart Mckenzie Papers, Mount Stuart House, Isle of Bute.

156. There is no surviving list of the Philosophical Society membership in these years and no minutes. A partial members list is given by me in articles in the *British Journal for the History of Science* (1979-1988) listed in the bibliography of this book.

157. Berkeley and Berkeley, *Mitchell*, pp. 120-21. One spin-off from this interest was the 'Argyll sauceboat' which the Duke designed. This sauceboat has a sleeve into which a hot iron can be inserted to keep warm whatever the dish contains.

158. Haggarty and Forbes, 'A-Marked Porcelain', p. 6.

159. Rock and Haggarty have argued that the fine porcelain produced there and marked with an 'A' may well indicate that Argyll had a financial interest in the Lind pottery which almost certainly produced the ware. Rock, 'The "A" Marked Porcelain', p. 69; Haggerty, personal communication.

160. Milton was also involved with this business. Argyll to Milton, 18 December 1750, NLS, 16671/133-34; see also Haggarty and Forbes, 'A-Marked Porcelain', pp. 5-6.

161. *Ibid*, p. 6

162. Lind to Milton, 10 April 1749; 26 April 1749, NLS, 16667/86; Haggarty and Forbes, *Ibid*, pp. 4-5.

163. *Ibid*, p. 6.

164. I thank Jonathan Kinghorn of the Glasgow Museums and Art Galleries for information about the offer of clay and the Duke's purchases of dishes.

165. Matthew Eddy, *The Language of Mineralogy: John Walker, Chemistry and the Edinburgh Medical School 1750-1800* (London, 2008), p. 108.

166. Jan Golinski, *Science as Public Culture: Chemistry and Enlightenment in Britain, 1760-1820*, (Cambridge,1992), 35-36; Donovan, *Philosophical Chemistry*, p. 85. Cullen sent the Duke a draft of a piece on the making of salt; Thomson/Cullen Papers, GUL, 2255/60, 61-66. The Duke would also have known that Cullen's lectures on chemistry, given in 1747-48 and afterwards, were 'calculate not only for medical students, but for the general students of the University [of Glasgow], and for the gentlemen engaged in any business connected with chemistry' such as potteries. Thomson, *Life of William Cullen*, I:25.

167. Drafts of a letter or letters mentioning the first and concerning the latter can be found in Correspondence with Pupils, GUL, Cullen Papers.

168. Ilay to Milton, 20 June 1741, NLS, 16580/41.

169. David Flint to Argyll, 10 September 1759, NLS, 16710/47.

170. *Ibid.*

171. Lind made a special putty and cement for the bason at The Whim. Ilay to Milton, ? March 1742, NLS 16587/71.

172. Other scholars used his library for their researches.

173. Golinski, *Science as Public Culture*, p. 12.

174. Robert Simson to William Hunter, 9 July 1761; I owe this reference to the late Dr. Helen Brock.

Chapter 8

1. The 2nd Duke had this built to designs by James Gibbs in 1728. Nearby were fine gardens at Rutland Lodge, Montrose House, Douglas House and across the Thames, Marble Hill House. If he owned Kenwood House at anytime, he maintained another fine garden there. Anonymous, *Middlesex, Biographical and Pictorial* (London, 1906) unpaginated. [p.45-46].

2. Argyll to Lord Milton, 12 November 1743, quoted by Ian Lindsay and Mary Cosh, *Inveraray and the Dukes of Argyll* (Edinburgh, 1973), p. 11-12.

3. Plants could cost a great deal. Two guineas for a rare import was not an uncommon price while a Greek strawberry tree sold at mid-century for £54.11.0; Andrea Wulf, *The Brother Gardeners: Botany, Empire and the Birth of an Obsession* (New York, 2009), p. 139.

4. Mark Laird, *The Flowering of the Landscape Garden English Pleasure Grounds 1720-1800* (Philadelphia, 1999), p. 98; Edmund and Dorothy Berkeley, *Dr. John Mitchell:The Man Who Made the Map* (Chapel Hill, 1974), pp. 131-32.

5. Ilay to Lord Milton, 2 August 1735, NLS, 16559/134.

6. Berkeley and Berkeley, *Mitchell*, p. 150. Dr. Henry Noltie of the Royal Botanic Garden, Edinburgh, tells me this is a very early Scottish instance of such work.

7. Deskford to James Grant of Grant, 22 February 1761, Seafield Papers, NRS, GD248/672/4.

8. The plans of the area from *The Survey of London* (Vol.31, p. 296) show the one at No. 7 as being 100' by 50'. *The Survey* is available on line.

9. Ilay to Milton, 2 August 1735, NLS, 16559/134. Cosh suggests that the property was bought with some of his profits from the South Sea Bubble. See: 'Lord Ilay's Eccentric Building Schemes', *Country Life*, 20 July 1972, pp. 142-145.

10. Berkeley and Berkeley, *Mitchell*, p. 110; Lindsay and Cosh, *Inveraray*, p. 10; Laird, *The Flowering*, p. 83. What follows relies heavily upon those accounts.

11. Argyll to Milton, 25 February 1748, NLS, 16656/79. Michael Symes, Alison Hodges and John Harvey, 'The Plantings at Whitton', *Garden History*, 14 (1986), pp. 138-172. The size of the place is differently estimated but their estimate of 55 acres may be correct.
12. Ilay to Lord Milton, NLS, 16531/15.
13. Ilay to Milton, 10 July 1725, NLS, 16531/23.Cosh, 'Lord Ilay's Eccentric Building Schemes', p. 143.
14. Symes, *et al.* 'The Plantings at Whitton', p. 143. It served as a guest house.
15. Laird, *The Flowering*, pp. 85, 88.
16. Ilay to Milton, October 1741, NLS, 16584/86. The fish were fed blood meal.
17. 'The Country Seat' has been edited by William Johnston and published on a compact disk in the Officina series of disks on the Scottish Enlightenment.
18. The Temple was eventually replaced with a three-sided Gothic Tower.
19. Sir John Clerk of Penicuik, journey to London in 1727, Clerk of Penicuik Papers, NRS, GD18 2107/8-9.
20. Cosh thought the frontage of 108' belonged to the unbuilt mansion; 'Lord Ilay's Eccentric Building Schemes', p. 144.
21. Sir John Clerk, A Tour into England, GD18/2110/1, p. 39.
22. 'The great walks round the Garden at Whitten 1386 yds wanting 373 yds of a mile viz 1760 yds.'; Andrew Fletcher's Diary, NLS, 17747/29.
23. The length is given in Symes, *et al*, 'Plantings', p. 143.
24. See, William Woollett, two engravings (Plates 8 and 9) showing the canal and tower in 1757 as seen from the Greenhouse and the bowling green behind the house.
25. See Plate 5.
26. T. F. Friedman, *James Gibbs* (New Haven, Conn., 1984), p. 163.
27. See Plate 5.
28. The eagle and crow came by ship, possibly from America; Ilay to Milton, 4 January 1732, NLS, 16548/89; Milton to Ilay, 22 December 1740, NLS, 16580/145. Ilay later sent crows to Scotland where they seem to have been meant to control pests.
29. The 1761-65 map of the garden shows it (Plate 5). Laird quotes Thomas Spence's account of the garden c.1760. Laird, *The Flowering*, p. 83. The Coutts 'Out book' shows payments for birds on 19 August 1724 of £0.1.6 and December 1727 of £ 1.11.6; their sale price is in the Coutts 'In book', 24 July 1761, £61.8.6.
30. The Duke asked an old friend, Cadwallader Colden, for a 'Bull & cow' and eventually got them in 1750. They seem to have been temporarily at Whitton but at least one was destined for Inveraray. Berkeley and Berkeley, *Mitchell*, pp. 136,147; Ilay to Milton, 7 July 1749, NLS, 17619/287; 'A Letter from John Mitchell to Caddallader Colden [25 March 1749]', ed. Theodore Hornberger, *Huntington Library Quarterly*, 10 (1947), pp. 411-417. This purchase was probably prompted by Mark Catesby's description of buffalo which pointed out: 'They have been known to breed with tame cattle, that were become wild and the calves being so too, were neglected; though it is the general opinion that if reclaiming these animals is impracticable (of which no trial has been made) to mix the breed with tame cattle, would much improve the breed, yet nobody has had the curiosity, nor have given themselves any trouble about it'. See *Catesby's Birds of Colonial America*, ed. Alan Feduccia (Chapel Hill and London, 1985), p. 157; The male bison was shipped to Inveraray but one hears nothing more of him. He presumably did not improve the breed of the Highland cattle raised in the vicinity, just as his mate did nothing for breeds in Surrey. Ilay to Milton, ? January 1733, NLS,16552/68.
31. He may have been thinking about more than mohair cloth since he sent Lord Milton an angora wig. Ilay to Milton, 6 November 1732, NLS, 17642/183.
32. Ilay to Milton, 21 September 1734, NLS, 16552/86.

33. The house by Roger Morris is depicted and described by Cosh, 'Lord Ilay's Eccentric Building Schemes', p. 145.
34. Laird, *The Flowering*, pp. 87-88.
35. One entrance to the considerable literature on this subject is found in Yu Liu, 'The Importance of the Chinese Connection: The Origin of the English Garden', *Eighteenth-Century Life*, 27 (2003), pp. 70-98.
36. Laird, *The Flowering*, p. 88. An earlier catalogue, now lost, had been made by John Mitchell by early 1749; 'A letter....', *Huntington Library Quarterly*, p. 415.
37. Berkeley and Berkeley give the number of trees and shrubs as 368; *Mitchell*, p. 132.
38. *Kalm's Account of his Visit to England...*, trans. Joseph Lucas (New York, 1892), pp. 57-59. How difficult it was to grow exotics in England has been emphasized by Laird, *The Flowering*, p. 86.
39. A. A. Tait, *The Landscape Garden in Scotland 1735-1835* (Edinburgh, 1980), p. 99.
40. Berkeley and Berkeley, *Mitchell*, p. 149.
41. Symes, 'Plantings', p. 150; the lists are on pp. 151-172. Sir Charles Lennox, 2nd Duke of Richmond; Robert, 8th Baron Petre and Charles Hamilton were friends of Ilay and among his dinner guests at Whitton. They were all fanciers of new shrubs and trees. Hamilton's garden and his innovations are frequently noticed by Laird in *The Flowering* which has views of it (Figures 1, 2, 5, 8, 9)
42. *Ibid*, pp. 85-88, *passim*.
43. *The Correspondence of John Bartram 1734-1777*, ed. Edmund and Dorothy Smith Berkeley (Gainesville, 1992), pp. 287, 288, 291, 311, 312, 319, 320, 421.
44. See, Wulf, *The Brother Gardeners, passim*.
45. When Pehr Kalm visited in 1748, he observed that 'the Duke comes out from London as often as he can find time from his duties'. *Kalm's Account*, p. 57.
46. Lisbet Koerner, *Linnaeus: Nature and Nation* (Cambridge, Mass., 1999); See chapters 4-8.
47. NLS, 17889/73-82. The Berkeley's believed that the essays on the cultivation of plants found in the Saltoun Papers were copies or versions of papers written by John Mitchell. Berkeley and Berkeley, *Mitchell*, pp. 133-136.
48. Symes, 'Plantings', pp. 170-172.
49. *Correspondence of John Bartram*, p. 312.
50. Like Bute, Stuart Mackenzie was a member of numerous scientific societies and knew many astronomers, agriculturists and naturalists. An inventory of some of his manuscripts is given by David Gavine, 'James Stewart Mackenzie (1719-1800) and the Bute MSS', *Journal of the History of Astronomy* 5 (1974), pp. 208-214.
51. Richmond, Petre, some of the nurserymen and others in this circle are discussed in Wulf, *The Brother Gardeners, passim*. Others can be found in Forbes Robertson, *Early Scottish Gardeners and their Plants 1650-1750* (East Linton, 2000).
52. Justice went bankrupt c.1749 but Milton and Argyll managed his withdrawal from his post as Principal Clerk of Session and arranged to pay his creditors 10s in the pound; NLS, 16664/21. See also, Priscilla I. M. Minay, 'James Justice (1698-1763): Eighteenth-Century Scots Horticulturalist and Botanist', *Garden History*, 2 (1974), pp. 51-74. For Naysmith or Naesmith see *HPHC 1715-1754*, II:289; D. J. Mabberley, *ODNB*, 40:103-04; R. M. Sunter, *Patronage and Politics in Scotland 1707-1832* (Edinburgh, 1986), pp. 148-59. I am told by Dr. Henry Noltie that Naysmith was unlikely to have studied in Sweden. Naysmith was another of Ilay's friends with a Jacobite past.
53. Tait, *Landscape Garden*, pp. 18-21, 40-44.
54. Hazel Le Rougetel, 'The Chelsea Gardener: Philip Miller 1691-1771'. (Natural History Museum Publications, London, 1990), pp. 9-10, 63-4;

____, 'Philip Miller/John Bartram: Botanical Exchange', *Garden History* 14:1 (1986), pp. 32-49. She thinks Ilay was something of a follower of Miller.

55. Laird believes some of the garden's oldest trees may have come from Catesby's collecting expeditions to America from 1712-1726. Laird, *The Flowering*, p.86. Symes, *et al.*, in 'Plantings', suggest that some might also have come from the collections made in Georgia by William Houston (1695-1733). A brief account of Houston's collecting activities is given in Nicolai Josephi Jacquin, *Selectarum Stirpium Americanarum Historia* (facsmile edition of the 1763 publication), edited and introduced by Frans A. Stafleu (New York, 1971), p. F23. Houston's work was known in Sweden and France and many of his seeds were raised by Philip Miller. Houston's brother, James, remained active in botanical and collecting circles for many years.

56. Le Rougetel, 'Philip Miller/John Bartram', pp. 32-49.

57. For Clayton, see, J, L. Reveal and J. S. Pringle, 'Taxonomic botany and floristics' in *Flora of North America North of Mexico*, ed. the Flora of North America Editorial Committee (Oxford, 1993), I:157-192; E. and D. Berkeley, *The Reverend John Clayton: A Parson with a Scientific Mind* (Charlottesville, 1965).

58. Berkeley and Berkeley, *Mitchell*, 127; Lisbet Koerner, *Linnaeus*, p. 89.

59. John Harvey, 'A Scottish Botanist in London in 1766', *Garden History* 9 (1981), pp. 40-74. I thank Dr. Alison Morrison-Low for this reference.

60. Ilay to Milton, 26 February, 22 and 31 December 1726, NLS, 16533/49, 150 and 153. Those letters record seeds from the Carolinas, Pennsylvania and perhaps northern colonies as well. Other seed contributors are noted by Berkeley and Berkeley, *Mitchell*, pp. 125-143, *passim*.

61. Margaret Riley, 'The club at the Temple Coffee House revisited', *Archives of Natural History* 33 (2006), pp. 90-100.

62. For an account of this club, see R. P. Stearns, *Science in the British Colonies of America* (Chicago, 1970), pp. 258-338 and Stearns and George Frederick Frick, *Mark Catesby, The Colonial Audubon* (Urbana, 1961), pp. 86-98.

63. *Catesby's Birds*, p. 137.

64. *Ibid*, pp. 37-38.

65. Collinson's botanical world can be mapped from, *"Forget not Mee & My garden..."* *Selected Letters, 1725-1768 of Peter Collinson, F.R.S.*, ed. Alan W. Armstrong (American Philosophical Society (Philadelphia, 2002).

66. Amy R. W. Meyers and Margaret Beck Pritchard, 'Introduction: Toward an Understanding of Catesby' in *Empire's Nature: Mark Catesby's New World Vision*, ed. Meyers and Pritchard (Chapel Hill, 1998), p. 23.

67. He had the two volumes published by subscription in 1731-35. The second edition of this work was finished only in 1747 by which time it had '220 plates, illustrating 109 birds, 33 amphibians and reptiles, 46 fishes, 31 insects, 9 quadrupeds, and 171 plants'; *Catesby's Birds*, p. 5. Ilay had subscribed to the collection by 1743 if not earlier. David R. Brigham, 'The Patronage of Natural History', in Meyers and Pritchard, *Empire's Nature*, pp. 141-46; 114. Brigham prints the list of the 105 known subscribers on pp. 141-45.

68. *Mark Catesby's Natural History of America; The Watercolors from the Royal Library,Windsor Castle*, ed. Henrietta McBurney (London, 1997), p. 17.

69. Therese O'Malley, 'Mark Catesby and the Culture of Gardens' in Meyers and Pritchard, *Empire's Nature*, pp. 147-183, especially, pp. 170-174.

70. Cochineal was the source for a red dye; rhubarb was a laxative in common use in Britain. A great deal of money and effort was expended to make it available at lower cost. See, Clifford M. Foust, *Rhubarb: the Wonderous Drug* (Princeton, 1992). Dr. Patrick Sinclair studied not at Leiden but Utrecht while Ilay was there. Sinclair later became an Army

Physician. See, Peter J. and Ruth V Wallis., *Eighteenth Century Medics*, Project for Historical Bio-bibliography (Newcastle upon Tyne, 1988).

71. Catesby to Sherrard, 20 November 1724, quoted by David Brigham, 'The Patronage of Natural History'. in Meyers and Pritchard, *Empire's Nature*, pp. 106-07.

72. I thank Dr. John Dixon for this information. See Colden's letter: 'An acct of some plants the seeds of which were sent to Brigadier Hunter at his desire for the Earl of Islay', October 1725, in 'Copy book of letters on subjects of Philosophy, Medicine, and Friendship, 1716-1721' in *Unpublished Scientific and Political Papers and Notes, Cadwallader Colden Papers* (New York Historical Society). The Coldens had long been associated with the Inveraray Campbells. Hunter, FRS, was an Argathelian who shared Ilay's interest in the theatre since he was also a playwright.

73. Alexander Lind was in London in late 1749 and early 1750 so this is probably not Dr. James Lind who took his M.D. degree at Edinburgh in 1748 and had recently ceased to be a surgeon.

74. Diary of Andrew Fletcher, NLS, 17745, 17746, 17747, 17750; also. See Appendix IV.

75. James Glen to Argyll, n.d. (after 1743), NRS, Dalhousie Papers, GD45/2/1. I thank Alexander Murdoch for this reference. The letter promised to send plants and seeds, birds and shells for the Duke's cabinet. The specimens were to show the uniqueness of the flora and fauna of America when compared with those of Britain and Europe. The cabinet is likely to have been extensive but little is known about it.

76. In the 1750s, he was in touch with three Carolinia planters (Dr. Alexander Garden, Henry Middleton, and an old Eton classmate named Kinlock) about grape vines and cork oaks which might improve the colonial economy and provide imports to Britain. Edmund and Dorothy Berkeley, *Dr. Alexander Garden of Charles Town* (Chapel Hill, 1969), pp. 156-7.

77. Roger L. Emerson, 'The Edinburgh Society for the Importation of Foreign seeds and Plants, 1764-1773', *Eighteenth-Century Life* 7, n.s. 2 (1982), pp. 73-95.

78. *Peeblesshire: An Inventory of the Ancient Monuments*, 2 vols (Edinburgh, 1969) II:326-331; NLS, 17642 contains documents about the lease and purchases.

79. NLS, 17612/220.

80. Ilay to Milton, 2 and 10 February 1738, NLS, 16572/77 and 85.

81. There is a modern edition of this edited by Annette Hope (Edinburgh, 1988).

82. Part of this sum was probably paid in meal to the 'Turfors'.

83. NLS, 17642/46. This was apparently surveyed by a Patrick Lindsay. What is likely to be a reference to another survey and set of estimates is found in the records for 1731; NLS, 17642/116.

84. NLS, 17642/77-80.

85. 'A Treatise Concerning the Manner of Fallowing Ground, Raising of Grass-Seeds and Training of Lint and Hemp ....' (Published by HIKAS, Edinburgh, 1724), pp. 18-24.

86. Ilay to Lord Milton, NLS, 165303/162. Other correspondence from about the same time shows the men sharing information on plows, mowing machines, cattle and crops.

87. NLS, 17646/193.

88. NLS, 17889/73-82.

89. In 1730, Ilay sent up alders, 'Abeles' [white poplars], black poplars, aspins, Dutch elms and willows. Ilay to Milton, 24 December 1730, NLS 16540/97. In 1731, he planted New England 'Scarlet Oak and Virginian cedars'. He noted, 'As the Spring comes forward I become A little Tree mad'. Ilay to Milton, 16 March and 5 July 1731, NLS, 16545/80,82 and 88; see also Robertson, *Scottish Gardeners*, p. 127

90. The 'I' of the essay is may be Argyll.

91. NLS, 17642/116.

92. Most of these plants are found in the seed bills rendered for 1749-1750 by the Edinburgh seedsman Patrick Drummond; NLS, 17619/139.
93. There are references from 1740, to the models of the 'Pidgeon house', which is described as not yet finished. NLS, 17645/266-267, 17646/86 and 185.
94. NLS, 17647/210-a-c.
95. Lindsay and Cosh, *Inveraray*, pp. 130, 132; NLS, 17650/245.
96. NLS, 17642/134.
97. Lindsay and Cosh *Inveraray*, p. 134. Such ponds go back to medieval monasteries. In his, the oysters died and the attempt to farm them was soon given up.
98. *Ibid*, pp. 121-143.
99. Horace Walpole, *On Modern Gardening* (London, 1975; written 1770 and first published in *Anecdotes of Painting*, 1780), p.24. Walpole went on to discriminate three kinds of gardens — gardens shading into parks, those appropriate to ornamental farms and those which went from gardens to a wild landscape. They corresponded roughly to the Duke's gardens at Whitton, The Whim and Inveraray.

Chapter 9

1. Ilay to ?, 22 November 1726, PRO, SP54/17, item 68.
2. 'As for prayers, intercessions, & remonstrations, they have effect only with the tender, the compassionate & the good, & are very faint in their effects on those of different dispositions', Argyll to Henrietta Howard, n.d. [1746], British Library Add. Ms. 22628/51.
3. Sir John Clerk. A Toure into England in the Year 1733, NRS, GD18/2110/1/p.47. Gordon was not only a deist and 'Commonwealthman' but a classical scholar who published translations of Tacitus and Sallust in 1728 and 1744. Those were subsidized by the government to keep him from writing against it.
4. See: Michael Hunter, ' "Aikenhead the Atheist": The Context and Consequences of Articulate Irreligion in the Late Seventeenth Century' in *Atheism from the Reformation to the Enlightenment,* eds. Michael Hunter and David Wooton (Oxford, 1992); pp. 221-254; Michael Graham, *The Blasphemies of Thomas Aikenhead* (Edinburgh, 2008). That book discusses the works available to students at Edinburgh. Glasgow University Library had most of the titles Graham mentions: see 'Catalogus Librorum Bibliothecae Universitatis Glasguensis anno 1691', GUL, Gen. 1312. The entries in that under-used catalogue run to at least 1718 and show what the University bought during a long generation.
5. James Wodrow, Cases Answered by the Society of Students of divinity under Mr. Ja[mes] Wodrow, GUL, MS Gen.343.
6. Aikenhead was a student at Edinburgh at about the same time as Thomas Halyburton was studying at Edinburgh and St Andrews (1692-96). Both knew the sceptics and atheistical thinkers. *The Memoirs of the Life of Mr. Thomas Halyburton* (Edinburgh, 1714), particularly Chapter 2, testify to his own temptations to scepticism and atheism. His posthumous and frequently reprinted *Memoirs* was aimed at deists and sceptics. By 1703, Edinburgh University had its heretical and atheistic books under lock and key; *Extracts from the Records of the Burgh of Edinburgh 1710-1718*, ed. Helen Armet (London, 1967), p. 49.
7. Wodrow, Cases of Conscience; for more on the theological teaching in these years see Anne Skoczylas, *Dr. Simson's Knotty Case: Divinity, Politics and Due Process in Early Eighteenth-Century Scotland* (Montreal, Kingston, London, Ithaca, 2001). Students

everywhere were exposed in this fashion to atheistical ideas. See Alan C. Kors, *Atheism in France 1650-1729: the Orthodox Sources of Disbelief*, Vol. I (Princeton, 1990).

8. Jonathan Israel, *Radical Enlightenment: Philosophy and the Making of Modernity* (Oxford, 2001); ____, *Enlightenment Contested; Philosophy, Modernity, and the Emancipation of Man 1670-1752* (Oxford, 2006). The first supersedes older accounts of the clandestinely circulated literature leading to some strands of the early enlightenment.

9. John W. Cairns, 'Alexander Cunningham's Proposed Edition of the Digest An Episode in the History of the Dutch Elegant School' *Tijdschrift voor Rechtsgeschiedenis*, vol. 69, (2001), pp. 81-117 and pp. 307-359.

10. For a discussion of all that see Frank E. Manuel, *The Eighteenth Century Confronts the Gods* (Cambridge, 1959), especially Chapters one and two, pp. 3-128.

11. NLS, 16531/59.

12. English deists tended to hold a conjectural history of religion which saw it as going through cycles, swinging from an original monotheism, which was moral and reasonable, to superstition and enthusiasm. Those phases they associated with periods of economic prosperity and political freedom oscillating with periods of oppression under tyrants. Everything varied together.

13. See Hugh Trevor-Roper, 'From Deism to History: Conyers Middleton' in *History and Enlightenment*, ed. John Robertson (New Haven, Conn. and London, 2010), pp. 71-119.

14. In 1757, Argyll made it a condition in the leases of his tenants on Iona that they 'should build a sufficient stone wall six foot high... at forty feet distance from the walls of its ruins on a line marked out by the Duke's factor'. Derek John Patrick, 'People and Parliament in Scotland 1689-1702', Unpublished Ph.D. dissertation, St Andrews University 2002, pp. 150-51; *Argyll: An Inventory of the Monuments*, Vol. IV, Royal Commission on Ancient and Historical Monuments in Scotland (Edinburgh, 1982), pp. 49, 150-51.

15. Stephen D. Snoblen, 'To Discourse of God: Isaac Newton's Heterodox Theology and His Natural Theology' in *Science and Dissent in England, 1688-1945*, ed. Paul B. Wood (Aldershot, England and Burlington, Vt.); see also Snoblen's entry, 'Newton', in T*he Oxford Encyclopedia of the Enlightenment*, 4 vols, ed. Alan C. Kors, (New York, 2002), 3:172-77.

16. One only has to look at a few of them to see this - Girolamo Cardano, Hugo Grotius, René Descartes, Thomas Hobbes, Jan de Wit, Jean LeClerc, and others. They found their way into collections such as the dictionaries of Louis Moreri, Pierre Bayle, Jeremy Collier, John Ward, or Giovanni Botero's *Detti memorabili di personaggi illustri* (1608), [*Memoirs of Illustrious People*], all of which Ilay owned.

17. A general discussion of this is contained in John Hedley Brooke, *Science and Religion: Some Historical Perspective* (Cambridge, 1991).

18. See the *Alciphron or the Minute Philosopher* (1732) in which Berkeley describes those men.

19. For Toland's writings on politics see Robert E. Sullivan, *John Toland and the Deistic Controversy: A Study in Adaptations* (Cambridge Mass., 1982).

20. John Calvin, *The Institutes of the Christian Religion*, 2 vols trans. and ed. Henry Beveridge (London, 1962), I:234-37.

21. What follows here draws heavily upon 'Professor John Simson and the Growth of Enlightenment in the Church of Scotland', Ph.D. thesis by Ann Skoczylas, University of Western Ontario, (1996) and from her book *Mr. Simson's Knotty Case*.

22. See 'John Anderson' in *Biographical Dictionary of Eminent Scotsmen*, 4 vols, ed. Robert Chambers (Glasgow, 1854), I:60-61. Ilay secured for John's grandson, another John, the Chair of Oriental Languages at Glasgow University. Professor Anderson described his grandfather as 'an eloquent preacher, a defender of civil and religious liberty, and a man of wit and learning;' *Ibid*.

23. 'Act for securing the Protestant Religion and Presbyterian Church government'.
24. The lists were printed in an annual pamphlet, 'The Principal Acts of the General Assembly of the Church of Scotland'. This contained an abbreviated set of minutes for the Assembly. The years in which he is not listed among the Commissioners to the General Assembly are more likely to contain errors of omission than to show him really absent from the list.
25. The intention of the English MPs was to make the established churches more alike and a future union more likely and less jarring to Scots.
26. Henry Sefton, 'Lord Ilay and Patrick Cuming: A Study in Eighteenth-Century Ecclesiastical Management', *Records of the Scottish Church History Society* 19 (1977), pp. 203-216, 203-04.
27. He probably had done so earlier when students at Glasgow appealed to his brother and him for aid in a legal case against the University. See, Roger L. Emerson, *Academic Patronage in the Scottish Enlightenment: Glasgow, Edinburgh and St Andrews Universities* (Edinburgh, 2008), pp. 67-70. That case also involved Lord Molesworth who circulated in c.1720 in the set of Henrietta Howard; British Library, Add. Ms. 22269.
28. Roger L. Emerson, *Professors, Patronage and Politics: the Scottish Universities in the Eighteenth Century* (Aberdeen, 1991), *passim*.
29. NLS, 17614/4.
30. 'Lord Isla subscribed the Formula, and sate as a member of the Commission. I think it's the first time he has sat in our church Judicatories, though often named'. Robert Wodrow, *Analecta or Materials for a History of Remarkable Providences Mostly Relating to Scottish Ministers and Christians*, 4 vols, ed. Matthew Leishman (Edinburgh 1842-43), II:243.
31. Alexander Carlyle reported that the Duke chid Alexander Webster, an evangelical minister, in an Assembly held during the 1740s for remarks made about Walpole in a 'satirical sermon'; *The Autobiography of Dr. Alexander Carlyle of Inveresk 1722-1805*, ed. John Hill Burton (Edinburgh, 1910), pp. 249-50, 263. Carlyle says Ilay spoke with 'dignity and force.'
32. That position was adopted in the Church of Scotland Act of 1921.
33. Wodrow, *Analecta*, IV:72. Among the Argathelian ministers were William Hamilton, the Professor of Divinity at Edinburgh, James Gowdie, a future Principle of Edinburgh appointed by Ilay, and George Logan, a powerful Edinburgh minister.
34. Ilay to Newcastle, 2 September 1729, NRS, SP54/19/90.
35. Quoted in Arthur Fawcett, *The Cambuslang Revival:The Scottish Evangelical Revival of the Eighteenth Century* (Edinburgh and Carlisle, Pa., 1996; 1st printing 1971), p. 197.
36. What follows relies on the parish entries for the presbyteries of Inveraray, Cowal, Kintyre, Lorn and Mull in the Synod of Argyll contained in Hew Scott, *Fasti Ecclesiae Scoticanae*, 8 vols (Edinburgh, 1915-30; 1st edn. 1866-71),and on the accounts of them in the *Statistical Account of Scotland,* 20 vols, ed. Sir John Sinclair (Edinburgh, 1791-1799; reprinted and rearranged with editorial comments by Donald Withrington, Ian Grant, *et al*, 20 vols, Wakefield, 1983).
37. The parish of Kilfinichin and Kilviceuen on Mull had one church. Worship took place 'at the side of a hill' in the other sections of the parish. *Statistical Account*, XX:318.
38. Leigh Eric Schmidt, *Holy Fairs: Scotland and the Making of American Revivalism* (Grand Rapids, 2001; 1st ed. Princeton, 1989), p. 261 n.31.
39. At Glasgow, Edinburgh, St Mary's College, St Andrews, and King's College, Aberdeen the principals were professors of divinity.
40. All this is nicely summarized by Richard B. Sher and Alexander Murdoch, 'Patronage and Party in the Church of Scotland, 1750-1800', in *Church Politics and Society: Scotland 1408-1929*, ed. Norman Macdougall, (Edinburgh, 1983), pp. 197-220.

41. Andrew L. Drummond and James Bulloch, *The Scottish Church 1688-1843*, (Edinburgh, 1973), pp. 39-40.
42. Quoted by Henry Sefton in 'Lord Ilay', pp. 203-216; 205.
43. Walter Stewart to Robert Wodrow, 31 December 1725, NLS, Wodrow Quarto Letters, XVI.
44. Emerson, *Academic Patronage*, p. 234.
45. Sefton, 'Lord Ilay,' p. 204.
46. M.A. Stewart, 'Principal Wishart (1692-1753) and the controversies of his day', *Records of the Church History Society* 30 (2000), pp. 60-102; 78-82.
47. It suggested biblical language was adjusted or accommodated to human capacities and knowledge in the time and place where something was revealed.
48. This view of him is shared by Laurence A. B. Whiteley, his biographer in *ODNB*, 14:626-27. Whitely stressed his conciliatory nature, his success as a politician and his willingness to see stipends raised in 1749. At the same time, he notes that he was dependent upon Ilay's support for his power. See also, John Ramsay of Ochtertyre, *Scotland and Scotsmen in the Eighteenth Century*, 2 vols, ed. Alexander Allardyce (Edinburgh and London, 1888), I:250-254. See also Ochtertyre MSS, NLS, 1635/1/344 and 1635/2/58.
49. *Letters of John Ramsay of Ochtertyre 1799-1812*, ed. Barbara L.H. Horn, Scottish Historical Society, 4th Series, 3 (1966), p. 34.
50. Sher and Murdoch (note 40 above) show how difficult Kirk management was.
51. Sefton, 'Lord Ilay', pp. 211-214.
52. Richard Sher's account of the Moderates in *Church and University in the Scottish Enlightenment: the Moderate Literati of Edinburgh* (Princeton, 1985) needs to be supplemented with less sympathetic accounts. The Moderates did not embody the Scottish Enlightenment as Sher seemed then to think, and they did much damage to the Kirk and to religious life in Scotland. A respectable 'opposition' book is John R. McIntosh, *Church and Theology in Enlightenment Scotland: The Popular Party, 1740-1800*, Scottish Historical Review, Monograph No.5 (East Linton, 1998). See also, Jonathan Yeager, *Enlightened Evangelicalism: The Life and Thought of John Erskine* (New York, 2011).
53. By the early or mid-1720s, Ilay recognized that his friends in the church were innovative men like John Simson of Glasgow, William Hamilton in Edinburgh, and younger men who had been taught by them or who had learned a modern and somewhat rationalist divinity in Holland. The Squadrone politicians in the teens and 1720s had patronised similar ministers.
54. *Acts of the Parliament of Scotland* XI, 402, c.6 (1707); quoted from W. Croft Dickinson and Gordon Donaldson, *A Source Book of Scottish History*, 3 vols (Edinburgh, 1954), III:493. The terms of subscription had been modified by the General Assembly in 1700 and again in 1711 when the Assembly demanded that those who signed the Confession 'believe the whole doctrine contained in the Confession of Faith to be the truths of God' which they were to hold as their own personal beliefs. Ilay would have signed this or the earlier version which demanded that one recognize the Confession as containing true beliefs to which the subscriber would adhere.
55. 'A Letter from a P - - - in North- Britain, to the Right Honourable the E. of I- - a' (London, 1716).
56. Edward Calamy, *An Historical Account of My Own Life*, 2 vols (London, 1829), II:451. The background to this included the Salter's Hall controversies of 1718-1719; see Duncan Coomer, *English Divines under the Early Hanoverians* (London, 1946), pp. 71-77.
57. William Dunlop, *A Preface to an Addition of the Westminster Confession, &c..*, (Edinburgh and London, 1720).
58. Calamy, *Historical Account*, pp. 71-77. The issue for Evangelicals like Robert Wodrow was whether or not those who did not wish to subscribe were trying to deny the Trinity. In 1725, he thought the English Dissenters who opposed subscription 'have lost much of

their reputation by their unhappy debates about Arrianism and Subscription'. Wodrow, *Analecta*, II:390. In the previous year, Wodrow said all this came from too great a reliance on reason in religious matters; II:171.

59. For Dunlop and his position see: Colin Kidd, 'Scotland's invisible Enlightenment: subscription and heterodoxy in the eighteenth-century Kirk', *Records of the Scottish Church History Society* 30 (2000), pp. 28-58; pp. 37-39.

60. I am relying throughout this section on Skoczylas's *Mr. Simson's Knotty Case.*

61. 'The Argathelians of consequence, favoured Mr. Webster in his prosecution of a court minister and professor of divinity, Simson'. James Erskine, Lord Grange, 'Letters of Lord Grange' in *The Miscellany of the Spalding Club*, vol 3 (Aberdeen, 1846), p. 27.

62. Skoczylas has summarized some of his positions: 'Simson continued to believe that a benevolent God gave man grace to seek the remedy for sin. His Creator was not vindictive; rather He displayed His glory in His creation and appointed a mediator for His fallen children. Since the Bible did not specify either the number of the elect, or to whom election would be granted, Simson saw no problem in considering the number large and the offer to be received by many. Grace would not be universally given, but could be freely offered. The Providence of God was indeed over all, but free will produced the reality of human sin, which, through grace, must be repented before the individual could accept the appointed Mediation. Rational beings would automatically glorify God through making the correct choices which would allow them to enjoy God and His glory for ever. The legalism of federal theology did not fit this pattern of unconditional grace extended to those who believed; nor did the notion of a prejudged soul. Simson's understanding of natural and divine law could not permit sinning in Hell; he therefore had to assume the divine restraint placed on the damned. On earth, grace would give the elect person the power to repent and obey God. It would then follow that the faith of the saved would indeed be made perfect by works, although they were in no way saved by works.': 'Professor John Simson', Ph.D. dissertation, University of Western Ontario, (1996), pp. 221-22.

63. Dr. Skoczylas returned to this case in 'The Regulation of Academic Society in Early Eighteenth- Century Scotland: The Tribulations of Two Divinity Professors', *The Scottish Historical Review*, 88 (2004), pp. 171-195.

64. Lord Milton to Ilay, 26 April 1729, NLS, 16582/30.

65. Skoczylas, *Mr. Simson's Knotty Case*, pp. 289-321.

66. Skoczylas, 'The Regulation of Academic Society', pp. 171-195.

67. Ilay secured this man's post. Campbell dedicated books to the brothers.

68. Ilay's very 'high church' cousin, Archibald Campbell, had just been elected Bishop of Aberdeen.

69. John Cunningham claimed that the 1712 Patronage Act had been 'almost a dead letter in the statute-book' until the late 1720s, a claim echoed by Drummond and Bullock in *The Scottish Church* (p. 58); Cunningham in *The Church History of Scotland* (Edinburgh, 1859), p. 418. The pamphlets are discussed by Sher and Murdoch, 'Patronage and Party in the Church of Scotland, 1750-1800', in *Church Politics and Society*, pp. 197-220.

70. Emerson, *Academic Patronage*, pp. 109-113.

71. Ilay was willing in 1743 to harass and oppose his political opponents who had supported the candidacy of William Leechman, an unsound Calvinist. James Coutts, *A History of the University of Glasgow* (Glasgow, 1909), pp. 236-39; Various letters to Lord Milton about opposing the installation of William Leechman appear in NLS, 16591.

72. David C. Lachman, *The Marrow Controversy* (Edinburgh, 1988), pp. 169-70.

73. Archibald Campbell's *An Enquiry into the Original of Moral Virtue* (1733), rooted morals in self interest and only secondarily in the word of God; Wilkie, notable as a poet and natural philosopher, gave his lordship a poem. John Home dedicated to him a play.

74. For the university men see, Emerson, *Academic Patronage*, pp. 225-25, 351-53.

Chapter 10

1. James Dalrymple, 1st Viscount of Stair, *The Institutions of the Law of Scotland*, ed. David M. Walker (Edinburgh, 1981), Book I: Title 1, section 16.
2. *Ibid*, p. 78-79; Book I, Title 1, 9-14.
3. Ilay to Newcastle, 21 October 1725, SP 54/16/53. See also, Andrew Mackillop, *"More Fruitful than the Soil": Army, Empire and the Scottish Highlands 1715-1815* (East Linton, 2000), pp. 15-16.
4. The same points were made by David Hume in his *Essays Moral, Political and Literary*, Part II (1752) and in the *History of England* (1754-62).
5. Sir James Fergusson, 'The Appin Murder Case' in *The White Hind* (London, 1963; reprinted Glasgow, 2004), p. 146.
6. Kames's ideas are discussed by Ian S. Ross, *Lord Kames and the Scotland of His Day* (Oxford, 1972), pp. 222-246. The sociology of the Scots rooted in such notions as did that of Montesquieu.
7. Ilay waited on the baronet's wife to offer his service and to tell her that his interest would be used for her husband. He then spoke to ministers and to the Attorney General who told him the case would be treated as a case of manslaughter since the dead man had been the aggressor. Eliott was promised the King's pardon. Ilay to Sir Gilbert Elliot, Lord Minto, 27 August 1727, Minto Papers, NLS, 11004/ 13-15; Walter Riddell Carre, *Border Memories or Sketches of Prominent Men and Women of the Border* (Edinburgh, 1876; reprinted Glasgow, 2012), pp. 146-477.
8. One Scottish historian who has seen clearly the disorder of the society is Christopher Whately whose *Scottish Society 1707-1830* (Manchester and New York, 2000) has many references to riots and disturbances over social, political and economic grievances; *e.g.*, pp. 187-188, 170-174. Another is the Marxist historian, Neil Davidson, whose *Discovering the Scottish Revolution 1692-1746* (London and Sterling, Va., 2003) mentions them but did not index them. It is not clear that Ilay had not been willing to use election rioters for his own ends.
9. Ilay to Newcastle, 7 October 1725, transcript copies in NRS, GD215/1657.
10. *The Lyon in Mourning...*, compiled by Bishop Robert Forbes; ed. Henry Paton, 3 vols (Edinburgh, 1975; 1st ed. 1896.), III:134.
11. Cited in Lee Holcombe, *Ancient Animosity: The Appin Murder and the End of Scottish Rebellion* (Bloomington, Indiana, 2004), p. 485.
12. The rioters had caused loss of life and much property was damaged. The organizers were art and part to those crimes and deserved to suffer for them.
13. He tried to make the punishment of some of them as severe as he could by sending them to Jamaica where he believed the climate would soon kill them. Ilay to Newcastle, 28 October 1725 and 6 November 1725, NRS, SP54/16/68.
14. He asked for mercy for one of them but would have tried them all on capital charges. Ilay to Newcastle, 16 and 23 September 1725, NRS, SP54/16/43, 20.
15. Ilay to Milton, 15 June 1738, NLS, 16572/94.
16. Stair, *Institutions*, IV:3:1.
17. Ilay to Lord Grange, 15 October 1720, NRS, GD124/15/1213.
18. NRS, GD124/15/1291.
19. The outcome of this case did not have that effect. In 1743, in another case of the same sort, Lovat Frasers had burned out one of their Mackenzie neighbours and killed a man. To one Highland lawyer it seemed 'ane Earnest of further Mischiefs if our great man don't distinguish himself by being a terror to bade men and cultivating friendship with his nebor families no of which at present Seem over fond of Him'. Alexander Mackenzie

to ?, 9 February 1743, NLS, 1342/44 and Yester Papers, NLS, 7057. The great man in question was either Lord Lovat or the 2nd Duke of Argyll.
20. Ilay to Newcastle, 30 September 1725, NRS, SP54/16/29.
21. Ilay to My Lord [?Newcastle], 20 September 1715, NRS, SP54/8/72.
22. It held incriminating evidence and had been taken by the Crown. *The Trial of Simon, Lord Lovat*, ed. David N. Mackay (Edinburgh, 1911), pp. liv; *JHL*, Vol IX, 17 December 1746 -19 March 1747.
23. Andrew Mitchell to Duncan Forbes, 27 May 1747, *More Culloden Papers*, ed. Duncan Warrand, 5 vols (Inverness, 1923-1930), V:149.
24. This case figures in several letters in 1730 and 1731, NRS, SP54/19/27- /20/55 and is also noticed by Leah Leneman, *Living in Atholl 1685-1785* (Edinburgh, 1986), pp. 164-65. Ilay thought it was almost impossible to prove cattle thefts in the Highlands since the cattle were not well marked and grazed freely over large areas. Ilay to Milton, 3 July 1731, NLS, 16542/90-92.
25. Ilay to Milton, 22 November and 30 December 1735, NLS, 16559/178 and 183. In the first letter, Ilay asked for the trial records and precedents since he was seeking their release.
26. Ilay to My Lord [?Mar], 26 December 1711, NRS, SP 54/41. Ilay had other thoughts about the relations of soldiers to civilian authorities. In 1718, he protested the Mutiny Bill because it did not adequately define the offence and did not keep military authority subject to civilian oversight. That may have been a move to annoy his opponents but it mirrored his own beliefs. Mutiny Acts were necessary because they were now customary and repeal 'would be a temptation towards committing crime', but he also thought many punishments were too severe both in the services and in civil life; *The Parliamentary History of England ... 1066 ... 1803*, ed. William Cobbett (London, 1813), XIV:459; *JHL*, XXI, 20 and 24 February 1718.
27. George Lockhart to John Hay of Cromlix, 13 October 1725, *Letters of George Lockhart of Carnwath*, ed. Daniel Szechi, Scottish Historical Society 5th Series, II (Edinburgh, 1989), p. 247.
28. Ilay to Milton, 3 July 1731, NLS, 16545/90.
29. Ilay to Newcastle, 21 September 1725, NRS, SP54/16/19.
30. Fergusson, *White Hind*, pp. 147-48, 161, 178.
31. Argyll seemed ready to prosecute the mad Duke of Douglas for murder if he returned to Scotland and sought to live outside his house and without restraints. The threat was enough to make his family restrain him.
32. He did this in the Glasgow rioters' case.
33 Quoted by Tobias Smollett, *The History of England from the Revolution in 1688 to ... [1727]* (London, 1810), II:541.
34. Lovat to Duncan Forbes of Culloden, 28 June 1716, *Culloden Papers*, no editor listed, (London, 1815), pp. 55-56.
35. His *amendments* to the 'sett' or constitution of the city were substantially modified only by acts governing the treatment of mobs. Those were provoked by the Porteous Riot, which Ilay deplored and whose after-effects he tried to mitigate. See, *Set of the City of Edinburgh with the Acts of the Parliament and Council Relative thereto* (Edinburgh, 1783). Ilay's 'Decreet' takes up pp. 39-51
36. Ilay to Delafaye, 12 November and 27 November 1730, NRS, SP54 230/30, 36.
37. Argyll to Milton, 29 May 1760, NLS, 16713/166.
38. *Trial of Lord Lovat*, p. 300.
39. Ilay to Newcastle, 30 September 1725, NRS, SP54/16/29.
40. Ilay sometimes skipped sessions when petitions and procedural questions were presented but not when cases were decided.

41. He of course voted on bills which dealt with England and did not apply in Scotland.

42. In 1722, a case was appealed from Scotland involving two people from Aberdeen. Ilay was the sole speaker for those who favoured reversal of the decision of the Scottish courts while the 2nd Earl of Aberdeen, a trained Tory lawyer from the Aberdeen area, spoke for those seeking to uphold the decision. Montrose described the legal debate: 'None spoak but ye the above named Earls wch I declare lasted ane hour & a half, each of em spoak verie [?well] & E[arl]. Il-a was for reversing & E[arl]. Ab. For affirming. There was a vote but no division demanded, for it carried to affirm Both E. Cupar & Ld Trevor [English Law Lords] were for affirming so they did not demand a division... E. Il-a lookt like the d ... l not being accustomed to meet wt such rubs, for he finds hereafter his law is no longer to pass for Gospel'. NRS, GD220/5/838/18. This was seen as a political case won by one who opposed the Peerage Bill.

43. Ilay's speeches were not always bare legal arguments. In one dealing with the Porteous Riots, 'Islay was full of Latin, he brought in Horace, but he left out Tully...'. *The Orrery Papers*, ed. The Countess of Cork and Orrery, 2 vols (London, 1903), I:257.

44. Delegates heard appeals from the Court of the Arches and the Court of Chancery of York and from their peculiars, from the Irish Probate courts and other courts using civil law procedures and laws.

45. *Country Journal or the Craftsman*, 10 June 1738.

46. *The Grenville Papers: Being the Correspondence of Richard Grenville Earl Temple...*, 4 vols, ed. William James Smith (London, 1852;reprinted NY, 1970), I:295; *The London Chronicle* (20 September 1759) and other papers carried the story.

47. How the members of committees were chosen is not clear from the Journals of the House of Lords. In some cases, every member present in the House save the presiding officer might be named; in others, it might be 27 out of 81 or some similar ratio. The quorum was often five with the time and place of meeting specified. Argyll seems never to have been named as the chairman of a committee. Those who were seem to have been junior members of the government or the oldest peer in attendance. Some committees demanded considerable work; others probably did their business in minutes.

48. *General Evening Post*, 18 June 1751; 'Annesley, James 1715-1760' in *thePeerage.com*.

49. Those dates come from various letters and from the dates given by Fergusson in 'The Appin Murder Case', p. 146.

50. Erskine Murray Correspondence, NLS, 5080/128.

51. What follows is largely dependent on Fergusson, 'The Appin Murder Case', pp. 133-179, and on Holcombe, *Ancient Animosity*.

52. Campbell of Glenure had evicted Camerons from Crown lands earlier that spring. George Malcolm Thomson, *A Kind of Justice: Two Studies in Treason* (London, 1970), p. 118.

53. Alexander Murdoch, *ODNB*, IX:432.

54. Fergusson, 'Appin Murder Case', p. 144. The claim that it was fair has been disputed by Ian Nimmo in *Walking with Murder on the Kidnapped Trail* (Edinburgh, 2005). He notes that two alleged Jacobites had recently been acquitted by Edinburgh juries and that Clan Campbell men would not have to be told to follow the lead of their Chief (p. 119). He believed that James Stewart was denied proper legal representation, that witnesses were pressed to testify in the right way (p. 12) and that character witnesses were improperly refused in an unfairly conducted trial (p. 121). He says Allan Breck Stewart may have been complicit (p. 181) but he believes him innocent and educed *post mortem* examination evidence to show that he did not shoot Glenure – a conclusion to which Holcombe also came (p. 529). Why that evidence was not presented at the trial remains unclear but the burden to do so lay with the defence.

55. Quoted by Fergusson, from the records of the trial, 'Appin Murder Case', p. 177. See also, MacKay, *The Trial of James Stewart*.

56. Holcolmbe, *Ancient Animosity*, p. 443.
57. Fergusson, 'Appin Murder Case', pp. 147-48, 161, 178.
58. There were no *verbatim* records of the proceedings made at the time.
59. Fergusson, 'Appin Murder Case', p. 186.
60. Fergusson, 'Appin Murder Case', p. 150.
61. *E.g.*, (on warrants) Ilay to Charles Delafaye, 20 January 1728, NRS SP54/19/4; (election warrants and proxies) Ilay to [? Delafaye], 27 September, 1730, 8, 10, 12, 17, 27, November 1730, NRS SP54/20/36; (wording of a pardon which will fit both English and Scots law), Ilay to Sir [Delafay?] 8 February 1734, NRS SP54/22/22.
62. NLS, 17610/37.
63. Alexander Tait to Milton, 28 January 1757, NLS, 16702/103. Kames's case against them is summarized in Ross, *Lord Kames*, p.343; Sir Alexander Cunningham Dick to Milton, 4 October 1759, NLS, 16709/228-29; Questions to be debated in the Select Society, Newhailes Mss, Acc. 7228/136.
64. Sir Alexander Cunningham Dick to Lord Milton, 27 October 1759, NLS, 16709/229. Elsewhere, Sir Alexander noted the many memos of this sort which he had produced in the 1750s and 1760s; see Sir Alexander to 3rd Earl of Bute, 23 February 1763, Uncatalogued Bute Papers, Mount Stuart House. See also, Ross, *Lord Kames*, pp. 211-13 which also contains a nice statement of the theory of legal development held by civilians.

Chapter 11

1. Colen Campbell, *Vitruvius Britannicus or the British Architect*, 3 vols (London, 1715-1725), I: Plates 53 and 53. Another set of house plates (I: Plates 29, 30) was dedicated to the Duke of Argyll. Campbell's dedication show the connexion between Ilay and the Burlington set at the time when Ilay was himself beginning to build. Joseph Rykwert thought Campbell's design was for Whitton but Ilay did not own his Whitton property in 1715-1717; Rykwert, *The First Moderns: The Architects of the Eighteenth Century* (Cambridge, Mass., 1980), p.255 n.396. Colen Campbell was of the Campbells of Cawdor and had trained as a Scottish lawyer. He was then Lord Burlington's favourite architect.
2. If Ilay ever lived there, it was presumably in the central block of the present house. This house owes nothing to him. It was redesigned and enlarged after 1754 by Robert Adam for William Murray,1st Earl of Mansfield. The House was notable in the eighteenth century for its orangery (possibly built c.1700) but the present orangery is by Robert Adam. The house had impressive gardens, including an American garden full of evergreens, but the present ones were rebuilt from Humphrey Repton's designs in the 1790s.
3. 'Declaration of Trust', London Metropolitan Archives, ACC/1/49/209, available on-line.
4. 'Marble Hill', ed. Julius Bryant (English Heritage, n.p., n.d.), pp. 1, 33. Rykwert reproduced a plate of the design for Marble Hill House published in *Vitruvius Britannicus*. p. 187. There, he says the design was by Campbell, Roger Morris and Lord Pembroke. *First Moderns*, pp. 185-195, *passim*.
5. Morris had trained as a mason and carpenter and worked some time in the office of Colen Campbell so he too was in touch with the Earls of Burlington and Pembroke. Morris designed and built with Lord Pembroke the notable Palladian Bridge at Wilton. John, 2nd Duke of Argyll, Master-General to the Board of Ordnance, made Morris the Board's Carpenter and Principal Engineer. The architect worked for several of the large investors in the South Sea Company and later (1731-32) made an Italian tour with one of them, George Bubb Dodington, MP, later 1st Baron Melcombe of Melcombe Regis

(1761). Emil Kaufmann said of Morris that 'many of his designs are on an average level, distinguished perhaps only by a definite predilection for plainness'. Kaufmann then went on to cite the value and interest of several of his buildings including Combe Bank built for the 2nd Duke of Argyll. Kaufmann, *Architecture in the Age of Reason* (New York, 1955), p. 22. See also, Ian Lindsay and Mary Cosh, *Inveraray and the Dukes of Argyll* (Edinburgh, 1973), p. 30-31; Hugh Phillips, *The Thames Around 1750* (London, 1952), p. 186; Rykwert, *First Moderns*, pp. 185-86, 189, 254 (n. 394).

6. Christopher Hussey, *English Gardens and Landscapes 1700-1750* (New York, 1967), p.36; 'Marble Hill', pp. 22-23.
7. Richmond (1701-1750) was associated with the 2nd Duke of Argyll in the Horse Guards and Army and with Ilay because of his interest in gardens, natural history and medicine. He lived nearby and later held an honorary MD from Cambridge University (1749). In the 1740s he was sometimes a guest at Ilay's Sunday dinners. Blanche Henrey, *British Botanical and Horticultural Literature before 1800*, 3 vols (Oxford, 1975), II: 647; Rykwert, *First Moderns*, pp. 185-190; Tracy Borman, *Henrietta Howard, King's Mistress, Queen's Servant* (London, 2007), p. 228.
8. The Coutts 'Out book', shows payments to Morris for £163.15.0 on 18 December 1728 and for £200 on 3 April 1730 and 12 November 1731. There are many later payments but those may be for work in London and not for this house.
9. Mary Cosh, 'Lord Ilay's Eccentric Building Schemes', *Country Life*, 20 July 1972, pp. 143-145. Whitton House is shown in Plate 8.
10. Lindsay and Cosh, *Inveraray*, p. 45; Cosh, 'Eccentric Building Schemes', pp. 143-145.
11. This relies on the description given by Cosh, *Ibid*. Marble Hill House had about twenty rooms plus halls and servants quarters. Its plan is given in Bryant, *Marble Hill*, p.41.
12. Much of the meat would have come garnished with vegetables. The 'fossils' are likely to have been mineral samples, not what we think of as fossils.
13. A Toure into England in the year 1733, Clerk of Penicuik Papers, NRS, GD18/2110/1.
14. Henrietta Pye, *A Short View of the Principal Seats and Gardens in and about Twickenham* (London, 1767), pp. 30-32.
15. Cosh, 'Eccentric Building Schemes', p. 145.
16. *Ibid*, p. 145; a somewhat different and less likely account of the house's fate is given by David G. Stuart, *Georgian Gardens* (London,1979), p. 245.
17. The Greenhouse with its apartment on the first floor may have been finished by 1725 when Ilay invited Lord Milton to stay with him 'in the Garden'. NLS, 16531/15.
18. Edmund and Dorothy Berkeley, *Dr. John Mitchell: The Man Who Made the Map* (Chapel Hill, 1974), p.110; Terry Friedman, *James Gibbs*, (New Haven and London, 1984), p. 163.
19. Friedman, *James Gibbs*, pp. 163, 317.
20. For the Tower, see Plates 5 and 9 and Lindsay and Cosh, Inveraray, p. 30. Lord Bathurst's Alfred's Hall was begun in 1721 but gothicized in the late 1720s or early 1730s. Maynard Mack, *Alexander Pope: A Life* (New Haven, London and New York, 1985), p. 380.
21. *Memoirs of the Life of Sir John Clerk...*, ed. John M. Grey, Scottish History Society, 1st Series,13 (1892), p. 143 n. 2.
22. John Gifford, *William Adam 1689-1748* (Edinburgh,1989), p. 160.
23. Alistair Rowan, 'William Adam's Library', *Architectural Heritage*, I (1990), pp. 8-33, 14-17.
24. Lindsay and Cosh, *Inveraray*, p. 351 n.62; NLS, 17851/63-64, John McGills opinion of ye Ague in Ld Ilay's case sent to him 27 Octr 1730.
25. John Fleming, *Robert Adam and his Circle* (Cambridge, Mass., 1962), p. 331; Lindsay and Cosh, *Inveraray*, p. 351 n. 62.
26. Until the 1720s, William Adam was known more as a builder and contractor than as an architect. His main works were done c.1720-48. The subscription list for his book,

Vitruvius Scoticus, had been opened in the late 1720s but the book appeared only in 1810. Adam knew a great deal about much else which interested Ilay – machinery, mines and the details of construction. His work as a builder is discussed in Lindsay and Cosh, *Inveraray* and by Gifford, in *William Adam* and in *Architectural Heritage,* I (1990).

27. Gifford, *Ibid,* p. 160. Scot was an Argathelian with political interests in Fife and was uncle to William Murray, 1st Earl of Mansfield.
28. *Ibid.*
29. Cosh, ' Eccentric Building Schemes', p. 145. Adam was from Kirkcaldy and had extensive business dealing in Fife; Annan is likely to have worked for him.
30. James Simpson, 'William Adam 1689-1748 A Tercentenary Exhibition', National Portrait Gallery (Edinburgh, 1989), p.2.
31. NLS, 17644/167.
32. NLS, 17651/167-8; plans for The Whim are held by the Royal Commission on Ancient Monuments, Edinburgh. Some of them are on its web site. See also 'Whim', Royal Commission on Ancient and Historical Monuments of Scotland, *Peeblesshire: An Inventory of the Ancient Monuments,* 2 vols (Edinburgh, 1967), pp. 326-332.
33. NLS, 17643/56-59.
34. National Monuments Record of Scotland, PBD 121B.
35. Plans for them were sent up from London in 1740; NLS, 17646/185.
36. Ilay to Milton, 8 March 1740, NLS, 16580/75. There were two other bridges which led to the lime quarry and to the coal seam which by 1739 had pumps in the mine. NLS, 17646/65.
37. NLS, 17643/4.
38. NLS, 17647/208.
39. A Toure into England in the year 1733, Clerk of Penicuik Papers, NRS, GD18/2110/1.
40. *Survey of London,* vol 31 (London, 1963), *British History Online* (see the web site). This gives maps of the area and a brief description of the house, its grounds and the surrounding area. Ilay would have consulted Roger Morris and perhaps James Gibbs since both were involved with the development scheme.
41. The *Survey* says this is taken from a watercolor of the house by T.H. Shepherd and from two undated plans held at Inveraray Castle which were probably made after Ilay's death. Neither fully described the layout of the house. The facade of the London Palladium Theatre, which now occupies the site, is a play on the original design but wider in frontage with differences in the fenestration and entrances.
42. This the *Survey* described as 'small... a room in the east wing measuring only 18 feet 6 inches by 17 feet 4 inches'.
43. The sauce boats are described in H. Newman, *An Illustrated Dictionary of Silverware* (London, 1987). They had sleeves into which a hot piece of iron could be inserted to keep warm what the service dish contained.
44. The *Survey* says the basement was 'a warren of service rooms and vaults' which makes it likely that the laboratory was somewhere else where the light was better.
45. Lindsay and Cosh, *Inveraray,* p. 42.
46. Quoted by Ian S. Ross in 'Aesthetic Philosophy: Hutcheson and Hume to Alison' in *The History of Scottish Literature,* 4 vols, ed. Cairns Craig (Edinburgh, 1989); II:253.
47. They were added after a disastrous fire in 1877 gutted the original building. Lindsay and Cosh, *Inveraray,* p. 338.
48. Englished it reads, 'October 15 1746 The Noble Duke, William of Cumberland Made This Building Possible'. Lindsay and Cosh, *Inveraray,* pp. 55-56. General Campbell sent it to Argyll – who corrected his Latin and that of Milton and Maule who had all emended it; General Campbell to Argyll, 8 September 1746, Campbell Papers, NLS, 3736/486. A notice of it was put in the Edinburgh papers.

49. Lindsay and Cosh, *Inveraray*, p. 352 n.9.
50. Milton to Argyll, 8 February, 1757, NLS, 16698/142. The Haddington market price for oats at that point was about £12 (Scots) so the cost would have been about £800 (sterling) and did not cover the whole year or his other building sites. A. J. S. Gibson and T. C. Smout, *Prices, Food and Wages in Scotland 1550-1780* (Cambridge, 1995), p. 150-51.
51. While there, Adam investigated the feasibility of opening old coal workings and, at Greenoch, limestone quarries. Lindsay and Cosh, *Inveraray*, pp. 48; 92; Gifford, *William Adam*, p. 37.
52. This was largely due to Milton's intercession but the Duke recognized the claim the family had on him. Were they to lose William's posts, they might well not be paid for outlays on government projects such as Fort George, a massive work near Inverness. Lindsay and Cosh, *Inveraray*, pp. 63, 67, 69-70.
53. His long relationship to Bubb Dodington rested on shared interests in politics and finance, gardens, architecture and *objets d'art*. Despite being opposed politically for many years, they appear to have remained friends. Rykwert, *First Moderns*, p.195; *HPHC 1715-1754*, I:500-503.
54. Lindsay and Cosh, *Inveraray*, pp. 87, 365 n.217; T. C. Smout, 'The landowner and the Planned Village' in *Scotland in the Age of Improvement*, ed. N. T. Phillipson and Rosalind Mitchison (Edinburgh, 1970), pp. 73-106; 86. Smout noted that the architect Robert Mylne was also involved in the building of Inveraray.
55. Milton too had interests in such things; see Lindsay and Cosh, *Inveraray*, p. 363 n. 197, and, Mr. Adam's paste for the walls at Inveraray, May 1759, NLS, Saltoun Papers Misc 54. That and other papers in this collection look like papers given at the meetings of the Philosophical Society of Edinburgh.
56. The Saltoun Correspondence in the NLS has materials on these topics.
57. 'I received your Graces... orders have sent you by model & by drawing the best methods of piecing timbers [1752]. As I did not know whither Your Grace wanted to truss Girders or make any high Building by adding one long piece of Timber to another, or to make plates to the Roof; I have sent you different methods, that your Grace's workmen may be competant judges by the Models & Drawings to perform either of the above mentioned works without any further Explanation'. NLS, 17685/49.
58. For descriptions of his Whitton garden, see above pp. 150-55. See also Rykwert, *First Moderns*, pp. 176, 245 n. 344. Sharawaggi was not quite so recent a discovery as is sometimes believed. Ilay may well have known the ancient, seventeenth-century, and recent accounts of order in disorder; see Yu Liu, 'Castell's Pliny: Rewriting the Past for the Present', *Eighteenth-Century Studies*, 43 (2010), pp. 243-57.
59. A. A. Tait, *The Landscape Garden in Scotland 1735-1835* (Edinburgh, 1980), pp. 47-56.
60. *Ibid*, pp. 75-76.
61. *Ibid*, pp. 45-53. Dalrymple's manuscript had circulated in Britain since the 1750s.
62. James Holloway, 'William Aikman 1682-1731', (Scottish Masters Series, Scottish National Galleries, 1988), pp. 9-10.
63. See Plate 2. That painting in 1800 was described as hanging in the Edinburgh Town Hall with 'full length portraits of King William III, Queen Mary his consort, and Queen Anne' by Kneller and portraits of George I and John Duke of Argyle by Aikman. Anon., *A New History of the City of Edinburgh, from the Earliest Periods to the Present Time* ... (4th edn, Edinburgh,1800). I thank Paul Wood for this information which puts the Dukes in the setting in which many eighteenth century Scots thought of them - next to royalty.
64. Neither is mentioned in Richard Saunders, *John Smibert, Colonial America's First Portrait Painter* (New Haven, Conn., 1995).
65. Alastair Smart, *Allan Ramsay 1713-1784* (Edinburgh,1992), pp. 10, 19; Alastair Smart,

The Life and Art of Allan Ramsay (London,1952), pp. 53, 55, 72, 184.

66. I owe this information to John Cairns who found the layout of the unreadable page to be that of the Mackenzie volume. See also, Smart, *Allan Ramsay* (1992), pp. 82-89.

67. George Fairfull-Smith, *The Foulis Press and The Foulis Academy*, (The Glasgow Art Index and Friends of Glasgow University Library, Glasgow, 2001), p. 51.

68. The printing of his library catalogue, *Catalogus Librorum A. C. D. A,* may have been a subsidy to them but the keeping of Alexander Wilson's type-foundry in Glasgow was a more important support for them and other Scottish printers. The art school advertised itself as for genteel scholars, men intending to pursue military careers, in which drawing was useful, and for those who would 'apply themselves to the Study of Manufactures'. NLS, 17603/42.

69. Fairfull-Smith, *The Foulis Press*, p. 51. That copy and the Ramsay portrait of 1749 show the Duke's neatly shod feet. He often wore Scottish-made clothing. Glasgow manufactured shoes. This is probably, in part, an advertisement for local products. It also is likely that Ilay supported the work of Richard Cooper, an English artist and engraver who produced a bit of everything from engraved silver to music and maps and anatomy plates. He probably had a hand in the decoration of the 'A' marked pottery thought to have been manufactured by his brother-in-law, Alexander Lind, at Preston Pans. Cooper was treasurer of the Academy of St Luke, the Edinburgh art school founded in 1729 which continued in various guises at least until the 1740s. That was a school of industrial design as much as one teaching the fine arts. Cooper was a successful businessman with several properties. See Joe Rock, ' "A" Marked Porcelain: Further Evidence for the Scottish Option', *Transactions of the English Ceramic Circle* 17 (1999), pp.69-78; ____, 'Richard Cooper, Senior (c.1696-1764) and His Properties in Edinburgh', *Book of the Old Edinburgh Club,* NS, 6 (2005), pp. 11-23.

70. Smart, *Ramsay* (1992), p. 76.

71. That is reproduced by Cosh, 'Eccentric Building Schemes', p. 141. This may indicate what the medallions on Gibbs's cenotaphs were like. See above p. 152

72. This is partly because many copies of his portraits exist.

73. There seems to be little on the Nories but see James Hollaway, *Patrons and Painter: Art in Scotland 16750-1760* (Edinburgh, 1989), pp. 145-46.

74. 'Inveraray Castle' (tourist brochure, Norfolk, 2000), p.12 and Lindsay and Cosh, *Inveraray*, pp. 95-96.

75. Sir John Clerk of Penicuik, Journey to London in 1727, and, A Toure into England in the year 1733. Clerk of Penicuik Papers, NRS, GD18/2107;18/2110/1.

76. For Cooper's career and his association with Argyll and his friends, see Rock's articles noted above (n. 69) The second article contains a reproduction of this print.

77. Lindsay and Cosh, *Inveraray*, p. 412. Despite believing in perpetual motion, Cumming later became an FRS and FRSE. The Duke is said to have educated him, brought him to London and patronized him there. Mary Cosh, 'Clockmaker Extraordinary: The Career of Alexander Cumming', *Country Life*, 1969, pp. 1528-1535.

78. Lindsay and Cosh, *Inveraray*, p. 428.

79. The world of the gem collectors into which he fitted is described by John Boardman, Diana Scarisbrick, Claudia Wagner and Erika Zwierlein-Diehl in *The Marlborough Gems Formerly at Blenheim Palace* (Oxford, 2010).

80. Smart, *Ramsay* (1992), p. 109.

81. Allan Ramsay sr. to Patrick Lindsay, Lord Provost of Edinburgh, 5 April 1735, *The Works of Allan Ramsay*, 6 vols, ed. Alexander M. Kinghorn, *et al*, (Edinburgh, 1945-1974), Scottish Text Society (1970), IV:199-200; 'Petition of Alan Ramsay', 8 December 1737, NLS, 17604/25.

82. Coutts, 'Out book', 11 December 1728. Seals and small cameos were included in that category.

83. *The Complete Letters of Lady Mary Wortley Montagu*, ed. Robert Halsband, 3 vols (Oxford, 1965-69), III:97, 176.

84. Rock, ' "A" Marked Porcelain', p. 172; George Haggarty and Sheila Forbes, 'Scotland: Lind and A-Marked Porcelain', The Northern Ceramic Society Journal, 20 (2003-04), pp. 1-10. The Victoria and Albert Museum has on display about fifteen pieces of 'A' marked porcelain. A few of Ilay's other porcelain objects are at Inveraray Castle including an Argyll sauce boat. The Delftfield works in Glasgow made more utilitarian products (see above p. 146).

85. She sent the same request to Lord Milton. NLS, 17604/93 and 95.

86. Adam Smith solicited Lord Milton's favour for Wilkie: [He is] 'a man whom we regard as undoubtedly the first poet as well as one of the most eminent Philosophers of the Present Age'; *Correspondence of Adam Smith*, ed. Ernest Campbell Mossner and Ian Simpson Ross (rev. ed., Indianapolis, 1987; 1st ed. 1977), pp. 22-24.

87. Wilkie to Lord Milton, 17 May 1759; Wilkie to Milton, n.d.; NLS, 16712/213, 216; those letters speak of jobs at St Andrews and Marischal College. Earlier, Wilkie and his relatives had sought places at Glasgow and Edinburgh through the intercession of Alexander Lind and Lord Milton; 11 April 1751; February 1752, 26 February 1752, NLS, 16675; 16676.

88. David Hume, writing on 15 October 1754 to Joseph Spence, called Argyll one of the 'best judges', ranking him with Sir George Lyttleton and Mr. Pitt. Joseph Spence, *Observations, Anecdotes, and Characters of Books and Men Collected from Conversations*, ed James Osborn, 2 vols (Oxford, 1966). I:204.

89. Colley Cibber's preface thanked the 2nd Duke for arranging benefits for him. The 1st Duke had been the dedicatee of Cibber's *Love's Last Shift* (1696). Ilay was helping an old family friend. *The Plays of Colley Cibber*, 2 vols, ed. Rodney L. Hayley (New York, 1980).

90. Kinghorn *et al.*, *Ramsay's Works*, IV:208-09.

91. Ilay had been castigating clerics for preaching that Captain Porteous's death was providential. The Earl and his brother were quarrelling and the 2nd Duke was about to go into opposition.

92. Sir Gilbert Elliot to his wife, Minto Papers, NLS, 11006/23.

93. Home to Sir Gilbert Elliot, 5 November 1756, NLS, 11008/17.

94. Home to Lord Milton, 9 April 1757, NLS, 16700/196-97.

95. Hume to Adam Smith, 12 April 1759, *The Letters of David Hume*, ed. J.Y.T. Greig (Oxford, 1932; reprinted 1969), I:302. Hume and Argyll, both good players, are said by Shirley Robin Letwin to have played whist together; *The Pursuit of Certainty: David Hume, Jeremy Bentham, John Stuart Mill, Beatrice Webb* (Cambridge, 1965; Indianapolis, 1998), p. 6. She sometimes erred on small facts but one would like this to be correct.

96. William Cullen to Smith, January-April 1751, *Correspondence of Adam Smith*, pp. 433-36.

97. *Ibid*, pp. 6, 59.

98. See, R. L. Emerson, *Academic Patronage in the Scottish Enlightenment* (Edinburgh, 2008), pp. 128-29, 340-41; M. A. Stewart, 'The Kirk and the Infidel, an Inaugural lecture delivered at Lancaster University 9 November 1994', (privately printed, 1995).

99. James to Robert Adam, 25 June 1758, NRS, GD18/4849. James Adam went on to say that Wilkie's dedication in *The Epigoniad* read in part,

> But if great Campbell, whose auspicious smile
> Bids Genius yet revive to bless our Isle,
> Who, from the toils of state & public cares
> Oft with the Muses to the shade repair,

> My numbers shall approve, I rise to fame;
> For what he praises, Envy dare not blame.

The verse is cited from a letter of George Stewart to Gilbert Elliot, MP, 17 February 1757, NLS, 11014/96. The Adam brothers decided dedicating their book to the Duke would look 'too nationall'; dedicating it to George II would be better for business. That was arranged.

100. Wilkie to Lord Milton, 17 May 1759 and n.d., NLS, 16712/213 and 216. Those letters speak of jobs at St Andrews and Marischal College. That Wilkie 'shou'd have the first professorship that fell' is a more complicated, story as I have shown elsewhere; Emerson, *Academic Patronage*, pp. 137, 138, 469-71.

101. In 1748, the London newspapers were advertising a new edition of Defoe's poem, 'Caledonia: a poem in honour of Scotland, and the people of that nation. In which The Scandalous and Groundless Imputations of Cowardice...'. This was dedicated to the 2nd Duke of Argyll whose brother is probably the Campbell named in it. Given the date, the republication may be implicitly comparing the heroism of the 2nd and 3rd Dukes to the disadvantage of the latter.

102. An anonymous 32 line poem, probably written after 1743 and published in part without translation, reads in part

> He's come in cheerful, friendly way To his people,
> He's spread bounty on each side of him Most humanely.
> You've laid the foundations of the loveliest court In your ancestral capital,
> May you have life and health To enjoy it.
> And as long as one stone's on another
> In Campbell's town, Your name and fame eternally Will be remembered.

This survives in several manuscripts found on the Isle of Canna and at NLS and in the archives of the Royal Highland and Agricultural Society. It was partially printed in Alexander Cameron's *Reliquiae Celticae* (2 vols, ed. Alexander MacBain and John Kennedy, Inverness, 1894), pp. 318-19. I thank Dr. Ronald Black for this information and the translation. The Inveraray Campbells had been determined to modernize the Highlands which may account for their lack of bards.

103. Ilay has been noticed in two lists of British mathematicians: Ruth and Peter Wallis, *Biobliography of British Mathematics and its Applications, 1701-1760*, (Letchworth, n.d., [1986]) and E.G.R Taylor, *Mathematical Practitioners of Hanoverian England* (London, 1966). The latter lists books dedicated to him; pp. 48, 58, 72, 118, 119, 131, 182. To that list can be added one more by Abraham de Moivre.

104. It was one of the two plates included in Sir John Hill's *System of Botany, with the latest improvements in which the Genera and Species plantarum of Linnaeus are connected into one...* (London, 1759-75). Hill, like James Lee, whom Argyll also patronized, was eager to make Linnaeus available in English. Blanche Henrey, *British Botanical and Horticultural Literature before 1800*, 3 vols (Oxford, 1975), II: 100-01, 354, 658.

105. Gordon to Clerk, 17 November 1727, NRS, GD18/5023/3/39.

106. Gordon to Clerk, 13 August 1728, NRS, GD18/5023/3/40.

107. Gordon to Clerk, 13 August and 7 September 1728, NRS, GD18/5023/3/41 and 44.

108. Gordon to Clerk, 24 September 1728, NRS, GD18/5023/3/42.

109. Gordon to Clerk, February 1729, NRS, GD18/5023, 7 September 1728; 24 September 1728; 15 October 1728; 13 August 1728, NRS, GD18/5023/3/41, 42, 43, 45.

110. Gordon to Clerk, n. d [1729], NRS, GD18/5023/3/46.

111. Gordon to Clerk, 13 October 1729, NRS, GD18/5023/3/49.

112. Gordon to Clerk, 13 October 1729; 3 April 1730, NRS, GD18/5023/3/50.

113. Gordon to Clerk, 5 December 1732, NRS, GD18/5023/3/59.

114. Gordon to Clerk, 9 January 1733, NRS, GD18/5023/3/61. The most recent account

of Gordon is found in Iain Gordon Brown, 'Archaeological Publishing in the First Half of the Eighteenth Century', *The Edinburgh History of the Book in Scotland, Vol. II, Enlightenment and Expansion*, ed. Stephen W. Brown and Warren McDougall (Edinburgh, 2012), pp. 510-527.

Chapter 12

1. Their system is described in a letter from James Erskine, Lord Grange, to Tweeddale, n.d. [1742], Yester Papers, NLS, 7044/46 and in Tweeddale to Thomas Hay, 3 March 1742, NLS, 7075/6-7.
2. Roger L. Emerson, *Professors. Patronage and Politics: the Scottish Universities in the Eighteenth Century* (Aberdeen, 1991), pp. 5-6.
3. See Plate 2.
4. The library of over 6,000 books belonging to Andrew Fletcher 'the patriot' was inherited by Lord Milton and has been partially reconstructed by P. J. M. Willerns in *Bibliographia Fletcheriana or, the extraordinary library of Andrew Fletcher of Saltoun*, (Privately printed, Wassenaar, 1999).
5. Milton may have owed his first post to the Earl Sunderland who had been friendly with Andrew 'the patriot'.
6. Kinloch had married a sister of the wife of Ilay's uncle. John Stuart Shaw, *The Management of Scottish Society 1707-1764* (Edinburgh, 1983), p. 64.
7. *Ibid*, p. 63.
8. Ilay, in 1725, was making lists of JPs and Sheriff-Clerks and advising the government that even the Writers to the Signet ought to have their commissions renewed when a new Keeper of the Signet was appointed as he had been in 1721. This was a threat to the Writers or solicitors in Edinburgh some of whom would have lost offices when their commissions lapsed. Ilay to Newcastle, 9 October 1725, NRS, SP54/16/41; 54/16/48.
9. The process was also started at St Andrews where in 1720 the Duke of Atholl was Chancellor. Ilay initially tried to assert some influence in that University by moving to get rid of Alexander Scrymgeour, the Professor of Divinity whose chair was in the gift of the crown. PRO, SP54/20 item 22. He later supported Scrymgeour. See Roger L. Emerson, *Academic Patronage in the Scottish Enlightenment* (Edinburgh 2008), pp. 424-25.
10. *Ibid*, pp. 85-106.
11. *Charters, Statutes, and Acts of the Town Council* [of Edinburgh] *and the Senatus 1583-1858*, ed. Alexander Morgan and Robert Kerr Hannay (Edinburgh and London, 1937), pp. 169-172.
12. I have made that case in 'The Founding of the Edinburgh Medical School: The Real Story', *Journal of the History of Medicine and Allied Sciences*, 59 (2004), pp. 183-218 and in *Academic Patronage*, pp. 273-324.
13. Earlier, all three had been active in Glasgow University affairs; Anne Skoczylas, 'The Regulation of Academic Society in Early Eighteenth-Century Scotland: The Tribulations of Two Divinity Professors', *The Scottish Historical Review*, 83 (2004), pp. 171-195; 185-6 and Emerson, *Academic Patronage, passim*. Scrymgeour came from a well connected Jacobite family and was *de jure* Earl of Dundee.
14. Ilay to Newcastle, 28 June 1728, NRS, SP54/36. In Ilay's mind, this applied to all the universities save Edinburgh. With the exception of Marischal College and University, the others had been ecclesiastical foundations which fell to the Crown at the Reformation. At Marischal, the chairs in the gift of the Lord Marischal had been forfeited to the Crown because of the treason of the 10th Earl so Marischal College and University was little

different. Only chairs founded by private patrons whose descendants enjoyed the right to appoint would have escaped royal control but even in those the Crown's appointed officials might have blocked a nominee from assuming office. Ilay was trying for effective control of the corporations.

15. There are in the Saltoun Correspondence at NLS many letters from Mackaile written during the 1720s.

16. That chair was filled by competitive examination and was not easy to influence since the Town Council had a say in its management and was assertive. In the Scottish universities, custom, long practice, and the toleration of that by Parliamentary or Royal Visitors had allowed the universities once headed by bishops to pick their Chancellors. Ilay had a case but not one which was as clear as he wished to make it.

17. Aberdeen Town Council Letter Books, Vol. 9 (1723-1739), p. 94-128, Aberdeen City Archives.

18. Emerson, *Academic Patronage*, pp. 596-614. That book discusses all those cases in its various sections.

19. There is correspondence about this and its relation to professorships and church living in Aberdeen in the Saltoun Papers for 1727-28; *E.g.*, NLS, 16538/180, 182, 184, 190, 192.

20. For Ilay's control of the burghs, see Shaw, *Management*, pp. 91-98.

21. Duncan Forbes to ? , 5 July 1726, NRS, SP54/17/35. In 1730, the Convention's Commissioners were closely divided and Ilay may not have had a majority on his side; Commissions to the Convention of Royal Burghs, ECA, SL 30 Moses Bundle 242.

22. Some burghs were represented by prominent politicians; others, virtually owned by local men, were represented by their relatives or lawyers who defended political interests.

23. Shaw, *Management*, pp. 87-88.

24. *Ibid*, pp. 60-62.

25. Grange was trying to buy back the confiscated family lands. See p. 432, n. 35 and Anne Skcozylas's forthcoming biography of Lord Grange; 'Thomas Erskine', *HPHC 1715-1754*, II: 17.

26. John Chamberlayne, *Magnae Britanniae Notitia: or the Present State of Great Britain....* (London, 1736), 'A List of the Offices and Officers in North-Britain or Scotland', Part II, p. 43; Shaw, *Management*, pp. 86-117.

27. *Ibid*, pp. 65, 120-21, 112.

28. Scott, Richard, 'The Politics and Administration of Scotland 1725-1748', unpublished Ph. D. Dissertation, Edinburgh University, 1982, p. 324-330.

29. On 16 September 1725, Ilay wrote to [? Newcastle] that he was watching the Edinburgh elections very closely and needed to have a job for one of his old friends, John McGill, the Edinburgh Surgeon-Apothecary. McGill became H. M. Apothecary for Scotland; Ilay carried the elections. NRS, SP54/16/16.

30. Milton and Ilay regularly concerned themselves with jobs worth as little as £5; not all of those places had perquisites which made them valuable.

31. Scott says a quarter of all Ilay's nominees to the offices in the gift of the Treasury were rejected. 'Politics and Administration', p. 59. Getting one's way 75% of the time was not bad.

32. This was well known since it was noticed several times by Robert Wodrow during the summer of 1729; *Analecta or Materials for a History of Remarkable Providences*, 4 vols, ed. Matthew Leishman (Edinburgh, 1842-43).

33. For an account of the Argathelian faction in the Presbytery of Glasgow see, Anne Skoczylas, *Dr. Simson's Knotty Case: Divinity, Politics and Due process in Early Eighteenth-Century Scotland* (Montreal, Kingston, London, Ithaca, 2001), *passim*.

34. Ilay to Milton, 21 April 1724 and 6 September 1724, NLS, 16529/55-58;16529/80.

35. ? to Ilay, n.d., (1724); NLS, 17614/4.

36. Wodrow, *Analecta*, IV:191. The Wodrow Quarto [manuscript] Letters at the NLS have many references to the increasing interference of the Argathelians in Kirk affairs after 1724. As early as 30 November 1715, Charles Morthland had written to Montrose that Ilay was mingling secular with religious politics; NRS, GD220/5/529/3.

37. *E.g.*, 'Pray speak to G[eorge] Drummond he to take care of the Elections for the general Assembly', Ilay to Milton, 21 April 1724, NLS, 16519/58.

38. Ilay to Milton, 18 December 1725, NLS, 16531/52.

39. Ilay to Milton, received 14 May, 1726, NLS, 16533/80.

40. *E.g.*, NRS, SP54/18/36; Ilay's recommendations can be found in SP54/18/57. The same source also has his list of suitable Lord-Lieutenants which reads like a list of the Argathelian peers.

41. 'The Moderate Man's Confession', (Leith, 173?). NLS, Broadside Collection,, Ry.iii.c.34. (53). It is a misconception that the term 'Moderate' was not used until the 1750s.

42. Relations between the brothers seem to have been frosty in 1712, 1714, 1722, 1727, 1728-29, 1736-38, 1740-1743.

43. Walpole to Townshend, 3 September 1725, in William Coxe, *Memoirs of the Life and Administration of Sir Robert Walpole...*, 3 vols (London, 1798), II:467-68.

44. John Stuart Shaw, *The Political History of Eighteenth-Century Scotland* (Basingstoke and New York, 1999), p.69.

45. *HPHC 1690-1715*, 5:567-68.

46. On 21 July 1722, William Stratford wrote Lord Harley, 'I hear Argyll and his brother Ilay quarrelled when they were last in Scotland, and that Argyll bid him begone out of his house, and told him he had been misled long enough by him'. *HMCR on the MSS of His Grace the Duke of Portland*, (London, 1899), VII:331. During such times Argyll and Ilay communicated through Stewart. Messages allowed them to quarrel and not see each other but to concert their political activities. Stewart had another use. David Scott quotes Robert Dundas of Arniston saying that the messenger had been given the place of King's Remembrancer in Exchequer 'on a Bargain with L Ila for naming [William] Bogle to be D[eputy] Remembrancer, whom L Ila wanted in the Exchequer that he might have every court in the hands of his tools', Richard Scott, 'Politics and Administration', p. 168. Scott believed Stewart was Ilay's secretary after 1726.

47. *Ibid*, p. 372.

48. There were sometimes rules imposed by the King, by custom and the practices of other ministers. See, Wherli, 'Scottish Politics in the Age of Walpole', Ph. D. dissertation, University of Chicago, (1983), pp. 271-72.

49. Ilay to Milton, 29 July 1735, NLS, 16559/129.

50. NLS, 16721/145.

51. NLS, 16580/99.

52. Ilay to ? Delafaye, 10 October 1730, NRS, SP54/20/38; Argyll to Milton, 23 April 1748, NLS, 16656/33.

53. Ilay to Milton, 29 May and 11 June, NLS, 16564/91 and 98; William Rouet to Robert Simson, 4 January 1756, GUA, 30485.

54. Emerson, *Academic Patronage*, pp. 240-42. Henry Mackenzie remembered Cuming as a man who 'enlivened by his Conversation, & delighted with his good humor'; Life of [John] Home, NLS 10686.

55. Carre was Lord Marchmont's nominee whom Argyll helped into his gown. NRS, GD158/2591/5.

56. Argyll to Marchmont, n.d. [1753], NRS, GD158/2591/1.

57. He somewhat inadvertently made Alexander Kincaid the King's Printer but the printer too was a polite and learned man helpful to Argyll in the '45. Henry Mackenzie, *The Anecdotes and Egotisms of Henry Mackenzie 1745-1831*, ed. Harold William Thompson

(London, and Oxford, 1927), pp. 181-82; Richard Sher, *The Enlightenment and the Book: Scottish Authors and Their Publishers in Eighteenth Century Britain, Ireland and America* (Chicago, 2006). p. 313. Ilay often promised more help than he was willing to give but did not resent outcomes to which he had assented although he had not really wanted them.

58. *E.g.*, GUA, 30485, on the problems of having too many relatives of Principal Stirling.
59. An example of such a choice is the appointment of Thomas Dundas at Edinburgh in 1732. NLS, 16548/96.
60. John Anderson to Robert Simson, 27 May 1756, GUA, 43160. Those appointments are discussed in Emerson, *Academic Politics*, pp. 133-34.
61. 'We were forced to agree to ye madmen's bringing in Mr. [Alexander] Webster to be minister of Edr. In order to secure Mr. Wisehearts [Wishart] being one'. Milton to Ilay, n.d. [1736], NLS, 16564/148.
62. *E.g.* Argyll to Milton, 2 June 1745, NLS, 16596/185.
63. Lady Mary to the Countess of Bute, 5 September 1749, *Complete Letters of Lady Mary Wortley Montagu*, 3 vols, ed. Robert Halsband (Oxford, 1967), II:441.
64. 'Some Account of John Duke of Argyll' in *The Letter and Journals of Lady Mary Coke* , 4 vols, ed. J. H. Horne (London 1970, facsimile of ed. 1889-1896); Vol. I:xxii-iii.
65. Christopher Whately, *The Scots and the Union* (Edinburgh, 2006), pp. 141-57; A. J. S. Gibson and T. C. Smout, *Prices, Food and Wages in Scotland 1550-1780* (Cambridge, 1995), pp. 166-71.
66. Many of those pamphlets are noticed in *Anglo-Scottish Tracts, 1701-1714: A Descriptive Checklist*, ed. W.R. and V. B. McLeod (Lawrence, Kansas,1979).
67. The Darien Company or the Company of Scotland Trading to Africa and the Indies was founded in 1695, the same year as the Bank of Scotland. The Darien Company was to revive Scotland's foreign trade, provide an American colony, and give work to the impoverished. In reality, between 1695 and 1700, it stripped the country of capital and hard cash which was then lost in ill-fated ventures in the Caribbean and the Far East. By the beginning of the new century, it was a failed venture which had left many in debt and the country bare of money.
68. *The Writings of William Paterson...*, 3 vols, ed. Saxe Bannister (London, 1859; New York, 1968), I:16. There was nothing new in the proposal for what Americans once termed 'an ever normal granary'. Nurnberg and other continental cities had such things in the late sixteenth century.
69. *Ibid*, 1:17.
70. *Ibid*, I:94.
71. *Ibid*, I:17-19.
72. *Ibid*, I:39-56.
73. *Ibid*, I:92.
74. *Ibid*, I:39.
75. *Ibid*, I:82-84.
76. *Ibid*, I:28.
77. *Ibid*, I:103.
78. *Ibid*, I:103-4.
79. *Ibid*, I:105.
80. Antoin Murphy, *John Law: Economic Theorist and Policy-maker* (Oxford, 1997).
81. John Law's *Essay on a Land Bank*, ed. Antoin Murphy (Dublin, n.d.), pp. 26-42.
82. Murphy denies that this was Law's intention in the *Essay* (p. 24) but the consequence of issuing bills against un-mortgaged land in Scotland would have had that effect since the value of land was worth more than the circulating money in that currency-poor country.

83. *Ibid*, p. 40. This paragraph also draws on my essay 'The Scottish Setting of Hume's Political Economy' in *Essays on David Hume's Political Economy*, ed. Carl Wennerlind and Margaret Schabas (New York, 2007), pp. 1-23.
84. *The Writings of William Paterson*; II:xliii-vii.
85. *Ibid*, II:vi.
86. Ilay to My Lord [Townshend], 28 September 1715, NRS, SP54/8/12.
87. *The Writings of William Paterson*, II:xlv-xlvi.
88. *Letters to and from Henrietta, Countess of Suffolk and her second husband...George Berkeley... 1712-1767*, ed. John Wilson Croker, 2 vols (London, 1824), I:43, no 4.
89. Anonymous, 'A Letter to Mr. Law Upon His Arrival in Great Britain', (2nd ed. London, 1721/2 [dated 11 November 1721 on the fly-leaf]).
90. In seventeenth-century Rome, paper money circulated within the Papal States where banks controlled the issue. Some of the men who debated the measures in the Scottish Parliament of 1705 would have known that – although it could not have helped much to have a Roman Catholic model for the reform of Presbyterian Scotland. A recent commentator states that 'it was the complete confidence they [the bank notes of the Banco di Santo Spirito and the Monte di Pieta] enjoyed that first gave the Scottish financier John Law the idea for his ill-fated system'; Hanns Gross, *Rome in the Age of the Enlightenment* (Cambridge, 1990), pp. 145-146.
91. *The Writings of William Paterson*, I:cxxviii.
92. Patricia Dickson, *Red John of the Battles: John Second Duke of Argyll and First Duke of Greenwich 1680-1743* (London, 1973), p. 208.
93. Murphy, John Law, *passim*, John P. Wood, *A Sketch of the Life and Projects of John Law of Lauriston* (Edinburgh and London, 1791), p. 5.
94. Larry Neal, ' "For God's Sake, Remitt me": The Adventures of George Middleton, John Law's London Goldsmith-Banker, 1712-1729', *Business and Economic History*, 23 (1994) pp. 27-60.
95. That was the result of wider discussions; see Henry Hamilton, *An Economic History of Scotland in the Eighteenth Century* (Oxford, 1963), p. 132-33.
96. Wodrow, *Analecta*, III:308.
97. Quoted from Shaw, *Management*, p. 59.
98. *Ibid*.

Chapter 13

1. John Stuart Shaw, *The Management of Scottish Society* (Edinburgh,1983), p. 126.
2. The best account of this is Shaw's, *Management*, pp. 124-132. The Improvers also sent their proposals to the Justices of the Peace in Fife, the freeholders of Perth and Kincardine and sought support from various burghs and among the weavers of Glasgow. The Improvers' proposals can be found in the Convention of Royal Burghs Papers in ECA, Bay D, Shelf 1C, items 1- 13 and in the Convention Minute Books, ECA, SL 30/1/1/ 10, p. 145 [8 November 1726].
3. [Petitions and memorials for a Board], ECA, Bay D, Bundle 6, 14 Items.
4. The sources of those funds may be best described by Henry Hamilton, *The Industrial Revolution in Scotland* (New York, 1966; 1st ed 1932), p. 78.
5. The Irish plan was in the mind of the founders as is shown by a pamphlet which advocated limiting the dispersion of funds to the linen trades and the fisheries. Anon., 'General Heads and Questions Concerning Manufactures and Fisheries in Scotland' (n. d., [?1727], n. p.)
6. There are also many references to the Board's chemists and technologist in Archibald and Nan Clow, *The Chemical Revolution* (London, 1952; reprinted Freeport, N.Y., 1970).

7. Shaw, *Management*, pp. 130-32.
8. He was answering a claim that the Board had wasted £20,000 in ten years; Copy of an Answere ...[to] Mr. Cockburn of arnistoune, 15 December 1738, NRS, GD18/5901.
9. Henry Hamilton, *An Economic History of Scotland in the Eighteenth Century* (Oxford, 1963), p. 113.
10. The subsidies were not always paid on time. On 10 July 1730, the Convention of Royal Burghs asked Ilay to look into the matter of subsidies unpaid since 1728. Minutes of the Convention of Royal Burghs, ECA, SL 30/1/1/10, pp. 365-67.
11. 'About the year 1744 [Campbeltown] had only two or three small vessels belonging to the port: at present there are seventy-eight sail, from twenty to eighty tuns burthen, all built for, and employed in, the herring fishery; and about eight hundred sailors are employed to man them. This town in fact was created by the fishery; for it was appointed the place of rendezvous for the busses; two hundred and sixty have been seen in the harbour at once...'. Cited from Thomas Pennant, *Tour in Scotland* (1772) in *Beyond the Highland Line: three journals of travel in eighteenth century Scotland; Burt, Pennant, Thornton,* edited and abridged by A. J. Youngson (London, 1974), pp. 78, 163-64.
12. Perhaps this was when Ilay invested in a fishing company which did not succeed. In a 1750 debate over a British Fisheries Bill, he said that there was need of a large regulated stock company. He went on to say that it would succeed only if it could survive several years with no profits while Britons accustomed themselves to herring instead of 'our French ragouts and kickshaws'. He said 'those who have never made the experiment may imagine that the herring fishery may be set on foot by private adventurers; but I am convinced it never will, because I have made the experiment' with others. They had lost half their capital. Salt duties had to be as low as those of the Dutch; inland counties had to develop a taste for salted fish; the distribution system had to improve. Campbeltown would be a proper western rendevous for the ships since the fish were there. William Cobbett, *Parliamentary History of England*, (London, 1813), XIV:781.
13. Pennant, *Tour*, p. 162.
14. Loretta Timperley, *A Directory of Landownership in Scotland in c. 1770*; Scottish Record Society N.S. 5 (Edinburgh,1976); pp. 29, 33.
15. Jackson, Gordon, 'Glasgow in Transition' in *Glasgow*, 2 vols, eds T. M. Devine and Gordon Jackson, (Manchester and New York, 1995), I:82-83.
16. Clow and Clow, *The Chemical Revolution*, p. 176.
17. *Ibid*, pp. 173-4.
18. Minutes of the Convention of Royal Burghs, 30 March 1736, ECA, SL 30/1/1/11, p. 104. The bill was to remove duties from materials used in bleaches.
19. John Law, *Money and Trade Considered with a Proposal for supplying the Nation with Money* (Edinburgh, 1705), pp. 116-7.
20. Sidney Checkland, *Scottish Banking: A History, 1695-1973* (London and Glasgow, 1975), p. 8.
21. Shaw, *Management*, pp. 118-125.
22. The investments of the early years can be traced in 'Ledger of the daily transactions of The Royal Bank of Scotland Kept at Edinburgh Commencing 1st January 1728' [ending 25 March 1731], RB/714/1. See also Ledgers E and F, 'Commencing 1 January 1727' [ending 28 Mar 1731], RB/763/9-10, Archives of the Royal Bank of Scotland [ARBS].
23. The exceptions are George Baillie of Jarviswood, (1727-1730) and John Hamilton, W. S. (1730-1739); both were ordinary directors elected by the stockholders which may suggest they were not good Squadrone men in those years. The list of Directors can be found in Neil Munro, *History of the Royal Bank of Scotland* (Edinburgh, 1928, reprinted Glasgow, 2011), pp. 397-415.

24. ARBS, Minutes of the Royal Bank of Scotland, RB/12/1. 31 July 1727- 14 March 1728, pp. 1-88.
25. Edna Healey, *Coutts & Co. 1692-1992 The Portrait of a Private Bank* (London, 1992), p. 58n.
26. Those were non-redeemable interest-bearing government bonds issued at the time of the Union with England to repay losses on the Darien Company, to redeem the Scottish national debt and to compensate Scots for the interest paid on the English national debt which they had not incurred.
27. That would have shifted its control away from its then stockholders to English and Argathelian investors.
28. Hamilton, *Industrial Revolution*, p. 256; Checkland, *Scottish Banking*, pp. 48-58.
29. Checkland, *Scottish Banking*, pp. 49, 59.
30. *Ibid*, p. 59.
31. Munro, *History of the Royal Bank*, pp. 36, 38.
32. *Ibid*, pp. 36-40, 397-415; Checkland, *Scottish Banking*, pp. 48-76; Hamilton, *Economic History*, p. 300; John Chamberlayne, *The Present State of Great Britain, A List....*, (London,1736), Part II, pp. 41, 59.
33. There are several letters about this in NLS, 16525 none of which is very clear.
34. Ilay to Milton, 25 January, 4 March, 11 April, 21 July 1724, NLS, 16529/12-13, 31-32, 67, 58.
35. Ilay to Milton, 25 January; 4 March; 21 July 1724, NLS, 16529/12-13; 16529/31-32; 16529/67.
36. ARBS, General Stock Journal, EQ/10/3; Ledger of the Daily Transactions, RB/14/1. It is interesting that neither the Duke of Argyll nor his man of business, Duncan Forbes, became stockholders in the RBS. The Duke may simply have lacked cash.
37. Middleton invested more than £9,000, Shaw, *Management*, p. 120; Healey, *Coutts & Co.*, p. 58.
38. Daranda became the chairman of the London 'Committee of Correspondence of the Members of the Royall Bank'. ARBS, RBS, Minutes, RBS/12/1, pp. 10, 11, 88, 314.
39. ARBS, General Stock Journal, EQ/10/3, EQ11/2/2 circled/1, p.42 and EQ 18/2/1 circled/ No. 81.
40. ARBS, Minutes, RBS/12/1 pp. 116-17, 192. The others so bound were Daranda, Benjamin Lanquet, Edward Harrison, John Merrill and James Campbell; NLS, 16538/83.
41. Ilay to Milton, 24 February 1729, NLS, 16540/25. The Old Bank sought to undermine confidence in it by questioning the RBS's charter, which had been given by the Crown not Parliament.
42. Ilay to Milton, 6 August 1728, NLS, 16538/65.
43. ARBS, Minutes, RBS/12/1/253.
44. Ilay to Milton, 6 August 1728, n.d. [autumn 1728], 23 November 1728, NLS, 16538/65, 75 and 83.
45. Ilay to Milton, 16 January 1729 and n.d. [1728-29], NLS, 16540/16 and 69.
46. ARBS, Minutes, 6 February and 26 March 1730, RBS/12/1, pp. 303, 314.
47. Ilay to Milton, 3 February 1732, NLS, 16548/98.
48. Checkland, *Scottish Banking*, p. 65; ARBS, Minutes, 13 March 1734, RB/12/ 2, p. 205. That meeting sent to Ilay and others the RBS proposals for the new charter which would be required.
49. ARBS, Minutes of 14 January 1732, RB/12/2, p. 45; Ilay to Milton, January 1733, NLS, 16552/70; Minutes of 10 May 1732, p. 69.
50. Ilay to Milton,? September 1732, NLS, 16548/114. The man Ilay sacked thought his Lordship did not have a proper regard for Campbells – but he belonged to the Campbells of Breadalbane. John Campbell to P[atrick] Campbell of Barcaldine, 28 October 1732. Barcaldine Papers, NRS, GD170/199/23. The writer was made Cashier of the Bank in

1745. 'The Diary of John Campbell', transcribed by J. S. Gibson (Edinburgh, The Royal Bank of Scotland Archives, 1995), p. 1.

51. Checkland, *Scottish Banking*, pp. 62-63.

52. The Town Council dominated by Ilay's friends became a large stockholder in the RBS owning £3,500 of stock by 1753. ECA, Memorial Querries for the magistrates & Council... 16 July 1753, Bay D, Bundle 5, Shelf 16, item 13. The burgh also borrowed money from the RBS.

53. ARBS, Ledger of the daily *Transactions...*, RB/714/3, f.51 and many entries 1734- 1736.

54. Ilay to Sir [?Charles Delafaye], 14 October 1731, NRS, SP54/20/57.

55. Shaw, *Management, passim.*

56. Ilay to Milton, 29 May, 2 and 5 June, 4 August 1739, NLS, 16576/100, 103, 107, 113.

57. Minutes of the Convention of Royal Burghs, 16 May 1729, ECA, SL 30/1/1/10 p. 315. Ilay in 1724 seems to have been similarly worried about 'coin'; NLS, 16529/10 and he may have been so again in 1731, Ilay to Milton, 18 November 1731, NLS, 16542/104.

58. Robert Maxwell, *Select Transactions of the Honourable the Society of the Improvers of the Agriculture in Scotland* (Edinburgh, 1743, reprinted Glasgow, 2003), pp. iii-xvii, 1-9.

59. *Ibid*, p. xii.

60. William Mackintosh of Borlum, 'An Essay on the Husbandry of Scotland with a proposal for the further improvement of it' (Edinburgh, 1732).

61. Maxwell, *Select Transactions*, p. vi.

62. Cochran started life as an officer in the dragoons before moving to a regiment of foot. By 1730, he held a Majority but was retired to the post of Commissioner of Excise thanks to the intervention of the Campbell brothers.

63. John Gifford, *William Adam, 1689-1748* (Edinburgh, 1989), p. 160.

64. NLS, 17642/49. The ms dates from c.1729/30.

65. NLS, 17617/285, 287.

66. NLS, 17747/71.

67. Robert Brisbane to Lord Milton, 14 February 1761, NLS, 16718/82.

68. I thank Professor T.C. Smout for this information.

69. NLS, 17645/175.

70. NLS, 17642/134.

71. NLS, 17651/ 170.

72. NLS, 17747/71.

73. Maxwell, *Select Transactions*, pp. vi-vii; see also Ian G. Lindsay and Mary Cosh, *Inveraray and the Dukes of Argyll* (Edinburgh, 1973), pp. 7, 11, 17.

74. Until after the mid-1750s, Scottish bleachers used sour milk, soap, washing and sunlight as their principal bleaching agents.

75. 'Whim', *Royal Commission on the Ancient and Historical Monuments of Scotland, Peeblesshire: An Inventory of the Ancient Monuments*, 2 vols (HMSO, Edinburgh, 1967), II:327.

76. NLS, 17646/15.

77. NLS, 17645/218.

78. NLS, 17680/128-130; 17650/159. At Salt Coats in Ayrshire, Ilay had salt pans and a mine to fire them. Those establishments were not large, employing only about a dozen men each. In 1736, he paid a coal bill in Edinburgh so the need for a mine was clear.

79. NLS, 17646/76; 108, 190; 17650/16. In 1761, twenty of those were 'foreign'. Cattle Inventory, 13 June 1761, NLS, 17650/205.

80. Ilay to Milton, 21 December 1726, NLS, 16533/145.

81. Tracy Borman, *Henrietta Howard King's Mistress, Queen's Servant* (London, 2007), pp.143-44, 167; Dickson, *Red John of the Battles: The Second Duke of Argyll and the First Duke of Greenwich 1680-1743* (London, 1970), p. 213.

82. *E.g.*, Original Letters ... to Henrietta Howard, Countess of Suffolk..., British Library, Add MSS 22625 (correspondence with Arbuthnot, Swift, Gay and others); Add MSS 22628/29-30, 31,40; 22629/177.

83. This may be *The Lady's Guide or the Whole Art of Dress* (c.1726) sometimes attributed to Elizabeth, Lady Hervey – in which case they would have been reading a book by one of their own set.

84. In December 1725, Ilay was 'making interest for Dr. Arbuthnot's book' and expecting Milton to do so as well, NLS, 16531/60.

85. NLS, 16531/50.

86. Mary Lepel to Mrs. Howard, n.d., Lothian Muniments, NSA, GD40/9/140/19; 20 21 and 28.

87. *The Correspondence of Alexander Pope*, ed. George Sherburn, 4 vols (Oxford, 1956), May 1729, III:34.

88. Maynard Mack, *Collected in Himself: Essays Critical, Biographical and Bibliographical on Pope and some of His Contemporaries* (Newark, London and Toronto,, 1982), p. 404.

89. *Correspondence of Pope*, I:379, 417; 3:34, 478; 4:21. In 'Bounce [Pope's bitch] to Fop [Mrs. Howard's dog] (1726-36), Pope referred to 'some of I 's hungry Breed', a line that suggests it was written after his Lordship had fallen out of favour because of his crass political patronage and his manipulations of the 1734 elections in Scotland. 'I 's' is given in some editions as 'J 's' but the 'I' makes more sense given Pope's disgust at Ilay's behavior in the 1734 Scottish elections. Alexander Pope, *The Twickenham Edition of the Poems of Alexander Pope*, ed. John Butt (London, 1994), Vol VI:366-371, I:53; Pope to the Earl of Marchmont, November 1740, *Correspondence of Pope*, IV:271.

90. Through Chesterfield, Voltaire met a long list of people; see, *An essay on epic poetry*, ed. David Williams in *The Complete Works of Voltaire*, Vol.3B, Voltaire Foundation (Oxford, 1996), pp. 131-40. As late as 1769, Voltaire, when visited by a daughter of the 2nd Duke, 'mentioned my father and the late Duke of Argyll [Ilay] with great incomiums'; *Letters and Journals of Lady Mary Coke*, III: 159.

91. In 1735 the Countess married George Berkeley, a follower of William Pulteney and an Opposition MP; *HPHC 1715-1754*, pp. I:456-7.

92. John Hervey, Baron Ickworth, *Memoirs of the Reign of of George the Second from His Accession to the Death of Queen Caroline*, ed. John Wilson Croker, 3 vols (New York, 1884), I:337.

93. The story of Curll's humiliation of the printer is told in *A Window in the Bosom: The Letters of Alexander Pope*, ed. James Anderson Winn (Hamdem, Conn., 1977), pp. 30-41, 203-221, 235-37 and in 'A Narrative of the Method By Which the Private letters of Mr. Pope have been Procur'd and Publish'd By Edmund Curll', *Correspondence of Pope*, III:458-467, 478.

94. Pope to Marchmont, ? October 1740, *Correspondence of Pope*, IV:271.

95. Robert Halsband, *Lord Hervey Eighteenth-Century Courtier* (Oxford, 1974), p. 93.

96. Joseph Spence, *Observations, Anecdotes, and Characters of Books and Men....* 2 vols, ed. James M. Osborn (Oxford, 1966), II:403.

97. Ilay to Milton, NLS, 16531/46. He seems never to have been hung over.

98. Ilay to Milton, 6 August 1731, NLS, 16545/96.

99. Marchmont Papers, NRS, GD158/1367/1, 2, 3. Malaria, from which he probably suffered, often flared up in the spring and autumn. He could have picked it up in Southern Europe but it was also endemic in England during this time. 'Ague' usually meant a high fever followed by chills often accompanied by tremors.

100. Ilay to Milton, NLS 16542/82-84. Other letters to Milton about his complaint are NLS 16542/36, 67, 79 and 92.

101. Ilay to Milton, 1 September and 17 October 1730, NLS, 16542/67and 82-84.
102. Ilay to Milton, 9 July 1731, NLS, 16545/77.
103. Ilay to Milton, 25 and 30 January 1735, NLS, 16559/89 and 92.
104. Ilay to Milton, 12 September 1735, NLS, 16559/149.
105. Ilay to Milton, ? May 1735, NLS, 16559/120.
106. Ilay to Milton, 17 November 1735 and n.d., NLS, 16559/170 and 177; Milton to Ilay, 8 January 1736, NLS, 16559/172; Ilay to Milton, 8 January 1736, NLS, 16564/66.
107. John Chamberlayne, *Present State of Great Britain...* (London, 1723), Book III, Part II, pp.11 (Lord Justice General 1710-1761, £ 1,000), 12 (Lord Privy Seal 1721-1733 and Lord Keeper of the Great Seal 1733-1761, £3,000).
108. He bought Champagne by the dozen, brandies, Arrick and Tokay by the gallon, White or Rhenish wine by the barrel [generally 30-40 imperial gallons], Burgundy and Claret by the hogsheads [52.5 imperial gallons], Port and Madeira by the pipe [105 imperial gallons]. For some years, there are no purchases recorded in the 'Out book'. His household also consumed home made drinks like orange and other cordials, cyder and gooseberry wine and probably ale or beer.

Chapter 14

1. HPHC *1715-1754*, I:159; Richard Scott, 'The Politics and Administration of Scotland 1725-1748', unpublished Edinburgh University Ph.D. thesis, 1982, p. 396.
2. This discussion is nicely summarized by Andrew Mackillop in *'More Fruitful than the Soil' Army, Empire and the Scottish Highlands 1715-1815* (East Linton, 2000), pp. 15-17.
3. Robertson to Thomas Kennedy, 9 January 1731, Kennedy of Dalquharran and Dunure, NRS, GD27/5/18 and 10.
4. Ilay's Memorandum for Newcastle, 2 September 1729, NRS, SP 54/19/114.
5. Ilay to Newcastle, 2 September 1729, NRS, SP54/19/90.
6. The sett was published in *Set of the City of Edinburgh with the Acts of Parliament and Council Relative Thereto* (Edinburgh, 1783), pp. 39-51.
7. Robert Wodrow noted the Earl's arguments in August in his *Analecta*; quoted in *Intimate Letters of the Eighteenth Century*, ed. George Campbell, 8th Duke of Argyll, 2 vols (London, n.d.), I:23.
8. *Ibid*, I:23.
9. The 'Baillies' to Milton, 11 July 1729, Aberdeen Town Council, Out letter Book 1729-1738.
10. Excise taxes paid only for about 75% of the costs. Scott, 'Politics and Administration', p. 123.
11. Scott, 'Politics and Administration', p. 86.
12. *More Culloden Papers*, ed. Duncan Warrand, 5 vols (Inverness, 1923-30), III: 61, 63, 73, 80, 87, 91, 94, 95; Seafield Papers, NRS, GD248/17/2/21; there is more on those conflicts in the Seafield MSS, NRS, GD248/47-171, *passim*.
13. Marchmont MSS, NRS, GD158/1183/1367/1 and 2.
14. There are several letters about this election in NRS, SP54/20/36.
15. A. S. Turberville, *The House of Lords in the XVIIIth Century* (Oxford, 1927) p. 199.
16. York to James Clavering, 27 February 1730 in *The Correspondence of James Clavering*, ed. H. T. Dickinson, Surtees Society, 178 (1968), p. 168.
17. Turberville, *House of Lords*, p. 199; William Cobbett, *Parliamentary History of England From the Norman Conquest, in 1066 to the Year 1803*, vols 6-15 (London, 1810-13), VIII:792.
18. E.g., his speech on the sinking fund, Cobbett, *Parl. Hist*, compiled by William Cobbett (London, 1810-13), Vols VI-XV. Microfilm produced by Fairview Park: Pergamon Press, Inc, n.d., IX:127-28.

19. *Ibid,* VIII:1051-1062. This had some relation to unpaid subsidies on exported fish about which the Convention of Royal Burghs complained on 10 July 1730; Minutes of the Convention of Royal Burghs, ECA, SL 3/1/1/10, pp. 365-67.
20. *Parl. Hist.,* VIII: 1051.
21. *Ibid,* VIII:1259.
22. Bolingbroke had been allowed to return to Britain but was barred from the House of Lords because of his earlier support of the Pretender.
23. 'Country party' arguments persisted in Scotland and show up in David Hume's political essays which reflected Scottish conditions as much as those in Britain generally. Hume's *Essays Moral and Political,* 2 vols (1741-42) fit this context. James Oswald offered to present the second volume of the *Essays* to the friends of the Prince of Wales. Hume's friends read his Opposition allegiance correctly; *Memorials of the Public Life and Character of the Right Hon. James Oswald of Dunniker* (Edinburgh, 1825), p. 21.
24. J. H. Plumb, *Sir Robert Walpole The King's Minister,* 2 vols (London, 1960), II:270.
25. Plumb, *Walpole,* II:270; John Hervey, Baron Ickworth, *Memoirs of the Reign of George the Second from His Accession to the Death of Queen Caroline,* ed. John Wilson Croker, 3 vols (New York, 1884), I:203.
26. Plumb, *Walpole,* II:276, 278; Cobbett, *Parl. Hist,* IX, (London, 1811), IX:97.
27. Plumb, *Walpole,* II:278.
28. *Parl. Hist.,* IX, (London, 1811), IX:146.
29. Roger L. Emerson, *Academic Patronage in the Scottish Enlightenment* (Edinburgh, 2008), pp. 93-95. It is almost surprising to find in October 1733 that the notable Argathelian and Squdrone politicians could gather at Dumbarton to celebrate the King's birthday and to drink toasts to each other. [London] *Daily Courant,* 30 October 1733.
30. Mar and Kellie Manuscripts, NRS, GD124/15/1424/3.
31. See Roger B. Manning, *An Apprenticeship in Arms* (Oxford, 2006). The Campbells belonged to an aristocratic warrior class but they had seen the advantages of professionally officered armies not led by the likes of Cobham and Bolton.
32. Turberville, *House of Lords,* pp. 208-09.
33. Ilay to My Lord ?, 19 July 1733, NRS, SP54/22/17/9.
34. 'If you want money for the 300 for Cromarty, Rea, & Rollo as I mentioned in last post, You may take it from the money the R. Bank owes me'. Those peers each received £100. Ilay to Milton, 30 November, 11 December 1733, NLS, 16556/111, 116. Most of the 1733 recipients were still being subsidized in 1740 and 1741; NLS,17615/183; NLS, 17616/38.
35. Ilay was involved over many years with James Erskine, Lord Grange, the brother of the attainted and forfeited John, Earl of Mar. They had been students in Holland (c.1700) and entered political life at about the same time, in Erskine' case c.1707 as an aide to his brother. He worked with Ilay then. After 1714, he was loyal to the Argathelian interest. His loyalty was rooted in hopes that Ilay would either be able to secure the reversal of Mar's attainder or have the Erskine estates restored to Mar's son. Grange tried to keep the family afloat and bought in as much of their confiscated lands as he could. He was going ever deeper into debt and found it increasingly hard to meet the payments on the money he had borrowed for his purchases. For years he lobbied Ilay and others about this. He was given fair words but little else. By 1728, Erskine had become desperate enough to try to kidnap Mar's unstable or lunatic wife. With her in his possession, he, not her sister, Lady Mary Wortley Montagu, would control Lady Mar's jointure of £1,000 a year. Grange's attempt at abduction failed. Her sister was not willing to grant Grange's request because she was looking after the deranged woman and needed funds to do that. Ilay, the friend of both, was asked to sort out the mess. He recommended to Grange that the affair be put 'in the hands of A third person unconcerned'. If things went well,

good; if not, then the break would not be laid to Grange's account. Lady Mary told Ilay that Grange had misrepresented her position and that she was willing to give him half the funds. (Lady Mary to Ilay, 20 February 1729, quoted in Robert Halsband, *The Life of Lady Wortley Montagu* (Oxford, 1956), p. 153.) Lawyers met and the affair was resolved by a division of the monies. (Ilay to Grange, 10 September 1728 and Lady Mary to Ilay, 20 February [1729], NRS, GD124/15/1338 and GD124/15/1351). The jointure was split equally between Lady Mary, who looked after her sister in London, and Grange, who used his share of the money to make payments on the Erskine estates. (Halsband, *The Life of Lady Mary Wortley Montagu* (London, 1961; 1st ed, Oxford, 1956), p. 135); *The Complete Letters of Lady Mary Wortley Montagu*, ed. Robert Halsband, 3 vols (Oxford, 1965), II:90. 'Anecdotes of Lady Mary Wortley Montagu', *The Yale Edition of Horace Walpole' Correspondence*, ed. Wilmarth S. Lewis, *et al.*, 48 vols (variously in New Haven, Conn., N.Y. and London, 1937-1963), IX:244. In 1731, Grange was refused a pension by Ilay. He opposed Ilay's position on the rights of patrons and heritors to call ministers. The expenses of the Earl of Mar's funeral in 1732 probably made Grange desperate. He had his own somewhat mad wife kidnapped by men directed by Lord Lovat. Argathelians were complicit in that venture. Milton wrote to Ilay, ' I am to meet wt my Lord at his desire to concert what is to be said on yt subject.', [n.d.,1731-32], NLS 16548/94). Grange sent his wife to the island of St Kilda where she could not threaten his physical safety, as she seems to have done, or spread rumours of his alleged Jacobitism. In 1732/3 Grange was on the fringes of the Opposition; by the end of 1733 he was one of its leaders. Grange's stated reasons for changing sides were those of the Opposition to Walpole. Having been a corrupter, his conversion made him so pure that he was willing to pillory his one-time friends. See Anne Skoczylas, *Life of Grange*, forthcoming

36. In March 1734, Tweeddale told Lord Grange that no letter had miscarried 'yett some of them appear to have been opened'. Party leaders were always concerned to have a reliable men in charge of the post offices. Tweeddale to Grange, 12 March 1734, NRS, GD124/15/1424/5; Walpole, *Correspondence*, IX:244.

37. Tweeddale to Grange, 12 March 1734, NRS, GD124/15/1424/5.

38. *Parl. Hist.,* IX:484-85.

39. The story is told by W. Ernest-Browning, *Memoirs of the Life of Philip Dormer fourth Earl of Chesterfield* (London, 1906), p. 40

40. Stair to Grange, 20 March 1734, NRS, GD124/15/1428/2.

41. Mr. Cleland to Grange, 20 or 21 March 1734, NRS, GD124/15/ 1431.

42. *Parl. Hist.,* IX:519, 550, 551.

43. Ilay to ?, 19 October 1732, NRS, GD248/167/1/21; Alexander Cunningham to ?, 31 December 1732, NRS, GD248/167/1/36. It was possible through the seeming transference of property to trustworthy dependants and friends to increase the number of voters in a county. Because the franchise was so limited, the creation of a few votes often determined an election.

44. Brodie of Brodie to Grant of Grant, 27 April 1733; Ilay to Sir James Grant, 13 September [1733], NRS, GD248/171/2/16 and 12.

45. Tweeddale to Grange, 23 February 1734, NRS, GD124/151424/4 and Stair to Grange, 2 March 1734, NRS, GD124/1428/1.

46. NLS, 7044/68-73.

47. Because English judges doubted the legality of Grange's resignation, it was not accepted for some time. Grange to Newcastle, 1 May 1734; Hardwicke to Newcastle, 19 May 1734; Harrington to Newcastle, 21 May 1734, NRS, SP54/22/26/28 and 29 and 30.

48. Minute Books of the Convention of Royal Burghs, 5 April 1734, ECA, SL30/1/1/11/ pp. 34-55.

49. Milton to Newcastle, 5 March 1734, NRS, SP 54/22/17/23.
50. *London Gazette*, 23 April 1734.
51. The figures are given by Scott, 'Politics and Administration', p. 396.
52. William Ferguson, *Scotland:1689 to the Present* (Edinburgh and London, 1968). p. 144.
53. Sir James Fergusson of Kilkerran, *The Sixteen Peers of Scotland: An Account of the Elections of the Representative Peers of Scotland 1707-1959* (Oxford, 1960), pp. 77-80. Much that follows is based on his account of this election.
54. William Robertson, *Proceedings Relating to the Peerage of Scotland from January 16. 1707, to April 29, 1788* (Edinburgh, 1788), pp. 152-53.
55. This is largely taken from the *London Evening Post*, 13 June 1734, but the same account appeared in other papers.
56. Grange, 'The Fatal Consequences of Ministerial Influence: Or, the Difference between Royal Power and ministerial Power Truly Stated....', pp. 34-35; Lord Hervey to Henry Fox, 10 February 1735, *Lord Hervey and His Friends*, 1726-38, ed. Giles Fox-Strangeways, 6th Earl of Ilchester (London, 1950), p. 221.
57. Names were omitted from the Appendix but they were given in a key bound with the pamphlet.
58. Grange, 'Fatal Consequences', Appendix, pp. 12-13.
59. Grange, *Ibid*, pp. 8-12. That the details of Ilay's dealings with Lords Garnock, Rae and Cromarty were widely known is shown by a letters in the Marchmont papers, *HMCR, Manuscripts of Lord Polwarth*, ed. Henry Paton, (London, 1940), 5:110, 111 162.
60. A third son, John Elphinstone, was an Army Engineer and cartographer.
61. Grange, 'Fatal Consequences', pp. 2-8.
62. Ilay obtained the Ensigncy at Stirling Castle for Elphinstone's son over the objections of the Squadrone Governor, Lord Rothes. He tried to get the other son a company but failed. He hoped his efforts would change Lord Elphinstone's mind but 'if it has not I shall only think that I have thrown away one of the King's favours on the son of a man, who certainly has merit whether he be a friend of mine or no, I heartily wish him and his family well independent of all political views'. Copy of a letter of Ilay to Lord Lovat, 19 December 1733, Marchmont Papers, NRS, GD158/2915. On wonders how Marchmont came by the letter.
63. Grange, 'Fatal Consequences', pp. 1-2. Glasgow and his family remained in Opposition. His son was later chosen as Rector of Glasgow (1754-56) when Ilay's fortunes were at a low ebb.
64. *Ibid*, p. 13.
65. Cromartie was made Collector of Crown Rents in Ross-shire, a job which paid £300; *HMCR, Report on Reginald Rawdon Hastings, Esq.*, ed. Francis Bickley (London, 1934), V:111.
66. NLS, 17615; Ilay was said to have bought up the mortgages and loans of the Earl of Home whose vote then became secure.
67. Fox-Strangeways, *Lord Hervey and His Friends*, pp. 199-200. Among the peers outed at the election were Montrose, Tweeddale, Marchmont, Stair, Haddington and Rothes and the unreliable Earl of Buchan.
68. Ilay to Milton, 30 January 1735, NLS, 16559/92.
69. W. Ernest-Browning, *Memoirs of the Life of Chesterfield*, pp. 86-87.
70. On the government's pension list, in 1734-35, were the Earls of Home, Dalhousie, Northesk, Cromartie, Kellie, Kilmarnock, and Barons Rea [Ray], Colville, Elibank, Rollo, Gray, Oliphant and Balcarres. Lord Milton paid them but Ilay kept their receipts. NLS, 17615/3.
71. Grange, 'Fatal Consequence', p. 34-35; Fox-Strangeways, *Lord Hervey, Ibid*.

72. I take that to be his meaning in a letter in which he says he is 'endeavouring to defend the Claim of Right', in which the oppressions of James II and VII had been detailed.

73. *Parl. Hist.*, IX:793-95.

74. *Ibid*, IX: 917-944. Not all of the reported speech is by him but its more technical portions and familiar arguments probably are.

75. *A Collection of Parliamentary Debates in England ... (1666-1803)*, compiled by John Torbuck *et al.*, 20 vols (Dublin or London, ?1741), XIII:147-58, 176.

76. Ilay to Milton, 31 July 1735, NLS, 16559/132.

77. The university cases are discussed in Roger L. Emerson, *Academic Patronage* or in *Professors, Patronage and Politics*: t*he Scottish Universities in the Eighteenth Century* (Aberdeen, 1991). The most important of those was the one which brought William Wishart II to the principalship of Edinburgh University in 1736.

78. Hervey to Henry Fox, 23 and 24 January 1735, Fox-Strangeways, *Lord Hervey and His Friends*, pp. 218-19; Coutts, 'Out book', 1735.

79. Turberville, *House of Lords*, p. 214-216; *Parliamentary Debates* (?Dublin, 1740), XIII:450, 524. He and his brother the Duke were unable to make this as lenient to the Quakers as they had hoped to do.

80. In 1736, Ilay opposed Hardwicke's bill which would made smuggling a more risky activity. Hervey, *Memoirs*, III:99.

81. Ilay to Milton, 5 August 1736 and ? September, NLS, 16564/109 and 115.

82. Sir Robert Walpole to Horace Walpole, 9 August and 1 October 1736, in William Coxe, *Memoirs of the Life and Administration of Sir Robert Walpole, Earl of Orford*, 3 vols (London, 1800), III:348, 365.

83. *Ibid*, III:348, 365. Lord Milton presided at Porteous's trial.

84. Ilay to Walpole, 16 October 1736 in Coxe, *Walpole*, III:367.

85. *Ibid*, III:367.

86. *Ibid*, I:494.

87. Ilay to Milton, 14 December 1736, NLS, 16564/135.

88. Hervey, *Memoirs*, III:107.

89. Coxe, *Walpole,* I:495; *Parl. Hist.*, X:198.

90. Hervey, *Memoirs*, III: 119.

91. *Ibid*, III:103.

92. *Ibid*, III:103.

93. *Ibid*, III:115- 117.

94. *The Autobiography of Alexander Carlyle of Inveresk 1722-1805*, ed. John Hill Burton (Edinburgh, 1910), pp. 45-46.

95. Hervey said that he, Ilay and the Queen had worked out the punishments of the city but that Ilay's silence was to protect his interests in Scotland. *Memoirs*, pp. 104-106.

96. Alexander Murdoch, *ODNB* IX:431.

97. 'The Country (say they) has been ill used, Lord Ilay no better and his friends continue to be dispised. And though they are told if it had not been for Sir R[obert Walpole] we should have been worse used, this has little Effect; they say, it is the same thing, both to the Country and them whether, it proceeded from want of inclination or Power in those upon whose protection they depended'. Richard Scott quoted by Alexander Murdoch in *ODNB*, IX:432.

98. Quoted by Jeremy Black in *British Foreign Policy in the Age of Walpole* (Edinburgh, 1985), pp. 52-53.

99. Basil Williams, *Carteret and Newcastle: A Contrast in Contemporaries* (London, 1966), p.104.

100. Coxe, *Walpole*, I:527-28, 541.
101. In 1737, Hervey reported that the Queen in a private interview told Ilay that she had told Newcastle to stop harassing him. She warned Newcastle that the King would not endure Ilay's mistreatment. *Memoirs*, III:290. John Shaw saw her as having blighted Ilay's career and prevented him from ever becoming Secretary of State for Scotland. John Shaw, *The Political History of Eighteenth-Century Scotland* (London and New York, 1999), p. 68.
102. Gwynn Vaughn to Duncan Forbes, 6 July 1737, Culloden Papers, NLS, 2968/ 63.
103. Argyll to Duncan Forbes, 9 October, 1737, Culloden Papers, NLS, 2968/64.
104. *Parl. Hist*, X (London, 1812), X:1034-35.
105. *Parliamentary Debates*, (?Dublin, 1740), XVII:218, 226.
106. *Ibid*, XVII:232.
107. *Ibid*, XVII:232-33; 345-365, 226.
108. 26 January and 3 March 1739, Coxe, *Walpole*, III: 514, 516; Ilay to Milton, 3 March, 1739, NLS, 16576/86.
109. *Parliamentary Debates* (?Dublin,1740), XVII:476-92; Cobbett, *Parl. Hist.*, (London, 1812), X:1230-1241.
110. The title contains a pun. It was printed by Patrick Ramsay in London. Archibald Stewart, Argyll's candidate, not Ilay's, was elected.
111. ' "The Speech of the D of A upon the State of the Nation," April 15 1740' in 'The conduct of His Grace the D-ke of Ar--le for the four last years review'd ... Together with His Grace's speech April 15th, 1740 Upon the state of the nation' (London, 1740).
112. The menu items come from the his secretary's Diary, NLS, 17615; 17616; 17617.
113. J. M. Simpson, 'William Steuart' in *HPHC 1715-1754*, II:447.
114. Various entries, NLS, 17615. Faber's c.1744 mezzotint shows him dressed in that fashion but without the gold (Plate 7).
115. There were periodic campaigns in Scotland to have people buy only locally manufactured items. This cause was taken up by the HIKAS 1725: eg. 'RESOLVE of the Honourable Society ...', a broadside (Edinburgh, 17 December 1725). The sheet says that it is intended to raise employment and the standards of production and to encourage the bleachers. In the 1750s, the Edinburgh Society was urging the same things, as did others whenever times were hard.
116. Those can be checked in A. J. S. Gibson and T. C. Smout, *Prices, Food and Wages in Scotland 1550-1780* (Cambridge, 1995).
117. Emerson, *Academic Patronage*, pp. 98-100.
118. Patricia Dickson, *Red John of the Battles, John Second Duke of Argyll and First Duke of Greenwich* (London, 1973), pp. 227-28. Lovat by 1741 had reverted to being a Jacobite. His secret re-conversion was but one sign of the revival of Jacobite hopes brought by the alliance of France and Spain and the initial success of their forces. Lovat's interest was thrown to Argyll. *HPHC 1715-1754*, I:387.
119. Quoted by Scott, 'Politics and Administration', p. 440.
120. Liam to Milton, 14 February 1741, NLS, 16580/51. One can infer from Cobbett's account of this debate that Ilay argued that such a motion presupposed Walpole's guilt of some crime without giving any evidence of criminal behaviour. The Duke of Argyll's retort to that was, 'attend the voice of the people!' *Parl. Hist.*, XI:1964.
121. Ilay to Milton, 20 June 1741, NLS, 16584/41.
122. He is not known personally to have been involved with this but his men in the House of Commons certainly were. He was also likely active in various measures recommended by the Convention of Royal Burghs to limit the impressment of seamen, the quartering of troops and the protection of Scottish shipping. Minute Books of the Convention of Royal

Burghs, ECA, SL 30/1/1/11, pp. 271, 274, 276, 310, 333. The entries cover the period January 1741 to August 1742.

123. *Parl. Hist.*, XI:701, 725-31.
124. *Ibid*, XI: 732.
125. *Ibid*, XI:1000, 1030; a week later he intervened in a foolish debate about assigning seats to lords saying that 'the question of good or bad places is nothing'; *Ibid*, 1041.
126. Scott, 'Politics and Administration', pp. 394-99.
127. *HPHC 1715-54*, I:46.
128. Coxe, *Walpole*, II:613.
129. Scott, 'Politics and Administration', p. 400.
130. Foord, *Opposition*, p. 276.
131. Ilay stayed on in London that summer to defend Walpole's interests. That did not stop Walpole's son Horace from thinking Ilay had betrayed his father. His belief was set out in a widely circulated 'ode' by Sir Charles Hanbury Williams. Among its lines are the following:
    [Walpole] trusted Islay, till it was too late...
    To trust a traitor that he knew so well
    (Strange truth! Betrayed, but not deceived, he fell! ...
    Trusted to one he never could think true,
    And perished by a villain that he knew.
    Horace Walpole continued to believe that. Hanbury Williams had earlier attacked Ilay and Argyll in other odes from 1740. *Walpole Correspondence*, 17 (1954), pp. 346-47.
132. Ilay to Milton, ?February 1742, NLS, 16584/55.
133. Ilay to Milton, ? July 1742, NLS, 16587/87.
134. John Drummond to Sir John Clerk of Penicuik, 25 March 1742, NRS, GD18/3228/1/5.
135. Ilay to Milton, 7 October 1742, NLS, 16587/104.
136. Argyll had mental breakdowns or strokes in 1730, 1738-39 and near the end of his life. Richard Glover, *Memoirs of A Celebrated Literary and Political Character from the Resignation of Sir Robert Walpole in 1742 to the Establishment of Lord Chatham's Second Administration in 1757* (London, 1813), pp. 11-12.
137. Glover, *Memoirs*, pp. 8-10. In the end, Duke John was so debilitated that he could not bring himself to sign the marriage settlement of at least one daughter. *Walpole Correspondence*, 17 (1954), pp. 479-80 n. 40.
138. Ilay to Milton, 15 October 1742; 19 March 1743; 2 April 1743, NLS, 16587/103; 16591/39; 43.
139. Murdoch, *ODNB*, IX:818.
140. *Parl. Hist.*, XII:707.
141. Thomas Hay to Tweeddale, 27 April 1742, NLS, 7046/100.
142. This is said in a Memorandum, n.d. [1754], NLS, 144226/143.
143. They went from Malta to Leghorne and were re-shipped to Britain where they arrived in the summer of 1742. Horace Mann to Horace Walpole, 22 April 1742, 6 May 1742 *Walpole Correspondence*, 17 (1954), p. 394; 419f; see also 1 July 1742; 17 (1954), pp. 338, 462, 464. By the time they were sent, Walpole seemed to have been more taken with them and regretted sending them to a man who 'would shut them up and starve them, and then bury them under the stairs with his wife' – which says much about Walpole and something about Ilay's reputation among those who disliked him. Walpole to Mann, 21 July 1742, *Walpole Correspondence*, 17 (1954), p. 506. Maltese cats were not and are not a breed but semi-feral animals known as good mousers. One of them can perhaps be seen in Woollett's 1757 engraving of the garden and canal at Whitton (Plate 9).
144. Baron Philip von Stosch, was a minor diplomat, antiquarian and dealer in coins and gems who functioned as a British spy, principally in Italy, from c.1721 until his death in 1757. Ilay may have dealt with him over gems, medals and coins.

145. He was also then very lame in his good leg perhaps because of his treatment of the problem. Ilay to Milton, 24 July 1742, NLS, 16587/89.
146. Scott, 'Politics and Administration', p. 474; see also Shaw, *Political History*, p. 71.
147. Horace Walpole to Horace Mann, 30 June 1742 OS, *Walpole Correspondence*, 17 (1954), p. 479; Dickson, *Red John*, pp. 238-241; Ilay to Milton, 9 October 1742, NLS, 16587/106.
148. Ilay to Milton, 6 October 1743, NLS, 16591/68; the existing seals are not very clear.
149. Ilay to Milton, 29 October, 9 November 1743, NLS 16591/83 and 92.
150. This is also the view of Shaw, *Political History*, pp. 67-68.
151. Ilay paid £1,213.7.6 for the land, a bit over £55 an acre. Laird, *The Flowering of the Landscape Garden English Pleasure Grounds 1720-1800* (Philadelphia, 1999), p. 83; Coutts, 'Out book', 16 November 1734.
152. This verse was widely circulated. The most convenient place to find it is *Walpole Correspondence*, 3 June 1742, 17 (1954):441.
153. His accounts in the early 1730s suggest that he was purchasing chemical apparatus and optical devices.
154. 'A Catalogue of the Library of the Honble Samuel Molyneux Deceas'd.... '(London, 1730) held at Houghton Library Harvard University, Ms. B 1827. S78*. I have used, with permission from Harvard University, a xerox copy supplied to me by the Whipple Library at Cambridge University.
155. See Appendix I.
156. A few years later, Ward moved it to Richmond where its smell annoyed fewer of the genteel. *Daily Gazetteer*, 31 March 1736; Archibald and Nan Clow, *The Chemical Revolution* (London, 1952; reprinted, Freeport, N.Y., 1970), p. 131-32.
157. Lord Milton once told Sir John Clerk that he and Ilay would dine with him (preferably at 2:00 pm) and gave instructions regarding his reception: ' ...if you have a mind to Regale his Lop do not make a feast for him nor come to meet him but let us have the pleasure of surprising you in some of your choisest amusements...' Then, with no formalities, they would talk about those. Milton to Clerk, n.d. [1732], NLS, GD18/5385/1.
158. *Daily Journal*, 14 August 1736.
159. Coutts, 'Out book', 28 December 1727.
160. Katharine Glover, ' "Polite London Children": Educating the Daughters of the Scottish Elite in Mid-Eighteenth-Century London' in *Scots in London in the Eighteen Century*, ed. Stana Nenadic (Lewisburg, 2010), pp. 253-271.
161. Halsband, *Lady Mary*, p. 155.
162. Coutts, 'Out book', 26 May 1739. It was notable for its gardens. Lady Mary in 1749 thought her daughter had 'fitted it up very well' and remembered it as an 'agreeable place' where she would 'with a great pleasure to me see my Grand children run about in the Gardens'. Halsband, *Letters of Lady Mary Wortley Montagu*, II:437-39.
163. I thank Alexander Murdoch for sending me this quotation which comes from an uncatalogued letter at Mount Stuart House. It is quoted with the permission of the Marquis of Bute.
164. Montagu, *Complete Letters*, II: 200; see also David Gavine, 'James Stewart Mackenzie, 1719-1800) and the Bute MSS', *Journal of the History of Astronomy* 5 (1974), pp. 208-214. This article gives an inventory of his scientific and other manuscripts then held at Mount Stuart House.
165. Ilay's relationship to Mrs. Williams bothered his brother who is supposed to have exclaimed at some point. "No whore's child shall inherit my estate'. To that Ilay replied with a reference to their father, 'Brother, shall I be the first of the family to have done so'. *Walpole Correspondence*, 26 (1971), Appendix, p. 11. Ilay's plans to make Mrs. Williams his heiress were known inside the family before 1743.

166. The story is also told by Horace Walpole; Walpole to Horace Mann, 3 March 1742 OS, *Correspondence*, 17 (1954), p. 358 and 30 (1961), p. 59 n. 5. Stuart Mackenzie challenged Hyndford to a duel but the latter laughed and threw his letter in the fire. Cf. Lady Louisa Stuart, *Letters and Journals of Lady Mary Coke*, I:liii.
167. Coutts, 'In book', 1736.
168. This estimate is based on the Coutts 'In' and 'Out' books for 1740 which seem complete enough to use.
169. Ilay seemed to have kept up with old friends like Henry Lowther, 3rd Viscount Lonsdale, who accompanied him to a reception for the Prince of Orange in the autumn of 1733. They had dealings during the period of the bubbles in the 1720s and were there partly because of their many Dutch contacts; *London Evening Post*, 8 November 1733.
170. Lindsay and Cosh, *Inveraray and the Dukes of Argyll* (Edinburgh, 1973), p. 10 n. 12.
171. Ilay to Milton, 26 November 1743, NLS, 166570/104. Ilay sought treatment from his Edinburgh physician, Dr. John Clerk.
172. *More Culloden Papers*, III:161. General Campbell and his oldest son were the next in line to inherit; Strichen was farther down the line but also a cousin.
173. He noted that he had now to regard Jack's sons as his own, which he pretty much did. *Ibid.*
174. NLS, 17610/98.
175. The sums are those given by 'Mr. Bolton' in *The Present State of Great Britain....* (London, 1745), Part II, Ch. XIII, pp. 395, 396. His places made him very like the old Scottish Chancellors who often were members of the courts, keepers of records, and general agents of the Crown. See, Alexander Murdoch, The *People Above: Politics and Administration of Mid-Eighteenth-Century Scotland* (Edinburgh, 1980), p. 37.
176. Feu duties were dues paid on land held of a feudal superior such as Argyll. Teinds are tithes.
177. Eric Cregeen, *Argyll Estate Instructions*, (Scottish History Society, Edinburgh, 1964), p. xii. Elsewhere, Cregeen estimated that in 1743-44 the estate rentals came to c.£7,500 but that after the '45 they fell to c.£4,000 in 1746-47 owing to the disruption and devastation caused by that conflict. Troops had ravaged the region destroying homes, cattle and utensils; 'The Tacksmen and their successors: A Study of Tenurial Reorganization in Mull, Morven and Tiree in the Early Eighteenth Century', *Scottish Studies*, 13 (1969), pp. 93-144, A.J. Youngson, *After the Forty-five* (Edinburgh, 1973), p. 21.
179. Eric R. Cregeen, 'Changing Role of the House of Argyll in the Scottish Highlands', in *Scotland in the Age of Improvement*, ed. N.T. Phillipson and Rosalind Mitchison, pp. 5-23; p. 15.
180. Thomas Pennant in 1772 noted improvements which almost certainly derive from Ilay who showed much interest in lime and its possibilities: '... his grace [the 4th Duke] does all in power to promote the useful arts, by giving a certain number of bolls of burnt lime to those who can shew the largest and best fallow; and by allowing ten per cent out of the rents to such farmers as lay out ready money in solid improvements; for example, in inclosing, and the like'. Excerpted in *Beyond the Highland Line: Three Journals of Travel in eighteenth century Scotland: Burt, Pennant Thornton*, ed. A. J. Youngson (London, 1974); p. 165. Improvements were also noticed in the *Statistical Account*'s entry for Campbeltown and in the records of Inveraray: 'As the greater part of the last leases were given by the Duke of Argyll, [the 5th Duke but the policy was Ilay's], on condition of making certain improvements, instead of paying an augmentation of rents, there is reason to hope that the face of the country will soon assume a better appearance.... His Grace also employs a skilful improver, to give his best advice and direction to the tenants, from which considerable benefit may in time be expected'. *Statistical Account of Scotland*, 20 vols, eds. Donald Withrington and Ian R. Grant (Wakefield, England, 1983; 1st edn. Sir John Sinclair, Edinburgh, 1791-1799), VIII:53-54.

181. Cregeen, *Argyll Estate Instructions*, p. x-xii; *The Clan Campbell Abstracts of Entries Relating to Campbell in the Sheriff Court Book of Argyll at Inveraray*, ed. Henry Paton (Edinburgh, 1913), 8 vols, I;160.

182. Lindsay and Cosh, *Inveraray*, 89-90; Charles W. J. Withers, *Geography, Science and National Identity Scotland since 1520*, Cambridge 2001, p.26- 28; ___, 'How Scotland came to know itself...', *Journal of Historical Geography*, 21 (1995), pp. 371-397.

183. Surveys had been made before 1720 by John Adair; Receipts to the 1st Duke of Argyll from John Oliphant dated 1 January 1720 for a map of the lands around Inveraray; another is dated 20 July 1720; NLS, RD12/60/292; CS 233/0/1/16. I thank Mr. John Moore for this information.

184. Despite that, Argyll wanted a 50 ton Clyde-built ship which would be used to bring deals from Norway and other things needed in his Inveraray building schemes. It is not known if this was the 'Peggy' which later appears in the record doing that — as well as delivering his male bison in 1749. Argyll to Milton, 22 December 1743, NLS, 16591/122; 1 July 1749, 17619/287. he chartered many other ships.

185. This paragraph relies on Lindsay and Cosh, *Inveraray*, pp. 121-127.

186. Cregeen, 'Changing Role', p. 17.

187. The number is given in Lindsay and Cosh, *Inveraray*, p. 158.

188. Eric Cregeen and Angus Martin, *Kintyre Instructions: The 5th Duke of Argyll's Instructions to his Kintyre Chamberlain 1785-1805* (Glasgow, 2011), p. 127.

189. Cregeen, 'Changing Role', p.11; *Scotland as It Was and Is*, ed. George Douglas Campbell, 8th Duke of Argyll, 2 vols (Edinburgh, 1882), II:46. Few peasants willingly changed things because their margin of subsistence was so narrow.

190. Quoted by Eric Cregeen, 'Changing Role', p .11.

191. Cregeen, *Argyll Estate Instructions*, pp. xviii-xix.

192. Among the letters of condolence received by Lord Milton after the Duke's death was one from Andrew Bathgate, the farm manager at Inveraray. He wrote, after Argyll's demise, 'maney of the people of this place will be very well pleased that It Should be so for I held them veray Short by the head'. They expected an easier regime to replace Bathgate's – he was let go but quickly hired by Lord Milton. Bathgate to Milton, NLS, 16718/55; Lindsay and Cosh, *Inveraray*, p. 359 n. 153.

193. Dobson had been made a Burgess and Gildbrother of Glasgow at the request of its Provost in 1753. It is likely that he had been useful to the Glasgow town fathers. Dobson, the Provost, a prominent merchant, and some others were all made freemen of Inveraray in 1754. The Duke's servants had found someone who could teach navigation and other subjects for perhaps £70 a year when fees were included. Dobson came with some boarding students which testifies to his reputation and value. Lindsay and Cosh, *Inveraray*, p. 163; *Extracts from the Records of the Burgh of Glasgow....* (Printed for the Corporation, Glasgow, 1911), VI: 381, *The Burgesses of Inveraray 1665-1963*, ed. Elizabeth A Beaton and Sheila MacIntyre, Scottish Record Society, New Series 14 (Edinburgh, 1990), p. 67.

194. Lindsay and Cosh, *Inveraray*, p. 12.

195. *Ibid*, pp. 145-6, 171-174.

196. *Ibid*, pp. 56-57.

197. *Ibid*; *Statistical Account of Scotland*, 8:146.

198. Scott, 'Politics and Administration', p. 491; Glover's *Memoirs* gave an unflattering character of the 2nd Duke whom, he said, quit politics in 1742 because he was ill received at court. The Duke's reason was that the Ministry created was not broad-bottomed enough. Glover also claimed that Ilay belonged to none of the English political factions; pp 11-12, 48.

Chapter 15

1. William Ferguson, for one, thought he had not 'over-exerted himself' and makes his conduct similar to Tweeddale's; *Scotland 1689 to the Present* (Edinburgh and London, 1968), p. 151.
2. In his entourage that summer were Lord Milton, Dr. Charles Stewart, John Maule, his secretary, and his architect, Roger Morris, and the Duke's map maker and valet, James Doritt. Another important member of the group was his servant Peter Ross, who could cook for them all on the road and at Inveraray which had a scanty and super-annuated staff. The group was later joined by the Duke of Atholl, also a patron of Morris and a man interested in the recruitment of the Highland companies which Argyll was urging the Ministry to raise; Ian G. Lindsay and Mary Cosh, *Inveraray and the Dukes of Argyll* (Edinburgh, 1973), pp. 11, 12, 17.
3. Yester Papers, NLS, 7063/137-8.
4. NLS, 14427/23-24.
5. Argyll to Milton, 14 January 1744, NLS, 16596/115. The bill was the 1742 Place Act (15 George II, c. 22; SL XVIII, 36) which barred some office holders from sitting in Parliament. Argyll probably also saw this as a threat to friends in office but any manager of a political interest would bridle at such an abridgement of the inducements he could offer.
6. Lindsay and Cosh, *Inveraray*, p. 11; Argyll to Milton, ? February 1742, NLS, 16584/55.
7. John Stuart Shaw, *The Management of Scottish Society 1707-1764* (Edinburgh 1983), pp. 125-26. That 1744 wish may mark his return to active politicking.
8. *The Parliamentary History of England from the Earliest Period 1066 to the Year 1803*, compiled by William Cobbett (London, 1810 -1813), Vols VI-XV. Microfilm produced by Fairview Park: Pergamon Press, Inc, n.d. XII:1239-1246; 1418-19. Ilay also sought to amuse his audience and told a story of a rapist who in the House of Commons backed a law which would have made him suffer. When asked why he did so, he said, that being for it made all women trust him. The story is probably about Ilay's sometime friend Col. Francis Charteris. *Parl. Hist.*, XI:1371.
9. *Parl. Hist.*, XI:1291-92.
10. Argyll to Milton, 24 November 1743, NLS 16591/104; 4 February 1744, NLS, 16596/130.
11. Maclaurin's and Hume's cases are discussed in Roger L. Emerson, *Academic Patronage in the Scottish Enlightenment* (Edinburgh, 2008), pp. 108-113, 339-341.
12. The *General Evening Post* reported this first on 24 November 1743.
13. John Inglis to Tweeddale, 3 August 1744, Yester Papers, NLS, 7063/72.
14. *Memoirs of the Life of Sir John Clerk of Penicuik, ... 1676-1755*, Scottish History Society, 13; (Edinburgh, 1892) p. 168.
15. Milton to Tweeddale, 22 February 1744, NLS, 14422/3 and 7.
16. Argyll to Milton, 4 February 1744, NLS, 16591/121.
17. *Parl. Hist.*, XIII:538-40.
18. The official estimate of clan manpower in 1725 was that between 22,100 and 24,100 men could be soldiers. Andrew Mackillop, *'More Fruitful than the Soil':Army, Empire and the Scottish Highlands 1715-1815* (East Linton, 2000), pp. 16, 25-28.
19. His role is traced by Mackillop in *'More Fruitful than the Soil'*, passim.
20. Lindsay and Cosh, *Inveraray* p. 16.
21. *Ibid*, p. 17.
22. Craigie to Tweeddale, 24 July 1744 and ? July 1744, NLS, 7063/56, 68. Craigie told Tweeddale that appointing the best lawyers would hurt the government since they were not Squadrone men – a testimony to Argyll's attraction to the talented and ambitious. Craigie to Tweeddale,10 November 1744, NLS, 7064/65.

23. John Inglis to Tweeddale, 3 August 1744, NLS, 7063/72.
24. Tweeddale to Argyll, 21 August 1744; Argyll to Tweeddale, ? September 1744, NLS, 7074/105; NLS, 7063/147.
25. Milton to Argyll, 16 August 1744, NLS, 16596/164. The Jacobites in France had hoped to sail for Britain on 9 January 1744; Alice Wemyss, *Lord Elcho of The '45* (Edinburgh, 2003), p. 52.
26. Argyll to Tweeddale ? September 1744, NLS, 7074/ 147. This was partly a response to local unrest and cattle raiding; Mackillop, '*More Fruitful than the Soil*', pp. 27-28.
27. Atholl and John Maule had been with Argyll at Inveraray just before the letter was written. See above, n. 2; NLS, 7063/123.
28. Henry Pelham to Argyll, 22 September 1744, quoted in William Coxe, *Memoirs of the Administration of the Right Honourable Henry Pelham...* 2 vols (London, 1829; New York, 1979), I:251.
29. *Ibid.*
30. Tweeddale told him that only two companies would be raised but asked him to recommend officers. The same letter told the Duke that Stair was to become a Representative Peer. Tweeddale to Argyll, 21 August 1744, NLS, 7074/ 105; Argyll to Tweeddale, ? September 1744, NLS, 7063/147.
31. A similar request went to the Duke of Gordon. Tweeddale to Argyll, 1 and 6 December 1744, NLS, 14427/155, 159. Argyll may have secured a Dutch company for Milton's son Henry. NLS, 16596/191.
32. Mackillop, '*More Fruitful than the Soil*', pp. 27-29; Tweeddale to Argyll, 1 December 1744, NLS, 14427/155.
33. Christopher Duffy, *The '45* (London, 2003), p. 44.
34. Craigie's choices were Charles Erskine for Dun and James Graham for Royston. NLS, 14427/152-6.
35. Robert Craigie to Tweeddale, 10 November 1744, NLS, 7064/65; Robert Dundas of Arniston to Tweeddale, 20 November 1744, NLS, 7064/89-92; George Brunton and David Haig, *An Historical Account of the Senators of the College of Justice... [to 1802]* (London, 1832), pp. 513-14.
36. Argyll to Milton, ? April 1744, NLS, 16596/146.
37. Craigie to Tweeddale, 22 September 1744, NLS, 7063/131/1.
38. Argyll to Milton, 1 November 1744, NLS, 16596/179.
39. Argyll to Milton, 29 November 1744, NLS, 16596/185.
40. Cope to Duncan Forbes, 29 November 1744, *More Culloden Papers*, ed. Duncan Warrand, 5 vols (Inverness, 1923-1930), III: 215; Argyll to Milton, ? April 1744, NLS, 16596/146.
41. Argyll to Milton, 11 November 1744, NLS, 16596/183.
42. Tweeddale was the sort of man who could forget to send his proxy for a peerage election. Thomas Hay to Tweeddale, 22 April 1742, NLS, 7046/91.
43. Argyll to Milton, 19 May 1745, NLS, 16596/182.
44. Duffy, *The '45*, p. 45.
45. *Ibid*, pp. 171, 174; Newcastle to the Duke of Richmond, 13 August 1745, *The Correspondence of the Dukes of Richmond and Newcastle 1724-1750,* ed. Timothy J. McCann, Sussex Record Society, 73 (1982-83), p. 173. The dispatch was noticed in the London papers by 24 August; later, his leaving for Scotland on 21 August was noted.
46. Newcastle to Argyll, 1 August 1745, Campbell Papers, NLS, 3733/2.
47. Charles celebrated his victory at Preston Pans on 21 September at Pinkie, Tweeddale's house near Musselburgh; Duffy, *The '45*, pp. 23, 125.
48. *Ibid*, pp. 174, 176.

49. The French initially planned to land at Maldon, Essex, but English soldiers thought sites in Sussex and Kent more likely. Wemyss, *Elcho*, p. 50; Duffy, *The '45*, pp. 369-379.
50. Jack's career is outlined in *HPHC 1715-1754*, I:526.
51. Initially, eight companies operated in northern Scotland under Loudoun. The companies were united by the winter of 1745-46 but four were separated and fought in the south under Jack's leadership.
52. Argyll to Archibald Campbell of Stonefield, 5 August 1745, Campbell of Stonefield Papers, NRS, GD/14/24. Argyll was not often angry but his temper when aroused could be formidable as episodes at Glasgow University showed. Emerson, *Academic Patronage*, p.139; William Rouet to Robert Simson, 11 March 1756, GUA, 30492.
53. Argyll to Archibald Campbell of Stonefield, 5 August 1745, NRS, GD14/24.
54. Milton to Archibald Campbell of Stonefield, 10 August 1745, NRS, Campbell of Stonefield Papers, GD14/26
55. Duffy, *The '45*, p. 563.
56. Lindsay and Cosh, *Inveraray*, p. 48; Alastair Campbell of Airds, *History of the Clan Campbell*, 3 vols (Edinburgh, 2000-2008), III: 124-25.
57. Original letters to Robert Craigie of Glendoick... 1745, NLS, 3036/1.
58. Lovat to Cope, 10 August 1745, NLS, 7069/50.
59. Craigie to Tweeddale, 10 September 1745, NLS, 7071/111.
60. Andrew Fletcher to Archibald Campbell of Stonefield, 10 August 1745, NRS, GD14/26.
61. Newcastle to Argyll, 1 August 1745, in Coxe, *Memoirs of Pelham*, I:253 and NLS, 3733/2.
62. Rupert C. Jarvis, 'The Lieutenancy and Militia Laws' in *Collected Papers on the Jacobite Risings*, 2 vols (Manchester and New York, 1971), 1:97-119; p. 104. Jarvis was another who thought Argyll did too little in the '45: 'He refused the government's proffered arms .... and went off to leave Scotland to her fate' because the Squadrone men were 'of the wrong faction'. *Ibid.*
63. It is estimated that the Duke's lands could have raised 3,000 men. Another 1,000 could have been supplied by Breadalbane and an equal number from the cadets of both houses. Duffy, *The '45*, p. 562; Andrew Fletcher to Archibald Campbell of Stonefield, 13 August 1745, NRS, GD14/27 .
64. Jarvis, *Collected Papers*, I:105.
65. Argyll to Craigie, 12 August 1745, NLS, 3036/3.
66. Jarvis, *Collected Papers*, I:104; There seem to have been only 200 stand of arms at Inveraray left over from the '15; A. Campbell, *A History*, III: 128.
67. Milton to Stonefield, 13 August 1745, NRS, Campbell of Stonefield Papers, GD14/27; Lindsay and Cosh, *Inveraray*, p. 48. The chronology of the following account relies heavily on Duffy, *The '45*.
68. John Robertson, *The Scottish Enlightenment and the Militia Issue* (Edinburgh, 1985), p. 52.
69. NLS, 14427/168.
70. Quoted by Jarvis, *Collected Papers*, I:104- 5.
71. Argyll to Cope, 13 August, 1745; Craigie to Tweeddale, 13 August 1745, NLS, 7069/5 and 13.
72. Thomas Hay to Tweeddale, 15 August 1745, NLS, 7069/31.
73. Alexander Watt, 11 August 1745, NLS, 7069/43.
74. Craigie to Tweeddale, 15 August 1745, NLS, 7069/53.
75. Argyll to Craigie, 12 August 1745, NLS, 3036/3.
76. Charles wanted Argyll on his side but would have settled for a hostage. Prince Charles to the Old Pretender quoted in *The Cochrane Correspondence Regarding the Affairs in Glasgow*, ed. James Smith (Maitland Club, Glasgow, 1836), p. xiv.
77. Robert Craigie to Tweeddale, 20 August 1745, NLS, 7069/178-81.

78. Cope to Tweeddale, 17 August 1745, NLS, 7069/74; Thomas Hay to Tweeddale, 17 August 1745, NLS, 7069/103.
79. Milton to Tweeddale, 18 August 1745, NLS, 7069/108.
80. Newcastle to Argyll, 21 August 1745, in Coxe, *Memoirs of Pelham*, I:259. Argyll's letters arrived in London on 11, 12, 13, and 17 August. See also Sir James Fergusson of Kilkerran, *Argyll in the Forty-Five* (London, 1951), p. 24.
81. 'I am also, in their Excellencies' name, to desire your Grace, to take such measures as you shall judge most proper, for the defense of the Kingdom against these attempts of his Majesty's enemies, and to acquaint your Grace, that they have ordered arms to be sent to Scotland, and have directed Sir John Cope to give them out to such persons as your Grace shall think proper, as your Grace will have seen by a former letter', Coxe, *Memoirs of Pelham*, I:256.
82. Henry Hastings wrote to the 9th Earl of Huntingdon on ? October 1745 that 'The Duke of A[gyll] wrote before he left Scotland to the M[arquess of T[weeddale] for leave to arm his clans, but had leave only to provide himself with arms'. *Report on the Manuscripts of the late Reginald Wawdon Hastings, Esq.*, ed. Francis Bickley (London, 1934), III:52-53.
83. Lord Glenorchy sent Cope a letter on 15 August 1745 saying that there were reports of 10,000 French troops having landed. NLS, 7069/76; Maule to General John Campbell of Mamore, 24 August 1745, NLS 3733/10. Archibald Campbell of Stonefield noted in the next letter in that collection that all the Campbell's old clan enemies were rising against them. By 22 August, Milton had concluded that such rumours of French troops were circulated by the rebels and were not to be believed. Milton to Tweeddale, 22 August 1745, NLS, 7070/21; Milton thought the Prince had a force of about 3,000 men. As late as 24 December 1745, Tweeddale told the Lord President that he did not believe the recent report that 10,000 French troops had landed. See also NLS, 16720/171.
84. Glenorchy to Craigie, 12 August 1745, and Alexander Campbell to Craigie and General Cope, n.d., NLS, 3036/7 and 22; Milton to Tweeddale, 22 August 1745, NLS, 7070/21.
85. Milton to Argyll, 29, 31 August 1745, NLS, 16604/197, 198.
86. W. S. Speck in 1981 said of him: 'The first thing he did when the rebellion broke out was to head south to London which showed his appreciation of where power ultimately lay'. Speck saw this as a self-serving dereliction of duty if not something less honourable. Speck, *The Butcher:The Duke of Cumberland and the Suppression of The '45* (Oxford, 1981), p. 12.
87. Drumcleugh to Arniston, 12 September 1745, NLS, 7071/121.
88. Hume's views were set out in a pamphlet, see: M.A. Box, David Harvey, and Michael Silverthorne, 'A Diplomatic Transcription of Hume's "volunteer pamphlet" for Archibald Stewart: Political Whigs, Religious Whigs, and Jacobites', *Hume Studies*, 29 (2003), pp. 223-266. Hume held some Argathelians responsible for the trial of his friend Lord Provost Stewart.
89. Drumsheugh to Arniston, 12 and 14 September 1745, NLS, 7071/121-129.
90. *Ibid*. The Disarming Act disarmed compliant Whigs but not their enemies.
91. Jarvis, *Collected Papers*, I:104.
92. Richard Scott, 'The Politics and Administration of Scotland 1725-1748'. Ph. D. Dissertation, Edinburgh University, 1982, p. 512.
93. Horace Walpole quoted in Lindsay and Cosh, *Inveraray*, p. 49.
94. Milton to Argyll, 22 November, NLS, 16604/220-21.
95. Quoted by Mackillop, *'More Fruitful than the Soil.'* pp. 43-44. He lists other manuscripts in the papers of Lord Milton where similar concerns are voiced.
96. *Cochrane Correspondence*, p. xiv.
97. Lindsay and Cosh, *Inveraray*, p. 49.

98. Craigie to Tweeddale, 10 September 1745, NL,S 7071/111. Newcastle at this time was suffering from shingles which could not have improved the efficiency of the London government. NLS, 16607/70.

99. Lord Glenorchy, Breadalbane's heir, said he could not raise his men for the government because they threatened to carry him to the rebels if he tried. Drumsheugh to Robert Dundas of Arniston, 14 September 1745, NLS, 7071/128-29. By then Milton advised against arming any dubiously loyal clans; Milton to Tweeddale, 16 September 1745, NLS, 7071/162. The same letter again points out the folly of not having armed more Highlanders to prevent this rebellion.

100. Thomas Hay to Tweeddale, 10 September 1745, NLS, 7071/100. Tweeddale's men underestimated the strength of the Prince's force which neither they nor Cope imagined would move as fast as it did.

101. Milton to Tweeddale, 7 September 1745, NLS, 7071/71. Jarvis says this prompted Sir Andrew Mitchell to write 'facetiously to Craigie'. Jarvis, *Collected Papers*, I:102.

102. Lindsay and Cosh, *Inveraray*, p. 51.

103. Milton to Tweeddale, 16 September 1745, NLS, 7071/161-64. That letter was a criticism of the Disarming Acts, of the failure to establish enough Independent Highland Companies and of the harsh policies applied in the region.

104. Fergusson, *Argyll in the Forty-Five*, pp. 47, 104; NLS 17617.

105. John B. Owen, *The Rise of the Pelhams* (New York and London,1971; 1st ed 1957), p. 278.

106. Duffy, *The '45*, p. 125.

107. Henry Hastings to the 9th Earl of Huntingdon, ? October 1745, *HMCR of the Hastings MSS*, III:52-53.

108. Provost James Morrison to Milton, 31 August 1745, Yester Papers, NLS, 7071/73.

109. *Cochrane Correspondence*, pp. 21 and 24.

110. Andrew Cochrane (1693-1777), a tobacco merchant and the founder of the Glasgow Arms Bank, was several times Provost of Glasgow and served Ilay in that city much as did George Drummond in Edinburgh. In the 1740s, he started a political economy club in Glasgow to which Adam Smith belonged in the 1750s. John Strang, *Glasgow and Its Clubs...* (Glasgow, 1864), pp. 25, 57; Nicholas Phillipson, *Adam Smith An Enlightened Life* (London, 2010), pp. 40, 129.

111. Edinburgh Castle was besieged but not taken. It was allowed food only when its commanders threatened to wreak destruction on the city beneath its guns.

112. Miscellaneous Jacobite Manuscripts, NLS, 3142/38, 44-74.

113. Duffy, *The '45*, pp. 204-207.

114. *St James Evening Post*, 7 November, 1745.

115. Argyll to Stonefield, Campbell of Stonefield Papers, NRS, GD14/49.

116. A. Campbell, *History*, III:130.

117. Argyll to Stonefield, 10 December 1745, NRS, GD14/50.

118. Argyll to Stonefield, NRS, GD14/48. This letter told Lt. Col Jack Campbell to be 'frugal' but that the government would reimburse all the debts he incurred. Sir George Mackenzie (d.1691) was to be Stonefield's guide on the raising of the militia. He was also instructed on how to make an invisible ink. The Duke sent sugar of lead to be dissolved in water. It would be readable if 'scorched a little before the fire'. Stonefield was warned to send nothing which could not be read to the ministers and the King.

119. Maule to General Campbell, 5 and 8 December 1745, NLS, 3733/35, 33.

120. Hume-Campbell to Marchmont, 30 October 1746, *HMCR of the Polwarth Papers* (London, 1911), V:184; NLS, 3733/14, 15.

121. Argyll to Milton, 5 and 17 December 1745, NLS, 16604/226-27, 292.

122. Chesterfield to General Campbell of Mamore, 10 December 1745, NLS, 3733/39; General Campbell to Argyll, 23 December 1745, NLS 3733/53. W. Ernst-Browning, *Memoirs of the Life of Philip Dormer fourth Earl of Chesterfield* (London, 1906), p. 273; *Private Correspondence of Chesterfield and Newcastle 1744-46*, ed. Sir Richard Lodge, Royal Historical Society (1930), p. 123. General Cope had complained of food shortages in September; Milton tried to alleviate them. Thomas Hay to Tweeddale, 3 September 1745, NLS, 7071/19-20.

123. General Campbell of Mamore to Argyll, 10 January 1746, NLS, 3733/78.

124. Maule to General Campbell of Mamore, 1 January and 28 January 1746; Mamore to Milton, 8 September 1746, NLS, 3733/118, 123 and 477. The 'Out books' at Coutts show no payments made from his account to the General but few were posted in this period. On 15 May 1747, £200 was paid into this account by General Campbell for a bill on the Duke he had drawn earlier. Coutts, 'In book'. In 1744-45, Argyll lent Major General John Campbell, Earl of Loudoun, a sum not shown on the Coutts accounts which may relate to the raising of troops. In 1745, that Earl was given a reduced interest rate when his land was pledged to the Duke. Argyll to Milton, 15 November 1744 and 12 January 1745, NLS 16596/183 and 16604/178. Argyll may have helped the war effort with those loans too.

125. John Maule to Campbell of Mamore, 18 February 1746; Argyll to Lt. Col. Jack Campbell, n.d., NLS, 3734/152 and 154.

126. John Maule to Campbell of Mamore, 18 February 1746; 1 March 1746, NLS, 3734/152 and 168.

127. Argyll to Milton, 6 15 and 17 March 1746, NLS, 16615/97, 99 and 105.

128. Argyll to Campbell Mamore, 14 January 1746, NLS, 3733/90.

129. Argyll to Milton, 2 and 9 January, NLS, 16615/75 and 77.

130. Argyll to Milton, n.d., NLS, 16615/118 and 121; Horace Walpole, *Memoirs of King George II*, 3 vols (New Haven, Conn., 1985), I:176;

131. Cochrane to Lord Milton, November 1745; Cochrane to Argyll, ? December 1745, *Cochrane Correspondence*, pp. 43-44; 86-87. Argyll had been irritated by the Provost who may have shown too much willingness to comply with Jacobite demands. Argyll to Milton, 9 January 1746, NLS, 16615/77.

132. Argyll had had by express an account of the battle from Lt. Col. Jack Campbell which he received on 20 January. NLS, 3733/105. The Duke worried that Jack and others to whom Argyll had given commissions had not done well. Jack assured him this was not the case. NLS, 3733/118, 119.

133. Maule to Campbell of Mamore, 2 and 9 January 1746, NLS, 3733/68, 75.

134. 'If I had less connection with my friends the resigners than I have, I could not with any reputation avoid quitting; all my apprehensions are that in that event the people of Argylshire may cool in their zeal for the public service, this must be prevented by all means possible, for I tremble to think of it for the sake of the Publick, my private interest, & what effects me in the highest degree, my Character'. The same letter says that the Pelhams would have forced Tweeddale to resign had he not done so. It concluded, 'The Pelhams play their game very ill'. Argyll to Milton, 18 January 1746, NLS, 16615/81.

135. Newcastle to Argyll, 10 and 18 February 1746, NLS, 3733/139 and 87.

136. Argyll to Milton, 11 February 1746, NLS, 16615/89.

137. Argyll to Campbell of Mamore, 11 February 1746, NLS, 3733/145.

138. John Maule to Campbell of Mamore, 13 February 1746, NLS, 3734/148.

139. Argyll to Milton, NLS,16615/87.

140. The Minutes of the Convention of Royal Burghs, ECA, SL 30/1/1/11/ p. 438.

141. Argyll to Milton, 23 February 1746, NLS, 16615/93; those may have been prepared by Alexander Lind who solicited lists to be sent to Cumberland, EUL Laing MSII.6205.

142. Campbell of Mamore to Argyll, 24, 27 and 30 March 1746, NLS, 3734/222, 223, 239, 253; Mamore to Newcastle, 30 March 1746, NLS, 3734/237. The London newspapers also noted several addresses sent to Argyll in May - July by the burgh of Aberdeen, Edinburgh University, the county of Lanark and the Convention of Royal Burghs. Those were for presentation to the King.
143. Newcastle to Campbell of Mamore, 8 February 1746, NLS, 3733/138.
144. *E.g.*, NLS, 3734/243, 256.
145. Maule to General Campbell of Mamore, 8 and 9 March1746, NLS, 3734/179.
146. Duffy, *The '45*, p. 458; NRS, SP54/30/4; A. Campbell, *History*, III:138-40.
147. Argyll to Stonefield, 5 April; 8 April; 10 April, NRS, GD14/76; 77; 79.
148. Fergusson, *Argyll in the Forty-Five*, p. 209. Those events, and the Jacobite reactions to them, were reported in the London papers which noted that Argyll had been a loser in the reprisals, *E.g.*, *Penny London Post or Morning Advertiser*, 18 April 1746.
149. Archibald Campbell to Argyll, 15 May 1746, NLS, 3735/339/ 37.
150. On 24 April, the Militia was praised by the King; A. Campbell, *History*, III: 142, 144.
151. Fergusson, *Argyll in the Forty-Five*, pp. 99-100.
152. Ilay to Newcastle, 30 September 1725, NRS, SP54/16/29.
153. He wrote to Argyll for protection in June 1746, *Correspondence of Horace Walpole*, 19 (1954), p.272; Wemyss, *Elcho*, pp. 131-32.

Chapter 16

1. The *Cochrane Correspondence Regarding the Affairs of Glasgow 1745-46*, ed. James Smith (Maitland Club, Glasgow, 1836), pp. 90-99.
2. John Campbell of the Bank to John Campbell of Barcaldine, 15 September 1746. NRS, GD170/1014/24.
3. Milton to Argyll, n.d. [May or June 1746], NLS, 16615/121.
4. Scott, Richard, 'The Politics and Administration of Scotland 1725-1748', unpublished Ph.D. Dissertation, Edinburgh University, 1982, p. 542; *HPHC 1715-1754*, I:398- 99. Argyll professed no concern with this election so long as the man was 'an uncontested Whig & no Patriot' which meant he opposed Drummond's candidacy. Argyll to Milton, 7 July 1747, NLS, 16641/68.
5. Milton claimed he was asked to accept this by the Pelhams; Milton to Stuart Mackenzie, 18 December 1764, NLS, 17730/154. The value of the Keepership of the Signet was increased by £400.
6. John Shaw saw Milton as the one man in Edinburgh who really did organize resistance to the rebels and started to do so before the Prince landed in Scotland; Shaw, *The Management of Scottish Society 1707-1764* (Edinburgh, 1983), pp. 164-69. The problem here, as always with Milton's actions, is to show that they were independent of Argyll's direction. Shaw's case is not convincing. There was no divergence in Milton's and Argyll's policies or in their attitudes. Like the Duke, he urged the appointment of Lord-Lieutenants, wanted arms sent up and sent, in particular, to Glasgow. He was eager to see the Army advised by men who knew the lay of the land. Both Milton and Argyll recommended leniency for the rebels and both saw in economic development the real cure for Scottish ills. None of the Squadrone men or the English saw him as other than Argyll's man. Neither group completely trusted him but the distrust was not usually of him personally but of him as an agent. His attitudes toward the settlements made in the late 1740s and beyond differed little from those of Argyll. Like the Duke, the '45 cost him a lot of money. His heirs asked for £1,899.4.6¾ and said there was more owing for which vouchers could not be found. NLS, SB Public Accounts, 1745-46.

7. His appointment had been suggested by Pelham in the deal which gave Milton the Signet and a place for his oldest son. Argyll would help Robert Dundas to his place on the Court of Session. Dundas had long been active in the Squadrone and became Lord President in 1748. Argyll to Milton, 9 February 1748, NLS, 16656/22.

8. Hume Campbell to the Earl of Marchmont, 31 January 1747, *HMCR on the Manuscripts of Lord Polwarth*, ed. Henry Paton (London, 1911), V:197.

9. Margaret S Bricke, 'The Pelhams vs. Argyll: A Struggle for the Mastery of Scotland, 1747-1748', *Scottish Historical Review*, 61 (1982), pp. 161-62

10. Alexander Murdoch, *The People Above: Politics and Administration in Mid-Eighteenth-Century Scotland* (Edinburgh, 1980), p. 35.

11. *Ibid*, p. 37.

12. Soon after the 1747 elections, he supported the internationally known Jacobite mathematician James Stirling, for the Edinburgh professorship of mathematics although he knew Stirling could not be chosen. The Duke's choices fell into a ranking based on international reputation and the utility of their work in practical life. Stirling had published important papers, was a mine manager and had invented machines. The Duke was willing to settle for others including Robert Simson and Matthew Stewart. He received the post. Argyll to Milton, 18 August 1747, NLS, 16641/82; Peter J. Wallis, 'James Stirling', in *Dictionary of Scientific Biography*, 16 vols, ed. Charles C Gillispie (New York, 1970-1980), 13:67-70.

13. Hume Campbell to Marchmont, 12, 17 and 31 March 1747, *Polwarth Manuscripts*, V:214-219, 221-228, 230.

14. Hume Campbell to Marchmont, 12 March 1747, *Polwarth Manuscripts*, V:212.

15. Argyll to Milton, 19 July 1747, NLS, 16641/74-75.

16. *Polwarth Manuscripts*, V:184.

17. Scott, 'Politics and Administration', pp. 532-539; *HPHC 1715-1754*, I:57.

18. Argyll to Milton, 23 June 1747, NLS, 16641/59.

19. Quoted by Murdoch, *People Above*, p. 35. William Robertson lists Argyll as present at the peerage election on 1 August 1747; Robertson, *Proceedings Relating to the Peerage of Scotland from January 16. 1707 to April 29, 1788*, (Edinburgh and London, 1790), p. 257.

20. Argyll to Milton, 7 July 1747, NLS, 16641/74-75; *HPHC 1715-1754*, I:397.

21. *HPHC 1715-1754*, I:473.

22. *HPHC 1715-1754*, II:261.

23. Marchmont to Cumberland, *Polwarth Manuscripts*, V:256.

24. Argyll to Milton, 9 June 1747, NLS, 16641/33.

25. Argyll to Bute, 23 June 1747, 16641/51.

26. John W. Wilkes, *A Whig in Power: The Political Career of Henry Pelham* (n.p. [Chicago], 1964), p. 87.

27. Murdoch, *People Above*, p. 35.

28. Hume Campbell to Marchmont, 17 and 31 March 1747, *Polwarth Manuscripts*, V:225-27, 231-32.

29. Robertson, *Proceedings*, p. 257.

30. Argyll to Milton, 5 December 1747, NLS, 16641/110.

31. Scott, 'Politics and Administration', pp. 513-526.

32. Argyll and Newcastle agreed on his appointment and on that of James Fergusson of Kilkerran to the Justiciary Court in April 1749. George Brunton and David Haig, *An Historical Account of the Senators of the College of Justice... [to 1802]* (London,1832), p.506; Argyll to Milton, 22 December 1748, NLS, 16656/87.

33. Argyll to Milton, 9 and 13 February 1748, NLS, 16656/22 and 27; n.d., [April or May, 1748], NLS 16656/46.

34. Argyll to Lord Justice Clerk, 16 June 1748 and 5 November 1748, NLS, 5087/24 and 34.

35. Various Letters of Alexander Hume Campbell to Marchmont and the Duke of Cumberland; Marchmont to Cumberland and Newcastle, *Polwarth Manuscripts*, V:214-261.

36. John Campbell to John Campbell of Barcaldine, 20 September 1748, NRS, GD170/1014/30.

37. Shaw, *Management*, pp. 171-176.

38. A. J. Youngson, *The Highlands After the Forty-Five* (Edinburgh, 1973), p. 37.

39. Argyll had thought him a good choice as Commander-in-Chief in 1746 but his views changed. Argyll to Milton, 7 October 1746, NLS, 16615/149.

40. Argyll had known Bland since their days as young officers. Bland's family invested heavily in South Sea Co. stock and the General married into the Dalrymple family in 1755. Argyll's recommendation was qualified. Bland, he said, 'would do as well or better than any other of his rank and quality'. General John Huske was probably Argyll's first choice. Pelham to Argyll, 22 September 1747, cited by William Coxe, *Memoirs of the Administration of the Right Honourable Henry Pelham...*, 2 vols (London, 1829; New York, 1979), I:376; Argyll to Milton, 24 October 1746, NLS, 16615/153; Margaret S Bricke','The Pelhams vs. Argyll', p. 163.

41. Bruce Lenman, *The Jacobite Risings in Britain 1689-1746* (London, 1980), pp. 261-264.

42. Youngson, *After the Forty-Five*, p. 24; Shaw, *Management*, p. 170; Milton to Argyll, 23 May 1746, NLS, 16615/119.

43. Milton to Argyll, 23 May 1746, NLS, 16615/119.

44. Those acts are all printed in the *Scots Magazine* in the relevant years.

45. Rents and duties were paid annually by those with feus; blench tenures [quitrents] owed a minimal annual payment which acknowledged the superiority of an overlord. Milton to Argyll, 17 and 23 May 1746, NLS, 16615/115 and 119. The change would raise rents.

46. *The Parliamentary History of England from the Earliest Period 1066 to the Year 1803*, compiled by William Cobbett (London, 1810-1813), Vols VI-XV. Microfilm produced by Fairview Park: Pergamon Press, Inc, n.d., XIII:1417, XIV; (London, 1813), XIV:2-3. The Scottish judges, while refusing to draft it, made suggestions including giving Sheriffs salaries and making all Scottish criminal trials come under the appellate jurisdiction of the Justiciary Court — one of Ilay's earlier recommendations (see above, p. 191). They also urged juries for civil trials, a recommendation realized only in 1816. Those ideas sound more like Argyll than Duncan Forbes who drafted the reply to Hardwicke.

47. Newcastle to the Duke of Richmond, 11 April 1747, in *The Correspondence of the Dukes of Richmond and Newcastle 1724-1750*, ed. Timothy J. McCann, Sussex Record Society, 73 (1982-83). *Correspondence*, p. 244.

48. Rex Whitworth, *William Augustus Duke of Cumberland: A Life* (London, 1992), p. 102.

49. *Memoirs and Speeches of James, 2nd Earl of Waldegrave 1742-1763*, ed. J.C.D. Clark (Cambridge, 1988), p. 247 n.12; Horace Walpole to Horace Mann, 10 April 1747, *The Yale Edition of Horace Walpole's Correspondence*, ed. Wilmarth. S. Lewis, *et al.*, 48 vols (variously in New Haven, Conn., New York and London, 1937-1963), 19: (1954), pp. 386-89.

50. *Walpole Correspondence*, 19 (1954), p. 388.

51. 'The Scotch Bill which was loudly, & universally called for by our Friends, & indeed by all Friends to England, & the Government, had like not to have had a seconde reading in the House of Commons. It was carried but by 25 & nobody spoke one Word for it, but my Brother [Henry Pelham], the Attorney, & Sollicitor genl & Advocate of Scotland, every one Friend of the D of Argyle against it, except one or two who were away'. *The Correspondence of the Dukes of Richmond and Newcastle*, p. 244.

52. Hume Campbell to Marchmont, 17 April and 12 May 1747, *Polwarth Manuscripts*, V:232, 235-36.

53. Murdoch, *People Above*, pp. 35-36. The appointments generally went to local men so he was not hurt as much as one might think. See, Ann E. Whetstone, *Scottish County Government in the Eighteenth and Nineteenth Century* (Edinburgh, 1981), pp. 4-5.
54. William Speck, *The Butcher: the Duke of Cumberland and the Suppression of the '45* (Oxford, 1981), p. 175. Argyll suffered from debilitating migraine headaches but this looks as if it were more a political than a medical condition.
55. Ilay was thanked by the Convention of Royal Burghs on 7 July 1747 for 'Saving and Reserving to all the Royal Burrows all Such Jurisdictions, Privileges & Immunities as by Law are Vested in them, or Competent to any of them Whether within or without the Royalties respectively'. They would give themselves the honour of waiting 'upon his Grace, how Soon he arrives in this Country' to give him their thanks. On 19 December 1747, the Convention appealed to him to intervene to prevent the Dutch from seizing Scottish ships trading to France. ECA, Minutes of the Convention of Royal Burghs ECA, SL 30/1/1/11, pp. 484, 505.
56. Argyll to Milton, 3 January 1747, NLS, 16641/28-29.
57. His comments on this provision included: 'If justice is done, far better for me that it should be done by the king's courts than my own. It would be better supported and enforced'; *Parl. Hist.*, XIV:53.
58. He happily reminded the English that many of those men had been ordained by English non-jurors after they had been given a *congé d'élire* from the Pretender. *Parl. Hist.*, XIV:286 –88.
59. *Parl. Hist.*, XIV:53-57.
60. Murdoch also quotes a different reaction: 'The D. of A mad the most exotic speech I ever heard .... had I not been informed before that he was to speak for the bill I should have thought from his facts and reasonings that he intended to vote ag't it'. Andrew Mitchell to Duncan Forbes, Lord Culloden, 22 May 1747, *People Above*, p. 35.
61. Bricke, 'The Pelhams', p.161; Coxe, *Pelham*, I:353.
62. Sir James Fergusson, 'The Appin Murder Case' in *The White Hind* (London, 1963, reprinted Glasgow, 2004), p. 146.
63. Waldegrave says that Argyll got the compensation for the heritable jurisdictions reduced. James, Earl Waldegrave, *Memoirs and Speeches of James, Earl Waldegrave 1742- 1763*, ed. J.C.D. Clark, (Cambridge, 1988). p. 247 n. 13.
64. *Scots Magazine*, February 1747, pp. 57-61; December 1747, pp. 582-589; March 1748, pp. 136-138.
65. *E.g., St James Evening Post*, 17 October 1747.
66. *Walpole Correspondence*, 2 December 1748, Vol 20 (1960), p.124. Argyll offended Bedford more deeply in April 1756 when he urged passage of the Paddington Road Bill and managed to make it a trial of strength between Grafton, Fox and Bedford. The road damaged Bedford by running through his property. Bedford, said Horace Walpole, 'was betrayed, was beaten, was enraged'. Waldegrave, *Memoirs and Speeches*, p. 275.
67. *Walpole Correspondence*, 2 December 1748. Vol 20 (1960), p. 5n; Wilkes, A *Whig in Power*, p. 146.
68. That was notable enough to be reported in the London papers; e.g., *General Evening Post*, 17 and 23 August 1748.
69. *General Evening Post*, 3 October and 5 November 1748; 1 December 1748.
70. Marchmont to Hume Campbell, 26 January 1748, *Polwarth Manuscripts*, V:267-68.
71. *The Autobiography of Alexander Carlyle of Inveresk 1722-1805*, ed. John Hill Burton (Edinburgh, 1910), pp. 272-73.
72. Ilay to My Lord [?Townshend], 20 September 1715, NRS, SP 54/8/78.
73. They were paid 9 d a week and lived on wheat, meal, eggs and butter which shows what

by 1738 was surplus there. NLS, 17645/171.
74. Shaw, *Management*, p. 155.
75. Alastair J. Durie, *The British Linen Company, 1745-1775*, Scottish History Society 5th Series, 9 (Edinburgh, 1996); Charles A. Malcolm, *The History of the British Linen Bank* (Edinburgh, 1950), p. 14.
76. Beckford, a West Indian merchant and financier, was later Lord Mayor of London. Mann was an active entrepreneur but one who hoped this venture would give work 'to many thousands of families [and] furnish the home market and the Colonies and plantations of America' - a suitably patriotic gloss. Malcolm, *British Linen Bank*, pp. 5-9 and 'Appendix 2, 'The Original Proprietors [of the British Linen Company]', pp. 234-236.
77. Shaw, *Management*, p. 157.
78. Malcolm, *British Linen Bank*, pp. 7-9; Durie, *British Linen Company*, p. 20.
79. Shaw, *Management*, p. 161.
80. Malcolm, *British Linen Bank*, p. 8.
81. Shaw, *Management*, p. 163.
82. I thank T. C. Smout for that insight.
83. Malcolm, *British Linen Bank*, p. 14.
84. *Ibid*, pp. 2, 5.
85. Christopher Whately, *Scottish Society 1707-1830* (Manchester and New York, 2000), p. 67.
86. The Society helped many who had left the Highlands for employment in Glasgow. It had been founded in 1727 and by the 1750s and 1760s included several men with chemical interests such as Robert Cowan, surgeon, Hector Maclean, surgeon, Peter Wright, M.D. and James MacGregor, manufacturer. See: Roger L. Emerson and Paul B. Wood, 'Science and Enlightenment in Glasgow, 1690-1802' in *Science and Medicine in the Scottish Enlightenment*, ed. Charles W. J. Withers and Paul Wood (East Linton, 2002), pp. 79-142.
87. Durie, *British Linen Company*, p. 8
88. The Post Office was used to watch the political activities of local politicians. John Watson [Argyll's Edinburgh 'doer'] to Milton, 17 September 1754, NLS, 16689/199-201
90. Argyll to Milton, 5 November 1747, NLS, 16641/98. As a result of the valuation, the Duke was sued by Duncan Omay of Kilchulmkill over the dues levied on his land. Omay claimed that the Duke had no title to it and so could not collect feu duties from him. Not all were awed by the Duke. NLS, Acc 7004.
91. 'A breaft acct. of the life of Archd Duke of Argyll', NLS, Acc 8168/1/3.
92. Lindsay and Cosh, *Inveraray*, p. 423.
93. Whately, *Scottish Society*, p. 249; Argyll to Milton, December 1750, 16669/114.
94. *General Evening Post*, 20 October 1750, 2 April 1751, *Public Advertiser*, 12 November 1756, 14 May 1757; *Lloyd's Evening Post*, 22 July 1757.
95. Minutes of the Convention of Royal Burghs, 18 January 1749; 6 July 1749, ECA, SL 30/1/1/11, p. 554; SL 30/1/1/12, p. 12.
96. Lindsay and Cosh, *Inveraray*, p. 356 n.94.
97. Argyll to Milton, NLS, 16664/74.
98. *The Grenville Papers: Being the Correspondence of Richard Grenville, Earl Temple .... and George Grenville ...*, ed. James Smith, 4 vols (London, 1852, reprint ed. New York, 1970), I:77.
99. Lord Leicester to Lady Mary, 1 January 1747 (copied to Henrietta Howard), British Library, Add. MSS, 22629/139.
100. British Library, Add. MSS, 22629/142; the letter has no date.
101. Lady Mary to Lady Marches, n.d. [1747], Brit. Lib., Add. MSS, 22629/148-9.
102. Horace Walpole to George Montague, 14 July 1748, *Walpole Correspondence*, 9 (1941), pp. 59-61.

103. This would have confirmed the views of those who charged Argyll with cowardice for leaving Scotland in the autumn of 1745. They forgot his military service, his wounds in 1715 and his willingness to brave mobs during the Sacheverell and Excise Tax crises. Walpole to Horace Mann, 2 December 1748, *Walpole Correspondence*, 20 (1960), p. 124.
104. Lady Mary Cook to Argyll, 27 November 1748, Brit. Lib., Add. MSS, 22629/159.
105. Viscount Leicester to Argyll, 27 January 1749, Brit. Lib., Add MSS, 22629/160-161.
106. *The Political Journal of George Bubb Dodington*, ed. John Carswell and Lewis Arnold Drolle (Oxford, 1965), p. 25 n. 3
107. *HPHC 1715-1754*, I:564. The Hon. Edward Coke remained a Whig but opposed the Scots in every measure brought to the House of Commons until he died in 1753.
108. When the Viscount died in 1753, Lady Mary was twenty-six. She lived a long life of eccentricity and extravagant actions. Lady Louisa Stuart in *The Letters and Journals of Lady Mary* [Campbell] *Coke*, 4 vols, ed. Lady Lousia Stewart (London, 1889-96; Facsimile, London, 1970), I:lxii-iv, cxxiv, cxxviii; Horace Walpole to Lady Mary Wortley Montagu, *Walpole Correspondence*, 9 (1941), pp. 59-61.
109. *The Survey of London*, XXXI:296. Surveys of London are available on the internet.
110. One copy exists in the hand of David Hume. Ilay is accused of cuckolding both Milton and 'T -m C- n', who, for power, acquiesced in their horning. One verse reads:

> The husbands consented, & now
> With their wives, and My Lord they command.
> To these five poor Scotia must bow,
> And all owe her woes to their hand.

'The Debate', Robertson-Macdonald Letters, NLS, 22159/133, 177-178 NLS, 3943/133; NLS, 23159. On the basis of the handwriting, M.A. Stewart has dated the Hume copy to c. 1732 and identified T-m C-n as Thomas Cochrane; see 'The Dating of Hume's Manuscripts' in *The Scottish Enlightenment: Essays in Reinterpretation*, ed. Paul Wood (Rochester, 2000), pp. 267-314; 276.
111. Lindsay and Cosh, *Inveraray*, pp. 11, 51.
112. Lindsay and Cosh suggest he did not go at all (*Inveraray*, p. 52) but he seems to have been at The Whim by 5 August and at Inveraray on the 12th. He would have left London after voting for the conviction of the peers on 28 July. See The Diary of Andrew Fletcher, NLS, 17746/5 and 12 August 1746.
113. Lindsay and Cosh, *Inveraray*, p. 76.
114. Argyll to Milton, 29 July 1751, NLS, 16673/146.
115. Some of that was probably attributable to the payment for his heritable jurisdictions.

Chapter 17

1. That was his way of referring to the irregular election of 1746 and another in 1750 which made George Drummond Lord Provost. Argyll to Milton, 25 December 1750, NLS, 16669/131.
2. Minutes of the Convention of Royal Burghs, 6 July 1749, ECA, SB 30/1/1/12, p. 19.
3. Ian G. Lindsay and Mary Cosh, *Inveraray and the Dukes of Argyll* (Edinburgh, 1973), pp. 356-57 n. 94. He continued to do this for several years.
4. *Whitehall Evening Post*, 2 June 1750. One suspects that such items were placed in friendly papers by Argyll or his friends.
5. Alexander Murdoch, *The People Above: Politics and Administration of Mid-Eighteenth-Century Scotland* (Edinburgh, 1980), pp. 52-84; John Stuart Shaw, *The Management of Scottish Society 1707-1764* (Edinburgh), pp. 80-82, 86-113.

6. Horace Walpole, *Memoirs of King George II*, 3 vols, ed. John Brooke (New Haven, Conn. & London, 1985), I:187 n.3. Murdoch says that the King first used this term derisively in 1747 when he had refused to see Argyll thinking him a disloyal Jacobite. Murdoch, *The People Above*, p. 35.

7. Argyll to Kames, 4 January 1752, Abercairny Manuscripts, NRS, GD24/1/556/2; Ian S. Ross, *Lord Kames and the Scotland of his Day* (Oxford, 1972), pp. 113-118.

8. *Ibid*, pp. 117-118.

9. See Roger L. Emerson, *Academic Patronage in the Scottish Enlightenment* (Edinburgh, 2007), pp. 115-149. The rectorial elections were annual local tests of the factional support for the Argathelians and Squadrone men.

10. Those were open-air revival meetings marked by what the sober thought of as wild enthusiasm. See, Arthur Fawcett, *The Cambuslang Revival: The Scottish Evangelical Revival of the Eighteenth Century* (Edinburgh, 1971; reprint edition Carlisle, Pa., 1996); John R. McIntosh, *Church and Theology in Enlightenment Scotland: The Popular Party, 1740-1800* (East Linton, 1998) and Leigh Eric Schmidt, *Holy Fairs: Scotland and the Making of American Revivalism* (2nd ed., Grand Rapids, Mich., and Cambridge, 2001).

11. Richard B. Sher, 'Witherspoon's Dominion of Providence and the Scottish Jeremiad Tradition', in *Scotland and America in The Age of the Enlightenment*, ed. Richard B. Sher and Jeffery R. Smitten (Edinburgh, 1990), pp. 46-64; McIntosh, *Church and Theology*, pp. 61-64.

12. Emerson, *Academic Patronage*, pp. 230-363.

13. Their efforts to secure university chairs is detailed in Emerson, *Academic Patronage*.

14. Robertson was brought to Edinburgh with the acquiescence of the Duke of Argyll; Robertson to Gilbert Elliot of Minto, 15 October 1755. Robertson promised in that letter not to 'disturb the town nor the Church with any irregular or Enthusiastic systems either in preaching or in Church politics'. He would, he said, continue to '[pursue] those moderate measures which have been promoted among us by the Duke of Argyle' from whom he expected favour. Elliot recommended him to Lord Milton on 10 October. Robertson was appointed. NLS, 16692/1; Harry Barclay of Colarnie to Milton, 12 May 1753. NLS, 16681/63.

15. Milton to Argyll [scroll], n.d. [1750], NLS, 16676/137.

16. This is clear from the *The Autobiography of Alexander Carlyle of Inveresk*, ed. John Hill Burton, (London and Edinburgh, 1910), *passim*.

17. Marchmont's brother, Alexander Hume Campbell was almost continually in opposition and the Duke's friendliness may have been to wean away a ministerial opponent and protect the Earl of Home and the Minto family. Gilbert Elliot, wished to sit as MP for Berwickshire; *HPHC 1754-1790*, II: 653-54.

18. Argyll to Marchmont, 17 August [1751], NRS, GD158/2591/1.

19. Letters between them exist about the appointments of Alexander Boswell of Auchinleck, George Carr of Nisbet, Andrew Macdowal of Bankton and Peter Wedderburn of Chesterhall to the Court of Session. The first three were appointed in 1754 and 1755; NRS, GD158/2915/3, 5, 6. For more, see Murdoch, *People Above*, pp. 53-62.

20. Marchmont to Argyll, ? August 1753, NLS, 16684/153.

21. With the Marquis of Tweeddale a reconciliation, accompanied by some distrust, came later (See pp. 325-27).

22. Argyll to Milton, 22 December 1750, NLS, 16669/127 and 16 February 1751, NLS, 16673/120.

23. He secured £2,000 from the government for that in 1755. ECA, City Muniments Vol 11, Bay D, Shelf 2, Bundle 108.

24. Hugh Arnot, *The History of Edinburgh*, (Edinburgh, 1779), pp. 574-75, 310, 313.

25. By the end of the year Drummond had alienated Henry Pelham. Argyll to Milton, 2 January and 1 March, 22 December 1753, NLS, 16681/109, 118 and 138.

26. Accounts of those developments can be found in A. J. Youngson, *The Making of Classical Edinburgh* (Edinburgh, 1966) and Andrew G. Fraser, *The Building of Old College: Adam, Playfair & The University of Edinburgh* (Edinburgh, 1989). Argyll was thanked by the Town Council on 15 May 1755 for getting the city £2,000 from the government for the Royal Infirmary. Seafield MSS, NRS, GD248/565/38.

27. Milton to Argyll, 8 March 1753, NLS, 16681/121; Argyll to Milton, 13 December 1753, NLS, 16681/131; William Alston to Milton, 1 May 1754, NLS, 16685/52.

28. Edinburgh Town Council to Ilay, 15 May 1755 and to Newcastle, 26 June 1755, ECA, Edinburgh City Muniments Vol 11, Bay D, bundle 108, shelf 2; Ilay to Milton, 4 March 1755 and 16 September 1755, NLS, 17625/29-30.

29. Argyll to Milton, 2 February 1751, NLS, 16673/118.

30. Argyll to Milton, 15 October 1753, NLS, 16681/127.

31. Alastair J. Durie, *The British Linen Company* 1745-1775, Scottish History Society, 5th Series, (Edinburgh, 1996), p. 9-11.

32. Argyll to Milton, ? December 1750, NLS, 16669/114; 2 December 1755, NLS, 16690/98; 14 April 1757, NLS, 16694/148.

33. Milton to Argyll, 5 July 1757, NLS, 16698/168.

34. Over the years, Argyll was appointed to Committees in the House of Lords which considered improvements to the ports of Haddington (1709), Inverness (1719), Dundee (1731), Dunbar (1737), Dysart (1753), Paisley (1753), Preston Pans (1753), Leith (1754) and to at least eight ports in England. He sat on three river improvement committees for Scotland: the Dee (1740, 1744) and the Cart (1753) and on at least thirty-one more appointed for England. He would have been interested in the technical aspects of those projects but whether he went to committee meetings is unknown. That he did so is suggested by his presence on most of the highway committees appointed while he served in the House (at least 164) and on most of other committees which dealt with scientific and technical projects such as the North-west Passage, repairs to the Parliament buildings, the building of the New London Bridge and other of the King's Works.

35. His efforts probably began in 1750, cf. Argyll to Milton, ? December 1750, NLS, 16669/114. He was supporting the Campbeltown Whale Fishery Co. and trying to placate English fellow-investors. Milton to Argyll, 25 November 1751, NLS, 16673/151-52. That venture failed (see p. 311). Among Argyll's other associates was likely to have been Alexander Lind of Gorgie who had a whaling boat built at Dunbar in 1752. George Haggarty and Sheila Forbes, 'Scotland: Lind and A-Marked Porcelain', *Northern Ceramic Society Journal* 20 (2003-04), p. 2.

36. ECA, SL 30/1/1/12, p. 154-57, 184.

37. The Duke sent them the secret recipe for Dr. James Fever Powders, a respected medicine of the times. NLS, 26223.

38. Some of those are to be found in NLS 16671. The proposals may relate to the work of Edinburgh Society for the Encouragement of Arts which flourished 1755-1761 and was designed to push improvements in Scotland. Argyll and Lord Hardwicke were opposed to entails but did not try to change the laws since there was no consensus on this issue. See p. 198 and Sir Alexander Cunningham Dick to Milton, 4 October 1759, NLS 16709/228-29. In 1755, Argyll tried to give a place on the Board of Police to Sir Alexander but was forced for political reasons to give it to Tweeddale's brother. Putting Sir Alexander on the Board would have insured that it did something. Argyll was impressed with the baronet's promise to spend some of his pension on 'the Publick [which] pleased me very much'.

Argyll to Milton, 25 August 1755, NLS, 16690/95. In 1758, Sir Alexander promised that £300 would be expended on the road to The Whim, NLS, 16703/154.

39. Quoted in John Stuart Shaw, *The Political History of Eighteenth Century Scotland* (New York and London, 1999), p. 34.

40. Milton later claimed sole credit for the civil scheme which means Bland approved a plan he was not competent to devise save in its military parts. Shaw, *Management*, p. 171. Others wanted the Board of Police to manage the estates but that was not liked by the Army and would have been opposed because the members of the Board were mostly Argathelian placemen. Argyll thought that the new board would be composed of three Englishmen and two Scots; Argyll to Milton, 4 February 1752, NLS, 16677/114. Inaction was prudent.

41. In 1715, Lord Ilay had advised the King to retain and not sell the confiscated estates. In 1747, this may still have been his choice. He had a personal interest in the question since he was a creditor of the estate of the attainted Lord Lovat. The Crown would pay the debts out of estate revenues.

42. For accounts of that, see Youngson, *After the Forty-Five*; Annette Smith, *Jacobite Estates of the Forty-Five* (Edinburgh, 1982); *Walpole Correspondence*, 20 (1985), p. 310; Horace Walpole, *Memoirs of King George II*, 3 vols (New Haven, Conn. and London, 1985), I:176-187; Argyll to Milton, 10 March 1752, NLS, 16677/116.

43. During that period, Argyll considered buying some of the forfeited properties such as the estate of Stewart of Ardsheal. Andrew Mackillop, *'More Fruitful than the Soil': Army, Empire and the Scottish Highlands 1715-1815* (East Linton, 2000), pp. 79-80.

44. Murdoch thought the delay was owing to the Treasury's hesitancy to pay the debts on the forfeited estates; *People Above*, p. 38. Shaw saw the delays as attributable, in part, to Argyll's political weakness at the time and to his general decline in activity and effectiveness due to age. Shaw, *Management*, pp. 175-180.

45. Quoted from Youngson, *After the Forty-Five*, p. 27.

46. Mackillop saw those as imitative of Lowland estate management policies; *'More Fruitful than the Soil'*, p. 81.

47. See Murdoch, 'Management or Semi-Independence? The Government of Scotland from 1707-1832' (unpublished paper given to the Association for Scottish Historical Studies, 1996). Murdoch's source is Byron F. Jewel, 'The Legislation Relating to Scotland After the Forty-Five', unpublished University of North Carolina Ph.D. dissertation, 1975, pp. 236-246.

48. Horace Walpole said 'none of his [Argyll's] people had attended the bill in the other House [the Commons]', *Walpole Correspondence*, 20:311.

49. William Coxe, *Memoirs of the Administration of the Right Honourable Henry Pelham...* 2 vols (London, 1829; reprint, N.Y., 1979), II:218; Argyll to Milton, 10 March, 1752, NLS, 16677/116.

50. Milton to Argyll, n.d. [1751], NLS, 16673/165. This letter says that the government wanted the window tax collected even if it yielded nothing above the costs of collection. The Duke was probably ridiculing the argument that the Annexing Act would cost the English taxpayers too much - something the window tax was said to do. *Walpole Correspondence* (1985), 20:310.

51. Argyll to Milton, 26 March 1752, NLS, 16677/119. In the end, Argyll secured money to pay the creditors of the estates - £70,000 in the case of the Perth estate once owned by Drummonds. Murdoch, *People Above*, pp. 82, 84.

52. Argyll to Milton, 26 March 1752, NLS, 16677/119.

53. Argyll to Milton, 6 April 1752, NLS, 16677/121.

54. Horace Walpole to Horace Mann, 23 March 1752, *Walpole Correspondence*, 20 (1960), pp. 310f. Walpole thought Argyll had been for colonizing the Highlands with British

ex-service men. Cobbett in his coverage of this bill records no speeches by Argyll: *The Parliamentary History of England from the Earliest Period 1066 to the Year 1803*, compiled by William Cobbett (London, 1810 -1813), Vols VI-XV (Microfilm produced by Fairview Park: Pergamon Press, Inc, n.d.) 16:1235-70.

55. Coxe, *Pelham*, II:214-5.
56. See: Roger L. Emerson, 'The Scottish Setting of Hume's Political Economy' in *Essays on David Hume's Political Economy*, eds. Margaret Schabas and Carl Wennerlind (N.Y., 2008), pp. 10-30.
57. George Ross to Lord Milton, 22 October 1754, NLS, 16689/75.
58. Shaw, *Management*, p. 78; Murdoch, *People Above*, pp. 76-80; Smith, *Jacobite Estates*, pp. 38-39, 239-41.
59. Shaw, *Management*, pp. 177-179.
60. 16 March 1751, *JHL*, Vol 27.
61. Naturalization was favoured by many of the Bishops and by most peers. It was carried in the Lords by a substantial majority of those voting.
62. Leah Leneman, 'The Scottish Case That Led to Hardwicke's Marriage Act', *Law and History Review* 17 (1999).
63. John Wilkes, *A Whig in Power: the Political Career of Henry Pelham* (n.p., 1964), p. 164.
64. *HPHC 1754-1790*, ed. Sir Lewis Namier and John Brooke, 3 vols (London, 1964), I:59-62, 469-512, *passim*. This says the cost came to £1,800.
65. Sir Lewis Namier, *The Structure of Politics at the Accession of George III*, (2nd ed. London, 1961), p. 200.
66. Argyll kept him out of sinecure offices in Scotland and forced him to relinquish his Aberdeenshire seat. Newcastle was also a loser in this scuffle. *HPHC 1754-1790*, III: 143.
67. NLS, 16685/183 and 185. Tweeddale at about the same time began referring place-seekers to Lord Milton and Argyll saying that because 'he was not employed in the Service of the Government...[he] meddled little in publick affairs'; 'favours were only to be obtain'd by application to the Duke of Argyle'. Left out, he now sided with Argyll. John Hay to Lord Milton, 22 March 1755, NLS, 16692/75.
68. Argyll to Milton, 19 December 1754, NLS, 16685/183.
69. Murdoch, *People Above*, p. 44.
70. Lord Deskford, son to the 4th Earl of Findlater to his father, ? 1727, Seafield Papers, NRS, GD248/ 571/6/29-31. I thank Dr. Joe Rock for that information.
71. Argyll to Milton, NLS 16690/96.
72. Christopher Whately, *Scottish Society, 1707-1830* (Manchester and New York, 2000), pp. 104-05.
73. Seafield Papers, NRS, GD248/562/55/18/15.
74. Argyll advertised his yacht, the *Princess Augusta*, as having belonged to Lord Baltimore, not to himself. The Irish Lord had been associated with the Admiralty but the purpose of this ruse is not clear. The vessel, a seventy-five ton ship armed with eleven brass guns, had been bought in 1751 and was sold to become a coast guard vessel. It would likely have had a single deck and a crew of twenty. Argyll to Milton 7 January 1755, NLS, 16690/70; Murdoch, *People Above*, p.65. Lindsay and Cosh, *Inveraray*, p. 67.
75. Seafield Papers, Dupplin to Deskford, June and July 1755, NRS, GD248/562/55/18/1, 2, 20, 24.
76. Yester Papers, NLS, 10 June 1755, 14422/128.
77. Seafield Papers,NRS, GD248/562/55/19.
78. Argyll to Milton, NLS, 16690/96.
79. Argyll to Milton, 2 November and 27 December 1755, NLS, 16690/96 and 100; Shaw, *Management*, p. 79.

80. Murdoch, *People Above*, p. 97.
81. This relies on the account given of those years by Murdoch, *People Above*, pp. 52-84.
82. Argyll to Lord Milton, ? February 1755, NLS, 16690/78.
83. *E.g.,* NLS, 16681/138, 16685/185; 16690/76, 80, 91.
84. Argyll to Milton, 2 December 1755, NLS, 16690/98; Murdoch, *People Above*, pp. 79-80.
85. Argyll wrote to Tweeddale on 10 November 1755 warning him that Charles Townshend's management of the estate of Lady Dalkeith's boy was 'absolutely impractable' and urged him to be a more active guardian; NLS, 14422/139-40. In January, he wrote again saying that Mr. John Craigie should manage the Buccleuch estate 'which I explained fully to Mr. Townshend', NLS, 14422/146. Appointing Craigie was favouring Robert Craigie, John's father-in law, now Lord President and a Squadrone man with whom Argyll had refused to work in 1746 (see p. 296). Shaw, *Management*, pp. 79-80.
86. Tweeddale thanked Argyll for agreeing to Andrew Mitchell's election from the Elgin Burghs. He wrote that Mitchell 'was pleased to inform me of Your Grace's friendly intimations toward my self. I can with truth affirm I was always naturally inclined to be in connection with your Grace, times and circumstances without any real cause given me may have given rise to some interuption. There are particulars which your Grace does not know too long & be now immaterial to be mentioned'. He promised to see him when Parliament met. Tweeddale to Argyll, n. d., NLS, 14426/143.
87. Argyll to Tweeddale, 27 August 1754, NLS, 14426/97. The place was probably the Glasgow Chair of Ecclesiastical History which Richard Betham had wanted and in which Argyll did meddle. In the end, the Duke let the College make a deal with Lord Hopetoun to get rid of the incumbent professor of history, William Rouet. About two weeks later, he assured the Marquis that he had let the Glasgow job drop since he was unlikely to be able to secure it against the wishes of the College men. Argyll later could have named a man to the Humanist's chair. The Masters pleaded with Argyll to nominate someone but he only gave his permission for them to chose George Muirhead. When he named no one, the masters quarrelled which in the long run strengthened Argyll's power in the institution. Muirhead was useful to the Foulis Press. Argyll to Tweeddale, 22 September 1754, NLS, 14426/107; Roger L. Emerson, *Academic Patronage in the Scottish Enlightenment* (Edinburgh, 2008), pp. 125-127.
88. Argyll to Tweeddale, 4 September 1755, NLS, 14422/134.
89. Hay in a letter to 'My Lord' [Tweeddale] on 4 November 1754 noted that his family was loyal but went to Episcopalian churches. He had been called a Jacobite by Sir James Steuart of Goodtrees and had employed Jacobite servants c.1749-50. He had a picture of the Pretender and his sons in his home until he was employed by Tweeddale c.1740; then, it was destroyed. His father had Jacobite leanings and may have been out in the '15. In an undated letter from 1754, he told Argyll that a brother had been out in 1745. NLS, 14426/142.
90. Tweeddale and Hay also approached Newcastle, Granville, Queensberry, Dupplin and his brother, then the Bishop of St Asaph's. NLS, 16688/20-30.
91. Thomas Hay to Tweeddale, 9 and 10 November 1754, NLS, 14426/125, 136.
92. That was the old friend from whom Argyll had bought The Whim but of whom Milton now said 'that the Major & the Duke were at bottom not friends & that the Duke considered him a fool & did not mind him'. NLS, 14426/131.
93. Hay claimed to have burned many of his papers from that period so that they would not fall into the hands of rebels. NLS, 14422/143.
94. Hay to Tweeddale, 10 November 1754, NLS, 14426/130-136.
95. Hay to Milton, 2 September 1754, NLS,16688/27. Hay's appointment may be related to Argyll's chats with George Bubb Dodington in the early 1750s when he a part of the

Leicester House set. The Leicester House agenda, in the 1750s, included the forming in a new reign of a Ministry which would include the Argathelians and the remnants of the Squadrone interest in Scotland. It was a naive aim but seriously pursued. Argyll, who hoped to survive with power into the next reign, might have been insuring against the loss of his position with some patronage given to Squadrone men. It is also interesting that in 1751 Argyll named his yacht *The Princess Augusta* for the wife or daughter of Frederick, Prince of Wales. Given Newcastle's prominence, but his likely unpopularity in the next reign, the Duke's moves were prudent. For the Leicester House plans, see *Leicester House Politics, 1750-60, From the Papers of John, Second Earl of Egmont*, ed. Aubrey N. Newman, Camden Society 4th series, 7, pp. 85-228.

96. Argyll to Tweeddale, 1 and 8 June 1756, Yester Papers, NLS, 14422/150, 152, 153, 155-7. Brown had once been driven from a parish for fornicating with a parishioner. Emerson, *Academic Patronage*, pp. 467-469. The same letters show the Duke soliciting a pension for one of Tweeddale's relatives.

97. Murdoch, *People Above*, pp. 44-46.

98. *Ibid*, p. 68.

99. Minute Books of the Convention of Royal Burghs, ECA, Sl30/1/1/12/157, 183, 189, 221, 223.

100. Shaw, *Political History*, p. 74.

101. Deskford opposed some provisions of the bill in 1754 which he thought would damage the Scottish linen trade. Whately, *Scottish Society*, pp. 108, 120.

102. Murdoch, *People Above*, p. 69.

103. Shaw, *Political History*, p. 74; Murdoch cites a letter in which Newcastle says he had but three Scottish votes in the Commons one of which belonged to Andrew Mitchell then in Brussels; Murdoch, *People Above*, p. 45.

104. Scott, 'Politics and Administration', p. 552.

105. Stormont to 10th Earl of Huntingdon, 2 March 1757, *HMCR on the Manuscripts of the late Reginald Rawdon Hastings*, Esq., 5 vols, ed. Francis Bickley (London, 1934), III:132.

106. Murdoch, *People Above*, p. 45.

107. Thad W. Riker, *Henry Fox First Lord Holland*, 2 vols (Oxford, 1911), II:23-24; Sir Lewis Namier, *England in the Age of the American Revolution* (London, 1963), p. 87. Riker said Argyll did 'scarcely more than broach the subject to the prospective Groom of the Stole' who rejected the King's offer of a pension and office. By September, Fox and William Barrington had convinced the King to appoint Bute to the office he sought. Alexander Murdoch, 'Lord Bute, James Stuart Mackenzie and the government of Scotland' in *Lord Bute: Essays in Interpretation*, ed. Karl W. Schweizer (Leicester, 1988), pp. 121-23.

108. Murdoch, *People Above*, pp. 47-49; Mackillop, '*More Fruitful than the Soil*', pp. 45-46, n. 16.

109. Cumberland was among those who made them. Rex Whitworth, *William Augustus Duke of Cumberland A Life* (London, 1992), p. 179.

110. He seems to have been willing to use subsidies to prevent Hanover from being attacked but those he approved would have subsidized the armies of allies. Giles Fox-Strangways, 6th Earl of Ilchester, *Henry Fox. First Lord Holland His Family and Relations*, 2 vols (London, 1920), I:275.

111. One of Argyll's reactions to this was to sell funds which he was sure would fall. Argyll to Milton, 7 August 1756, NLS, 16694/105.

112. It was about this time that a confident Argyll insisted that the English and Scottish Annexed Estates Commissions be treated equally. When Lord Cadogan refused in the House of Lords to explain what the Scottish reports meant, Argyll moved to have the reports of both Commissions read in the House 'to prevent any particular distinction,

& to give time to send for our friends'. He was bearding a man whose family had a long record of contempt for Scots. Argyll to Lord President Dundas, 13 July ? [1756], Dalrymple Papers, NRS, GD110/1292.

113. Argyll to Milton, 21 August 1759, NLS, 16708/176. The best clue as to Argyll's views on imperial and European affairs then may well be found in Dr. John Mitchell's *The Contest in America between Great Britain and France with Its Consequences and Importance...* (London, 1757). This was written about the time two men became close. Mitchell argued for the defense and development of the American colonies, support for the Iroquois and the extirpation of the French which would allow Britain to balance their power in Europe. Mitchell's map and political writings are discussed at length by Edmund and Dorothy Berkeley, *Dr. John Mitchell: The Man Who Made the Map* (Chapel Hill, 1974), pp. 174-230, passim.

114. Copy of a Letter, 23 October 1756, NLS, 16694/107.

115. Argyll to Milton, 16 November 1756, NLS, 16694/108.

116. Murdoch says that Argyll suggested to Pitt that Highlanders would do nicely in America but the idea had been pitched before. Murdoch, *ODNB* 9:733.

117. Mackillop, '*More Fruitful that the Soil*'. p. 45.

118. Argyll had few expectations for it, writing to Milton on 11 June 1757, that 'Lester House' and the Duke of Newcastle would not 'long agree'. A week later, he noted that he had friends in the new Chancellor of the Exchequer, the Hon. Henry Legge, an old Walpolean, and in his niece's husband, Charles Townshend. Lord Bute, however, was then avoiding him. NLS, 16698/162; Argyll to Milton, 11 and 18 June 1757, NLS, 16698/162.

119. Mackillop, '*More Fruitful than the Soil*', p. 45-46.

120. Argyll to ?, 4 February 1756, NLS, 2521/20.

121. Argyll to Milton, 9 April 1757, NLS, 16694/147.

122. Argyll to Milton, ?November 1756, NLS, 16694/110.

123. Argyll to Milton, 23 December 1756, NLS, 16694/115.

124. Argyll blocked his earlier attempt to enter Parliament; *HPHC 1754-1790*, II:471.

125. Mackillop, '*More Fruitful than the Soil*', pp. 4-48. This increased the number of the Duke's collectors of seeds and plants; *E.g.*, Dr. Richard Huck to General John Loudoun, 30 November 1758, Loudoun Papers, Huntington Library, LO 5969. I thank the Rev. Dr. Alexander Campbell for a copy of this letter.

126. St. Clair to Charles Erskine, Erskine-Murray Correspondence, NLS, 5079/111. They had known each other since at least 1715.

127. John Campbell to John Campbell of Barcaldine, 10 and 12 September 1759, NRS, GD170/1014.

128. Argyll in 1759 was involved with George Ross, MP, in appointing commissaries at the Highland forts. Ross was a former clerk of Duncan Forbes who had acted as solicitor for three of the Jacobite Lords tried in 1746. He became Argyll's 'military secretary' as well as agent for the Convention of Royal Burghs and a 'fixer' who dealt in many things; *HPHC 1754-1790*, III:378-79; Gordon Bannerman, *Merchants and the Military in Eighteenth Century Britain* (London, 2008), pp. 113, 117-8.

129. The Duke had been advancing Gordon's career since at least 1754; NLS, 16685/26; Mackillop, '*More Fruitful than the Soil*', p. 51 which cites more evidence.

130. *Ibid*, p. 48.

131. Fencible regiments were raised to defend only the areas in which they had been recruited; they were not to be used abroad. Militia troops were not part of the regular establishment but could be sent out of the country.

132. Murdoch, *People Above*, p. 89.

133. This paragraph is based on material contained in John Robertson, *The Scottish Enlightenment and the Militia Issue* (Edinburgh, 1985) and in *HPHC 1754-1790*, II:653-55.

134. Milton to Argyll, 24 November 1759 and 23 February 1760, NLS, 16708/176 and 16713/147; Horace Walpole to Horace Mann, 28 February 1760, *Walpole Correspondence*, 21 (1960), pp. 371-72. Thurot's voyages are noticed by Robertson, *Militia Issue*, pp. 106-107.

135. Daniel Campbell to ?Charles Erskine, 13 July 1759, NLS, 5080/138; 5081/42. Minutes of the Convention of Royal Burghs, 8 April 1760, ECA, SL 30/1/1/12, p.423.

136. That elite debating club flourished 1754-c.1762 and enrolled all the important intellectuals of the city and many of its fashionable young men. Roger L. Emerson, 'The Social Composition of Enlightened Scotland', *Studies on Voltaire and the 18th Century*, Vol. 114 (1973), pp. 291-329 and Roger L. Emerson, 'Select Society of Edinburgh' in *ODNB*, 39:705-708.

137. Robertson, *Militia Issue*, pp. 108-10, 124.

138. Argyll to Milton, 8 March 1760, NLS, 16713/153.

139. Walpole, *George II*, III:198.

140. What follows relies principally on John Brooke, *King George III* (London, 1972).

141. Murdoch, *People Above*, p. 85.

142. Riker, *Henry Fox*, 1:23-26; Namier, *England in the Age of the American Revolution* (London, 1963), p. 87. Namier cited a letter of William Murray to Newcastle, 10 July 1756.

143. Waldegrave, *Memoirs*, p. 216.

144. This relies on the splendid entry on Townshend by Sir Lewis Namier in the *HPHC 1754-1790*, III:539-548.

145. *Ibid*, I:502.

146. *Ibid*, I:493-94.

147. *Ibid*, I:471.

148. This and the following paragraph rely mainly on Murdoch, *People Above*, pp. 93-94.

149. Argyll, after talking to Newcastle, advised Erskine, on 1 March 1760, to tell Newcastle and the Lord Chancellor that the recently dead Lord President Craigie had been put in 'over your head'. Argyll was sure that Robert Dundas wanted the post but said he would do 'every thing in the best manner for your service Being your old friend & humble servant'. Argyll made this into a complex deal involving the succession to the Lord Justice Clerk's office and the coming elections. Argyll, in the end, may not have supported Erskine. Lord Hardwicke wrote frankly to Erskine telling him that, because he was too old for the work, the King had given it to Dundas 'who has health & strength to undergo the fatigues of this laborious situation'. Erskine told Hardwicke on 15 May that he had not applied for the job. NLS, 5081/44, 50, 52. Erskine, after Argyll died, applied for the Lord Justice General's position vacated by the Duke but was told that it had gone immediately to Tweeddale 'at the instance of his Father in law, my Lord president'. Erskine to Hardwicke, 20 April 1761 and Hardwicke to Erskine 28 April 1761, NLS, 5081/120.

150. Argyll to Erskine, 7 July 1760, Erskine Muray Papers, NLS, 5087/26 [this undated letter possibly refers to events in 1753-4].

151. Namier, *Age of the American Revolution*, p. 139. He cites the list as Newcastle MSS, The British Library, MS 32999 ff. 15-17; see also NLS, 5081/103, 107, 113.

152. *E.g.*, Argyll to Charles Erskine, 23 February 1760, NLS, 5081/36.

153. This affair generated a number of letters and involved Newcastle, Hardwicke and Holderness. NLS, Erskine Murray papers, 5081/36, 44.

154. ECA, SL 30/1/1/12, 443.

155. Namier, *Age of the American Revolution*, p. 139.
156. NLS, 5081/105, 107, 113.
157. Elliot to Bute, 16 December 1760, quoted by Murdoch, *People Above*, pp. 94-95.
158. Argyll to Milton, 26 December 1760, NLS, 16713/195.
159. Murdoch, *People Above*, p. 95; *The Political Journal of George Bubb Dodington*, ed. John Carswell and Lewis Arnold Dralle (Oxford, 1965), p. 409.
160. NLS, 16713/190-95; *HPHC 1754-1790*, I:502.
161. Ilay to Milton, 28 March, Milton to Argyll, March, 28 March, 2 April 1761, NLS, 16718/141, 146, 152.
162. Namier, *Age of American Revolution*, pp. 161-62.
163. Lord Justice Clerk to Hardwicke, 20 April 1761, NLS, 5081/120.
164. Gilbert Elliot to Charles Erskine, LJC, 1 May 1761 NLS, 5081/128; George Ross to Colonel William Williams, 29 August 1761, NLS, 5081/166.
165. Namier, *Age of American Revolution*, p. 162.
166. Lindsay and Cosh, *Inveraray and the Dukes of Argyll* (Edinburgh, 1973), p. 88.
167. Among those appointed in this period were John Anderson, James Beattie, Joseph Black, George Campbell, William Cullen, Adam Smith, William Wilkie, and Alexander Wilson.
168. Argyll to Lord Milton, 7 August 1756, NLS, 16694/104-05. It is impossible to say what he was personally worth c.1750 but it must have been well over £60,000 – more if real estate and moveables are included .
169. Bubb Dodington, *Journal*, pp. 25-244. *passim*.
170. Fairholm to Lord Milton, 5 April 1761, NLS, 16719/120.
171. The bubbles in his came from the 'first Fermentation', and not from that in a bottle to which sugar had been added, but it was still very expensive.
172. Minutes of the meetings of Trustees' Standing Committee 1754, The British Museum Archives [BMA], Microfilm CE 3, reel 1-2.
173. One of the men employed was Roger Morris's son James. Argyll turned out to look after a man whom he had befriended and who was still working for him.
174. BMA, Minutes of Trustees' General Meetings, Microfilm CE 1 1753- 1761, reel 1.
175. *Ibid*, 3 April 1754, 8 May 1755, 16 June 1755.
176. *Ibid*, 3 June 1756.
177. BMA, Committee Minutes; Book of Presents, Microfilm CE 30, reel 1.
178. Argyll to Milton, 8 February and 8 March 1750, NLS, 16669/97 and 102-03. For London reactions to these events see T.D. Kendrick, *The Lisbon Earthquake* (Philadelphia and New York, 1957), pp. 11-44, 101-02.
179. He had dismissed 'the Great Couture' [unidentified] and had hired 'a Professor of a very good Character and much cheaper'. Argyll to Milton, 10 November 1755, NLS, 16690/96.
180. Edmund and Dorothy Berkeley, *Dr. John Mitchell: The Man Who Made the Map* (Chapel Hill, 1974), p. 219.
181. Argyll to Milton, 28 December 1751, NLS, 16673/161. This is one of several letters dealing with missing silver instruments carried in a shagreen case. He was becoming forgetful and, like many men in their seventies, misplaced keys, books and other things.
182. BMA, Original Papers, Microfilm CE 4, OP 1 Vol. 1; 14 August 1761.
183. William Strahan to Franklin, 23 November 1748, *The Paper of Benjamin Franklin*, 20 vols, eds Leonard W. Labaree, *et al.* (New Haven, Conn., 1961), III:327
184. Lindsay and Cosh, *Inveraray*, p. 365 n. 217.
185. Berkeley and Berkeley, *Mitchell*, pp. 175-213.
186. In a letter from October 1756 that shows not a concern for his venison but for starving beasts, Argyll touchingly lamented the condition of his roe deer in Inveraray: 'sure they

might feed them some how or other, hay, oats, or even bread may be given them in any covered Trough railed from other cattle'. NLS, 16694/102. He seems always to have had cats and dogs and in his zoo more beasts and birds.

187. 9 July 1752.

188. Lindsay and Cosh found that his expenses from Glasgow to Inveraray in 1744 amounted altogether to £41.7. 3½. *Inveraray*, p. 235 n. 47. He would have entertained many in Glasgow and the towns down the Clyde.

189. By preference (as shown by his vintner's bills), Argyll drank Claret, Madeira and Port, Burgundy, and Champagne in that order. Robert Brisbane to Milton, 2 April 1761, NLS, 16718/87.

190. NLS, 17628/80. Many of the meat dishes came garnished with vegetables and some with sippets – bread to soak up the juices.

191. NLS, 17629/219.

192. In 1760, it took seven to nine men nine days to shear them. NLS, 17662/38. In some years he sold 200 lambs.

193. NLS, 17629/115, 219, 236.

194. Day books of the Gardiners at Whim, NLS, 17657- 17661. The ordinary labourers were paid about 5d per day – 2s 6d a week. Those were good wages only if they worked all year and had cottages and small plots of their own. The plowman in 1760, who had those, got about £3 a year cash and a pair or two of shoes. See, A. J. S. Gibson and T. C. Smout, *Prices, Food and Wages in Scotland 1550-1780* (Cambridge, 1995), p. 323.

195. See p. 194.

196. Carlyle, *Autobiography*, p. 418.

197. John Davidson, W. S., became Crown Agent. He was also a legal historian, antiquary and collector of art objects.

198. This dispute interested nearly all the *literati* of Edinburgh and many of its businessmen. See: Alastair Smart, *Allan Ramsay: Painter, Essayist and Man of the Enlightenment* (New Haven and London, 1992), pp. 135-138; Ramsay Garden Papers, 'Letters Relating to the Dispute with John Davidson, W.S. Concerning the property at Ramsay Garden 1757-1760', NLS, 3417/98-99. Argyll had been asked to serve as a mediator in disputes since at least 1721; *Culloden Papers*, NLS, 2966/79.

199. He offered to give 'such curious and exotic Trees and Shrubs as our Soil and Climate will bear'. A. D. Boney, *The Lost Gardens of Glasgow University* (London, 1988), pp. 87-90.

200. Those are discussed in Roger L. Emerson, 'The Philosophical Society of Edinburgh 1748-1768', *British Journal of the History of Science*, 14 (1981), pp. 133-176 and Emerson and Paul B. Wood, 'Science and Enlightenment in Glasgow, 1690-1802' in *Science and Medicine in the Scottish Enlightenment*, ed. Charles W. J. Withers and Paul Wood (East Linton, 2002), pp. 79-142.

201. Lindsay and Cosh, *Inveraray*, pp. 144-181, *passim;* 'A Breaft acct. of the life of Archd Duke of Argyll', NLS, Acc. 8168/1/3.

202. Records from the salt pans, NLS, 17680.

203. In 1754, Argyll paid his butcher £2.11.6 for slaughtering for the use of those at Inveraray 23 cows and stots, 60 sheep, 11 lambs, 5 veals, 14 deer, and '8 fowls for the Yacht'; NLS 17624/145. He and his guests went through a lot of meat but some of that was perhaps for his workmen.

204. Carlyle, *Autobiography*, pp. 399-400.

205. Franklin's visit, about which nothing is known, is noted by Lindsay and Cosh, *Inveraray*, p. 365 n. 217. Their note mentions the Franklin stoves the Duke possessed.

206. Argyll to Milton, 6 February 1759, NLS,16708/158.

207. John Adams account for the 'New Library'[c.1760], £158.18.5; NLS, 17650/164.

208. NLS, 17629/115, 219, 236.
209. This post is valued at £1,000 in Guy Miège's *Present State of Great Britain* (10th edn. London, 1745), II:329. There do not seem to be entries in his Coutts ledgers for payments. The other sums come from Miège.
210. Eric R. Cregeen, *Argyll Estate Instructions: Mull, Morvern, Tiree 1771-1805*, Scottish History Society, 4th Series, vol. 1 (Edinburgh, 1964), p. xii. Immediately after the '45, his rents dipped to something like £4,000 a year.
211. A paper among the Saltoun Papers says that his income from land and offices in 1761 was £15,191.18.5; NLS, 17612/223. This record can be compared with the finances of Newcastle who started life with an income much like that and ended up poor. See, Ray A. Kelch, Newcastle *A Duke without Money: Thomas Pelham-Holles 1693-1768* (Berkeley and Los Angeles, 1974).
212. Coutts 'Out book', 15 July 1760.
213. Coutts 'Out book', 7 May 1760.
214. Argyll to Charles Erskine, 29 July 1754, NLS, 5087/28.
215. Argyll to Charles Erskine, 5 August 1758, NL,S 5080/22.
216. Argyll to Charles Erskine, 4 January 1759, NLS, 5079/22.
217. Montrose to ?, reference lost.
218. In December 1756, he warned off Grants who were trying to buy lands once belonging to the Maules of Panmure. Argyll called their efforts a 'wicked measure' – 'a 'selfish scheme' bound to have 'mischevious consequences' among which would be the 'perpetual hatred' of the Maules and their friends and relations. Argyll to Charles Erskine, n.d. [December 1756], NLS 5079/106.
219. *E.g.*, (1724) NLS, 16529/21-2; (1737) NLS, 16569/84; (1742) NLS, 16584/55; (1755) NLS, 16690/55.
220. This does not show in the Coutts accounts.
221. This figure has been arrived at by summing the payments of interest and dividends shown in his 'In book' and treating those as 3% of the value of the capital. It agrees well with the £41,700 and the £2,000 of British Linen Co. Stock he would have held at the time of his death since he was still its Governor.
222. The Duke earlier had given Maule £500 as a gift. Argyll to Milton, NLS 1754; Archibald Campbell to Milton, 4 July 1761, NLS, 16718/204. Maule, knowing the cost of keeping this place, had by then made the property over to John, 4th Duke of Argyll who sold it in 1763.
223. Many people were paid something after his death but it is unclear who was given a legacy or a year's wages and who was paid for an outstanding debt. Pujolas received £444.8.2 'for Sundry acct of taxes, wages Legacy etc.' The 'major domo' had served the Duke since at least 1714.
224. *Scots Magazine*, 23, May 1761, p. 278; that account of his will is confirmed by a copy of the Duke's will among Milton's papers, NLS 17612/178-80. Other published versions of his will say he left his servants only a week's wages which seems unlikely.
225. His joint executors were Mrs. Williams, their son, Col. Williams, James Coutts, banker and MP and George Ross, London Agent for the Convention of Royal Burghs and MP. Mrs. Williams died soon after leaving her son to act as the principal executor. The will was proved in the Prerogative Court at Canterbury, 2 June 1762, with William Williams named (in a document I have not seen) as sole executor. London Municipal Archives, ACC/1149/194.
226. Probably James Coutts, the London banker who had George Campbell as a partner. Their bank was in the Strand – as the Coutts Bank still is.

227. Lindsay and Cosh, *Inveraray*, pp. 77-78.
228. This was also done for his Scottish papers at Rosneath and Inveraray; Archibald Campbell to Milton, 4 July 1761, NLS, 16719/24.
229. When Argyll's old friend, Lord Dundonald, deplored the terms of the will which left so much to his mistress and illegitimate son, he was told by Alexander Forrester, that it 'becomes not those who lie under such solide obligations to his Grace to joyn in reflexions upon his memory'. Forrester to ?, 7 May 1761, NRS, GD214/717.
230. He, too, was a successful investor, an antiquary and collector, a gardener and a man of many interests and probably more taste than the 3rd Duke.
231. Archibald Campbell to Milton, 4 July 1761, NLS, 16718/204.
232. Murdoch, 'Lord Bute', pp. 124-25.

Chapter 18

1. Lindsay and Cosh, *Inveraray and the Dukes of Argyll* (Edinburgh, 1973), p. 179.
2. 4th Duke of Argyll to Lord Milton, June 1761, NLS, 16718/25.
3. NLS, 16719/40.
4. NLS, 16718/219.
5. Lindsay and Cosh, *Inveraray*, p. 177.
6. Sir Harry Erskine to Lord Milton, 24 April 1761, NLS, 16719/103.
7. Andrew Cochrane to Lord Milton, 25 March [April] 1761, NLS, 16718/141.
8. Lord Adam Gordon, the Commander-in-Chief in Scotland, to Lord Milton, 23 April 1761, NLS 16720/188
9. Dick to Milton, 30 April 1761, NLS, 16719/193.
10. Anonymous [Patrick Cuming] in NLS, 17612/218-220.
11. *Scots Magazine*, 22, April 1761, p. 223.
12. NLS, Acc 8168/1/(3).
13. Other accounts made it as high as eight: presumably in Latin and Greek, English, French, Italian, Dutch and German or Spanish. Andrew Henderson, 'Considerations on the Question, Relating to the Scots Militia... with a faithful Character of Archibald late Duke of Argyll' (2nd edn., London, 1761), p. 42.
14. Anonymous, 'A Letter to the Author of the North Briton with a Striking Character of Lord Bute, and of Archibald, late Duke of Argyll', (London, 1763), pp. 41-43.
15. Nicholas Tindal, *The Continuation of Mr. Rapin's History of England From the Revolution to the Present Times*, 8 vols (London, 1759), VIII:260. Tobias Smollett also left a character written about that time in which Ilay appears learned, 'artful', 'enterprising' and 'invariably true to his own interests'. *Complete History of England*, 4 vols (London, 1757-1758), III:344.
16. Stana Nanadic. 'The Enlightenment in Scotland and the popular passion for portraits', *British Journal for Eighteenth-Century Studies*, 21 (1998), pp. 175-192; 179.
17. There is no documentary evidence that it was a political parade in aid of his friends as some have suggested.
18. Eric R. Cregeen, *Argyll Estate Instructions*, Scottish History Society (Edinburgh, 1964), p. xxxvi. Cregeen in a later unpublished manuscript noted that Argyll exercised a 'draconic and detailed control of the [Kintyre] estate' and was rigorous in his exaction of rents and arrears. He showed 'a decided tendency to take legal action against any tenant in debt to the estate and to recover what is owed by poinding his goods and distress'. Cregeen and Angus Martin, *Kintyre Instructions: The 5th Duke of Argyll's Instructions to his Kintyre Chamberlain 1785-1805* (Glasgow, 2011), p. 185.

19. He kept looking for positions for Stamp Brooksbank who had been sent up from England to watch the Scots from his post as Secretary of the Forfeited Estates Commission. With his encouragement, Brooksbank eventually departed for a better job. In the universities Ilay wished to appoint only one real Englishman, a distinguished astronomer who later became Astronomer Royal.

20. Anonymous, 'A Letter to the Author of the North Briton ... with a Striking Character of Lord BUTE and of Archibald, late Duke of Argyll' (London, 1763).

21. For lists, see below, note 23.

22. The Edinburgh doctors were unsalaried but after 1733 they divided the £100 salary given to the King's Physician in Scotland. NLS, 16552/50. The Glasgow medical men were salaried but had smaller classes and fees; they later divided the stipend of the Physician to the Prince of Wales in Scotland.

23. In making these comparisons, I have identified faction members using principally the following works: Alexander Murdoch, *The People Above: Politics and Administration in Mid-Eighteenth-Century Scotland* (Edinburgh,1980), John Stuart Shaw, *The Management of Scottish Society 1707-1764* (Edinburgh, 1983); ____, *The Political History of Eighteenth-Century Scotland* (New York, 1999); Eric G.J. Wehrli, 'Scottish Politics in the Age of Walpole', unpublished Ph.D. dissertation, Edinburgh University, 1983. The club members have been found in The Honourable the Improvers of the Knowledge of Agriculture of Scotland, the Select Society of Edinburgh and its subsidiary group, the Edinburgh Society; the Edinburgh Poker Club and the Philosophical Society of Edinburgh. There is no complete list of the members of the first but see the list contained in *Select Transactions of the Honourable The Society of Improvers ...*, ed. Robert Maxwell (Edinburgh, 1743; reprinted Glasgow, 2003). That can be supplemented by additions from the partial copy of the Society's minutes held in the Library of the Royal Highland Society. The list of Select Society members is given in Roger L. Emerson, 'The Social Composition of Enlightened Scotland', *Studies on Voltaire and the 18th Century*, 114 (1973), pp. 291-329. There is no comparable list of the Edinburgh Society membership which did include all the members of the Select. Some members of the Poker Club are listed in John Robertson, *The Scottish Enlightenment and the Militia Issue* (Edinburgh, 1985), pp. 188-192. For the Philosophical Society, see Roger L. Emerson, 'The Philosophical Society of Edinburgh 1737-1748', *British Journal for the History of Science*, 12, (1979), pp. 154-91; ____, 'The Philosophical Society of Edinburgh 1748-1768', *British Journal for the History of Science*, 14, (1981), pp. 133-176; ____, 'The Philosophical Society of Edinburgh 1768-1783', *British Journal for the History of Science*, 18, (1985), pp. 255-303.

24. Roger L. Emerson, *Academic Patronage in the Scottish Enlightenment* (Edinburgh, 2008), pp. 540-41

25. See, Anne Skoczylas, *Dr. Simson s Knotty Case: Divinity, Politics and Due Process in Early Eighteenth-Century Scotland* (Montreal, Kingston, London, Ithaca, 2001), *passim*.

26. Emerson, *Academic Patronage*, pp. 116-19; John Cairns, *The Teaching of Law in Eighteenth Century Scotland* (forthcoming).

27. Roger L. Emerson, 'Medical Men, Politicians and the Medical Schools at Glasgow and Edinburgh 1685-1803' in *William Cullen and the Eighteenth Century Medical Worlds*, eds A. Doig, J.P.S. Ferguson, I.A. Milne and R. Passmore, (RCPE, Edinburgh, 1993), pp. 186-215.

28. He may have remembered Hutcheson from dealings with him ten years earlier but his name was sent to Ilay by someone in Scotland. Ilay chose him out of a field of four. His friends at the College voted to make this appointment by election and not by a 'comparative trial'. This created a precedent for future appointments to be made in the

same manner. Charles Morthland to Mungo Graham of Gorthy, 22 December 1729, NRS, GD220/5/1081/34; GUA, Faculty Minutes, 12 December 1729.

29. David Hume to Henry Home, 24 July 1746, *New Letters of David Hume*, ed. Raymond Klibanski and Ernest C. Mossner (Oxford, 1954; reprinted N.Y.,1983 in an edition prepared by Lewis White Beck), p. 21 n. 2. That identifies Williamson as another man. But, since James Williamson became Professor of Mathematics and was a favoured student of Robert Simson, and was old enough to be appointed, it is more likely to be him and not the Rev. John Williamson.

30. Wilson trained as an apothecary-surgeon but became an inventor and type-founder. One of his papers on sunspots won a prize from the Royal Academy at Copenhagen in 1769. Argyll had been patronizing Wilson since c.1737. The chair was created for him partly to enable the University to use its fine new instrument collection and to teach navigation and astronomy.

31. Ian Simpson Ross, *Life of Adam Smith* (Oxford, 1995), p. 12.

32. *Ibid*, p. 110.

33. For his views and teaching accomplishments see, David B. Wilson, *Seeking Nature's Logic: Natural Philosophy in the Scottish Enlightenment* (University Park, 2009), pp. 171-200.

34. John Butt, *John Anderson's Legacy: The University of Strathclyde and Its Antecedents 1796-1996* (East Linton, 2000), pp. 3-4.

35. Roger L. Emerson, *Professors Patronage and Politics: The Aberdeen Universities in the Eighteenth Century* (Aberdeen, 1992), pp. 61, 63; Ilay to Delafaye, 10 October 1730, NRS, PRO, SP54/20/38. Gordon was unanimously recommended by the professors at King's. Local men, including Col. John Middleton, wanted this chair made into a professorship of mathematics but charity prevailed over political and intellectual interests. Middleton to Milton, 2 September 1730, NLS, 16554/54.

36. The hyper-Calvinism of the older men is discussed by Anne Skoczylas, in *Mr. Simson's Knotty Case* and in her 'The Regulation of Academic Society in Early Eighteenth-Century Scotland: The Tribulations of Two Divinity Professors', *Scottish Historical Review*, 83 (2004) pp. 171-195.

37. The classic expression of this was the often reprinted *Ecclesiastical Characteristics* (1753) by John Witherspoon. That pamphlet was followed by *A Serious Apology for the Ecclesiastical Characteristics* which answered Argyll's claim that the Kirk was a church established by law and thus controllable by the state. Witherspoon argued that the Treaty of Union protected a Church which was free of any tie to the state and exercised in its own courts a control of its affairs which was not to be abridged. The Kirk was not established but only acknowledged to be protected by the Treaty. Witherspoon went on to tax the Moderates and their friends with simony, a parsimonious refusal to raise stipends and with pluralism, which, 'as power follows property' would dazzle some with expectations of worldly success unbecoming in ministers. In a veiled reference to the Squadrone and Argathelians, Witherspoon said that their fault was making clerical affairs the matter of state parties. *Characteristics*, pp. 191-210.

38. *The Rev. Dr. John Walker's Report on the Hebrides of 1764 and 1771*, ed. Margaret M. McKay (Edinburgh, 1980).

39. Andrew Mackillop, *'More Fruitful than the Soil': Army, Empire and the Scottish Highlands 1715-1815* (East Linton, 2000), p. 49.

40. A recent discussion of this can be found in T. M. Devine, *Scotland's Empire 1600-1815* (London, 2003), pp. 290-319.

41. There were perhaps 5,500 trained Scottish medics in the eighteenth century with about

8,400 non-Scots medically educated or partially trained in the country's universities. All that was worth to the country somewhere around a million pounds. See, Roger L. Emerson, 'Numbering the Medics' in *Essays on David Hume, Medical Men and the Scottish Enlightenment* (Farnham, Surrey, 2009), pp. 163-224.

42. It was said in one of the Duke's obituaries that he also had found £8,000 sterling in invalid money for the Royal Infirmary of Edinburgh. That too contributed to medical education and defrayed hospital costs to the benefit of others not in the services. Patrick Cuming's obituary for the Duke, NLS, 17612.

43. T. M. Devine, *Scotland's Empire*, p. 269.

44. *Ibid*, p. 305.

45. Ilay to Milton, 22 November 1731, NLS, 16545/106.

46. Devine, *Scotland's Empire*, p. 269.

47. Some of those have been noticed by John Michael Dixon in his forthcoming study of Cadwallader Colden.

48. Ilay to Milton, ? September 1732, NLS, 16548/112.

49. For a brief account of the relations between agriculture, chemistry and improvement and improvers, see Matthew D. Eddy, *The Language of Mineralogy: John Walker, Chemistry and the Edinburgh Medical School 1750-1800* (Farnham, Surrey; Burlington, Vt., 2008), pp. 110-113. Some of Walker's work was done under the aupices of the Board of Annexed Estates.

50. Walker belonged to the Moderate Party in the Kirk and became Moderator in 1790. About that time, he sought appointment to the new Chair of Agriculture. Earlier he had been one in the botanical network to which the Duke had belonged.

51. Roger L. Emerson, 'Hume and Art: Reflections on a man who could not hear, sing or look' in *Rivista di Storia della Filosofia Special Issue on Hume*, ed. by Emilo Mazza and Emanuele Ronchetti (Milan, 2007); Johanne Wolfgang von Goethe, *Faust*, Part II, Act V, Scene vi.

52. The plate contrasts old and new agricultural methods.

53. Creegan, *Argyll Estate Instructions*, p. xxii.

54. Roger L. Emerson, 'The Scottish Setting of Hume's Political Economy', in *Essays on David Hume's Political Economy*, eds. Margaret Schabas and Carl Wennerlind (New York, 2005), pp. 10-30.

55. Board of Trustee to Argyll, 19 February 1758, NLS, 16698/156.

56. Two such wrights were Andrew and Robert Meikle, Lindsay and Cosh *Inveraray*, p. 360 n.166; Minutes of the Board of Trustees, NRS, NG 1/1/11/81, 116, 183; NG 1/11/12/141.

57. See Sidney G. Checkland, *Scottish Banking: A History; 1695-1973*, pp. 3-52.

58. Eric Richards, 'Agriculture and Animal Husbandry' in *Encyclopedia of the Enlightenment*, 4 vols ed. A. C. Kors, *et al.*, (New York, 2003), I:32-38.

59. Denina was wrong about Hutcheson and Glasgow. Hutcheson, brought to Glasgow by Lord Ilay, was less important to the intellectual history of eighteenth-century Scotland than Denina thought. Many who have believed him have been misled by his account. Glasgow University was not treated better by Argyll than Marischal College or Edinburgh University. Denina was correct about the Duke's patronage and the Enlightenment in Scotland. Carlo Denina, *An Essay on the Progress of Learning Among the Scots...* (London, 1771; Italian edn.1763), pp. 275-277. Denina's book did not appear in a full English translation until 1771 but the flattering parts on Scotland were translated and published in a separate pamphlet and in the *Caledonian Mercury* and the *Scots Magazine*. I thank R. B. Sher for this information.

60. Denina, *An Essay*, p. 277

61. His reference was probably to James Ferguson, the London astronomer and lecturer on

science and mathematics, not Adam Ferguson. In 1763 Adam Ferguson was a professor of natural philosophy who had no reputation outside Edinburgh. He was retired as a joint-professor of mathematics; it was a way to give him a retirement income.

62. Denina, *An Essay*, pp. 279-80.
63. Roger L. Emerson, 'The Organization of Science and its Pursuit in Early Modern Europe' in *Companion to the History of Modern Science*, ed. R.C. Olby, G. N. Cantor, J. R. R. Christie and M. J. S. Hodge (London and New York, 1990), pp. 960-979.
64. This has been well documented by C. C. Gillispie, *Science and Polity in France at the End of the Old Regime* (Princeton, 1980).

.

Bibliography

[Publishers' names have been omitted except in those cases where the work would be otherwise obscure. Dissertations, pamphlets, articles and other short works are not italicized but put in quotation marks.]

I. Manuscripts

ABERDEEN

Town Council Archives
    Council Registers.
    Council Letter Books.
    Council Out Letter Books.

 ISLE OF BUTE: MOUNT STUART HOUSE
    Uncatalogued papers of the 3rd Earl of Bute.
    Uncatalogued papers of James Stuart Mackenzie.
    Uncatalogued papers of John Campbell, 4th Earl of Loudoun.

EDINBURGH

National Records of Scotland
    Abercairny Manuscripts, GD24.
    Board of Trustees Minutes, NG/1/1/2-14.
    Campbell of Barcaldine Manuscripts, GD170.
    Campbell of Stonefield Papers, GD14.
    Clerk of Penicuik Papers, GD18.
    Dalhousie Papers, GD45.
    Dalrymple Papers, GD110.
    Kennedy of Dunure, GD27.
    Lothian Muniments, GD40.
    Mackay Family of Bighouse, GD87.
    Maclaine of Lochbuie, GD174.
    Mar and Kellie Papers, GD124.
    Marchmont Papers, GD158.
    Montrose-Lennox Papers, GD220.
    Morton Mss, GD150.
    Scottish Papers, SP54.
    Seafield Papers, GD248.
    Transcript Copies of Letters from Lord Ilay to the Duke of Newcastle, GD215.

National Library of Scotland: Advocates Manuscripts
    Thomas Kincaid's Diary, Adv Mss. 22.2.10.
    Argyll Papers, Adv. Mss 29.3.5.
    James Anderson Papers, Adv Mss 29.5.1; 29.5.11
    Murray of Stanhope, Adv. Ms 29 [includes Papers of John Spottiswoode].

National Library of Scotland Manuscripts
  Anonymous, A Character of His Grace Archibald Duke of Argyll 1761, 17612/218-22.
  Campbell Papers, 3733-3736.
  [Craigie] Original Letters to Robert Craigie of Glendoick, 3036.
  Culloden Papers, 2521, 2965-8.
  [Davidson], Ramsay Garden Papers, 3417.
  Dunlop Papers, 9252.
  Elliot of Minto Papers, 11004-12.
  Hay of Yester Papers, 7044-7074; 14427.
  David Hume Papers, 23159.
  Melville Papers, 17604.
  Miscellaneous Jacobite Mss, 3142.
  Mure of Caldwell, 4945-5006.
  Robertson-Macdonald Letters, 1777-1788, 3943.
  William Rouet (Ruat) Mss, 4992.
  Spottiswoode Papers, 658, 2933, 2937.
  Saltoun Manuscripts
        Correspondence, 16501-16723;
        Miscellaneous, SB;
        Papers Dealing with The Whim, 17642-51; 17819.

National Library of Scotland Broadside and Pamphlet Collection
  'The Moderate man's Confession' (Leith, c.1739) in Ry.111.c.34 (53)/51.
  'E[dinburg]h s Instructions to their Member' (London, 1739).

Royal Commission on Ancient Monuments, Edinburgh
  National Monuments Record of Scotland: Peeblesshire, Whim, Various Plans of Whim
  House, PBD/286/43, PB/508- 10, A66188CN.

Library of the Royal College of Physicians
  William Cullen, Letters and Cases.
  Papers of Francis Home.

Royal Highland Society
  Transcript Minutes of the Honourable the Improvers in the Knowledge of Agriculture in
  Scotland, APS 4.9632; AS, 1731-36.

Edinburgh City Archive
  Acc 289, Box 13, Bundle 4.
  Board of Trustees: 14 petitions for a Board of Trustees, Bay D, Bundle 6.
  City Muniments, Volume 11, Bay D.
  Papers of the Convention of Royal Burghs
        Minute Books of the Convention of Royal Burghs, SL 30/1/8-12 (1705-1760).
        SL 30, Bundle 224.
        Moses Bundles 234, 242, 244.

Edinburgh University Library
  Papers of David Gregorie, Edinburgh University Library, EUL Dk.1.2. 21 /B/23 -28.

The Royal Bank of Scotland Archives
   General Stock Journals, EQ/10/2 - 3.
   Stock Ledgers No. 1727-1784, EQ 11/2/2/1; EQ/18/1; EQ/ 18/2/1.
   Ledger of the daily transactions of the Royal Bank, 1st January 1728 [to 1750], RB/714/1-8.
   Ledgers 1727-1750, RB/736/9- 10.
   Minute Book of the Court of Directors, RB/12/1 -4[1727- 1744].
   Private Papers of John Campbell [1719-1762] 1st Cashier, RB/1480/0- 1.

GLASGOW

Glasgow University Library
   Murray Manuscripts
         Letters of Principal John Stirling of Glasgow, 650-653.
   Letters to Professor Robert Simson, 660.
   Thomsom/Cullen Papers, Ms. 2255.
   Robert Simpson Correspondence, Ms Gen. 196.
   Stirling Letters, 3 vols, Ms 204 [a copy of the GUL 650-653].
   James Wodrow, Cases Answered by the Society of Students of Divinity under Mr. Ja[mes]
   Wodrow, Ms Gen. 343.

Glasgow University Archives
   Faculty Minutes [those are extensive and listed under variously names], Ms. 27115.

LONDON

Public Record Office
   Scottish Papers, SP54. [Those are listed in the NAS under a separate number series which
   also gives the London call numbers. I have used the latter.]

British Library
   Papers of Henrietta Howard, Add Mss 22625-22629.
   Additional MS 6861/66.

British Museum Library [all on microfilms]
   Book of Presents, CE 30.
   Minutes of Meetings of Trustees Standing Committee 1754-1963, CE 3 Vols I-VI.
   Original Letters and Papers, OP1 Vol I, 1743-1784; CE4.

Coutts Bank
   Typescripts of the Accounts of Archibald Campbell, Earl of Ilay and 3rd Duke of Argyll
   (1713-1762) ['In' and 'Out' books supplied by the Bank].

UNITED STATES OF AMERICA
   Harvard University Library
         A[n annotated] Catalogue of the library of the Honble Samuel Molyneux... (London,
         1730).

II. Unpublished Dissertations

Ph.D.s
Dixon, John, 'Cadwallader Colden and the Rise of Public Dissension: Politics and Science in Pre-Revolutionary New York', University of California, Los Angeles, 2007.
B.F. Jewell, 'Legislation Relating to Scotland after the Forty-Five', University of North Carolina, 1975.
Patrick, Derek John, 'People and Parliament in Scotland 1689-1702', St Andrews University, 2002.
Scokzylas, Anne, 'John Simson and the Growth of Enlightenment in the Church of Scotland', University of Western Ontario, 1996.
Scott, Richard, 'The Politics and Administration of Scotland 1725-1748', Edinburgh University, 1982.
Wehrli, Eric G. J., 'Scottish Politics in the Age of Walpole', Edinburgh University, 1983.

M.A.s.
Roberts, Alonso D., 'St Andrews Mathematics Teaching 1765-1858', St Andrews University, 1970.

III. Periodicals

Scottish
　The Bee, 1794-96 [various issues].
　Caledonian Mercury, 1761 [various issues].
　Edinburgh Evening Courant, 1761 [various issues].
　Scots Magazine, 1737-1761 [various issues].

English
　The Christian Magazine (1767).
　The Freeholder [edited by James Leheny (Oxford, 1979).
　Gentleman's Magazine (various issues, c. 1740-1761).
　Many other English periodicals have been searched using the 17th and 18th Century Burney Collection of Newspapers (Gale Cengage Learning, 2010).

IV. Printed Books and Articles

[Aberdeen] Officers and Graduates of University & King's College Aberdeen, ed. Peter John Anderson (The New Spalding Club, Aberdeen, 1893).
[Adam] William Adam 1689-1748 A Tercentenary Exhibition, ed. James Simpson, National Portrait Gallery, (Edinburgh, 1989);
　John Gifford, William Adam 1689-1748 (Edinburgh, 1989);
　William Adam, Architectural Heritage, 1 (1990, a special issue);
　[See Fleming below].
Adam, Rev. William, Essay on Mr. Hume's Essay on Miracles (London, 1752).
Anderson, R. G. W., J. A. Bennet and W. F. Ryan, eds, Making Instruments Count: Essays on Historical Instruments presented to Gerard L'Estrange Turner (Cambridge, 1993).
Anderson, William, The Scottish Nation; or the Surnames, Families, Literature, Honours, and Biographical History of the People of Scotland, 3 vols (Edinburgh, 1863).

Anonymous:
'A Copy of Three Letters, giving an Account of the total Defeat of the Rebels at Preston in Lancashire' (Edinburgh, 16 November 1715).

'A letter to the Author of the North Britain... with a Striking Character... of the late Duke of Argyll' (London, 1763).

'A Letter from a Gentleman in Fife to his Friends in Edinburgh' (found in NRS, SP 54/9/80).

'A Letter from a P _ _ _ in North-Britain, to the Right Honourable the E. of I _ _ a.', (London 1716).

'A New History of the City of Edinburgh, from the Earliest Periods to the Present Time ...', (4th edn Edinburgh, 1800).

'A Treatise Concerning the manner of Fallowing Ground, Raising of Grass-Seeds and Training of Lint and hemp ...' (Edinburgh, 1724).

'General Heads and Questions Concerning Manufactures and Fisheries in Scotland' (c.1727).

Middlesex, Biographical and Pictorial (London, 1906).

[Argyll, see also entries for Campbell, Inveraray. Royal Commission on Ancient and Historical Monuments of Scotland, Royal Historical Manuscripts Commission Reports.]

The Argyll Papers, ed. Thomas G. Stevenson (Edinburgh, 1834).

Arkell, R. L, Caroline of Ansbach, George the Second's Queen (Oxford, 1939).

[Arnot, See Edinburgh.]

Ault, Norman, New Light on Pope with some additions to his poetry hitherto unknown (London, 1949).

Baker, C. H. Collins and Muriel I. Baker, The Life and Circumstances of James Brydges First Duke of Chandos (Oxford, 1949).

Balfour-Melville, Barbara, The Balfours of Pilrig (Edinburgh, 1907).

[Balmerino] Letters of Lord Balmerino to Henry Maule, ed. Clyve Jones, Scottish History Society Miscellany 12, 1994, pp. 99-168.

Bannerman, Gordon, Merchants and the Military in Eighteenth Century Britain (London, 2008).

[Bartram] The Correspondence of John Bartram 1734-1777, ed. Edmund and Dorothy Smith Berkeley (Gainesville, 1992).

Berkeley, Edmund and Dorothy, The Reverend John Clayton: A Parson with a Scientific Mind (Charlottesville, 1965);

Dr. Alexander Garden of Charles Town (Chapel Hill, 1969);

Dr. John Mitchell: The Man Who Made the Map (Chapel Hill, 1974).

Blackwell, Elizabeth, A Curious Herbal, 2 vols (London, 1737-39).

Boardman, John, Diana Scarisbrick, Claudia Wagmer and Erika Zwierlein-Diehl, The Marlborough Gems: Formerly at Blenheim Palace (Oxford. 2010).

Boney, A. D., The Lost Gardens of Glasgow University (London, 1988).

Boyle, see Orrery.

[Box, See Hume].

Bricke, Margaret S., 'The Pelhams vs. Argyll: A Struggle for the Mastery of Scotland, 1747-1748', Scottish Historical Review, 61 (1982), pp. 157-165.

Brigham, David R, 'The Patronage of Natural History' in Empire s Nature: Mark Catesby's New World Vision, ed. Amy R. W. Meyers and Margaret Beck Pritchard (Chapel Hill and London, 1998), pp. 91-146.

British Book Sale Catalogues 1676-1800: A Union List, compiled and ed. A.N.L. Munby and Lenore Coral (London, 1977).

Brooke, John, King George III (London, 1972).

Brooke, John Hedley, Science and Religion: Some Historical Perspectives (Cambridge, 1991).

Brown, Horatio F., Inglesi e Scozzesi all Universit... dall annon 1618 sino al 1765. Monografie Storiche sullo Studio di Padova (Venezia, 1922).

Brown, Stephen and Warren McDougall, The Edinburgh History of the Book in Scotland, Vol. 2, Enlightenment and Expansion (Edinburgh, 2012).

Browning, Reed, The Duke of Newcastle (New Haven, Conn. and London, 1975).

Brunton, George and David Haig, An Historical Account of the Senators of the College of Justice... [to 1802] (London, 1832).

Bryant, Julius, 'Marble hill' (English Heritage, n.p., n.d.).

Bryden, David, 'James Short and His Telescopes', (Royal Scottish Museum exhibition catalogue, Edinburgh, 1968);
'Scottish Scientific Instrument makers, 1600-1900 '(Royal Scottish Museum booklet, Edinburgh, 1972);
'A Dictionary of Mathematical Instruments' in Making Instruments Count: Essays on Historical Scientific Instruments presented to Gerard L Estrange Turner, ed R. G. W. Anderson, JA Bennet, WF Ryan (London, 1993), pp. 365-382.

Bubb Dodington, The Political Journal of George Bubb Dodington, ed. John Carswell and Lewis Arnold Dralle (Oxford, 1965).

Burton, John Hill, History of Scotland, 8 vols (Edinburgh and London, 1898).

Butt, John, John Anderson's Legacy: The University of Strathclyde and Its Antecedents 1796-1996 (East Linton, 2000).

Cairns, John, 'George Mackenzie, The Faculty of Advocates and the Advocates' Library' in Oratio Inauguralis ... ed John Cairns and A.M. Cain (Edinburgh, 1989), pp. 18-86;
'John Spotswood, Professor of Law: A Preliminary Sketch' in Stair Society, Miscellany 3, ed. W.M. Gordon, (Edinburgh 1992), pp. 131-159;
'Alexander Cunningham's Proposed Edition of the Digest: An Episode in the History of the Dutch Elegant School of Roman Law', Tijschrift voor Rechtsgeschiedenis 69 (2001), pp. 81-117, 307-59;
The Teaching of Law in Eighteenth Century Scotland (forthcoming).

Calamy, Edmund, An Historical Account of My Own Life..., 2 vols (London, 1829).

Cameron, Alexander, Reliquiae Celticae, 2 vols, ed. Alexander MacBain and John Kennedy (Inverness, 1894).

[Campbell], The Clan Campbell Abstracts of Entries relating to Campbell in the Sheriff Court Book of Argyll at Inveraray [and other places], 8 vols, ed. Henry Paton (Edinburgh, 1913).

Campbell of Airds, Alastair, A History of the Clan Campbell, 3 vols (Edinburgh, 2000, 2002, 2004).

Campbell, Archibald, Marquis of Argyll, Instructions to a Son... (1661; republished by the Foulis Press, Glasgow, 1743).

Campbell, Archibald, 3rd Duke of Argyll
'Abstract and Condescendance of His Grace the Duke of Argyll's Titles' (Edinburgh, 1747);
Catalogus Librorum A[rchibald]. Campbell]. D[uke]. A.[rgyll], compiled by Alexander MacBean (Glasgow, 1758);
'The Decreet-Arbitral' of Lord Ilay in Set of the City of Edinburgh: with the Acts of Parliament and Council Relative thereto, ed. John Robertson (Edinburgh, 1783).

Campbell, Colen [or Colin], Vitruvius Britannicus or the British Architect, 3 vols (London, 1715-1725).

Campbell, George, 8th Duke of Argyll, ed. Intimate Letters of the Eighteenth Century, 2 vols (London, n.d.);
Scotland as It Was and Is, ed. George Douglas Campbell, 8th Duke of Argyll, 2 vols, (Edinburgh, 1882).

Campbell, John, 2nd Duke of Argyll, 'A Speech of the Duke of Argyll upon the State of the Nation , April 15 1740' in 'The conduct of His Grace the D_ke of Ar_ _ le for the last four years reviewed...' (London, 1740).

[Campbell, Lady Mary Coke, see Coke].

Campbell, Robert, The Life of the Most Illustrious Prince, John, Duke of Argyll and Greenwich... (London, 1745).

Cannon, Richard, Historical Record of the Thirty-sixth or the Hertford Regiment of Foot ..1701...1852 (London, 1853).

Carlyle, Alexander, The Autobiography of Alexander Carlyle of Inveresk, ed. John Hill Burton, (London and Edinburgh, 1910).

[Carstares] State-Papers and Letters Addressed to William Carstares... edited by Joseph M'Cormick (London and Edinburgh, 1774).

Carswell, John, The South Sea Bubble (London, 1960).

[Catalogus], See Archibald Campbell, 3rd Duke of Argyll].

[Catesby, see Myers and Frick].

Catesby's Birds of Colonial America, ed. Alan Feduccia (Chapel Hill and London, 1985); Mark Catesby's Natural history of America; The Watercolors from the Royal Library, Windsor Castle, ed. Henrietta McBurney (London, 1997).

Chamberlayne, John, Magnae Britanniae Notitia of the Present State of Great Britain... (London, 1723) and 1736; [see Miège].

Chambers, Robert, ed. A Biographical Dictionary of Eminent Scotsmen, 4 vols (Glasgow, 1856).

Checkland, S.G., Scottish Banking: A History 1695-1973 (Glasgow and London, 1975).

[Chesterfield], W. Ernest-Browning, Memoirs of the Life of Philip Dormer Fourth Earl of Chesterfield (revised ed., London, 1906).

Chesterfield to Newcastle, Private Correspondence of Chesterfield and Newcastle 1744-1746, ed. Sir Richard Lodge, Royal Historical Society/The Camden Society, 3rd series, 44, (1930).

[Church of Scotland], The Principal Acts of the General Assembly of the Church of Scotland, 2 vols (Edinburgh, 1721-1766; [Printed yearly in an abridged form and here bound in a unique collection.]

Clarke, T. N., A.D. Morrison-Low and A.D.C. Simpson, 'James Short the Optic', in Brass & Glass (National Museums of Scotland, catalogue, 1989), pp. 1-6.

[Clavering] The Correspondence of James Clavering, ed. H. T. Dickinson, Surtees Society, 178 (1968); [See Cowper].

[Clerk, Sir John of Penicuik], 'Scottish Law Students in Leiden at the End of the Seventeenth Century: The Correspondence of John Clerk, 1694-1697', eds. Kees Van Strien and Margreet Ahsmann, LIAS 19 (Leiden, 1992), pp.271-330, LIAS 20 (1993), pp. 1-.65; Memoirs of the Life of Sir John Clerk of Penicuik ..., ed. John M. Gray, Scottish History Society, 1st Series, 13, (1892); History of the Union of Scotland and England, ed. Douglas Duncan, Scottish History Society, 5th Series, 6 (1993); 'Sir John Clerk s Observations on the present circumstances of Scotland, 1730', ed. T. C. Smout, Scottish History Society Miscellany, 4th Series, 2 (1965); 'The Country Seat', ed. William Johnston, Officina Educational Publications [Compact disk] (Livingston, Scotland, 2003).

Clow, Archibald and Nan, The Chemical Revolution (London, 1952; reprinted, Freeport, N.Y., 1970).

[Cobbett, William], The Parliamentary History of England from the Earliest Period, 1066 to the Year 1803, compiled by William Cobbett (London, 1810 -1813), vols VI-XV (on a Microfilm produced by Fairview Park: Pergamon Press, Inc, n.d.).

[Cochrane] The Cochrane Correspondence Regarding the Affairs of Glasgow 1745-46, ed. James Smith (Maitland Club, Glasgow, 1836).

[Coke] The Letters and Journals of Lady Mary [Campbell] Coke, 4 vols, ed. [Lady Louisa Stewart] and J. H. Horne (London, 1889-96; Facsimile, London, 1970).

[Collinson, Peter], "Forget not Mee & My Garden... Selected Letters 1725- 1768 of Peter Collinson, FRS, ed. Alan W. Armstrong (American Philosophical Society, Philadelphia, 2002).

The Coltness Collections, ed. James Dennistoun, Maitland Club 58, (Edinburgh, 1842).

Coomer, Duncan, English Divines under the Early Hanoverians (London, 1946).

Connor, R. D. and Allan Simpson, Weights and Measures in Scotland: A European Perspective, ed. by Alison Morrison-Low, (Edinburgh, 2005).

Constantin, L.-A., Manuels-Roret, Bibliotheconomie ou Nouveau Manuel Complet pour L Arrangement, La Conservation et L'Administration des Bibliotheques (Paris, 1841).

Cosh, Mary, 'Clockmaker Extraordinary: The Career of Alexander Cumming', Country Life, 12 June 1969, pp.1528-35;
' Lord Ilay's Eccentric Building Schemes', Country Life, 20 July 1972, pp. 142-145.

Coutts, James, A History of the University of Glasgow (Glasgow, 1909).

[Cowper] Diary of Mary [Clavering], Countess Cowper.... 1714-1720, ed. ? (London, 1864).

Coxe, William, Memoirs of the Life and Administration of Sir Robert Walpole, Earl of Orford, 3 vols (London, 1800);
Memoirs of the Administration of the Right Honourable Henry Pelham..., 2 vols (London, 1829; New York, 1979).

Craig, William, History of the Royal College of Physicians, Edinburgh (Edinburgh, 1976).

Cregeen, Eric R. Argyll Estate Instructions, Scottish History Society, 4th Series, 1 (1964);
'The Tacksmen and their Successors: A Study of Tenurial Reorganization in Mull and Morvern and Tiree in the Early Eighteenth Century', Scottish Studies, 13, (1969), pp. 93-144;
'Changing Role of the House of Argyll in the Scottish Highlands', in Scotland in The Age of Improvement, ed. N.T. Phillipson and Rosalind Mitchison, (Edinburgh, 1970), pp. 5-23.

Cregeen, Eric R., and Angus Martin, Kintyre Instructions: The 5th Duke of Argyll's Instructions to his Kintyre Chamberlain, 1785-1805 (Glasgow, 2011).

Croft Dickinson, W. and Gordon Donaldson, A Source Book of Scottish History, vol 3, (Edinburgh, 1954).

Cruickshanks, Eveline, Political Untouchables, (New York, 1979).
editor, Ideology and Conspiracy: Aspects of Jacobitism 1689-1759 (Edinburgh, 1982).

[Cullen] William Cullen and the Eighteenth Century Medical World, ed. Andrew Doig et. al (Edinburgh, 1993).

[Culloden, See Forbes]

Cunningham, John, The Church History of Scotland from the Commencement of the Christian Era to the Present Century, 2 vols (Edinburgh, 1859).

Dalrymple, James, 1st Viscount Stair, The Institutions of the Law of Scotland, ed. David M. Walker (Edinburgh, 1981).

Denina, Carlo, An Essay on the Revolutions in Literature, trans. John Murdoch (London, 1771; Italian ed. 1763) [The Scottish sections can be found in the Scottish Historical Review, 7 (1910)].

Devine, T. M., Scotland's Empire 1600-1815 (London, 2003).

Devine, T. M. and Gordon Jackson, Glasgow, 2 vols, I:Beginnings to 1830 (Manchester, 1995).

Dickson, Patricia, Red John of the Battles: John Second Duke of Argyll and First Duke of Greenwich 1680-1743 (London, 1973).

Donovan, Arthur, Philosophical Chemistry in the Scottish Enlightenment (Edinburgh, 1975).

Douglas, Sir Robert, The Peerage of Scotland, containing An Historical & Genealogical Account of the Nobility of that Kingdom, 2 vols (2nd edn revised & corrected with a continuation by J.P. Wood; Edinburgh, 1813).

Drummond, Andrew L. and James Bulloch, The Scottish Church 1688-1843 (Edinburgh, 1973).

Duffy, Christopher, The '45 (London, 2003).

Dunlop, William, A Preface to an Addition of the Westminster Confession.... (Edinburgh and London, 1720).

Durie, Alastair J., The British Linen Company, 1745-1775, Scottish History Society, 5th Series, 9 (1996).

Eddy, Matthew, The Language of Mineralogy: John Walker, Chemistry and the Edinburgh Medical School 1750-1800 (London, 2008).

[Edinburgh and the University]

Extracts from the Records of the Burgh of Edinburgh 1710-1718, ed. Helen Armet, (London, 1967);

The Lord Provosts of Edinburgh 1296-1932, compiled by Sir Thomas Whitson, (Edinburgh, 1932);

Set of the City of Edinburgh with the Acts of the Parliament and Council Relative thereto (Edinburgh, 1783);

Arnot, Hugo, History of Edinburgh (Edinburgh and London, 1779);

Charters, Statutes, and Acts of the Town Council and the [University] Senatus 1583-1858, ed. Alexander Morgan and Robert Kerr Hannay, (Edinburgh and London, 1937);

Andrew G. Fraser, The Building of the Old College: Adam, Playfair & The University of Edinburgh (Edinburgh, 1989).

[Egmont] Leicester House Politics 1750-60, From the Papers of John [Wyndham], Second Earl of Egmont, ed. Aubrey N. Newman, Camden Miscellany, 4th series, (1969), 7, pp. 55-228.

Emerson, Roger L., 'The Philosophical Society of Edinburgh 1737-1747', British Journal of the History of Science, 12 (1979), pp. 154-191;

'The Philosophical Society of Edinburgh 1748-1768', British Journal of the History of Science, 14 (1981), pp. 133-176;

'The Edinburgh Society for the Importation of Foreign seeds and Plants, 1764-1773', Eighteenth-Century Life, VII, n.s. (1982), pp. 73-95;

'Natural philosophy and the problem of the Scottish Enlightenment' , Studies on Voltaire and the Eighteenth Century, 242 (1986), pp. 243-291;

'Sir Robert Sibbald, Kt., The Royal Society of Scotland and the Origins of the Scottish Enlightenment, Annals of Science, 45 (1988), pp. 41-72;

'The Organization of Science and its Pursuit in Early Modern Europe' in Companion to the History of Modern Science, ed. R. C. Olby, G. N. Cantor, J. R.R. Christie and M.J.S. Hodge (London and New York, 1990), pp. 960-979;

Professors, Patronage and Politics: the Scottish Universities in the Eighteenth Century (Aberdeen, 1991);

'Medical men, politicians and the medical schools at Glasgow and Edinburgh 1685-1803' in William Cullen and the Eighteenth Century Medical World, ed. Andrew Doig, Joan P.S. Ferguson, Iain Milne, Reginald Passmore (Edinburgh, 1993);

'Catalogus Librorum A.C.D.A.: the library of the 3rd Duke of Argyll in The Culture of the Book in the Scottish Enlightenment, ed. Philip Oldfield (Thomas Fisher Rare Book Library, University of Toronto, 2000), pp. 12-39;

'The Scientific Interests of Archibald Campbell, 1st Earl of Ilay and 3rd Duke of Argyll', Annals of Science, 59 (2002), pp. 21-56;

'The Founding of the Edinburgh Medical School: The Real Story', Journal of the History of Medicine and Allied Sciences, 59 (2004), pp. 183-218;

'The Scottish Setting of Hume's Political Economy' in Essays on David Hume's Political Economy, eds Margaret Schabas and Carl Wennerlind (New York, 2005), pp. 1-32;

Academic Patronage in the Scottish Enlightenment (Edinburgh, 2008);

Essays on David Hume, Medical men and the Scottish Enlightenment, (Farnham, Surrey and Burlington, Vt., 2009).

Emerson, Roger L. and Paul B. Wood, 'Science and Enlightenment in Glasgow,1690-1802' in Science and Medicine in the Scottish Enlightenment, ed. Charles W. J. Withers and Paul Wood (East Linton, 2002), pp. 79-142.

Encyclopaedia Britannica, ed. William Smellie, 3 vols (Edinburgh, 1771, reprinted in
    facsimile, Chicago, c.1970).
Encyclopedia of Library and Information Science, 64 vols (New York, 1968-1995).
[Ernest-Browning, see Chesterfield].
Erskine, James, The Fatal Consequences of Ministerial Influence ....With an Appendix...
    (London, 1736; published anonymously);
    Extracts from the Diary of a Senator of the College of Justice [James Erskine, Lord
    Grange] M.DCC.XVII-- M.DCC.XVII (Edinburgh, 1843);
    'Letters of Lord Grange' in The Miscellany of the Spalding Club, 3 (Aberdeen, 1846).
Essays and Observations Physical and Literary, eds. Alexander Monro and David Hume,Vol.
    II (Edinburgh, 1766).
[Fairfull-Smith, George, See Foulis].
Fawcett, Arthur, The Cambuslang Revival: The Scottish Evangelical Revival of the
    Eighteenth Century (Edinburgh and Carlisle, Pa., 1996; 1st printing 1971).
Ferguson, William, Scotland:1689 to the Present (Edinburgh and London, 1968).
Fergusson, Sir James of Kilkerran, Argyll in the Forty-Five (London, 1951);
    'The Appin Murder Case' in Fergusson's The White Hind (London, 1963; reprinted
    Glasgow, 2004), pp. 133-79.
    The Sixteen Peers of Scotland: An Account of the Elections of the Representative Peers of
    Scotland 1707-1959 (Oxford, 1960)
Fleming, John, Robert Adam and his Circle (Cambridge, Mass., 1962).
Foord, Archibald S., His Majesty s Opposition 1714-1830 (Oxford, 1964).
Forbes, Bishop Robert, compiler of The Lyon in Mourning..., ed. Henry Paton, 3 vols
    (Edinburgh, 1975; 1st ed. 1896).
[Forbes of Culloden], Culloden Papers, no editor, (London, 1815);
    More Culloden Papers, ed. Duncan Warrand, 5 vols (Inverness, 1923-1930).
[Foulis, Press and Academy]
    Fairfull-Smith, George, 'The Foulis Press and The Foulis Academy', (The Glasgow Art
    Index and Friends of Glasgow University Library, Glasgow, 2001);
    Gaskell, Philip, A Bibliography of the Foulis Press (London, 1964);
    Johnston W.T., A Bibliography of the Foulis Press with Corrections (Officina Compact
    Disk, 2002).
Foust, Clifford M., Rhubarb The Wondrous Drug (Princeton, 1992).
Fox-Strangways, Giles, 6th Earl of Ilchester, Henry Fox, First Lord Holland His Family and
    Relations, 2 vols (London, 1920);
    [See Hervey].
[Fraser, Andrew; see Edinburgh.]
[Fraser, Simon, 12th Baron Lovat] Trial of Simon, Lord Lovat of the '45, ed. David N. Mackay
    (Edinburgh and Glasgow, 1911).
Frick,George Frederick and Raymond Phineas Stearns, [Mark Catesby] The Colonial
    Audabon, (Urbana, 1961).
Friedman, T. F., James Gibbs, (New Haven, Conn., 1984).
Fry, Michael, The Union: England, Scotland and the Treaty of 1707 (Edinburgh, 1707).
Garnier, P. J., Systema bibliotheca collegii parisiensis (Society of Jesus, Paris, 1678).
Gavine, David, 'James Stewart Mackenzie (1719-1800) and the Bute MSS', Journal of the
    History of Astronomy 5 (1974), pp. 208-214.
Gibson, A.J.S. and T.C. Smout, Prices, Food and Wages in Scotland 1550-1780 (Cambridge,
    1995).
Gillispie, Charles C., Science and Polity in France at the End of the Old Regime (Princeton, 1980).
[Gifford, John, see William Adam.]
Gifford, John, Colin McWilliam, David Walker and Christopher Wilson, Edinburgh in The
    Buildings of Scotland series (London, 1984).

[Glasgow], Extracts from the Records of the Burgh of Glasgow....vols 5 and 6 (1708-1760) (Printed for the Corporation, Glasgow, 1911).

[Glasgow Trades], The Records of the Trades House of Glasgow A.D. 1713-1777, ed. Harry Lumsden (Glasgow, 1934).

[Glasgow University], Munimenta alme universitatis glasguensis: Records of the University of Glasgow from its Foundation till 1724, 4 vols ed. Cosmo Innes, The Maitland Club, (Glasgow, 1854);
[See, J. D. Mackie.]

Glover, Katharine, 'Polite London Children: Educating the Daughters of the Scottish Elite in Mid-Eighteenth-Century London' in Scots in London in the Eighteen Century, ed. Stana Nenadic (Lewisburg, 2010), pp. 253-271.

Glover, Richard, Memoirs of A Celebrated Literary and Political Character from the Resignation of Sir Robert Walpole in 1742 to the Establishment of Lord Chatham's Second Administration in 1757 (London, 1813).

Golinski, Jan, Science as Public Culture: Chemistry and Enlightenment in Britain, 1760-1820 (Cambridge, 1992).

Grabiner, Judith; See Maclaurin.

Graeme, William, 'An Essay on the Method of Acquiring Knowledge in Physic' (London, 1729).

Graham, Michael, The Blasphemies of Thomas Aikenhead (Edinburgh, 2008).

Grange, Lord, See James Erskine

The Grenville Papers: Being the Correspondence of Richard Grenville, Earl Temple, K.G. and the Right Hon: George Grenville, their Friends and Contemporaries, 4 vols, ed. William James Smith (London, 1852; New York, 1970).

Gross, Hanns, Rome in the Age of the Enlightenment (Cambridge, 1990).

Haggarty, George and Sheila Forbes, 'Scotland: Lind and A-Marked porcelain', The Northern Ceramic Society Journal, 20 (2003-4), 1-10.

Halsband, Robert, The Life of Lady Mary Wortley Montagu (London, 1961; 1st ed, Oxford, 1956).

Halyburton, Thomas, Memoirs of the Life of Mr. Thomas Halyburton (Edinburgh, 1714).

'Ham House Surrey', (no ed. given; National Trust, 1995).

Hamilton, Henry, The Industrial Revolution in Scotland (New York, 1966; 1st ed. 1932);
An Economic History of Scotland in the Eighteenth Century (Oxford, 1963).

Harris, Joseph, 'The Description of the Use of the Globes, and the Orrery...' (10th edn., London, 1768).

Harvey, John, 'A Scottish Botanist in London in 1766', Garden History, 9 (1981), pp. 40-74.

Hatton, Ragnhild, George I Elector and King (Cambridge, Mass., 1978).

Healey, Edna, Coutts & Co. 1692-1992 The Portrait of a Private Bank (London, Sydney, Auckland, 1992).

Heilbron, J, L., Electricity in the 17th and 18th Centuries: A Study in early Modern Physics (Mineola, NY, 1999).

Henderson, Andrew, The Life of John Earl of Stair...(London, c.1748);
'Considerations on the Question, Relating to the Scots Militia... with a faithful Character of Archibald late Duke of Argyll' (2nd edn. London, 1761).

Henrey, Blanche, British Botanical and Horticultural Literature before 1800, 3 vols (London, New York and Toronto, 1975).

Hervey, John, Baron Ickworth, Memoirs of the Reign of of George the Second from His Accession to the Death of Queen Caroline, ed. John Wilson Croker, 3 vols (New York, 1884);
Some Materials Towards Memoirs of the Reign of King George II, ed. Romney Sedgwick (London, 1931);
Lord Hervey's Memoirs, ed. Romney Sedgwick (London, 1952);

Lord Hervey and His Friends, 1726-38, ed. Giles Fox-Strangways, 6th Earl of Ilchester (London, 1950).

Hirschmann, A. O., The Passions and the Interests (New York, 1977).

Historical Manuscripts Commission Reports [HMCR]
Fourth Report of the Royal Commission on Historical Manuscripts, Part I. Report and Appendix... 'The manuscripts of His Grace the Duke of Argyll, K.T.', ed. William Fraser (London, 1874);
HMCRReport 5, Bute MSS (London, 1876);
HMCR on the Manuscripts of the late Reginald Rawdon Hastings, Esq., ed. Francis Bickley (London, 1934), Vol. 1-5;
HMCR on the Muniments of the Duke of Montrose and other Scottish Papers (London, 1872);
HMCR on the Manuscripts of Lord Polwarth, ed. Henry Paton (London, 1911);
HMCR on the Manuscripts of His Grace the Duke of Portland (London, 1891).

History of Parliament: The House of Commons [HPHC]
History of Parliament: The House of Commons 1690-1715, 6 vols, ed. D. W. Hayton (Cambridge, 2002);
History of Parliament: The House of Commons 1715-1754, 2 vols, ed. Romney Sedgwick (New York, 1970);
History of Parliament: The House of Commons 1754-1790, 3 vols, ed. Sir Lewis Namier and John Brooke (London, 1964).

History of Parliament: House of Lords
Journals of the House of Lords 1707-1761, vols 18-30 (London, 1709-1763);
House of Lords Manuscripts, New Series 1712-1714, vol 9, ed. M.F. Bond, Historical Manuscripts Commission, (London, 1949);
[House of Lords, Debates]: See Cobbett and Parliamentary Debates.
House of Lords Sessional Papers, ed. F. William Torrington (Dobbs Ferry, N.Y., 1978) Vols 1-8, Sessions 1714-1760;
Turberville, A. S, The House of Lords in the XVIIIth Century (Oxford, 1927).

Holbrook, Mary, W.G. R. Anderson and David Bryden, eds., Science Preserved (London, 1992).

Holcombe, Lee, Ancient Animosity: The Appin Murder and the End of Scottish Rebellion (Bloomington, Indiania, 2004).

Holloway, James, Patrons and Painters: Art in Scotland 1650-1760 (Scottish National Portrait Gallery, Edinburgh, 1989);
'William Aikman 1682-1731', (Scottish Masters, Scottish National Galleries, 1988).

Holmes, Geoffrey, The Trial of Doctor Sacheverell (London, 1973).

Holmes, Geoffrey and Clyve Jones, The London Diaries of William Nicolson, Bishop of Carlisle 1702-1718 (Oxford, 1985).

Home, John, Douglas: A Tragedy - with contemporary commentaries, edited and introduced by Ralph McLean (Glasgow, 2010)

[The Honourable the Improvers of Knowledge of Agriculture of Scotland], 'RESOLVE of the Honourable Society...' (Edinburgh, 1725).

Hopkins, Paul, Glencoe and the End of the Highland War (Edinburgh, 1986).

Howard, Henrietta Hobart, Countess of Suffolk, 1688(?)-1767, Letters to and from Henrietta, Countess of Suffolk and her Second Husband, The Hon. George Berkeley, From 1712 to 1767, ed. John Wilson Croker (London, England, 1824).

Hume, David, The Letters of David Hume, 2 vols, ed. J.Y.T. Greig (Oxford 1969; 1st ed. 1932);
Box, Mark, David Harvey and Michael Silverthorne, eds., 'A Diplomatic Transcription of Hume's volunteer pamphlet for Archibald Stewart: Political Whigs, Religious Whigs, and Jacobites', Hume Studies, 29 (2003), pp. 223-266.

Hunter, Michael, 'Aikenhead the Atheist: The Context and Consequences of Articulate Irreligion in the Late Seventeenth Century' in Atheism from the Reformation to the Enlightenment, ed. Hunter and David Wootton (Oxford, 1992), pp. 221-254.

Hussey, Christopher, English Gardens and Landscapes 1700-1750 (New York, 1967).

Ilchester, 6th Earl of, See, Fox-Strangways,

Inveraray
    Inveraray Papers, ed. Duncan C. MacTavish (Oban, 1939);
    The Burgesses of Inveraray 1665-1963, ed. Elizabeth A Beaton and Sheila MacIntyre, Edinburgh, Scottish Record Society, New Series, 14, (1990).

Jackson, Gordon, Glasgow in Transition in Glasgow, 2 vols, eds T. M. Devine and Gordon Jackson, (Manchester and New York, 1995), I:82-83.

Jacquin, Nicolai Josephi, Selectarum Stirpium Americanarum Historia, introduction by Frans A. Stafleu (New York, 1971).

Jarvis, Rupert C., Collected Papers on the Jacobite Risings, 2 vols (Manchester and New York, 1971).

Justice, James, The Scots Gardener's Director (Edinburgh, 1754).

Kalm, Pehr, Kalm s Account of his Visit to England..., Joseph Lucas, trans., (New York, 1892).

Kaufmann, Emil, Architecture in the Age of Reason (New York, 1955).

Kelch, Ray A., Newcastle A Duke Without Money: Thomas Pelham-Holles 1698-1768 (Berkeley and Los Angeles, 1974).

Kendrick, T.D., The Lisbon Earthquake (Philadelphia and New York, 1957).

Kidd, Colin, 'Scotland's invisible Enlightenment: Subscription and heterodoxy in the eighteenth-century Kirk', Records of the Scottish Church History Society, 30 (2000), pp. 28-58.

[Kincaid, Thomas], 'An Edinburgh Diary', ed. Henry Meikle, Book of the Old Edinburgh Club 27 (1949), pp. 111-154.

Koerner, Lisbet, Linnaeus: Nature and Nation (Cambridge, Mass.,1999).

Kors, Alan Charles, Atheism in France 1650-1729, 2 vols., [only volume I has been published] (Princeton, 1990).

Lachman, David C., The Marrow Controversy (Edinburgh, 1988).

Laird, Mark, The Flowering of the Landscape Garden English Pleasure Grounds 1720-1800 (Philadelphia, 1999).

Law, John, Money and Trade Considered with a Proposal for supplying the Nation with Money (Edinburgh, 1705);
    John Law's Essay On A Land Bank, ed. Antoin E. Murphy (Dublin, n.d.).

Leneman, Leah, Living in Atholl 1685-1785 (Edinburgh, 1986).

Lenman, Bruce, The Jacobite Risings in Britain 1689-1746 (London, 1980).

Le Rougetel, 'The Chelsea Gardener: Philip Miller 1691-1771' (Natural History Museum Publications, London, 1990);
    'Philip Miller/John Bartram: Botanical Exchange', Garden History, 14 (1986), pp. 32-49.

Letwin, Robin Shirley, The Pursuit of Certainty ... (Cambridge, 1965; Indianapolis, 1998).

Lin, Yu, 'The Importance of the Chinese Connection: The Origins of the English Garden', Eighteenth-Century Life, 27 (2003), pp. 70-98;
    'Castell's Pliny: Rewriting the Past for the Present', Eighteenth-Century Studies, 43 (2010), pp. 243-57.

Lindsay, Ian G. and Mary Cosh, Inveraray and the Dukes of Argyll (Edinburgh, 1973).

[Lockhart] Letters of George Lockhart of Carnwarth 1698-1732, ed. Daniel Szechi, Scottish History Society, 5th Series, 2 (1989);
    Memoirs of the Affairs of Scotland, (Edinburgh, 1714);
    The Lockhart Papers, 2 vols, ed. Anthony Aufrere (London, 1817).

[The Lyon in Mourning, see Forbes].

McGeachy, Robert A. A., Argyll 1730-1850: Commerce, Community and Culture (Edinburgh, 2005).

McInnes, Angus, Robert Harley Puritan Politician (London, 1970).

Mackintosh, William of Borlum, 'An Essay on the Husbandry of Scotland with a proposal for the further improvement of it' (Edinburgh, 1732).

McIntosh, John R., Church and Theology in Enlightenment Scotland: The Popular Party, 1740-1800, Scottish Historical Review, Monograph No.5 (East Linton, 1998).

Mack, Maynard, Alexander Pope: A Life (New Haven, Conn., and London, 1985).

Mackay, David N., The Trial of James Stewart (The Appin Murder) in Notable Scottish Trials (London, 1908);
   The Trial of Lord Lovat of the '45 (Edinburgh and London, 1911).

Mackenzie, Henry, The Anecdotes and Egotisms of Henry Mackenzie 1745-1831, ed. Harold William Thompson (London and Oxford, 1927).

Mackie, J.D., The University of Glasgow 1451 to 1951 (Glasgow, 1954);
   The Short History of Scotland (Edinburgh and London, 1962).

Mackillop, Andrew,"More Fruitful than the Soil": Army, Empire and the Scottish Highlands 1715-1815 (East Linton, 2000).

[Maclaurin,] The Collected Letters of Colin Maclaurin, ed. Stella Mills (Nantwich, 1982);
   An Account of Sir Isaac Newton's Philosophical Discoveries, facisimile of the 1st edn, ed. L. L. Laudan (New York and London, 1968; 1st ed. London, 1748);
   Grabiner, Judith, ' "Some Disputes of Consequence": Maclaurin Among the Molasses Barrels', Social Studies of Science, 28 (1998), pp. 139-168;
   'Maclaurin and Newton' in Science and Medicine in the Scottish Enlightenment, eds. Charles Withers and Paul. B. Wood,(East Linton, 2002).

McLeod, W. R. and V. B. McLeod, Anglo Scottish Tracts 1701-1714: A Descriptive Checklist (Lawrence , Kansas, 1979).

[Daniel MacQueen] Letters on Mr. Hume s History of Great Britain (Edinburgh, 1756.) Inveraray Castle (Derby, 1982).

Mactaggart, Col. Charles, 'The Limecraig Duchess'. Kintyre Antiquarian & Natural History Society Magazine, WebEdition, 13 January 1998:

Malcolm, Charles A., The History of the British Linen Bank (Edinburgh, 1950).

Manning, Roger B., An Apprenticeship in Arms (Oxford, 2006).

Manuel, Frank E., The Eighteenth Century Confronts the God, (Cambridge, 1959);
   Isaac Newton Historian, (Cambridge, Mass., 1963);
   The Changing of the Gods, (Hanover, N.H. and London, 1983).

The Marlborough-Godolphin Correspondence, 3 vols, ed. Henry L. Snyder, (Oxford, 1975).

Martin, Peter, Pursuing Innocent Pleasures, The Gardening World of Alexander Pope (Hampden, Conn.,1984).

Massue, Melville Henry, Marquis de Ruvigny & Raineval, The Jacobite Peerage... compiled and annotated with an introduction by Roger Arat (facsimile edn, (London, 1974; 1st ed. 1904).

Maxwell, Robert, Select Transactions of the Honourable the Society of the Improvers of the Agriculture in Scotland (Edinburgh, 1743; reprinted Glasgow, 2003).

Melville, Lewis, The South Sea Bubble (London 1921).

Meyers, Amy R. W. and Margaret Beck Pritchard, eds. Empire's Nature: Mark Catesby's New World Vision (Chapel Hill, 1998);
   'Introduction: Toward an Understanding of Catesby' in Meyers and Pritchard, Empire's Nature, pp. 1-33.

Miège, Guy, The Present State of Great Britain and Ireland... (3rd edn., London, 1715);
   Ibid., compiled by Mr. Bolton, (10th edn, London, 1745).

Minay, Priscilla, 'James Justice (1698-1763): Eighteenth-century Scots Horticulturalist and Botanist', Garden History (1974), pp.51-74.

Mitchell, John, 'A Letter from John Mitchell to Caddwallader Colden' [25 March 1749], ed. Thedore Hornberger, Huntington Library Quarterly 10 (1947). pp. 411-417;

The Contest in America between Great Britain and France with Its Consequences and Importance... (London, 1757).

Mitchison, Rosalind, A History of Scotland (London, 1970; 2nd edn, London, 1982)
'Elizabeth Murray, Duchess of Lauderdale' in ODNB, 39: 892-93.

[Molyneux], A Catalogue of the Library of the Honable Samuel Molyneux... (London, 1730).

[Montagu], The Complete Letters of Lady Mary Wortley Montagu, ed. Robert Halsband, 3 vols (Oxford, 1965-1967);
The Selected letters of Lady Mary Wortley Montagu, ed. Robert Halsband (London, 1970).

Munby, A.N.L. and Lenore Coral, compilers and eds, British Book Sale Catalogues 1676-1800: A Union List (London, 1977).

Munro, Neil, History of the Royal Bank of Scotland (Edinburgh, 1928; reprinted Glasgow, 2011).

Murdoch, Alexander, The People Above: Politics and Administration of Mid-Eighteenth-Century Scotland (Edinburgh, 1980);
'Management or Semi-Independence? The Government of Scotland from 1707-1832', (unpublished paper given to the Association for Scottish Historical Studies, 1996;
'Archibald Campbell, 1st Duke of Argyll', ODNB, 9:725;
'John Campbell, 2nd Duke of Argyll', ODNB 9 :814-18.

[Murdoch, Patrick] 'An Account of the Life and Writings of the Author' in An Account of Sir Isaac Newton s Philosophical Discoveries... by Colin Maclaurin, ed. Patrick Murdoch (London, 1748; New York and London, 1968).

Murphy, Antoin, John Law: Economic Theorist and Policy-Maker (Oxford, 1997); see Law.

Musson, A. E. and Eric Robinson, Science and Technology in the Industrial Revolution, (Manchester, 1969).

Namier, Sir Lewis, The Structure of Politics at the Accession of George III (2nd edn, London, 1961);
England in the Age of the American Revolution (London, 1963).

Naudé, Gabriel, Advice on Establishing a Library, trans. Archer Taylor (Berkeley and Los Angeles, 1950).

Neal, Larry, ' "For God's Sake, Remit me" : The Adventures of George Middleton, John Law's London Goldsmith-Banker, 1712-1729', Business and Economic History, 23 (1994) pp. 27-60;
' "I am not master of events", John Law's Bargains with Lord Londonderry, 1717-1729', unpublished seminar paper, University of California at Riverside, 17 November 2008.

Nenadic, Stana, 'The enlightenment in Scotland and the popular passion for portraits', British Journal of Eighteenth-Century Studies, 21 (1998), pp. 175-192;
ed. Scots in London in the Eighteenth Century, (Lewisburg, Pa., 2010).

Newman, Aubrey N. 'Leicester House Politics 1750-1760 From the Papers of John [Percival], Second Earl of Egmont', Camden Society Miscellany 23, 4th Series, 7 (1969), pp. 85-228.

Newman, Harold, Illustrated Dictionary of Silver (London, 1981).

Nickson, M.A.E, 'Books and Manuscripts', in Sir Hans Sloane: Collector, Scientist, Antiquary, ed. Arthur MacGregor (London, 1994), pp. 263-294.

Nimmo, Ian, Walking with Murder on the Kidnapped Trail (Edinburgh, 2005).

O'Malley, Therese, 'Mark Catesby and the Culture of Gardens' in Meyers and Pritchard, Empire's Nature, pp. 147-183.

Omand, Donald, ed., The Argyll Book (Edinburgh, 2004).

[Orrery], The Orrery Papers ed. by [Emily de Burgh Boyle] The Countess of Cork and Orrery (London, 1903).

[Oswald, James] Memorial of the Public Life and Character of the Right Hon. James Oswald of Dunniker, no ed. (Edinburgh, 1825).

Owen, J.B., The Rise of the Pelhams (New York and London, 1971; 1st ed. 1951).

Oxford Dictionary of National Biography: From the Earliest Times to the Year 2000, 60 vols., eds H. C. G. Matthew and Brian Harrison (Oxford, 2004).

Parliamentary Debates, ed. John Torbuck, vols 6-17 (1736-1741) [some volumes were
 printed in London, some in Dublin, but the places are not always noted,]; [A Collection
 of Parliamentary Debates in England ... (1666-1803), compiled by John Torbuck *et al.* 20
 vols (Dublin or London, 1743-1774].

[Paterson] The Writings of William Paterson..., 3 vols, ed. Saxe Bannister (London 1859;
 reprinted New York, 1968).

Peters, B. J., 'Coutts & Co.: a Bank of Information', Scottish Archives 3 (1997), pp. 44-48.

Phillips, Hugh, The Thames About 1750 (London, 1951).

Phillipson, Nicholas, 'The Making of an Enlightened University', pp. 51-101 in The University
 of Edinburgh: An Illustrated History, eds. Robert Anderson, Michael Lynch, Nicholas
 Phillipson (Edinburgh, 2003);
 Adam Smith: An Enlightened Life (London, 2010).

Phillipson, N. T. and Rosalind Mitchison, eds, Scotland in the Age of Improvement,
 (Edinburgh, 1970).

Plumb, J. H, Sir Robert Walpole The King s Minister (London, 1960);
 The Growth of Political Stability in England 1675-1725 (London, 1967).

[Pope] Correspondence of Alexander Pope, 4 vols, ed. George Sherburn (Oxford, 1956);
 The Poems of Alexander Pope, ed. John Butt, (New Haven, Conn., 1963);
 A Window in the Bosom: The Letters of Alexander Pope, ed. James Anderson Winn,
 (Hamdem, Conn., 1977).

Potter, Paul, ' "Taste Sets the Price:" Mead, Askew, and the Birth of Bibliomania in
 Eighteenth-Century England', Canadian Bulletin of Medical History, 12 (1995), pp. 241-257.

Pye, Henrietta, A Short Account of the Principal Seats and Gardens in and about Kew
 (London, c.1767).

[Ramsay] The Works of Allan Ramsay, 6 vols, eds, Alexander M. Kinghorn, *et al*, Scottish
 Text Society (Edinburgh, 1945-1974).

Ramsay, John, Scotland and Scotsmen in the Eighteenth Century, 2 vols, ed. Alexander
 Allardyce (Edinburgh and London, 1888);
 Letters of John Ramsay of Ochtertyre 1799-1812, ed. Barbara L.H. Horn, Scottish
 Historical Society, 4th Series, 3, (Edinburgh, 1966);
 'John Ramsay' by Laurence A. B. Whiteley, ODNB, 14:626-27.

Real, Herman J, 'Two Swift Autographs Rediscovered', Swift Studies 11 (1996), pp. 5-15.

Realey, Charles B., Early Opposition to Walpole, in Humanistic Studies, 6, Nos. 2 and 3,
 (Lawrence, Kansas, 1931).

Reveal, J.L. and J.S. Pringle, 'Taxonomic botany and floristics', in Flora of North America
 North of Mexico, eds Flora of North America Editorial Committee (Oxford, 1993).

Reid, John, The Scots Gard'ner, a facsimile edited and introduced by Annette Hope
 (Edinburgh, 1988).

[Richmond, Duke of] The Correspondence of the Dukes of Richmond and Newcastle 1724-
 1750, ed. Timothy J. McCann, Sussex Record Society, 73 (1982-83).

Riker, Thad W., Henry Fox First Lord Holland, 2 vols (Oxford, 1911).

Riley, Margaret, 'The Club at the Temple Coffee House revisited', Archives of Natural History
 33 (2006), pp. 90-100.

Riley, P. W. J., English Ministers and Scotland 1707-1727 (London,1964);
 The Union of England and Scotland (Manchester, 1978);
 King William and the Scottish Politicians (Edinburgh, 1979).

Robertson, John, The Scottish Enlightenment and the Militia Issue (Edinburgh, 1985).

Robertson, Forbes W., Early Scottish Gardens and their Plants 1650-1750 (East Linton, 2000).

Robertson, William, Proceedings Relating to the Peerage of Scotland from January 16. 1707
 to April 29, 1788, (Edinburgh and London, 1790).

Robinson, John Robert, The Princely Chandos: A Memoir of James Brydges... (London, 1898).

Rock, Joe, 'The "A" Marked Porcelain: Further Evidence for the Scottish Option',
Transactions English Ceramic Circle 17 (1999), pp. 69-78;
'Richard Cooper Senior (c. 1696-1764) and His Properties in Edinburgh', Book of the Old
Edinburgh Club, N.S. 6 (2005), 11-23.

Rocque, Jean. An Exact Survey of the CITY'S of London and Westminster...Begun in 1741,
finished in 1745, and publish'd in 1746 (London, 1746); [also on line];
Survey of London, vol. 31 (London, 1963), British History Online [contains material in the
previous book].

Royal Commission on Ancient and Historical Monuments of Scotland:Peeblesshire: An
Inventory of the Ancient Monuments (with the Seventeenth Report of the Royal Commission
on Ancient and Historical Monuments of Scotland, 2 vols, (HMSO, 1967);
Argyll: Inventory of the Ancient Monuments, (with the Twenty-second Report of the
Commission, HMSO, 1982).

Ross, Ian Simpson, Lord Kames and the Scotland of his Day (Oxford, 1972);
'Aesthetic Philosophy: Hutcheson and Hume to Alison' in History of Scottish Literature, 4
vols, ed. Cairns Craig (Edinburgh, 1989), II: 239-257;
The Life of Adam Smith (Oxford, 1995; rev. ed. 2010).

Rowan, Alistair, 'William Adam s Library', Architectural Heritage, 1:8-33;

Ruestow, Edward G., Physics at Seventeenth- and Eighteenth-Century Leiden: Philosophy
and the New Science in the University (The Hague, 1973).

[Ryder] The Diary of Dudley Ryder 1715-1716, ed. William Matthews (London, 1949).

Rykwert, Joseph, The First Moderns: The Architects of the Eighteenth Century (Cambridge,
Mass., 1980).

Saunders, Richard, John Smibert Colonial America s First Portrait Painter (New Haven,
Conn., 1995).

Saville, Richard, Bank of Scotland: A History 1695-1995 (Edinburgh, 1996);
'Banking Archives and Scottish History', Scottish Archives, 3 (1997), pp. 12-19.

Scattola, Merio, 'Before and After Natural Law: Models of Natural Law in Ancient and
Modern Times ' in Early Modern Natural Law Theories: Contexts and Strategies in the
Early Enlightenment, eds. T.J. Hochstraser and P. Schröder (Dordrecht, 2003).

Schmidt, Leigh Eric, Holy Fairs: Scotland and the Making of American Revivalism, (2nd ed.,
Grand Rapids, Michigan, and Cambridge, 2001).

Schweizer, Karl W., Lord Bute: Essays in Re-interpretation (Leicester, 1988).

Scott, Hew et al., Fasti Ecclesiae Scoticanae, 8 vols, (Edinburgh, 1915-30; 1st edn. 1866-71).

Scott, W. R. The Constitution and Finance of English, Scottish and Irish Joint Stock
Companies to 1720, 3 vols (Cambridge, 1911).

Sefton, Henry. 'Lord Ilay and Patrick Cuming: A Study in Eighteenth-Century Ecclesiastical
Management', Records of the Scottish Church History Society, 19 (1977), pp. 203-216.

Sellar, W. D. H., 'The Earliest Campbells: Norman, Briton or Gael?', Scottish Studies, 17
(1973), pp. 109-125.

S'Gravesande, Willem Jacob Storm, Physices elements mathematica, experimentis
confirmata, sive introductio ad philosophiam Newtoniam, 1720-21 (2d ed. 1725; 3d ed.
enlarged 1742).

Shaw, John Stuart, The Management of Scottish Society 1707-1764 (Edinburgh, 1983);
The Political History of Eighteenth Century Scotland (New York and London, 1999);
'Archibald Campbell' in the ODNB, 9:716-24.

Shepherd, Christine King, 'Newtonianism in the Scottish Universities in the Seventeenth
Century' in The Origins and Nature of the Scottish Enlightenment, ed. R.H. Campbell and
Andrew Skinner (Glasgow, 1982).

Sher, Richard B., Church and University in the Scottish Enlightenment: the Moderate
    Literati of Edinburgh (Princeton, 1985);
    'Witherspoon's Dominion of Providence and the Scottish Jeremiad Tradition' in Scotland
    and America in the Age of the Enlightenment, eds. Richard B Sher. and Jeffery R. Smitten
    (Edinburgh, 1990);
    The Enlightenment and the Book: Scottish Authors and Their Publishers in Eighteenth
    Century Britain, Ireland and America (Chicago, 2006).
Sher, Richard B. and Alexander Murdoch, 'Patronage and Party in the Church of Scotland,
    1750-1800', in Church Politics and Society: Scotland 1708-1929 (Edinburgh, 1983).
Simpson, Donald, Twickenham Past: A Visual History of Twickenham and Whitton (London,
    1993).
Simpson, John M., 'Who Steered the Gravy Train, 1707-1766?' in Scotland in the Age of
    Improvement, eds. Rosalind Mitchison and N.T. Phillipson (Edinburgh, 1970).
Skoczylas, Anne, Dr. Simson's Knotty Case: Divinity, Politics and Due process in Early
    Eighteenth-Century Scotland (Montreal Kingston, London, Ithaca, 2001);
    'The Regulation of Academic Society in Early Eighteenth-Century Scotland: The
    Tribulations of Two Divinity Professors', Scottish Historical Review, 83 (2004), pp. 171-195;
    The Life of James Erskine, Lord Grange, (forthcoming).
[Sloane], Sir Hans Sloane: Collector, Scientist, Antiquary, ed. Arthur Macgregor (London, 1994).
Smart, Alastair, The Life and Art of Allan Ramsay (London, 1952);
    Allan Ramsay 1713-1784 (Edinburgh, 1992).
[Smith] Correspondence of Adam Smith, eds. E.C. Mossner and I. S. Ross, (Liberty Classics,
    1987; 1st ed. 1977, 2nd ed. 2010).
Smith, Robert, A Compleat System of Opticks, 2 vols (London, 1738).
Smollett, Tobias, The History of England from the Revolution in 1688 to the death of George
    II..., 6 vols (London, 1810).
Smout, T. C., History of the Scottish People 1560-1830 (2nd ed., London, 1970);
    'The Landowner and the Planned Village' in Scotland in the Age of Improvement, ed. N.T.
    Phillipson and Rosalind Mitchison (Edinburgh, 1970), pp. 73-106;
    [see Gibson].
Snedden, Ian N., 'Robert Simson' in Dictionary of Scientific Biography, 16 vols, ed. C.C.
    Gillispie (New York, 1970-1980).
Snoblen, Stephen D., 'Sir Isaac Newton' in The Oxford Encyclopedia of the Enlightenment,
    ed. Alan C. Kors, et al. (New York, 2002);
    'To Discourse of God: Isaac Newton s Heterodox Theology and His Natural Theology'
    in Science and Dissent in England, 1688-1945, ed. Paul B. Wood (Aldershot, U.K. and
    Burlington, Vt., 2004), pp. 39-66.
Somerville, Thomas, My Own Life and Times, 1741-1814 (Edinburgh, 1861).
[Sotheby's] Sale Catalogue 1395 (1999).
Speck, William, The Butcher: the Duke of Cumberland and the Suppression of the '45
    (Oxford, 1981).
Spence, Joseph, Observations, Anecdotes, and Characters of Books and Men Collected from
    Conversations, ed James Osborn, 2 vols (Oxford, 1966).
Statistical Account of Scotland, 20 vols, ed. Sir John Sinclair (Edinburgh, 1791-1799;
    reprinted and rearranged with editorial comments by Donald Withrington and Ian Grant,
    et al, 20 vols Wakefield, 1983).
Steele, Victoria, 'The First Italian Printing of Leonardo da Vinci's Treatise on Painting: 1723
    or 1733?', Notiziario vinciano, 13 (1980), pp. 3-24.
Stewart, Lady Lousia, See Coke.
Stewart, Larry, The Rise of Public Science: Rhetoric, Technology, and Natural Philosophy in
    Newtonian Britain, 1660-1750 (Cambridge, 1992);

'The Edge of Utility: Slaves and Smallpox in the Early Enlightenment', Medical History, 19 (1985), pp. 54-70.

Stewart, M. A., 'The Kirk and the Infidel, an Inaugural lecture delivered at Lancaster University, 9 November 1994' (privately printed);
'Principal Wishart (1692-1753) and the controversies of his day', Records of the Church History Society, 30 (2000), pp. 60-102; 78-82.

[Stuart] Calendar of Stuart Papers Belonging to His Majesty The King preserved at Windsor Castle [no editor listed] (London, 1902).

Stuart, David G., Georgian Gardens (London, 1979).

Sullivan, Robert E., John Toland and the Deist Controversy (Cambridge, Mass., 1982).

Sunter, Ronald M., Patronage and Politics in Scotland 1707-1832 (Edinburgh, 1986).

Symes, Michael, Alison Hodges and John Harvey, 'The Plantings at Whitton', Garden History, 14 (1986), pp. 138-172.

Szechi, Daniel, George Lockhart of Carnwath 1681-1731: A Study in Jacobitism (East Linton, 2002);
1715 The Great Jacobite Rebellion (New Haven and London, 2006).

Tait, A. A., The Landscape Garden in Scotland 1735-1835 (Edinburgh, 1980).

Tayler, Henrietta, 'John, Duke of Argyll and Greenwich' , Scottish Historical Review, 26 (1947), pp. 64-74.

Taylor, E.G. R., Mathematical Practitioners of Hanoverian England (London, 1966).

Thomson, George Malcolm, A Kind of Justice: Two Studies in Treason (London, 1970).

Thomson, John, An Account of the Life, Letters, and Writings of William Cullen, M.D.', 2 vols, (I: Edinburgh,1832; I and II: Edinburgh, 1859).

Thorpe, Nigel, ed., The Glory of the Printed Page (London, 1987).

Timperley, Loretta, A Directory of Landownership in Scotland c. 1770, Scottish Record Society, N.S. 5 (1976).

Tindal, Nicholas, The Continuation of Mr. Rapin's History of England From the Revolution to the Present Times, 8 vols (London, 1759).

Trevelyan, G. M., England Under Queen Anne, 3 vols (London, 1930-34).

Trevor-Roper, Hugh [Baron Dacre of Glanton], History and the Enlightenment ed. John Robertson (New Haven, Conn. and London, 2010).

Turberville, A. S., The House of Lords in the XVIIIth Century (Oxford, 1927).

Turner, A. Logan, Story of a Great Hospital: The Royal Infimary of Edinburgh 1729-1929, (Edinburgh, 1937; facsimile reprint Edinburgh, 1979).

Underwood, E. Ashworth, Boerhaave s Men at Leyden and After (Edinburgh, 1977).

[Voltaire, François Marie Arouet, de], An essay on epic poetry, ed. David Williams, in The Complete Works of Voltaire, vol. 3B (Voltaire Foundation, Oxford, 1996).

[Waldegrave] Memoirs and Speeches of James, Earl Waldegrave 1742- 1763, ed. J.C.D. Clark (Cambridge, 1988).

Wallis, Peter J. and Ruth V., Biobliography of British Mathematics and its Applications, 1701-1760 (Letchworth, n.d. [1986]);
Eighteenth Century Medics (Project for Historical Bio-bibliography, Newcastle upon Tyne, 1988).

[Walker] The Rev. Dr. John Walker's Report on the Hebrides of 1764 and 1771, ed. Margaret M. McKay (Edinburgh, 1980).

[Walpole, Horace] The Yale Edition of Horace Walpole's Correspondence, ed. Wilmarth. S. Lewis, *et al.*, 48 vols, (variously in New Haven, Conn., N.Y. and London, 1937-1963;
Memoirs of King George II, 3 vols; ed. John Brooke (New Haven & London, 1985);
On Modern Gardening, n. ed. (London, 1975; excerpted from Anecdotes of Painting in England, Vol. IV, 1780).

Walsh, Patrick, 'The Bubble on the Margins: The South Sea Bubble in Ireland and Scotland', forthcoming.

Wentworth Papers 1705-1739... , ed. James J. Cartwright (London, 1883).

Whately, Christopher. Scottish Society 1707-1830 (Manchester and New York, 2000); The Scots and the Union, (Edinburgh, 2006).

Whetstone, Ann E., Scottish County Government in the Eighteenth and Nineteenth Centuries,(Edinburgh, 1984).

Whiston, William, Memoirs of ..., 2 vols (London, 1753).

White, Dennis B., Exploring Old Duddingston and Portobello (Edinburgh, 1990).

Whitworth, Rex, William Augustus Duke of Cumberland: A Life (London, 1992).

Wilkes, John, A Whig in Power: The Political Career of Henry Pelham (n.p., 1964).

Wilkinson, Vicki, 'Hidden treasures: a brief insight into the Scottish archives of the Royal Bank of Scotland', Scottish Archives, 3 (1997), pp. 37-43.

Willems, P. J. M., Bibliographia Fletcheriana or, the extraordinary library of Alexander Fletcher of Saltoun (Privately printed, Wassenaar, 1999).

Williams, Basil, Stanhope: A Study in Eighteenth-Century War and Diplomacy (Oxford, 1932).

[Wilson], 'Biographical Account of Alexander Wilson M.D.', The Edinburgh Journal of Science, 10 (1829) 1-17 [probably by his son but perhaps edited by David Erskine, Earl of Buchan.]

Withall, Mary, Villages of Northern Argyll (Edinburgh, 2004).

Withers, Charles W. J., 'William Cullen's Agricultural Lectures and Writings and the Development of Agricultural Science in Eighteenth-Century Scotland', The Agricultural History Review, 37 (1989), pp. 144-156;
'How Scotland came to know itself...', Journal of Historical Geography, 21 (1995), pp. 371-97;
Geography, Science and National Identity: Scotland since 1520 (Cambridge, 2001).

Withers, Charles W. J. and Paul B. Wood, eds. Science and Medicine in the Scottish Enlightenment (East Linton, 2002).

Wodrow, Robert, Analecta or Materials for a History of Remarkable Providences Mostly Relating to Scottish Ministers and Christians, 4 vols, ed. Matthew Leishman (Edinburgh, 1842-43);
The Correspondence of the Rev. Robert Wodrow, 3 vols, ed Thomas McCrie, (Edinburgh, 1842).

Wood, John P., A Sketch of the Life and Projects of John Law of Lauriston (Edinburgh and London, 1791).

Wulf, Andrea, The Brother Gardeners: Botany Empire and the Birth of an Obsession (New York, 2009).

Yeo, Richard, Encyclopaedic Visions: Scientific Dictionaries and Enlightenment Culture (Cambridge, 2007).

Youngson, A. J., The Making of Classical Edinburgh with photographs by Edwin Smith (Edinburgh, 1966);
After the Forty- five (Edinburgh, 1973);
Beyond the Highland Line: Three Journals of Travel in eighteenth century Scotland: Burt, Pennant, Thornton, ed. A.J. Youngson (London, 1974).

Plate 11. Study for a portrait of the Duke of Argyll by Allan Ramsay, c.1757, Scottish National Gallery, Edinburgh.

Appendix I: Argyll in the House of Lords

Table 1: Attendance in the House

This Table is based on the sessions recorded in the published Journals of the House of Lords. It counts as missed days, the meetings to prolong the prorogations; those he seldom attended. He also missed every sermon preached on fast days and those to the memory of the blessed Charles, the Martyr. He usually avoided the opening and closing sittings of the House. Argyll's attendance at sessions doing business was thus somewhat higher than the percentage figures would suggest. The bolded dates indicate a new Parliament elected in that year. [The new Parliament often did not sit until the next calendar year.]

Dates	Absent	Present	Total	%	Committees
1707 23 /10/07- 1/4/08	24	79	103	78	19
1708 16/11/08- 21/4/09	23	63	86	73	23
15/11/09- 21/9/10	21	74	95	78	23
1710 25/11/10- 12/6/11	14	105	119	88	27
7/12/11- 21/6/12	33	84	117	74	21
9/4/13- 16/7/13	31	36	67	54	7
1713 16/2/14- 9/7/14	Absent	because he was unelected		in 1713	
1/8/14/- 25/8/14	Absent	because he was unelected		in 1713	
1715 17/3/15-21/9/15	24	90	114	79	15
9/1/16-26/6/16	34	61	95	64	3
20/2/17-15/7/17	13	6	19	32	9
21/11/17-21/3/18	13	58	71	82	8
11/11/18-18/4/19	12	76	88	86	23
23/11/19-11/6/20	51	49	100	49	13
18/12/20-29/7/21	23	111	134	83	29
31/7/21-10/8/21	3	3	6	50	3
19/10/21-7/3/22	9	66	75	88	22
1722 9/10/22-27/5/23	30	88	118	75	20
9/1/24-24/4/24	23	51	74	69	16
12/11/24-31/5/25	22	103	125	82	34
20/1/26-24/5/26	28	40	68	59	20
17/1/27-5/5/27	19	57	76	75	21
26/6/27-7/2/27	3	8	11	73	1

Dates	Absent	Present	Total	%	Committees
1727 23/1/28-/5/28	13	55	68	81	29
21/1/29-4/5/29	16	62	78	80	30
13/1/30-15/5/30	19	60	79	76	29
21/1/31-7/5/31	13	59	72	82	26
13/1/32-1/6/32	9	71	80	89	36
16/1/33-3/6/33	16	75	91	82	37
17/1/34-16/4/34	10	50	60	83	25
1734 14/1/35-15/5/35	20	58	78	74	19
15/1/36-20/5/36	10	58	68	85	27
1/2/37-21/6/37	10	80	90	89	29
24/1/38-20/5/38	13	54	67	81	30
1/2/39-14/6/39	10	70	80	88	33
15/11/39-29/4/40	11+	58+	69+	c.84	c. 20
18/11/40-25/4/41	10	67	77	87	32
1741 1/12/41-15/7/42	24	66	90	73	31
16/11/42-21/4/43	19	48	67	72	20
1/12/43-12/5/44	21	66	87	76	28
27/11/44-2/4/45	36	38	74	51	18
17/10/45-12/8/46	43	79	122	65	14
18/11/46-17/6/47	28	65	93	70	22
1747 10/11/47-13/5/48	35	45	80	56	16
29/11/48-13/6/49	26	60	86	70	26
16/11/49-12/4/50	26	44	70	63	22
17/1/51-25/6/51	23	64	87	74	28
14/11/51-26/3/52	28	43	71	61	25
11/1/53-7/6/53	27	56	83	67	32
15/11/53-6/4/54	28	38	66	58	21
1754 31/5/54- 5/6/54	4	0	4	0	4
14/11/54-25/4/55	44	41	85	48	19
13/11/55-27/5/56	53	50	103	49	21
2/12/56-4/7/57	53	58	111	52	27
1/12/57-20/6/58	41	61	102	60	25
23/11/58-2/6/59	60	32	92	35	17
13/11/59-22/5/60	48	40	88	45	22
26/10/60-29/10/60	3	1	4	25	0
18/11/60-19/3/61	40	22	62	35	11
Totals	1343	3199	4545	70	1205

Table 2 : Argyll's Committee Assignments by Type for Sessions Falling Principally in the Given Years

Dates Committees	1708-21	1722-41	1742-47	1748-1756	1757-61	Totals
Addresses and Representations to the Crown [1]	8	14	1	8	2	33
Rights, Privileges and Procedures of the House of Lords [2]	4	0	1	1	0	6
Customs, Rules, Privileges	14	16	8	6	1	45
Standing Orders	2	3	0	0	2	7
Journals and Records [3]	10	15	2	5	2	34
Housekeeping [4]	1	5	0	1	0	7
Conference Committees with the House of Commons	3	8	1	1	1	14
Appeals, Judicial Processes [5]	11	18	1	1	0	31
Other Legal Rulings and Business	8	22	4	7	1	42
Misc. Bills and Petitions	8	5	2	5	0	20
Marriage Settlements, Portions and Divorces [6]	8	26	14	7	2	57
Minors, guardians and Trustees	13	7	2	10	2	34
Estate Settlements	53	65	8	8	9	143
Sales for Debt and Others Actions Breaking Entails	26	47	24	16	5	118
Name changes	1	22	11	12	3	49
Naturalization [7]	15	31	16	14	4	80
Military/Naval	5	3	0	0	0	8
Civil Administration	5	2	0	1	0	8
Customs and Excise	1	0	0	0	0	1
Public Order	1	0	1	0	0	2

Dates Committees	1708-21	1722-41	1742-47	1748-1756	1757-61	Totals
Urban Improvements	3	14	4	4	3	28
Work Houses, Jails and hospitals	1	5	2	1	0	9
Poor Relief	0	0	0	1	0	1
Parishes, Churches, Glebes, Cemeteries [8]	9	21	7	2	1	40
Schools and Colleges and Universities	4	1	0	2	3	10
Enclosures	4	50	26	11	25	116
Drainage	0	3	0	1	2	6
Roads, Highways and Bridges [9]	11	60	10	51	24	156
Rivers, Bridges and Harbours	4	21	1	11	3	40
Ports and Docks	3	4	1	0	0	8
Reports from the Office of Works	1	0	0	0	0	1
Trade	8	19	2	0	3	32
Lunacy and Lunatics	2	1	1	2	3	9
Other	2					2
Totals	249	508	150	189	101	1197

Notes on Table 2.

1. This committee is one on which he served when he was securely in place. He did not serve on it in 1742, 1743, 1744, 1745 and 1746 when he was effectively out of office. His absences in 1753, 1755, 1759, 1760 or 1761 may be due to ministerial instability and in the end to old age.

2. Customs, Rules, Privileges and Standing Orders are sometimes conflated in the Journals so these categories can be treated as one. Doing that has resulted in a lower total for the number of committees than is give in Table 1. Another source of the discrepancy is confusion in 1727 over several committees dealing with a workhouse, breaking an entail, a road bill and one or two miscellaneous bills.

3. The committee dealing with the Journal was technically a sub-committee but its importance was control of the official record of the House of Lords.

4. This is a collection of *ad hoc* committees which dealt with the refurbishment of the House, appointment of clerks and keeping order.

5. It is difficult for a layman to discriminate between a process leading to a trial and one which was designed to make regulations either by a ruling or legislation. This and the following category strive to make that distinction but I am not sure I have done so.

6. The categories from marriage to sales for debt might all be put in one category since most of them involved creating or destroying legal arrangements which tied up property as did entails. It is not hard to see why he opposed entails and wished to see them abolished or made easier to change.

7. Some of the naturalization bills involved Dutch (perhaps Jewish) merchants and bankers in London.

8. About half of those committees dealt with the building of new churches and the better funding of others.

9. The Duke's technical knowledge and inclinations seem to have landed him on the committees dealing with enclosures and engineering projects.

Appendix II: The Library of Archibald Campbell, 3rd Duke of Argyll

Table 1 : The estimated distribution of books by centuries when their Publication Dates are Known from the Catalogus

Note. This table is based on sampling equal numbers of pages of catalogue entries for folios, quartos and octavos.

	15th	%	16th	%	17th	%	18th	%	Total N
Theology			8	6	71	55	50	39	129
History			16	8	95	47	90	45	201
Jus Publicum			7	4	125	64	63	32	195
Juridici			12	7	94	54	68	39	174
Greek & Latin	4	1	79	28	137	48	66	23	286
Philologi	2	1	38	15	123	49	86	34	249
Medici, chemici, &c.			14	8	107	60	57	32	178
Philosophici			21	11	83	44	86	45	190
Mathematici			19	10	118	60	59	30	196
Miscellanei			23	10	121	50	96	40	240
Totals	6	0	237	12	1074	52	721	35	2038

Table 2: The Duke of Argyll's Bibles, Dictionaries, and Grammars

+ means that the Duke had one or more items in this category, including partial bibles.

Language	Dictionary	Grammar	Texts in	Bibles	Works on the language
1. Hebrew	+	+	+	+	+
2. Greek[1]	+	+	+	+	+
3. Latin	+	+	+	+	+
4. Chaldean	+	+	+	+	+
5. Syriac	+	+	+	+	+
6. Aramaic	+	+	+	+	+
7. Amharic[2]	+	+		+	
8. Ethiopian	+	+		+	
9. Coptic	+		+	+	
10. Arabic	+	+			
11. Turkic	+	+			
12. Georgic	+				
13. Armenian		+			
14. Persian	+	+			
15. Chinese	+				+
16. Japanese	?	+			
17. Malabaric		+			
18. Malaico-Latin		+			
19. Malay		+			
20. Singalese		+			
21. Italian	+	+	+	+	+
22. Spanish	+	+	+	+	+
23. Portugese	+	+	+	+	+
24. French	+	+	+	+	+
25. Romansch				?	

Language	Dictionary	Grammar	Texts in	Bibles	Works on the language
26. Celtic - French	+				
27. Irish				+	
28, Scots Irish				+	
29. Welsh	+				
30. English	+	+	+	+	+
31. Anglo-Saxon	+	+		+	
32. Danish				+	
33. Swedish		+			
34. Gothic	+			+	
35. German	+	+	+	+	
36. Bohemian	+				
37 Illyrican	+				
38.Slavonic-Latin-Greek	+				
39. Polish		+			
40. Russian	+			+	
41. Algonkwin[3]				+	
42. Peruana		+			

Notes

1 He also had a dictionaries for more than one dialect of Greek.
2 The catalogue lists Ethiopian, Coptic, and Amharic which may have all been one language or they may have been somewhat different forms of a single tongue.
3 This was the famous bible of John Eliot, Apostle to the Indians. He also possessed *The Key to the Language of America* by Roger Williams.

Table 3. Outline of the Cataloguing System used for Ilay's Library

8951+ titles, 12,177+ volumes

Theology

462 titles, 630 volumes

Bibles
  Polyglot
  New Testament
    Greek
    Other languages
  Old Testament
    Hebrew
    Other Languages
  Psalms and parts of Bibles
    Hebrew
    Latin
    Other languages
  Bibles in other languages

Concordances, glosses and commentaries

Fathers of the Church
  Ante-Nicene Fathers
  Post-Nicene Fathers

Councils

Theology
  Christian thinkers by period
  Apologetics and Moral theology
  Pagans and Atheism
  Natural Religion (Deism)
  Dogmatic theology
  Controversy
  Doctrine of the church
  Islam

Church History

Sermons

Deists and Free-thinkers

History

1472 titles, 1512 volumes

Chronology and Universal History
Providential History
General Civil History

Historical Methods

Ancient Histories
  General
  Roman
  Medieval

Ecclesiastical
  General
  The Primitive Church
  Heresies

National History
  General
  Ancient
  Modern

Hebraic

Britain
  Scotland
  England
  Ireland
  Wales

France

Netherlands

The Empire

Eastern Europe

Germany
  Brandenberg

Saxony
Sweden
Denmark
Poland
Hungary
Croatia
Trieste
Russia

Spain

Portugal

Italy
  The Papacy
  Council of Trent
  Florence
  Milan
  Genoa
  Venice

The Turks

The Moguls

Persia

China

Japan

Aethiopia

The New World
  Spanish- Mexico, Peru, Florida,
  French- Canada
  English

Bibliography and methods

Jus Publicum

546 titles, 718 volumes

Moral Philosophy or the Law of Nature and
  of Nations
Natural Law Writers (Suarez, Grotius,
  Cocceii, etc.)

Controversy (e.g., Bodin, Hooker, Locke,
  Sydney, Harrington, Machiavelli, Hobbes)

Document Collections
Treaties
Constitutions
Political Memoirs and Accounts of Great
  Events such as the Thirty Years' War
Rights and Interests of Princes
Divine Right Theorists

Public Law
  British
  English political history
  The Low Countries
  The Empire
  Eastern Europe
  France
  Italy
  Spain
  Poland/Livonia
  Tartaria

Miscellaneous Political Theories
  Republican
  Classical
  Monarchomachi
  Royalist
  Divine Right Theories
  Secular

Political Testaments

Judici

868 titles, 1035 volumes

Dictionaries and Handbooks

Roman Law
  Corpus juris civilis
  Commentaries
  Pandects, Institutes, Practice
  Civilians
  Civil Law
  Criminal Law
  Canon Law

European Law
  Feudalisms

French
Civil
Canon
Commercial
Ecclesiastical and Canon

Laws of the Scots
  Ancient: Civil and Criminal
  Modern
  Acts of parliament
  Case law and Decisions
  Style Books

Laws of the English
  Statutes
  Common Law Courts
  Equity Courts
  Criminal Law
  Ecclesiastical Law
  Other Courts and Laws
  Maritime
  Prerogative
  Law in New England

Rights and Powers of Parliament and the
  Crown

Indices to Records, Abridgements, reports

Autores Graeci et Latini

1080 titles, 1554 volumes

Greek (by genres and periods)
  Historians from Herodotus to the
  Byzantines
  Other Classical prose writers
  Philosophy
  Politics
  Oratory
  Satires
  Fables
  Letters
  Poetry
  Playwrights
  Tragedy
  Comedy

Roman (repeats all categories)

Philogici

1074 titles, 1512 volumes

Works by Humanists and Learned Men

Works on Antiquity and the Modern Periods
  Greek
  Roman
  Other – Egyptians , Asiatics, Celts, etc.

General Reference Books
Dictionaries of Languages
Etymologies
Dictionaries of Arts and Sciences and
  General Knowledge: Moreri, Bayle, etc.
Other Reference Works

Antiquities
  Numismatics, Seal and Gems
  Weights and Measures
  Architecture
  Art

Miscellaneous Learned Works – (e.g.,
  Memoires of the Academie des
  Inscriptiones)

Bibliographies and books on books

Works on Religion and Myth
  Gentiles
  Christians
  Others

Critical Writings on Poetry, Letters, Orations
  etc.

Methods of Study and Learning

Sceptics

Journals and Periodicals
  English
  French
  Latin
  Italian

Book Catalogues
Libraries

Sales

Grammars and Dictionaries in all languages

Medici, Chimici &c.

1096 titles, 1284 volumes

Botany
    General
    Places
    Plant Anatomy
    Physiology
    Systems

Pharmacy
    History of materia Medica
    Materia Medica

Chemistry
    General
    Systems
    Airs
    Waters
    Salts
    Metals
    Specific Compounds
    Applied Chemistry

Medicine
    History and Theories in Works
    Ancient
    Modern
    Systems
    Specialities (*e. g.* , fevers)
    Diseases
    Plagues and epidemics by time and place

Anatomy

Physiology
Surgery

Journals and Serials

Philosophici &c.

795 titles, 1077 volumes

Natural History
General Science (Cosmology)
General Physics
Space and Time
Body
    Forces and Powers (electricity, magnetism, fire, gravity, etc.)
    Statics
    Dynamics
        Aero-
         Hydro-
    Optics
    History of the Earth – geology

Controversies

Journals

Mathematici

1164 titles, 1276 volumes

Mathematics
    Pure
    Geometry - plane, solid, spherical, Arithmetic
    Probablity theory
    Algebra
    Trigonometry
    Fluxions
    Logarithms
    Uses in surveying, fortification, machines, hydraulics, etc.

Newton and His Commentators

Theory of the Earth
    Longitude, navigation, ships

Mixed
    Astronomy
    Instruments
    Optics, Dioptics, Catoptics
    Theory
Practical – observations, tables, ephemerides, etc.

Pneumatics
Geodesy
Dialing
Horology
Stereography,
Cartography
Navigation
Magnetica
Mechanics
Machines
Architecture
    History
    Military:Fortification (and Gunnery)
    Civic
    Domestic
    Landscape
Music Theory

Miscellanei

1024 titles, 1570+ volumes

Geography
Atlases and Maps
Travels
Choreography, Topographical and Natural
    and Civil Histories

Modern Literature

French: Works by Author and kind
Prose: heraldry, novels, biography, art of
    war, history, manners and conduct,
    funeral sermons, education, etc.

Poetry
Other genres: letters criticism, plays
Philosophy
Proverbs
Literature
    Italian
    Spanish
    Portugese
    Dutch
    Old English
    Middle English
    Modern English
    British

Economics, Commerce, Trade
    Trade in General
    Money and finance
    Treatises
    Specific Topics
        Money, coin, paper
        Banking
    Trade
    General
        Colonial and Imperial
            General
                By Nations and Places
    Specific Trades
Regulation of Trade and Monopoly
    companies

Debt
Public Finances: debt, taxes, sinking funds

Agriculture

Fisheries

Trades

Trade in Italy
        France,
        Holland
        The Empire etc.

Table 4: Marks Denoting Special Provenances, Editions and the Names of Editors, Printers and Publishers Noticed in the *Catalogus Librorum*.

Abbreviation	No.of entries	Name
Agryph		See Gryphus
Ald	31	Aldine Press, Venice
Aldus	5	Aldus Minutius (1450-1515), Paulus Minutius (1512- 1574), Aldus II (1547-1597)
Ant Delrii	1	Delrii Martini Antonii Delrii, S.J., (1551-1608, author, classical editor and annotator
AntMureti	1	Marc Antoine Muret (1526-1585) , Rome
Ant St	1	?
Ant Vincent	1	16th century Genevan and French merchant/printer of Protestant books.
Benenat	1	Parisian publisher of legal works c.1570
B.n.	1	?
Burlandi	1	?
ch.m.	207	Special paper or formats
Chronic	1	?
Cock	1	17th century Dutch bookseller/editor
Colin	7	Simon de Colines (?- 1540)
Commellini	1	? Joanis Commellini, 17th century gardener at Amsterdam
Coutures	1	?
CSt	2	? Charles Estienne, Parisian printer 1550s [See Stephen]
de Ghini	1	Luca Ghini (1490 -1556), Italian physician and botanist, creator of the first herbarium
Agryph	1	See Gryphus
DuPin	1	?
Elz	59	Louis Elzivir (c. 1540-1618), Louis II (1604-1670), Daniel (1626-1680), Bonaventure (1583-1652), Abraham (1592-1652) John (fl. c.1660), Louvain , Leiden, Amsterdam
Fabratti	1	Raphael Fabretti (1618-1700) Italian antiquary and classical editor
Florent	1	Florent Chrestien (1541 – 1596), poet and editor of classical works
JoFlorianus	1	Joannes Florianus 16th Italian geographic writer
Floridi	1	?
Fr Gryph	5	See Gryphus
Frob	2	Johannes Froben (1460-1527)
Gadovini	1	?
Gagnier	1	?
Galeot a Prato	1	Galeotum A' Prato, Parisian printer c.1550s
Gifani	1	?
Giunt [or Junta]	4	Jacque (1486-1546) or Lucantonio or Filippo, Venice, Florence, Lyons, Rome, London, Salamanca, Bruges

Gori	1	? 16th century Italian printer
Gr Lat	1	Probably a bilingual edition in Greek and Latin
Gronovii	3	Jacobi Gronovii, Leiden publisher of classics, c. late 17th to early 18th centuries
Agryph	1	Anthoine Gryphus, Lyons printer 1550s
Fr Gryph	5	Gryphus Parisian Printer. c.1530s
SebGryph	4	Sebastian Gryphus (1493-1556), Lyons and Germany bookseller printer and humanist
Guillard	2	Charlotte Guillard (1480s-1557) first well known woman publisher in France
Hamilton	2	Gavin Hamilton (1704-1767), Edinburgh
HeinReinoldus	1	See Reinold
Helvetius	1	? John Fredrick Schweitzer, called Helvetius 1625-1709, German alchemist
HST	33	Henri Estienne (c.1460-1520), Paris
HenSt	1	Henri II (1528-1598), Paris
HenStephen	12	
PSt	1	? Paul Estienne Robert Etienne (1499-1559), Robert II (?- 1570), Paris
Jan de Wit	1	?
JaniPlanci	1	?
Jel	2	?
JohParv	1	?
JoPena	1	?16th century German or Swiss printer
Junt	4	See Giunt
JVVondel	1	See Vondel
Lambini	2	? Dionysii Lambini Monstroliensis (1455-?), classics editor
Lister	1	Martin Lister (1639-1712), naturalist, FRS
JoLoccen	1	?
Lubini	1	?
Marolles	2	?
Mattaire	6	Michael Mattaire (1668-1747), classics editor
Meurs	2	?Meurs, Jacob van, (1619-1680), printer
Montani	1	Joannis Montani, mid 16th century medical and pharmaceutical writer
Morelli	2	16th century Italian printer
Mours	2	?
N. Visscher	1	Nicholas Visscher (163?-1702) Amsterdam map maker
Nasson	1	Jean Papire Nasson, (1544-1611)
Olearii	1	Adam Olearius (1600-1671 and Nicolas Olearius (1600–1667)
Olivet	1	?Pierre Robert Olivétan (c.1506-1538)
PhLabbe	18	Phillip Labbe, S.J. (1607- 1667) writer on history and geography
Pii	2	?
exbibli Pithae	1	?
Plant	23	Christopher Plantin (c. 1530-1589)
Portl	1	?
Potter	1	?

PSt	1	? See Stephen
Rebuff	1	?
HeinReinoldus	1	?
Riccoboni	1	?
RobSt	5	? See Estienne
RSt	23	? See Estienne
Rodelini or Rodeli	3	?
Ross	1	?
Rouil	1	
Sanby	1	Paul Sandby (1731 – 1809) , mapmaker and engraver
Scaletti	1	?
Scaligeri	1	Julius Caesar Scaliger (or Giulio Cesare della Scala) (1484 – 1558) of Joseph Justus Scaliger (1540 – 1609)
SebGryph	4	See Gryphus
Schoettyenii	1	?
Sgr	1	?
Sike	1	?
Strebaei	3	Iacobi Lodoici Strebaei (16th century) classical Editor
Strykii	2	Samuelis Strykii, late 17th and early 18th century jurist and legal writer
Thirlbii	1	Styan Thirlby (1686-1753), annotator and editor of patristic sources
Th Johnston	2	Thomas Johnston , the Hague
Tonson	1	Jacob Tonson (1656-1736), London
TR	5	
TypR	17	The Papal Press, 1566 (run by Paulus Manuitius)
Turnebi	4	Adrian Turnebus, 1512-1565, editor of classics and commentator on Cicero
Vanderwater	3	Willem Van der Water , Utrecht printer and bookseller with whom Ilay may have lived c.1702
Vascosan	7	Michel de Vascon, (c.1500 -1576) Paris bookseller and publisher
Villende	1	?
Viviani	1	(1622 -1703) Italian mathematician and scientist.
Vol. Mediol	1	?
JVVondel	1	? Joost van der Vondel, 17th century Dutch engraver
Von Fried	1	?
Vossii	2	Gerrit Janszoon Vos (Gerardus Vossius, 1577 –1649) and or Isaac Vossius (1618-1689)
Wendelini	1	Johann and Wendelin of Speyer (also known as Giovanni and Vendelino da Spira) German printers in Venice Mainz and Speyer 1468 to 1477.
Wech	4	?
Wechel	2	Christian Wechel (c. 1500-after 1572), Basle
Wolfii	4	Georg Wolf (?- c.1500) ; Reyner or Reginald Wolfe c.1505- 1530, London

Inevitably incomplete. Approximately 100 presses and editors accounting for 386 titles + 207 ch.m.=593 titles.

Appendix III

Selected Instruments, Machines and Models Owned by the Duke of Argyll

The following abbreviations have been used below:

AI	Adams Inventory
BBM	Edmund and Dorothy Berkeley and Berkeley, *John Mitchell: The Man who Made the Map*
CIB	Coutts 'In book', 1762
L&C	Ian Lindsay and Mary Cosh, *Inveraray and the Dukes of Argyll*
MC	Molyneux Catalogue

Other entries can be identified from the bibliography
W = used at The Whim; I = used at Inveraray

Mathematical Instruments

Cases of Instruments	MC, p57; many entries in NLS, *e.g.* 16569/195
"Box Zograscope, Deal Coloured; the double Convex Broke"	AI
Pantograph	AI

Navigational Instruments

Argyll around 1744 may have purchased a 50-ton Clyde built ship to be used to import deals for Inveraray (NLS, 16591/122). In the 1750s, he owned a snow used in whaling and trade to America and an armed yacht of seventy tons which carried eight brass cannon (see above p. 323). He almost certainly owned navigational instruments but we do not know what or how many.

Surveyor's Equipment

Surveyor's Equipment	Various entries in NLS, 17642-17650
Compasses	"
Surveyor's chains and rods	"
Waywiser	NLS, 17617/141
A 'road measure'	NLS, 17617/141
plane table	AI
Theodolite	NLS, 17617/271/7

Circumferentor   NLS, various entries
Semi-Circle for Fortifications, and to take
      the Internal and External Angles of Buildings   MC, p.60

Meteorological Instruments

Thermometers

2 Ordinary thermometers in London, 1 by Sisson   AI
1 Boiling thermometer by Bird   AI
1 Thermometer/barometer by Haukesbee   AI
Some in-door and outdoor thermometers
      in Scotland,   NLS, various entries

Barometers

1 Diagonal Barometer   AI
1 Diagonal Double Barometer frame and level
      made by Sisson   AI
Static Barometers   AI
1 Barometer with an open Cistern   AI
1 Portable Measuring Barometer   AI; BBM, p.147.
Other Barometers   NLS, various entries
                                                       not noted
1 Conical Hydrometer in Silver   AI

Weathervanes shone on the plans for his outbuildings

Astronomical Instruments and Clocks

Orrery made by Thomas Wright before 1745   AI
Armillary Sphere by Thomas Wright   AI
Equinoctial Standing Ring-dial c. 1720 made
for Ilay by Richard Glynn of London   *Sotheby's Sale*
                                                       Catalogue 7395

Clocks

Sundial bottoms   AI
Sundials   Various garden plans
1725,"Thre freanch horrys and other mometers"[sic]   NLS, 17650/204)
Alarm Clocks, before 1744   NLS, 17617/141
Other Clocks   NLS, 17613/71, 17650/203
c. 1758 longcase clock by Cumming   Mary Cosh, *Country Life*,
                                                       1969, p. 1531

Various watches	NLS, 17614/71
Astronomical clock by Tapping	CIB, 1762
Astronomical Clock	MC, p. 61
Tools to repair clocks	BBM, p. 147

Telescopes

Before 1730, 'A reflecting telescope of Newton's design' made by Samuel Molyneux	MC, p. 66
Before 1730, 'A Meridian telescope with regulator with a Swiveling and rising chair'	MC, p. 66.
1733, 15 inch Gregorian by James Short	*Maclaurin Letters*, p. 252
1745, little telescope shipped from London, I	NLS, 17617/141
1749, telescope from London to Rosneath	NLS, 17619/286
1749, telescope, W	NLS, 17619/286
n.d., a telescope, 3' 9"	NLS, 17617/141
Transit instrument at London 3'9"on mahogany supports and so 5'6" from the ground	AI
Equatorial Telescope with a glass case and on a pedestal	AI
'An Annalemma 2 feet diamtr. on a Table & Claw'	AI
A paper Annalemma on a Board with Box Indexes	AI
A 'spiral line 2 feet. 4. Inches. Diamtr. on a Do.'	AI
A paper Instrument for 'the Epocha' of the Moon	AI
Two Astronomical Rotola' [by James]Ferguson	AI
An Old Brass Quadt. Lett into Wood with two Brass Telescopes'	AI
Various telescope mounts	*E.g.* MC, p.60

Optical Instruments

1 Spy glass	NLS, entry lost
2 Camera obscura 1744 sent to Scotland	NLS, 17617/141
1 Pocket Camera Obscura Mahogeney No Glasses	AI
3 Sci-optick Balls [mounts for lenses for camera obscura]	AI
1 Small Wainscot Camera	AI
1 Wainscot Camera 12 inch	NLS, entry lost
2 Microscopes sent to Scotland 1745	NLS, 17617/271/7
2 Microscopical spectacles sent to Scotland in 1745	BBM, p.147; NLS MS.
1 Double [compound] microscope by Villet	MC, p. 60

Philosophical Instruments

Compasses	[inferred]
Loadstone and magnets	NLS, 17617/271/7
'A large Needle to find the Variation of the Compass in a wooden box'	MC, p.57

Chemical Instruments

Mortars and Pestles, W	Various entries in NLS
Glass Phials, Tubing and Vessels, W	
2 Swans Necks, W	NLS, 17646/282
Crucibles, W	NLS, 17642/47
7-10 Furnaces, W	NLS, 17646/284
1 Ore Furnace, W	NLS, 17646/283
1 Sand Heat, W	NLS 17646/283
1 Plate and Pot, W	NLS, 17646/284
Thermometers (boiling, ordinary mercury, spirit), W	AI and various NLS MSS
2 Glass Stills (Whim and Brunstane)	NLS, 16580/107
Another still	NLS, 16584/49
2 Copper Stills	NLS, 17646/286
More Stills at Whitton,	NLS, 16584/55
2 Worms of Pewter	NLS, 17646/282
1 Copper Worm and tube	NLS, 17646/286
1 Iron Press [inferred from]	NLS, 16585
2 Pewter Pipes, W	NLS, 17646/282
Medicine Chest and Instruments, W	Various sources now lost

Miscellaneous

Marshal Saxe's House or Campaign Waggon, I	L&C, p.99
Large pipe organ, I	L&C, p.88
Scales and steelyards ?	E.g. MC, p.61
Guns and Pistols, W	NLS, L&C, p.16
'Three steel joints' [devices for swivels?] ?	NLS, 17620; BBM, p.147

Pumps

?7 Portable Pumps from Leith, W	NLS, 17646/84
Waterscoop, W	L&C, p. 16.

[Ilay in 1740 seems to have been
interested in a pump for his coal mines
but there is no indication that he got
the one he considered. This was said
to be able to lift water from a depth
of over 100 feet. NLS, Ms. 17646/175]

Wooden Pipes to bring spring water to the
Whim and the 1"augers to bore the pump logs   NLS, 17650/261

Miscellaneous Tools and Machines and Tools

Miscellaneous Farm Equipment and all sorts of utensils used in dairies, brewhouses, lint yards, lime kilns, salt pans, and much more. Those items were often made on site by local smiths and wrights. Among the more notable of those were the following:

Oyster Grates, I	Source not noted
[Probably a crane designed by William Crow	
and made by ? Robert Meikle	NLS, 16669/153]
Pulleys and blocks	NLS, 17642/ ?
'A Pair of Stilyards for weighing heavy Bodies'	MC, p. 61
Windmill with Vertical Vanes at Whitton	*Gentleman's Magazine*, 19 (1749), pp. 249-50
Limestone Crusher	*ibid*, p. 242
? A press to compact peat into bricks	NLS, 17619/286/8
Water Wheels, a steam engine and milling machines for wood, iron and cloth	NLS, numerous entries.

Other Tools and Devices

Chest of Tools (Rosneath)	NLS, 16718/717
Three steel joints'[devices for swivels?]	NLS, 17620; BBM, p.147
Guns and Pistols W NLS, various letters;	L&C, p. 16

Models Mentioned in the Papers and Works Dealing with the 3rd Duke of Argyll. Works based on these models seem to have been built.

1740, 'a Gothic Tour', W	NLS, 17645
1740, a Classical Pidgeon House, W	"
1743, Water screw, W	NLS, 16591/47
1744, ' of a Pump', W	NLS, 17617/141
'lint mill', I	?
windmill for corn or malt, I	"
water mill for spinning thread, I	"
(All made by Robert MacKell)	
1744-45, engine for slitting iron, I	L&C, p. 423.
engine for slitting and chipping iron and rolling hoops, I	", p. 360 note 166
1745, 'Modell of a Gate', W	NLS, 17617/271/7
'Modell of a Bridge', W	NLS, 17617/271/20
'Modell of a Stable' ,W	NLS, 17617/21
'an Engine' ,W	NLS, 17617/21
1745, 'of a [?summer] House, W	NLS, 17617/269

1745, Models for Laboratory	
(Made by Robert MacKell), W	NLS, 17617/21
1747, model of Inveraray Castle, by Morris, I	L&C, pp. 60, 109
1749, Moveable hurdles or Flakes	NLS, 17747/72,
(sent to Whim 11 May 1751), W	NLS, 17746, entry for 11 May 1751
1749, mill made for Marquis of Belle Isle	NLS, 16656/33.
with a smaller one for Scotland, I	
1750, Model of the Whitton Rabbit Warren	
and Summerhouse	NLS, 17747/53
1751, ' wheeld low Carriages for removing	NLS, 17747, entry for 11 May 1751
Stones, or loggs of wood', W	
1751, Several scientific models, I	NLS, 17747, entry for 11 May 1751
Others seem to date from 1758	
1752, 3 Models of "the best method of piecing	NLS, 17680/49
Timbers", I	
1756, Bridges and Casemates made by Robert	L&C, p. 86
Mackell, I	
1758, Model of Marshall Saxe' "campaign caravan",	
probably made by Alexander Cumming, I L&C, pp 98, 364, note 208 1758	

Other Known Toys and Models Owned by Argyll

Model of a gate, W	NLS,17617/271/7
Models of Grain Mill, W	Various Saltoun Papers
Model of Stocking Mill, I	"
Model of a Bridge, I	"
Model of a Cart, W	"
Model of the escapement of a pendulum	
– cited above ?	AI, p .61
? Archimedes' Water Screw	NLS, 16591/47
Pump, W	NLS, 17617/141
Steam engine ?	NLS, 16694/108

Appendix IV

Table of Botanical Transactions 1749

(mostly taken from NLS 17747)

* = sent from Whitton. All other entries concern materials sent to Whitton.

In Entry 2, Walker's list of seeds and cones included at least fifteen American trees, shrubs and plants: "pines, larx, hornbeam, fir, cypress, sweet cheery, evergreen oak, acacia, baum of Gilead, pyracanthia berries, mesereon berries, sweet briar, laburnum, 'Va Bladden Nat. Laimes Tinus' berries and lucern seed."

Dealers	Scottish Friends	English Friends	Europeans	Americans and Others	Sent or Received
1	Maj T.Cochran*				balm of gilead, firs
2	Ld. Milton* (from Mr. Walker)				16 American plants including balm of Gilliad, pryacanthia berries, mesereon berries, acacia, evergreen oak, sweet briar, 'Va. Bladden Nat.' and Laimes Tinus.
3				John Bartram	box of tree and shrub seeds
4				Dr. Mitchell, Barbadoes& Jamaica	24 shrubs, flowers and seeds including Gully Plums, Lignam vitae, Fr. Physic nuts, Soap berry, box tree and 'the Moabite Virgin's Bower'.
5	Lord Deskford*				seeds
6	Mr. Mackay*				seeds
7	Ld Milton*				45 seed packets
8	Ld Milton*				62 seeds
9		Duke of Richmond* to Crafts			Alpine pine cones, seeds, 13 plants
10				Mr. Crocatt, mer in South Carolina* sent to Whitton and Saltoun	plants
11	Gen.James Sinclair				seeds / pine cones from the Alps / seeeds
12 Mr. Croft or Craft*					pine cones, seeds and plants
13	Milton*				seeds

Dealers	Scottish Friends	English Friends	Europeans	Americans and Others	Sent or Received
14			Mr. Vilay*		seeds
15	Inveraray*				seeds
16	Ld. Milton*				plants
17	Ld Loudoun*				seeds
18		Dr. Mitchell from Oxford			7 kinds of seeds
19 Collinson's gardener, Mr. John Finlay*					2 letters and scarlet summach
20		Ld Hardwick			plants
21 Mr. Home?					letter on seeds
22 James Gray					letter on seeds
23				Walter Paterson*	36 seeds of Carolina swamp Pine
24 Mr. James Gordon of Mile End to Mr. Craft*				Walter Paterson*	44 kinds of seeds
25 Dr. Mitchell					6 kinds of seeds
26		Ld Petre*			23 kinds of plants
27				[Mr. Drummond at Alexandretta*]	report of his seeds which have come up from seeds sent by Drummond
28 Mr. Crofts				[?*]	Large Carolina potatoes
29	Maj. Cochran				1 tulip tree seed
30				Walter Paterson*	scarlet summach, etc
31		Ld Hardwick			N.E. pine
32	Alex. Brodie				N.E. pine and hornbeam
33 Mr. Hewitt					14 kinds of plants

Dealers	Scottish Friends	English Friends	Europeans	Americans and Others	Sent or Received
34	William Campbell at Liston Hall*				16 N.E. pines
35		Mr. [James?] West at Lincoln Fields			plants
36		Mr. Robert Nugent			plants
37	Ld Milton				letter on planting Carolina seeds
38 Mr. Frederick's seeds sent to Crofts					Seeds
39	Mr. Miller				4 kinds of tobacco
40				Mr. Rutherford, N.Y.	List of 18 kinds of seeds sent
41	Mr. Hepburn*				List of 24 flower seeds sent
42	Mr. Kinloch of Gilmerton*				List of 15 seeds sent
43	Ld Milton at Brunstane*				26 kinds of seeds
44	Ld Milton Saltoun*				63 kinds of seeds
45	Box to Inveraray				seeds
46				Consul Pringle in Spain*	seeds
47 Mr. Frederick					20 kinds of seeds
48 Crofts*					a bag of triple thorned accacia seed
49		Ld Petre*			? triple thorned acacia seed

Dealers	Scottish Friends	English Friends	Europeans	Americans and Others	Sent or Received
50		Ld Petre*			
51	Ld Bute*				seeds
52		Dr. Sibthorpe, Oxford*			seeds
53				Capt. Frotheringham from Connecticut*	18 kinds of seeds, 1/2 peck of chestnuts, 1/2 bushel walnuts 64 sassafrass plants
54 Mr. Crofts*					various seeds
55	Inveraray				box of Connecticut seeds
56	Maj Cochrane*				box of Connecticut seeds
57	Ld Milton at Saltoun*				box of Connecticut seeds
58	Ld Milton at Saltoun*				box of Connecticut seeds
59	Ld Milton*				clover seeds, etc.
60		Duke of Richmond			3 cuttings
61		Mr. North?			11 kinds of plants
62	Inveraray				report of seeds which have come up
63 Mr. Crofts*					ine cones from Switzerland & Carolina
64 Col. Mr. Gordon					List of 38 plants
65				Mr. Heylen at Canton*	3 kinds of plants
66	Ld Milton at Saltoun				Syrian onion seeds

Dealers	Scottish Friends	English Friends	Europeans	Americans and Others	Sent or Received
67	Ld Home*				Gathered 52 kinds of seeds at Whitton
68					9 kinds of seeds
69				Gen. Campbell at Allepo	4 kinds of seeds
70	Inveraray				5 kinds of seeds
71		Peter Collinson (See 72 below)			7 kinds of nuts from Germany
72 and sent to Crofts					7 kinds of nuts from Germany
73				John Bartram, Penn.*	list of 38 kinds of seeds sent
74	Ld Milton*				trees for Inveraray, Rosneath, Saltoun
75				Dr. Alexander Mitchell, Jamaica* and sent (see 76 below)	16 kinds of seeds
76 Mr. Crofts*					some or all of Mitchells seeds from Jamaica
77				Mr. Kinloch of S.C.	Kinloch sent a list of seeds to be had in America (a want list)
78 Patrick Drummond seed merchant in Edinburgh					28 vegetable seeds for the garden at Whim?

Appendices

Plate 12. The Duke of Argyll, attributed to Allan Ramsay, Scottish National Portrait Gallery, Edinburgh, with permission of the Gallery.

Index I - Archibald, Earl of Ilay and 3rd Duke of Argyll

Index I is devoted to Archibald Campbell, Earl of Ilay and 3rd Duke of Argyll. Here and elsewhere, he is referred to as Ilay and his brother John, as the 2nd Duke, as Argyll.

Index II is a Subject Index and Index III is an Index of Names. In Indices II and III, some entries have references with an '*'. Those point the reader to appropriate sections of Index I where those or related topics also appear.

The Table of Contents should also be consulted since the sub-sections of its chapter list many topics.

There are no entries for the 2nd Duke's political views in Index III unless they differed from those of his brother, Ilay – which they increasingly did after 1736.

Place] and 24 Argyll St, 3, 37, 203-4, 313, 340; New Town and Castle at Inveraray, 204-6, 271, 339, 341; Marble Hill House, 82, 199; others, 203, 204;

Results of his building, 205-6

v. Virtuoso and collector, 336;

Numismatics, 207-8;

Porcelain collection, 107, 142, 151, 200, 202, 208, 273, 336, 343, [see above 2.ii] and Cullen, A Lind, F. Home, in Index III];

'Gems', 273

vi. Uninterested in music, 207, 209; paintings, 206-8

3. Career [For his Political Career, See 4 below]

i. Offices and Titles: 28, 31, 39, 50, 59, 71, 219, 265, 270, 271, 276;

In Scotland,
1705-6, Lord Treasurer of Scotland, 29, 32; Governor of Dumbarton Castle, 33, 52, 368 n.75;
1706-07, Scottish Privy Councillor, 33; Commissioner to Negotiate the Union, 32; created Earl of Ilay, 33-34, 39;
1707, Governor of Blackness Castle, 33, 370 n.18;
1708- 61, Extraordindary Lord of Session, 58;
1710-61, Lord Justice General, 44, 48;
1714-16. Lord Register 43, 54;
1715- 61, Lord Lieutenant of Midlothian, 59;
1721-33, Keeper of the Scottish Privy Seal, 91, 254;
1737-61, Lord Lieutenant of Haddington;
1733-61, Keeper of the Great Seal of Scotland, 334, 342;
1743-61, 3rd Duke of Argyll and MacCailein Mor, etc., 275-77;
[He was never Chancellor of a university as is sometimes claimed.];

In Great Britain,
Representative Peer in every Parliament through 1761 save that elected in 1713, 34, 35, see *4 below, Peerage elections 1711- 61;
British Privy Council, 44

ii. Nicknames, 257, 266, 302, 316

iii. Army service (?-c. 1711), 28-29, 40, 168; in the '15, 59, 61-64, 65

iv. As Lawyer and judge, Training, 25-6;

Views of the law, 117, 187-92, 307; Procedures and processes, 191-4, 196, 436 n.120, 449 n.46; Entails, 198, 264, 454 n. 38, see Appendix I, Table 2 n.6; 'the common law', 188, 348;

As lawyer, 36, 74, 246;

As judge, 90, 94-97,194-7, 314, 450 n.57;

Roles in Scottish Courts, 316;
Justiciary and Circuit Courts, 65, 70, 190, 191-4; Appin Murder Trial, 194-97, 339;
Court of Session, 39, 90, 94-6, 194, 339;
Scottish Admiralty Courts, 193;
J.P. and Quarter Sessions, 94-5;
Feudal Courts, 187, 197;
Roles in British courts: 219-20;
House of Lords, 47, 50, 191-4, *passim*;
1710, Sacheverell impeachment, 41-42;
1715, Stafford's impeachment, 192;
1717, Oxford's impeachment, 74, 75;
1718, Forfeited Estates bill, 193;
1725, Macclesfield's impeachment, 193;
1733, Edmund Curll, 193, 244;
1746, Jacobite Peers' Trials, 313;
1747, Lovat's Trial for Treason, 193;
1760, Lord Ferrers' murder trial, 193;

Court of Delegates, 193;

Lord Commisssioner in Admiralty, 193;

As an arbitrator, 250, 339, 432 n.35, 462 n.198

525

Index II - Subjects

Spain, 1705- 15, 28, 46, 48, 58; 1718- 61, 76, 157, 265-6, 268, 368 n.72, 436 n.118

Squadrone [see Clans and families above and *4.i, Elections and Politicking];
Aims and views: (To 1725), 32, 35, 43, 51, 52, 55, 67, 72-3, 88-90; (To 1745), 94-95, 233, 253, 258, 261; (After 1745), 286;

Geographical base, 66, 69, 269, 291;

Lacked strength in towns, 65;

Leaders of, 21, 34-5, 66, 69, 213, 238, 251, 254, 270, 323;

Miscellaneous, 39, 98, 192, 209, 222, 302, 303, 351;

Relations with Kirk, 67, 171, 174, 180, 183, 184

Sweden, 76, 119, 122, 157, 243, 381 n.89

T

Temple Coffee House Botany Club [London], 156

Tolerance and Toleration [*4.i, Managing the Kirk]

Tories, English [*4,iv, Ministries], 40-48 *passim*, 51, 52, 56, 57,59, 74, 128, 286; Scottish Tories [See Jacobites, above]

U

Union of England and Scotland, 43 [See *I. 4.i]

Universities, English, 72-3, 366 n.42; Cambridge, 211, 133; Oxford, 156

V

Virtuosi, 24-6 *passim*, 106, 128, 131, 151, 358

W

Wars (outside Britain) [*3.ii Army Service, and *4.v, Foreign Affairs], 19, 115, 168, 243, 284, 398 n.86

Whale Fishing [*5.iii, Commercial Interests]

X/Y/Z

York Buildings Company [*5.iii, Commercial Interests]

Index III - Names

E

F

X/Y

CPSIA information can be obtained
at www.ICGtesting.com
Printed in the USA
BVHW071326030620
580775BV00005B/171